3/97

HUXFORD'S

COLLECTIBLE

Advertising

THIRD EDITION

SHARON & BOB HUXFORD

COLLECTOR BOOKS
A Division of Schroeder Publishing Co., Inc.

On the Cover:
Coca-Cola, cardboard sign, 1951, 36x20", NM, A, $575.00 (Photo courtesy Gary Metz)

Pabst Extract, calendar, 1907, 37x10", NM, A, $330.00 (Photo courtesy Lynn Geyer, Advertising Auctions)

NEHI, cardboard stand-up sign, 41", EX, A, $990.00 (Photo courtesy Bill Bertoia Auctions)

Buster Brown Shoes, die-cut tin sign, 25x40", EX, A, $12,000.00 (Photo courtesy Noel Barrett Antiques & Auctions)

Van Camp's Concentrated Soups, die-cut tin stand-up sign, 32x23", EX, A, $5,720.00 (Photo courtesy Bill Bertoia Auctions)

Editorial Staff:
Editors:
Sharon and Bob Huxford

Research and Editorial Assistants:
Nancy Drollinger and Donna Newnum

Cover Design:
Beth Summers

Book Design:
Michelle Dowling

Searching For A Publisher?

We are always looking for knowledgeable people considered to be experts within their fields. If you feel that there is a real need for a book on your collectible subject and have a large comprehensive collection, contact Collector Books.

The current values in this book should be used only as a guide. They are not intended to set prices, which vary from one section of the country to another. Auction prices as well as dealer prices vary greatly and are affected by condition as well as demand. Neither the Authors nor the Publisher assumes responsibility for any losses that might be incurred as a result of consulting this guide.

Additional copies of this book may be ordered from:

COLLECTOR BOOKS
P.O. Box 3009
Paducah, Kentucky 42002-3009

@$24.95. Add $2.00 for postage and handling.

Copyright: Bob & Sharon Huxford, 1997

Printed in the U.S.A. by Image Graphics

Introduction

The field of collectible advertising is vast and varied. Offering an almost infinite diversity of items, it has the obvious potential to appeal to nearly anyone, with any interest, within any budget. With this in mind, we have attempted to compile a guide that would be beneficial to all collectors of advertising memorabilia. This book includes over ten thousand descriptive listings and hundreds of photos. The format has been kept as simple as possible, by using an alphabetical sequence starting with product or company name.

Items are sorted primarily by alphabetizing the product name as worded on each specific sign, tray, tin, etc. For instance, you'll find listings for Papst Blue Ribbon Beer, others under Pabst Brewing Co., still another under Pabst Malt Extract. Each variation indicates the primary, most obvious visual impact of the advertising message. There are some exceptions. Even though many examples of Coca-Cola advertising are simply worded 'Coke,' all have been listed under the title 'Coca-Cola.' The advertising message as it actually appears is given in the description. There are several other instances where this applies — Cracker Jack and Pepsi-Cola, for example. When appropriate, cross references have been added.

After the product (or company) name, the form of the item is given, i.e. sign, tin, mug, ashtray, etc. Following phrases describe materials, graphics, colors, and sizes. When only one dimension is given, it is height; and height is noted first when two or more are noted. Dates are given when that information was available. Condition is indicated by standard abbreviations: NOS for new old stock, M for mint, NM for near mint, EX for excellent, VG for very good, and G for good. Plus and minus signs were used to indicate levels in between. See the section 'Condition and Its Effect on Value' for more information.

We have given actual sizes when that information was available to us, otherwise sizes are approximate.

Because our listings have been compiled from many sources, we have coded each line to indicate that the suggested value is (A), an auction result or a price actually realized by another type of sale, or (D), a dealer's 'asking' price. As everyone is aware, auction prices are sometimes higher than dealers' prices, but they are just as apt to be lower. At any rate, they are legitimate prices for which merchandise actually changed hands and have always been used by dealers as a basis for their evaluations. This edition contains listings with codes identifying the dealer, collector, or auction house who provided us with that information. Feel free to contact these people if you are interested in buying or selling, or need information about specific items. Many dealers tend to specialize in specific areas of advertising, and even if they no longer have the item in question, they may be able to locate it for you. We'll tell you how to decipher the codes in the following pages. Please remember, as you should regard any price guide, this one is offered as only a tool to be used in addition to your own personal observations of market dealings, show sales, and tradepaper ads.

Acknowledgments

We are indebted to the following dealers, collectors, and auction galleries who contributed photographs that help make this guide a success:

Autopia Advertising Auctions	Darryl Fritsche	Duane Nycz
Noel Barrett Antiques and Auctions Ltd.	Lynn Geyer's Advertising Auctions	Postcards International
Bill Bertoia Auctions	Henry Hain III	Sandy Rosnick
Ann Brogley	David Hirsch	Steve Sourapas
Buffalo Bay Auction Co.	James D. Julia Inc.	Nate Stoller
Collector's Auction Service	Allan Licht	Kelly Wilson
Dunbar's Gallery	Gary Metz	David Zimmerman
Fink's Off the Wall Auctions	Mike's General Store	
Donald Friedman	Wm Morford	

Identification of Coded Auctions and Dealers

Our listings contain 2-character codes indicating the dealer, collector, or auction house who provided us with the description and value. These codes are located at the very end of the line. These codes give the reader an invaluable network of dealers, collectors, and auction houses from which to buy, sell, trade, or inquire about specific advertising collectibles.

As all collectors know, lapse time between data entry and the actual release date of a price guide can involve several months. During that time dealers may buy and sell identical or very similar advertising items several times, and since they must sometimes pay more to restock, their prices will fluctuate, so don't regard the prices they sent us as though they were etched in stone! Over the months that elapse, market values may appreciate, and if you're an advertising collector, you should hope that this is the case. An active market is healthy for both dealers as well as collectors. But even if the item you want to purchase is no longer in stock, as I'm sure you're aware, there is a nationwide network of dealer connections, and the contact you make may be able to steer you to someone else that will be able to help you.

Please, if you make an inquiry by mail, send the dealer or auction gallery a self-addressed, stamped envelope. This is common courtesy. In the long run it not only makes the transaction more convenient for the dealer, but it assures you that his response will make its way back to the proper address. Handwritten addresses are often difficult to make out. If you call and get his answering machine, when you leave your message and your number, tell him by all means to call you collect with his response.

If you're a dealer who regularly or even occasionally puts out a 'for sale' list of advertising items and would like to be involved in our next edition, please contact us at Huxford Enterprises, 1202 7th Street, Covington, Indiana 47932.

Auction Directory

(A1)
Autopia Advertising Auctions
15209 NE. 90th St.
Redmond, WA 98052
FAX (206) 867-5568
Automobilia and General advertising

(A2)
Bill Bertoia Auctions
2413 Madison Ave.
Vineland, NJ 08360
(609) 692-1882; FAX (609) 692-8697
General advertising

(A3)
Buffalo Bay Auction Co.
Lawrence Manos
5244 Quam Circle
Rogers, MN 55374
(612) 428-8879 or (612) 428-8480
General advertising

(A4)
Marc Cardelli
25 Phillips St.
Weymouth, MA 02188
(617) 337-3314
Coca-Cola, Pepsi-Cola and other soft drinks

(A5)
Cerebro
P.O. Box 327
East Prospect, PA 17317-0327
(800) 695-2235; FAX (717) 252-3685
Cigar box labels

(A6)
Collector's Auction Service
RR#2 Box 431; Oakwood Rd.
Oil City, PA 16301
(814) 677-6070; FAX (814) 677-6166
Automobile, gasoline and general advertising

(A7)
Frank's Antiques
P.O. Box 516
Hillard, FL 32046
(904) 845-2870; FAX (904) 845-4888
General advertising

(A8)
Lynn Geyer's Advertising Auctions
300 Trail Ridge
Silver City, New Mexico 88061
(505) 538-2348
Breweriana and general advertising

(A9)
James D. Julia Inc.
P.O. Box 830
Fairfield, ME 04937
(207) 453-7125; FAX (207) 453-2502
General advertising

(A10)
Bob Kay
P.O. Box 1805
Batavia, IL 60510-1805
(708) 879-6214
Beer labels

(A11)
Kurt R. Krueger
P.O. Box 275
Iola, WI 54945-0275
Pin-back buttons and pocket mirrors

(A12)
Mapes Auctioneers and Appraisers
1729 Vestal Parkway West
Vestal, NY 13850
(607) 754-9193; FAX (607)786-3549
General advertising

(A13)
Gary Metz's Muddy River Trading Company
263 Key Lakewood Dr.
Moneta, VA 24121
(540) 721-2091; FAX (540) 721-1782
Coca-Cola, Pepsi-Cola and other soft drinks

(A14)
Mike's General Store
52 St. Anne's Rd.
Winnipeg, Manitoba, Canada R2M-2Y3
(204) 255-3463
General advertising

(A15)
Wm Morford
RD #2
Cazenovia, NY 13035
(315) 662-7625; FAX (315) 662-3570
General advertising

(A16)
Nostalgia Publications
Allan J. Petretti
21 South Lake Dr.
Hackensack, NJ 07601
(201) 488-4536 (evenings)
Coca-Cola and other soft drinks

(A17)
Postcards International
Martin J. Shapiro
P.O. Box 2930
New Haven, CT 06515
(203) 865-0814
Vintage postcards

(A18)
Sandy Rosnick
15 Front St.
Salem, MA 01970
Tins and general advertising

(A19)
Fink's Off the Wall Auctions
108 East 7th St.
Lansdale, PA 19446
(217) 855-9732; FAX (217) 855-6325
Breweriana

(A20)
Dave Beck
P.O. Box 435
Mediapolis, IA 52637
(319) 394-3943
Signs, fobs, pin-backs and mirrors

(A21)
Noel Barrett Antiques and Auctions Ltd.
P.O. Box 1001
Carversville, PA 18913
General advertising

Dealer Directory

(D1)
Ann Brogley
P.O. Box 16033
Philadelphia, PA 19114
(215) 824-4698
Cracker Jack

(D2)
Dave Beck
P.O. Box 435
Mediapolis, IA 52637
Signs, fobs, pin-backs, mirrors

(D3)
Cairn's Antiques
P.O. Box 44026
Lemon Cove, CA 93244
(209) 597-2242
Crate labels

(D4)
Marc Cardelli
25 Phillips St.
Weymouth, MA 02188
(617) 337-3314
Soft drink and automotive collectibles

(D5)
Cerebro
P.O. Box 327
New Prospect, PA 17317-0327
(800) 695-2235
Cigar box labels

(D6)
Dennis and George Collectibles
3407 Lake Montebello Dr.
Baltimore, MD 21218
General advertising

(D7)
David B. DuBrul II
500 Pine St. 1C
Burlington, VT 05401
(802) 860-2976 (evenings)
Beer-related items

(D8)
Dunbar's Gallery
Howard and Leila Dunbar
76 Haven St.
Milford, MA 01757
(508) 634-8697; FAX (508) 634-8698
Signs

(D9)
Frank's Antiques
Box 516
Hillard, FL 32046

(904) 845-2870 or (904) 845-4888);
FAX (904) 845-4000
General advertising

(D10)
Donald Friedman
660 W. Grand Ave.
Chicago, IL 60610
(708) 656-3700 (day); (312) 226-4741
    (evenings and weekends)
Advertising puzzles

(D11)
Darryl's Old Advertising Signs
Darryl Fritsche
1525 Aviation Blvd.
Redondo Beach, CA 90278
(310) 376-3858
Signs

(D12)
Gaylord's Mercantile
Bill Gaylord
1015 Second St.
Sacramento, CA 95814
(919) 444-5738
Crate labels

(D13)
Charles Goodman
636 W. Grant Ave.
Charleston, IL 61920
Advertising paperweights

(D14)
Henry Hain III Antiques and Collectibles
2623 Second St
Harrisburg, PA 17110
General advertising

(D15)
Roy R. and Linda M. Hartman
13139 Country Ridge Dr.
Germantown, MD 20874
De Laval and Crawford Cooking Ranges

(D16)
Jan and Linda Henry
RR#2 Box 193
Galesville, WI 54630
Root Beer

(D17)
Hesson Collectibles
Judy Hesson
1261 S. Lloyd
Lombard, IL 60148
(708) 627-3298
Mail-order catalogs

(D18)
Charles E. Kirtley
P.O. Box 2273
Elizabeth City, NC 27906
(919) 335-1262
*Pin-backs, pocket mirrors and general
    advertising*

(D19)
Allan Licht
1512 Lady Anne
Streetsboro, OH 44241
(216) 626-1429
Signs

(D20)
Gary Metz's Muddy River Trading Co.
263 Key Lakewood Dr.
Moneta, VA 24121
(540) 721-2091
Coca-Cola, Pepsi-Cola and other soft drinks

(D21)
Mike's General Store
52 St. Anne's Rd.
Winnipeg, Manitoba, Canada R2M-2Y3
(204) 255-3463
General advertising

(D22)
Wm. Morford
RD#2
Cazenovia, NY 13035
(315) 662-7625; FAX (315) 662-3570
General advertising

(D23)
Paper Pile Quarterly
Ada Fitzsimmons
P.O. Box 337
San Anselmo, CA 94979-0337
Paper collectibles

(D24)
John and Sheri Pavone
29 Sullivan Rd.
Peru, NY 12972
(518) 643-8152
General advertising

(D25)
Judy Posner Collectibles
RD #1 Box 273
Effort, PA 18330
(717) 629-6583 FAX (717) 629-0521
Black Americana

(D26)
Postcards International
Martin J. Shapiro
P.O. Box 2930
New Haven, CT 06515
(203) 865-0814
Vintage postcards

(D27)
Jim Rash
135 Alder Ave.
Pleasantville, NJ 08232
(609) 646-4125
Dolls and figures

(D28)
Bill Retskin
P.O. Box 18481
Ashville, NC 28814
(704) 254-4487
Matchcovers and related ephemera

(D29)
Don Shelly
P.O. Box 11
Fitchville, CT 06334
(203) 887-6163
Bread end labels

(D30)
Signs of Age
Robert and Louise Marshall
115-117 Pine St.
Catasauqua, PA 18032
(215) 264-8986
Signs

(D31)
Steve Sourapas
810 W. Blaine St.
Seattle, WA 98119
Hires Root Beer

(D32)
Craig and Donna Stifter
P.O. Box 6514
Naperville, IL 60540
(708) 717-7949
Soft-drink collectibles

(D33)
Nate Stoller
960 Reynolds Ave.
Ripon, CA 95366
(209) 599-5933
Pre-WWII Maytag collectibles

(D34)
The Sign Sez
Larry and Nancy Werner
P.O. Box 188
Winfield, IL 60190
(708) 690-2960
Tin and porcelain signs

(D35)
Tobacco Road
Chris Cooper
Rt. 2 Box 55
Pittsburg, TX 75686
(903) 856-7286
Tobacco collectibles

(D36)
Kelly Wilson
P.O. Box 41006
2271 Pembina Hwy.
Winnipeg, Manitoba, Canada R3T-5T1
(204) 275-6438; FAX (204) 275-6438
Coca-Cola and other signs

(D37)
David Zimmerman
6834 Newtonsville Rd.
Pleasant Plain, OH 45162
(513) 625-5188
Small and sample tins

(D38)
Duane Nycz
P.O. Box 923
Soap Lake, WA 98851
(509) 246-0672
Denim-related advertising and pre-1940 tin and porcelain signs

Condition and Its Effect on Value

Condition, more than any other consideration, is very important when assessing the value of advertising collectibles. On today's market items in good to very good condition are slow to sell unless they are extremely rare. Mint or near mint examples are high.

The following criteria are generally used by most dealers and auction galleries when describing condition (corresponding numbers are sometimes used instead of letter codes; these are also given).

Mint (M) (10) — Unused, absolutely no wear, like new.

Near Mint (NM) (9) — Appears new, but on closer examination minor wear, a few very light scratches, or slight dullness can be seen.

Excellent (EX) (8) — General appearance is very pleasing with only a few very minor dents, scratches, and loss of paint to distract.

Very Good (VG) (7) — Still attractive to display, but with more defects than one in excellent condition; has some rust, pitting, and fading.

Good (G) (6) — Used, faded; has paint wear, dents, scratches, and rust. Generally not collectible unless the item is especially hard to find.

Good- (G-) (5) — Has serious problems; heavily rusted, scratched, pitted; has little if any value.

To help you arrive at values for items in conditions other than those specifically given, we suggest the following guidelines. These are only in general, and there are of course exceptions to the rule.

Using excellent as a basis, equate the same item in mint condition at 2X; NM at 1.5X; VG at ½X; and G at ¼X. For instance, an item in EX condition worth $100 used as a basis makes the same in M condition $200; NM, $150; VG, $50 (or less).

A Gettelman, tray, deep-dish, green with hand-held frothy mug encircled by product name & Milwaukee Wis on red band, G+, A19 ....$10.00

A Michaels Perique Mixture, tin, green with product lettering & graphics, 5x3½x2½", EX, A18................$50.00

A No 1 Chocolates, sign, cardboard, yellow with red Assorted Penny Goods surrounded by molded chocolate forms, 11x9", rare, G-, A2.....................$170.00

A No 1 Marshmallows, tin, pictures child's hand with mouse on each fingertip, rhyme above, hinged lid, ca 1910, 6x4x2", VG+, A3.....................................$110.00

A Paul & Co Resilient Mainsprings, tin, flat, gold & yellow with lettering & image of coiled spring, rectangular, rounded corners, ¾x2¾x5", EX, D37 ....$40.00

A Raymond & Co Mens Outfitters, letter folder, tin, Adam & Eve on 1 side & New York men's clothier descriptions on reverse, 12x3", G+, A9............................$155.00

A&P, trade card, 'Birds Tea Party,' multicolored litho, 1885, EX, D6...$50.00

A&P, see also Atlantic & Pacific Tea Co

A&W Root Beer, baby mug, glass, red logo with solid circle, A&W Ice Cold Root Beer Trade Mark..., M, D16 ....$10.00

A&W Root Beer, baby mug, plastic, brown oval logo, NM, D16...$10.00

A&W Root Beer, coupon, round logo left of product name & advertising, 2x3", NM, A7.............................$10.00

A&W Root Beer, mug, glass with applied label, A&W Ice Cold Root Beer, black, red & white, NM, D16 ....$10.00

A-Merry-Christmas, cigar box label, outer, encircled portrait of Old St Nick, VG, A5............................$135.00

A-Penn Motor Oil, can, Guaranteed 2500 Miles on speedometer in center, red, cream & black, screw cap & handle, 2-gal, 11x8", VG+, A6 ....$10.00

A-Treat Finer Beverages, sign, die-cut cardboard, product name on banner above reindeer pulling Santa in sleigh, 22x28", EX, D30...$50.00

A-Treat Finer Beverages, sign, porcelain, Take Home A-Treat Finer Beverages, It's A Treat & glass on circle at top, 10x20", EX+, D30 ....$120.00

A-Treat Finer Beverages, sign, tin flange, Take Home A-Treat Finer Beverages, It's A Treat & glass on circle at top, 14x18", NM, D30..$145.00

A-1 Pilsner Beer, sign, glass, Authorized Dealer above product name & eagle, One Of America's... below on cloud-like field, 15x21", EX, A8...........................$185.00

A-1 Pilsner Beer, tray, deep-dish, Judged The Finest, medals on circular band, ...Pilsner A Premium Beer & eagle above, 13" dia, NM, A8 ....$40.00

A-1 Premium Beer, menu board, The Western Way To Say Welcome & product name on red with western symbols above board, 24x16", NM, A19....................$35.00

AA-1 Motor Oil, can, product name on front & various vehicles on sides, shades of silver on blue, 1-qt, rare, EX, A1..$500.00

AAA Campground, sign, porcelain, Approved above triple-A logo, oval, 2-sided, 23x30", NM+, D11...........$175.00

AAA Emergency Service, sign, porcelain, AAA on oval center, Emergency Service above & below, blue & white, oval, 17x22½", EX, A6 ....$90.00

AAA Emergency Service, sign, porcelain, inverted triangle with rounded corners, red, white & blue, 2-sided, 28x26", VG, A1 ....$50.00

AB Chase Piano, bookmark, celluloid, multicolored carnation at top, 5", EX+, A11 ....$10.00

Abaco Cigars, box label set, Indian in profile, 2 pcs, G, A5 ....$155.00

Abbey Rough Cut Tobacco, see Tuckett's

Abbotts Ice Cream, brush, celluloid, factory image, blue & red, 3" dia, EX, D22....................................$80.00

Abbotts Ice Cream, flavor board, tin & aluminum, woman in profile & product name in oval atop row of 11 flavor slots, 29x12½", EX+, A1 ....$45.00

ABC Beer, sign, reverse-painted glass, Thank You, Please Pay When Served... in silver on red & black panels, 12x20", VG, A8 ....$75.00

ABC Beer, tray, stamped aluminum, product name above & below initial logo, 15" dia, G, A8..........................$40.00

ABC Beer, see also American Brewing Co

ABC Oil Burners, sign, die-cut cast metal, ABC in bold letters on flames above Oil Burners in silver letters, 8x11", EX, A6..$150.00

AC Fire Ring Spark Plugs, clock, plastic, bold product name surrounds Change Now & numbers, black, orange, yellow & cream, 16" dia, VG, A6...........$150.00

AC Fire Ring Spark Plugs, radio, Admiral, red, white & blue, 5½x9½", EX+, A6.......................................$120.00

AC Oil Filters, towel dispenser, metal, product name in circle above Keep Oil Clean, yellow & black, 8x8", VG+, A6 ....$25.00

AC Spark Plug Cleaning Station, sign, die-cut tin flange, winking horse taking a shower atop Registered... & spark plug graphic, 15x11", VG, A6....................**$190.00**

AC Spark Plugs, display rack, metal wire cage holds 2 spark plugs, yellow, red & white sign reads These Birds Were Caught..., 7", EX, A6.................................**$185.00**

AC Spark Plugs, sign, embossed tin, Ask For..., orange, blue & cream, 13x41", VG, A6 ....**$120.00**

AC Spark Plugs, sign, tin, product name on circle below spark plug graphic, 18x10", M, D11.......................**$75.00**

AC 1075 for Fords, display, metal canister shape, Ask For..., yellow, orange, cream & blue, cardboard guide on back, 12x11" dia, EX+, A6.............................**$650.00**

Ace Combs, display case, wood with 3 mirrored sides & 7 decals, 14", G+, A13......................................**$85.00**

Ace CX2 Motor Oil, can, red, white & black, 5½x4" dia, 1-qt, NM, A6...**$30.00**

Ace High Cocoa, tin, sample, shows airplane, rectangular, EX, D37...**$120.00**

Ace High Motor Oil, can, product name with race car & plane against clouds on 'sunburst' oval, red, white & blue, 1-qt, NM, A1...**$300.00**

Ace High Motor Oil, can, product name with race car & plane against clouds on 'sunburst' oval, red, white & blue, 5-qt, VG, A6 ....**$70.00**

Ace High Motor Oils, sign, Ace High & 100% Pure logo above car & airplane flanked by 35¢ Per Quart, framed, 21½x40", rare, G, A6..........................**$385.00**

Ace Motor Oil, can, Ace above gas station scene, Ace of the Hi-Way & Motor Oil below, blue & white, 1-qt, EX, A1...**$405.00**

Ace Motor Oil, can, red, white & black, 5½x4" dia, 1-qt, NM, A6..**$135.00**

Ace Stores, sign, porcelain, airplane & white lettering on green, yellow & red emblem, 3650 Southport Ave..., 16x48", NM, D8......................................**$1,125.00**

Ace Wil-Flo 10W-30 Motor Oil, can, red, blue, green & brown graphics with car, red & white lettering, 5½x4" dia, 1-qt, NM, A6..**$110.00**

Acme Beer, calendar, 1944, cardboard stand-up, illuminated lady with glass above full pad, company name below, 7x3", NOS, EX, A8..**$35.00**

Acme Beer, sign, cardboard hanger, product name upper right of Uncle Sam holding up full glass, Let's Go America! below, VG+, A19 ....**$125.00**

Acme Beer, sign, die-cut cardboard, America's Favorite Beer, Non Fattening, sandwich tray with 2 bottles & glasses, 26x19", G, A8..**$20.00**

Acme Beer, sign, self-framed tin over cardboard, octagonal shape with game birds hanging above bottle & glass, EX, A8 ....**$275.00**

Acme Beer, sign, tin, America's Favorite in script upper left of product & company name on yellow, red border, VG+, A19 ....**$105.00**

Acme Beer, tap knob, chrome with celluloid cover, red, yellow & black lettering on white, 2" dia, EX+, A8 ....**$75.00**

Acme Bull Dog Ale, can, flat-top, rolled, 12-oz, EX, A19 ....**$25.00**

Acme Bulldog Beer, bottle stopper, plaster, molded bulldog head with red embossed Bulldog Beer, VG+, A8 ..**$25.00**

Acme Light Beer, label, Light above Acme on wood sign, Healthfull Beverage on ribbon over colorful image, 21-oz, EX, A19 ....**$20.00**

Acme No 2 Repair Kit, tin, Bonus Brand logo left of product name, decorative border, rectangular, rounded corners, ½x2¼x3½", EX, D37...........................**$100.00**

Acme Pickles, jar, stoneware, barrel shape, J Weller Co arched above product name, Cincinnati Ohio below, late 1800s, 13", VG, A6......................................**$90.00**

Acme Quality Motor Car Finishes, sign, celluloid over tin, stand-up, man brush-painting Ford car, color samples below, 1910, 14½x10", VG, A1....................**$220.00**

Acorn Brand Peanut Butter, pail, acorn surrounded by product name in center, gold background, press lid & bail, 1-lb, EX, D22....................................**$125.00**

Acorn Stoves, sign, embossed tin, facsimile of actual warranty issued with stove when purchased, 13½x19½", VG, A21..**$60.00**

Acrobat, strip label, citrus, acrobat & dog, M, D3........**$2.00**

Action 5¢ Cigar, pocket mirror, tin with paper insert, Smoke...Seed & Havana Long Filled, white on blue, round, EX, A11...**$35.00**

Adam Scheidt Brewing Co, match safe, Lotos Export in red, black & gold on green on cream, brewery in script & brands on reverse, EX, A8 ....**$110.00**

Adam Scheidt Brewing Co, see also Valley Forge Special Beer

Adams Assorted Tutti-Frutti Chewing Gum, printer's proof, Victorian boy eyeing gum display through store window, 1880, 14x11", EX+, A3.........................**$165.00**

Adams Black Jack Chewing Gum, ad card, 1880s, Belle of the South on front, various gum products & medical testimonials on back, EX, D23 ....**$100.00**

Adams Spearmint Chewing Gum, display box, tin, depicts gum packs on all 4 sides with product name & 'Chicle' logo, green, white & black, 6x7", EX, A2 ....**$385.00**

Adams Sweet Fern Chewing Gum, box, product name above & below bust image of smiling girl, 9x4½", VG, A7...**$190.00**

Adams Tutti-Frutti Pepsin Gum, sign, die-cut cardboard, Chew... arched above elegant girl surrounded with flowers, 14x10", NM, A9.................................**$2,100.00**

Adirondacks, cigar box label, outer, sepia & white image of deer herd, early, 4½x4½", EX, D5....................**$40.00**

Admiral Appliances, bank, George Washington-type figure, vinyl, 1980s, 7", M, D27...............................**$20.00**

Admiral Rough Cut, tin, round with product name above & below encircled admiral, ship beyond, gold trim, knob lid, NM, A18...**$245.00**

Admiration Cigars, sign, plaster, product name above winking moon face with cigar, Mild & Mellow To The Last Inch below, 15x11", VG, A9..........**$275.00**

Adolph Betz Farm Implements Buggies, sign, embossed die-cut, girl looking through diagonal gold frame with floral decoration, framed, 17x13", EX, A8.........$100.00

Adolphus Busch, dance program, Golden Wedding Anniversary, embossed A & eagle logo with oval bust portraits, March 7, 1911, VG+, A8......................**$140.00**

Advance Machinery Dealers, sign, farm scenes, The Golden Grain Of A Continent From An Advance Thresher To The Sea, 1895, framed, 22x28", EX, A3 ....**$330.00**

Advance Thresher Co, match safe, celluloid, features Advance Compound Traction Engine, black & white, 2¾x1½", EX, A11 ....**$140.00**

Aerio Gas, gas globe, product name above & below airplane ready to land, green rippled Gill body, 13½" dia, rare, NM+, A6...**$8,500.00**

Aero Club Pale Select Beer, can, cone-top, logo above Aero Club in script on center band, Pale Select (in script) Beer below, unopened, EX+, A8...............**$25.00**

Aero Eastern Motor Oil, can, Super Refined above encircled airplane & product name, 2500 Mile Guarantee below, 1-qt, round, NM, A1...............................**$245.00**

Aero Eastern Motor Oil, can, Super Refined above encircled airplane & product name, 2500 Mile Guarantee below, screw cap, 2-gal, 11x8", EX, A6 ....**$200.00**

Aero Mayflower Transit Co, display, counter-top, light-up, golden oak case with colored glass front, lettering above moving van, 23x17x6", NM, A6 ....$600.00

Aero Mfg Co Windmills, salesman's sample, tin replica of windmill with red name & trim, 18", M, A2 ....**$250.00**

Aero Motor Oil, can, Super Refined & plane above product name on oval, 2500 Mile Guarantee below, 1-qt, EX, A1..**$150.00**

Aero Motor Oil, can, Super Refined & plane above product name on oval, 2500 Mile Guarantee below, 2-gal, VG+, A6...**$100.00**

Aeroshell Lubricating Oil, sign, die-cut porcelain, winged shell atop sign, ...Stocked Here, 2-sided, 15x28", rare, EX+, A6...**$1,600.00**

Aeroshell Oil, can, product name above winged Shell logo, cream, red & yellow, 1-qt, EX+, A1.............**$90.00**

Aetna Brewing Co, tray, porcelain, red & blue circular logo left of company name on white, blue trim, oval, 11x14", EX+, A19...**$205.00**

Aetna Dynamite, paperweight/mirror, celluloid, pictures large stick of dynamite, 3" dia, EX, D22 ....**$190.00**

Aetna Insurance Co, sign, paper, trademark image of Mt Vesuvius erupting on fancy oval inset, Stobridge Litho Co, 25x31", G, A9..**$250.00**

Aetna Life Insurance Co, scorekeeper, celluloid, mechanical, Play Games & Enjoy Life at top, red & black, 1½x3", EX, A11...**$30.00**

Aetna Life Insurance Co, stamp holder, circular logo above ...Hartford Conn, Accident, Health & Liability Insurance, blue & red, 2x1", EX, A11...................**$35.00**

Africora, cigar box label, outer, woman walking through jungle, 1905, 4½x4½", M, D5 ....**$3.00**

Agalion Motor Oil, can, lion's face on square inset above product name, Northern Oil & Fuel Corp, screw cap & handle, 1-gal, 11x8", EX, A6 ....**$325.00**

Agency Tansill's Punch 5¢ Cigar, sign, embossed tin, trademark image of caricatured Punch head, 23½" dia, rare, G-, A9...**$650.00**

Air Float Talcum Powder, tin, sample, name above & below floral oval portrait of lady, red & green on white, ¾x1¼x2", EX, D37 ....$120.00

Air Race/Deep-Rock Aviation Quality Motor Oil, can, Air Race above plane, Motor Oil with Deep-Rock in curved letters below, off-white, red, blue & gold, 1-qt, VG+, A1 ....**$170.00**

Air Race/Deep-Rock Motor Oil, can, Air Race above plane, Motor Oil with Deep-Rock in curved letters below, yellow, white, red & blue, 1-qt, VG+, A1..................**$160.00**

Air-India, display, composition, bowing figure in native costume on carpet lettered Air-India, 12", EX, A8 ....**$40.00**

Airline 41, tap knob, black ball with blue on orange metal insert, VG+, A8................................**$280.00**

Airship, crate label, California orange, old 4-prop commercial plane on royal blue, Fillmore Citrus Assoc, 1940s, 10x11", M, D3..........................**$15.00**

Airway Motor Oil, can, sea plane above oval Airway logo, Motor Oil below, green, yellow & black, 1-qt, EX+, A1.....................**$480.00**

Ajax Cleanser, container, sample, cardboard & tin, lady on her knees with sign reading New Type Foaming Cleanser..., 2-oz, EX, D37.....................**$18.00**

Akerley Hair Brush, sign, tin, large hair brush flanked by lettering in center, encircled woman in upper left, 9x9", EX, A9.....................**$300.00**

Akron Brewing Co, sign, shows factory scene through black shading, name & triangle logo below, ornate wood frame, 22½x31", NM, A19..........**$500.00**

Akron Sewer Pipe Co, letter folder, tin, factory scene on 1 side, various products on reverse, Somero's Rose, 10½x3", G+, A9.....................**$150.00**

Al's Lager Beer, label, Bloomer Brewery Inc, Internal Revenue Tax Paid statement, 1933-50, 64-oz, M, A10.....................**$15.00**

Alabama National AA Motor Club, sign, porcelain, elongated diamond shape, diamond flanked by stars in center, 2-sided, 17x23", NM+, D11.............**$125.00**

Alabama Stean Baking Co, calendar, 1908, die-cut caricature image of baker dumping a variety of breads & muffins into basket, 12x8", EX, D38...........**$250.00**

Aladdin Redi-Cut Homes, catalog, 1936, 64 pgs, EX, D17.....................**$50.00**

Alaska Lager Beer, label, Pilsener Brewing Co of Alaska, U-type permit number, Internal Revenue Tax Paid, 1933-36, 11-oz, M, A10.....................**$22.00**

Alber's Flapjack Flour, container, sample, cardboard, round with product name on black bands above & below round image, slip lid, EX, A18.............**$120.00**

Aldens, catalog, Christmas, 1950, EX, D17.............**$100.00**

Alexander Kielland, crate label, Washington apple, 2 red apples on green background, yellow logo, Cashmere, 9x11", M, D12.....................**$12.00**

Alhambra Casinos, sign, cardboard, Very Mild Imported Hand Made above product name & open box with 5¢ over tropical scene, 36x27", VG+, A1.............**$20.00**

Alice Foote MacDougall Coffee, tin, product name above silhouette portrait on emblem, lined background, 1-lb, EX+, A3.....................**$65.00**

Alka-Seltzer, bank, Speedy, vinyl, 1960s, 5", EX, D27..**$250.00**

Alka-Seltzer, dispenser, metal & plastic with cardboard sign behind bottle picturing Speedy & Bless That... on oval, 17x8", NM, A1.....................**$275.00**

Alka-Seltzer, figure, Speedy, vinyl, 1960s, 8", M, D27..**$500.00**

Alka-Seltzer, figure, Speedy, vinyl, 1960s, 8", VG, A21..**$245.00**

Alka-Seltzer, sign, reverse glass with silver & gold foil, silver Alka-Seltzer above gold Be Wise — Alkalize on black, 10x18", EX, A2.....................**$175.00**

"Listen to it Fizz"

Alka-Seltzer, sign, self-framed cardboard, 'Listen to it Fizz,' elderly gent with glass of Alka-Seltzer, 29x30", EX, A6.....................$130.00

All American Draught Beer, label, Columbus Brewing Co, U-type permit number, Internal Revenue Tax Paid statement, 1933-36, 1/2-gal, NM, A10...........**$12.00**

All American 2500 Mile Motor Oil, can, product name above & below map of North America, Deco-style border with cars, pour spout & handle, 2-gal, EX, A1........**$40.00**

All Jacks Cigarettes, sign, metal, All Jacks above open pack, Hard To Beat below, 3-color background, red, black & gold, 14x10", EX+, A8.............**$45.00**

All Year, crate label, California lemon, palm trees over fertile valley with purple hills beyond, Fillmore, 9x12", M, D12.....................**$4.00**

Allcock's Porous Plaster, newspaper ad, New York Herald, December 5, 1895, 2 black women using product on children's backs, 12x15½", G, A9...........**$95.00**

Allen & Ginter Tobacco, sign, paper, American Indian... & Indian hunting buffalo surrounded by 50 portraits, framed, image: 29x21", rare, G, A9.............**$1,100.00**

Allen & Ginter's Cigarettes, insert cards, Flags of All Nations series, 1887, set of 11, all VG-EX, A5......**$25.00**

Allen & Ginter's Cigarettes, insert cards, World Champion Billiard Players series, 1888, set of 5, all G-EX, A5..**$95.00**

Allen & Ginter's Dixie Cigarettes, insert card, features actress Marie Pierval, 1887, G, A5.............**$8.00**

Allen & Ginter's Imperial Cube Smoking Mixture, canister, portrait at left of lettering & scroll design, round, NM, A3.....................**$25.00**

Allen Bros Co, store bin, pictures black workers picking coffee beans & leading mule cart flanked by coffee branches, VG+, A3.....................**$385.00**

Allen's (Steel Cut) Coffee & Dainty Tea, toy airplane, Airking JR8 Monoplane, balsa with rubber band launcher, advertising on wings, 1930s, NMIB, A3 ....$90.00

Allen's Ice Cream, tray, stock image of kids eating ice cream & little girl feeding dog with spoon, lettering on rim, 13½" dia, G, A9 ....$130.00

Allen's Red Tame Cherry, drinking glasses, set of 12 with flared tops & name etched on each, includes original box, NM, A13 ....$525.00

Alliance Girl, tobacco tag, embossed, large, EX, D35..$5.00

Allied Mills Inc, sign, porcelain, red & white striped feed sack with black silhouette of soldier on horse, 34x21", EX, A6 ....$250.00

Allied Van Lines, doll, Buddy Lee, green uniform & hat with red patches, EX, A13 ....$300.00

Allis-Chalmers, watch fob, nickel-plated, shaped like front of tractor, M, A20 ....$65.00

Allstate Tire, menu board, embossed lettering & tire image above Today's Special on chalkboard, 1930s, 35x22½", VG, A6 ....$75.00

Almond Smash, sign, die-cut cardboard, Drink Almond Smash surrounded by floral wreath above It's Good!, 11x13", NM, D30 ....$18.00

Alpen Brau, foam scraper, blue & red on ivory, EX, A8..$35.00

Alpine Coffee/Nestle Product, tin, Alpine scene with houses in center, EX, A3.......................................$50.00

Alt Heidelberg, sign, celluloid, Alt Heidelberg, Here's To You, uniformed man with tankard on half circle, 9", G, A8 ....$50.00

Alta Crest Farms Certified Milk, sign, porcelain, No Milk Can Be Too Good For Your Baby...Ask Your Doctor-He Knows, white on blue, 6x18", EX+, A13.............$240.00

Alta Crest Farms Certified Milk, sign, porcelain, No Milk Can Be Too Good For Your Baby...Ask Your Doctor-He Knows, white on blue, 6x18", M, A1 ....$400.00

Alta Ginger Ale, sign, self-framed tin, girl in green dress pointing to ad, 19½x13½", EX+, A9 ....$1,000.00

Altes Lager, sign, cardboard, Enjoy Aged-In Sealed-In Flavor above Altes Lager left of bottle & glass, 1940s, framed, 12x17", EX, A8 ....$60.00

Altweiser Pale Beer/Auto City Brewing Co, label, product name above & below Conestoga wagon, company name on black band below, 12-oz, EX+, A19 ....$12.00

Alumni Burley Cut, pocket tin, vertical, concave, white with gold lid, name above & below red oval image of graduate, rare, NM, A18..................................$1,935.00

Amalie Motor Oil, clock, metal & glass, Amalie on oval in center, product cans at 12-3-6-9, red, black & white, 15" dia, NM, A6...$275.00

Amalie Motor Oil, sign, porcelain, product name & 100% Pure logo on emblem, red, white & black, 2-sided, EX, A6..$325.00

Amalie Motorcycle Oil, can, waxed cardboard, oval product name on checkered flag above motorcycle rider, 1-qt, 5½x4" dia, NM, A6......................................$40.00

Amalie Outboard Oil, chalkboard & sign, tin, product name & can above chalkboard, The Oiler Oil below, red, white & black, 22x17", NM, D8 ....$250.00

Amalie Pennsylvania Motor Oil, display rack, product name on oval in center of red, white & black sign above rack, 38", VG, A6..$20.00

Amami Bouquet Talcum, tin, sample, name flanks girl looking up, shaker top, ¾x1¼x2⅛", EX, D37 ....$100.00

Ambassador Beer, sign, Becco, Ambassador Escort Brewed Beer In Bottles, red, blue & gold, curved corners, 7x10", EX, A8..$25.00

America Dry Ginger Ale, sign, embossed tin, Ask For...Best Ginger Ale Your Money Can Buy, tilted bottle at right, 14x29", G, A6...$30.00

America's Pride Beer, label, Terre Haute Brewing Co, U-type permit number, Internal Revenue Tax Paid statement, 1933-36, 12-oz, M, A10 ....$20.00

American Ace Coffee, tin, bust image of pilot with coffee cup at left of product name, blue background, key-wind lid, 1-lb, NM, A3 ....$275.00

American Airlines, sign, porcelain, trademark eagle in center, red, white & blue, 10" dia, NM, D22 ......$225.00

American Automobile & Supply Co, catalog, 1920, 100 pgs, EX, D17 ....$75.00

American Beauty Fine Mixture, tin, cream with product name & red rose, red decorative border, rectangular with rounded corners, EX, A18 ....$60.00

American Br'wg Co/ABC Bohemian, trade card, 3 women & a man pop-up from box with company & product name on front, patriotic logo on side, 1894, VG+, A8 ....$75.00

American Brew Co Beer & Ales, sign, embossed tin & reverse-painted glass, Statue of Liberty at right of lettering, framed, image: 24x36", EX+, A9 ....$750.00

American Brewing Co, drinking glass, stem with embossed eagle & shield logo, NM, A8................$45.00

American Brewing Co/St Louis ABC Beers, mug, ceramic, company name above patriotic eagle logo, product name below, EX, A8 ....$275.00

American Central Insurance Co/Saint Louis, sign, brass, Automobile Insurance arched above company name & early car, 10x14", NM, D8.............................$1,300.00

American Central Life Insurance Co, pocket mirror, company name & lettering surrounded by birthstone border, round, EX, A20 ....$30.00

American Chewing Tobacco, box, small rectangular silver-tone metal with embossed name above & below eagle on lid, 1x1¾x3½", EX, A18 ....$50.00

American Crown, cigar box label, salesman's sample, patriotic image with crown, sword & shield, VG, A5 ....$65.00

American Deluxe Coffee, tin, product name on shield flanked by lettering, National Tea Co, key-wind lid, NM, A3 ....$30.00

American Eagle Fire Insurance Co, sign, tin, eagle atop US map with company name in black, wood frame, 26½x20½", EX, A6 ....$875.00

American Eagle Tobacco, pocket tin, sample, flat, dark blue, canted corners, EX, A18 ....$85.00

American Eagle Tobacco, pocket tin, sample, flat, green, diagonal corners, VG+, A18.........................$65.00

American Exports, cigar box label, outer, eagle & Statue of Liberty, VG, A5 ....$65.00

American Express, clock, reverse-painted glass, square with circular clock image, American Express Money Orders Sold Here, 13x13", EX, A18.....................$165.00

American Flyer Lines, toy water tower, tin, EX, D6 ..$70.00

American Gas, post lamp, cast iron with red, white & blue lens, 1930s, 32x17", EX, A6 ....$600.00

American Gasoline & Motor Oils, sign, metal, patriotic shield flanked by Sunlight Kerosene & Motor Oils, 100% Pure... below, 10½x35", VG, A6................$225.00

American Home, cigar box label, outer, large home with people on front porch, 1895, EX, A5 ....$85.00

American Home Fresh Roasted Coffee, tin, product name above & below house image on paper label, pry lid, 1920s, 1-lb, EX+, A15.................................$190.00

American Interinsurance Exchange, basset hound figure with plaque, plastic, Breyer, 7½", NM $25.00

American Lady Shoe, sign, reverse glass, name in gold script shadowed in black on green above $3. $3.50 $4. Shoe, gold frame, 9x37", EX, A2 ....$230.00

American Lager Beer, label, Congress Brewing Co Ltd, pre-prohibition, M, A10 ....$20.00

American Line, pocket mirror, lettering above & below ocean liner, round, VG+, A8 ....$50.00

American Line, tip tray, lettered & decorative border around image of steamship, round, EX, A18......$145.00

American Maid, crate label, California pear, blue silhouette of lady in bonnet on orange background, 8x11", M, D12.$2.00

American Mills Mocha & Java Coffee/JS Silvers & Bro, tin, cream with product lettering around Samson opening lion's mouth, rectangular with rounded corners, 4x6x4", NM, A18...$200.00

American Queen Shoes, pocket mirror, celluloid, multi-colored image of a woman, oval, EX+, A11.......$160.00

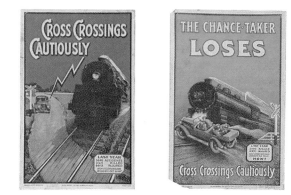

American Railway Association, poster, paper, Cross Crossings Cautiously & lightning bolt above car approaching train, 1928, 22x14", EX+, A1 ...$310.00

American Railway Association, poster, paper, The Chance-Taker Loses above image of touring car trying to beat speeding train, 1929, 22x14", VG, A1 ...$220.00

American Red Cross, poster, nurse reaching out above Join American Red Cross & cross symbol, flood disaster scene beyond, 30x20", NM, A1.............................$80.00

American Rubbers, sign, die-cut cardboard hanger, elegant girl draped in banner on swing, gray, white, brown & pink, 1900, 25x12", VG, A6.................$150.00

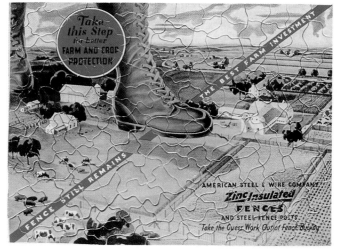

American Steel & Wire Co, jigsaw puzzle, Take This Step For Better Farm & Crop Protection, giant boots walking over farmland, 1933, 9x12", EX, D10 ....$65.00

American Steel & Wire Company's Banner Steel Posts, sign, tin, post at left of We Sell above company & product name, The Post With A Backbone at bottom, 24x11", EX, A1...$32.00

American Stores Co, sign, 'The Younger Generation,' farm scene with little boy showing girl a chick, framed, 18x14", EX, A6 ....$90.00

American Stores Co Asco Coffee, sign, paper, oval image of girl with thoroughbred, plantation scenes in corners, ca 1930, framed, 14x11", NM, A3 ....$110.00

American Suspender Company, box label, harnessed circus elephant tearing up tree trunk, 7½x15½", VG+, A9 ....$175.00

American Telephone & Telegraph Co & Associated Companies, sign, flange, name around bell marked Local & Long Distance Telephone, Bell System below, blue & white, 18", EX, A8 ....$165.00

American Wringer Co, display rack, wood with black lettering, 54x14x5", G, A6 ....$35.00

American-Maid Bread, fan, die-cut cardboard, woman with pink, green & blue hat, 9x8½", EX, A6 ....$30.00

Americana Grapes, lug box label, ornate blue lettering on red, white & blue banner, Kettleman, M, D12 ....$2.00

Amherst Stoves & Furnaces, paperweight, glass, Amherst above stove flanked by Stoves & Furnaces, Buffalo Cooperative Stove Co, rectangular, M, D13 ....$65.00

Ammens Powder, tin, sample, with contents, 2¾", NM, A7 ....$12.00

Amoco Anti-Freeze, thermometer, porcelain & tin, Amoco in white on blue band with red oval background in center, oval, 11x15", EX+, A1 ....$350.00

Amoco 586, bank, can shape, 2¼" dia, NM, A7 ....$15.00

Amortia, tin, pictures sailboat, horizontal rectangle, VG+, A18 ....$55.00

Amrico Violet Talcum Powder, tin, product name with floral image, slanted sides, shaker top, EX+, A18 ....$70.00

Amstutz Hatcheries, sign, porcelain in iron holder, chicks & company name above Pedigreed Sired Chicks, St Johns Mich, 28x30", EX, A6 ....$75.00

Anchor Brand Clothes Wringers, display rack, wood with black lettering & anchor, 57x17", EX, A6 .....$30.00

Anchor Brand Clothes Wringers, replica of clothes wringer, wood & metal with rubber wringers, fully functional, 7½" wide, VG+, A21.........................$330.00

Anchor Nutmeg, can, tin & cardboard, product name above & below encircled anchor, 2¾", NM, A7...$25.00

Anderson Equipment, catalog, 1950, 365 pgs, EX, D17..$50.00

Anderson-Prichard, gas globe, Challenge on center circle, red, white & blue, plastic body, 13½" dia, NM+, A6 ....$130.00

Andes Stoves & Ranges, sign, tin, ...Best On Earth, orange & black lettering, 7x20", EX, A6 ....$40.00

Andrew Curtin 5¢ Cigar, sign, cardboard hanger, oval with Agency For... above portrait, 5¢ Cigar & company name below, 2-sided, 9x12", EX, A8 ....$45.00

Andrews' American Queen, sign, paper, 'Society News of the Continent,' vignettes of ships, polo players, lawn tennis, etc, 1881, 16x22", VG, A9 ....$400.00

Angelus Marshmallows, pocket mirror, cherub with trumpet & product, oval, 3", EX+, A3 ....$60.00

Angola Maid, cigar box label, printer's proof, colorful image of maiden surrounded with scroll design, NM, A5 ....$45.00

Anheuser-Busch, ashtray, copper, irregular shape made for cigars with embossed A & eagle logo, 6½", VG+, A8 ....$95.00

Anheuser-Busch, booklet, 'Epoch Marking Events Of American History,' historical paintings & fold-out factory scene, 1914, 24 pgs, VG, A8 ....$50.00

Anheuser-Busch, bottle, amber, embossed eagle with wings tucked in A, applied crown top, EX, A8..$45.00

Anheuser-Busch, bottle, amber, embossed early eagle with wings extended from A, Consumers... embossed on back, applied crown top, VG, A8..................$30.00

Anheuser-Busch, bridge set, leather-type Amity case holds 2 decks of cards, score pad & 2 cases of miniature bottles, 1973, VG+, A8...$50.00

Anheuser-Busch, charm bracelet, gold-plated A & eagle charm with rhinestones, gold-plated chain, EX, A8.............$100.00

Anheuser-Busch, cigar cutter/corkscrew, Compliments of... on reverse, with 2 blades, G+, A8...............$100.00

Anheuser-Busch, corkscrew, metal bottle shape, 2¾", EX, A6 ....$75.00

Anheuser-Busch, desk plaque, metal A & eagle logo atop wood base, commemorating 50 million barrels, EX, A8 ....$100.00

Anheuser-Busch, drinking glass, stemmed goblet, dimple & facet design with embossed name (no hyphen), 7", rare, NM, A8 ....$260.00

Anheuser-Busch, drinking glass, straight-sided with pink-toned etched A & eagle logo, 3½", NM, A8 ....$65.00

Anheuser-Busch, lighter, embossed barrel shape with A & eagle logo, Ceramarte, EX, A8.........................$245.00

Anheuser-Busch, mug, Budweiser girl on oval with filigree border, 3 different versions, EX, A8, each..........$535.00

Anheuser-Busch, mug, embossed clear glass, slight barrel shape with thick fluted bottom, eagle with both wings in wide A, 5", NM, A8 ....$65.00

Anheuser-Busch, mug, embossed clear glass, straight-sided with thick fluted bottom, eagle with both wings in narrow A, 5", EX+, A8 ....$60.00

Anheuser-Busch, note holder, brass with embossed A & eagle logo, 6x4", EX, A8 ....$40.00

Anheuser-Busch, plate, buxom lady encircled by decorative border, 10" dia, EX, A19 ....$90.00

Anheuser-Busch, plate, pewter, stamped A & eagle logo in center, raised 2-banded rim, 9½", VG, A8........$40.00

Anheuser-Busch, plate, shows the Champion Clydsdale team on white background, Sabin China, 9" dia, EX+, A8 ....$50.00

Anheuser-Busch, pocketknife, 2 blades, corkscrew & opener, features stanhope & Adophus Busch, dated Jan 1, 1900, VG, A8 ....$415.00

Anheuser-Busch, pocketknife, 2 blades & corkscrew, company name on 1 side, embossed A & eagle logo on reverse, VG, A8 ....$100.00

Anheuser-Busch, postcards, 'The Relief Train,' 'Attack on the Emigrant Train' or 'The Father of Waters,' VG+, A8, each..$45.00

Anheuser-Busch, print, 'Custer's Last Fight,' panoramic image of General & troops, 1896, original frame, image: 30x40", VG+, A9 ....$675.00

Anheuser-Busch, print, paper litho, pictures rider leading pack mules along trail at water's edge, matted & framed, VG+, A19................**$85.00**

Anheuser-Busch, print, pictures the Budweiser team coming through arched gate on Grants Farm, framed, 20x30", EX, A8................**$105.00**

Anheuser-Busch, salt & papper shakers, ceramic, white stein shape with A & eagle logo, NM, A8.............**$25.00**

Anheuser-Busch, sign, cardboard, Budweiser Girl above golden image of draped nude on rock with A & eagle emblem, 28½x15½", G, A21 ....$120.00

Anheuser-Busch, sign, paper, Budweiser Girl in red dress standing in front of tree, 1907, matted & framed, image: 28x14", EX+, A9................**$600.00**

Anheuser-Busch, sign, tin hanger, Anheuser-Busch arched above A & eagle logo above cherubs with different brands, oval, VG, A8................**$220.00**

Anheuser-Busch, stein, 35-year safety stein with A & eagle logo, company name below, 15", M, A8................**$340.00**

Anheuser-Busch, trade card, Crowned Again above allegorical factory scene, A & eagle logo with 1898 gold medals & text, 7x4½", VG, A8................**$90.00**

Anheuser-Busch, see also Adophus Busch, Bevo, Budweiser, or Cotton Club Syrup

Anheuser-Busch Brewing Ass'n, token, penny size with A & eagle logo & date, company name on reverse, 1880, EX, A8 ....**$75.00**

Anheuser-Busch Brewing Ass'n, tray, A & eagle logo encircled by red band with company name & city, decorative border, round, G+, A19................**$210.00**

Anheuser-Busch Brewing Ass'n, tray, colorful image of Victory surrounded by cherubs holding variety of products, oval, 13½x16½", EX, A6................**$650.00**

Anheuser-Busch Incorporated/Budweiser, tray, repro of 100 Years Anniversary, 3 oval portraits on labeled ribbon above vignettes, 13x19", NM, A19................**$40.00**

Anheuser-Busch Malt Nutrine, bottle, amber with front & back label, side label reads Pure Food & Drug Act of 1906, VG, A8 ....**$100.00**

Anheuser-Busch Malt Nutrine, sign, tin, oval image of draped nude with oversized bottle & cherubs, self-framed, 26x18", G+, A21................**$440.00**

Anheuser-Busch Malt Nutrine, sign, tin on cardboard, 'A Hurry Call,' doctor in buggy following stork in flight, 8x13", NM, A19................**$75.00**

Anheuser-Busch Malt Nutrine, sign, tin on cardboard, 'Coming Events Cast Their Shadows Before,' doctor on path with stork shadow, 8x13", EX, A19 ....**$55.00**

Anheuser-Busch's Malt Nutrine, sign, cardboard, nypmh at water's edge blowing horn, cherubs & birds watch, advertising on reverse, 1903, round, EX, A19 ....**$170.00**

Ann Page Allspice, tin, paper label, 2¾", NM, A7 ......**$6.00**

Anna Bacon's Millinery Store, pocket mirror, If Your Hat Pleases You, Tell Your Friends It Came From..., round, EX, A20 ....**$35.00**

Annette's Perfect Cleanser, tin, sample, ...Cannot Leave A Ring, Trial Size 10¢, shaker top, 2x1½" dia, EX, D37..**$10.00**

Annie Laurie, crate label, California orange, Scottish lassie on bright plaid background, Strathmore, 10x11", M, D3 ..**$4.00**

Ansco Camera Co, catalog, 1916, 64 pgs, EX, D17...**$50.00**

Ante-Bellum Smoking Tobacco, cigarette papers, EX, A7 ....**$150.00**

Anthony & Kuhn Beer, drinking glass, side curves in & out at middle, etched letters & logo, NM, A8.....**$110.00**

Anthony & Kuhn XXX Brewing Co St Louis, drinking glass, stem with embossed lettering, NM, A8.......**$50.00**

Anti Hi-Test Knock, gas globe lens, black & red on white, 15" dia, EX, A6................**$25.00**

Antikamnia Tablets, calendar, 1906, features 2 novice nuns with tablets, calendar & prescription information on back, framed, 10x8", EX+, A3................**$135.00**

Antique Bourbon, display, ceramic, weight lifter with arms crossed & lettered chest stands on base with bottle display, 11", EX, A8................**$20.00**

Antiseptic Ready Shavor, tin, canister type with slip lid, light green with dark green lettering, 2⅜x1½" dia, EX, D37, minimum value **$415.00**

Antler, crate label, Washington apple, 6-point buck on dark blue background, Chelan, 9x11", M, D12 ....**$10.00**

Anvil Brand Work Clothes, sign, light-up, reverse glass, product name above & below oval anvil logo, red & black on white, 1950s, 9x13", EX, A13 ....**$40.00**

AP Little Satin Finish Typewriter Ribbon, tin, flat, gray with lid appearing to be peeled back around image of black boy, square, rounded corners, EX, D37 ..$100.00

AP Little Satin Finish Typewriter Ribbon, tin, flat, orange & black with oval image of black boy, Since 1888, square, rounded corners, EX, D37 .....$100.00

Apache Trail Tobacco, tin, product name above Indian scout on horse with valley beyond, blue background, slip lid, NM, A18 ....**$2,005.00**

Apollo Chocolates, sign, porcelain, ...The Distinctive Chocolates, portrait on shield at right, 16x24", VG+, D11 ....**$225.00**

Apollo Chocolates, sign, porcelain, A Holiday's Apollo Day, silhouette image of man presenting chocolates to woman, 12x32", G+, A9.......................................$135.00

Appleton, crate label, California apple, 1915 design with Art Nouveau lady, vista & apples, Watsonville, 9x11", M, D12..$8.00

Approved Red Hat Motor Oil, can, encircled top hat logo, checked design top & bottom, cream, black & red, screw lid & handle, 1-gal, 11x8", EX+, A6..........$900.00

Arabela Cigars, sign, cardboard, By Far The Greatest... 5¢ Each, Pocket Pack Of Five 25¢, close-up of man with cigar, 11x21", EX, A18..............................$20.00

Arboleda, crate label, California lemon, surf, groves & mountains on oval in center, Goleta, 9x12", M, D12..........$3.00

Arbuckles' Ground Coffee, sign, embossed tin, product name & 'It Smells Good Daddy' flanked by dad & daughter with steaming cup, 11x27", VG+, A13 ..$475.00

Arcadia Lager Beer, label, Arcadia Brewing Co, Internal Revenue Tax Paid statement, 1933-50, 12-oz, M, A10...$10.00

Arcadia Mixture, tin, yellow with embossed & embellished lettering, rectangular, square corners, EX, A18..$25.00

Archer Household Oil, can, Indian shooting bow & arrow at top, plastic squirt top, 4-oz, 5", EX, A6.............$35.00

Archer Lubricants, can, waxed cardboard, with contents, pictures Indian with bow & arrow, 1-qt, 5½x4" dia, EX+, A6...$30.00

Archia's Seed Store Corp, pocket mirror, Bulbs, Plants & Seeds arched above large rose, round, EX, A20 ..$18.00

Arden Fresh Churned Buttermilk, sign, red Arden above black Fresh Churned & Buttermilk on wood-grain background, horizontal, EX, A3 ....$15.00

Arden Ice Cream, sign, die-cut aluminum, Arden boy in uniform carrying carton of ice cream, 36x15", NM, A1 ....$1,700.00

Argo Corn Starch, recipe booklet, 'Soup To Souffle,' 1960s, 7x4", NM, D24 ....$5.00

Argonaut Beer, label, Regal Products Co, Internal Revenue Tax Paid statement, 1933-50, 11-oz, EX, A10 ....$30.00

Arm & Hammer, tobacco tag, die-cut, red, EX, D35 ..$4.50

Arm & Hammer Baking Soda, box, red or blue label, 2-oz, NM, A7, each..$30.00

Arm & Hammer Baking Soda, sign, paper, happy black lady holding biscuit in 1 hand & product box in the other, green ground, framed, 16x25", EX, A2 ....$550.00

Arm & Hammer Baking Soda, tin, pry lid, 2-oz, NM, A7..$35.00

Arm & Hammer Soda, sign, cardboard, 1908, robin snipe standing in swamp, lettering on frame, 11½x14½", EX, A6...$70.00

Armour Star Franks, sign, light-up, boy's face above fire, Buy..., With The 'Open-Fire' Flavor!, 6x12", VG, D30...$25.00

Armour's Grape Juice, sign, self-framed tin, Drink... 100% Pure, colorful image of bottles & full glasses with snack bowl, 13x19", G, A21 ....$275.00

Armour's Lighthouse Cleanser, watch fob, lighthouse scene, contest number on reverse, oval, EX, A20...$60.00

Armour's Rolled White Oats, container, cardboard, gold with blue lettering above & below image of an elf holding stalk of grain, 3-lb, EX, A3 ....$85.00

Armour's Shield Brand Lard, sign, cardboard, I Forgot To Get above chef running in street, product & name on blue below, 1915, 30x15", EX+, A13 ....$85.00

Armour's Star Ham, pin-back button, Heads The Parade & stars on border around large star with product name, EX, A20 ....$10.00

Armour's Veribest Peanut Butter, pail, product name on oval above nursery rhyme vignettes, 1-lb, lid missing, EX+, A3 ....$80.00

Armour's Veribest Root Beer, mug, black logo, 6x3½", NM, D16...$55.00

Armour's Vigoral, cup, china, floral motif, 3½x3", NM, D16..$25.00

Armour's Vigoral, dispenser, china, white urn shape with floral motif & Vigoral in gold script, 6 cups with name on inside lip, EX, A2..$1,210.00

Armstrong Cork Co, ruler/cork gauge, celluloid, circular logo at right, company name in center, black & white, 6½", EX, A11...$10.00

Armstrong's Livestock, sign, cardboard, pictures farmer spraying cows, field beyond, 8x12", VG, D22.......$75.00

Army & Navy Coffee, tin, red, white & blue with sailor & soldier holding shield flanked by American flags & eagle, round, 1-lb, EX, A2 ....$635.00

Arnold's 'Perfect' Ribbons, tin, vertical, lime green name on fancy emblem, Keep The Type Clean, slip lid, 2x1⅝x1⅝", EX, D37, minimum value $45.00

Around The World Motor Oil, can, Around The World above ringed planet Earth, Motor Oil below, white, green & orange, 1-qt, G, A1 .... **$125.00**

Arrow Beer, sign, cardboard, Matchless Body Arrow Beer below Earl Moran nude on draped stool, framed, 34x22", EX+, A13 .... **$250.00**

Arrow Brand Pure Ginger, tin, 4", NM, A7 .... **$18.00**

Arrow Collars, display case, wood & glass with 3 spindles displaying collars, 33½x21½x9", EX, A9 .... **$800.00**

Arrowhead, tobacco tag, die-cut, red, EX, D35 .... **$8.00**

Arthur Donaldson, cigar box label, outer, man sitting at desk enjoying cigar, 4½x4½", M, D5 .... **$4.00**

Arthur Donaldson Pilsen, sign, die-cut cardboard stand-up, open cigar box with embossed inner-lid label, 9x11", NM, A8 .... **$85.00**

Arthur Donaldson Pilsen Cigars, sign, die-cut cardboard stand-up, open box of cigars with inner label showing the 'Prince Of Pilsen,' 1895, NM+, A3 .... **$25.00**

Arthurettes, sign, cardboard hanger, You Can't Get Enough... above man with many cigars & flanked by 5¢, 1890s, 15x12", EX, A3 .... **$275.00**

Artic Ice Cream, tray, polar bear on iceberg, ...The Cream Supreme on rim, 13½" dia, G-, A9 .... **$80.00**

Artiste Cigars/Goulet Bros, sign, paper, Smoke... above image of demure-looking girl holding lilac sprig, framed, 20x15", EX, A18 .... **$200.00**

Ashland Kerosene, gas globe, red & blue lettering on white, plastic body, 13½" dia, NM, A6 .... **$170.00**

Askeys Cone, display, papier-mache, young man in tuxedo & top hat holding onto oversized ice-cream cone on red base, EX, A2 .... **$1,375.00**

Associated Gasoline, sign, porcelain, More Miles To The Gallon on pitcher in center, red ground with green & white border, 28" dia, VG+, A1 .... **$700.00**

Associated Oil Co, restroom sign, porcelain, features actuated spring mechanism with time that restroom was serviced, 14x8½", NM+, A1 .... **$510.00**

Associated Oil Co, sign, etched brass, Our Creed arched above serviceman on circle, list of qualities below, black ground, 11x8", VG, A8 .... **$50.00**

Athlete, crate label, California orange, 3 runners reaching finish line in stadium, Claremont, 1930s, 10x11", M, D3 .... **$5.00**

Athletic Smoking Mixture, tin, shows product name right of boxer in landscape, rectangular, rounded corners, EX, A18 .... **$175.00**

Atlantic & Pacific Tea Co, calendar, 1905, embossed cardboard, 12 months surround round image of little girl drinking tea, 10x8", NM, A3 .... **$160.00**

Atlantic & Pacific Tea Co/Thea Nectar Tea, sign, cardboard, oval profile image of lady seated & sipping Thea Nectar Tea, 1888, 9x7", EX+, A3 .... **$75.00**

Atlantic Ale & Beer, matchbook, Full Of Good Cheer, 20 strike, front strike, NM, D28 .... **$5.00**

Atlantic Ale & Beer/Steinerbru Ale & Beer, contest sheet, Atlantic ad above football player flanked by rules & prizes, Steinerbru ad below, 1938, 15", EX, A8 .... **$40.00**

Atlantic Beer, tap knob, black plastic with gold & blue insert, round, EX+, A8 .... **$275.00**

Atlantic Beer, tray, Atlantic The Beer Of The South above visitors arriving at southern mansion, scalloped rim, 13½x18½", EX, A8 .... **$100.00**

Atlantic Coast Line & Railway, sign, paper, snow scene with 2 railway workers hanging sign, framed, image: 21x13½", VG+, A9 .... **$1,200.00**

Atlantic Gasoline, gas globe, Atlantic in bold letters on wide center band, red, white & blue, Gill body, 13½" dia, NM, A6 .... **$220.00**

Atlantic Gasoline, gas globe lens, black lettering with red, white & blue logo in center, 15" dia, VG+, A6 .. **$130.00**

Atlantic Imperial, gas globe, product name on shield, gold, red, blue & yellow, 3-pc glass with blue metal bands, 13½" dia, NM, A6 .... **$400.00**

Atlantic Imperial Motor Oil, sign, metal, tilted oil can at left of In A Class By Itself, marked AM Enc Lynchburg, VA, 10-66, 10½x17½", EX+, A6 .... **$45.00**

Atlantic Motor Oil, sign, porcelain, company logo with product name above & below, red, white & blue, 52x35½", EX, A6.................................**$230.00**

Atlantic Motor Oil For Fords, can, oval image of parrot on a branch with product name arched above, For Fords below, 1-qt, 8x3¼" dia, VG, A6 ....**$90.00**

Atlantic NC Motor Oil For Fords, blotter, product name flanked by parrot & oil cans, Special Offer 5-gal Can-$4.00... upper right, 3x6", EX+, A6.......................**$50.00**

Atlantic Paraffine Base Aviation Motor Oil, can, product name above plane flying up & through the word Aviation, red & blue on white, 1-qt, EX, A1.............**$100.00**

Atlantic Premium Gasoline, bank, tin, gas pump, 5x1½", NM, A7 ....**$65.00**

Atlantic Premium Motor Oil, bank, tin, can shape, 2" dia, NM, A7 ....**$15.00**

Atlantic Refining Co, sign, porcelain, Atlantic on crossed arrows surrounded by lettering, red, black & white, 2-sided, 10x10", VG+, A6.................................**$190.00**

Atlantic Refining Co Gasoline, Polarine, Oils..., sign, porcelain, ...For Sale Here, scroll design in each corner, white on blue, 1904-06, EX+, A6......**$925.00**

Atlantic White Flash, license plate attachment, painted metal, image of singing trio with lettering on hats, red jewel in center, 5", VG+, A6 ....**$55.00**

Atlantic White Flash, pump sign, porcelain, Atlantic above round White Flash logo, red, white & blue, marked IR 50, 17x13", VG+, A6.....................................**$100.00**

Atlantic White Flash Gasoline, bumper tag, red reflector in center of 3 Atlantic men in top hats, NM with original envelope, D22..**$60.00**

Atlantic White Lead, string holder, die-cut tin, Dutch boy in swing painting sign above, bucket below, chain hanger, G-, A2...**$855.00**

Atlantic White Lead, string holder, die-cut tin, Dutch Boy painting window frame, bucket below, chain hanger, 30", EX, A2 ....**$1,980.00**

Atlas Batteries, bank, shaped like 6-volt battery, red & silver on black, 3x3x2", EX, A1.............................**$40.00**

Atlas Beer, drinking glass, inside fluting, multicolored oval decal with Colon Panama on arched banner above globe, 4½", NM, A8...**$30.00**

Atlas Colder Anti-Freeze, tester, metal & glass with rubber pump & hose, product name above 'A' logo, Protects Against... below, 18", EX+, A6...........................**$60.00**

Atlas Explosives & Atlas Farm Powders, sign, painted tin, globe logo with product lettering above & at right, dealer name on white panel below, 14x20", EX, A1...........**$70.00**

Atlas Ginger, tin, paper label, 4", NM, A7.................**$20.00**

Atlas Prager Beer, tap knob, chrome ball shape with white on red enamel insert, EX, A8.............................**$55.00**

Atlas Prager Beer, tray, deep-dish, encircled red Atlas & castle above product name, Slow-Brewed on ribbon below, red rim, 12" dia, EX, A19.........................**$45.00**

Atlas Wiper Blades, thermometer, degrees arched above product name on emblem, 8x14", M, D11...........**$75.00**

Atwood's Private Brand Fresh Coffee, tin, Atwood's in script, key-wind lid, EX+, A3.............................**$25.00**

Auborn & Saxon Automobiles, fan, cardboard, 2 autos flank girl in yellow hat on white background, wooden handle, 1916, EX, A15.....................................**$130.00**

Audi, radio, AM-FM transistor, repeated logos on perforated front, hand strap & sliding antenna, 4x3", EX, A6...**$15.00**

Aug Wolf & Co Works Machinery, sign, paper, illuminated factory scene, matted & framed, image: 22½x32½", VG, A9.......................................**$100.00**

Augsburger Bavarian Style, drinking glass, pilsener with red & white graphics, 8", NM, A8.........................**$25.00**

August Schell, see Willfommen Thr Bruder

Ault Deutcher Beer, label, St Marys Beverage Co, Internal Revenue Tax Paid statement, 1933-50, 12-oz, M, A10 ....**$10.00**

Aultman & Taylor Machinery Co, sign, paper, name above images of 2 machines, 'The Eureka' & 'The Hercules,' 'The Dixie,' below, framed, 28x19", EX, A8 ....**$465.00**

Aultman-Taylor Thresher, sign, paper, The Grain Waisting Machine Of The Past...The Thresher Of The Period above threshing scene, 18x40", VG+, A2...........**$495.00**

Auman's Root Beer, mug, glass with red logo, 4½x3", NM, D16...**$25.00**

Aunt Dinah Molasses, can, oval image of Aunt Dinah in center, cream & black on red, 5x5" dia, EX, A6...**$70.00**

Aunt Jemima, alarm clock, Aunt Jemima on white numbered face, bell atop nickel-plated footed case, US Alarm, Pat 1907, EX, A2................................**$200.00**

Aunt Jemima, alarm clock, Aunt Jemima Time lettered at right of 3-quarter image of Aunt Jemima on round dial, ca 1930, 5", EX, A2................................**$215.00**

Aunt Jemima, pancake forms, metal, 4 cut-out animal shapes within handled round form, scarce, EX+, A18...**$135.00**

Aunt Jemima, sign, paper, 6-part hanger, cut-out letters attached to product boxes flanked by plates of food, EX, A12...**$4,700.00**

Aunt Jemima Flour, sign, curved porcelain, product name above & below portrait, Excels For All Baking Purposes, 1910s, 22x18", EX, A13 ....$6,000.00

Aunt Jemima Pancake Flour, sign, die-cut cardboard hanger, copyright 1917, Aunt Jemima on swing with pancakes in her lap, 17½x9½", VG, A9 ....**$5,400.00**

Aunt Jemima Pancakes, banner, Here Today!...In Person Serving Her Famous Pancakes, her image & stack of cakes on red & white, 34x54", EX, A21 ....**$135.00**

Aunt Sue's French Dry Cleaner, can, oval image of woman using product, red, black & white, screw lid & handle, 1-gal, 10½x6½", VG, A6 ....**$50.00**

Aunty, crate label, Florida citrus, smiling black woman holding branch of citrus blossoms, 3x8", M, D3.....**$2.00**

Aurora Invincible/Geo Burghart Maker, tip tray, Aurora above standing draped nude, lettering on rim, Sold 2 For 25¢, Now 10¢ Straight, 4" dia, VG+, A8 ....**$65.00**

Auto City Queen Bee Cigar Co, box label, outer, passengers in early convertible with city scene beyond, 1905, EX, A5 ....**$220.00**

Auto Cycle Union Hotel, sign, porcelain, ACU logo in center of 4-leaf clover with lettered border, 20x20", VG+, D11 ....**$185.00**

Auto-Lite Spark Plugs, display case, metal & glass, 6 plugs displayed, yellow & cream lettering, 18½x13x7", VG+, A6..**$130.00**

Auto Strop Razor, sign, tin stand-up, product name above & below oval image of hands sharpening razor, beveled edge, 9x9", VG+, A2 ....**$75.00**

Auto-Lite, sign, porcelain flange, Auto-Lite on red band across blue ring lettered Official Service, 1920s, 14", EX+, A13..**$400.00**

Auto-Lite Spark Plugs, sign, painted tin, yellow Auto-Lite Spark Plugs above white Ignition Engineered... on blue, dated 1939, 13x28", EX+, A1 ....**$190.00**

Auto-Lite Speedometer Service, sign, glass light-up with metal frame, Authorized..., yellow & white lettering on blue & red background, 11x21", EX, A6............**$225.00**

Auto-Magic Picture Gun, display gun, plywood, advertises toy gun that acts as filmstrip projector, red on silvertone, 1940s, 40", EX, A21...................................**$440.00**

Autobacco, pocket tin, vertical, red with product & company name above & below image of pipe-smoking man behind wheel, EX, A18 ....$190.00

Autobacco, pocket tin, vertical, red with product name above image of pipe-smoking man behind wheel, gold lid, EX, A18..**$480.00**

Autocrat Coffee, tin, bird with steaming cup of coffee at left of product name, A Swallow Will Tell You... below, key-wind lid, NM, A3...**$50.00**

Autoline Oil XP, can, product name in bold letters above Triple Protection in script, red, black & cream, 1-qt, 5½x4" dia, VG, A6..**$40.00**

Automobile Club of New York Inc, sign, porcelain, red, white & blue, 5½x22½", VG+, A6.........................**$75.00**

Avalon Cigarettes, sign, paper, You'd Never Guess... They Cost You Less!, woman in flat brim hat in seductive shoulder pose, 15x10", NM, A7............................**$15.00**

Avenue, crate label, California orange, early auto on avenue shaded with eucalyptus & palm trees, Riverside, 10x11", M, D3..**$2.00**

Avery Mf'g Co, pin-back button, celluloid, Teeth Talk above dog showing his teeth, ...Peoria, Ill's, round, EX, A11 ....**$85.00**

Avon, dealer catalog, features Christmas gifts, 1954, 34 pgs, EX, D17..**$75.00**

Ayer's Cathartic Pills, sign, paper, product name above cherubs putting pills into boxes, Safe, Pleasant & Reliable... below, 13x10", VG, A9...........................**$400.00**

Ayer's Cathartic Pills, sign, tin, winged maiden sprinkling pills to cherubs in clouds, Safe, Pleasant... below, ornate frame, 29x16", G-, A9............................**$400.00**

Ayer's Cherry Pectoral, sign, paper, product name above little girl with cherries, For The Cure Of Coughs, Colds... below, 13x10", VG+, A9.......................**$325.00**

Ayer's Sarsaparilla, sign, die-cut cardboard, 'The Old Folks At Home,' shows elderly couple in rocking chairs, 11x8", EX, A21 ....**$80.00**

Ayrshire Cattle For Sale, sign, porcelain, Ayrshire Cattle at left of For Sale on circle, red on white, 6x24", NM, D22 ....**$125.00**

⁓ B ⁓

B&B Blue=jay, display box, encircled blue jays flank B&B above Blue=jay & Stops Pain/Removes Corns, drawers on 1 side, EX, A18...**$85.00**

B&L Oysters, tin, Delicious... above image of sailing ship at night, pry lid, EX, A3 ....$44.00

B-K Root Beer, baby mug, glass, white logo, M, D16 .$8.00

B-K Root Beer, mug, glass, orange oval logo, 4x3", NM, D16 ....$12.00

B-K Root Beer, mug, glass, orange sign logo, 6x3", NM, D16 ....$10.00

B-L (Buchanan & Lyall's) Blue Label Cut Plug, pocket tin, flat, cream with Blue Label on scrolled ribbon on B-L seal over plugs of tobacco, rounded corners, EX, A18 ....$60.00

B-1 Lemon-Lime Soda, sign, cardboard, Here Comes Pleasure above hands holding tray with bottle, Plus Vitamin B1 below, 11x28", NM+, D30 ....$20.00

B-1 Lemon-Lime Soda, sign, cardboard, Life Of The Party, couple at buffet, Vitamized Refreshment below, wood frame, 18x30", EX, A13 ....$240.00

B-1 Lemon-Lime Soda, sign, tin, Drink... & tilted bottle left of encircled product name, 2-sided hanger with wrought-iron bracket, NM, A16.......................$145.00

B-1 Lemon-Lime Soda, sign, tin, Drink...Plus Vitamin B1, tilted bottle at left, black ground with red diagonal band at top, 18x32", NM, D30 ....$155.00

B-1 Lemon-Lime Soda, soda glass, red & white logo on red circle, 5x2½", NM, D16..................................$15.00

B-1 Lemon-Lime Soda, soda glass, white logo, Drink B-1 For Better Tomorrows..., tapered, 4x2", NM, D16..$15.00

Bab-O Cleanser, can, sample, cardboard & tin, NM, A7 .$30.00

Babbitt's Cleanser, see BT Babbitt's Cleanser

Babcock's Corilopsis of Japan Talc Powder, tin, sample, Oriental motif, shaker top, 2x1½x⅞", EX, D37 .$120.00

Baby Rose Allspice, tin, paper label, baby's image above product name, 2½", NM, A7 ....$40.00

Baby Ruth, beanbag, 1971, Hasbro, shaped like a candy bar, VG, D27...$30.00

Baby Ruth, display figure, hard rubber, blond boy pointing to candy bar at base, Curtiss NRG Candies on shirt, 15", VG, A9 ....$275.00

Baby Ruth, matchbook, Curtiss Candies...Rich In Pure Dextrose, The Energy Sugar, 20 strike, front strike, NM, D28 ....$3.00

Baby Ruth, sign, tin, large image of candy bar in red & white on bright yellow background, 1930s, 16x35½", scarce, VG, D19...$250.00

Baby Ruth, whistle, 2¾", NM, A7.................................$25.00

Baby Stuart Cloves, tin, paper label, product name above & below portrait, 3", NM, A7.............................$50.00

Baby's Own Powder, container, paper on cardboard, baby sucking his fingers above product name, JB Williams Co, full, 4x2" dia, NM, A3..............$100.00

Bachelor Cigars, display box, tin with reverse-painted glass marquee, slanted hinged glass top, 12x10½", EX, A21 ....$305.00

Badger, cigar box, 5½x8¼", EX, A7.............................$25.00

Bagdad Coffee, pail, product name above & below arched doorway image of 3 Arabs, straight-sided, screw lid, bail handle, 5-lb, EX, A18............$190.00

Bagdad Coffee, pail, product name above & below arched doorway image of 3 Arabs, straight-sided, screw lid, bail handle, 5-lb, NM, A18.................................$285.00

Bagdad Short Cut Pipe Smoking, pocket tin, vertical, 2-tone blue with name above & below encircled profile image of man in red fez, short, EX+, A18.........$125.00

Bagdad Tobacco, humidor, ceramic, Bagdad above portrait of man in red fez, fancy border, blue shaded glaze, 6½x5" dia, NM, A6..$130.00

Bagdad Tobacco, humidor, ceramic, Bagdad above portrait of man in red fez, fancy border, blue shaded glaze, 6½x5" dia, EX, A18 ....$85.00

Bagley's Burley Boy Pipe or Cigarette, pocket tin, vertical, White Man's Hope lettered in red O with photo image a boy boxer, white background, NM, A3...........$1,200.00

Bagley's Burley Boy Pipe or Cigarette, pocket tin, vertical, White Man's Hope lettered in red O with image of boy boxer, white background, VG+, A18..........$690.00

Bagley's May Flower, pocket tin, sample, flat, blue & gold, rounded corners, Somers, VG, A18....................$115.00

Bagley's Old Colony Mixture Smoking Tobacco, pocket tin, vertical, silver with red oval portrait of lady in profile, EX+, A18...$215.00

Bagley's Old Colony Mixture Smoking Tobacco, pocket tin, vertical, white with red oval portrait of lady in profile, profile, VG+, A18.............................$100.00

Bagley's Old Colony Mixture Smoking Tobacco, pocket tin, vertical, white with yellow oval portrait of lady in profile, G, A18..$75.00

Bagley's Old Colony Tobacco, whetstone, celluloid, multi-colored tobacco tin in center, oval, EX+, A11......$40.00

Bagley's Sweet Tips, pocket tin, vertical, oval, black & gold paper label with name & image of fanned-out tobacco leaves, EX+, A18.................................$75.00

Bagley's Sweet Tips, pocket tin, vertical, oval, black & gold paper label with product name & image of fanned-out tobacco leaves, VG+, A18...................$40.00

Bagley's Turkish Patrol, pocket container, vertical, cardboard & tin, black with gold name above & below crescent moon & star logo, VG+, A18.........................$85.00

Bagley's Wild Fruit Flake Cut Smoking & Chewing Tobacco, tin, red, yellow, white & blue with gold trim, rounded corners, 4x6", EX, A18 ....$75.00

Bair Motor Car Company, calendar, 1918, colorful image of romantic couple in car, complete, 16x9", VG+, A6...$75.00

Baker's, see also W/WH Baker or Walter Baker & Co

Baker's Breakfast Cocoa/Walter Baker & Co Ltd, tip tray, 'A New England Homestead' & full-length profile image of chocolate girl flanked by lettering, 6" dia, VG+, A3 ....$200.00

Baker's Century Vanilla Chocolate, tin, sample, lid shows embossed oval image of chocolate girl & product lettering, 2⅜x1⅛", EX, D37 ....$45.00

Baker's Cocoa Butter, tin, sample, oval with product name above & company name below chocolate girl, ⅝x2¾x1¾", EX, D37 ....$35.00

Baker's Talcum Powder, tin, blue & white with photo image of woman in profile, cylindrical, 4", EX, A2 ....$60.00

Bala Club Cola, can, cone-top, 12-oz, EX+, A19 .....$125.00

Bala Club Ginger Ale, can, cone-top, 12-oz, G+, A19 ..$25.00

Bala Club Root Beer, can, cone-top, 12-oz, EX, A19 ..$100.00

Balboa Bock Beer, label, Balboa Brewing Co, U-type permit number, Internal Revenue Tax Paid statement, 1933-36, M, A10...$20.00

Bald Eagle Beer, label, JH Velott/Koch's Brewery, Internal Revenue Tax Paid statement, 1933-50, 12-oz, M, A10 ....$35.00

Baldwin Locomotive Works/Burnham Williams & Co, sign, paper, black & white image of locomotive & tender reading Southern, company name below, framed, 16x30", VG+, A2...$253.00

Baldwin Locomotive Works/Burnham Williams & Co, sign, paper, black & white image of locomotive & tender reading Denver & Rio Grande, name below, framed, 16x30", EX, A2...$330.00

Baldwin's Herbal Blood Pills, sign, paper, ...Cures Blackheads, Pimples, Blotches, Boils, Scurvy, Irritation Of The Skin, Bad Legs..., 27x20", VG+, A8................$55.00

Ball Fruit Jars, sign, cardboard, Preserve Health with above Kellogg's Corn Flakes box & other food items, name below, 24x20", VG+, A21..........$310.00

Ballantine & Co's Export Beer, sign, glass, name above & below 3-circle logo on Celebrated Newark NJ emblem, black on gold, framed, 42x29", VG+, A8.........$1,200.00

Ballantine Ale, sign, embossed tin, America's Largest Selling Ale, large green bottle bursting through paper, 53x17½", EX, A8....................................$100.00

Ballantine Ale & Beer, sign, light-up, 3-circle logo & product name on glass panel in metal trapezoid-shaped frame, 10½x32½", NM, A19...............................$250.00

Ballantine Beer, sign, embossed tin, Beba Cerveza Ballantine, La Preferida En La Ciudad & frothy glass, beveled edge, 7x10", VG, A8...............................$20.00

Ballantine Beer, song book, 1939 NY World's Fair, shaped like frothy mug of beer with intertwined 3-circle logo, 16 pgs, 10½", EX, A8..........................$20.00

Ballantine Beer, tap knob, black ball shape with intertwined 3-circle logo above name, EX, A8 ....$30.00

Ballantine Draught Beer, can, pictures product name on keg with glasses of beer, 1-gal, EX, A19...............$35.00

Ballantine's Export Beer, sign, embossed tin, oval shape with product lettering on black around 3-circle logo on red, pre-1920s, 118x26", EX+, A19 ....$450.00

Ballantine's On Tap, sign, reverse glass, We Recommend above 3-circle Purity, Body & Flavor logo, America's Finest..., 15x18", VG+, A19 ....$160.00

Balm of Tulips, display box, cardboard, advertising marquee atop upright compartment box holding 6 bottles, 8" long, NM, A2...$250.00

Bang Up Cigars, box label, salesman's sample, nude boy with top hat riding a cigar, VG, A5 ....$100.00

Bangle, tobacco tag, EX, D35 ....$4.00

Bank Note Cigars, counter display, 3-D die-cut cardboard, gentlemen enjoying cigars above fold-out box flanked by 5¢ & name, EX, A18 ....$255.00

Bank Note Cigars, pocket tin, vertical, cream with Bank Note above red Five Cents on band, green border, Federal Tin Co, EX+, A18 ....$55.00

Bank Note Cigars, sign, die-cut cardboard stand-up, 2 gentlemen enjoying product above full box flanked by 5¢, name below, 21x14", EX, A21 ....$85.00

Banko Beverages, drinking glass, slightly tapered with Enjoy Banko Beverages on emblem above repeated dot design, M, A16 ....$30.00

Banner Buggies, sign, paper, First, Last & All Time... lettered on brim of red hat of illuminated lady, framed, 22x16", NM, A8...............................$450.00

Banner Buggies, sign, paper, girl in violet & cream dress & large hat holding violets, logo in center of dress, framed, 26x14", EX, A8 ....$280.00

Banneret, cigar box label, outer, child holding banner, 4½x4½", M, D5 ....$15.00

Banquet Tea, tin, black & white on bright orange, McCormick & Co, pry lid, copyright 1939, 3x3", EX, D14 ....$15.00

Baranger Studios' Advertising Automaton, 'Alice in Wonderland,' 15x22½x12", EX, A9 ....$1,650.00

Baranger Studios' Advertising Automaton, 'Animal Orchestra,' 14x16x13", EX, A9 ....$4,000.00

Baranger Studios' Advertising Automaton, 'Balance Wheel,' 21x19x11", EX, A9 ....$2,200.00

Baranger Studios' Advertising Automaton, 'Barber Shop Quartet,' 15x25x14", EX, A9 ....$3,250.00

Baranger Studios' Advertising Automaton, 'Casey Jones,' 17½x22½x10", EX, A9 ....$1,250.00

Baranger Studios' Advertising Automaton, 'Clown With Dog Jumping Through Hoop,' 19x20x12", EX, A9 ....$1,000.00

Baranger Studios' Advertising Automaton, 'Cowboy,' twirling lasso, 18x15" dia, EX, A9 ....$2,500.00

Baranger Studios' Advertising Automaton, 'Dan Cupid Information Dept,' 18x22x12", EX, A9............$2,950.00

Baranger Studios' Advertising Automaton, 'Deep Sea Divers,' 19½x26x9", EX, A9.......................$3,500.00

Baranger Studios' Advertising Automaton, 'Diamond Cleaner,' 17x13½x13½", EX, A9...................$3,500.00

Baranger Studios' Advertising Automaton, 'Diamond Inspectors,' 10½x14x14", EX, A9....................$700.00

Baranger Studios' Advertising Automaton, 'Diamond Polishers,' 14x15x15", EX, A9......................$750.00

Baranger Studios' Advertising Automaton, 'Diamond Setters,' 18x12x9", EX, A9........................$1,250.00

Baranger Studios' Advertising Automaton, 'Dutch Mill,' 16x18x11", EX, A9..............................$800.00

Baranger Studios' Advertising Automaton, 'Elopement,' 23x25½x14", EX, A9............................$1,450.00

Baranger Studios' Advertising Automaton, 'Fish Wedding,' 13x17x15", EX, A9 ....$2,700.00

Baranger Studios' Advertising Automaton, 'Fortune Teller,' 17x13x9", EX, A9..........................$850.00

Baranger Studios' Advertising Automaton, 'Gay 90's Photo Gallery,' 19x25x12", EX, A9................$3,250.00

Baranger Studios' Advertising Automaton, 'Grandfather's Clock,' 20x21x11", EX, A9.................$2,700.00

Baranger Studios' Advertising Automaton, 'Honeymoon Rocket,' 19x15½x13", EX, A9..................$2,750.00

Baranger Studios' Advertising Automaton, 'Horse & Buggy,' 16½x23½x13", EX, A9....................$2,500.00

Baranger Studios' Advertising Automaton, 'Knight Hood,' 21x24x11", non-working, VG, A9 ....$300.00

Baranger Studios' Advertising Automaton, 'Lighthouse,' 18x25x13", EX, A9............................$3,500.00

Baranger Studios' Advertising Automaton, 'Little Church,' 20x24x12", EX, A9..........................$1,600.00

Baranger Studios' Advertising Automaton, 'Merry-Go-Round,' 21x25x11", EX, A9......................$3,000.00

Baranger Studios' Advertising Automaton, 'Military Wedding,' 23x28x17", EX, A9......................$2,950.00

Baranger Studios' Advertising Automaton, 'Noah's Ark,' 15x23x14", EX, A9...........................$4,450.00

Baranger Studios' Advertising Automaton, 'Old King Cole,' 15x21x14", EX, A9.........................$1,250.00

Baranger Studios' Advertising Automaton, 'Old Mill,' 17x20x14", EX, A9.............................$1,500.00

Baranger Studios' Advertising Automaton, 'Organ Grinder,' 21x25x12", EX, A9........................$2,100.00

Baranger Studios' Advertising Automaton, 'Racehorse,' 17x17x9", EX, A9.............................$2,100.00

Baranger Studios' Advertising Automaton, 'Rodeo Rider,' 13½x21x12", EX, A9.........................$2,000.00

Baranger Studios' Advertising Automaton, 'See-Saw,' 19x25x9", EX, A9...............................$2,250.00

Baranger Studios' Advertising Automaton, 'Serenade,' 23x25x12", EX, A9.............................$1,400.00

Baranger Studios' Advertising Automaton, 'Seven Dwarfs,' 18x23x11", EX, A9.........................$2,450.00

Baranger Studios' Advertising Automaton, 'The Drum,' 17x15" dia, EX, A9.............................$1,350.00

Baranger Studios' Advertising Automaton, 'The Saw Mill,' 14½x23x10", EX, A9.........................$750.00

Baranger Studios' Advertising Automaton, 'Their First Auto,' 21x25x14", EX, A9......................$4,500.00

Baranger Studios' Advertising Automaton, 'Trolley Car,' 16x19x½x13", non-working, VG, A9 .... **$1,050.00**

Baranger Studios' Advertising Automaton, 'Walrus & Carpenter,' 13x21x13", EX, A9 .... **$1,250.00**

Baranger Studios' Advertising Automaton, 'Wedding Book Frame,' 16x24x14½", EX, A9 .... **$2,200.00**

Baranger Studios' Advertising Automaton, 'Wedding Cake,' 14x15" dia, EX, A9 .... **$1,000.00**

Baranger Studios' Advertising Automaton, 'Wedding Chapel,' 21x25x14", EX, A9 .... **$2,350.00**

Baranger Studios' Advertising Automaton, 'Wells Fargo Coach,' 14x25½x13", EX, A9 .... **$3,000.00**

Barbarossa, sign, cardboard, library scene with bottle & glass on tray with stein, Barbarossa on bookend, wood frame, G+, A8 .... **$20.00**

Barbarossa, tap knob, black with gold, red & black enameled insert, VG+, A8 .... **$30.00**

Barbarossa Bock Beer, sign, cardboard, Barbarossa above ram & crown logo flanked by Bock Beer, red, black, brown & yellow, 11x14", EX, A8 .... **$20.00**

Barber Shop, sign, curved metal, white Barber Shop on blue with diagonal red, white & blue stripes, 1930s-40s, 24x16", EX+, A13 .... $220.00

Barber Shop, sign, porcelain, Barber arched above Shop above striped pole, shouldered top, red, white & blue, 29x6", EX+, A13 .... **$275.00**

Barber Shop, sign, porcelain flange, Barber arched above Shop on center rectangle bordered by stripes, 12x24", VG+, A13 .... **$190.00**

Bardahl, clock, Ask For Bardahl, Makes Cars Run Better, features the Bardahl man, TW O'Connell Co, 12" dia, EX+, A1 .... **$125.00**

Bardahl, sign, tin, Bardahl For The Farm, tractor image, 10x15", NM, D11 .... **$50.00**

Bardahl, sign, tin, Stops Valve Lifter Clatter left of man with can inside of his coat, 17x20", EX, D19 .... **$75.00**

Bardwell's Root Beer, canteen, elk on 1 side & product name on the other, M, D16 .... **$500.00**

Bardwell's Root Beer, canteen (reproduction), elk on 1 side & product name on the other, blue, M, D16 .... **$50.00**

Bare Foot Boy Tomatoes, can label, product name above & below large tomato & barefoot boy, 4½x13½", NM, A7 .... **$2.00**

Barker's Brand Linen Collars & Cuffs, sign, tin, name & Barco Shrunk, 2 For 25 Cts around image of dog with collar in its mouth, 20" dia, G-, A21 .... **$245.00**

Barking Dog Cigarettes, cigarette carton, pictures bulldog & open pack left of product lettering, EX+, A18 .. **$28.00**

Barnes White Flyer/EC Bald, pin-back button, name around head-on image of bicyclist, EX, A20 .... **$35.00**

Barnum's Animals/National Biscuit Co, tin, product name above 4 caged animals, company name below, slip lid, 1979, NM, A7 .... **$8.00**

Barq's, sign, tin flange, bottle at left of Drink Barq's It's Good in red & white on blue with red border, oval, 14x22", NM, A1 .... $275.00

Barq's, sign, tin over cardboard, Barq's in diagonal script above bottle & glass with food, 14x11", NM, A13 .... **$150.00**

Barq's, thermometer, metal, Drink Barq's 'It's Good' above large bottle & bulb, black, red, cream & orange, 25", EX, A6 .... **$100.00**

Barrington Hall Coffee, tin, oval image of Barrington Hall in center, key-wind lid, EX, A3 .... **$45.00**

Bartels, scoreboard/sign, tin on cardboard, The Professor Says, 'Bartels There Is None Better' above scoreboard, 10x29", EX+, A19 .... **$95.00**

Bartels, tap knob, orange ball shape with orange lettering on buff insert, EX, A8 .... **$30.00**

Bartels Beer, sign, metal with wood backing, round with Bartels Beer encircling initial logo, C Shonk litho, 18" dia, EX+, A8 .... **$110.00**

Bartels Brewing Co, sign, self-framed tin, 2 elegant couples being served, BB Co logo on sign above, 28x22", VG, A9 .... **$2,700.00**

Bartels Lager, Ale & Porter, tip tray, bearded lancer holding up frothy stein, product names & city lettered on rim, 4" dia, VG+, A8 .... **$70.00**

Bartels Malt Extract, sign, tin on cardboard, An Ideal Tonic above product & company name right of bottle, pre-1920s, 6x13", EX+, A19 .... **$65.00**

Bartels Pilsner Crown Beer, label, yellow & white lettering on shades of blue, brown & black, 12-oz, EX, A19 .. **$5.00**

Bartholomay, calendar, 1897, die-cut, girl on winged wheel above calendar pad, wooden oval framed with curved glass, 7½", VG+, A8 .... **$100.00**

Bartholomay Beers, Ales & Porter, tip tray, deep-dish, trademark image of girl on winged wheel, ...In Kegs & Bottles above & below, 4" dia, EX, A8 .... **$100.00**

Bartholomay Rochester Beer & Ale, drinking glass, barrel shape with applied white logo, NM, A8 .... **$20.00**

Bartholomay's Rochester, mug, ceramic, tan glaze with winged wheel above name on scrolled banner, Mettlach, 1887, EX+, A8 .... **$90.00**

Bartles Bonded Motor Oils, blotter, For Better Lubrication Use... on large sign in front of trees & stream, EX+, D21 .... **$12.00**

Bartlett Spring Mineral Water, tray, girl pointing to large bottle flanked by lettering, ...Bartlett Springs Co San Francisco on rim, 13" dia, G-, A9.....................**$150.00**

Bartosz Beer, label, Auto City Brewing Co, Internal Revenue Tax Paid statement, 1933-50, 12-oz, M, A10...........**$18.00**

Baskin Robbins, spoon figure, pink plastic with embossed 31 logo on handle body, movable arms & legs, white hands & feet, 4½", M $5.00

Bassett's Egg Shampoo, tin, decorative egg shape, 1¾x2¾", EX, D37 ....**$35.00**

Bassick Casters, display, metal & wood, ...For Any Furniture On Any Floor above rows of castors, 13x13", EX, A6 ....**$30.00**

Bat Phila Athletics Plug Chewing Tobacco, tin, red with white product name above & below oval image of ball & bat, round, gold slip lid, EX, A18.....................**$250.00**

Bata Super Bullets Shoes, display shoe, painted plaster replica of the classic black high-top basketball shoe, 12x23", EX, A21 ....**$145.00**

Batavaia Brand Rolled Oats, container, cardboard, dark blue & white lettering with gold trim on white, 3-lb 7-oz, VG+, A3 ....**$40.00**

Battle Ax Plug Tobacco, newspaper ad, cartoon image, 1896, matted & framed, 5x7", EX, D3 ....**$30.00**

Battle Axe Grapes, lug box label, knight in armor & ancient weapon with red ribbon, Sanger, M, D12 ..**$2.00**

Battle Leaders Cigars, box label, salesman's sample, 2 oval portraits flanked by flags, eagle & vignettes below, G, A5.....................**$100.00**

Battleship Coffee, tin, name above head-on image of battleship on orange vertical label against white, round, pry lid, 3-lb, EX, A18 ....$110.00

Baum's Auto Soap, sign, metal on oak board frame, Buy Here & product name above can & Saves The Paint-Cleans Brighter, 11x17", EX, A6 ....**$80.00**

Baum's Polish, sign, die-cut cardboard stand-up, Shines Like Magic..., pictures front end of car with girl driver, 13x9", NM, A6.....................**$110.00**

Bausch & Lomb Microscopes & Scientific Instruments, catalog, 1929, 318 pgs, EX, D17 ....**$90.00**

Bavarian Master Beer, label, Bavarian Brewing Co, Internal Revenue Tax Paid statement, 1933-50, 32-oz, EX, A10.....................**$15.00**

Bavarian Premium Beer, sign, tin on cardboard, man & hops above name & 'In 8 Ounce Splits,' gold on white, beveled edge, 6x9", VG+, A8 ....**$35.00**

Bavarian's Old Style Beer, tray, deep-dish, circular logo above product name, 12" dia, EX+, A19.....................**$85.00**

Bay Horse Ale/Heidelberg Brewing Co, label, black with Pale & Sparkling above product name & 3 horse heads, Aged In Oaken Casks below, 32-oz, VG, A19......**$40.00**

Bazooka Bubblegum, briefcase, Bazooka Deal, $2.98 Briefcase Free!, NMIB, A7 ....**$40.00**

BB American Mainsprings/Bogle Bro's Co, tin, flat, blue & gold with decorative border around lettering, square with rounded corners, ¾x3x3", EX, D37 ....**$40.00**

BB Special High Grade Coffee, milk can, blue with red & blue label, bail handle, 5-lb, 12", VG, A2...........**$255.00**

Beacon 'Radiant' Kerosene, sign, porcelain, product lettering above line with Caminol Product lettered below, red on yellow, 18x21", NM, A1 ....**$100.00**

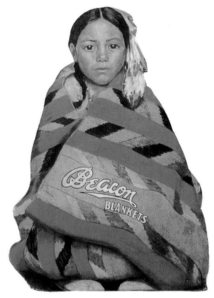

Beacon Blankets, sign, die-cut, Indian child wrapped in colorful blanket, 29x19", EX, D8 ....$750.00

Beacon Security Motor Oil, can, lighthouse logo with 100% Pure Paraffin Base above product name, yellow, blue & red, no bottom, EX+, A1 ....**$410.00**

Beacon Shoes For Men, sign, paper, sailing ship passing lighthouse at night, framed, 24x19½", EX, A9.....................**$300.00**

Beadleston & Woerz, see Gold Label

Bear Wheel Balancing Service, sign, die-cut tin, smiling bear holding sign, yellow, red & black, 40x28", VG, A6 ....**$275.00**

Beatty's California Grapine, sign, paper, Thirsty? Try... above girl smelling rose, framed, image: 20x15", G, A9 ....**$150.00**

Beauty Bright Cigarettes, insert cards, features actresses Pauline Hall & Mary Engle, G/VG, A5 ....**$25.00**

Beauty Maid Bob Pins, tin, cylinder with name on side, 2½" dia, EX, D37 ....**$6.00**

Beaver State Beer, tap knob, black ball shape with cream lettering on brown celluloid insert, very rare, EX+, A8 ....**$240.00**

Beaver-Penn Motor Oil, can, yellow & blue with oval image of a beaver atop lettered emblem, bulldog lower left, 5-gal, VG+, A1 ....**$50.00**

Beaverhead Brewery, tip tray, Costs Less-Worth More-Dillon Beer, bust of girl with red poppies in hair, lettered rim, 4" dia, VG+, A8 ....**$750.00**

Beck's Beer, sign, painted glass, Brewing The Best... above product name & Naturally Smooth with eagle logo, framed, 8x16", EX, A8 ....**$75.00**

Beck's Bottled Beer, tip tray, company name above patriotic eagle, Buffalo's Best... on rim, Magnus Beck Brewing Co, 4" dia, NM, A8 ....**$90.00**

Beck's Hunting Tobacco, cigarette papers, NM, A7 ..**$105.00**

Becker's Best Beer, can, flat-top, instructional, 12-oz, G+, A19 ....**$7.00**

Bee Hive Overalls, pocket mirror, lettering around image of shirtless girl in overalls, metal open handle & rim, 2¾", VG, A21 ....**$190.00**

Beech-Nut Chewing Gum, alarm clock, shows girl's face with advertising on forehead, round red footed case with bell atop, 1900, 5½", EX, A2 ....**$525.00**

Beech-Nut Chewing Gum, counter container, Fruit Stripe tub, ...Five Flavors & logo against striped background, NM, A7 ....**$20.00**

Beech-Nut Chewing Gum, dispenser, metal, 5¢, It's Delicious..., shows blond woman in hat, 2 slots, 1940-early 50s, no key, VG, A6 ....**$275.00**

Beech-Nut Chewing Gum, display box, oval Beech-Nut logo on cover, NM, A16 ....**$40.00**

Beech-Nut Chewing Gum, display box, shaped as a pack of Peppermint gum, 2½x4x15", NM, A7 ....**$80.00**

Beech-Nut Chewing Gum, figure, Fruit Stripe Gum Man, bendable wire arms & legs, 1967, 7½", VG, R3 .**$150.00**

Beech-Nut Chewing Tobacco, sign, die-cut tin, image of unopened pack, 14x11", EX+, A18 ....**$185.00**

Beech-Nut Chewing Tobacco, sign, porcelain, pictures product at left of lettering, red, white & blue, 12x24", VG, D35 ....**$175.00**

Beech-Nut Chewing Tobacco, store bin, medium green with red, white & blue product label & pack with white lettering, slant top, EX+, A18 ....**$325.00**

Beech-Nut Coffee, tin, sample, key-wind, 4-oz, EX, A7 ..**$15.00**

Beech-Nut Coffee, tin, sample, slip lid, 2⅛", NM, A7 ...**$20.00**

Beech-Nut Oralgene Chewing Gum, box, ...For The Teeth, With Dehydrated Milk Of Magnesia, lettering on receding background colors, bordered, EX+, A13 ....**$45.00**

Beechies, counter container, shaped like cottage cheese tub, Refreshing 1¢ Beechies above open pack on oval, 5", NM, A7 ....**$15.00**

Beefeater Gin, display, composition, figural English guard with staff on lettered wood base that displays bottle, 17x9", VG+, A8 ....**$25.00**

Beeman's Pepsin Gum, display, cardboard, product name above image of the Great Chicago Fire, 2-pc, 24½x35½", VG, A1 ....**$500.00**

Beeman's Pepsin Gum, pocket mirror, Chew Beeman's above oval portrait flanked by Pepsin & Gum, Good For Digestion below, 2" dia, EX, A21 ....**$255.00**

Beeman's Pepsin Gum, sign, tin, lettering around image of gum pack on yellow background, 6x9", G, A21 ...**$95.00**

Beethem Chewable Breath Mints, tin, flat, lady's head at left facing 5¢ dot above product name, rectangular with rounded corners, EX, A7 ....**$15.00**

Belding Brothers & Co Spool Silk, spool cabinet, oak, 6 glass-front drawers & 1 solid-front bottom drawer, 21½x20¼x18¼", EX, A12 ....**$575.00**

Belfast Old Fashioned Mug Root Beer, matchbook, pictures frothy mug, 20 strike, front strike, NM, D28 ..**$3.00**

Belfast Old Fashioned Mug Root Beer, mug, tan, M, D16 ....**$25.00**

Belinda, tobacco box label, name above oval portrait of lady holding up stemmed glass, fancy detailed border, 1874, 14", NM, D9 ....**$50.00**

Bell System, sign, porcelain, Public Telephone above & below center bell marked Bell System, blue & white, 1940s-50s, 7" dia, EX, A6 ....**$125.00**

Bell System, sign, porcelain, Public Telephone above & below center bell marked Bell System, blue & white, 1940s-50s, 7" dia, NM, A13 ....**$200.00**

Bell System, sign, porcelain flange, bell surrounded by New England Telephone & Telegraph Co..., blue on white, 16x16", EX, A6 ....**$125.00**

Bell System, sign, porcelain flange, bell surrounded by New England Telephone & Telegraph Co..., blue on white, 16x16", NM+, D11 ....$235.00

Bell Telephone, paperweight, nickel-plated silver, horseshoe shape, New Bell Telephone Building St Louis MO on shield at top, M, D13 ....$50.00

Bella Hess, catalog, Spring/Summer, 1950, EX, D17 . **$30.00**

Belle of Virginia, tobacco box label, name above lady smoking cigarette, fancy detailed border, 14", NM, D9 ....**$15.00**

Belle Plaine Candy Kitchen, calendar, 1916, die-cut paper, garden scene with couple embracing in gazebo, full pad, framed, EX, A6 ....$110.00

Bellevue Ice Cream, tray, little kids eating ice cream & little girl feeding dog from her spoon, lettering on rim, 13½" dia, G-, A9..$100.00

Bellingham Bay Beer, drinking glass, straight-sided with etched product name arched above factory scene, 3½", NM, A8 ....$50.00

Bellis Bicycles, pin-back button, pictures boy on bicycle, EX, A20 ....$25.00

Belmont Brewing Co, mug, ceramic, barrel shape with 1897 BPOE logo with elk's head, Mettlach, EX+, A8........$65.00

Belmont Brewing Co, mug, ceramic, bell with leaf & hops design above company name, Martin's Ferry O below, gold trim, EX+, A8..$190.00

Belmont Cube Cut Smoking Tobacco, pocket tin, vertical, metallic blue-green with gold name above & below gold initial emblem, gold lid, EX+, A18 ....$495.00

Bem, mug, Serve Bem, embossed couple at barrel, Ceramarte, Rio Negrinho green mark, 1974, 6½", EX, A8...$45.00

Ben-Brew Beer/Franklin Brewing Co, label, image of Ben Franklin in red circle on blue, 12-oz, EX+, A19 ....**$5.00**

Ben-Hur 5¢ Cigars, sign, tin, oval image of charging chariot pulled by 4 horses with scrolled border, 18x26", VG+, A9 ....**$400.00**

Bengal Gin, display, plaster, roaring tiger on lettered bottle base, ...Imported (And Undomesticated!), 7x9x5", EX, A8 ....**$25.00**

Benjamins Horehound Cough Drops, tin, tan with black graphics & lettering, vertical square with smaller round lid, Somers, 5-lb, VG+, A18 ....**$85.00**

Bennett Manufacturing Co, replica of trash recepticle, painted pressed steel, green with Help Keep Our City Clean in white, 7", NM, A21 ....**$210.00**

Benson & Hedges, ball-point pen, gold color, B&H logo on clip, 1970s, NM, D23 ....**$10.00**

Benson's Toffee, display, animated nodding Benson's Toffee man on rectangular base with product name, clockwork, EX, A2 ....$2,310.00

Benson's Toffee, tin, red with image of Benson's Toffee man & name on front, pry lid, 9x6", EX, A2 ......**$155.00**

Benton Mixture Smoking Tobacco, tin, deep yellow with embellished name left of bust image of elderly gent, rectangular, square corners, EX+, A18...............**$150.00**

Benton Mixture Smoking Tobacco, tin, gold with product lettering left of man's portrait, rectangular with square corners, EX+, A18 ....**$155.00**

Bergner & Engel Brewing Co's Celebrated Beer, sign, paper litho, girl in golden curls wearing top hat, product name below, 1888, matted & framed, 14x9", EX, A19 ....**$75.00**

Bergner & Engel Brewing Co's Celebrated Beer, sign, paper litho, girl in golden curls wearing top hat, product name below, 1888, matted & framed, 14x9", NM, A19 ....**$135.00**

Bergner & Engel Brewing Co's Tannhaeuser, sign, reverse-painted glass, lettering on blue, framed, 15x26", VG, A19 ....**$595.00**

Berkshire Brewery Ass'n, calendar, 1913, cowgirl beside horse, full pad in lower left corner, framed, image: 20x15½", VG, A9..**$1,100.00**

Berma Choice Mountain Grown Coffee, tin, product name lettered on mountain scene, 1-lb, EX+, A3..**$40.00**

Bermarine Quinine Pomade, tin, name above & below encircled lady in profile, floral band across center, diamond ground, 3x2½x1⅜", EX, D37 ....**$30.00**

Bermarine Quinine Pomade, tin, sample, pictures original can with Free Sample arched above, floral band across center, ¼x1½" dia, EX, D37 ....**$45.00**

Berry Brothers Celebrated Varnishes, sign, celluloid, boy in product box reining dog to stop for train, 15x21", EX+, A9 ....$1,300.00

Berry Brothers Celebrated Varnishes, sign, embossed tin, When You See Varnishes & Hard Oil Finishes...They Are The Best, product can at left, 20x28", G, A6..**$150.00**

Berry's Beverages, sign, 'Tops In Quality' & emblem with BB logo above Berry's With Beverages on ribbon banner, vertical, EX, A16.................................**$80.00**

Best Beer, label, Kalispell Malt & Brewing Co, pre-prohibition, NM, A10 ....**$60.00**

Best Bros Keene's Cement, postcard, photo image of the First National Bank of Cleveland, 1910, VG, D26 ..**$45.00**

Best Dog, tobacco tag, die-cut bone, EX, D35 ....**$10.00**

Best Gum Co, pencil sleeve, celluloid, 'If You Love Your Sweetheart Chew Best,' EX, A7 ....**$90.00**

Best Hats, display, chalkware, figural boy's head wearing hat on base reading Why Under The Sun Don't You Wear One?, 16", EX, A2 ....**$320.00**

Best Pickens/Gravely & Miller, tobacco pouch, cloth with label, EX, A7 ....**$25.00**

Best Value Brand Coffee, tin, shows product name & scale, Weideman & Co litho, 1-lb, EX+, A15......**$250.00**

Bestyet Drip Grind Coffee, tin, Bestyet in script on elongated oval above steaming cup, key-wind lid, 1-lb, NM+, A3 ....$75.00

Betsy Ross Bread, toy spinner, 1½" dia, NM, A7 ......**$20.00**

Betsy Ross Orange Pekoe & Pekoe High Grade Tea, container, cardboard with tin base & pry lid, red with Queen Of All arched above portrait image, EX+, A3 ....**$20.00**

Betsy Ross 5¢ Cigar, sign, self-framed tin, oval image of Betsy Ross holding flag on wood-grain background, gold lettering, 24x20", EX, A6...........................**$450.00**

Betty Ann Baking Powder, can label, little redheaded girl in pink dress skipping rope on white with gilt border, 1920s-30s, 6-oz, M, D3 ....**$3.00**

Betty Zane Pop Corn, box, allover star design, 2-oz, 7¾x4¾", A7 ....**$5.00**

Between The Acts All Tobacco Cigarettes, sign, paper, sign on post behind girl on fence with photo album, Thos Hall New York lower left, framed, 34x18", EX, A21 ....**$200.00**

Betz Beer, tray, B logo in center flanked by Betz & Beer on scrolled ribbon, decorative border, 14" dia, EX, A19 ..**$20.00**

Betz Bock Beer, label, John F Betz & Son, U-type permit number, Internal Revenue Tax Paid statement, 1933-36, 12-oz, M, A10..**$15.00**

Betz Light Beer, label, John F Betz & Son, U-type permit number, Internal Revenue Tax Paid statement, 1933-36, 12-oz, M, A10..**$15.00**

Betz Old Stock Lager, label, John F Betz & Son, U-type permit number, Internal Revenue Tax Paid statement, 1933-36, 12-oz, M, A10..**$10.00**

Beverly Peanut Butter, tin, product name in multicolored letters above girl & boy facing each other, pry lid, 5x5" dia, EX+, D21 ....$32.00

Beverwyck Beer-Ales, sign, composition, black, red Beverwyck above gold quadruple B logo, red Beer-Ales below, gold frame, 8x12", NM, A19 ....**$85.00**

Beverwyck Famous Lager, tip tray, shows colorful factory scene, lettering around rim, 4" dia, EX, A21 .....**$330.00**

Beverwyck Lager, tray, 'The Invitation,' demure girl with bouquet holding glass to lips, VG+, A8..............**$145.00**

Bevo/Anheuser-Busch Inc, trade card, 'The Home Of Bevo' with facts & figures below large building, fancy vining border, 7x11", VG, A8 ....**$140.00**

Bevo/Anheuser-Busch Inc, tray, product name on red rim bordering horse-drawn wagon in country scene, 10x13", VG+, A19 ....**$110.00**

Bewitching Cigars, box label, salesman's sample, girl relaxing on hammock surrounded by flowers, EX, A5...**$55.00**

Beymer-Bauman White Lead, string holder, die-cut tin, name on panel above figure of the Dutch boy on window frame with bucket, 28x14x5", G, A9 ....**$2,800.00**

BF Goodrich, see also Goodrich

BF Goodrich Tires, sign, die-cut porcelain, BFG logo above lettering, blue background, 16x36", VG, D21 ....**$100.00**

BF Gravely & Sons Special Crimp Cut Pipe Tobacco, pocket tin, vertical, light blue with red, yellow & black lettering above & below man in turban, full, EX, A18 ....$365.00

BF Gravely & Sons Special Crimp Cut Pipe Tobacco, pocket tin, vertical, product name above & below image of person pointing to yellow paper, rare, 4½", VG+, A18 ....$265.00

BH Douglass & Sons Perfected Capsicum Cough Drops, tin, green, vertical square with 2 concave sides, slip lid, Ginna, EX, A18...$125.00

BHC & S Co's Choice Quality Coffee, milk can, red & white, bail handle, 5-lb, 12", G-, A2....................$230.00

Big Ben, canister, with Specimen coupon, product name above horse, Valuable B&W Coupons Inside This Tin... below, EX, A3...$30.00

Big Ben, cigarette papers, NM, A7......................$5.00

Big Ben Pipe & Cigarette Smoking Tobacco, pocket tin, red & yellow with image of Big Ben tower, Big Ben repeated on yellow band above, M, A18 ....$2,150.00

Big Ben Smoking Tobacco, sign, cardboard, product name on band above rider on horse & pocket tin, Save Big Ben Coupons, 14x20", EX, A7 ....$20.00

Big Boy, ashtray, smoked glass, white & gold image of Big Boy in center with outline border, curved sides, 1970s, 2x2", M, D25 ....$35.00

Big Boy, bank, Big Boy figure, soft molded vinyl with removable head, 1973, 9", M $30.00

Big Boy, figure, Big Boy, Dakin, 1974, M, D27........$100.00

Big Boy Beer, label, Bloomer Brewery Inc, Internal Revenue Tax Paid statement, 1933-50, 12-oz, M, A10 ....$30.00

Big Boy Cola, sign, tin, Drink...Because It's Better, BB logo & tilted bottle at right, red with black border, 18x30", G, A6 ....$85.00

Big Boy Grape-Ju, sign, cardboard, ...In The Big Bottle, 2 clusters of grapes flanking bottle, 1920s-30s, 20x12", EX+, A13 ....$120.00

Big Boy New Orange, sign, tin, product name above bottle against oranges & leaves, Made From..., orange on blue, 1920s-30s, 20x12", EX+, A13 ....$120.00

Big Boy Pale Dry, sign, tin, bottle left of Big Boy Pale Dry & 5¢ dot, In Green Bottles Only on band below, 9x19", NM, A7 ....$70.00

Big Boy Red Head Spark Plugs, tin, pictures boy holding logo, flat-sided with checkered slip lid, 4¼x2x1⅞", EX, D37...$150.00

Big Boy Soft Drink, sign, embossed tin, A Real Drink, boy with bottle above Big Boy on yellow background, black & red border, 35", G, A21......................$95.00

Big Chief/Quachita Coca-Cola, bottle, EX, A7........$20.00

Big City Asparagus, crate label, skyline & tall buildings on orange background, M, D12 ....$2.00

Big City Tomatoes, lug box label, city skyline on orange background, Sacramento, M, D12 ....$2.00

Big Giant Cola, sign, tin, product name above comical image of bottle lifting weights, For A Real Lift..., 24x12", EX+, D30 ....$100.00

Big Jo Flour, pocket mirror, celluloid, Riverside Mills arched above Our Best Big Joe Flour, Wabasha Minn, round, EX, A11 ....$20.00

Big Noise, cigar box label, outer, girl yelling in megaphone above pile of sporting equipment, 1911, NM, A5 ..$75.00

Big Patch, crate label, vegetable, little boy in patched overalls gazing at fields with dog at his feet, 7x9", M, D3.......$3.00

Big Sky Beer, sign, product sign above plastic cowboy & calf on metal sky background, From The Big Sky Country below, 19", VG+, A8 ....$160.00

Big Wolf, cigar box label, outer, green wolf showing his teeth, 4½x4½", M, D5 ....$2.00

Bigger Hair Chew or Smoke Tobacco, pack, profile image of black person on yellow, full, NM, A18..............$65.00

Bigger Hair Smoke or Chew Tobacco, container, all cardboard, profile image of black person on yellow, slip lid, 7x5" dia, scarce, EX+, A18.................................$200.00

Bigger Hair Smoke or Chew Tobacco, container, cardboard with tin bottom, profile image of black person on yellow paper label, slip lid, round, EX+, A18 .....$150.00

Bill's Culmbacher Beer, label, Independent Milwaukee Brewery, U-type permit number, Internal Revenue Tax Paid statement, 1933-36, 12-oz, NM, A10 ....$25.00

Billings-Chapin Finest Paints, Enamels & Varnishes, sign, porcelain flange, Bill Chape Says: Use..., painter leaning on large paint can, orange, blue & white, 24", VG, A6 ....$200.00

Billings-Chapin Flexo Flint Finish, light fixture, 4-sided glass paneled fixture with colorful decals, 8½x6x6", EX, A9 ....$500.00

Billy Buster Shoes, stickpin, oval plastic end with image of young boy, EX, A11...$90.00

Biltrite Heels & Soles, thermometer, tin, We Rebuild Like New above bulb on sole of shoe, product name below, 15", NM+, D30 ....$85.00

Binder's Beverages, sign, embossed tin, Binder's lettered above bottle, Beverages 'They're Better' below, 28x20", NM, A13 ....$45.00

Bing's Resilient Mainsprings/OH Bingenheimer Co, tin, flat, lettering within decorative border, rectangular, rounded corners, ⅞x2¾x5⅛", EX, D37 ....$40.00

Bingo/Holister Co, label, Bingo in 'icy' letters, EX+, A19 ....$15.00

Bininger's Festive Whiskey, barrel label, comical image of bears in woodland scene, framed, image: 15" dia, VG, A9 ....**$1,050.00**

Binzel Beer, label, Binzel Brewing Co, Internal Revenue Tax Paid statement, 1933-50, 12-oz, NM, A10 ......**$25.00**

Birchola, sign, flange, Ice Cold Birchola Sold Here in white & red on green & white, EX, D30......................**$125.00**

Birchola, sign, tin, Drink Birchola In Bottles flanked by bottles, red, cream & green, 1930s, 10x28", EX+, D19 ....**$65.00**

Birchola, syrup dispenser, ceramic, ball shape with tall flared base, Drink... & leaf design, original pump, 15", EX, A2 ....**$880.00**

Bird Valley, crate label, apple, blue crow perched on shield, orange background, M, D3.........................**$2.00**

Birds Golden Raising Powder, tin, English, 4-oz, A7 ..**$6.00**

Birdseye Frosted Foods, sign, glass light-up with metal frame, Birdseye on dove, red, white & blue, 15x30", EX, A6 ....**$250.00**

Bireley's, door push plate, glass, Ice Cold above Bireley's & tilted bottle, Please Keep Door Closed below, 1950s, 6x3", NM+, A4 ....**$25.00**

Bireley's, thermometer, Drink... on red, black, white & blue circle design above bottle & bulb, 28", NM+, D30..**$135.00**

Bireley's Beverages, sign, metal, Drink above Bireley's on blue design, Non-Carbonated Beverages below, yellow background, 10x28", EX, A6..............................**$40.00**

Bireley's Orangeade, sign, tin, glass with straw at left of product name in white on red, 1937, 32x56", VG, D19 ....$200.00

Bischoff's Breakfast Cocoa, tin, sample, red & white product name & emblem with decorative border, RG Collas, round, slip lid, 3¾x2½", EX, D37 ....**$60.00**

Bishops Rough House Chocolates, sign, die-cut porcelain shield, 18x16½", G, A9 ....**$125.00**

Bismark Cafe Special Brew, drinking glass, stemmed goblet, etched name above & below bust portrait, H Weinhard Portland below, 7", NM, A8 ....**$50.00**

Bisonoil, can, buffalo on grassy hill lettered It's More Than Oil — It's Bisonoil..., white, red & black, 1-qt, EX+, A1 ....**$165.00**

Bissell's Carpet Sweepers, rack, wood with cardboard sign at top, Bissell's 'Cyco' Bearing...Are The Best, 6 wooden pegs, 47x16½", VG, A6 ....**$100.00**

Bit-O-Honey, sign, embossed tin, product name above candy bar with bunch of almonds & 5¢, 9x20", EX, A13 ....$650.00

Bixby's Royal Polish, sign, paper, The Old Woman Who Lived In A Shoe Always Used..., children playing around shoe, 20x13", VG+, A9...........................**$250.00**

Black & White Roll Cut Smoking Tobacco, pocket tin, vertical, black & white diagonal background with reversed black & white lettering, tall, EX, A18...**$350.00**

Black Bear, tobacco tag, oval, EX, D35 ....**$6.00**

Black Bear Motor Oil, can, bear leaning on lettered barrel, orange & black, easy pour, wire handle with wood grip, 5-gal, 22x11" dia, VG+, A6......................**$135.00**

Black Beau Candy, tin, pictures black boy holding bouquet of flowers, EX, D6 ....**$70.00**

Black Bird, tobacco box label, name above bird on branch & stream, 1886, 14", NM, A7................................**$35.00**

Black Brewing Co, print on board, bust image in profile of Chief Blackhawk, framed, 24x21½", VG+, A8....**$265.00**

Black Cat Cigarettes, sign, Give Me Black Cat Every Time! above woman holding black cat & smoking a cigarette, 1950s, framed, 32x22", EX, D8 ..$200.00

Black Crook Habana, box label, salesman's sample, ballet recital, EX, A5..**$340.00**

Black Dallas Bock Beer, label, Schepps Brewing Co, U-type permit number, Internal Revenue Tax Paid statement, 1933-36, 12-oz, M, A10 ....**$25.00**

Black Draught, dispenser, porcelain, open front on white vertical container with black lettering, 6 original packages, 24", NM, A2..................................$190.00

Black Eagle Beer/Class & Nachod Brewing Co, sign, tin, man at table by hearth with product, product label below, pre-1920s screened over in 1933-34, 19x13", VG+, A8................................$355.00

Black Eagle Beer/Poth Brewing Co, label, Internal Revenue Tax Paid statement, 1933-50, 12-oz, NM, A10.........$12.00

Black Jack Chewing Gum, jigsaw puzzle, woman forcing gum into mouth of man with armfull of packages, advertising below, 1933, 10x7", EX, D10.........$40.00

Black Kow, sign, tin, product name on white oval flanked by cow with bottle & In Bottles 5¢, red background, 12x28", EX, D30....................................$135.00

Black Label Beer/Carling Brewing Co, can, pull-tab, Boston Bruins Stanley Cup Champions 1969-70, NM, A19..$30.00

Black Maria, tobacco tag, oval, EX, D35.....................$4.00

Black Oak, tobacco box label, name below drummer with street scene beyond, 14", NM, A7 ....$15.00

Black Sea, cigarette papers, NM, A7 ....$5.00

Black Swan Fine Twist/Watson & McGill, label, product & company name around cameo image of girl bordered by flowers, 1873, matted & framed, 12x12", EX, A21..$35.00

Black-Draught, dispenser, porcelain, 3-sided vertical container, dispenses from bottom, 1940s, 24x3", NM, A13..$190.00

Black-Draught, dispenser, porcelain, 3-sided vertical container, dispenses from bottom, 1940s, 24x3", EX, A13..$130.00

Blackbird Spices, tin, paper label, 2½", NM, A7.......$30.00

Blackhawk Mills Our Leader Coffee, tin, red with gold graphics & lettering, round & shouldered with round lid, VG+, A18................................$220.00

Blackhawk Topping Beer, matchbook, pictures an Indian, 20 strike, front strike, NM, D28 ....$4.00

Blackwell's Durham, premium catalog, Catalogue Of Premiums above soft pack of tobacco, pipe & cigarettes, Save... below, 1904, 8 pgs, NM, A7.......................$70.00

Blair Feed Mills, whetstone, celluloid, 'A Feed For Every Need' arched above Honey Bee Feeds..., pink & black, round, EX+, A11......................................$18.00

Blanke-Wenneker Candy Co, calendar, 1916, elegant lady in purple dress & plumed headband, yellow floral background, framed, 36x10", VG+, A8 ....$155.00

Blanke's World's Fair Coffee, tin, red with vertical oval image of 1903 St Louis, tall tubular shape, VG, A2.............$190.00

Blatz Beer, display, flocked pot metal, ...It's Draft-Brewed Blatz At Local Prices on plaque above running waiter, 19", EX, A8..$60.00

Blatz Beer, display, light-up, banjo player with Blatz barrel body singing 'I'm From Milwaukee' next to bottle on stage, EX, A8 ....$100.00

Blatz Beer, display, plaster, Bartender Joe standing on marked base holding bottle, EX+, A8 ....$90.00

Blatz Beer, sign, die-cut porcelain, ...Made In Milwaukee, white on blue with white border, pre-1920s, 35x45", VG, A19..$60.00

Blatz Beer, sign, tin on cardboard, ...Milwaukee's Most Exquisite Beer 15¢ A Bottle, Pale Dry, bottle & glass, 14x11", NM, A13................................$160.00

Blatz Brewing Co, sign, tin, shows table with product bottles & a full glass in elegant setting, pre-1920s, matted & framed, VG+, A19................................$355.00

Blatz Brewing Co, see also Val Blatz Brewing Co

Blatz Milwaukee, drinking glass, slightly flared rim with applied raised white lettering & star logo, NM, A8..$20.00

Blatz Old Heidelberg Beer, sign, 3-D plaster, colorful image of barmaid dancing atop barrel, 1933, 36x22", EX, A6..$475.00

Blatz Old Heidelberg Brew Milwaukee, drinking glass, straight-sided, etched lettering, NM, A8................$45.00

Blatz Pilsner Beer, can, cone-top, NM, A8.............$40.00

Blatz-Milwaukee Old Heidelberg Beer, drinking glass, pilsner, etched star encircled with product name, 8", NM, A8..$20.00

Blazing Star, crate label, California pear, yellow flower in center box on blue background, Kelseyville, 8x11", M, D12..$5.00

Bliss Native Herbs, match holder, product name above image of Capitol Hill on red, yellow holder with text, ca 1915, 6½x4½", NM, A13 ....$260.00

Blitz Weinhard, display, plaster, Better But Blitz! above mountain next to winking 'Bavarian' gent holding up frothy mug, 9x9", VG+, A8 ....$100.00

Blitz Weinhard, sign, Blitz Weinhard on oval above Always In Good Taste! in script, blue & gold, 13x13", VG+, A8 ....$20.00

Blitz Weinhard, sign, reverse-painted glass, product name on oval with Light & Lively ribbon on striped background, 8x12", VG, A8...............................$55.00

Blondie Paints, sign, litho tin, head shot of Blondie looking down on Dagwood 'the artist,' red ground, 1946, 5x6", NM, A3 ....$35.00

Blood Orange Pellets, tin, red with black graphics & lettering, vertical square with smaller round lid, VG+, A18...............................$105.00

Blood's Pure Ground Cloves, tin, product name above & below beehive, 3", NM, A7...............................$35.00

Blu-Green, poster, paper on masonite, Blu-Green diagonally above 2 lightning bolts leading to Fights Carbon, 46x34", EX+, A1...............................$40.00

Blue Badge Fine Cut, pocket tin, vertical, embossed name on red emblem with blue ribbon, VG+, A18 ..$2,000.00

Blue Beacon Coal, sign, tin, Your Guide To Fuel Economy in graduated letters at right of lighthouse, product name in blue, 12x15", NM, D30 ....$175.00

Blue Bird, sign, cardboard hanger, Let's Drink... More Delicious Than Grape Juice above Armstrong girl & bluebirds, 12x9", EX, A16 ....$140.00

Blue Bird, sign, tin & cardboard, Let's Drink Blue Bird, More Delicious Than Grape Juice!, red on yellow, no image, 9x10", EX, D30 ....$75.00

Blue Bird Cinnamon, tin, paper label with bird's image above Blue Bird lettered on center band, NM, A7 ..$45.00

Blue Bird Marshmallows, tin, triangular with lid showing blue birds perched in tree watching group roast marshmallows, 7", EX, A18...............................$115.00

Blue Boar Tobacco, humidor, porcelain, pictures tavern, coach & cottage scenes, 8x6", NM+, A3 ....$95.00

Blue Boar Tobacco, tin, sample, round with embossed top, 1¼x1¾" dia, EX, A18 ....$140.00

Blue Bonnet Coffee, tin, product name above & below lady's head on 2-color background flanked by Vacuum & Packed, key-wind, 1-lb, G, A7...............................$20.00

Blue Buckle OverAlls for Boys, sign, die-cut cardboard, young boy sitting on fence atop sign, 13½x9½", G, A2...............................$30.00

Blue Chelean, crate label, Washington apple, arched 3-D lettering on light blue, brown & dark blue background, Chelan, 9x11", M, D12...............................$2.00

Blue Eagle Guaranteed Motor Oil, can, product lettering above & below eagle logo, metallic blue & silver, pour top & handle, 2-gal, VG+, A1 ....$50.00

Blue Heron, crate label, Florida citrus, blue heron stalking through cattails & reeds, red background, Brooksville, M, D12...............................$3.00

Blue Jewel Cream of Tarter, tin, paper label, 1¾", NM, A7 ....$20.00

Blue Jewel Ginger, tin, paper label, 2½", NM, A7 ....$22.00

Blue Label Beer, label, Pittsburgh Brewing Co, Internal Revenue Tax Paid statement, 1933-50, 12-oz, M, A10...............................$15.00

Blue Larkspur, crate label, apple, bay racehorse with blue winner's neck wreath, M, D3...............................$5.00

Blue Ribbon Bourbon, oleograph, colorful image of the distillery with product name on roof, framed, 38x48", EX, A6 ....$525.00

Blue Ribbon Brand Coffee, tin, cream lettering on blue, 1-lb, EX, A3...............................$35.00

Blue Ribbon Dental Cream, full tube, NMIB, A7.....$20.00

Blue Ribbon Vehicles, sign, wood, ...Made By Durant-Dort Carriage Co, Flint, Mich, 12x72", EX, D8.........$1,100.00

Blue Rock, tobacco tag, die-cut bird, EX, D35.........$10.00

Blue Sunoco, gas globe, product name in blue on elongated yellow diamond, yellow metal body, 15" dia, NM, A6...............................$375.00

Blue Sunoco 200, sign, porcelain, Blue Sunoco in yellow on blue diamond with red arrow over yellow vertical diamond, 21x15", EX, A6...............................$140.00

Blue Wagon Staple Cotton, flue cover, celluloid, product name arched above wagon & Will Pay More Dollars Per Acre, red, white & blue, EX+, A11 ....$130.00

Blue-Jay Corn Plasters, display, die-cut tin, Don't Whittle Corns, grandpa in rocking chair whittling, ad panel on front of legs, 14", VG+, A1 ....$280.00

Blue-Jay Corn Plasters, display, die-cut tin, Sakes Alive Everbody Uses..., grandma in rocking chair, ad panel on front of legs, 14", G+, A9 ....$200.00

Bluebird Ground Mustard, tin, 3¼", NM, A7 ....$50.00

Bluff City Brewery Inc/Bock Beer, sign, cardboard, Draught & In Bottles above ram's head in profile, Bock Beer in bold letters, 18x12", G+, A8...............................$20.00

Bluhill Coffee, milk can, light blue with blue lettering & steaming cup on white label, bail handle, 5-lb, 12", EX, A2...............................$205.00

Blushing Melons, lug box label, girl at beach with wind blowing her yellow dress, M, D12 ....$5.00

BMC Best Roller Flour, sign, flange, black flag shape with Buy above end of wooden barrel showing name on red & blue shield, 12x18", EX, A2 ....$185.00

Boardman's Allspice, tin, paper label, 3¼", NM, A7 ..$40.00

Bob White Baking Powder, tin, product name above & below image of a bobwhite on paper label, with contents, 4-oz, NM, A7 ....$90.00

Bock Beer, label, Auto City Brewing Co, Internal Revenue Tax Paid statement, 1933-50, 12-oz, M, A10.........$20.00

Boeing Building Defense, license plate attachment, die-cut tin, keyhole shape with 4-engine bomber, early 1940s, red, white & blue, 4x7", EX, A1.............$130.00

Bohemian Beer, sign, plaster, 'Wanted' poster, gun & sherrif's badge applied to wood-look plaque, Big Reward..., 1950s, 13x11", VG+, A8.........................$40.00

Bohemian Club Bock Beer, label, Moose Brewing Co, Internal Revenue Tax Paid statement, 1933-50, 12-oz, M, A10.........................$12.00

Bolivar, cigar box label, outer, portrait flanked by medallions, M, A5.........................$75.00

Bols Liqueurs, display, plaster, lettered oval & Dutch gent holding cordial on bottle base, Since 1575, 29 Delicious..., 17", VG+, A8.........................$85.00

Bomb-Buster Pop Corn, can, product name & 'exploding' graphics on paper label, with contents, 5", NM, A7 ..$20.00

Bon Ton, tobacco tag, round, EX, D35.........................$3.00

Bon Voyage, cigar box label, inner lid, sailing ship & images of Mercury, 1920, 6x9", EX, D5.................$25.00

Bon-Air Smoking Mixture, pocket tin, cream with black lettering, red lid & 3 red stripes at bottom, EX+, A18 ....$175.00

Bon-Ami Cleanser, tin, cardboard & tin, flat-sided, pry lid, 2½", NM, A7 ....$15.00

Bond Bread, blotter, The Lone Ranger Says...'Let Safety Be Your Rule For The Honor Of Your School,' NM, A16.........$25.00

Bond Bread, broom holder, metal, Fresh Bond Bread on red circle with serrated edge on white panel, blue legs, 1930s-40s, EX+, A13.........................$210.00

Bond Bread, end label, black & white photo image of Hopalong Cassidy on Topper, red border, EX, D29.........$12.00

Bond Bread, end label, black & white photo image of James Bond in card game, white border, EX, D29.............$20.00

Bond Bread, end label, colorful image of Hopalong Cassidy shooting at bank robbers, red border, EX, D29......$6.00

Bond Bread, matchbook, Navy Planes series, Helldiver, 20 strike, front strike, NM, D28.........................$6.50

Bond Bread, sign, paper, Easter Greetings above girl watering pot of lilies, loaf of bread & name below, 1930s, 38x13", NM+, A13.........................$210.00

Bond Bread, sign, porcelain, Bond Bread, The Home-Like Loaf in black on yellow with white border, 14x19", VG, A6.........................$60.00

Bond Bread, sign, porcelain, Fresh Bond Bread, red & black lettering with red line border, 1940s, 4x18", EX+, A13.........................$65.00

Bond of Union Smoking Mixture, tin, name above & below image of 3 gents lying on grass, soldiers beyond, rectangular, rounded corners, EX, A18.............$145.00

Bond Street Pipe Tobacco, pocket tin, sample, vertical, pictures building with large Bond Street sign, reads Trial Size, 2x3", VG, A7.........................$35.00

Bond Street Pipe Tobacco, pocket tin, sample, vertical, pictures building with large Bond Street sign, reads Trial Size, 2x3", NM, A18.........................$100.00

Bonner & Marshall Brick Co, pocket mirror, company name on white emblem on brick wall, round, EX, A11.........................$20.00

Bonnie Rolled Oats, container, Scottish girl dancing in center, Quaker Oats Co, 3-lb, NM+, A3 ....$100.00

Bonnie True, cigar box label, printer's proof, portrait surrounded by flowers, EX, A5.........................$55.00

Booster Cigar/Stirton & Dyer, sign, paper, dapper cigar-smoking black man observing lady adjusting her garter, framed, image: 24x16½", EX+, A18.........$525.00

Booster Motor Oil, can, product name above Guaranteed 100% Pure logo, red, white, black & gray, screw cap & handle, 2-gal, 11x8", EX, A6.........................$20.00

Boot Jack Chewing Tobacco, sign, reverse-painted glass, mountain climber admiring view above product name, Costliest..., 1905-10, 12x8", NM, A13.........$550.00

Booth's Creamy Root Beer, can, cone-top, G, A16.$25.00

Boothbys Shore Diners, mechanical toothpick, fish shape, blue & white, EX, A11.........................$85.00

Borax Extract of Soap, sign, porcelain, Use...For Washing Everything, white, blue & orange, white border, 1900-15, 10x14", EX, A13.........................$250.00

Borax Soap, sign, porcelain, Save Wrappers From Premiums, Welcome..., colorful image of clothes on clothesline, 10x27½", EX, A6.........................$675.00

Borden's, pamphlet, 'The Story Of Elsie The Cow,' ca 1975, 8x3", NM, D24.........................$5.00

Borden's, pin-back button, Elsie's Bagel & Cream Cheese, Junior Member arched above Elsie's image, 1¼", NM, A7.........................$70.00

Borden's, sign, Borden's products & lettering on front, reference on history, nutrition, etc on back, 1924, framed, 25x19", NM, A3...$165.00

Borden's, sign, die-cut cardboard stand-up, Borden's Have One Now, pictures float in glass & pie a la mode, 17x21", EX, A7...$35.00

Borden's, sugar bowl & creamer, Elsie & Beauregard head figures, F&F Plastic, M, pair $65.00

Borden's, toy horse-drawn milk wagon, wood with paper litho details, A Rich Toy, 1930s-40s, 20" long, EX, A13 ....$325.00

Borden's, toy horse-drawn milk wagon, wood with paper litho details, A Rich Toy, 1930s-40s, 20" long, G, A13 ....$175.00

Borden's Ice Cream, sign, reverse-painted glass countertop, You Know It's Pure! on ribbon banner above product name, NM+, A16 ....$140.00

Borden's Malted Milk, container, aluminum with imprinted black Borden's above red Malted Milk in script, EX+, A18...$110.00

Borden's Malted Milk, jar, flat-sided clear glass with tall round neck, knobbed lid, painted label with product name & eagle, 7", VG, A1...$85.00

Borden's Malted Milk, tip tray, girl in maid's uniform with serving tray, ...In The Square Package on rim, 4½" dia, G, A9 ....$85.00

Borden's Milk, can, cardboard & tin, product name above & below 'Silver Cow,' 2¼", NM, A7 ....$20.00

Borden's Milk, can, cardboard & tin, product name above & below Elsie's portrait, 2¼", NM A7 ....$25.00

Born & Co Pale XX, drinking glass, straight-sided with flat bottom, etched name & Columbus Ohio with fancy diamond logo, 3½", NM, A8...$40.00

Boscul Coffee, tin, sample, Vaccum Packed above & It's Minus The Chaff below name flanked by diamond images, 2¼x2¾", EX, D37 ....$90.00

Boston Daily & Sunday Globe, sign, tin, jolly fat man with Largest Circulation In New England on his belly, For Sale Here below, 17½x11", EX, A6 ....$650.00

Boston Garter, display case, wood with gold lettering, glass front with paper litho inserts, 6x14x9", EX, A12...$130.00

Boston Herald, tip tray, lettering on red rim around newsboy hawking papers, yellow background, 3½" dia, VG, A21 ....$145.00

Boston Stock Ale, can, cone-top, multicolored oval logo on silver-tone can, 1-qt, M, A8.................................$495.00

Bostonians Shoes for Men, shoehorn, black with engraved shield & crest emblem, 4" long, VG, D24..............$15.00

Botl'O Orange, sign, tin, Call For... at left of tilted bottle, And Other Flavors below, 12x24", NM+, D30 ....$120.00

Bounty Cigarette Case/Blended Turkish & Domestic Tobacco, pocket tin, vertical, blue with name above & below cigarette lettered Roll Your Own, EX+, A18...$60.00

Bounty Cigarette Tobacco, cigarette papers, NM, A7 ..$6.00

Bournville Cocoa, tin, sample, lid shows round can above Made By 'Cadbury,' rectangular with rounded corners, ½x1¾x2½", EX, D37.........$75.00

Bower & Bartlett's 'Blue Ribbon Brand' Coffees, store bin, red with gold & blue lettering & ribbon graphics, gold trim, slant top, 19x18", EX, A2....................$550.00

Bowes Seal Fast Tire & Tube Repairs, sign, die-cut tin, logo flanked by Patent Process on tire above Tire & Tube Repairs, 27x22", EX, A1..............................$425.00

Bowl of Roses Pipe Mixture, pocket tin, vertical, name above & below bowl of roses on table next to man smoking pipe by fireplace, tall, EX, A18......$180.00

Bowl of Roses Pipe Mixture, pocket tin, vertical, name above & below bowl of roses on table next to man smoking pipe by fireplace, short, EX, A18.........$170.00

Bowl of Roses Pipe Mixture, pouch, paper, name above & below bowl of roses on table next to man smoking pipe by fireplace, unopened, EX+, A18................$50.00

Bowl of Roses Pipe Mixture, tin, name above & below bowl of roses on table next to man smoking pipe by fireplace, round, pry lid, 5", NM, A18...................$35.00

Bowl of Roses Pipe Mixture, tin, name above & below bowl of roses on table next to man smoking pipe by fireplace, square, slip lid, 1-oz, EX+, A18..........$110.00

Bowl of Roses Pipe Mixture, tin, paper label, name above round image of bowl of roses by pipe & product can, round, unopened, EX+, A18................................$50.00

Bowles Live Stock Commission Co, whetstone, For Salesmen 'Sharp As A Razor' Try..., blue & white, oval, EX, A11 ....$18.00

Boy-O-Boy! Hot Popcorn, box, boy's head above product name, 5½x3¼", NM, A7 ....$8.00

Boye Patent Spring Curtain Holder, display case, metal, pictures a bed on front, ...For Beds, Windows & Doors, yellow, brown & rust, 8x9x7½", VG, A6 ....$115.00

Boylston Bock, sign, paper litho, product name above & below ram's head, Erie Litho Co, 37x25", VG+, A19 ....$130.00

BPS Lumber Paint, sign, porcelain, BPS encircled in lower left corner, Lumber Paint in bold letters, 2-sided, 24x48", G, A6 ....$55.00

Brabo Brand Coffee, tin, red Brabo above oval image of a grove, white Coffee on black band below, round, gold screw lid, 1-lb, VG+, A18.................................$200.00

Bracelet, cigar box label, inner lid, early, hand holding bundle of cigars, 6x9", VG, D5...........................$30.00

Bradbury's Equalizer for Horses, bottle, with contents, NM, A7 ....$20.00

Braems Bitters, sign, aluminum, Drink... above bottle, For Appetite below, 1906 Pure Food Statement, 13½x7", VG+, A8 ....$35.00

Brandimist, sign, tin, Drink... First For Thirst, 2-color background with bottle at left, 1928, framed, horizontal, EX+, A16 ....$130.00

Brandreth Pill, booklet, The Beautiful Brandreth Pill above surreal image of Egyptian woman, 1880s, 20 pgs, EX, D23 ....$35.00

Braumeister Beer, sign, composition, Ask & For flank portrait above scrolled banner, Milwaukee's Choicest..., self-framed, 11x13", EX, A19 ....$40.00

Braumeister Special Pilsener Beer, sign, glass, foil on blue, We Suggest above product name, 'Milwaukee's Choicest' below, metal frame, 8x12", VG+, A8.....$45.00

Brazier's Chocolates, sign, self-framed tin, Chrysanthemum Girl, Choice Of Cultured Tastes below, American Artworks, ca 1910, 14x12", VG+, A9 ....$475.00

Brazil Beer, sign, curved porcelain, Quaker man encircled by Brazil Brewing Co... in center, red, white & blue, 20x13", EX+, A9..$700.00

Brazilla, dispenser, stoneware, white barrel shape with blue stripes & red lettering, Drink Brazilla 5¢, 11½x8" dia, NM, A6...$900.00

Breakfast Belle, crate label, Florida citrus, black maid serving breakfast, 9x3", M, D3.................................$2.00

Breakfast Cheer Dripco Coffee, tin, coffeepot in lined oval on side, key-wind lid, NM, A3 ....$35.00

Brehm's Brew, label, 1933-34, Baltimore Brewing Co, U-type permit number, Internal Revenue Tax Paid statement, 12-oz, M, A10 ....$16.00

Breidt's, tap knob, black ball with gold & white on red enamel insert, EX+, A8.....................................$75.00

Breidt's Draught Beer, label, 1933-50, Internal Revenue Tax Paid statement, 64-oz, NM, A10 ....$28.00

Brew 66 Special Draught, bank, plaster, upright barrel with cork in bung, 2-sided embossed lettering, gold banded, 12", VG+, A8.......................................$35.00

Brew 66 Special Draught, display, molded composition, barrel behind bartender with frothy mug on bar, Sicks' Century Brewery, 20x14", A8................................$85.00

Brewers' Best, sign, die-cut metal, round logo left of Brewers' Best in cut-out letters atop base, The New Big Name In Beer, VG+, A8.......................................$70.00

Brewers' Best, tap knob, large chrome ball shape with B/B logo encircled by Brewers' Best, Peter Breidt Brewing Co, NM, A8..$95.00

Breyers Ice Cream, sign, metal, Breyers in script on green leaf above Ice Cream in curved lettering, white background, 58", VG+, A21....................................$60.00

Breyers Ice Cream, soda glass, green logo, tapered & footed, 6x3", M, D16 ....$5.00

Briar Pipe or Cigarette Tobacco, cigarette papers, NM, A7...$60.00

Briardale Quick Cooking Rolled Oats, container, cardboard, sheath of wheat above name in script & white Rolled Oats on red oval, 3-lb, EX+, A3 ..$22.00

Bricks Jubilee Beer, can, cone-top, Internal Revenue Tax Paid statement, 12-oz, NM, A19 ....$90.00

Bridge Club Coffee, tin, product name lettered across playing card marked Vacuum Packed, key-wind lid, NM, A3 ....$55.00

Bridgestone Tires, tire rack, BS logo on black tire design above red & black product name, yellow background, 10x15x9", NM, D8 ....$95.00

Briggs Pipe Mixture, pocket tin, vertical, product name above hand-held pipe, 'When A Feller Needs A Friend' below, dark brown, EX, A3 ....$25.00

Brillo, sign, die-cut cardboard, open box of Brillo pads on handle of skillet showing hand scrubbing with pad, 14", VG, A2 ....**$85.00**

British Consols Navy Cut Extra Mild Pipe Tobacco, tin, blue-green with cream name above diagonal image of navy ship, gold screw lid, 5x4" dia, EX+, A18 ....**$40.00**

Broadcast Gramophone Needles, tin, flat, red with gold trim, lightning bolt & globe logo above lettering, rounded corners, ½x1¼x1½", EX, D37 ....**$40.00**

Broadmoor Hotel, flier, 'Gentile Clientele,' illustrated, 1940, 4 pgs, EX, D23 ....**$25.00**

Brockton Cut Plug, tin, black lettering & high-top shoe on red rectangular shape with rounded corners, pre-1901, EX+, A18 ....**$55.00**

Bromo-Seltzer, dispenser, blue glass with metal base & stand, original bottle, 8½", EX, A3 ....**$75.00**

Bromo-Seltzer, sign, cardboard, product name & Is Sweet Relief For Overworked Nerves... above girl with glass, 18x16", G-, A9 ....**$375.00**

Bronco Artichokes, crate label, cowboy on bucking bronco fanning with hat on blue background, Castroville, M, D12 ....**$6.00**

Brookdade Orange Soda, sign, die-cut tin, bottle shape, EX+, A16 ....**$70.00**

Brooks Soft Finish Machine Cotton, spool cabinet, wood, 4-drawer with cut-out sides, 13½x22½x15", EX, A12 ....**$775.00**

Brotherhood American Yeoman, pocket mirror, shows home office encircled by lettered band, dated 1912, round, VG+, A8 ....**$20.00**

Brotherhood Tobacco, sign, cardboard, 2 workmen flank locomotive, ...Chewing & Smoking below, framed, image: 38x28", VG, A9 ....**$2,600.00**

Brown, Forman Co Distillers, sign, tin, A Pleasant Reminder..., salesman at bar getting shot of whiskey, framed, image: 19x27", VG+, A9 ....**$2,200.00**

Brown & Bigelow, calendar, 1953, shows bathing beauty, incomplete, 32x16", EX, D8 ....**$90.00**

Brown & Haley Chocolates, product box, circular bird graphic on vertical stripes with product name, orange with black, white & yellow, 10", EX, A1 ....**$15.00**

Brown Beauties, cigar box, paper on wood, pictures Indians holding shield with logo on inner lid, ca 1900, EX, A3 ....**$20.00**

Brown Derby Pilsner Beer, can, flat-top, instructional, blue, black & silver, 12-oz, EX+, A19 ....**$75.00**

Brown's Jumbo Bread, sign, die-cut tin elephant, 12½x15", EX+, A9 ....**$295.00**

Brownie Brand Salted Peanuts/United Fig & Date Co, tin, blue with white lettering around oval image of a Brownie figure on yellow, pry lid, 10-lb, EX, A2 ....**$220.00**

Brownie Chocolate Soda, sign, cardboard, If You Like Chocolate Soda above image of brownie with bottle, Drink Brownie below, 60x20", EX+, A13 ....**$280.00**

Brownie Chocolate Soda, sign, tin, If You Like Chocolate Soda Drink..., In Bottles Only, brownie pouring from bottle at left, 10x28", G+, A9 ....**$150.00**

Brownies, crate label, California orange, cute image of brownies preparing orange juice, blue ground, Lemon Cove, 10x11", M, D3 ....**$4.00**

Browning Gun Oil, container, tin, orange & brown with small oval portrait & rifle, 4¾", NM, A3 ....**$50.00**

Browning Gun Oil, tin, brown & metallic gold graphics & lettering on deep yellow, NM, A3 ....**$110.00**

Brucks Beer, drinking glass, pilsener with red graphics, logo above Brucks in diagonal script, 7½", NM, A8 ....**$50.00**

Brucks Jubilee Beer, display, plaster wall sconce, stein with lid on base marked Cincinnati's Oldest, 18", VG, A8 ....**$75.00**

Brundage Star Made Salted Peanuts, tin, maid with tray in front of star with rays in center, VG+, A3 ......**$165.00**

Brunswick, bank, Bowling Man, 1960s, EX, D27 ......**$95.00**

Brunswick Standard Regulation Bowling Alleys, plaque, embossed bronze, large lettered bowling pin left of text, 1910, 11x7", EX+, A13 ....**$125.00**

Brunswick Tires, sign, die-cut porcelain flange, product name on sign above Service Depot on band across tire, 25x15", EX, A6...**$3,750.00**

Bryan & Stevenson Cigars, box label set, oval portraits of Bryan & Stevenson, 2 pcs, EX, A5 ....**$395.00**

BT Babbitt's Cleanser, can, sample, cardboard & tin, 3", NM, A7 ....**$35.00**

BT Babbitt's Cleanser, trolley sign, cardboard, product can over split image of lady cleaning by day & out for the evening, 11x21", EX+, A1 ....**$270.00**

BT Babbitt's Soap Powder, sign, posterboard, little girl sitting atop boxes playing with fishing net, copyright 1894, 20x15", EX, A6.............................**$85.00**

BT Babbitt's 1976 Soap Powder, trolley sign, cardboard, Use It Every Day... on bottom half of circle & box flanked by hands cleaning, 11x21", NM, A1........**$30.00**

Bub's Beer, label, Peter Bub Brewery, Internal Revenue Tax Paid statement, 1933-50, ½-gal, M, A10........**$15.00**

Bubble Balloon Chewing Gum, sign, paper, product name flanks circular image of boy blowing bubble, red, white & blue, framed, 4x14", NM, A2 ....$145.00

Bubble Up, paper cup, red, white & green, sample-size, D16 ....$2.00

Bubble Up, sign, tin, arrow pointing toward bubble logo, Drink..., A Kiss Of Lemon, A Kiss Of Lime, 12x32", EX, D30 ....$85.00

Bubble Up, soda glass, red, white & blue bubble logo, tapered, 5x3", NM, D16 ....$18.00

Bubble Up, soda glass, red & green logo with allover bubbles, tapered, 5x3", NM, D16 ....$15.00

Buck, sign, embossed tin, Drink Buck, 'The Beer-y Beverage,' National Beverage Sales Co, green & red on yellow, 10x20", VG, A8 ....$50.00

Buck-Eye Cigars, tin, light blue & yellow with pink roses above & below Buck-Eye lettered in black, gold trim, square corners, VG+, A18 ....$40.00

Buck-Skin Typewriter Ribbon/FW Neely Co, tin, flat, lettering & company logo on deer skin, decorative border, rounded corners, ¾x2½x2½", EX, D37 ....$25.00

Buck-Skin Typewriter Ribbon/FW Neely Co, tin, vertical, lettering & logo on deer skin, 2½x2½", EX, D37 ....$45.00

Bucket Syrup, bucket, embossed tin, wood-look with red product name above & below framed image of product, 5x4" dia, EX+, A18 ....$90.00

Buckeye Beer, display, illuminated bottle on arched backdrop on round stepped base, 1940s, 14x8", EX+, A13 ....$400.00

Buckeye Beer, door push bar, Months In Brew-Then Served To You flanked by 2 running waiters, 3x13", EX+, A19 ....$25.00

Buckeye Beer, sign, self-framed tin, Months In Brew..., animated bar scene with Bucky serving, red & green on gold, 12x18", VG+, A8 ....$120.00

Buckeye Harvesting Machines, trade card, 3 hearts with images of 3 different women unfolds to form a fan, EX, D8 ....$60.00

Buckeye Root Beer, jug & 2 mugs, ceramic, lettered with name, NM, 16 ....$360.00

Buckeye Root Beer, mug, black logo, tail of Y forms circle around Buckeye Root Beer, regular handle, footed, 6x3½", M, D16 ....$45.00

Buckeye Root Beer, mug, black logo, tail of Y forms circle around Buckeye Root Beer, V-shaped handle, footed, 6x3½", NM, D16 ....$30.00

Buckeye Root Beer, syrup dispenser, ceramic tree stump, NM+, A4 ....$500.00

Buckeye Root Beer, syrup dispenser, ceramic urn shape, ...5¢ encircled above dancing 'centres,' original pump, 16", scarce, EX, A2 ....$2,530.00

Buckeye Root Beer, syrup dispenser, ceramic urn shape, arched lettering above foaming mug & nut-bud decor, replaced pump, 16x8", EX, A9 ....$1,200.00

Buckeye Root Beer, syrup dispenser, ceramic urn shape, black with product name on circle, no pump, 11½x8", VG, A9 ....$250.00

Buckeye Root Beer, see also Goldenmoon

Buckhorn Cigarette Case, pocket tin, vertical, red with white name above & below head image of buck, NM+, A18 ....$60.00

Buckingham, crate label, California pear, cowboy riding bucking pig, California Bartletts, Vacaville, 1920s, 7x11", M, D3 ....$3.00

Buckingham Ale, coaster, palace guard calling 'Ale! Ale! The Gang's All Here!,' yellow, red & brown, 3½" dia, VG, A8 ....$20.00

Buckingham Bright Cut Plug, see also Half & Half

Buckingham Bright Cut Plug Smoking Tobacco, pocket tin, sample, vertical, colorful lettering & graphics on black, yellow border, marked Trial Size, VG, A18 ....$120.00

Buckingham Bright Cut Plug Smoking Tobacco, pocket tin, vertical, colorful lettering & graphics, gold slip lid, EX+, A18 ....$75.00

Buckingham Bright Cut Plug Smoking Tobacco, pocket tin, vertical, colorful lettering & graphics, pry lid, NM+, A18 ....$85.00

Buckingham Bright Cut Plug Smoking Tobacco, tin, colorful lettering & graphics, pry lid, 5x5" dia, NM, A18 ....$60.00

Buckingham Bright Cut Plug Smoking Tobacco, tin, yellow with colorful lettering & graphics, slip lid, small round, EX, A18 ....$65.00

Buckskin Rubber Boots, sign, tin, product name flanked by large duck boot & boy on swing, For Sale Here below, framed, image: 16x22", G, A9 ....$225.00

Bud Light, display, light-up, molded plastic, Spud MacKenzie in red sweater with Bud Light emblem & name, dated May '87, EX, A8 ....$100.00

Budd's Baby Shoes, sign, paper, product name & text above 2 girls in pink & red, 1 playing mandolin, 1900, matted & framed, EX+, A13 ....$425.00

Budweiser, calendar, perpetual, self-framed tin, Budweiser above bottle & glass on tray, date holder below, 23x12", VG+, A1 ....$95.00

Budweiser, calendar, 1941, view of St Louis plant being compared to Chicago business district, full pad, 23x18", EX, A8 ....$130.00

Budweiser, can/bottle opener, can shape, 2½", EX, D23 ....$15.00

Budweiser, Certificate of Priority, dated April 7, 1933, issued to proprietor after prohibition, framed, VG, A8 .....$90.00

Budweiser, charger, 'Say When,' couple with man at left pouring beer into chafing dish, 16" dia, VG+, A19 ....$220.00

Budweiser, clock, Genuine...King Of Beers label with gold Clydsdale team & wagon, 13½x13½", EX, A8......$25.00

Budweiser, clock, mantel-type clock atop clear rectangular case holding a wagon & team of Clydsdales on base, 16x17", EX, A8..$85.00

Budweiser, cookie jar, glass barrel shape, A & eagle logo above wagon pulled by the Champion Clydsdales, wooden lid, 9", EX, A8 ....$120.00

Budweiser, display, 2 stacked cardboard 6-packs with top 6-pack moving up & down to expose hand (missing), 1950s, EX, A19..............................$90.00

Budweiser, drinking glass, fluted pilsener with red & black graphics, Anheuser-Busch logo above Budweiser, 8½", A8..$25.00

Budweiser, ice scraper, Have You Made The Budweiser Beer Test? above A & eagle logo, Anheuser-Busch..., trapezoid shape, EX, A8..$65.00

Budweiser, jewelry case (man's), wood with mirrored etched label on lid, 1974, 8½x10½x3½", EX, A8 ..$95.00

Budweiser, mug, ceramic, CS-22, 1876-1976 logo on field with ragged edges, regular handle, EX, A8 ....$260.00

Budweiser, mug, ceramic, CS-22, 1876-1976 logo on field with ragged edges, angled twig handle, EX, A8 ..$470.00

Budweiser, mug, clear glass, Budweiser & King Of Beers arched above & below A & eagle logo, '68 Cardinal schedule, 1968, NM, A8 ....$20.00

Budweiser, mug, CS-1, shaped as Bud Man with name embossed on chest, hollow head, EX, A8..........$280.00

Budweiser, mug, CS-19, A & eagle logo above horse-drawn wagon, inscribed St Louis Mo, Budweiser, Champion Clydsdales, EX, A8 ....$65.00

Budweiser, mug, CS-26, embossed barrel shape with A & eagle logo, product name on band below, EX, A8..$95.00

Budweiser, mug, CS-9, A & eagle logo & horse-drawn wagon, inscribed St Louis Mo, Budweiser, Champion Clydsdales, smooth lid, EX, A8 ....$250.00

Budweiser, mug, CS-9, A & eagle logo & horse-drawn wagon, inscribed St Louis, Budweiser, Champion Clydsdales, hammered lid, VG, A8 ....$175.00

Budweiser, musical coin or stamp box, 100th Anniversary, 1976, EX, A8..$165.00

Budweiser, plaque, embossed foil on masonite, 'Los Famosos Caballos...,' Clydsdales pulling wagon, Mexican colors, 12x22", VG+, A8 ....$30.00

Budweiser, plaque, etched faux marble, 100th Anniversary..., history vignettes of Budweiser, limited edition, 19x24", EX+, A8..$125.00

Budweiser, pocketknife, embossed team of Clydsdales, gold on silver, MIB, A8....................................$55.00

Budweiser, salt & pepper shakers, Bud Man figures, NM, A8..$215.00

Budweiser, salt & pepper shakers, commemorating US Bicentennial, 1 marked 200 years & the other marked 100 years, NM..$250.00

Budweiser, sign, Budweiser King Of Beers On Draught, encircled A & eagle logo above, gold on red, Becco, self-framed, 8x12", EX, A8 ....$75.00

Budweiser, sign, light-up, circle & bar emblem with A & eagle logo above Budweiser Beer, clear plastic lettered base, EX, A8 ....$70.00

Budweiser, sign, light-up, plastic with metal frame, A & eagle logo above Budweiser, Preferred Everywhere below, 10x20", VG+, A8....................................$55.00

Budweiser, sign, light-up, reverse-painted glass, logo above ...King Of Beers, For Those Who Know on base, 5x5x10", EX, A1 ....$85.00

Budweiser, sign, paper litho, Budweiser Girl (Hamilton King), A & eagle logo upper right of girl in orange, 1913, framed, EX, A19 ....$1,500.00

Budweiser, sign, porcelain, Drink Budweiser, A & eagle logo below, white on red, 2-sided, 36x72", EX, A21.....$110.00

Budweiser, sign, reverse-painted glass, We Feature in script above product name, company name below, bordered, 4x12", VG, A8 ....$55.00

Budweiser, sign, tin, Budweiser Preferred Everywhere above & below bottle & glass on tray, beveled edge, 1950s, 15x12", EX+, A8 ....$150.00

Budweiser, sign, tin on cardboard, We Feature...King of Bottled Beer, 15¢ A Bottle, bottle & glass on bull's-eye, 14x12", G+, A19 ....$85.00

Budweiser, telephone, can shape, EX, D25..............$48.00

Budweiser, tray, anodized aluminum, shows 'Budweiser Clock Tower,' scalloped rim, 14" dia, VG+, A8....$65.00

Budweiser, tray, deep-dish, Ask Your Customers To Make The Budweiser Test, bottle, glass & can on half circle, 13" dia, VG, A8..$40.00

Budweiser, tray, shows colonial hunters around hearthside table, Budweiser lettered on rim, pre-1920s, 13x18", EX, A19..$125.00

Budweiser, tray, shows the Robert E Lee steamboat at busy dockside, lettered rim, 1930s, 13x18", G-, A.........$45.00

Budweiser, tray, shows the Robert E Lee steamboat at busy dockside, lettered rim, 1930s, 13x18", VG+, A8 ..**$140.00**

Budweiser, see also Anheuser-Busch

Budweiser Barley Malt Syrup, bank, can shape with eagle logo above Hop Flavored, product & company name below, with original mailing tube, EX+, A8 ....**$165.00**

Budweiser Barley Malt Syrup, lamp shade, red, green & black over milk glass shade, 7x5" dia, VG, A9...**$250.00**

Budweiser Bottled Beer, sign, light-up, reverse-painted glass on metal footed base, We Feature...Preferred Everywhere, 11x17", EX, A8 ....**$300.00**

Budweiser Draught Beer, sign, light-up, reverse-painted glass on metal footed base, We Feature...Preferred Everywhere, 11x17", EX, A8 ....**$300.00**

Budweiser Draught Beer, sign, reverse-painted glass, We Feature...Preferred Everywhere, gold & black, framed, 8x14", EX, A8 ....**$150.00**

Budweiser Lager, can, flat-top, instructional, 12-oz, EX+, A19 ....**$15.00**

Budweiser Lager Beer, label, Anheuser-Busch Brewing Assoc, pre-prohibition, M, A10 ....**$60.00**

Budweiser Malt Syrup, syrup dispenser, union label on cylinder on black round base, NM, A19 ....**$95.00**

Budweiser/Field & Stream, mugs, ceramic, set of 4 depicting fish, bear, elk & duck scenes, Field & Stream lettered on band below, MIB, A8 ....**$200.00**

Buffalo, crate label, California apple, buffalo head in circle with shaded white logo, Watsonville, 9x11", M, D12..**$3.00**

Buffalo, tobacco tag, die-cut B, EX, D35 ....**$4.00**

Buffalo Brand Salted Peanuts, jar, glass, octagonal with red & yellow decal labels on 2 sides, knob lid, 11x10" dia, EX, A2 ....**$385.00**

Buffalo Brewing Co, tip tray, 1915 San Francisco Expo, shows figures bowing to lady at head of steps, decorative lettered rim, EX, A8 ....**$120.00**

Buffalo Club Whiskey, tray, shows bottle with black & gold label, 2 glasses & corkscrew on table, C Shonk litho, 12" dia, VG, A8 ....**$25.00**

Buffalo Evening News, news wagon, Yes Sir 'Skippy' Carries A Knife Every Day In The... on blue wood box, red wheels, black frame, EX, A2 ....**$1,540.00**

Buffalo Forge Co, sign, paper, pictures several men working in forge shop with company name upper right, 13½x16½", VG, A2 ....$145.00

Buffalo Tobacco, cigarette papers, NM, A7 ....**$7.00**

Buffalo Tobacco, pouch, cloth with paper label, ⅞-oz, NM, A7 ....**$20.00**

Bugler, cigarette papers, 25 leaves, NM, A7 ....**$4.00**

Buick, poster, litho, Don't Take Chances..., motorcycle cop scolding 2 boys riding double on bike, framed, 36x23", NM+, A1..**$70.00**

Buick, poster, litho, Tough On Tires, 2 boys on homemade car trying to stop before hitting dog & cat, framed, 36x23", M, A1..**$45.00**

Buick, poster, litho, Vacation Check-Up, Best Time Of The Year!, family in sedan, canoe atop, 1950s, framed, 36x23", NM+, A1..**$180.00**

Buick, sign, porcelain, Buick in diagonal script & Valve In Head in white on red circle with white border, 20" dia, NM, A1..**$400.00**

Buick, tire pressure gauge, bluish-green with blue & red lettering, blue & cream logo, 2x3", EX+, A6........**$75.00**

Buick Authorized Sales & Service, sign, porcelain, ...Value In Head, red, white and blue, 36" dia, EX, A6...**$850.00**

Buick Motor Cars, thermometer, porcelain, Buick lettered diagonally on square above bulb, Quinn Auto Co below, ca 1915, 27", VG, A6......................**$200.00**

Buick Motor Cars, thermometer, porcelain, Buick logo above bulb, Motor Cars & Olar Buick Co below, white on black, 27", VG, D8..**$200.00**

Buick Quick Service, sign, tin, white & black on red, white & blue bands, 16x26", EX, D8.............$250.00

Bull Dog Cut Plug De Luxe, pocket tin, vertical, product name above & below oval image of bulldog with ornate border, VG+, A3 ....**$330.00**

Bull Dog Lager Beer, sign, stick-on, 'A Man's Beer!' says Jack Dempsey, his image with bulldog & product, includes autographed photo, EX, A8.................**$100.00**

Bull Dog Malt Liquor/Drewreys Ltd, can, flat-top, 8-oz, EX+, A19..**$10.00**

Bull Dog Overalls, pocket mirror, bulldog image surrounded by advertising, red & black on white, oval, 2¾", EX, A8..**$50.00**

Bull Dog Smoking Tobacco, pocket tin, vertical, black with gold product name above & below oval image of red elephant, EX+, A18......................................**$415.00**

Bull Durham, cigarette papers, NM, A7 ....**$5.00**

Bull Durham, postcard, Panama, from the 'Trip Around The World' series of 33, NM, A16 ....**$65.00**

Bull Durham, see also Durham Smoking Tobacco

Bull Durham Plug Tobacco, label, bull standing behind fence lettered Rich & Rare Flavor, G, A5.............**$95.00**

Bull Durham Smoking Tobacco, sign, cardboard, Genuine... above bull against sunrise & Statue of Liberty, Smoking... on scroll banner, 37x28", VG, A13 ...**$325.00**

Bull Durham Tobacco, pouch, cloth with paper label, drawstring closure, NM & sealed, D35 ....**$15.00**

Bully, cigar box label, inner lid, oval image of frog smoking, 1880s, 6x9", VG, D5.................................$70.00

Bulova Watches, sign, die-cut cardboard, panoramic fairy tale image looking at castles through arch, 17½x20", G, A9...$225.00

Bulwark Cut Plug, tin, yellow with red, white & blue vertical stripes flanking bulldog & leaf logo, rectangular, rounded corners, EX+, A18........................$85.00

Bumble Bee Water Pack Royal Cherries, can label, 4½x13½", NM, A7...$3.00

Bunte Diana 'Stuft' Confectioners, tin, red & white product name on cream above & below vertical oval image of Diana with dog, 9x5" dia, EX, A18.............$55.00

Bunte Fine Confections, canister, tin, inset of girl with her dog surrounded by flowers, slip lid, NM, A3.......$40.00

Bunte Marshmallows, store tin, pictures boy with hands full of marshmallows next to lettering, factory on reverse, 9x13" dia, VG, A21.........................$255.00

Burdan's Ice-Cream, tray, product name above oval image of ice-cream soda & flowers on table, copyright 1925, 13x13", EX, A6.......................................$300.00

Bureau-Penn Motor Oil, can, product name above & below Co-op logo, United Co-operative Inc, screw cap, 2-gal, 11x8½", EX, A6................................$40.00

Burger Beer, clock, A Finer Beer Year After Year, rectangular with numbers surrounding oval Burger emblem, wood frame, 14x19", VG, A8...........................$95.00

Burger Beer, plaque, hammered copper on wood, Burger Beer, A Finer Beer — Year After Year, shows 2 hunting dogs, 11x14", EX, A8......................................$20.00

Burger Beer, plaque, hammered copper on wood, Burger Beer, What More Could A Man Ask For, shows dog's head, 14x10", EX+, A8......................................$30.00

Burger Beer, sign, tin hanger, Burger Beer, Cincinnati's Famous Beer, shows panoramic view of city, gold raised rim, 8x14", VG, A8.............................$220.00

Burger Brewing Co, ashtray, ceramic, factory scene above company name, gold rim, 4 rests, ceramic, 1964, 7" dia, EX, A8...$25.00

Burgermeister Ale, label, burgermeister left of product name on black against yellow, San Francisco Brewing Co, 11-oz, VG+, A19.......................................$16.00

Burgermeister Beer, display, plaster, metallic gold-colored burgermeister bust holding up frothy mug on lettered base, 16x14x7", EX, A8..............................$130.00

Burgermeister Beer, sign, paper, The Beer That's Made The Long Slow Natural Way!, burgermeister with tankard, 1950, 17x31", VG+, A8..........................$50.00

Burgermeister Pale Beer, plaque, copper-colored stamped metal, bust of burgermeister holding stein with name & hops on rim, 16" dia, NM, A8................$20.00

Burgermeister Pale Beer, sign, paper, 'It's Marvelous' Says Carmen Davis..., framed image of black entertainer with glass, 1950s, 19x24", VG+, A8....................$25.00

Burgermeister Pale Beer, sign, paper, Enjoy... A Truly Fine Pale Beer, black musical star Dorothy Dandrich with glass, 1952, 19x23", VG+, A8.................$25.00

Burgess Batteries, thermometer, tin, ...For Sale Here in yellow & red above bulb, factory & Uniform Power... below, 13x5", EX, D8..............................$350.00

Burgess Flashlight Battery, display, metal, product name above arrows with various sizes pointing to slots, red & black on white, 12x8x4", NM, D21..................$75.00

Burgie!, decanter, cartoon image of man holding Burgie! sign, Ceramarte, dated on base, 1971, EX, A8......$80.00

Burgie!, mug, cartoon image of man holding Burgie! sign, Ceramarte, EX, A8...................................$55.00

Burgie!, sign, porcelain, Burgie man standing with cane and raising stein, no advertising, 40x16½", VG, A8...$105.00

Burkardt's Beer & Mug Ale, display, plaster relief, product name at right of man standing at bar with bartender, 9x13", EX, A8..................................$110.00

Burley Boy, see Bagley's Burley Boy

Burma-Shave Blades, sign, wood, orange & black, 11½x41", EX, D11.....................................$175.00

Burnard & Algers Manures For All Crops, sign, porcelain, Use...Well-Known Special Manures For All Crops lettered on turnip, Plymouth below, 19½x12", VG, A6...$275.00

Burr Oak, tobacco tag, die-cut acorn, EX, D35..........$3.00

Bursley's Coffee, tin, steaming cup of coffee above Bursley's in script, key-wind lid, EX, A3.....................$50.00

Burto, box label, outer, man holding knife in his teeth, 4½x4½", M, D5...$15.00

Bus Station, sign, porcelain, frontal silhouette view of passengers boarding Bus, Station below, 1940s-50s, 16" dia, EX+, A13...$425.00

Bus Station, sign, porcelain, white Bus Station (Deco lettering) on blue above blue Flag Stop Only on white, 2-sided, 24x18", VG+, A1...................................$145.00

Busch Gardens, stein, Los Angeles & Tampa, incised parrot logo with zigzag border, Delft, EX, A8........$110.00

Busch Gardens, stein, Los Angeles & Tampa, incised parrot logo with zigzag border, Ceramarte, Rio Negrinho green mark, EX, A8.....................................$250.00

Busch Gardens, stein, The Old Country, castle scenes with lettering top & bottom, Americana, EX, A8........$145.00

Busch Gardens, stein, The Old Country, castle scenes with lettering top & bottom, Ceramarte, Rio Negrinho green mark, EX, A8..$225.00

Busch Gardens, stein, Williamsburg, embossed logroll & jungleboat rides, Ceramarte, Rio Negrinho green mark, EX, A8...$105.00

Busch-Lager Beer, tray, deep-dish, product name on trapezoid emblem in center, lime green, 14" dia, NM, A19...$45.00

Bushkill Lager Beer, baseball uniform, gray wool shirt & pants with red lettering, late 1930s, NM, A19.....$135.00

Buss Clear Window Fuses, display case, metal, Why Be Helpless... above lady changing fuses, storage racks on backside, 1930s, 16x14", EX, A1.........................$80.00

Buss Fuses For Autos & Radio, display case, metal, Why Be Helpless... above confused man & text, front slides up, with 15 fuse boxes, 1930s, VG, A6................$35.00

Buster Brown Bread, match holder, pictures Buster having a party with children, 6¾x2⅛", EX, A2..........$1,350.00

Buster Brown Bread, sign, embossed tin, Buster & Tige flank Golden Sheaf Bakery advertising, 1915-20, framed, image: 20x28", G+, A9.........................$300.00

Buster Brown Cigar, tin, elderly man blowing smoke at Buster & Tige, signed RP Outcult, slip lid, 5x5" dia, scarce, EX, A18 ....$2,420.00

Buster Brown Hose Supporter, pin-back button, tin, round, NM, A7 ....$15.00

Buster Brown Knitwear, sign, die-cut cardboard stand-up, Buster Brown & Tige playing tug of war with sock, ...For Wear! 12x18", EX, A16 ....$65.00

Buster Brown Mustard, tin, paper label, small pry lid, 2½", VG, A21 ....$90.00

Buster Brown Quality Children's Shoes, sign, die-cut particle board, ...Since 1904...Quality... flanked by Buster & Tige playing tug of war, 43" long, VG, A21 ....$120.00

Buster Brown Shoe Game, ring toss, cardboard, lettering above rules flanked by Buster & Tige & 2 kids, dealer name below, complete, NOS, A1 ....$70.00

Buster Brown Shoes, doll, Buster Brown, cloth, 1974, 14", NM, A7 ....$35.00

Buster Brown Shoes, pin-back button, Brown Bilt Club arched above image of Buster & Tige, product name below, EX, A20 ....$10.00

Buster Brown Shoes, sign, die-cut tin, image of Tige pulling Buster in shoe, ...For Boys-For Girls lettered on wheels, 25x40", EX, A21 ....$12,100.00

Buster Brown Shoes, whistle, tin, pictures Buster & Tige, rectangular, EX+, A16 ....$32.00

Buster Brown Shoes, wrapping paper, 30x18", EX, A7 ..$25.00

Buster Brown Vacation Days Carnival, pocket mirror, head images of Buster & Tige, yellow & light green background, copyright 1945, EX+, A8 ....$40.00

Buster Chew or Smoke, tobacco tag, EX, D35 ....$5.00

Buster Cola, bottle display, die-cut cardboard, Buster Cola on arrow pointing to space for bottle, Bigger & Better, 5¢, EX, A16 ....$40.00

Busy Biddy Allspice, tin, product name above & below hen, 3", NM, A7 ....$170.00

Busy Biddy Mustard, tin, product name above & below hen, 3½", NM, A7 ....$200.00

Butler Bros, catalog, Spring/Summer, 1934, 178 pgs, EX, D17 ....$60.00

Butter Krust Bread, sign, die-cut porcelain, smiling boy holding up slice of bread, product name on bib, 1930s, 18½x14", NM, A13 ....$2,100.00

Butter Krust Bread, toy spinner, Whistle For..., 1½" dia, EX, A7 ....$25.00

Butter-Kist Peanuts, box, shows kids fishing, 5½x3½", NM, A7 ....$12.00

Butter-Nut Bread, door push, porcelain, Butter-Nut Bread on red flanked by proprietor's name on white ovals, 1930s, 4x30", EX+, A13 ....$100.00

Butter-Nut Bread, sign, die-cut cardboard, girl at lunch table taking bite of bread, 1940s, framed, image: 13x10", NM, A13 ....$70.00

Butter-Nut Bread, sign, litho on canvas, baker boy standing with loaf of bread under each arm, name below, 1890, framed, 38x18", EX, A3 ....$385.00

Butter-Nut Bread, sign, paper, The Jolly Baker Presents upper left of baker with loaf above name & Rich As Butter..., 22x16", EX, A7 ....$45.00

Butter-Nut Bread, sign, 2 young girls carrying large loaves of bread flank bright pink oval sign on gray ground, framed, 10x20", EX, A2 ....$60.00

Butter-Nut Salad Dressing, jigsaw puzzle, plate of food & variety of dressings in front of flower vase, original envelope, 1920, 14x11", NM, A3 ....$22.00

Butterfinger/Koko Nut Roll, sign, tin, Butterfinger on 1 side & Koko Nut Roll on reverse, Curtiss Candies...Rich In Dextrose, 10x28", G, A9 ....$150.00

Butterfly, tobacco label, die-cut, EX, D35 ....$5.00

Butterfly Quality Bread, door push, porcelain with wrought-iron brackets, product name in diagonal script, 1930s, EX, A13 ....$170.00

Buvez Orange Miami, sign, embossed tin, bottle at left of Un Breuvage De Qualite, 29x14", M, D11 ....$70.00

Byrd Antartic Expedition 1933, cigarette papers, NM, A7 ....$30.00

Byron B Fowler Dry Goods, match holder, die-cut cardboard, image of young girl in plumed hat against white scalloped background, 7x5", EX, A21 ....$145.00

Byrrh Tonic Water, postcard, nude woman with satyr man & boy, 1 of 113 in series depicting Art Nouveau ads for Byrrh, NM, A16 ....$70.00

C Maggio, lug box label, color photo of various fruit, Lodi, M, D12...**$2.00**

C Pfeiffer Brewing Co Famous Beers, tip tray, Famous Beers above & below initial logo with company name on outer rim, gold, red & black, VG+, A8 ....**$50.00**

C&C Super Cola Root Beer, can, cone-top, 12-oz, NM+, A19 ....**$65.00**

C&C Super Root Beer, can, cone-top, VG+, A16......**$20.00**

C&O Railroad, calendar/thermometer, die-cut cardboard, circular calendar atop thermometer, floral decor, framed, EX, A16 ....**$65.00**

C-W-I Beer, label, initial crest flanked by lions above Beer on blue band against red background, 11-oz, NM, A19 ....**$4.00**

Cabela's, catalog, Spring/Summer, 1972, 220 pgs, EX, D17 ....**$15.00**

Cadillac, clock, neon, Cadillac Service, octagonal, **emblem on black dot, yellow border, metal frame, 18", EX, A6** **$950.00**

Cadillac, sign, porcelain, Authorized Service, crown emblem in center, white lettering on blue ground, 2-sided, 42" dia, NM, A6 ....**$2,000.00**

Cadillac, sign, tin on cardboard, Guaranteed Cadillac Parts, emblem above, 1910, square, VG+, A15 ....**$375.00**

Cadillac Beer, label, Cadillac Brewing Co, Internal Revenue Tax Paid statement, 1934-36, 12-oz, M, A10...........**$16.00**

Cadillac Sweet Tips, cigar box, cardboard with paper labels, name on inner lid above crown emblem, Very Mild below, 5¢ upper left, VG, A6......................**$150.00**

Cadillac-La Salle Motor Cars, bulb kit, tin box, oval logo in center of lid, ...Part No 42677, orange, blue & beige, 1½x3½", VG+, A6.....................................**$75.00**

Cafe President Coffee/Quebec Preserving Limited, tin, white name over colorful image of crossed flags & coffee plants, company name on scolled banner, tall, 1-lb, EX, A18 ....**$150.00**

Cal-Neva, see Wild Indian Slot Machines

Calabash Smoking Mixture, pocket tin, vertical, flat lid, orange with name encircled by decorative border, EX+, A18..**$470.00**

Calabash Smoking Mixture, pocket tin, vertical, flip lid, orange with name encircled by decorative border, EX+, A18..**$500.00**

Calabash Smoking Mixture, sign, paper, man seated in distance smoking exaggerated close-up image of pipe resting in tobacco box, 20x14", EX+, A18 ....**$240.00**

Calderwood's Mother's Bread, sign, porcelain flange, white product name on orange, 6½x13", EX+, A13 ....**$75.00**

Caledonia, crate label, California orange, Scotch thistles on plaid background, Placentia, 10x11", M, D12........**$2.00**

California Brand Root Beer Schnapps, mug, glass, orange logo, 8x4", M, D16.....................................**$15.00**

California Dream, crate label, California orange, castle & 2 peacocks, gilt highlights, Placentia, 10x11", M, D3 ..**$15.00**

California Fig Co, tin, sample, with contents & original box, EX, A7...**$12.00**

California Gold Label Beer, sign, self-framed cardboard, shows western street scene with cowboys & goat, horizontal, EX+, A19.....................................**$65.00**

California Nugget Tobacco, pocket tin, flat, G, D35 ..**$30.00**

California Prunes, lug box label, stone litho of prunes, apricots & a peach, San Jose, M, D12.................**$15.00**

California Wine House, sign, paper, Compliments of... above Indian papoose strapped to reed cradle, metal strips, ca 1904, 20x15", G+, A9.....................**$375.00**

Callison Truck Lines, sign, porcelain, Callison on banner above Truck Lines, Eureka, East Bay, San Francisco, ICC..., 16x24", NM, D11 ....**$100.00**

Calso Supreme Gasoline, gas globe, white lettering on red & black, Gill body, 13½" dia, EX+, A6.........**$325.00**

Calumet Baking Powder, bank, paper on tin, boy insert at top wiggles back & forth when coin is dropped in slot, EX, A3..**$110.00**

Calumet Baking Powder, clock, tilted can of Calumet & advertising below Benrus Watch Time clock numbered 1-12, electric, 18½x15", EX, A1 ....**$240.00**

Calumet Baking Powder, clock, wood with glass front, Time To Buy Calumet Baking Powder, 'Best By Taste' in gold lettering, 38x18", EX+, A6.......................**$350.00**

Calumet Baking Powder, thermometer, painted wood, Call For...Best By Test...Trade Here & Save, orange can, boy & bulb on yellow, 21", EX, A2........$440.00

Calumet Baking Powder, tin, sample, ...Calumet The Double-Acting Baking Powder, shows Indian in full headdress, 4-oz, NM, A3...**$40.00**

Calumet Baking Powder, tin, sample, ...Calumet The Double-Acting Baking Powder, shows Indian in full headdress, 4-oz, EX, A7 .... $25.00

Calumet Beer, drinking glass, straight-sided with flat bottom, red lettering, 1934-42, NM, A8 .... $50.00

Calumet's Pride/Calumet Brewing Co, label, shows bust of Indian chief with decorative border, product name below, pre-1920s, 1-pt 14-oz, VG, A8 .... $25.00

Calvert, sign, self-framed tin, Clear Heads Call For Calvert, cigarette on ashtray with 2 bottles & jigger, 1930s, 9x13", NM, A8 .... $90.00

Camden Beer, sign, paper, None Better & product name on sign above girl with glass encircled by rope, 21x24", EX, A19 .... $30.00

Camden Beer, tray, deep-dish, 'None Better,' shows lady drinking from pilsner glass, product name below, 12" dia, EX, A19 .... $85.00

Camden Pilsner, tap knob, red ball shape with white lettering on blue celluloid insert, EX, A8 .... $55.00

Camel, crate label, California pear, camel & driver in desert sunrise & Arab kneeling, Loomis, 8x11", M, D12 ... $3.00

Camel Brand Cigars, tin, Egyptian on camel flanked by 5¢ & product name on triangle, Camel lettered above, 5½x6", EX, A18 .... $155.00

Camel Cigarettes, box, flat, cardboard, holds 50 cigarettes, with contents, unopened, M, A18 .... $100.00

Camel Cigarettes, can cooler, molded vinyl head of Camel Joe in sunglasses & smoking a cigarette, 1991, 4", M $15.00

Camel Cigarettes, cigarette carton, unformed, sides picture desert scene, top shows couples on veranda at night & unopened pack, EX, A18 .... $100.00

Camel Cigarettes, sign, paper, Smoke Camels above pack of cigarettes flanked by So Mild & So Good, red background, 24x30", M, D30 .... $25.00

Camel Cigarettes, sign, tin, For Smoking Enjoyment above Camel & unopened pack, white, yellow & red, 12x32", EX+, A18 .... $60.00

Camel Cigarettes, sign, tin, Smoke Camel Cigarettes lettered diagonally above open pack on circle, 18x12", NM, A7 .... $55.00

Camel Cigarettes, thermometer, tin, Camels For Mildness & Flavor above open pack with bulb, Sold Here below, red background, EX, A18 .... $40.00

Camel Cigarettes, tin, camel in desert scene, Turkish & Domestic Blend below, RJ Reynolds Tobacco Co, 1950s, 3x3½" dia, EX, A6 .... $30.00

Camel Cigarettes, tumbler, plastic, colorful images of Camel Joe at Joe's Place, 1994, 4½", M $5.00

Camellia, crate label, California orange, red camellias on white satin background, Redlands, 10x11", M, D3 .... $12.00

Cameron's Gold Medal, tin, product name above portrait surrounded by flags, Columbian World's Fair lettered below, EX, A18 .... $140.00

Cameron's Private Stock, tin, name & other lettering on torn corner of piece of paper with tasseled seal, rectangular, square corners, EX+, A18 .... $140.00

Campbell Brand Coffee, pail, yellow round shape with red product & company name above & below campsite with camels, slip lid, 4-lb, NM, A18 .... $75.00

Campbell Brand Coffee, tin with built-in grinder & pourer, product name on inverted triangle by Arab on camel, tall cylinder shape, EX+, A18 .... $155.00

Campbell's Soups, alarm clock, pictures large soup can, dial spins to read Soup & Crackers, round dial, square case, German, EX, A2 .... $40.00

Campbell's Soups, display, tin, ...M'm! M'm! Good! on red band above Campbell Kid & list of flavors, 3 rows of cans below, 20x16", VG, A8 .... $100.00

Campbell's Soups, doll, vinyl, Campbell boy or girl, Product People, 1974, 10", EX, D27, each $30.00

Campbell's Soups, doll, vinyl, Campbell Kid as chef holding towel & spoon, white with blue & red C on hat, 8", A21 .... $50.00

Campbell's Soups, sign, tin, Campbell Kid left of product name & Ready In A Jiffy! above 18 varieties of soups, 20x18", G+, A9 .... $35.00

Campbell's Soups, sign, tin, Campbell's Soups 6 Plates For 10¢ on banner above American flag made up of soup cans, 27x33", EX, A2 .... $46,200.00

Campbell's Soups, spoon, porcelain, yellow with Campbell's on handle, Campbell Kid pictured in bowl, 7" long, EX, A6 .... $35.00

Campbell's Soups, see also Reader's Digest

Campbell's Tomato Soup, sign, porcelain, can shape, 22½x14" dia, VG, A21 .... $375.00

Campbell's Tomato Soup, thermometer, porcelain, can shape with center circular window showing thermometer, 12x7x1¼", restored, NM, A13 ...$2,100.00

Campbell's Tomato Soup, trolley sign, cardboard, Can't You Just Taste It?, pictures can, tomatoes & bowl of soup, 11x21", EX, D8 ....$265.00

Campbell's Tomato Soup, trolley sign, cardboard, Our Suggestion For Dinner Today, pictures can, tomatoes & bowl of soup, 11x21", G, A6 ....$110.00

Campbell's Vegetable Soup, sign, porcelain, can shape, 22½x14", EX, A9 ....$2,200.00

Campbell's Vegetable Soup, trolley sign, cardboard, Fifteen Tempting Vegetables... above steaming bowl at left of can & vegetables, 11x21", NM, D8 ......$265.00

Canada Dry, clock, square glass face with plastic lens, metal frame, 12-3-6-9 & dots in between surround crown logo, 15x15", NM+, A1 ....$95.00

Canada Dry, drinking glass, frosted with image of fairy kneeled on rock looking into water, M, A16........$15.00

Canada Dry, mug, frosted glass with white logo, 4½x3", EX, D16..$10.00

Canada Dry, pin-back button, large winking eye in center, lettering around, NM, A16 ....$18.00

Canada Dry, push plate, embossed tin, The Best Of Them All, Canada Dry emblem above & behind hand with bottle, vertical, NM, A $100.00

Canada Dry, sign, die-cut tin, Canada Dry embossed on crown emblem, 14½x15", EX, A6..........................$80.00

Canada Dry Beverages, sign, porcelain, logo at left of product name, 7x24", M, D11...............................$65.00

Canada Dry Bourbon, lighter, with box, M, A16 .....$15.00

Canada Dry Ginger Ale, ashtray, green glass, crown logo & ...For The Sake Of Your Scotch in center, Emigrate To... on rim, 8" dia, NM, A16..................................$20.00

Canada Dry Ginger Ale, door push, tin, Canada Dry 5¢ above tilted bottle, It's Everything below, green on white, 1950s, EX, A13 ....$110.00

Canada Dry Grapefruit Beverage, matchbook, 20 strike, front strike, NM, D28..$4.00

Canada Dry Spur, postcard, Drink Spur lettered on airship hovering just above the ground, NM, A16...........$15.00

Canada Dry Spur, sign, embossed tin, Drink... Ice Cold & bottle on white, It's A Finer Cola on green below, 1947, 30x14", NM+, A13..$110.00

Canada Dry Spur, sign, tin, Drink Canada Dry Spur, Zip In Every Sip!, green & red on white with green border, 8x18", EX, D30..$45.00

Canadian Ace Brand Beer, can, cone-top, silver, NM, A8 ....$30.00

Canadian Brand Cream Ale, corkscrew, wood & metal, bottle shape with paper label, 4¼", EX, A6.........$15.00

Canadian Club 5¢ Cigar, sign, cardboard, Different From All Others..., oval portrait at left, yellow, blue, red & cream, 13½x21", VG, A6......................................$15.00

Canadian Home Assurance Co, sign, tin, logo above ...Fire, Automobile, Casualty, light green background, 13x19", NM+, D21 ....$50.00

Canandaigua Premium Beer-Pale Ale, tray, deep-dish, No Finer In America & Canandaigua on arched band above product names over map, 12" dia, VG+, A19 ....$85.00

Candy Bros Fruit Juice Tablets, tray, multiple jars of tablets, ...Always Fresh, butterflies & flowers surround rim, oval, 17x14", G, A9.....................................$350.00

Cannon's Aromatic Irish Sliced Plug Flake Smoking Blend, pocket tin, vertical, white with red Aromatic lettered diagonally across blue product name, EX+, A18..$150.00

Cantona, cigar box label, outer, man & woman within fancy border, NM, A5...$55.00

Cap'n Crunch Cereal, doll, Cap'n Crunch, vinyl, 7", EX, A21 ....$35.00

Capitan Parlube Motor Oil, can, ...The Peak of Quality above image of car on mountain road, screw lid & handle, 1-gal, 11x8½", EX, A6....................................$120.00

Capitol Fuel Co, paperweight, bronze, lettering surrounds capitol building, round, M, D13 ....$50.00

Capitol Milwaukee Beer, coaster, Capitol & Milwaukee on diagonal band with Capitol building above & Beer below, red, white & blue, 4", EX, A8....................$65.00

Captain Alippo Cigars, box label, salesman's sample, fancy scroll design around portrait with castle beyond, M, A5..$35.00

Caravelle Candy Bar, figure, Caravelle Candy man, bendable wire arms & legs, 1967, EX, D27 ....$150.00

Card Seed Co, display, wood with paper label, contains various colorful seed packets, 24½x15", EX, A6.......$275.00

Cardinal Beer/Standard Brewing Co, tray, porcelain, Costs 25% More To Brew... & company name around product name in center, red on white, 12" dia, EX, A8 ....$220.00

Cardinal Cherry, syrup dispenser, ceramic, ball shape embossed with cherries & leaves, flared base, original pump, 14", EX, A2 ....$3,740.00

Cardinal Cut Plug, pocket tin, vertical, product name above & below image of cardinal, 4½x3", EX, A15........$855.00

Cardinal Cut Plug, tin, sample, metallic gold with red name above & below image of red cardinal, slip lid, VG, A18 ....$525.00

Cargray Gold, sign, porcelain, winged logo, black & yellow, 10" dia, NM+, A6................$120.00

Carling's Ale, sign, tin on cardboard, 'Nine Points Of The Law,' 9 English bobbies sitting in a row, beveled edge, 13x20", EX, A8................$25.00

Carling's Amber Cream Ale, sign, silk-screened wood, Carling's above emblem, Amber Cream Ale below, yellow & red lettering, EX, A8 ....$100.00

Carling's Black Label, see also Black Label Beer

Carling's Black Label Beer, sign, tin on cardboard, Hey Mabel! with musical notes above product name, red, white on black, 12x18", EX, A8................$35.00

Carling's Red Cap Ale, matchbook, Cleveland, O, 20 strike, front strike, NM, D28 ....$4.00

Carlisle Force Draft Ventilator, pocket mirror, ventilator image surrounded by lettering, blue & white, round, EX, A20 ....$35.00

Carlton Club Mixture, pocket tin, vertical, product name & logo above 'A Perfect Blend Of Choicest Tobaccos For The Pipe,' NM, A3 ....$135.00

Carlton Club Mixture, pocket tin, vertical, product name & logo above 'A Perfect Blend Of Choicest Tobaccos For The Pipe,' VG+, A18 ....$75.00

Carmelo Cigars, tin, round with product name above lady's portrait, Made In Tampa below, paper label, slip lid, VG+, A1................$50.00

Carmen Cigarettes, tin, flat, photo image of Carmen with walking stick under arm, holds 20 cigarettes, VG+, A18................$40.00

Carmen Complexion Powder, bill clip, celluloid, product name above oval portrait of girl, round, EX, A11................$30.00

Carmen Complexion Powder, pocket mirror, product name above oval bust portrait of girl, round, EX, A8................$25.00

Carnation Baby Ruth Ice Cream, container, paper on cardboard, 1930, 1/2-gal, NM, A3 ....$35.00

Carnation Evaporated Milk, cow, black & white plush with red T-shirt, 7", NM, D24 ....$10.00

Carnation Fresh Milk, sign, porcelain shield, white Carnation on red above milk bottle & Fresh Milk on white, green border, 23x22", NM, A1................$500.00

Carnation Hair Tonic/J Sarubi Co, sign, flange, product & company name on sign with barber posts, red & green on white, 7x18", EX, A8 ....$45.00

Carnation Ice Cream, sign, die-cut tin, pictures dish of ice cream on divided 2-color background, bordered, 2-sided, 35x36", NOS, D11................$195.00

Carnation Milk, ad, paper, Keep Him Progressing On Milk, toddler on trike looking at sign, product name & can at bottom, 22x37", EX+, A1.......$275.00

Carnation Milk, bookmark, celluloid, Souvenir Of The Panama-Pacific Exposition... & carnation above can & dairy cow, 6x1", EX, A11 ....$25.00

Carnation Wheat Flakes, container, Free Trial Size, Cooks In 5 Minutes on band across 4 red carnations, ca 1922, 5", EX+, A3................$32.00

Caro Pepsin Gum, jar, glass, paper label, with wood shipping box stamped The Key To Good Digestion & name on key image, rare, EX+, A16 ....$550.00

Carson Pirie Scott, catalog, 1924, 344 pgs, EX, D17..$125.00

Carta Blanca, tray, bottle & full glass in front of pretty girl posed with chin on hands, Spanish lettering on rim, 13", EX, A8................$125.00

Carter Hall Tobacco, ashtray, tin, embossed image of tobacco, 3½" dia, NM, D35................$5.00

Carter's Knit Underwear, display, papier-mache, armless male figure with Carter's printed on forehead standing on lettered box, 33½", EX, A12................$725.00

Carter's Liver Bitters, trade card, ...Will Make You Eat above image of Sarah Bernhardt, ca 1880, EX, D23................$85.00

Carter's Union Suits For Men, sign, die-cut cardboard stand-up, man standing in long underwear against blue sign with white lettering, 19", EX, A2................$145.00

Caruso's, matchbook, piano keyboard on sticks, Chicago, 30 strike, front strike, NM, D28 ....$8.00

Casaday Furniture Co, sign, embossed tin, cute little girl holding roses, oval, 19x13", VG, A9 ....$275.00

Cascadian, crate label, Washington pear, winter scene with river & mountains, 8x11", M, D11................$4.00

Cascarets, pocket mirror, All Going Out-Nothing Coming In above cherub on commode, They Work While You Sleep, round, VG, EX, A3 ....**$55.00**

Cascarets, pocket mirror, Best For The Bowels above woman sleeping on tail of C in Cascarets, round, EX, A11 ....**$75.00**

Cascarets Candy Gathartic, tin, 25¢, Laxative For Constipation, rectangular with rounded corners, ½x1⅝x2½", EX, D37 ....**$12.00**

Cascarets Laxative Tablets, tin, 50¢, rectangular with rounded corners, ½x2¼x3¾", EX, D37 ....**$18.00**

Case, sign, porcelain, **Case lettered on world globe, 33½" dia, EX, A6** **$400.00**

Case, sign, porcelain & neon (missing), eagle atop world globe, rounded top, 40x18", EX+, A6 ....**$650.00**

Case, see also JI Case

Case Centennial Tractor Plow, watch fob, lettering above plow & 1837-1937, octagon, NM, A20 ....**$42.00**

Case Power Farming Machinery, sign, embossed tin, Case Power Farming Machinery & eagle logo on black above dealer's name on yellow, 14x20", EX, A1 ....**$150.00**

Cashmere Bouquet, tin, sample, product & company name on circular inset with decorative border, NM, A3 ....**$30.00**

Cashmere Bouquet, see also Colgate

Casilda, cigar box label, printer's proof, encircled portrait flanked by medallions, EX, A5 ....**$25.00**

Caspar Motor Oil, can, Caspar lettered on globe, Motor Oil on base, 1-qt, NM, A1 ....**$130.00**

Caspar Super Oil, can, Caspar lettered on globe, Super Oil on base, full, 1-qt, VG+, A6 ....**$30.00**

Casper Beer, label, Casper Brewing Co, Internal Revenue Tax Paid statement, 1933-50, 12-oz, M, A10 ....**$12.00**

Castle-Brew Beer/Deluth Brewing & Malting Co, label, product name on red band above view of castle, company name below, 12-oz, EX+, A19.....................**$25.00**

Castoria, sign, cardboard, 35 Doses above small girl in coat, hat & hand muff, Castoria 35 Cents below, 13x6", EX+, A15 ....**$500.00**

Castrol Motor Oil, can, green, red & cream pitcher-type with handle & exaggerated spout, 10½", VG+, A6..........**$65.00**

Castrol Motor Oil, thermometer, dial-type, Castrol in red on white emblem, green background, 12" dia, NM+, D30...**$40.00**

Caswell Blend Coffee, tin, The Caswell Blend on band above Coffee in script over poppies, company name below, slip lid, 3-lb, EX, A18..........................**$100.00**

Caswell's Coffee, tin, product & company name above & below oval image of lady in profile on diagonally striped ground, round, EX+, A18 ....**$195.00**

Caswell's Kona Coffee, tin, gold with product name against sunrise graphics, round, slip lid, 2½-lb, EX, A18..**$45.00**

Caswell's National Crest Brand Coffee, tin, tan with product name above & below eagle, gold lid, NM, A18..**$195.00**

Caswell's National Crest Brand Coffee, tin, tan with product name above & below eagle, slip lid, 2½-lb, VG+, A3 ....**$75.00**

Caswell's Yellow & Blue Brand Coffee, tin, blue background, gold slip lid, 1-lb, NM, A18................**$75.00**

Caswell's Yellow & Blue Brand Coffee, tin, diagonally striped background, gold slip lid, 1-lb, NM+, A18................**$85.00**

Caswell's Yellow & Blue Brand Coffee, tin, diagonally striped background, gold slip lid, 3-lb, EX, A18..**$75.00**

Cat-Tex Soles, clock, light-up, reverse-painted glass border in red with white letters, cat with paw up on face, 14" dia, EX, A6...**$425.00**

Catac Mixture, tin, gold on yellow, square corners, VG+, D35...**$60.00**

Catcher Rough Cut Pipe Tobacco, canister, product name above burning pipe, EX+, A3 ....**$50.00**

Caterpillar, watch fob, pictures 3 different farm machines, EX, A20..**$22.00**

Cattataugus Cutlery Co, display case, oak with glass sides & 3-tier round revolving shelves, gold name on black pediment, 33x15", EX, A12..................................**$600.00**

Cattataugus Cutlery Co, display case, wood & glass inverted trapezoid shape, holds straight razors, 12x17x4", EX, A2..**$300.00**

Cavalier, cigar box label, outer, smiling muskateer holding stein, 1886, 4½x4½", M, D5................................**$25.00**

Cavalier Cigarettes, sign, paper, New at left of cigarette pack above The Smoke Feels As Good As It Tastes! on blue & yellow, 24x30", M, D30.............................**$25.00**

Cavalier Plug Tobacco, tin, green with product lettering around circular image of cavalier on horse, rectangular with square corners, EX+, A18.............$125.00

CC (Carhart's) Scotch Snuff, tin, red & white with paper label, unopened, D35 ....$12.00

CD Kenny Co, see Mammy's Favorite Brand Coffee

Celluloid Starch, sign, die-cut cardboard, ...Destroys Germs For All Laundry Work on apron of girl, product name on hat, x15", G-, A9 ....$80.00

Centlivre Brewing Co, see also CL Centlivre Brewing Co

Centlivre's Nickel Plate Bottled Beer, sign, paper, couple in dining car being served by black waiter, 1915, framed, 21x15", EX+, A3 ....$210.00

Central City Cigar, box label, inner lid, building & busy street scene, 6x9", M, D5 ....$150.00

Central Union Cut Plug, cigarette papers, #8, NM, A7..$6.00

Central Union Cut Plug, lunch box, red with gold lettering & trim around face in crescent moon logo, rounded corners, brass catch, EX, A18 ....$130.00

Central Union Cut Plug, lunch box, red with gold lettering & trim around face in crescent moon, square corners, EX+, A18..$145.00

Central Union Cut Plug, sign, cardboard hanger, hand pointing to The 'Stamp' Of Approval on unopened pack, Union Made Price 5¢, 11x13", EX, A2.......$176.00

Century Bottled Beer/Ph Schneider Brewing Co, sign, Cardboard, 'A Social Drink,' oval image of couple toasting with a beer, framed, 14x10", NM, A3 ....$135.00

Century Bottled Beer/Phil Schneider Brewing Co, tip tray, 'A Social Drink,' oval image of couple toasting with a beer, 4" dia, VG+, A8.................................$50.00

Century Smoking Tobacco, pocket tin, flat, silver-tone with engraving around 3 combination locks, rounded corners, EX+, A18...$100.00

Cer-ola, sign, cardboard hanger, oval beach scene with bottle & glass on tray, A Triumph In Soft Drinks..., 18x11", EX+, A8..$40.00

Cer-ola, sign, cardboard hanger, oval beach scene with bottle & glass on tray, A Triumph In Soft Drinks..., 18x11", VG+, A8..$20.00

Ceresota Flour, match holder, die-cut tin, Ceresota boy slicing bread atop barrel holder, Prize Flour Of The World, 6x3", NM, A3...$330.00

Ceresota Flour, match holder, die-cut tin, Ceresota boy slicing bread atop flour box holder, Prize Bread Flour..., 6x3", EX, A2...$230.00

CF&I Coals, sign, porcelain, product name above 3 devils carrying coal buckets, Sold Here below, red, black & cream, 16x20", NM, D8 ....$550.00

Challenge Lemon-Ade, soda glass, red logo, tapered, with syrup line, 5x3", NM, D16...................................$25.00

Challenge Milk, sign, die-cut metal milk carton, 27x14", NM, D11...$95.00

Challenge Root Beer, soda glass, orange logo, 5x3", M, D16..$8.00

Challenge Safety Razor, tin, flat, green with lettering around & over large walnut, rounded corners, ½x1⅜x2", EX, D37, minimum value $225.00

Chamberlain Cigars, case, photo image of man seated in chair, fancy embossed border, rectangular, embossed square corners, EX, A18.......................................$50.00

Chamberlains Cough Remedy, corner window sign, paper litho, Pleasant & Safe To Take, shows baby opening box surrounded by pink flowers, NM, A15 ..$160.00

Champagne Sparklets/Falk Tobacco Co, tin, blue square shape with gold product & company name above & below image of bottle surrounded by grapes, 3", EX, A18 ....$65.00

Champagne Velvet, sign, composition, We Do Not Serve Minors above animated bartender scrutinizing young man entering bar, 10x14", EX, A8 ....$55.00

Champagne Velvet Beer, charger, tin, colonial people toasting cherubs, Terre Haute Brewing Co, 24" dia, G+, A9...$250.00

Champagne Velvet Beer, sign, tin on cardboard, depicts fishing scene, beveled edge, 14x19", EX, A19.....**$85.00**

Champagne Velvet Brand Beer, can, cone-top, full, EX, A8 ....**$65.00**

Champion Harvesting Machines, calendar top, 1910, shows ox-driven covered wagons crossing the prairie, framed, image: 16x15", VG+, A3 ....**$65.00**

Champion Spark Plug Service, sign, tin flange, black & white lettering & emblem on red & black background, Canadian, 12x18", EX, A6 ....**$75.00**

Champion Spark Plug Service, sign, tin flange, black & white lettering & emblem on red & black background, Canadian, 12x18", NM, D21.....................**$125.00**

Champion Spark Plugs, ashtray, sillimanite ceramic (used in spark plug mfg), chrome-plated spark plug in center, 1920s, 3x5" dia, EX+, A1.....................**$100.00**

Champion Spark Plugs, cologne decanter, Avon, original box, EX, D24 ....**$6.00**

Champion Spark Plugs, radio, gray & white plastic plug on black base, AM, 14", VG+, A21 ....**$40.00**

Champion Spark Plugs, sign, die-cut cardboard stand-up, Champion on banner around glove with plane & spark plug, 38x21", VG, A1 ....$200.00

Champion Spark Plugs, sign, embossed tin, Champion on arrow pointing to spark plug, Costs Less, More Power below, 6x15", EX+, A6 ....**$375.00**

Champion Spark Plugs, sign, metal flange, Dealer Service above spark plug logo, Checked & Cleaned below, red, black & white, 12x18", VG, A6.....................**$165.00**

Champion Spark Plugs, thermometer, die-cut wood, black & white spark-plug shape, Champion Dependable..., 21", VG, A6.....................**$300.00**

Champions, sign, tin, We Clean & Check & Recommend Champions right of spark plug on diamond, 2-color ground, 14x30", NOS, EX+, A1.....................**$380.00**

Chancellor Cigar, sign, cardboard, girl in pink feathered hat with fan above The Cigar of Quality in script, 35½x19", G, A9 ....**$225.00**

Chandler's Laxative Tablets, display, cardboard, for 10¢ Trial Size boxes, EX+, A3.....................**$16.00**

Chanticleer Ice Cream, sign, embossed tin, crowing rooster logo above product name & 'A Pal For Your Palate,' framed, image: 28x19½", G+, A9 ....**$100.00**

Charles Dickens, cigar box label, outer, portrait of Charles Dickens within fancy border, 1906, EX, A5.....................**$140.00**

Charles the Great, cigar box, 5x10", VG, A7.....................**$15.00**

Charles Williams Stores, catalog, Spring/Summer, 1920, 926 pgs, EX, D17.....................**$125.00**

Charms Fruit Tablets, trolley sign, cardboard, Raspberry — A Specially 'Tasty'... right of spilled fruit box & product pack, 11x21", NM, A1 ....**$110.00**

Chartres Indian Head Typewriter Ribbon, tin, flat, shows product name & Indian Head, rounded corners, ⅞x2½x2½", EX, D37, mimimum value,.....................**$30.00**

Chas Neubert & Co Oysters, tin, label shows mermaid, fish & oysters with red sky, pry lid, 1-gal, EX, A18 ...**$120.00**

Chase & Sanborn Choice Blended Coffee, milk can, orange with bold white lettering, bail handle, 4½-lb, 12", G, A2 ....**$175.00**

Chase & Sanborn Seal Brand Coffee, cup, heavy porcelain with detailed molding on handle, EX, D25...**$30.00**

Chase & Sanborn's High Grade Coffee, tin, sample, slip lid, 2¼", NM, A7.....................**$50.00**

Chase & Sanborn's High Grade Teas & Coffees, display, metal, name on panel above Recognized/Standards Of Quality/Teas & Coffees on shelves, Pat's 1908, 33", EX, A12.....................**$260.00**

Chase & Sanborn's Seal Brand Coffee, tin, logo flanked by Seal & Brand, key-wind lid, EX+, A3.....................**$45.00**

Chase & Sanborn's Superior Coffee, milk can, blue with bold white lettering, bail handle, 4½lb, 12", G-, A2.....................$200.00

Chastan, cigar box label, printer's proof, oval portrait, EX, A5 ....**$30.00**

Chaussures F Pinet Paris, French shoe ad, elegant woman with shoe box, 'L'economie par la Qualite' below, 21x14", EX, D8 ....**$150.00**

Cheatham Electric Switching Device Co, pocket mirror, celluloid, company name arched above 'Cheatham Switch' & other lettering, round, EX, A11.....................**$20.00**

Check Cigars, tin, light blue with red Check outlined in gold above factory scene, Good As Gold below, slip lid, round, 5", EX, A18 ....**$65.00**

Checkers Cut Plug Finest Virginia Tobacco, tin, round with black lettering on white shield & banner on black & white checked background, slip lid, 4x4", EX+, A18 ....**$55.00**

Checkers Granulated Plug, sign, cardboard hanger, yellow diamond shape with red & black checked can bordered by red & black text, EX, A15 ....**$275.00**

Cheer Up, soda glass, red & white logo, Drink Cheer Up with music notes, 4x2", M, D16....................**$20.00**

Cheer Up, soda glass, red logo, Drink Cheer Up on circle, 4x2", M, D16..**$15.00**

Cheerwine, sign, tin, For Health & Pleasure, blue & gray diamond shape with red & white oval, 1948, 48x48", EX+, A13....................................**$180.00**

Chef Boy-Ar-Dee Grated Cheese, tin, sample, pictures the chef with product name, pry lid, EX, D37............**$25.00**

Chef's Pride Pepper, tin, product name above & below portrait of chef on paper label, 4¼", NM, A7.......**$40.00**

Chelan Butte, crate label, Washington apple, yellow & red logo over scenic view, Chelan Falls, 9x11", M, D12...**$3.00**

Chemical Rubber Co, catalog, 1924, 324 pgs, EX, D17 ....**$75.00**

Cher-ola, sign, cardboard hanger, bottle & glass on tray before oval image of beach couple under umbrella, 17x11", EX+, A3....................................**$22.00**

Chero-Cola, blotter, Drink...There's None So Good on oval within 8-sided border on rectangle, VG, A16.......**$12.00**

Chero-Cola, bottle opener, metal, girl figure, Drink... 5¢, G+, A16....................................**$25.00**

Chero-Cola, sign, Bracing-Cooling above baseball player visiting with female spectator, ...Ice Cold — Sold Here, 17x11", EX+, A3....................................**$60.00**

Chero-Cola, sign, die-cut cardboard, Drink... There's None So Good 5¢ on oval above elegant fountain scene, 14½x12¼", EX, A7 ....**$130.00**

Chero-Cola, sign, paper, Keep Cool With Bracing Chero-Cola Served Here, bathing beauty at the beach with bottle, 16x11", NM+, A3................$45.00

Chero-Cola, tray, oval image of bottle on wood-grain background, rectangular, EX+, A16 ....**$200.00**

Cherokee Brewing Co, mug, ceramic with blue embossed detail, shows Indian in full headdress with bow & arrow, EX, A19....................................**$110.00**

Cherry Blossoms, sign, tin, In Bottles Only & A Blooming Good Drink above & below product name, bottle at left, 1920s-30s, 9x20", EX, A13 ....**$275.00**

Cherry Cheer, sign, cardboard hanger, Cheer Up Drink...5¢ It's Good, girl holding glass, 1920s, 11x7", NM, A13....................................**$210.00**

Cherry Smash, bottle topper, features colonial gent offering a full glass, logo below, 1910-20s, NM+, A13.........**$70.00**

Cherry Smash, hanger card, Drink Cherry Smash above logo & text, recipes on reverse, EX+, A16............**$35.00**

Cherry Smash, postcard, Cherry Smash lettered on Geo Washington's Mount Vernon lawn with black man serving him & Martha, VG, D26....................**$100.00**

Cherry Smash, sign, cardboard hanger, Always Drink above Cherry Smash & logo, Pleases Everybody & Everywhere 5¢, 5x11", VG, A16 ....**$175.00**

Cherry Smash, sign, paper, Lunch With Us Today above club sandwich left of Always Drink above logo, Our Nation's Beverage, EX+, A16....................**$115.00**

Cherry Smash, sign, tin on cardboard, Drink...In Bottles below animated colonial man, red, black & white, 1940s, 9", EX, A13....................................**$50.00**

Cherry Smash, syrup dispenser, ceramic potbelly, Always Drink above cherry branch & Our Nation's Beverage, 14x9", VG+, A9....................................**$1,400.00**

Cherry Smash, syrup dispenser, ceramic potbelly, Always Drink above cherry branch & Our Nation's Beverage, 14x9", G, A2....................................**$990.00**

Cherry Smash, syrup jug & dispenser, inverted gallon jug fits atop glass dispenser, white ceramic base, NM+, A13....................................**$160.00**

Cherry-Julep, see Howel's Cherry Julep

Chest-O-Silver Rolled Oats, container, pictures a treasure chest on 1 side & Purity Orchid & logo on the other, NM, A3....................................**$95.00**

Chesterfield Cigarettes, bridge pad, cameo image of woman above lit cigarette, They Satisfy..., 1930s, EX, D14 ....$25.00

Chesterfield Cigarettes, carton, ...For A Happy Holiday on banner above large group of people & name tag, EX, A18....................................**$10.00**

Chesterfield Cigarettes, carton, Happy Birthday, red with Arthur Godfrey, Bing Crosby & Perry Como holding up packs, EX, A18....................................**$10.00**

Chesterfield Cigarettes, push plate, porcelain, cigarette pack & They Satisfy on rectangle, -And The Blend Can't Be Copied below, 9x4", EX, A6 ....**$235.00**

Chesterfield Cigarettes, sign, cardboard, Father's Day June 21 above America's Best Cigarette Buy! & carton with 2 packs, 1953, 22x21", NM, A7....................**$10.00**

Chesterfield Cigarettes, sign, die-cut tin flange, Buy Chesterfield Here on oval above King-Size & Regular pack, red background, NM+, A3 ....$95.00

Chesterfield Cigarettes, sign, die-cut tin flange, Buy Here on red oval above large unopened pack, Regular & King-Size on band, 17x12", EX+, A18 ....$35.00

Chesterfield Cigarettes, sign, tin, 21 Great Tobaccos above 20 Wonderful Smokes left of tilted unopened pack, They Satisfy!, 18x24", NM, A7 ....$30.00

Chesterfield Cigarettes, tip tray, They Satisfy — And The Blend Can't Be Copied, unopened pack above gold lettering & trim on blue, 6x4", EX, A3 ..$110.00

Chesterfield Super Motor Oils, can, Chesterfield arched above silhouette of man in top hat, Aristocrat of... above 100% Pure logo, 10x10", EX, A6 ....$90.00

Chevrolet, banner, cloth, First Showing Master Deluxe Models For 1935, blue & orange on tan, 15x36", EX, A1 .....$150.00

Chevrolet, box, wooden, end shows Chevrolet logo above group of money bags & stacked coins, hinged lid, 5½x6¾x8", VG, A6..........................$110.00

Chevrolet, brochure, 'Chevrolet Trucks For 1942,' EX, D8 ....$50.00

Chevrolet, calendar, 1920, Chevrolet Motor Cars, touring car in front of farm house, incomplete, 27½x14½", VG, A9 ....$200.00

Chevrolet, clicker, Chevrolet Steel Turret Top, tin, 2", EX, A7 ....$15.00

Chevrolet, clock, neon, metal & glass, Ipswich Motor Sales Co above logo in center, blue, yellow, white & black, 21" dia, VG+, A6..........................$650.00

Chevrolet, clock, plastic & metal, logo at top, numbered 12-3-6-9, blue & cream, 16½x16½", VG, A6.......$130.00

Chevrolet, mirror, deer scene with mother & fawn at top, Courtesy... below, green border with pine branches, 22x12", EX+, A6..........................$125.00

Chevrolet, pin-back button, tin, I've Seen The 1953 above Chevrolet emblem, It's Great! below, serrated border, 1¾" dia, NM, A7 ....$16.00

Chevrolet, pin-back button, tin, New Chevrolet Six, shows bust portrait of pretty lady, 1" dia, EX, A7............$10.00

Chevrolet, pin-back button, tin, Watch The Leader, ¾" dia, EX, A7 ....$10.00

Chevrolet, pocketknife, Chevrolet Parts & Accessories, metal, embossed opalescent pearl sides, VG+, A6.............$20.00

Chevrolet, sign, embossed tin, For Economical Transportation above logo on blue, dealer's name on white below, 12x24", VG+, A1 ....$145.00

Chevrolet, sign, light-up, embossed plastic die-cut with pressed board back, ...Over The Years America's 1st Choice, 23x28", VG, A6 ....$160.00

Chevrolet, sign, porcelain flange, We Use Genuine Chevrolet Parts, yellow, red, black & cream, 18" dia, VG+, A6 ....$335.00

Chevrolet, thermometer, painted wood, logo above bulb & For Economical Transportation, dealer below, sharp corners, 10", EX, A1 ....$250.00

Chevron, pin, Chevron Dealer Service Award, red, white & blue cloisonne on 10k gold emblem with 1 star above, ¾", NM, A1 ....$85.00

Chevron, pin, Chevron Dealer Service Award, red, white & blue cloisonne on 10k gold emblem with 2 stars above, ¾", NM, A1 ....$100.00

Chevron, sign, heavy porcelain, Chevron shield shape with the word Chevron above 2 chevrons on white ground, 26x24", NM, A1..........................$330.00

Chi-Namel Shine-Easy Furniture Polish/Work Easy Dust Mop, sign, embossed tin on cardboard, piano flanked by product name, bottle & mop with advertising below, 9x13", EX, A8..........................$100.00

Chicago Cubs Chewing Tobacco, tin, blue with Chicago Cubs on white banner against eagle & 2 flags, Chewing Tobacco below, rectangular, 4x4x6", EX, A18 ...$600.00

Chicago Cubs Chewing Tobacco, tin, yellow with Chicago Cubs on banner against eagle & 2 flags, Chewing Tobacco below, round, slip lid, EX+, A18 ...$165.00

Chicago Packing & Provision Co's Cooked Meats..., sign, paper, company name above Victorian picnic scene, Cooked Meats & 'None Such' Hams below, 20x26", EX+, A9 ....$2,500.00

Chicago Stove Works, see Gold Coin Stoves and Ranges

Chicago-Bohemian Beer, label, Garden City Brewery, Internal Revenue Tax Paid statement, 1933-50, 1-qt, M, A10 ....$15.00

Chicken Dinner Candy, sign, die-cut cardboard stand-up, black & white rooster against yellow dot reading Get Your...5¢ Here!, 24", EX, A2..............$220.00

Chicken in the Rough Restaurant, desert plate, Syracuse China, M, D25....................................$25.00

Chicken in the Rough Restaurant, platter, Syracuse China, oval, 7", M, D25..........................$40.00

Chiclets, display box, cardboard with design of winterberries & gold medallions on green, lettering inside lid, 8x10x2", VG, D14 ....$110.00

Chiclets, display box, round Chiclets emblem with serrated edge on see-through top, rectangular, VG, A16...$80.00

Chicos 5¢ Spanish Peanuts/Curtiss, jar, square glass body with rounded corners on yellow, red & black tin base, yellow, red & black lid, 11x8x8", VG, A2...........$495.00

Chief, tobacco label, die-cut, EX, D35 ....$3.00

Chief Beer, label, Montgomery Brewing Co, U-type permit number, Internal Revenue Tax Paid statement, 1933-36, 64-oz, M, A10..$18.00

Chief Lotta Pop, display, plaster bust of Indian chief which holds lollipops that form headdress, 10", EX, A2 ....$275.00

Chief Lubricants, can, Indian chief in profile with product lettering, red, white & blue, pry lid, VG, A1 ....$70.00

Chief Oshkosh Beer, tap knob, plastic ball with white arrow (gold lettering) on red enameled insert, VG+, A8...$35.00

Chief Paints, sign, tin, Indian in full headdress at left of product name in yellow, black background, 12x28", EX+, D30..$65.00

Chieftain Dark Beer, label, Fort Pitt Brewing Co, U-type permit number, 1933-36, 12-oz, EX, A10 ....$30.00

Children's Hickory Garters, store display, die-cut wood, boy holding umbrella while girl reveals her garters, 19½x13x5½", G+, A9 ....$500.00

Chilton Paint, sign, neon, metal with glass front, orange & black, 10½x26½", EX, A6 ....$150.00

Chin Ekee, sign, cardboard, Indian girl & Drink A Real..., It Will Make You Cheerful, 5¢ Sold Everwhere 5¢, 1917, 9x14", EX+, A16..$132.00

Chippewa Salt, sign, paper, ...All Grades, Look For The Indian, encircled Indian at left, 24x61", VG, A6..$150.00

Chisca Brand Peanut Butter/Maury Cole Co, pail, gold with product & company name above & below encircled portrait on red oval, bail handle, pry lid, 48-oz, EX, A3..$25.00

Chocolate Cream Coffee, tin, Chocolate Cream in diagonal script above Steel Cut Brand & Coffee on emblem, small slip lid, 3-lb., EX+, A3 ....$90.00

Chocolate Cream Coffee, tin, Chocolate Cream in diagonal script above Steel Cut Brand & Coffee on emblem, key-wind lid, 1-lb, NM, A3 ....$50.00

Chocolate Soldier, sign, cardboard, Drink... above soldier in front of castle, orange, brown & yellow, 12x9", EX, A6..$40.00

Chocolate Soldier, sign, tin, Drink...Hot/Cold, tilted bottle on 2-color background, horizontal, EX, A16........$65.00

Chocolate Soldier, sign, embossed tin, pictures soldier & Drink at left of Sterilized...In Bottles on large bottle cap, 19x27", NM, A19..$38.00

Chocolate-Crush, sign, tin, Drink...A Rich Creamy Chocolate Soda In A Bottle, brown & white on yellow, 1930s, 14x20", EX+, A13 ....$180.00

Choctaw Machinery Sales, sign, porcelain, Rentals-Service above encircled Indian & Choctaw emblem, orange, black & white, 10x10", EX, A6 ....$145.00

Christian Feigenspan Breweries, tip tray, bust of 'Asti' girl in profile, lettering on bottom rim, 4" dia, NM, A8......$165.00

Christian Moerlein, booklet, features the story of Barbarosa, M logo above lettering bordered by fancy hops border, 1911, 12 pgs, EX, A8..............................$100.00

Christmas Brew Beer, label, Auto City Brewing Co, Internal Revenue Tax Paid statement, 1933-50, 12-oz, M, A10 ....$40.00

Christmas Seals, poster, cardboard, Buy... above Santa & child displaying 1924 seal, Fight Tuberculosis below, framed, 14x11", NM, A7 ....$70.00

Christmas Seals, trolley sign, Christmas Seal Your Christmas Mail above boy & dog with sled, 17th Annual Seal Sale, 21x11", NM, A7..$65.00

Christo Cherry Drink, syrup dispenser, ceramic barrel shape with product name, no pump, EX, A16...$350.00

Christo Ginger Ale, syrup dispenser, ceramic barrel shape, brown with chrome bands, 5¢ Drink 5¢ above Christo, original pump, 15", EX, A2................................$690.00

Chrysler, bank, Mr Fleet figure, vinyl, 9", EX, D27 .$350.00

Chrysler Plymouth Sales & Service, sign, porcelain, 2-sided, 18x35", EX+, D11 ....$295.00

Chunk-E-Nut Popcorn, box, Crispy & Delicious above couple & product name, NM, A7 ....$12.00

CIL 'Imperial' Shotshells/Dominion Center-Fire Cartridges, sign, paper, 'Hunting' Is Spoken Here in script above CIL logo left of product graphics, 15x26", NM, A7 ....$10.00

CIL 'Imperial' Poly-Kor Slugs, sign, paper, product name flanked by cut-away views of cartridges, 8x28", NM, A7..**$10.00**

CIL Ammunition, sign, cardboard fold-out, 'Two Firsts,' name above hunters & dogs flanked by 'Imperial' & 'Chanuck' Game Loads, NM, A7......................**$175.00**

CIL Ammunition, sign, cardboard fold-out, name above pheasants in flight with hunters taking aim, shotshell ad at right, 27x30", EX+, A7............................**$85.00**

CIL Ammunition, sign, cardboard stand-up, displays 5 rows of ammunition with listings below, 26x30", G, A7..**$10.00**

CIL Ammunition, sign, cardboard stand-up, name above close-up image of geese in flight over marsh, 26x15", G, A7..**$10.00**

CIL Ammunition, sign, cardboard stand-up, pictures 2 deer in snowy field with hills beyond, 27x20", NM, A7..**$95.00**

Cincinnati Burger Brau, drinking glass, stem with inside fluting, green & red with name above bust image of man drinking, 7", NM, A8............................**$40.00**

Cincinnati Cream Ale, label, Jackson Brewing Co, Internal Revenue Tax Paid statement, 1933-50, 12-oz, M, A10..**$22.00**

Cinelli's Extra Virgin Olive Oil, tin, full, 1/2-pint, EX+, A18..**$20.00**

Circle G, crate label, Washington apple, large white G on blue in white circle, red background, Seattle, 9x11", M, D12..**$2.00**

Circus Club Marshmallows, tin, cylinder with lithographed image of bulldog in blue coat & tie, blue hat lid, 7", EX, A6 ....$210.00

Circus Club Marshmallows, tin, cylinder with lithographed image of bulldog in blue coat & tie, blue hat lid, 7", G, A21....................................**$75.00**

Circus Salted Peanuts, tin, Circus above circus elephant on fancy inset, Peanuts on band below, striped background, ca 1946, EX, A3..........................**$30.00**

Cities Service, see also Trojan Motor Oil

Cities Service, gas globe, cloverleaf shape, black on white, glass body & lens, 16", NM, A6............................**$450.00**

Cities Service, poster, Season's Greetings above colorful image of serviceman & 3 reindeer, 38x50", EX, A6...**$40.00**

Cities Service, sign, porcelain, green logo above Clean Rest Rooms in bold red letters on cream, 24x23", NM, D8..**$415.00**

Cities Service, thermometer, metal & glass dial-type, logo in center, red, green & white, 12" dia, NM, A6..**$150.00**

Cities Service Koolmotor, gas globe, cloverleaf shape with black & yellow lettering, 16", NM, A6........**$750.00**

Cities Service Motor Oil, can, stripes above lettered emblem, Motor Oil below, If It's Cities Services... at bottom, white on green, 1-qt, NM, A1..................**$50.00**

Cities Service Motoring, map rack, green & white metal rack with maps of Florida, Delaware, Virginia, Vermont..., 18½x13½", EX+, A6 ....**$275.00**

Cities Service Oils, pump sign, porcelain, product name above clover & triangle logo & Once-Always on emblem, black & white, 11" dia, VG, A6...........**$135.00**

Cities Service Petroleum Products, pocketknife, opalescent pearl handle with green lettering, 1 blade missing, A6..**$25.00**

Cities Service Premium Koolmotor, bank, tin, can shape, 2" dia, NM, A7 ....**$18.00**

Cities Service 5D, bank, tin, can shape, 2" dia, NM, A7..**$18.00**

City Club, cigarette papers, NM, A7............................**$45.00**

City Club, sign, die-cut cardboard, Make The Happy Choice!..., lady with groceries standing behind stacks of cases, 22", VG+, A8..**$125.00**

City Club, sign, embossed tin, Drink City Club 'The Better Brew' right of bottle on oval, multicolor on dark green, 10x28", VG, A8..**$105.00**

City Club Crushed Cubes, pocket tin, vertical, man reading newspaper & smoking, The Pride Of Our Factory, 4½", EX, A9 ....**$200.00**

City Club Crushed Cubes, pocket tin, vertical, man reading newspaper & smoking, The Pride Of Our Factory, 4½", VG, A18 ....$160.00

City Cousin Cigars, box label, salesman's sample, farm girl resting on bale of hay, EX, A5..............................**$75.00**

City Hall, cigar box label, inner lid, sepia image of City Hall with horse-drawn carriages in the foreground, EX, A5..**$45.00**

City of Lakes Coffee, tin, product name & image on 3 bands, key-wind lid, 1-lb, G+, A3........................**$80.00**

City of Saint Paul, cigar box label, outer, aerial view of the city, FW Tuchelt's Sons Makers, 1906, M, A5.......**$55.00**

CL Centlivre, calendar, 1900, 'Century Bells,' die-cut bust of young girl encircled by bells & flowers, framed, 23x22", VG+, A8..**$550.00**

CL Centlivre Brewing Co, sign, paper litho, panoramic factory view with company name & portrait below, 25x37½", NM, A8..**$405.00**

Clabber Girl Baking Powder, sign, metal, Clabber Girl The Healthy Baking Powder lettered on white, outlined border, 2-sided, 12x34", EX, A8..............................**$20.00**

Clabber Girl Baking Powder, tin, sample, paper label, 4¾-oz, EX, A7...**$25.00**

Clapp & Jones Steam Fire Engines, sign, paper, horse-drawn fire pumper in center, 4 oval insets of other equipment in corners, image: 20x24", G, A9......**$650.00**

Clark & Courts, paperweight, glass, Texas House flanked by Manufacturing Stationers on center band, Galveston, Texas below, oval, M, D13 ....**$50.00**

Clark Bar, squeeze toy, Clark Candy boy holding candy bar, vinyl, 1960s, 8½", M, D27 ....**$200.00**

Clark Bar, thermometer, wood, 4PM Clark Bar O'Clock with candy bar & clock above bulb, curved top, 1910s-20s, 22x6", NM, A13..........................**$1,550.00**

Clark's Coffee, tin, Full Flavor Packed above steaming cup on center band, pry lid, EX, A3............................**$45.00**

Clark's Mile End Spool Cotton, calendar, 1886, roll-down, elegant girl with parasol looking at ocean view, full pad, framed, 30x20", NM, D8 ....**$325.00**

Clark's ONT, spool cabinet, wood, 2-drawer, Clark's on top drawer panel & ONT on bottom drawer, 8x15x23", appears restored, EX, A13 ....**$180.00**

Clark's Teaberry Gum, box insert, Mountain Tea & 5¢ above mountains & lake with large pack of gum, 3½x6", NM, A7 ....**$15.00**

Clark's Teaberry Gum, matchbook, 20 strike, front strike, NM, D28...**$2.00**

Clark's Teaberry Gum, note pad with 1927-28 calendar, fold-over book-type with pack of gum on cover, 5½x2½", VG, A7..**$12.00**

Clark's Teaberry Gum, sign, tin, A Happy Thought! upper left of diagonal gum pack, That Mountain Tea Flavor below, 1930s, 9x12", NM+, A13........................**$550.00**

Clarke's Pure Rye, plate, china, name above man with bottle, Bottled By The Government, brown on white, 1910s-20s, 11" dia, NM, A13 ....**$35.00**

Clarkson Chemical & Supply Co, pocket mirror, celluloid, features Buddy Brand, ...Manufacturing Chemists arched above, black & white, round, EX, A11 .....**$20.00**

Clarkson's Book Bargains, catalog, 1945, 196 pgs, EX, D17...**$15.00**

Clay Robinson & Co Live Stock Commission, calendar, 1919, 4 scenes depicting 4 stages of a fox hunt & showing all 12 months, 35x11", VG+, A3 ....**$82.00**

Clayton's Grape Smack, sign, tin, Clayton's in script above Grape Smack on red cross, Purity First below, 12" dia, EX, D30 ....**$195.00**

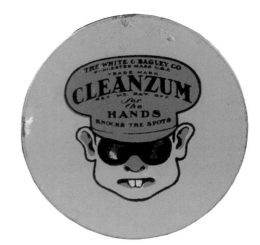

Cleanzum Antiseptic Hand Cleaner, tin, product lettering with buck-toothed Cleanzum man on lid, ca 1907, 2½x3", EX, A1 ....**$1,200.00**

Cleanzum Antiseptic Hand Cleaner, tin, sample, buck-toothed Cleanzum man with lettered hat, Antiseptic... around lower part of face, ⅝x1½", EX, D37 ......**$550.00**

Cleanzum Hand Cleaner, can, Cleanzum man with lettering on hat above product name & text, metallic orange, black & gold, 3-lb, VG+, A1 ....**$130.00**

Cleanzum Hand Cleaner, tin, orange & black, slip lid, White & Bagley Co, 2½x3¼" dia, VG, A6 ....**$55.00**

Clear Havana Cigars, tray, Aquilas & Habana above & below eagle flanked by medallions, product name on decorative rim, 10" dia, EX+, A3 ....**$165.00**

Clem's Cola, sign, embossed tin, Drink in diagonal letters above bottle cap & bottle on oval, red & yellow, 24x36", NM, A13..............................**$180.00**

Cleo Cola, sign, die-cut tin, Drink...For Goodness Sake, 28x28", EX+, D30 ....**$130.00**

Cleo Cola, soda glass, white shield logo, 4x2", NM, D16 ....**$25.00**

Cleveland & Buffalo, tip tray, name & 'The Great Ship Seeandbee' on decorative rim around image of passenger ship, oval, 4x6", NM, A18............................**$300.00**

Clicquot Club Beverages, sign, paper, product name above & below Pronounced Klee-Ko in black on yellow, 10x12", NM+, D30.....................................**$10.00**

Clicquot Club Beverages, thermometer, Drink... above bottle & bulb, white background, 15", EX, D30 ....**$55.00**

Clicquot Club Ginger Ale, bank, plaster, half-figure of Eskimo boy holding large bottle, coin slot on top of head, 1930s, 7x5½x4", M, A4 ....**$420.00**

Clicquot Club Ginger Ale, calendar, 1942, complete, 24x14", EX, A30 ....$90.00

Clicquot Club Ginger Ale, calendar, 1942, complete, 24x14", NM, A16 ....$130.00

Clicquot Club/Cyc-Kola, drinking glass, embossed, curved sides, NM+, A16 ....$55.00

Cliff, crate label, apple, river scene with old car approaching bridge over gorge, M, D3 ....$4.00

Climax Peanut Butter, tin, red with white & gold oval emblem, round, pry lid, 1-lb, EX, A18 ....$50.00

Climax Plug, tobacco label, EX, D35 ....$2.00

Climax Plug, tobacco pouch, leather, EX, A7 ....$17.00

Clipper, crate label, Florida citrus, sailing vessel & flying gull, 7x7", M, D3 ....$2.00

Clipper Baking Powder, tin, product name above & below clipper ship, 3½", NM, A7 ....$90.00

Clipper Brand Coffee & Chicory, tin, sample, yellow with red lettering above & below filigreed image of sailing ship, slip lid, 3x3¼" dia, G, D37 ....$175.00

Close Shave, tobacco pouch, cloth, VG, A7 ....$15.00

Cloth of Gold, can label, Golden Bantam Corn, early, big red bird, gilt highlights, M, D3 ....$3.00

Clover Brand Grinding Compound, tin, sample, with contents, 2-oz, VG, A7 ....$5.00

Clover Ice Cream, neon sign, clover-shaped tubing above Clover & Ice Cream tubing, 2-color, 20x18", NM, A13 ....$210.00

Clover Ice Cream, sign, reverse glass, Clover on black ribbon & clover plant above Ice Cream on blue, chain hanger, 1930s, 5x9", EX+, A13 ....$550.00

Cloverdale Soft Drinks, menu board, framed border with Drink...Soft Drinks on white panel above 7 menu inserts, 20x10", EX, A13 ....$110.00

Cloverdale Soft Drinks, sign, tin on cardboard, Cloverdale arched above 4-leaf clover & Soft Drinks on white oval inset on green, 9x13", EX, A19 ....$40.00

Club Chewing Tobacco, pocket tin, vertical, name in bold letters above Always Replace The Lid, EX+, A3...$40.00

Club House Beer, label, Ambassador Brewing Co, U-type permit number, Internal Revenue Tax Paid statement, 1933-36, 11-oz, NM, A10...............................$15.00

Club House Brand Peanut Butter, pail, name on enlarged fence board against western scene with cows behind fence, bail handle, slip lid, 4-lb, EX, A18 ....$145.00

Club Lido Smoking Mixture, pocket tin, vertical, white & black with red lettering & graphics, short, EX, A18 ..$200.00

Club Special Beer/Maier Brewing Co, can, pull-tab, blue & red on white, 12-oz, NM, A19 ....$40.00

Clubb's Dollar Mixture, tin, Half Pound 50¢...A Clubb & Sons, 4x6", VG+, D21...............................$35.00

Clysmic Table Water, tray, oval image of deer & nymph with large bottle at water's edge, lettering on rectangular rim, 13", VG+, A21 ....$120.00

Co-op, gas globe, single cobalt blue lens with white lettering, silver low-profile body, 15" dia, NM lens/VG body, A1 ....$295.00

Co-Re-Ga Denture Adhesive, tin, sample, 2¼", NMIB, A7 ....$15.00

Coach & Four English Pipe Blend, pocket tin, vertical, pictures horse-drawn coach, product name in yellow on black & red, VG+, A18 ....$140.00

Coach & Four English Pipe Blend, pocket tin, vertical, pictures horse-drawn coach, product name in yellow on black & red, EX+, A18 ....$175.00

Coal Castle, cigar box label, outer, black castle & coal mining scenes, 1903, 4½x4½", M, D5 ....$15.00

Coaline Electric Cleanser, sign, paper, product name above vignettes & text, Western Coaline Co, Chicago Ill below, 16½x21½", VG, A9 ....$250.00

Cobra Boot Polish, tin, image of smiling cobra with product name at right, 3" dia, VG, D21 ....$50.00

Coca-Cola, advertising price list, illustrations of advertising from the period, full color cover, 1941, EX+, A13 .$325.00

Coca-Cola, apron, Enjoy Ice Cold Coke on bib with Drink Coca-Cola on large front pocket, EX, A16............$50.00

Coca-Cola, apron, salesman's sample, Drink... In Bottles on bib-type with pockets to hold change, M, A16 ....$55.00

Coca-Cola, ashtray, glass, round with gold Enjoy Coca-Cola on black center, NM, A16 ....$20.00

Coca-Cola, ashtray, glass, round with white Coca-Cola on red button, white border, M, A16...............................$20.00

Coca-Cola, ashtray, glass, square with Drink...In Bottles on red diamond in round center, 1950s, EX, A16 ...$100.00

Coca-Cola, ashtray, glass, square with Drink...In Bottles The Pause That Refreshes & JJ Flynn Co on red round center, 1950s, M, A16............................$60.00

Coca-Cola, ashtray, tin, rectangular with applied key shape reading Support Your Firemen, Compliments Of Coca-Cola..., EX+, A16 ....$210.00

Coca-Cola, ashtrays, ruby glass, set of 4 shaped as heart, club, diamond & spade, 1950s, MIB, A16 ....$600.00

Coca-Cola, badge holder, metal & celluloid, Bottlers Conference, Drink... flanked by bottles above space for name, 1943, VG, A8 ....$40.00

Coca-Cola, Ball Of Fame, baseball-shaped card gives information on the game of baseball from 1901-1960, VG+, A13 ....$80.00

Coca-Cola, bank, red battery-operated vending machine with white lettering, 3 drinking glasses, Marx, 1950s, EX+, A4 ....$500.00

Coca-Cola, bank, red can shape with white diamond reading Coca-Cola, Canadian, 1960, VG, A16 ....$100.00

Coca-Cola, bank, red can shape with white diamond reading Coca-Cola, Canadian, EX+, 1960, A16.........$175.00

Coca-Cola, bank, red metal cooler shape, white lettering, Reg Phil Pat Off under Drink... logo on front, 1940s, 5x5x4", VG+, A13.................................$1,000.00

Coca-Cola, bank, wooden truck, early van with stamped Drink... logo, driver & cases of bottles, Toystalgia Inc, 1980s, 7", M, A16.....................................$25.00

Coca-Cola, banner, Atlanta & Coca-Cola Welcome You To Super Bowl XXVIII, Coca-Cola above hand-held bottle, 102x34", NM, A7...$60.00

Coca-Cola, banner, Be Really Refreshed ...Around The Clock!, features clock at right of seafood, barbecue & bottle, 1950s, M, A16.................................$45.00

Coca-Cola, banner, canvas, Take Coke Home in green & red above image of wooden case & price spot on yellow & white, 9-ft, NM, A13.........................$145.00

Coca-Cola, baseball counter, keeps runs, hits & errors of both teams, 1907, VG+, A13.............................$130.00

Coca-Cola, belt buckle, chrome plate with applied gold truck, 'Year 5 Record No Accident,' NM, A16 ....$130.00

Coca-Cola, bicycle, 1950s-style (reproduction ?) with Coca-Cola logo on crossbar, whitewall tires, NM+, A13 ..$300.00

Coca-Cola, billfold, inside shows gold-stamped straight-sided bottle, When Thirsty Try A Bottle, pre-1910, rare, EX+, A16 ....$105.00

Coca-Cola, blotter, 1906, Restores Energy, Strengthens The Nerves, Drink... on fancy emblem in center, EX, D8 ....$105.00

Coca-Cola, blotter, 1913, Pure & Healthful Drink...Delicious & Refreshing 5¢ Everywhere on oval flanked by bottles, G, A16 ....$50.00

Coca-Cola, blotter, 1915, Drink...Delicious & Refreshing All Soda Fountains 5 Cents, shows 2 ladies & soda jerk, VG, A16 ....$170.00

Coca-Cola, blotter, 1915, Pure & Healthful Drink...Delicious & Refreshing 5¢... on emblem flanked by bottles, bordered, VG, A13.......................................$120.00

Coca-Cola, blotter, 1927, So Refreshing Keep On Ice, couple leaning over cooler with door lettered Have A Case Sent Home, G+, A16 ....$50.00

Coca-Cola, blotter, 1929, The Pause That Refreshes, couple toasting with bottles, receding Drink... logo upper right, VG, A16...$45.00

Coca-Cola, blotter, 1930, The Pause That Refreshes, man in striped jacket relaxes with bottle, Drink... on receding logo, VG+, A13......................................$30.00

Coca-Cola, blotter, 1931, The Pause That Refreshes, shows lady seated with bottle in front of fan, EX+, A16 ....$230.00

Coca-Cola, blotter, 1935, Carry A Smile Back To Work-Feeling Fit, girl with hands behind her head, NM, A13 ....$100.00

Coca-Cola, blotter, 1936, 50th Anniversary on round dot left of bottle, Drink... on right dot, 1886-1936 on ribbon, EX, A16...$55.00

Coca-Cola, blotter, 1937, Cold Refreshment, Drink... on diamond left of tilted bottle, EX+, A6........$25.00

Coca-Cola, blotter, 1938, Stop For A Pause & Go Refreshed, policeman with bottle, EX+, A16........$60.00

Coca-Cola, blotter, 1939, The Drink Everybody Knows, hand holding bottle, red disk logo upper left, NM+, D21 ....$28.00

Coca-Cola, blotter, 1940, Le Meilleur Repos Qui Soit, clown with bottle, red disk logo at right, Canadian, NM+, D21 ....$40.00

Coca-Cola, blotter, 1940, The Greatest Pause On Earth, clown with bottle, red disk logo at right, green background, NM, D32..$65.00

Coca-Cola, blotter, 1940, The Greatest Pause On Earth, clown with bottle, red disk logo at right, green background, EX+, A16..$35.00

Coca-Cola, blotter, 1942, Completely Refreshing, bathing beauty lying on her stomach on beach, Drink... disk upper left, NM, A16.....................................$30.00

Coca-Cola, blotter, 1942, I Think It's Swell, girl lying on her stomach, red disk logo upper left, EX, A7.............$5.00

Coca-Cola, blotter, 1942, I Think It's Swell, girl lying on her stomach, red disk logo upper left, M, D21..........$15.00

Coca-Cola, blotter, 1942, Wherever Thirst Goes at left of girl in rowboat with bottle, Drink disk upper right, NM+, A16...$30.00

Coca-Cola, blotter, 1942, Wholesome Refreshment, 2 Boy Scouts enjoying bottles from cooler, EX, A7 ....**$5.00**

Coca-Cola, blotter, 1942, Wholesome Refreshment, 2 Boy Scouts enjoying bottles from cooler, NM, D21 .....**$12.00**

Coca-Cola, blotter, 1944, How About A Coke, shows 3 girls with bottles, Coca-Cola disk at right, NM, A16 .....**$35.00**

Coca-Cola, blotter, 1947, button logo at left of Sprite boy peering from behind tilted bottle, Belgium, NM+, A16 ....**$95.00**

Coca-Cola, blotter, 1948, Coke Knows No Season, snow scene with hand holding bottle, NM+, D21 ....**$12.00**

Coca-Cola, blotter, 1950, Be Prepared Be Refreshed, shows Boy Scout handing out bottles from cooler full of ice, NM, A7 ....**$5.00**

Coca-Cola, blotter, 1951, Drink Coca-Cola on arrow pointing to Sprite boy behind upright bottle, Delicious & Refreshing, NM, A16 ....**$30.00**

Coca-Cola, blotter, 1953, Canadian, Good!, Sprite boy with large bottle in snow, disk logo upper left, NM+, D21 ....**$25.00**

Coca-Cola, blotter, 1956, Friendliest Drink On Earth & Drink... on pennant left of hand-held bottle against globe, VG, D21 ....**$10.00**

Coca-Cola, blotter, 1956, Friendliest Drink On Earth & Drink... on pennant left of hand-held bottle against globe, M, A16 ....**$50.00**

Coca-Cola, blotter, 1957, 58 Million A Day, NM, A7 ....**$5.00**

Coca-Cola, blotter, 1960, Over 60 Million A Day, NM, A7 ....**$5.00**

Coca-Cola, book, 'Bottle Manufacturer,' showing & describing the making of bottles, 1954, 39 pgs, M, A16 ..**$92.00**

Coca-Cola, book, 'Illustrated Guide To The Collectibles Of Coca-Cola,' by Cecil Munsey, black & white, 1972, 333 pgs, NM+, A1 ....**$70.00**

Coca-Cola, book, 'The Six-Bottle Carton For The Home,' features 25¢ 6-pack on green cover, illustrated, 1937, NM, A13 ....**$230.00**

Coca-Cola, book, 'The Wonderful World Of Coca-Cola,' softcover, 350 color & black & white photos, NM, A16 ....**$75.00**

Coca-Cola, book, '100 Best Posters,' hardcover, 1941, EX+, A16 ....**$40.00**

Coca-Cola, booklet, 'Profitable Soda Fountain Operation,' fountain scene & title, Your Profit Leader... on back, 1953, EX, A13 ....$75.00

Coca-Cola, booklet, 'The Charm Of Purity,' 1920s, EX+, A16 ....**$16.00**

Coca-Cola, bookmark, 1899, celluloid heart, Drink... Delicious... Refreshing 5¢ around lady contemplating letter, EX+, A16 ....**$1,089.00**

Coca-Cola, bookmark, 1900, celluloid heart, Drink... Delicious... Refreshing 5¢ around lady with pen in hand & glass, EX+, A16 ....**$500.00**

Coca-Cola, bookmark, 1905, heavy paper, Drink Coca-Cola 5¢ above Lillian Nordica standing between embossed pillars, 5x2", NM+, A13 ....$1,500.00

Coca-Cola, bottle, see also seltzer bottles and syrup bottles

Coca-Cola, bottle, amber, straight-sided, LA in fancy script, logo on bottom, rare, EX, A15 ....**$165.00**

Coca-Cola, bottle, amber, straight-sided, marked Made At Williamstown New New Jersey..., 1905-10, 3¼", EX+, A13 ....**$3,200.00**

Coca-Cola, bottle, amber, straight-sided, Nashville, logo on bottom, EX+, A16 ....**$70.00**

Coca-Cola, bottle, amber (light), straight-sided, embossed LA Wolcott Co Hunington W VA, logo on bottom, rare, NM+, A16 ....**$170.00**

Coca-Cola, bottle, blue glass, straight-sided, Canadian, EX, D21 ....**$25.00**

Coca-Cola, bottle, green glass, straight-sided, Canadian, scarce, EX+, D21 ....**$80.00**

Coca-Cola, bottle, green (light), curved sides, brass tag & bottle charm around neck, full, 1955, M, A16 ....**$115.00**

Coca-Cola, bottle, green (light), straight-sided, block logo, Woonsockett RI, VG, A16 ....**$25.00**

Coca-Cola, bottle carrier, aluminum, lift handle, holds 12 bottles, 1950s, NM, D32 ....**$110.00**

Coca-Cola, bottle carrier, aluminum, wood handle, holds 6 bottles, 1950s, VG, D32 ....**$30.00**

Coca-Cola, bottle carrier, cardboard, Family Size, 1950s, EX, A16 ....**$15.00**

Coca-Cola, bottle carrier, cardboard, Regular Size on dot & across top of handle, 1950s, EX+, A16 ....**$18.00**

Coca-Cola, bottle carrier, cardboard, Season's Greetings, Drink... on red band over holly decor, holds 6 bottles, 1941, G+, D21 ....**$25.00**

Coca-Cola, bottle carrier, cardboard, shows 6-pack, receding logo & French text, 1934, VG+, A13 ....**$120.00**

Coca-Cola, bottle carrier, cardboard, Six Bottles Coca-Cola above Serve Ice Cold, Easy To Carry Home on handle, 1920s, EX, A16 ....**$85.00**

Coca-Cola, bottle carrier, cardboard, 6 For 25 Cents, holds 6 bottles, 1950s, EX, D32 ....**$20.00**

Coca-Cola, bottle carrier, metal, Drink... on side panels with individual wire holders, wire handle with wood grip, 1930s, VG, A16 ....**$205.00**

Coca-Cola, bottle carrier, wood, natural, wire handle, no dividers, wood grip, 1930s-40s, VG, A16.............**$55.00**

Coca-Cola, bottle carrier, wood, natural with wing logo on ends, wire handle, wood grip, with dividers, 1930s-40s, NM, A13.............**$375.00**

Coca-Cola, bottle carrier, wood, red with wing logo on ends, wire handle, wood grip, with dividers, 1930s-40s, EX+, A13.............**$450.00**

Coca-Cola, bottle carrier, wood, yellow with hand-held bottle & wing logo on each end, cut-out handle, 1940s, G+, A13.............**$195.00**

Coca-Cola, bottle carrier, wood, rectangular with rope handle, Drink Coca-Cola on side, G, A16.............**$22.00**

Coca-Cola, bottle carrier sleeve, cardboard, Christmas Greetings, bust of Santa & receding Drink... logo, 1930s, NM+, A13 ....**$1,900.00**

Coca-Cola, bottle case, waxed cardboard, ...In 6 Bottle Cartons, divided top with cut-out handles, 1950s, 8x10x16", M, NOS, A1.............**$50.00**

Coca-Cola, bottle opener, brass with black & red enamel, Drink...In Bottles, 1910-20, NM, A16.............**$100.00**

Coca-Cola, bottle opener, metal, bottle-cap end, 1920s-50s, VG, A16.............**$20.00**

Coca-Cola, bottle opener, metal, Coke stamped on hand shape with thumb & index finger forming circle, MIB, A16.............**$35.00**

Coca-Cola, bottle opener, metal, eagle head, engraved Drink Coca-Cola, 1912-late 1920s, EX, A16.............**$150.00**

Coca-Cola, bottle opener, metal, lion head, Drink Coca-Cola, plain back, 1910-30, NM+, A16.............**$165.00**

Coca-Cola, bottle opener, metal, loop end with band on handle reading Drink Bottled Coca-Cola, 1908, rare, NM, A16.............**$155.00**

Coca-Cola, bottle opener, metal, solid handle lettered Shirts For The Coke Set, EX+, A16.............**$25.00**

Coca-Cola, bottle opener, plastic & metal turtle shape with Enjoy Coke & Trade Mark on turtle's shell, NM, A16.............**$25.00**

Coca-Cola, bottle opener, wall mount, white metal with white Drink...In Bottles on red dot, EX, A16.............**$85.00**

Coca-Cola, bottle opener/spoon, Happy Days stamped on spoon, 1930, EX+, A16.............**$220.00**

Coca-Cola, bottle topper, Bathing Girl seated holding bottle on arrowhead-shaped emblem, receding logo above, 1929, 9x7", EX, A13 ....**$1,800.00**

Coca-Cola, bow tie, red with white Coca-Cola in script repeated across middle, NM, A16.............**$40.00**

Coca-Cola, bowl, green with embossed Drink Coca-Cola Ice Cold on all 6 sides, Vernonware, 1930s, 4x10", NM, A3.............**$525.00**

Coca-Cola, bracelet, Rock 'N' Roll Charm Bracelet, Things Go Better With Coke logo, 4 charms, 1965, MIB, A16.............**$60.00**

Coca-Cola, calendar, 1899, cardboard, oval image of girl at desk with rose border, months scattered below, 13x7", G+, A13 ....**$7,200.00**

Coca-Cola, calendar, 1904, top only (small), Lillian Nordica standing with plumed fan, VG+, A16 ....**$220.00**

Coca-Cola, calendar, 1909, top only, girl at table with 2 glasses, St Louis World's Fair beyond, 11¾x9¾", rare, VG, A13.............**$2,200.00**

Coca-Cola, calendar, 1909, top only, girl at table with 2 glasses, St Louis World's Fair beyond, 14x11", rare, EX+, A13.............**$5,500.00**

Coca-Cola, calendar, 1911, The Coca-Cola Girl, by Hamilton King, complete, matted & framed, 19½x17½", NM, A13 ....**$5,200.00**

Coca-Cola, calendar, 1912, girl standing in profile with hand on hip, Hamilton King illustration, incomplete, 20x10", EX, A16.............**$3,795.00**

Coca-Cola, calendar, 1914, top only, Betty in a bonnet, VG, A16.............**$240.00**

Coca-Cola, calendar, 1915, Elaine with glass & folded parasol at knee, landscape in the distance, VG, A13...$1,300.00

Coca-Cola, calendar, 1915, top only, Elaine with glass & folded parasol at knee, landscape in the distance, G, D21..$75.00

Coca-Cola, calendar, 1916, Elaine leaning on hand looking over her shoulder while holding bottle, incomplete, EX+, A16.................................$1,435.00

Coca-Cola, calendar, 1916, top only, Elaine leaning on hand looking over her shoulder while holding glass, G, A16..$440.00

Coca-Cola, calendar, 1916, top only, Pearl White leaning against tree while holding up a glass, very rare, G, A16..$440.00

Coca-Cola, calendar, 1918, oval image of June Caprice holding glass, complete, EX, A16.....................$300.00

Coca-Cola, calendar, 1918, oval image of June Caprice holding glass, complete, EX+, D32...................$350.00

Coca-Cola, calendar, 1922, girl in pink dress & hat at ballpark lifting glass, bottle on ledge, complete, EX+, A13..$1,700.00

Coca-Cola, calendar, 1922, top only, girl in pink dress & hat at ballpark lifting glass, bottle on ledge, VG, A16..$330.00

Coca-Cola, calendar, 1923, girl in blue dress & white stole with closed parasol holding up bottle, full pad, VG, A13 ....$500.00

Coca-Cola, calendar, 1924, girl in pink seated on ledge with glass & bottle by garden pond, EX+, A13..$550.00

Coca-Cola, calendar, 1925, pad only, incomplete, G, A16 ....$50.00

Coca-Cola, calendar, 1925, profile of girl in blue turban & white fox stole looking at full glass, complete, EX+, A16..$1,300.00

Coca-Cola, calendar, 1927, top only, seductive lady with glass, bottle in lower left corner, framed, VG, D21..........$100.00

Coca-Cola, calendar, 1928, girl in gold gown seated with glass resting in lap, incomplete, G-, A16............$210.00

Coca-Cola, calendar, 1928, lady in gold gown seated with glass resting in lap, incomplete, G+, A16..........$360.00

Coca-Cola, calendar, 1931, fishing boy resting under tree with sandwich & bottle of Coke while dog watches, incomplete, EX, A16 ....$650.00

Coca-Cola, calendar, 1932, The Old Oaken Bucket, boy seated at edge of well with bucket full of Coke bottles, dog watches, EX+, A3.............................$450.00

Coca-Cola, calendar, 1933, Village Blacksmith, blacksmith & schoolboy enjoying a Coke, complete with cover, framed, 24x12", NM, A1......................................$440.00

Coca-Cola, calendar, 1934, Carry Me Back To Old Virginia, period couple sitting on porch enjoying Coke, complete, EX+, A16.............................$720.00

Coca-Cola, calendar, 1935, Out Fishin', boy with bottle perched on tree stump fishing, complete with cover sheet, EX, A16 ....$660.00

Coca-Cola, calendar, 1936, pad only, incomplete, VG+, A16..$40.00

Coca-Cola, calendar, 1936, top only, old clam digger resting on red rowboat enjoying Coke with small girl, G+, A16..$220.00

Coca-Cola, calendar, 1940, The Pause That Refreshes, girl with bottle in lap, complete with cover sheet, EX+, A16 ....$605.00

Coca-Cola, calendar, 1941, ice skater on log with bottle, disk logo lower right, complete 2-month pad, EX+, A13 ....$350.00

Coca-Cola, calendar, 1942, Thirst Knows No Season, couple building snowman, disk logo lower left, complete, VG+, A13 ....$260.00

Coca-Cola, calendar, 1944, The Pause That Refreshes, bare shouldered girl with bottle before Capitol Building, complete, EX+, A13 ....$230.00

Coca-Cola, calendar, 1946, Sprite boy cover, complete, NM, A13...$1,250.00

Coca-Cola, calendar, 1947, girl hugging skis & poles, bottle & disk logo lower left, complete, EX+, A13.......$325.00

Coca-Cola, calendar, 1948, girl with bottle, red disk logo, complete, EX+, D32 ....$150.00

Coca-Cola, calendar, 1949, complete, EX+, A16......$285.00

Coca-Cola, calendar, 1949, incomplete, EX+, A3.....$105.00

Coca-Cola, calendar, 1952, Coke Adds Jest!, complete, EX, A16..$100.00

Coca-Cola, calendar, 1953, 3 Boy Scouts before the Liberty Bell, Norman Rockwell illustration, complete, NM, A13..$575.00

Coca-Cola, calendar, 1953, Talk About Being Good!, Dec 1952 cover page of smiling Santa holding up Coke bottle, 22x13", NM, D8 ....$200.00
Coca-Cola, calendar, 1954, girl putting on skates while being offered a bottle, complete, VG, A4..........$100.00

Coca-Cola, calendar, 1955, Work Better Refreshed, working girl with bottle surrounded by other workers, NM, D8 ....$200.00
Coca-Cola, calendar, 1955, Work Better Refreshed, working girl with bottle surrounded by other workers, complete, VG+, A16 ....$132.00
Coca-Cola, calendar, 1956, There's Nothing Like A Coke, complete, VG+, A16................................$185.00
Coca-Cola, calendar, 1957, There's Nothing Like A Coke, Canadian (English version), EX+, A4.................$150.00
Coca-Cola, calendar, 1959, The Pause That Refreshes, basketball scene with girl being offered a bottle of Coke, complete, VG+, A16................................$80.00

Coca-Cola, calendar, 1963, Reference Calendar, shows Santa with bottle playing with helicopter & train, complete, 7x12", EX, A7 ....$25.00
Coca-Cola, calendar, 1967, For The Taste That You Never Get Tired Of, complete, VG, A16.........................$35.00
Coca-Cola, calendar, 1979, complete, EX, A16 ....$26.00
Coca-Cola, calendar holder, Drink...In Bottles on red button atop with Have A Coke tab, rounded bottom, 1950s-60s, 20x8", EX, A13...................................$275.00
Coca-Cola, calendar holder, tin, Coke Refreshes You Best!, Drink on fishtail above, date pad below, 1963, 13x10", VG+, A4 ....$231.00
Coca-Cola, calendar holder, tin, It's The Real Thing above contour logo, number pages below, 1970s, vertical, EX+, A13 ....$60.00
Coca-Cola, can, red & white alternating diamonds with red Coca-Cola flanking white Coke on center diamond, 1960s, VG+, A16..$50.00
Coca-Cola, can, shaped to feel like bottle, red with white Coca-Cola logo, experimental, not produced, 1970s, 12-oz, NM+, A16...$368.00
Coca-Cola, can, shaped to feel like bottle, white with Coke contour logo, experimental, not produced, 1970s, 12-oz, EX+, A16...$242.00
Coca-Cola, card set, 'Flowers Of America,' set of 20 in original envelope, 1923, D32 ....$60.00
Coca-Cola, carton insert display sheet, 'Match The Orioles,'...For Fun & Prizes, collector sheet for 35-cap display, 1967, EX+, A16...$17.00
Coca-Cola, catalog, 'The All-Star Mechanical Pencil Line,' shows Coke, Pepsi, Dr Pepper, 7-Up & others, 1941, M, A16..$42.00
Coca-Cola, catalog sheet, 'Gifts In Fine Jewelry,' shows display of Roy G Booker Coca-Cola jewelry, 1940, NM, A16..$65.00
Coca-Cola, change purse, Drink...In Bottles Delicious & Refreshing gold-stamped on front, 1919, VG, A16..$65.00
Coca-Cola, cigarette box, 50th Anniversary logo on frosted glass top, 1936, rectangular, rare, NM, A16........$500.00
Coca-Cola, clock, Baird, composition, figure-8 shape with Roman numerals, The Ideal Brain Tonic..., ca 1891-95, 30½", VG, A13 ....$12,500.00
Coca-Cola, clock, Gilbert regulator, reproduction, Coca-Cola on face, Delicious & Refreshing at bottom, battery, NM+, A16...$175.00
Coca-Cola, clock, Gilbert regulator, wood case with round face numbered 1-12, Gibson girl decal on glass below, 1910, EX+, A13..$6,000.00
Coca-Cola, clock, Ingraham store regulator, wood case with with faded lettering on clock face, 1905-07, VG, A13..$300.00
Coca-Cola, clock, leather bottle shape with round clock face in center, Drink Bottled Coca-Cola... below, 1910, 8x3", G+, A13..$725.00
Coca-Cola, clock, light-up, counter-top, Have A Coke on base with numbered clock left of Drink...In Bottles, 1936, EX+, A13..$575.00
Coca-Cola, clock, light-up, counter-top, Please Pay When Served on base with round clock left of Drink..., 1950s, NM, A13..$525.00

Coca-Cola, clock, light-up, Drink Coca-Cola & bottle on octagon in center, yellow border, metal frame, 1942, 15x15", NM, D8 ....**$1,350.00**

Coca-Cola, clock, light-up, Drink Coca-Cola on red fishtail logo surrounded by numbers & dots, 1960s, square, NOS, NMIB, A13 ....**$240.00**

Coca-Cola, clock, light-up, Drink Coca-Cola in red on white, black numbers alternating with dots, metal frame, 1950s, 24" dia, VG+, A13 ....**$550.00**

Coca-Cola, clock, light-up, Drink Coca-Cola Sign Of Good Taste on red rainbow-shaped panel atop round clock, 1950s, 36" dia, EX+, A13 ....**$2,700.00**

Coca-Cola, clock, light-up, red Drink Coca-Cola & bottle on white background, green numbers, 1950s, round, EX, A13 ....**$400.00**

Coca-Cola, clock, light-up, red Drink fishtail logo surrounded by numbers alternating with dots, white background, square, EX, A4............................**$110.00**

Coca-Cola, clock, light-up, round with Drink... above bottle on yellow dot, numbered 1-12, metal frame, 1950s, EX+, A16 ....**$605.00**

Coca-Cola, clock, light-up, plastic, square face above 2 rows of repeated designs, Drink Coca-Cola below, 1960s, EX, A16 ....**$98.00**

Coca-Cola, clock, light-up, plastic, square face above 2 rows of repeated designs, Frozen contour logo below, 1960s, EX+, A16 ....**$110.00**

Coca-Cola, clock, light-up counter, Please Pay When Served, clock & Drink sign atop base, 1948-early 50s, NMIB, A16 ....**$1,309.00**

Coca-Cola, clock, light-up counter-top, Serve Yourself, square clock & Drink... sign atop base, 1948-early 50s, EX+, A16 ....**$849.00**

Coca-Cola, clock, neon, Drink... logo with bottle on octagon, yellow border on gold-tone metal case, 1942, 16x16", EX+, A13 ....**$950.00**

Coca-Cola, clock, neon, Ice Cold Coca-Cola & silhouette girl logo on center dot, 1941, octagonal, 18" dia, VG+, A13 ....$1,600.00

Coca-Cola, clock, plastic, square face above 2 rows of repeated designs, Drink Coca-Coal below, 1960s, vertical rectangle, EX+, A16 ....**$45.00**

Coca-Cola, clock, plastic & metal, Things Go Better With Coke in place of 10 & 11, disc logo at 4 & 5, 16x16", VG, A6 ....**$60.00**

Coca-Cola, clock, plastic front with gold-colored frame, red, green & beige pocket watch shape, Drink Coca-Cola, 14" dia, EX, A6............................**$55.00**

Coca-Cola, coin changer, Have A Coke, Get Your Nickels Here, overall restoration, Vendo, 1950s, 15x12", NM+, A13 ....**$625.00**

Coca-Cola, cooler, airline, red-painted stainless steel, white Drink... on side, top handle, side opener, 1940s, 12x17x7", EX, A13 ....**$450.00**

Coca-Cola, cooler, airline, stainless steel (unpainted), Drink... on side, top handle, side opener, 1940s, 12x17x7", NM+, A13 ....**$1,700.00**

Coca-Cola, cooler, floor-type in the shape of a large picnic cooler, red with Drink..., 1950s, 39", restored, NM, A13 ....$3,100.00

Coca-Cola, cooler, Glascock Junior (single case), 4 legs with castors, oval Coca-Cola logos, 1929, EX, A13 ...**$1,100.00**

Coca-Cola, cooler, picnic, Hemp Model 9022, red body with white Drink...In Bottles, white lid with metal handle & latch, NOS, A1............................**$900.00**

Coca-Cola, cooler, picnic, red, decal showing hand-held bottle, large swing handle, small lid handle, 1940s-50s, 13x12x8", VG, A13 ....**$100.00**

Coca-Cola, cooler, picnic, red vinyl box-type with fold-over top & strap, white fishtail logo, ...Refreshing New Feeling, NM, A16 ....**$40.00**

Coca-Cola, cooler, rectangular with double lids, red with Drink... Ice Cold on front, plastic insulated liner, 15x20x14", VG+, A16 ....**$300.00**

Coca-Cola, cooler, see also wet box

Coca-Cola, coupon, pre-1900, This Card Entitles An Adult One Glass Of...At The Fountain Of Any Dispenser Of Coca-Cola, EX+, A16............................**$220.00**

Coca-Cola, coupon, 1901, Hilda Clark leaning over bouquet, reverse reads This Card Entitles You... Free At The Fountain..., EX, A16............................**$200.00**

Coca-Cola, coupon, 1930s, Drink...In Bottles, Serve It In Your Home... with image of 6-pack on reverse, M, A16............................**$20.00**

Coca-Cola, cue sticks, features contour logo, EX+, A13, pair **$70.00**

Coca-Cola, cup, tin, inside bottom of cup lettered with advertising, Green Castle Ind, EX+, A16............**$112.00**

Coca-Cola, cups, plastic, set of 4 Santa cups in box reading Things Go Better With Coke, 1960s, NM, A16 .....**$40.00**

Coca-Cola, cutout, Athletic Games, 1932, EX, D8..**$50.00**

Coca-Cola, cutout, Toonerville Town, 1930, G, A16....**$85.00**

Coca-Cola, cutout, Toy Town, 1927, EX, D8.............**$70.00**

Coca-Cola, decal, Drink Coca-Cola fishtail logo flanked by sprig of leaves above Please Pay When Served, foil, NM, A16 ....**$25.00**

Coca-Cola, decal, Drink Coca-Cola Ice Cold, 1960, M, D32 ....**$30.00**

Coca-Cola, decal, Drink Coca-Cola In Bottles, white & yellow on red, yellow border, rounded corners, 1950s, framed, 8x15", NM, A13 ....**$85.00**

Coca-Cola, decal, Drink fishtail logo in center with chevron on cut-out design above & below, foil, NM, A16..**$20.00**

Coca-Cola, decal, Enjoy That Refreshing New Feeling, fishtail logo, M, D32 ....**$30.00**

Coca-Cola, decal, Have A Coke on disk with Sprite boy peeking around large Coke bottle, framed on glass, 13x13", NM, A13 ....**$375.00**

Coca-Cola, decal, Ice & Cold flank bottle above Drink emblem on triangle with fancy rounded corners, 1934, 18x15", unused, NM, A13 ....**$130.00**

Coca-Cola, decal, Thank You Come Again on bow-tie emblem, Drink Coca-Cola on tab below, foil, 1950s, NM, A16 ....**$25.00**

Coca-Cola, decal, Things Go Better With Coke (receding words), 1960s, NM, A16......................**$16.00**

Coca-Cola, dispenser, dispenses both Coca-Cola & root-beer, box shape with chrome lid & red sides, double taps, 1930s, NM, A16............................**$715.00**

Coca-Cola, dispenser, metal, Drink Coca-Cola, Ice Cold, red with embossed cream letters, top lifts to refill, 22x10½", VG, A6................................**$350.00**

Coca-Cola, dispenser, red with white Drink Coca-Cola Ice Cold, Have A Coke on tap, 1940s-50s, EX+, D32 ....**$700.00**

Coca-Cola, dispenser plaque, steel, embossed white Drink... on red rectangle with step corners, 1930s, 3x7", NN, A13 ....**$80.00**

Coca-Cola, dispenser/paper bag rack, tin sign above rack, For Home Refreshment above Sprite boy, red ground, 1949, 14x37", VG+, A1..............................**$300.00**

Coca-Cola, display, cardboard, large clown with bottle overseeing 3-D circus scene with many pieces, 1932, EX+, A13..**$4,600.00**

Coca-Cola, display, cardboard, Free Easy Recipe Ideas, Take One & Pick Up The Fixins', Enjoy Coke..., 14x20", 1957, NM, A16 ....**$25.00**

Coca-Cola, display, cardboard, Santa in rocket ship, Festive Holidays, Serve Coca-Cola on cone top, 33", 1957, EX+, A13..**$260.00**

Coca-Cola, display bottle, clear-glass 1923 bottle with tin lid, silver-painted logos, EX+ (worn cap), A13 ..**$260.00**

Coca-Cola, display bottle, glass, with cap & instruction tag, NM, A16..**$325.00**

Coca-Cola, display bottle, glass with painted Coca-Cola, no cap, NM+, A16....................................**$85.00**

Coca-Cola, display bottle, inflatable, 1960s, 36", M, A4...**$55.00**

Coca-Cola, display bottle, inside painted to appear full, unmarked cap, 1953, M, A16............................**$55.00**

Coca-Cola, display bottle, plastic, red base, ca 1953, 20", EX+, A13..**$210.00**

Coca-Cola, display bottle, rubber, 1948, 42", EX, A13 ..**$675.00**

Coca-Cola, display bottle, rubber, 1948, 48", EX, A13..**$900.00**

Coca-Cola, display bottle, styrofoam, 1961, 42", VG+, A13 ....**$210.00**

Coca-Cola, display bottle carrier, red with white Coke & Coca-Cola, white dots at corners, could hold 6 20" bottles, 1950s, EX, A13............................**$180.00**

Coca-Cola, display bottle case, wood, yellow with red lettering, 1950s, oversized, EX+, A13......................**$170.00**

Coca-Cola, display rack, cardboard, oval Drink... logo & Take Home A Carton above 2-step base, Six Bottles 25¢..., 1930s, VG, A13......................**$725.00**

Coca-Cola, doll, Buddy Lee, plastic, in uniform, no hat, 1950s, VG+, A16................................**$400.00**

Coca-Cola, doll, Buddy Lee, plastic, in uniform, with hat, 1950s, EX+, A13................................**$650.00**

Coca-Cola, doll, Santa, holding bottle & white book, white boots, 1950s-60s, VG, A16................................**$45.00**

Coca-Cola, door handle, plastic bottle on metal door mountings, Have ACoke, VG+, A16....................**$150.00**

Coca-Cola, door palm press, porcelain, Have A Coca-Cola, yellow & white on red, 1930s, 3½x6½", NM, A13.......**$260.00**

Coca-Cola, door plate, porcelain, Come In! Have A Coca-Cola in yellow & white on red, 1930s, 11½x3½", NM, A13 ....$290.00

Coca-Cola, door plate, porcelain, Entrez Et Buvez Un Coca-Cola in yellow & white on red, French Canadian, 11½x4", NM, D21 ....**$140.00**

Coca-Cola, door plate, porcelain, Iced Here in yellow flanks Coca-Cola in white, red background, 31", EX+, A13 ....**$150.00**

Coca-Cola, door plate, porcelain, Merci Revenez Pour Un Coca-Cola in yellow & white on red, French Canadian, 11½x4", NM+, D21 ....**$160.00**

Coca-Cola, door plate, porcelain, Prenez Un Coca-Cola in yellow & white on red, French Canadian, 3¼x6½", NM, D21 ....**$160.00**

Coca-Cola, door plate, porcelain, Thanks Call Again For A Coca-Cola in yellow & white on red, 1930s, 13½x3½", NM+, A13 ....**$325.00**

Coca-Cola, door plate, porcelain, Thanks Call Again For A Coca-Cola in yellow & white on red, 1930s, 11½x4", NM, A13 ....**$210.00**

Coca-Cola, door plate, tin, Drink... contour logo above bottle on white, square corners, 1970s, 20x4", EX+, A13 ....**$100.00**

Coca-Cola, door plate, tin, Pull/Push on white above Refresh Yourself & red disk on green, 1940s-50s, 6x3", NM+, A13, from $250 to **$330.00**

Coca-Cola, door push bar, porcelain, Buvez Coca-Cola Glace in yellow & white on red, 3x30", EX, D21 ....**$125.00**

Coca-Cola, door push bar, porcelain, Come In! Have A Coca-Cola, yellow & white on red with yellow border, 1930s, 11½x4", VG, A1 ....**$200.00**

Coca-Cola, door push bar, porcelain, Drink... on red with white trim, wrought-iron brackets, 1930s, EX, A13.**$260.00**

Coca-Cola, door push bar, porcelain, Iced Coca-Cola Here in yellow & white on red, 1950s, 3x30", EX, D21 .....**$150.00**

Coca-Cola, door push bar, porcelain, red Ice Cold & In Bottles flank red Drink... panel with curved ends on white, 35" NM, A13 ....**$255.00**

Coca-Cola, door push bar, porcelain, Thanks Call Again For A Coca-Cola in yellow & white on red, 11½x4", EX, A6 ....**$170.00**

Coca-Cola, door push bar, tin, red with silhouette girl left of Drink... & Delicious/Refreshing, 1939-41, 3½x33", EX+, A13 ....**$375.00**

Coca-Cola, drinking glass, bell-shaped, gold-dipped, 50th Anniversary, with plastic stand, 1950, large, EX, A13 ....**$250.00**

Coca-Cola, drinking glass, bell-shaped, NM, A7 ....**$10.00**

Coca-Cola, drinking glass, flared top, syrup line, Drink Coca-Cola, NM, A16 ....**$285.00**

Coca-Cola, drinking glass, modified flared top, Coca-Cola, 1923-27, NM+, A16 ....**$140.00**

Coca-Cola, drinking glass, plastic, Things Go Better With Coke repeated in slanted vertical rows around glass, EX+, A16 ....**$30.00**

Coca-Cola, drinking glass holder, silver with Coca-Cola logo, vertical bars, angled handle, early 1900s, NM, A13 ....**$1,300.00**

Coca-Cola, fan, Drink Coca-Cola, geisha girl in garden, Keep Cool Drink... with arrow pointing to 5¢ on reverse, 1911, 14", EX+, D8 ....**$150.00**

Coca-Cola, fan, Drink... above bottle against yellow dot on 2-color background, Sprite boy on reverse, 1930s, EX+, A16 ....**$65.00**

Coca-Cola, festoon, Icecicles, The Pause That Refreshes..., 1930s, 5 pcs with envelope, EX+, A13 ....**$775.00**

Coca-Cola, festoon, Petunia, Thirst Stops Here & glass flanked by ladies drinking from glasses, 1939, 5 pcs, EX, A6 ....**$1,000.00**

Coca-Cola, festoon element, center section of lady in hat & green gloves with glass, 1950, framed on green ground, 20x30", VG, A13 ....**$625.00**

Coca-Cola, festoon element, College Kids, The Pause That Refreshes, 2 girls & a guy with glasses & C pennant, 1940s, G, A16 ....**$115.00**

Coca-Cola, festoon element, Square Dance, Puts You At Your Sparkling Best, shows 2 girls & guy with full glasses, VG+, A16 ....**$275.00**

Coca-Cola, Fiftieth Anniversary Promotional Material, boxed set with various items, 1936, rare, M, A16..........**$275.00**

Coca-Cola, flyer, Toy Soda Fountain Dispenser & Miniature Glasses..., 1950s, NM, A16 ....**$20.00**

Coca-Cola, folder, features the Glasscock cooler, Why The Coca-Cola Cooler Excels, ...The Best Salesman Dealers Can Hire, NM, A16 ....**$35.00**

Coca-Cola, folder for Roy G Booker service emblems, full-color images with descriptions & prices, 1945, NM, A16 ....**$95.00**

Coca-Cola, frame, for cardboard sign, gold, 1940s, 20x36", EX, A13 ....**$225.00**

Coca-Cola, frame, gold reproduction for cardboard sign, 27x16", M, A16...**$95.00**

Coca-Cola, game, Bingo set, complete, original box, VG+, A16 ....**$45.00**

Coca-Cola, game, checker board, G, A16.................**$20.00**

Coca-Cola, game, cribbage board, complete, NMIB, A16 ....**$50.00**

Coca-Cola, game, Horse Race Game, complete, original box, EX, A16...**$305.00**

Coca-Cola, game, Shanghai, MIB, A16 ....**$20.00**

Coca-Cola, game, Steps To Health, 1938, complete with envelope, NM+, D21..........................**$120.00**

Coca-Cola, game, Streamlined Darts, original box, EX+, A16 ....**$35.00**

Coca-Cola, game, Table Tennis, complete, original box, EX+, A16...$40.00

Coca-Cola, game, Tower Of Hanoi, Compliments Of The Coca-Cola Company on lid, EX+, A16...............**$250.00**

Coca-Cola, game set, Checkers & Dice & Backgammon, complete, original box, VG+, A16........................**$40.00**

Coca-Cola, game set, 2 decks of cards, cribbage, dice, dominos & checkers, original box, EX+, A16....**$330.00**

Coca-Cola, game set, 2 decks of cards, cribbage board, dominos & checkers, Milton Bradley, 1943, complete in original box, VG, A13 ....**$130.00**

Coca-Cola, game set, 2 decks of cards, cribbage board, dominos & checkers, Milton Bradley, 1943, complete, NMIB, D36 ....$450.00

Coca-Cola, hat, soda jerk's, white cloth with red stripe & Drink Coca-Cola on side, M, A16......................**$42.00**

Coca-Cola, ice pick, wood handle reading Drink..., in box reading Drink...Delicious & Refreshing, 1960s, NM, A16...**$22.00**

Coca-Cola, ice pick/bottle opener, metal, wood handle, loop on end, box showing 2 bottles & Compliments Of..., 1940s-50s, NM, A16......................................**$40.00**

Coca-Cola, information kit, 1964 NY World's Fair, 'The Coca-Cola Company Pavilion'/'See-The-Fair,' NM, A16 ....**$60.00**

Coca-Cola, knife, wood handle with black Drink Coca-Cola logo, stainless steel A&J blade, early, EX+, A16 ....**$90.00**

Coca-Cola, knife, bone handle, with blade & opener, Delicious & Refreshing, 1920s, VG, A13...................**$100.00**

Coca-Cola, light fixture, milk glass with Coca-Cola & tassel design, metal hangs from bottom, 1930s, 100% original, NM+, A16...**$4,392.00**

Coca-Cola, light fixture, milk glass with red Drink Coca-Cola logo repeated below thin green band, 1930s, NM+, A13...**$1,250.00**

Coca-Cola, light fixture, octagonal with 8 lettered milk glass panels framed in a Deco motif, 1930s, 24x20" dia, EX+, A13 ....$1,800.00

Coca-Cola, light fixture, 4 insert panels with roof-like top, 3 red panels with Drink..., 1 Popcorn panel, 1960s, 18x18", NM+, A13..**$525.00**

Coca-Cola, lighter, flip-top, red & white enamel Enjoy... contour logo, M, A16...**$45.00**

Coca-Cola, lighter, flip-top, silver with embossed bottle, MIB, D21...**$40.00**

Coca-Cola, lighter, flip-top, 14k gold plate, Enjoy Coca-Cola on bottom, M, A16.......................................**$75.00**

Coca-Cola, lighter, flip-top with red Drink..., in original box, NM, A7 ....**$40.00**

Coca-Cola, lighter, musical, red with red Drink... on white dot, 1963, EX+, A16 ....**$162.00**

Coca-Cola, lighter, silver with red logo, executive award, 1984, NM, D21...**$28.00**

Coca-Cola, lighter, stands up on base, gold-tone with red Coca-Cola lettered diagonally, 1962, EX+, A13 ..**$140.00**

Coca-Cola, magazine, Human Life, 1909, color ad, Come In!, Soda Fountain above text encircled by arrow, NM, A13 ....**$60.00**

Coca-Cola, magazine, Human Life, 1909, color ad, Scortching Hot Day, 'Hott' sun & man above text encircled by arrow, EX+, A16 ....**$40.00**

Coca-Cola, magazine, Human Life, 1910, June, color ad featuring Human Life & lady in profile above text encircled by arrow, NM, A16......................................**$75.00**

Coca-Cola, magazine, Woman's Home Companion, 1905, features full-color Coca-Cola fountain scene on back, EX+, A16 ....**$210.00**

Coca-Cola, magazine, Woman's World, 1920, ad features oval image of girl in yellow with glass, Drink... below, EX+, A16 ....**$45.00**

Coca-Cola, magazine ad, 1917, features Coke glass on ledge with Drink... oval, busy cityscape beyond, EX+, A16 ....**$15.00**

Coca-Cola, magazine ad, 1923, color ad, flowers above head of girl wearing muffler & hat, Drink... below, NM, A16 ....$25.00

Coca-Cola, match striker, porcelain, Drink Coca-Cola/Strike Matches Here, square with rounded corners, 1939, 4x4", NM, A13 ....$500.00

Coca-Cola, match striker, porcelain, Drink Coca-Cola/Strike Matches Here, square with rounded corners, 1939, 4x4", NOS, M, A6 ....$610.00

Coca-Cola, match striker, porcelain, Drink Coca-Cola/Strike Matches Here, square with rounded corners, 1939, 4x4", EX+, D21 ....$235.00

Coca-Cola, matchbook cover, A Distinctive Drink In A Distinctive Bottle/Drink...Delicious & Refreshing, 1922, EX, A16 ....$115.00

Coca-Cola, matchbook cover, 1838-1938 Sequin Centennial, EX+, A16 ....$65.00

Coca-Cola, mechanical pencil, Coca-Cola Bottling Co in script, mother-of-pearl (?) handle, pocket clip, EX, A16 ....$45.00

Coca-Cola, mechanical pencil, Coca-Cola on side, pocket clip, eraser tip, early, NM, A16 ....$85.00

Coca-Cola, menu board, cardboard stand-up, Refreshing You Best flanked by 2 bottles below, Drink... marquee above, 1950s, VG+, A16 ....$100.00

Coca-Cola, menu board, Drink... disk with full glass flanked by menu slots, gold-tone, Kay Displays, 1940s-50s, 12x36", EX+, A13 ....$2,400.00

Coca-Cola, menu board, light-up, 1960s, EX, D32 ..$115.00

Coca-Cola, menu board, porcelain, Drink...Be Refreshed oval atop board, Have A Coke 5¢ below, yellow trim, 1950s, rare, NM, D36 ....$150.00

Coca-Cola, menu board, silver-tone metal, red disk logo with bell-shaped glass flanked by menu slots, Kay Displays, 1940s, VG+, A13 ....$500.00

Coca-Cola, menu board, tin, Drink Coca-Cola on panel above board, Delicious & Refreshing with silhouette girl below, 1940, G-, A16 ....$185.00

Coca-Cola, menu board, tin, Drink Coca-Cola on panel above board, Delicious & Refreshing with silhouette girl below, 1940, EX+, A13 ....$300.00

Coca-Cola, menu board, tin, Specials To Day, Drink... panel above board with red, yellow & green line design, 1934, 28x20", EX, A13 ....$350.00

Coca-Cola, menu board, tin, Specials To-Day, embossed board with rope-like border & bottle, Refresh Yourself, 1929, 28x20", G, A13 ....$150.00

Coca-Cola, Merchandising Kit for selling the Glasscock cooler & others, ca 1930, 27 pgs, M, A16 ....$90.00

Coca-Cola, mileage meter, red breadbox style with white lettering, Marion Coca-Cola Bottling Co, Crescent Beach SC, 1950s, EX, A13 ....$1,000.00

Coca-Cola, miniature puzzle in box, diagonal image of Refreshment lettered over bottle against Cold in 'icy' letters, 1983, NM, A16 ....$15.00

Coca-Cola, miniature 6-pack, fishtail logo on side of carton, Drink... on white front panel, NM+, A4 ....$50.00

Coca-Cola, mirror, Coca-Cola Memos at right of hand-held bottle, 50th Anniversary below, framed, vertical rectangle, 1936, EX+, A16 ....$90.00

Coca-Cola, mirror, Drink... In Bottles, Delicious & Refreshing on red above mirror, 1930s, 12x8", VG, A13 ....$130.00

Coca-Cola, mirror, pointed top with Deco design flanking Coca-Cola, bottle & more advertising at bottom, 1930s, 18x8", VG, A13 ....$160.00

Coca-Cola, money clip with knife & file, metal, engraved Drink... logo with Trade Mark below, rectangular, NM, A16 ....$80.00

Coca-Cola, nail clippers, sample set with advertising clip-ons, MIB, A16 ....$30.00

Coca-Cola, nail file, embossed metal, fold-up (pocketknife) type, Coca-Cola In Bottles in early script, EX+, A16 ....$253.00

Coca-Cola, name tag, Drink... flanked by bottles on panel above space for name, Bottlers Convention below, 1943, NM+, A16 ....$70.00

Coca-Cola, name tag, Drink... on red disk flanked by bottles & branches of leaves above space for name, EX, A16 ....$50.00

Coca-Cola, napkin, rice paper, arrow encircles text & points to girl with bottle, 1914, framed, EX+, A13 ....$50.00

Coca-Cola, napkin holder, chrome body with Sprite boy & 5¢ glass insert on 1 side, straw box on reverse, EX+, A13 ....$700.00

Coca-Cola, negative to 1946 cardboard sign, glass, shows tennis girl at cooler, 24x20", VG+, A13.............**$100.00**

Coca-Cola, No-Drip Protector, 1930, In Bottles, shows 2 bottles above receding logo, NM, A7......................**$5.00**

Coca-Cola, No-Drip Protector, 1936, The Pause That Refreshes, disk logo above lady with 3 bottles, NM, A7 ....**$5.00**

Coca-Cola, No-Drip Protector, 1936, The Pause That Refreshes, shows backside of man tipping bottle, NM, A7 ....**$4.00**

Coca-Cola, No-Drip Protector, 1938, A Great Drink...With Good Things To Eat, NM, A7 ....**$4.00**

Coca-Cola, No-Drip Protector, 1944, So Refreshing With Food, shows lady with tray, NM, A7.......................**$3.00**

Coca-Cola, No-Drip Protector, 1946, Take A Minute To Refresh, shows dancing couple, NM, A7 ....**$5.00**

Coca-Cola, No-Drip Protector, 1946, Take A Minute To Refresh, shows lady in rocker with bottle, NM, A7..**$3.00**

Coca-Cola, No-Drip Protector, 1946, The Taste That Always Charms, shows girl in profile tipping bottle, NM, A7..**$3.00**

Coca-Cola, No-Drip Protector, 1948, Every Bottle Refreshes, shows disk logo, NM, A7 ....**$3.00**

Coca-Cola, oil painting, encircled portrait of girl with glass in mittened hand, by Hayden Hayden (?), ca 1940, 24x28", NM, A13 ....**$4,000.00**

Coca-Cola, paper cup, Things Go Better With Coke in red on white square in center, red background, 1960s, 3½", NM+, D21...**$3.00**

Coca-Cola, pen, sample, 'Hava' & bottle on clip, quantity & prices on barrel of pen, M, A16 ....**$50.00**

Coca-Cola, pencil, bullet type with white Drink... on red fishtail logo, eraser tip, M, A16................................**$45.00**

Coca-Cola, pencil box, pencil shape, The Coca-Cola Bottling Co, shows Sprite boy & large bottle, cork end comes off, 1948, NM, A16.....................................**$175.00**

Coca-Cola, pencil holder, ceramic, 75th Anniversary, shaped like th 1896 syrup dispenser, M, A16.....**$165.00**

Coca-Cola, perfume bottle, with cap, M, A16 ....**$45.00**

Coca-Cola, pin, 10 Years Of Service, 10k gold, oval, NM+, D21 ....**$30.00**

Coca-Cola, pin, 15 Years Of Service, 10k gold, oval, NM+, D21 ....**$35.00**

Coca-Cola, pin, 25 Years Of Service, 10k gold, NM, D21 ....**$55.00**

Coca-Cola, pin-back button, club pin depicting hand-held bottle, , G+, A16 ....**$15.00**

Coca-Cola, pitcher, glass with Coca-Cola painted in red, painted rim & 4 rings around bottom, M, A16 .....**$70.00**

Coca-Cola, plate, Drink Coca-Cola/Good With Food on scalloped rim, marked Sample on back, Wellsville, 1940s-50s, 7½", NM, A13 ....**$750.00**

Coca-Cola, plate, Drink Coca-Cola/Good With Food on smooth rim, marked Sample on back, Wellsville, 1940s-50s, 6½", NM, A13..**$700.00**

Coca-Cola, plate, Drink Coca-Cola/Refresh Yourself on decorative rim, glass & bottle in center, Knowles China, 1931, 7", EX, A13..**$475.00**

Coca-Cola, plate, Drink...Delicious & Refreshing/Refresh Yourself, smooth rim, bottle & glass in center, 1930s, 8", rare, EX+, A13................................**$1,200.00**

Coca-Cola, play dollar bill, Refresh Yourself At The Bar..., advertises the Chesterman Co for a promotional event, NM, A13 ....**$100.00**

Coca-Cola, playing cards, 1915, Elaine seated with folded parasol, framed border, single card, G+, A16.......**$40.00**

Coca-Cola, playing cards, 1943, Coke bottle before girl in circular inset surrounded by leaves, complete in original box, EX, D21 ....**$60.00**

Coca-Cola, playing cards, 1943, silhouette girl with service girl on reverse, complete, M/NM box, A16........$110.00

Coca-Cola, playing cards, 1951, close-up of cowgirl with bottle, complete in original box, NM, D21 ....**$60.00**

Coca-Cola, playing cards, 1951, party girl with bottle, complete in original box, EX+, D21......................**$60.00**

Coca-Cola, playing cards, 1951, party girl with bottle, complete in original box, NM, A16......................**$100.00**

Coca-Cola, playing cards, 1958, 'Ice Man' holding bottle & Coca-Cola button, complete in original box, VG+, A16 ....**$80.00**

Coca-Cola, playing cards, 1959, Sign Of Good Taste, close-up of girl on pool with bottle, complete in original box, NM+, A16 ....**$70.00**

Coca-Cola, playing cards, 1960, Be Really Refreshed, shows costume party, complete in original box, EX, A16..**$80.00**

Coca-Cola, playing cards, 1961, Coke Refreshes You Best!, shows girl holding bottle & score pad, complete in original box, NM+, A16......................................**$50.00**

Coca-Cola, playing cards, 1961, pictures girl with bowling ball, MIB, D32 ....**$60.00**

Coca-Cola, playing cards, 1963, Things Go Better With Coke, couple resting under unplanted tree, complete, sealed, MIB, A16 ....**$70.00**

Coca-Cola, playing cards, 1971, It's The Real Thing, shows girl sitting in field, contour logo, complete, sealed, MIB, A16 ....**$30.00**

Coca-Cola, playing cards, 1971, It's The Real Thing, shows party food around bottle, complete in original box, NM, A16 ....**$25.00**

Coca-Cola, pocket mirror, 1906, Juanita sipping from glass, oval, G+, A13..**$85.00**

Coca-Cola, pocket mirror, 1907, bare-shouldered girl lifts glass, Drink Coca-Cola above, oval, VG+, A13..**$325.00**

Coca-Cola, pocket mirror, 1908, Victorian lady at fountain drinks from glass, Drink Coca-Cola above, oval, VG+, A13...**$600.00**

Coca-Cola, pocket mirror, 1909, lady at table with glass, St Louis World's Fair beyond, Drink Coca-Cola below, oval, EX, A13..$500.00

Coca-Cola, pocket mirror, 1910, The Coca-Cola Girl in wide-brimmed at with rose, Drink Coca-Cola below, oval, VG+, A13...$225.00

Coca-Cola, pocket mirror, 1910, The Coca-Cola Girl in wide-brimmed at with rose, Drink Coca-Cola below, oval, G+, A13..$70.00

Coca-Cola, pocket mirror, 1911, girl in wide-brimmed hat with 2 flowers, Drink Delicious & Refreshing, oval, VG, A13..$145.00

Coca-Cola, pocket mirror, 1911, girl in wide-brimmed hat with 2 flowers, Drink Delicious & Refreshing, oval, EX+, A16...$225.00

Coca-Cola, pocket mirror, 1914, lady looking over shoulder & lifting glass, Drink Coca-Cola 5¢, green background, oval, EX, A13 ....$450.00

Coca-Cola, pocket mirror, 1916, garden girl looking over her shoulder & holding bottle with straw, Drink... below, oval, EX+, A13 ....$375.00

Coca-Cola, pocket mirror, 1920, girl in yellow dress & hat leaning on chair holding bottle, Drink Coca-Cola below, oval, EX+, A13 ....$725.00

Coca-Cola, pocket mirror, 1920s, die-cut cardboard cat's head opens to round mirror & red bottle with logo, NM+, A13...$375.00

Coca-Cola, pocketknife, Drink Coca-Cola In Bottles, Delicious & Refreshing on reverse, bone handle, 1915-25, VG+, A8 ....$95.00

Coca-Cola, pocketknife & corkscrew, pearl with red Drink... & Sample No 501, NM, A16 ....$70.00

Coca-Cola, popcorn bag, Jungleland on oval & Drink... disk above tiger's head & Pop Corn against striped ground, 14x5", NM, A7............................$15.00

Coca-Cola, postage stamp carrier, celluloid, features lady in plumed hat sitting at dresser, 1902, 2½x1½", EX, A13..$550.00

Coca-Cola, postcard, 'Motor Girl' with bottle, Drink Bottled...Delightfully Carbonated So Easily Served, 1911, unused, NM+, A16 ....$1,300.00

Coca-Cola, postcard, black & white photo of Joplin MO plant & employees, NM, A16.........................$30.00

Coca-Cola, postcard, pictures DuQuoin, Illinois bottling plant, NM+, A16 ....$30.00

Coca-Cola, postcard, shows the Coca-Cola building in Kansas City, MO, NM, A16 ....$30.00

Coca-Cola, pot holder, yellow diamond shape with red Drink Coca-Cola, Every Bottle Sterilized, green border, 1910s-20s, VG, A13 ....$275.00

Coca-Cola, pretzel dish, aluminum, 1930s, EX, D32..$225.00

Coca-Cola, printing mat, cardboard, 1858, NM, A16..$40.00

Coca-Cola, proof for cardboard sign, paper, ca 1912, All Over The World It's..., tennis couple atop the world, 49x38", VG, A13.............................$16,500.00

Coca-Cola, puzzle, jigsaw, Crossing The Equator, with box, EX+, A16...$150.00

Coca-Cola, puzzle, jigsaw, Hawaiian Beach, very rare, NMIB, A16 ....$182.00

Coca-Cola, puzzle, jigsaw, Teen Age Party, NMIB, A16..$90.00

Coca-Cola, puzzle, jigsaw, 2000 Pieces, a collage of Coke items including a bicycle & vending machine, MIB (shrink wrapped), A13.............................$55.00

Coca-Cola, puzzle, jigsaw, 2000 Pieces, a collage of Coke items including bottle, fan, toy truck, can, cup, sign, etc, NMIB, A16 ....$20.00

Coca-Cola, puzzle, see also miniature puzzle

Coca-Cola, puzzle, wooden blocks, "15" Puzzle, spells out Ice Cold Coca-Cola with Drink Coca-Cola disk logo, rare, NMIB, A16.....................................$310.00

Coca-Cola, radiator plate, Drink Coca-Cola In Bottles in die-cut script, 1920s, 17" long, EX+, A13...........$275.00

Coca-Cola, radio, brown bottle shape, has had some modifications, 1933, EX, A13..................................$3,500.00

Coca-Cola, radio, red cooler form with white Drink Coca-Cola Ice Cold, 1950, restored, NM, A13..$625.00

Coca-Cola, radio, upright vending machine, red & white with row of bottles, leather case with handle, 1960s, EX+, A16...$330.00

Coca-Cola, radio, upright vending machine, red Drink... on white upper panel, red lower panel, with antenna, 1950s, EX, A16..$140.00

Coca-Cola, record, 'Buy The World A Coke' by The New Seekers, M, A16..$15.00

Coca-Cola, record carring case, vinyl, Hi-Fi Club logo on front, plastic handle, 1960s, NM+, A13 ....$75.00

Coca-Cola, roller skates, clamp-on type with leather straps, embossed Drink Coca-Cola In Bottles, marked Pat Aug 16 1914, VG+, A13 ....$900.00

Coca-Cola, saleman's sample, red cooler with Drink...Ice Cold in white lettering, open bottom, 1939, no case, EX+, A13...**$2,600.00**

Coca-Cola, salesman's sample, counter-top dispenser with original case & 'The Dole Director' cover, 1960s, 6¾", EX+, A13...**$2,500.00**

Coca-Cola, salesman's sample, storage display rack with 6 plastic cases & bottles, 1960s, 13x12x6", NM, A13 ......**$4,500.00**

Coca-Cola, seltzer bottle, Circle Beverages around silhouette image of cowboy on rearing horse, Miles City Mont, rare, NM, A16..**$495.00**

Coca-Cola, seltzer bottle, Coca-Cola Bottling Co Richmond Ind under bust image of Quaker man, NM, A16 .**$400.00**

Coca-Cola, sheet music, 'Juanita,' 1906, NM, D32 ...**$900.00**

Coca-Cola, sheet music, 'Rum & Coca-Cola,' EX+, A16..**$20.00**

Coca-Cola, sheet music, 'The Coca-Cola Girl,' 1927, EX, A16 ....$175.00

Coca-Cola, sign, arrow, 1920s, tin, Ice Cold Coca-Cola Sold Here, 2-sided hanger, 7¾x30", VG, A13.............**$200.00**

Coca-Cola, sign, arrow, 1920s, tin, Ice Cold Coca-Cola Sold Here, 2-sided hanger, 7¾x30", EX/EX+, A16 .....**$850.00**

Coca-Cola, sign, arrow, 1933, wood, Drink...emblem on inverted triangle with Ice Cold & bottle on arrow, 28x23", NM+, A16...**$990.00**

Coca-Cola, sign, arrow, 1939, wood, applied silver bottle above Drink...Ice Cold on red disk with silver arrow, 17" dia, G+, A13 ....**$400.00**

Coca-Cola, sign, arrow, 1940s, masonite, Ice Cold Coca-Cola above bottle on yellow dot on red disk, gold arrow, 17" dia, EX+, A13 ....$800.00

Coca-Cola, sign, arrow, 1940s, masonite, red die-cut cooler with Drink... Ice Cold, Sprite boy arrow missing otherwise EX, A13 ....**$260.00**

Coca-Cola, sign, bottle, 1954, die-cut tin, Trade Mark lettered under Coca-Cola, appears wet looking, 72", NM, A13..**$575.00**

Coca-Cola, sign, bottle, 1960s, die-cut tin, Trade Mark Registered lettered under Coca-Cola, appears wet looking, 36", EX+, A13...**$350.00**

Coca-Cola, sign, button, 1950s, bottle (hand-held) on white, 24", EX, A13 ....**$275.00**

Coca-Cola, sign, button, 1950s, bottle on white, 24", EX+, A13..**$400.00**

Coca-Cola, sign, button, 1950s, bottle on white, 24", M, D8..**$675.00**

Coca-Cola, sign, button, 1950s, Coca-Cola lettered over bottle, red, 24", EX+, A13..............................**$450.00**

Coca-Cola, sign, button, 1950s, Coca-Cola lettered over bottle, red, 24", M, D8.................................**$675.00**

Coca-Cola, sign, button, 1950s, Coca-Cola lettered over bottle, red, 36", EX, A13 ....**$325.00**

Coca-Cola, sign, button, 1950s, Coca-Cola lettered over bottle, red, 36", NM, A13 ....**$550.00**

Coca-Cola, sign, button, 1950s, Drink Coca-Cola, Sign Of Good Taste, red, 36", EX, A13.............................**$250.00**

Coca-Cola, sign, button, 1950s, Drink Coca-Cola, Sign Of Good Taste, red, 16", NM, A13...........................**$375.00**

Coca-Cola, sign, button, 1950s, Drink Coca-Cola In Bottles, red, 24", M, D8..$750.00

Coca-Cola, sign, button, 1950s, Drink Coca-Cola Sign Of Good Taste, red, 16" dia, G, A16 ....**$225.00**

Coca-Cola, sign, button, 1950s, 2-sided, electric, white Drink... on red, Have A Coke Here sticker on reverse, 16" dia, EX, A16 ....**$250.00**

Coca-Cola, sign, button with arrow, 1950s, Drink Coca-Cola, red, silver arrow, 12" dia, M, D8................**$675.00**

Coca-Cola, sign, button with arrow, 1950s, Drink Coca-Cola, red, silver arrow, 24" dia, NM, D8.............**$600.00**

Coca-Cola, sign, cardboard, die-cut, 1911, It's Time To Drink..., couple under umbrella leaning on sundial, 36x29", G, A2 ....**$3,520.00**

Coca-Cola, sign, cardboard, die-cut, 1913, Drink... ovals flank cameo girl, floral garland swag above, trifold, 34x60", VG, A13..**$5,200.00**

Coca-Cola, sign, cardboard, die-cut, 1938, Drink Coca-Cola, image of girl drinking from bottle, 22x15", G, A16 ....**$800.00**

Coca-Cola, sign, cardboard, die-cut, 1944, WWII battleship & disk logo with lettered banner, 14x26", EX+, A1 .**$1,300.00**

Coca-Cola, sign, cardboard, die-cut, 1946, Greetings From Coca-Cola, Santa with bottle, 12", EX, D32 ....**$125.00**

Coca-Cola, sign, cardboard, die-cut, 1950s, hand-held bottle, 9", M, A16 ....**$85.00**

Coca-Cola, sign, cardboard, die-cut, 1952, Take Home, sailor girl with signal flags, red Drink... button in center, 7x11", NM, A13 ....$375.00

Coca-Cola, sign, cardboard, die-cut, 1952, Take Home Enough! on panel with ribbon border above hand-held bottle, NM, A13 ....$160.00

Coca-Cola, sign, cardboard, die-cut, 1958, Santa standing holding bottle of Coke in each hand, 32", G, A16..........$500.00

Coca-Cola, sign, cardboard, die-cut, 1960s, Be Really Refreshed, 2-sided fold-out of girl with glass, red fishtail, 13x17", EX, A13..........................$425.00

Coca-Cola, sign, cardboard, die-cut hanger, 1930s, receding billboard logo & Ice Cold with bottle on green dot, 9", VG, A21 ....$285.00

Coca-Cola, sign, cardboard, die-cut hanger, 1931, My Hats Off To The Pause That Refreshes, shows Santa, 20x10", EX, D32..........................$400.00

Coca-Cola, sign, cardboard, die-cut hanger, 1933, Claudette Colbert Invites You To The Pause That Refreshes, 20x10", NM, A13 ....$3,400.00

Coca-Cola, sign, cardboard, die-cut hanger, 1940, Drink Coca-Cola, bathing beauty with bottle on blue diamond, 23x24", EX+, A13......................$1,000.00

Coca-Cola, sign, cardboard, die-cut hanger, 1940, Drink Coca-Cola, bathing beauty with bottle on blue diamond, 23x24", M, D32......................$1,500.00

Coca-Cola, sign, cardboard, die-cut hanger, 1950s, Serve... on circle behind Regular Size & Sign Of Good Taste bells, M, A16......................$20.00

Coca-Cola, sign, cardboard, die-cut hanger, 1955, Serve...Regular Size, Sign Of Good Taste, Chirstmas bulbs & bells, M, A16......................$20.00

Coca-Cola, sign, cardboard, die-cut stand-up, 1939, Drink...With Good Things To Eat above food tray with Coke, 42x31", EX, A13......................$350.00

Coca-Cola, sign, cardboard, die-cut stand-up, 1950s, A Merry Christmas Call For Coke, Santa in chair with elves, EX+, A16 ....$180.00

Coca-Cola, sign, cardboard, die-cut stand-up, 1954, Eddie Fisher, 19", EX, D32 ....$250.00

Coca-Cola, sign, cardboard, die-cut stand-up, 1956, Extra Bright Refreshment, Coke & Food..., girl with cart, 60", EX+, A13......................$900.00

Coca-Cola, sign, cardboard, die-cut stand-up, 1962, Season's Greetings, boy dreams of Santa, helicopter, and train, 24x16", NM+, A13......................$425.00

Coca-Cola, sign, cardboard, die-cut stand-up, 1962, Season's Greetings, child dreams of Santa, helicopter & train, 24x16", NM, A13......................$310.00

Coca-Cola, sign, cardboard, die-cut stand-up, 1962, Seasons Greetings, child dreams of Santa, helicopter & train, 47x32", VG, D32......................$150.00

Coca-Cola, sign, cardboard, hanger, 1930s, Our...Is Below 40°, It's Delicious, thermometer & hand-held bottle, 9x12", A16......................$785.00

Coca-Cola, sign, cardboard, hanger, 1943, B-26 bomber over enemy targets, bottle & button lower right, 13x15", VG, A6 ....$100.00

Coca-Cola, sign, cardboard, stand-up, Zing For Your Supper Ice Cold Coke, Refreshing New Feeling!, shows bottles & food, NM+, A16......................$160.00

Coca-Cola, sign, cardboard, stand-up, 1960s, For Extra Fun Take More Than One, 2 girls on tandem bike, 27x16", NM, A13......................$30.00

Coca-Cola, sign, cardboard, trolley, 1912, Have A Drink Of Coca-Cola, Deliciously Refreshing, girl in hammock, restored, EX, A13 ....$3,100.00

Coca-Cola, sign, cardboard, trolley, 1920s, Drink Coca-Cola above Delicious & Refreshing, bordered, matted & framed, G-, A16......................$135.00

Coca-Cola, sign, cardboard, 1928, Drink... Delicious... on receding sign above draped bathing girl with bottle, 31x21", VG+, A2......................$1,760.00

Coca-Cola, sign, cardboard, 1930s, Ice Cold...As Always Five 5 Cents, yellow & white on red, yellow & green border, 12x15", NM, A13 ....$275.00

Coca-Cola, sign, cardboard, 1930s-40s, Drink... Delicious & Refreshing on disk above ski couple, gold frame, 18x36", VG, A13 ....$625.00

Coca-Cola, sign, cardboard, 1934, Drink..., swim couple with bottles leaning on red blanket draped over railing, 50x29", EX, A13......................$2,700.00

Coca-Cola, sign, cardboard, 1935, Drink..., man wrapping red beach blanket around beauty in white swimsuit, 50x29", VG+, A13......................$1,400.00

Coca-Cola, sign, cardboard, 1936, Drink... above lady in white silk gown reclining on arm of chair with glass, 50x30", G+, A13 ....$700.00

Coca-Cola, sign, cardboard, 1936, Drink... above lady in white silk gown reclining on arm of chair with glass, 50x30", EX+, A13 ....$2,100.00

Coca-Cola, sign, cardboard, 1936, 50th Anniversary bathing beauties sitting atop red blanket, 50x30", G+, A13..**$800.00**

Coca-Cola, sign, cardboard, 1937, Drink... above bathing beauty seated with legs crossed holding bottle, 50x30", EX, A13...**$1,700.00**

Coca-Cola, sign, cardboard, 1937, Face The Sun Refreshed, girl with bottle shielding her face from sun, 50x29", VG, D32..**$200.00**

Coca-Cola, sign, cardboard, 1937, girl in yellow swimsuit & white cape running on beach with 2 bottles, 30x14", EX, D32..**$400.00**

Coca-Cola, sign, cardboard, 1938, bathing beauty with bottle, 22" dia, EX+, D32 ....**$1,800.00**

Coca-Cola, sign, cardboard, 1939, Drink... Delicious..., group in touring car being served by carhop, gold frame, 27x16", G+, A16....................................**$1,200.00**

Coca-Cola, sign, cardboard, 1940, Drink... disk logo above lady in red with fur stole holding bottle at ballpark, 50x30", EX+, A13 ....**$1,400.00**

Coca-Cola, sign, cardboard, 1940, Thirst Knows No Season, ski girl with bottle leaning on Coke case, horizontal, EX, A13..$450.00

Coca-Cola, sign, cardboard, 1940s, All Set At Our House, smiling boy holding up 6-pack, 27x56", NM, A16........**$970.00**

Coca-Cola, sign, cardboard, 1940s, Talk About Refreshing, 2 girls facing each other in beach chairs with bottles, 27x56", VG, A16 ....**$800.00**

Coca-Cola, sign, cardboard, 1940s, They All Want Coca-Cola, waitress with tray of burgers, 20x36", VG+, A13...**$130.00**

Coca-Cola, sign, cardboard, 1941, Entertain Your Thirst, spotlight on lady with bottle singing into microphone, 20x36", VG, A16 ....**$425.00**

Coca-Cola, sign, cardboard, 1941, It's A Family Affair, shows mother, father & son with bottles, disk logo, 20x36", NM, A13..**$675.00**

Coca-Cola, sign, cardboard, 1941, Refreshment Right Out Of The Bottle, girl with skates by cooler tips bottle, 27x16", EX+, A13 ....**$750.00**

Coca-Cola, sign, cardboard, 1941, Refreshment Right Out Of The Bottle, girl with skates by cooler, gold frame, 27x16", NM+, A16..**$985.00**

Coca-Cola, sign, cardboard, 1941, So Refreshing, encircled autumn girl with bottle, Drink... below, 27x16", G+, A13...**$425.00**

Coca-Cola, sign, cardboard, 1941, The Pause That Refreshes At Home, girl by flower bed, 25¢ 6-pack, gold frame, 27x56", EX+, A13 ....**$1,000.00**

Coca-Cola, sign, cardboard, 1941, They All Want Coca-Cola, waitress with tray of hamburgers holding up hand, 20x36", G, A16 ....**$100.00**

Coca-Cola, sign, cardboard, 1941, They All Want Coca-Cola, waitress with tray of hamburgers holding up hand, 20x36", VG+, A16 ....**$400.00**

Coca-Cola, sign, cardboard, 1942, Accepted Home Refreshment, couple by fireplace enjoying popcorn & Coke, 27x56", EX, A13..**$725.00**

Coca-Cola, sign, cardboard, 1942, America's Favorite Moment, couple in booth eating & enjoying Coke, 20x36", G+, A13 ....**$250.00**

Coca-Cola, sign, cardboard, 1942, At Ease...For Refreshment, nurse with bottle, gold frame, 25x56", NM+, A13...**$1,000.00**

Coca-Cola, sign, cardboard, 1942, Coca-Cola Belongs, couple having picnic against golden sky, 27x56", NM, A16..**$750.00**

Coca-Cola, sign, cardboard, 1942, Entertain Your Thirst, 2 ballerinas with bottles, vertical, VG, A13...........**$600.00**

Coca-Cola, sign, cardboard, 1942, Happy Ending To Thirst, girl in easy chair, 6-pack on yellow dot below, 27x16", G-, A13..**$250.00**

Coca-Cola, sign, cardboard, 1942, Hello Refreshment, bathing beauty eyeing bottle on diving board, 20x36", NM+, A13...**$1,700.00**

Coca-Cola, sign, cardboard, 1942, Hello Refreshment, bathing beauty eyeing bottle on diving board, 20x36", VG, A13..**$750.00**

Coca-Cola, sign, cardboard, 1942, I'm Heading For Coca-Cola, army girl at door of plane, 27x16", EX, A13...........**$600.00**

Coca-Cola, sign, cardboard, 1942, I'm Heading For Coca-Cola, army girl at door of plane, 27x16", G, A13 ....**$220.00**

Coca-Cola, sign, cardboard, 1942, Refreshment Right Out Of The Bottle, girls with bottles at car talking, 29x50", G, A16 ....**$425.00**

Coca-Cola, sign, cardboard, 1942, Talk About Refreshing, girl with umbrella & bottle standing next to cooler, 27x16", NM+, A16..**$800.00**

Coca-Cola, sign, cardboard, 1942, The Drink They All Expect, party couple getting bottles from bowl, 6-pack below, 27x16", VG, A13...................................**$350.00**

Coca-Cola, sign, cardboard, 1942, The Drink They All Expect, party couple getting bottles from bowl, 6-pack below, 27x16", NM+, A16..................................**$860.00**

Coca-Cola, sign, cardboard, 1942, The Drink They All Expect, 6-pack at left of party couple getting bottles, 27x16", NM, A13 ....$700.00

Coca-Cola, sign, cardboard, 1942, The Pause That Refreshes, girl with bottle in chaise lounge, 20x36", G-, A13 ....$90.00

Coca-Cola, sign, cardboard, 1942, We Sell... Part Of Every Day Served Ice Cold, glowing bottle, self-framed, NM, A13 ....$350.00

Coca-Cola, sign, cardboard, 1942, Wherever Thirst Goes, girl with bottle in rowboat, horizontal, EX+, A13..$475.00

Coca-Cola, sign, cardboard, 1942, You Taste Its Quality, Drink... disk logo left of lady tipping bottle, framed, 20x36", NM, A1..$625.00

Coca-Cola, sign, cardboard, 1942, You Taste Its Quality, Drink... disk logo left of lady tipping bottle, framed, 20x36", EX, A1..$485.00

Coca-Cola, sign, cardboard, 1943, All Set At Our House, smiling boy holding up 6-pack, horizontal, EX+, A13 ....$650.00

Coca-Cola, sign, cardboard, 1943, Coke Time, couple seated on step enjoying a sandwich & Coke, gold frame, vertical, EX+, A13 ....$950.00

Coca-Cola, sign, cardboard, 1943, Have A Coke, girl at cooler offering a bottle, 27x16", G+, A13 ....$260.00

Coca-Cola, sign, cardboard, 1943, Have A Coke, girl at cooler offering a bottle, 27x16", VG, A13...........$325.00

Coca-Cola, sign, cardboard, 1943, Lunch Refreshed, lady & 2 men having lunch, horizontal, NM, A13 ......$1,150.00

Coca-Cola, sign, cardboard, 1943, Nothing Refreshes Like A Coke, girl & soldier on bikes with bottles, vertical, NM, A13..$1,700.00

Coca-Cola, sign, cardboard, 1943, Pause... Go Refreshed & hand holding bottle behind wings on red dot, framed, VG, D8................................$130.00

Coca-Cola, sign, cardboard, 1943, Start Refreshed, navy officer lacing up roller skates of girl with bottles, 27x16", VG, A13 ....$300.00

Coca-Cola, sign, cardboard, 1943, The Best Is Always The Better Way, girl with sack of groceries & 6-pack, 27x16", EX, A13..$975.00

Coca-Cola, sign, cardboard, 1943, The Pause That Refreshes, overhead view of lady & navy man with bottles, 29x50", EX, A13..$775.00

Coca-Cola, sign, cardboard, 1943, The Rest-Pause That Refreshes, 3 Wacs seated with bottles, 20x36", EX, A13..$400.00

Coca-Cola, sign, cardboard, 1943, The Rest-Pause That Refreshes, 3 Wacs seated with bottles, 20x36", G-, A13..$80.00

Coca-Cola, sign, cardboard, 1944, Coke Belongs, teen couple, she with bottle, gold frame, 20x36", EX+, A13.......$950.00

Coca-Cola, sign, cardboard, 1944, Coke Belongs, teen couple, she with bottle, 20x36", EX, A13 .....$700.00

Coca-Cola, sign, cardboard, 1944, Coke Belongs, teen couple, she with bottle, 20x36", VG, A13.................$300.00

Coca-Cola, sign, cardboard, 1944, Coke Belongs, teen couple, she with bottle, 20x36", G-, A13 ....$90.00

Coca-Cola, sign, cardboard, 1944, For People On The Go, soldier & girl in sunsuit with bottles on boardwalk, 50x29", NM+, A13..$1,250.00

Coca-Cola, sign, cardboard, 1944, Have A Coke, large bottle tilted on iceberg against frosty glow, 20x36", G, A13..$160.00

Coca-Cola, sign, cardboard, 1944, Have A Coke, sideways view of smiling girl with bottle tilted towards head, 20x36", G, A13..$250.00

Coca-Cola, sign, cardboard, 1944, He's Coming Home Tomorrow, lady in coat & scarf taking Coke bottles from basket, 27x56", NM, A13.........................$1,250.00

Coca-Cola, sign, cardboard, 1944, Hello Coke!, young teen boy surprising girl with bottle of Coke, 20x36", G, A13 ....$325.00

Coca-Cola, sign, cardboard, 1944, Here's To Our GI Joes, 2 girls seated with bottles flank globe, 20x36", EX+, A13..$750.00

Coca-Cola, sign, cardboard, 1944, Here's To Our GI Joes, 2 girls seated with bottles flank globe, 20x36", G+, A13..$275.00

Coca-Cola, sign, cardboard, 1944, Home Refreshment, soldier & girl with bottle leaning on railing, 50x29", NM, A13..$1,800.00

Coca-Cola, sign, cardboard, 1944, Welcome Home, couple getting bottles of Coke from fridge, 20x36", G+, A13 ....$200.00

Coca-Cola, sign, cardboard, 1944, Welcome Home, couple getting bottles of Coke from fridge, gold frame, 20x36", EX, A13 ....$450.00

Coca-Cola, sign, cardboard, 1944, Yes!, smiling lady being offered a bottle of Coke, 20x36", G, A13...........$300.00

Coca-Cola, sign, cardboard, 1945, Coke Belongs, soldier & girl with bottles holding hands at table, 20x36", G, A13..$150.00

Coca-Cola, sign, cardboard, 1945, For The Party, soldier & girl on tandem bike with bottles in basket, 27x16", VG, A13.............................$475.00

Coca-Cola, sign, cardboard, 1945, For The Party, soldier & girl on tandem bike with bottles in basket, 50½x29", G, A6 ....**$325.00**

Coca-Cola, sign, cardboard, 1945, Home Refreshment On The Way, woman with basket of food & Coke, framed, 50x24½", EX, A6.........................$260.00

Coca-Cola, sign, cardboard, 1945, Just Like Old Times, soldier & girl on love seat with bottles, 27x16", NM, A13..............................**$1,400.00**

Coca-Cola, sign, cardboard, 1945, Just Like Old Times, soldier & girl on love seat with bottles, 27x16", G+, A13 ..**$300.00**

Coca-Cola, sign, cardboard, 1945, Merci Bien, girl in scarf being offered bottle of Coke, vertical, G, A13......**$50.00**

Coca-Cola, sign, cardboard, 1945, The Answer To Thirst, girl with bottle at desk, 20x36", G-, A13.....................**$70.00**

Coca-Cola, sign, cardboard, 1945, Why Grow Thirsty, gardening girl bent over flowers, hat propped on disk logo, 20x36", G-, A13.................**$150.00**

Coca-Cola, sign, cardboard, 1946, — And Coke Too, mother opening bottles schoolgirl leaning on table, 27x16", NM, A13.................**$325.00**

Coca-Cola, sign, cardboard, 1946, — And Coke Too, mother opening bottles, schoolgirl leaning on table, 27x16", G, A13...................**$90.00**

Coca-Cola, sign, cardboard, 1946, -Et Coke Aussi, mother opening bottles, schoolgirl leaning on table, Canadian, 27x16", EX, A13.............................**$220.00**

Coca-Cola, sign, cardboard, 1946, Coke For Me Too, couple with bottles, he with hot dog, she with opener, 20x36", G+, A13 ....**$180.00**

Coca-Cola, sign, cardboard, 1946, Coke For Me Too, couple with bottles, he with hot dog, she with opener, 20x36", NM, A13............................**$725.00**

Coca-Cola, sign, cardboard, 1946, Have A Coke, cheerleader with megaphone & bottle, disk logo at right, 20x36", G, A13...............................**$275.00**

Coca-Cola, sign, cardboard, 1946, Have A Coke, cheerleader with megaphone & bottle, disk logo at right, 20x36", NM, A1.............................**$400.00**

Coca-Cola, sign, cardboard, 1946, Have A Coke, unopened bottle in snow, 20x36", G-, A13 ....**$125.00**

Coca-Cola, sign, cardboard, 1946, Have A Coke, unopened bottle in snow, 20x36", EX, A1...........................**$305.00**

Coca-Cola, sign, cardboard, 1946, I'll Bring The Coke, girl leaning on bottom stair talking on phone, 20x36", G, A13......................**$210.00**

Coca-Cola, sign, cardboard, 1946, I'll Bring The Coke, girl leaning on bottom stair talking on phone, 20x36", EX+, A1 ....**$850.00**

Coca-Cola, sign, cardboard, 1946, Let's Have A Coke, majorette posed on cooler with bottle, 27x16", VG, A13................................**$230.00**

Coca-Cola, sign, cardboard, 1946, Let's Have A Coke, majorette posed on cooler with bottle, 27x16", G, A13................................**$140.00**

Coca-Cola, sign, cardboard, 1946, Right Off The Ice, female skater posed against rail with bottle, skaters beyond, 27x16", G, A16.................................**$145.00**

Coca-Cola, sign, cardboard, 1946, Right Off The Ice, female skayer posed against rail with bottle, skaters beyond, 27x16", VG, A13........................**$210.00**

Coca-Cola, sign, cardboard, 1946, Voici La Touche Finale, girl getting bottle from fridge, Canadian, 27x16", VG+, A13..................................**$30.00**

Coca-Cola, sign, cardboard, 1946, Welcome Pause, tennis girl at cooler with a bottle, 27x16", VG+, A13....**$260.00**

Coca-Cola, sign, cardboard, 1946, Welcome Pause, tennis girl at cooler with a bottle, 27x16", G-, A13 ....**$50.00**

Coca-Cola, sign, cardboard, 1946, Yes, smiling sunbather being offered a Coke, disk logo at right, 20x36", EX+, A1 ....**$375.00**

Coca-Cola, sign, cardboard, 1947, Coke Headquarters, couple getting bottles from fridge, 27x16", EX, A13 ..**$350.00**

Coca-Cola, sign, cardboard, 1947, En Roulant Mon Coke Roulant, couple with wheelbarrow, Canadian, vertical, EX+, A13.................................**$210.00**

Coca-Cola, sign, cardboard, 1947, Join Me, lady fencer leaning against cooler with bottle, replaced gold frame, NM+, A13..................................**$775.00**

Coca-Cola, sign, cardboard, 1947, Party Pause, girl in clown suit being offered bottle, 20x36", VG+, A16.........**$165.00**

Coca-Cola, sign, cardboard, 1947, Refreshing, blond holding sunglasses & bottle, horizontal, reproduced gold frame, NM, A13 ....**$675.00**

Coca-Cola, sign, cardboard, 1947, Talk About Refreshing, girl in raincoat with umbrella standing beside cooler, 27x16", NM, A13............................**$700.00**

Coca-Cola, sign, cardboard, 1947, The Pause That Refreshes, girl resting bottle on knee, replaced gold frame, EX+, A13 ....**$900.00**

Coca-Cola, sign, cardboard, 1948, Coke...For Hospitality, family enjoying outdoor barbecue, 20x36", G+, A16 ....**$375.00**

Coca-Cola, sign, cardboard, 1948, girl with tulips, 36x20", EX, D32...............................**$180.00**

Coca-Cola, sign, cardboard, 1948, La Pause Pour Un Coke, archery couple by target having a Coke break, Canadian, vertical, EX, A13........................**$100.00**

Coca-Cola, sign, cardboard, 1948, Servez Coke Chez-Vous, shows Sprite boy with 36¢ 6-pack, Canadian, vertical, G-, A13..............................**$80.00**

Coca-Cola, sign, cardboard, 1948, Shop Refreshed, girl with bottle putting bag on cooler, 27x56", NM, A13.....**$1,400.00**

Coca-Cola, sign, cardboard, 1948, To Be Refreshed, smiling girl with bottles, disk logo, replaced gold frame, 27x56", VG+, A13..**$325.00**

Coca-Cola, sign, cardboard, 1949, Coke Is Coca-Cola, Coca-Cola Is Coke..., white & yellow on red, gold frame, 20x36", NM, A13 ....$675.00

Coca-Cola, sign, cardboard, 1949, Play Refreshed, tennis girl seated on red cooler, 27x16", NM+, A13......**$750.00**

Coca-Cola, sign, cardboard, 1949, Play Refreshed, tennis girl seated on red cooler, reproduced gold frame, 27x16", EX, A13..**$475.00**

Coca-Cola, sign, cardboard, 1949, Serve Yourself, Ice Cold on red button, hand-held paper cup, aluminum frame, 11x13", NM, A13...................................**$350.00**

Coca-Cola, sign, cardboard, 1950, Hospitality In Your Hands, lady with tray of bottles, original gold frame, 20x36", EX, A16...**$365.00**

Coca-Cola, sign, cardboard, 1950, Pause!, clown handing bottle to ice skater, gold frame, 27x16", NM, A13 ....$1,850.00

Coca-Cola, sign, cardboard, 1950s, Delicious With Ice Cold..., spilled popcorn box & button logo, 12x15", EX+, A13..**$200.00**

Coca-Cola, sign, cardboard, 1950s, Let's Watch For 'Em, policeman with School Zone sign & schoolgirl's silhouette, 32x66", NM, A13 ....**$800.00**

Coca-Cola, sign, cardboard, 1950s, Let's Watch For 'Em, schoolgirl's silhouette at cross road, button & bottle, 32x66", NM+, A13...................................**$800.00**

Coca-Cola, sign, cardboard, 1950s, Prenz Un Coke/Glace, hands with bottles/Old Man Winter with bottle, 2-sided, Canadian, vertical, NM+, A13.......................**$150.00**

Coca-Cola, sign, cardboard, 1950s, Transcontinental Mileage & Driving Time chart, US map & traveling vignettes, 18x24", EX+, A16................................**$300.00**

Coca-Cola, sign, cardboard, 1950s-60s, Talk About Good, cowboy enjoying a Coke, bronco rider & button logo below, 36x20", NM, A1 ....**$760.00**

Coca-Cola, sign, cardboard, 1951, Play Refreshed, lasso image of cowgirl with bottle, button logo below, 36x20", NM, A13 ....$575.00

Coca-Cola, sign, cardboard, 1952, features Reece 'Goose' Tatum Star Of The Fabulous Globe Trotters..., EX+, A13 ....**$700.00**

Coca-Cola, sign, cardboard, 1952, Refreshment Ahead/Work Refreshed, sailing couple/blacksmith, 2-sided, 27x16", G-, A16 ....**$132.00**

Coca-Cola, sign, cardboard, 1952, Serve Yourself, girl's face flanked by paper cup & button, aluminum frame, 11x13", NM, A13 ....**$650.00**

Coca-Cola, sign, cardboard, 1953, What I Want Is A Coke, beach beauty on stomach reaching for bottle, gold frame, 20x36", EX+, A13.................................**$1,250.00**

Coca-Cola, sign, cardboard, 1954, Drink Coca-Cola, So Easy, party scene, reproduced frame, horizontal, EX+, A13 ....**$225.00**

Coca-Cola, sign, cardboard, 1954, Drink... Delicious & Refreshing on button, skiers descending hill around bottle, 27x16", EX+, A16 ....**$455.00**

Coca-Cola, sign, cardboard, 1954, So Delicious, ski girl with bottle next to red button logo, 2 skiers beyond, 20x36", EX, A13.................................**$575.00**

Coca-Cola, sign, cardboard, 1955, Coke Time, branding symbols border cowgirl, hand-held bottle & dinner triangle, 27x16", NM+, A13 ....**$750.00**

Coca-Cola, sign, cardboard, 1956, The Best Of Taste/The Quality Taste, winter girl/beach girl, 2-sided, 26x56", VG, A13 ....**$220.00**

Coca-Cola, sign, cardboard, 1957, Sign Of Good Taste, Drink... on snowflake above couple & snowman, gold frame, 27x16", G+, A16..........................**$175.00**

Coca-Cola, sign, cardboard, 1959, Be Really Refreshed!, man helping lady from boat left of bottle & logo, 20x38", EX+, A13...............................**$45.00**

Coca-Cola, sign, cardboard, 1960, A Merry Christmas Calls For Coke above Santa in chair with elves, Stock Up..., 27x16", VG, A16.......................**$100.00**

Coca-Cola, sign, cardboard, 1960s, Big Refreshment, King Size Coke, bowling girl & bottle, red background, 32x66", NM, A13............................**$650.00**

Coca-Cola, sign, cardboard, 1960s, Coke In Big 12oz Cans above Sprite boy & drinking glass, rectangular outline, vertical, EX+, A16....................**$50.00**

Coca-Cola, sign, cardboard, 1960s, Enjoy That Refreshing New Feeling!, lady with menu & bottle, red button logo, 32x66", NM, A13..................**$650.00**

Coca-Cola, sign, cardboard, 1960s, It's Twice Time, Twice The Value, beach couple with canoe over their heads, 32x66", NM+, A13.................**$800.00**

Coca-Cola, sign, cardboard, 1964, Things Go Better With Coke, skating couple/girl in captain's hat, 2-sided, 27x16", EX+, A16......................**$105.00**

Coca-Cola, sign, celluloid, Trink Coca-Cola Koffeloholfig, hand holding bottle, Eis-Kalt on emblem below, 16x6½", VG+, A13.......................**$170.00**

Coca-Cola, sign, celluloid, 1940s, Delicious & Refreshing Coca-Cola, red with gold border, 9" dia, EX, A13..**$180.00**

Coca-Cola, sign, celluloid, 1950s, Coca-Cola lettered over bottle, red with gold border, original envelope, 9" dia, NM. A13......................................**$230.00**

Coca-Cola, sign, celluloid, 1950s, Coca-Cola lettered over bottle, red with gold border, 9" dia, EX, A16 ..$170.00

Coca-Cola, sign, flange, Drink Coca-Cola on button above Ice Cold & bottle, 22½x18", EX, A1.................**$375.00**

Coca-Cola, sign, flange, 1930s, Ice Cold Coca-Cola Sold Here, green/red/green background, 12x16", EX+/VG+, A4...**$640.00**

Coca-Cola, sign, flange, 1930s, Refresh Yourself!..., colonial-style emblem, yellow & white on red, green border, EX+, A13..**$800.00**

Coca-Cola, sign, flange, 1940, Drink...Here, colonial-style emblem with yellow & white lettering, yellow border, restored, NM, A13........................**$650.00**

Coca-Cola, sign, flange, 1941, Drink... on red panel above cut-out design & bottle on yellow dot, 21x24", EX, D8..**$425.00**

Coca-Cola, sign, flange, 1941, Have A Coca-Cola, yellow & white on red, yellow border, 18x18", EX, D21 ..**$295.00**

Coca-Cola, sign, flange, 1950s, Drink Coca-Cola Ice Cold, pictures bottle & button logo, NM, D32 ....**$450.00**

Coca-Cola, sign, flange, 1950s, Drink... on button sign, Ice Cold & bell-shaped glass on white arrow flange, 16" dia, VG, A13..**$725.00**

Coca-Cola, sign, flange, 1952, Iced Coca-Cola Here, yellow & white on red, yellow border, vertical, rounded corners, NM, A13 ....$500.00

Coca-Cola, sign, flange, 1952, Iced Coca-Cola Here, yellow & white on red, yellow border, Canadian, oval, 20x18", EX, A13..**$190.00**

Coca-Cola, sign, flange, 1956, Drink... on red disk above green Ice Cold & bottle on arrow-shaped flange, NM, A13..**$475.00**

Coca-Cola, sign, flange, 1960s, Refreshes You Best under Coca-Cola fishtail, green lines on white, rounded outer corners, NM, A16...................................**$255.00**

Coca-Cola, sign, flange, 1960s, Sign Of Good Taste under Coca-Cola fishtail, green lines on white, rounded outer corners, NM, A16...................................**$255.00**

Coca-Cola, sign, flange, 1962, Enjoy The Refreshing New Feeling, red fishtail logo on green-lined white panel, 15x18", NM+/EX+, A13.......................**$230.00**

Coca-Cola, sign, glass, hanger, 1948, Please Pay Cashier, Coca-Cola on inverted trapezoid shape, chain hanger, EX+, A16...**$715.00**

Coca-Cola, sign, glass, 1920s-30s, Please Pay Cashier & Thank You above red band marked Drink..., oak frame, 11" dia, NM, A13...........................**$1,100.00**

Coca-Cola, sign, glass, 1930s, Drink...At Our Fountain on receding logo above bell-shaped glass, black wooden frame, 10x6", NM, A13........................**$2,000.00**

Coca-Cola, sign, glass, 1948, Please Pay When Served, Coca-Cola on inverted trapezoid shape, chain hanger, EX+, A16...**$700.00**

Coca-Cola, sign, glass, 1948, Please Pay When Served, Coca-Cola on trapezoid shape atop lettered wood base, EX+, A16...**$630.00**

Coca-Cola, sign, glass, 1970s-80s, stained-glass image of white Coca-Cola on red with green border, wood frame, 17x42", NM+, A13...........................**$525.00**

Coca-Cola, sign, light-up, cash register topper, 1948-50s, Drink..., Lunch With Us, ribbed frame, 6x11", NM, A1...**$400.00**

Coca-Cola, sign, light-up, counter-top, 1950s, Pause & Refresh, Drink...In Bottles, Have A Coke, waterfall motion, NM+, A13...$1,150.00

Coca-Cola, sign, light-up, 1950s, Have A Coke, Refresh Yourself, red arrow points to cup, red case, glass front, 10x17", NM, A13 ....$1,400.00

Coca-Cola, sign, light-up, 1950s, metal wall basket with Drink Coca-Cola on disk, NM, A16....................$305.00

Coca-Cola, sign, light-up, 1950s, Shop Refreshed on revolving 2-sided globe, Take Home Enough on base, 21", EX+, A13..$525.00

Coca-Cola, sign, light-up, 1950s, Work Safely Work Refreshed over man's image, cup & Work Safely below, 16x16", NOS, NMIB, A13 ....$675.00

Coca-Cola, sign, light-up, 1950s-60s, Drink Coca-Cola on red 2-sided globe hanger, clear rim, 16" dia, EX, A13 ....$450.00

Coca-Cola, sign, light-up, 1960s, Beverage Department in green on white panel, fishtail logo in center, 14x50", NOS, NM, A13 ....$300.00

Coca-Cola, sign, light-up, 1960s, Pause... Refresh, Things Go Better... left of Drink... disk, With Crushed Ice below, NM, A16 ....$445.00

Coca-Cola, sign, masonite, 1930s-early 40s, Fountain Service, Drink Coca-Cola flanked by fountain taps, die-cut, 14x27", EX+, A13...........................$1,200.00

Coca-Cola, sign, masonite, 1940s, die-cut image of girl with daisies draped over shoulder & in hair holding glass, 42x40", EX, A13 ....$450.00

Coca-Cola, sign, masonite, 1940s, Drink upper left of Coca-Cola, bottle on yellow dot lower right, framed, 19x54", EX+, A16....................................$485.00

Coca-Cola, sign, masonite, 1940s, Drink... above girl with bottle, 'Delicious & Refreshing' (diagonal script) below, 48x8", G, A13....................................$80.00

Coca-Cola, sign, masonite & wood, 1950s, Beverage Department & Sprite boy flank red button logo on white panel, 90", NM, A13....................$1,350.00

Coca-Cola, sign, mirror, 1920s-30s, Please Pay When Served above red band, Thank You below, reverse-painted, 11" dia, EX, A13....................................$250.00

Coca-Cola, sign, neon, rectangular tubing around Coca-Cola with contour design, M, A16....................$626.00

Coca-Cola, sign, neon, The Official Soft Drink Of Summer surrounds Coca-Cola over palm tree, NM, A13...$1,100.00

Coca-Cola, sign, neon, With Ice above drinking glass with Coke lettered sideways, M, A16........................$550.00

Coca-Cola, sign, neon, 1930s, Coca-Cola sits atop housing with In Bottles on front, some restored & replaced parts, NM, A13 ....$1,200.00

Coca-Cola, sign, neon, 1939, Drink...In Bottles on red footed panel with chrome trim, curved top corners, 14x17", VG+, A13 ....$1,700.00

Coca-Cola, sign, neon, 1940s-50s, Drink Coca-Cola, 18x28", old repair, EX+, A13....................................$600.00

Coca-Cola, sign, neon, 1950s, Drink...Sign Of Good Taste, 2-sided plastic & metal disk, neon around rim, 16" dia, NM/VG+, A13....................................$550.00

Coca-Cola, sign, neon, 1980s, Coke With Ice, drinking-glass shape with Coke lettered vertically, With Ice arched above, NM, A13....................................$350.00

Coca-Cola, sign, paper, die-cut, Drink Coca-Cola on rim of glass with foamy head, 20x12", VG+, A13 ......$1,800.00

Coca-Cola, sign, paper, Let Us Put A Case In Your Car, large case on red carpet leading to house, 20x36", NM+, A13....................................$230.00

Coca-Cola, sign, paper, The Pause That Refreshes, elf serves Santa in easy chair left of 2 elves with Enjoy... drum, 12x24", NM, A7....................................$60.00

Coca-Cola, sign, paper, 1912, All Over The World It's...Delicious & Refreshing..., tennis couple atop the world, 49x38", G+, A13....................$16,500.00

Coca-Cola, sign, paper, 1920s, Drink... Delicious & Refreshing, flapper girl eyeing bottle with straw, 20x12", G-, A9 ....$175.00

Coca-Cola, sign, paper, 1920s, Drink... Delicious & Refreshing, flapper girl eyeing bottle with straw, 20x12", VG+, A13 ....$475.00

Coca-Cola, sign, paper, 1920s, Drink... Delicious & Refreshing, flapper girl eyeing bottle with straw, 20x12", EX+, A16 ....$750.00

Coca-Cola, sign, paper, 1920s, Pause A Minute/Refresh Yourself, girl in profile admires bottle, metal strips, 20x12", G, A9 ....$450.00

Coca-Cola, sign, paper, 1920s, Pause A Minute/Refresh Yourself, girl in profile admires bottle, metal strips, 20x12", EX+, A13 ....$1,800.00

Coca-Cola, sign, paper, 1920s, That Taste-Good Feeling, boy eating hot dog while holding bottle, metal strips, 20x14", G-, A9 ....$200.00

Coca-Cola, sign, paper, 1920s, That Taste-Good Feeling, boy eating hot dog while holding bottle, 20x12", VG, A16 ....$685.00

Coca-Cola, sign, paper, 1920s, Treat Yourself Right, Drink Coca-Cola, man opening bottle, metal strips, 20x12", G-, A9 ....$300.00

Coca-Cola, sign, paper, 1920s, Treat Yourself Right, Drink Coca-Cola, man opening bottle, metal strips, 20x12", VG, A16 ....$755.00

Coca-Cola, sign, paper, 1930s, Cold in light blue & green above tilted bottle & button logo on iceberg, 20x58½", EX, A6 ....$600.00

Coca-Cola, sign, paper, 1930s, Let's Have A Coke, military couple with books, 20x57", NM, A13 ....$850.00

Coca-Cola, sign, paper, 1930s, Such A Friendly Custom, 2 military ladies at fountain with dispenser, horizontal, NM, A13 ....$350.00

Coca-Cola, sign, paper, 1940s, Come In...We Have Coca-Cola 5¢, Sprite boy pointing to row of receding glasses, 8x25", EX+, A13 ....$300.00

Coca-Cola, sign, paper, 1940s, Home Refreshment arched above 6-pack flanked by 2 triangles with product images, 3-pc, NM+, A13 ....$200.00

Coca-Cola, sign, paper, 1940s, We Have Coca-Cola, Sprite boy pointing to banner, 5¢ below, framed, NM+, A13 ....$500.00

Coca-Cola, sign, paper, 1950s, Hospitality Coca-Cola, woman lighting candle at left, Coke bottle at right, 30x59", EX, A6 ....$700.00

Coca-Cola, sign, paper, 1950s, Now! Family Size Too!, Sprite boy & bottle, disk below, yellow background, 27x17", EX, D8 ....$115.00

Coca-Cola, sign, paper, 1950s, Plastic Cooler For Picnics & Parties & product image, Keeps 12 Bottles Ice-Cold..., 27x16", NM, A3 ....$40.00

Coca-Cola, sign, paper, 1960s, Take Along Coke In 12 oz Cans, Buy A Case left of diamond can & men by boat, 19x35", NM, A16 ....$155.00

Coca-Cola, sign, plastic, Buvez Coca-Cola on oval atop wood base, 8x11", NM+, A16 ....$260.00

Coca-Cola, sign, plastic, Delicious With Ice-Cold Coca-Cola, overflowing popcorn box, 7x24", EX, A7 ...$40.00

Coca-Cola, sign, plastic, 1940s-50s, Drink... on red oval atop lettered wooden block, Canadian, 9x11", NM, A13 ....$260.00

Coca-Cola, sign, plastic, 1950s, Drink... In Bottles on red plastic insert, white bent wrought-iron frame top & bottom, NM+, A13 ....$160.00

Coca-Cola, sign, porcelain, die-cut, 1930s, Fountain Service, Drink..., sign flanked by fountain taps, black base, 14x27", EX+, A13 ....$1,200.00

Coca-Cola, sign, porcelain, die-cut, 1930s, Fountain Service above Drink... on emblem with diagonal 2-color field, 26x22", VG, A9 ....$500.00

Coca-Cola, sign, porcelain, die-cut, 1930s, white Drink Coca-Cola in cut-out script outlined in black, EX, A16...$750.00

Coca-Cola, sign, porcelain, die-cut bottle shape, 1950s, 16", NM+, A13 ....$275.00

Coca-Cola, sign, porcelain, 1930s, Drink... above Delicious & Refreshing on red, yellow outline, green self-frame, 36x60", VG+, A13 ....$450.00

Coca-Cola, sign, porcelain, 1930s, Drink...Delicious & Refreshing in white & yellow, green self-frame, 4x8 ft, NM, A13 ....$1,300.00

Coca-Cola, sign, porcelain, 1930s, Fountain Service in yellow on green above Drink... in white on red, 14x27", NM, D8..$1,300.00

Coca-Cola, sign, porcelain, 1930s, Fountain Service upper right of Drink... on diagonal 2-color ground, 1-sided, 26x22", EX+, A16 ....$715.00

Coca-Cola, sign, porcelain, 1930s, Fountain Service upper right of Drink... on diagonal 2-color ground, 2-sided, 26x22", NM, A16 ....$1,320.00

Coca-Cola, sign, porcelain, 1930s, shows hand pulling tap on dispenser filling glass, rounded corners, 24x26", G, A16 ....$400.00

Coca-Cola, sign, porcelain, 1930s(?), Drug Store on green above Drink...Delicious & Refreshing in white on red, 60x90", EX, D8 ....$600.00

Coca-Cola, sign, porcelain, 1940s, Coca-Cola Sold Here Ice Cold, white & yellow on red, yellow border, 12x29", EX, D21 ....$160.00

Coca-Cola, sign, porcelain, 1940s, Coca-Cola Sold Here Ice Cold, white & yellow on red, yellow border, 12x29", EX+, D21 ....$200.00

Coca-Cola, sign, porcelain, 1940s, Coca-Cola Sold Here Ice Cold, yellow & white on red, 12x29", NM, D21..$260.00

Coca-Cola, sign, porcelain, 1940s, Come In! Have A Coca-Cola, yellow & white on red, yellow border, rounded ends, 54", NM, D21 ....$1,050.00

Coca-Cola, sign, porcelain, 1950s, Delicious & Refreshing in green flank bottle, white background, 24x24", EX, D8 ....$250.00

Coca-Cola, sign, porcelain, 1950s, Drink & Fountain Service on ribbon around Coca-Cola panel with slanted ends, 18x28", NM, A13............................$700.00

Coca-Cola, sign, porcelain, 1950s, Drink Coca-Cola on disk above bottle, Ice Cold below, 48x16", EX+, A13 .$550.00

Coca-Cola, sign, porcelain, 1950s, Drink Pause Refresh on ribbon, Lunch on band below, 2-sided, 28x26", NM, A13...$3,100.00

Coca-Cola, sign, porcelain, 1950s, Drink...Ice Cold on image of fountain dispenser with full glass, 2-sided, 28x28", NM, A13 ....$1,600.00

Coca-Cola, sign, porcelain, 1950s, Drink...Ice Cold on image of fountain dispenser with full glass, 28x28", EX, D32...$650.00

Coca-Cola, sign, porcelain, 1950s, Fountain Service left of Drink Coca-Cola on red dot, lined center band, 12x34", NM+, A13...$450.00

Coca-Cola, sign, porcelain, 1950s, vertical courtesy panel with bottle on bracket above Drink... button, 2-sided, 60x24", NM, A13 ....$3,200.00

Coca-Cola, sign, porcelain, 1950s-60s, Drink... fishtail on white with faint green stripes, ends turned under, 16x44", NOS, NM, A13..$275.00

Coca-Cola, sign, tin, die-cut, 1930s, Drink Coca-Cola on red emblem with bottle on yellow dot, 2-sided hanger, 48x60", VG+, A13......................................$300.00

Coca-Cola, sign, tin, die-cut, 1930s, Drink...Ice Cold & bottle on triangle, filigree design atop, 2-sided hanger, EX+, A13...$600.00

Coca-Cola, sign, tin, die-cut, 1930s, 6 Bottles 25¢ on dot atop Drink & Take Home A Carton, 2-sided, 10x13", NM, A13...$150.00

Coca-Cola, sign, tin, die-cut, 1950s, Beverage Department flanked by bottles with Coca-Cola button logo in center, EX+, A16 ....$500.00

Coca-Cola, sign, tin, die-cut, 1950s, Sign Of Good Taste in red on yellow ribbon, 36", NM, A13 ....$210.00

Coca-Cola, sign, tin, die-cut, 1950s, Stop, Emergency Vehicles Only, policeman on round base, red disk/bottle on back, 60", VG, A13..........................$1,400.00

Coca-Cola, sign, tin, die-cut, 1950s, 6-pack, Delicious & Refreshing, red, NM+, A13...............................$750.00

Coca-Cola, sign, tin, die-cut, 1950s, 6-pack, 6 For 25¢, red, wire handle, EX+, A13....................................$500.00

Coca-Cola, sign, tin, die-cut, 1960s, Coca-Cola fishtail, 12x26", G+, A16 ....$220.00

Coca-Cola, sign, tin, die-cut, 1960s, 6-pack, King-Size, Coca-Cola on white panel, red & gold background, NM, A13...$700.00

Coca-Cola, sign, tin, die-cut, 1960s, 6-pack, King-Size, white fishtail logo, 36x30", NM+, A13................$725.00

Coca-Cola, sign, tin, 1899, Drink Delicious Refreshing 5¢ Coca-Cola, Hilda Clark at table, embossed, 28x20", EX, A13...$10,500.00

Coca-Cola, sign, tin, 1903, Coca-Cola, Hilda Clark holding glass & folded fan on oval, floral border, 19½x16¼", G+, A1 ....$3,700.00

Coca-Cola, sign, tin, 1907, Drink Coca-Cola In Bottles 5¢ flanked by straight-sided bottles, framed, 12x34½", VG, A6...$400.00

Coca-Cola, sign, tin, 1908, Drink Coca-Cola In Bottles 5¢ at left of straight-sided bottle, bordered, 12x36", G-, A16...$260.00

Coca-Cola, sign, tin, 1910s, Drink Coca-Cola with Trade Mark on tail of C, red with white line border, 12x30", EX, A13...$575.00

Coca-Cola, sign, tin, 1914, Drink Coca-Cola Delicious & Refreshing left of straight-sided bottle, bordered, 14x39", rare, G+, A16...............................$1,865.00

Coca-Cola, sign, tin, 1914, Ice Cold Coca-Cola Sold Here on red & green at right of straight-sided bottle on white, 20x28", G-, A13.......................$225.00

Coca-Cola, sign, tin, 1916-20s, Drink Coca-Cola In Bottles on red at right of 1916 bottle on green, embossed, 12x35", G+, A13 ....$150.00

Coca-Cola, sign, tin, 1920s, Coca-Cola, girl offering a glass on red oval on green rectangle, gold beveled edge, 8x11", VG, A13 ....$900.00

Coca-Cola, sign, tin, 1920s, Drink Coca-Cola, Trade Mark... on tail of C, embossed, 6x18", NM+, A16...........$550.00

Coca-Cola, sign, tin, 1920s, Drink Coca-Cola in white on red, green border, embossed hanger, 4x8", NM, A13 ..$900.00

Coca-Cola, sign, tin, 1920s, Drink Coca-Cola with Trade Mark on tail of C, self-framed border, 10½x32", NM, A13...$725.00

Coca-Cola, sign, tin, 1920s, Drink...Delicious & Refreshing, white on red, bottle on white at left, green border, 11x35", VG+, A13..$400.00

Coca-Cola, sign, tin, 1920s, Refresh Yourself! (script) Drink...Sold Here Ice Cold, yellow/white on red, green trim, 29x28", NM+, A16.............................$1,400.00

Coca-Cola, sign, tin, 1920s, Refresh Yourself! (script) Drink...Sold Here Ice Cold, yellow/white on red, green trim, 29x28", VG, A13 ....$350.00

Coca-Cola, sign, tin, 1920s, Refresh Yourself! Drink...Sold Here Ice Cold, yellow & white on red, green border, 29x28", G, A13...$150.00

Coca-Cola, sign, tin, 1930s, Coca-Cola lettered over center of bottle on red background, green & yellow border, 45" dia, EX, A6 ....$400.00

Coca-Cola, sign, tin, 1930s, Drink above & Coca-Cola below bottle on white background, green, yellow & red border, 13x5", EX, A13....................................$325.00

Coca-Cola, sign, tin, 1930s, Drink above & Coca-Cola below bottle on white background, green, yellow & red border, 13x5", NM+, A13...................................$625.00

Coca-Cola, sign, tin, 1930s, Drink Coca-Cola, Trade Mark Reg under tail of C, embossed, Dasco, 6x18", NM, A16 ....**$550.00**

Coca-Cola, sign, tin, 1930s, Drink Coca-Cola, Trade Mark... on tail of C, bottle image at left, 12x35", NM, A13 ......**$350.00**

Coca-Cola, sign, tin, 1930s, Drink Coca-Cola above bottle on circle, octagonal with gold ribbed border, 10" dia, VG, A4 ....**$330.00**

Coca-Cola, sign, tin, 1930s, Drink Coca-Cola above bottle on circle, octagonal with gold ribbed border, 10" dia, EX+, A16..**$525.00**

Coca-Cola, sign, tin, 1930s, Drink Coca-Cola on red at left of bottle on white field, yellow & green border, 12x35", NM+, A13 ....**$625.00**

Coca-Cola, sign, tin, 1930s, Drink Coca-Cola 5¢ Ice Cold, red with tilted bottle on yellow dot, self-framed, 54x18", VG+, A13 ....**$350.00**

Coca-Cola, sign, tin, 1930s, Drink..., yellow & white on red, 3 receding bottles & black shadow on green at left, 18x54", EX, A13 ....**$800.00**

Coca-Cola, sign, tin, 1930s, Drink... on red above Ice Cold on black, bottle on light green at left, embossed, 20x28", NM, A13 ....**$800.00**

Coca-Cola, sign, tin, 1930s, Drink...Ice Cold, white on red & black, bottle on green at left, silver border, 28x20", VG+, A13 ....**$375.00**

Coca-Cola, sign, tin, 1930s, Drink...Ice-Cold on red disk with bars above Delicious & Refreshing on green, 28x20", EX, A13 ....**$300.00**

Coca-Cola, sign, tin, 1930s, Drink...In Bottles, Delicious & Refreshing on red at right of bottle on white field, 10x27", NM, A13 ....$1,350.00

Coca-Cola, sign, tin, 1930s, Fountain Service, Drink..., die-cut colonial-type emblem with green & red diagonal background, VG, A13 ....**$650.00**

Coca-Cola, sign, tin, 1930s, Ice Cold...Sold Here, yellow & white on red, bottle on white at left, green border, 20x28", NM, A13..**$950.00**

Coca-Cola, sign, tin, 1930s, Ice Cold...Sold Here, yellow & white on red, bottle on white at left, green border, 20x28", VG+, A13 ....**$450.00**

Coca-Cola, sign, tin, 1930s, Ice Cold...Sold Here on green receding logo left of bottle on red, 19x28", VG+, A13.......**$475.00**

Coca-Cola, sign, tin, 1930s, Pause, Drink Coca-Cola, red with tilted bottle on yellow dot, self-framed, 54x18", EX, A13 ....**$220.00**

Coca-Cola, sign, tin, 1930s-40s, Take Home... above Coca-Cola, Bottles 25¢ Plus Deposit below, 2-sided rack sign, 13" dia, NM, A13 ....**$200.00**

Coca-Cola, sign, tin, 1940s, Candy, Ice Cream, Soda above Drink Coca-Cola & bottle on yellow dot, EX, D8 ..**$325.00**

Coca-Cola, sign, tin, 1940s, Come In! Have A Coca-Cola, yellow & white on red, door-push style, 54x18", NMIB, A13 ....**$1,700.00**

Coca-Cola, sign, tin, 1940s, Drink Coca-Cola, Delicious & Refreshing, couple with bottle, green self-frame, 20x28", NM, A13..**$850.00**

Coca-Cola, sign, tin, 1940s, Drink Coca-Cola Ice-Cold on button above Delicious & Refreshing, green background, 28x20", EX, A6....................................**$200.00**

Coca-Cola, sign, tin, 1940s, Drink Coca-Cola in yellow & white on red, bottle on yellow dot, silver self-frame, 18x54", NM+, A4 ....**$275.00**

Coca-Cola, sign, tin, 1940s, Drink Coca-Cola on red above bottle on yellow dot, silver self-frame, 20x28", NM, A13 ....**$340.00**

Coca-Cola, sign, tin, 1940s, Drink Coca-Cola upper left of smiling girl tipping bottle, self-framed, 20x28", NOS, NM, A13..**$425.00**

Coca-Cola, sign, tin, 1940s, Drink upper left of Coca-Cola in center, tilted bottle on yellow dot lower right, 20x28", EX+, A16..**$325.00**

Coca-Cola, sign, tin, 1940s, Drink... above tilted bottle on yellow dot, 5¢ Ice Cold below, silver self-frame, 54x18", NM, A16..**$660.00**

Coca-Cola, sign, tin, 1940s, Drink... Delicious & Refreshing at left of couple with he offering her a bottle, 20x28", A16 ....**$675.00**

Coca-Cola, sign, tin, 1940s, Drink...In Bottles on red emblem below plain white panel, wrought-iron-looking trim, 48", VG+, A13 ....**$425.00**

Coca-Cola, sign, tin, 1940s, embossed silver bottle on red background, original silver-tone wood frame, 48x24", EX, A13..**$250.00**

Coca-Cola, sign, tin, 1940s, Have A Coke, red with tilted bottle on yellow dot, Coca-Cola below, silver self-frame, 54x18", EX, A13 ....**$350.00**

Coca-Cola, sign, tin, 1940s, Have A Coke, red with tilted bottle on yellow dot, Coca-Cola below, silver self-frame, 54x18", NM, A16 ....**$475.00**

Coca-Cola, sign, tin, 1940s, Pause Drink Coca-Cola on red, bottle on yellow center dot, silver self-frame, 54x18", VG, A13 ....**$185.00**

Coca-Cola, sign, tin, 1940s, Pause...Drink Coca-Cola above & right of tilted bottle on yellow dot, red ground, 32x68", EX+, A13..**$350.00**

Coca-Cola, sign, tin, 1940s, Pause...Drink Coca-Cola right of image of cooler on yellow dot, silver self-frame, 18x42", EX+, A13 ....$2,400.00

Coca-Cola, sign, tin, 1940s, Serve Coke At Home, 16" red Drink... button atop white panel with 6-pack, rolled rim, 41x16", NM, A13..**$525.00**

Coca-Cola, sign, tin, 1940s, Take A Case Home Today & $1.00 dot above ...Delicious & Refreshing, white, yellow on red, 28", NM, A13 ....**$220.00**

Coca-Cola, sign, tin, 1940s, Take Home A Carton in yellow on green below 25¢ 6-pack on yellow dot with 3 bars, 28x20", NM+, A13 ....**$375.00**

Coca-Cola, sign, tin, 1950s, bottle image on white background, 36x18", EX+, A13 ....**$170.00**

Coca-Cola, sign, tin, 1950s, Coke bottle on white background, original wood frame, 36x18", EX+, A13..**$225.00**

Coca-Cola, sign, tin, 1950s, Deli, image of salomi, cheese & olives at left, Drink Coca-Cola on red dot at right, 15x50", NM, D8 ....**$450.00**

Coca-Cola, sign, tin, 1950s, Drink Coca-Cola Ice Cold on red field pointing to bottle on white, 20x28", EX+, A4 .**$180.00**

Coca-Cola, sign, tin, 1950s, Drink... button next to bottle on white with green-striped lower half, green border, 20x28", EX+, A13 ....$450.00

Coca-Cola, sign, tin, 1950s, Drink... on red field pointed toward bottle on white field, silver self-frame, 18x54", EX+, A13 ....**$170.00**

Coca-Cola, sign, tin, 1950s, It's A Natural! Coca-Cola In Bottles superimposed over bottle on red, round, 16" dia, EX+, A16 ....**$555.00**

Coca-Cola, sign, tin, 1950s, Serve Coca-Cola At Home, red with tilted bottle on yellow dot, yellow border, 54x18", EX, A13 ....**$350.00**

Coca-Cola, sign, tin, 1950s, Serve Coca-Cola At Home, 6-pack on yellow dot, red with yellow border, curved corners, 54x18", NM, A13 ....**$300.00**

Coca-Cola, sign, tin, 1950s, Take A Case Home Today, Quality Refreshment, yellow case of Coke on red carpet, 28x20", NM, D32 ....**$350.00**

Coca-Cola, sign, tin, 1950s, Take Home A Carton & 6-pack on 2-color background, 28x20", EX, A16............**$320.00**

Coca-Cola, sign, tin, 1950s, Take Home A Carton above 6-pack, yellow ground, curved corners, embossed, Canadian, 53x35", NM, A13 ....**$625.00**

Coca-Cola, sign, tin, 1960s, Candy-Cigarettes above Coca-Cola fishtail logo left of bottle, raised rolled rim, 20x28", EX+, A16 ....**$235.00**

Coca-Cola, sign, tin, 1960s, Cold Drinks in light blue above Drink... fishtail, With Crushed Ice on black below, 15x24", NM+, A13 ....**$200.00**

Coca-Cola, sign, tin, 1960s, Drink & Coca-Cola fishtail above Refreshes You Best at left of bottle, raised rim, 20x28", EX+, A16 ....**$215.00**

Coca-Cola, sign, tin, 1960s, Enjoy Coca-Cola on red left of bottle on white inset, white rolled rim, horizontal, NM+, A13 ....**$200.00**

Coca-Cola, sign, tin, 1960s, Enjoy That Refreshing New Feeling on fishtail at left of bottle, green raised rim, 12x32", NM, D8 ....**$175.00**

Coca-Cola, sign, tin, 1960s, Enjoy That Refreshing New Feeling vertical fishtail above bottle, green rolled rim, 54x18", NM+, A13 ....**$325.00**

Coca-Cola, sign, tin, 1960s, Gas & Oil flank fishtail logo & Good With Food on white ground, green raised rim, 16x96", NM, D8 ....**$450.00**

Coca-Cola, sign, tin, 1960s, Grocery in bold above bottle outline on diamond Coke can left of fishtail & bottle, 20x28", EX+, A16 ....**$400.00**

Coca-Cola, sign, tin, 1960s, Ice Cold & fistail above Enjoy That Refreshing... left of bottle, green raised rim, 20x28", EX+, A16...**$225.00**

Coca-Cola, sign, tin, 1960s, Ice Cold Drinks on green above disk logo & cup against snowflakes, Serve Yourself, 22x27", NM, A13 ....**$250.00**

Coca-Cola, sign, tin, 1960s, Sign Of Good Taste below fishtail logo left of Ice Cold & bottle, green raised rim, 32x56", NM, A13 ....**$225.00**

Coca-Cola, sign, tin, 1960s, Sign Of Good Taste on fishtail logo at left of bottle, green raised rim, 11x28", NM+, A13 ....**$240.00**

Coca-Cola, sign, tin, 1960s, Sign Of Good Taste on fishtail logo at left of bottle, raised rolled rim, 11x32", VG, A16 .**$155.00**

Coca-Cola, sign, tin, 1960s, Sign Of Good Taste on fishtail logo left of bottle & Ice Cold, green raised rim, 18x54", EX+, A13 ....**$240.00**

Coca-Cola, sign, tin, 1960s, Sign Of Good Taste on vertical fishtail above bottle on white, green rolled rim, 54x18", NM+, A13...................................$275.00

Coca-Cola, sign, tin, 1960s, Take Home A Carton & fishtail above Big King Size & 6-pack on white, green border, 28x20", EX, A13...**$250.00**

Coca-Cola, sign, tin, 1960s, Things Go Better With Coke at left of bottle, white background, raised rim, 24x24", EX+, A16 ....**$225.00**

Coca-Cola, sign, tin, 1960s, Things Go Better With Coke right of center bottle, Drink... disk logo far left, 11x32", EX+, A16 ....**$250.00**

Coca-Cola, sign, tin, 1960s, Things Go Better... & bottle flanked by disk logo & Ice Cold, white raised border, 18x54", EX+, A13.....................................$200.00

Coca-Cola, sign, tin, 1960s, Things Go Better... right of disk logo & center bottle on white, red outlined rim, 12x32", NM, A13.....................................$180.00

Coca-Cola, sign, tin, 1960s, Whatever You Do, English saddle, wire frame hanger, 18x14", NM, A13...........$170.00

Coca-Cola, sign, tin, 1960s, Whatever You Do, fish, wire frame hanger, 18x14", EX+, A16...........................$80.00

Coca-Cola, sign, tin, 1960s, Wherever You Go, pine cone & skier on slope, wire frame hanger, 18x14", NM, A13.....................................$170.00

Coca-Cola, sign, tin, 1960s, Wherever You Go, western saddle, wire frame hanger, 18x14", NM+, A13...$200.00

Coca-Cola, sign, tin, 1980s, Drink Coca-Cola in white above bottle over white wavy band, red background, 18x24", EX+, D21 ....$35.00

Coca-Cola, sign, tin, 1982, Enjoy...All The Year Round, giant Earth & hand-held bottle above swimmer & ice skater, 33x24", NM+, A13.....................................$120.00

Coca-Cola, sign, wood, Drink Coca-Cola on red left of bottle against the D in Delicious, metal hangers, Kay Displays, 32", EX, A16 ....$260.00

Coca-Cola, sign, wood, Yes, mini billboard showing girl swimming to hand-held bottle, disk logo, EX+, A16.......$110.00

Coca-Cola, sign, wood, 1930s, Drink..., 2 bell glasses atop red emblem on plaque, metal filigree atop, Kay Displays, 11x9", M, D32 ....$850.00

Coca-Cola, sign, wood, 1930s, Drink... above gold bottle with leaf design on inverted triangle, leaf decor atop, 23x23", VG, A16 ....$985.00

Coca-Cola, sign, wood, 1930s, Please Pay Cashier on 2 boards, filigree on ends, red emblem below, Kay Displays, 13x22", VG, A13 ....$1,950.00

Coca-Cola, sign, wood, 1930s, Quick Service on board with filigree border, red Drink... emblem below, Kay Displays, 3x10", VG+, A13.....................................$2,100.00

Coca-Cola, sign, wood, 1930s, While Shopping on board with filigree border, red Drink... emblem below, Kay Displays, 3x10", G+, A13 ....$1,500.00

Coca-Cola, sign, wood, 1940s, Here's Refreshment on board with applied silver bottle & horseshoe, Kay Displays, 15x17", EX, A13 ....$450.00

Coca-Cola, sign, wood, 1940s, Ye Who Enter Here... on rustic board with bottle, emblem below, Kay Displays, 11x39", rare, VG, A16.....................................$485.00

Coca-Cola, sign, wood, 1950s, Please Pay Cashier, cut-out marquee with stars atop Coca-Cola, rope hanger, 15x19", VG, A16 ....$225.00

Coca-Cola, sign, wood, 1950s, Slow School Zone/Resume Safe Speed, silhouette schoolgirl/bottle, 2-sided, 48x16", VG, A13 ....$350.00

Coca-Cola, sign, wood, 1950s, Sundaes/Malts flank button logo with gold bars on board, Sprite boy on rounded ends, 12x78", EX, A13.....................................$1,050.00

Coca-Cola, sign, wood, 1960s, Slow School Zone/...Resume Speed on diamonds, Drive Safely/Drive Refreshed, 2-sided, 48", EX+, A13.....................................$950.00

Coca-Cola, string holder, curved panels featuring Take Home above 25¢ 6-pack on dot above In Cartons, 1930s, NM, A13.....................................$1,100.00

Coca-Cola, syrup bottle, clear glass with red Drink... on white & gold fired-on label, metal jigger cap, 1920s, NM, A13.....................................$775.00

Coca-Cola, syrup bottle, Drink Coca-Cola with fancy painted filigree border, 1920s, no cap otherwise EX+, A16.....................................$276.00

Coca-Cola, syrup bottle, labeled Coca-Cola in block letters, jigger cap, EX, A13.....................................$375.00

Coca-Cola, syrup bottle, 1920s, labeled Coca-Cola in script, jigger cap, EX+, A13.....................................$665.00

Coca-Cola, syrup can, Fountain Syrup around top, encircled logo in center, red & white with silver highlights, 9x6" dia, EX, A6.....................................$55.00

Coca-Cola, syrup can, green with round paper label, drinking glass & logo bordered by names of major cities, 1940s, 1-gal, EX, A13 ....$525.00

Coca-Cola, syrup can, red, white & green paper label, red Coca-Cola & white dot with bars, 1940s-50s, 1-gal, EX, A13.....................................$275.00

Coca-Cola, syrup can, red with Coca-Cola/Coke on white dot, One Gallon lettered at top, VG, A16...........$100.00

Coca-Cola, syrup dispenser, rubber, 1950s reproduction of 1896 ceramic urn, EX+, A13 ....$700.00

Coca-Cola, syrup jug, paper label with Coca-Cola/Coke above image of a white paper cup & full glass of Coke, 1960s, 1-gal, EX, A16.....................................$50.00

Coca-Cola, syrup jug, stoneware with paper label, cork stopper, early 1900s, 10", VG+, A13 ....$2,600.00

Coca-Cola, syrup keg, wood with paper label, 1930s, VG, A13.....................................$100.00

Coca-Cola, thermometer, desk-type, self-standing leather case with round dial, 1930s, 3¼x3¼", rare, EX+, A13.....................................$1,600.00

Coca-Cola, thermometer, dial, Drink Coca-Cola, Sign Of Good Taste, 1957, 12" dia, NM+, D11 ....$150.00

Coca-Cola, thermometer, dial, Drink Coca-Cola fishtail, Be Really Refreshed!, 1960s, 12" dia, NM, A13 ....**$500.00**

Coca-Cola, thermometer, dial, Drink Coca-Cola In Bottles, white on red, glass lens, 1950s, 12" dia, NM+, A4 ....**$200.00**

Coca-Cola, thermometer, dial, Drink Coca-Cola over white outline of bottle, 1948, 12" dia, EX+, A13..........**$425.00**

Coca-Cola, thermometer, dial, Things Go Better With Coke, 1960s, 12" dia, EX+, A13 ....**$170.00**

Coca-Cola, thermometer, dial, Things Go Better With Coke, 1960s, 18" dia, NM+, A13 ....**$300.00**

Coca-Cola, thermometer, liquid crystal, Enjoy... on red dot with circular read-outs on square surface, 1970s, 10x10", NM, A13 ....**$120.00**

Coca-Cola, thermometer, masonite, Thirst Knows No Season, Drink... above bottle & slanted bulb, rounded ends, 1944, 17x7" EX+, A13 ....**$300.00**

Coca-Cola, thermometer, masonite, Thirst Knows No Season, Drink... above bottle & slanted bulb, rounded ends, 1944, 17x7", NM+, A4 ....**$440.00**

Coca-Cola, thermometer, molded gold bottle on panel with raised rolled rim, vertical, NM, A16.....................**$60.00**

Coca-Cola, thermometer, porcelain, La Soif N'a De Saison, Buvez... above, silhouette girl below, Canadian, 1942, 18", VG, A13 ....**$230.00**

Coca-Cola, thermometer, porcelain, Thirst Knows No Season, Drink... above, silhouette girl below, Canadian, 1942, 18", EX, A13 ....**$400.00**

Coca-Cola, thermometer, porcelain, Thirst Knows No Season on green, Drink... on red above, silhouette girl below, 1939, 18", NM+, A13 ....**$1,700.00**

Coca-Cola, thermometer, porcelain, Thirst Knows No Season on green, Drink... on red above, silhouette girl below, 1939, 18", EX+, A13 ....**$625.00**

Coca-Cola, thermometer, tin, bottle shape, marked Coca-Cola with small Trade Mark, 1958, 30", NM, A3...**$60.00**

Coca-Cola, thermometer, tin, bottle shape, 1923 Christmas bottle, 1931, 17", EX, D32.....................**$175.00**

Coca-Cola, thermometer, tin, die-cut, 2 embossed Coke bottles flank bulb atop Drink... on rectangular emblem, 1941, 16", NM, A9......................................**$400.00**

Coca-Cola, thermometer, tin, Drink Coca-Cola, Coke Refreshes, red & white, rounded ends, 1950s, 36x6", NM+, A13...**$3,300.00**

Coca-Cola, thermometer, tin, Drink...Sign of Good Taste on red above bulb & Refresh Yourself on white, 1950s, 29", M, D8..**$450.00**

Coca-Cola, thermometer, tin, Quality Refreshment, Drink... In Bottles button above bulb flanked by stripes, 1950s, 9", EX+, A13 ....**$250.00**

Coca-Cola, thermometer, tin, 2-sided emblem that fits on screen door, In Any Weather.../Thanks Call Again, 1930s, 6x10", NM, A13........................**$2,100.00**

Coca-Cola, thermometer, wood, Drink Coca-Cola, Delicious & Refreshing above bulb, curved top, 1915, 21", VG+, A1 ....**$400.00**

Coca-Cola, thermometer, wood, Drink... Delicious & Refreshing with lines above tube, arched top, square bottom, 1915, 21x5", G, A16.......................**$150.00**

Coca-Cola, thermometer, wood, Drink... 5¢ above tube, Delicious & Refreshing below, rounded top, square bottom, 1910, 21x5", G, A16..............................**$145.00**

Coca-Cola, tip tray, 1901, Hilda Clark leaning over bouquet of roses, bean & leaf decorated rim, 6" dia, G-, A16..**$400.00**

Coca-Cola, tip tray, 1903, Hilda Clark with glass, Coca-Cola & floral border, flat brown rim, 6" dia, EX, A13 .....**$2,300.00**

Coca-Cola, tip tray, 1903, Hilda Clark with glass, Delicious & Refreshing on rim, 4" dia, rare, VG, A16 ....**$675.00**

Coca-Cola, tip tray, 1903, Hilda Clark with glass, floral border, gold rim, 6" dia, G, A9 ....**$900.00**

Coca-Cola, tip tray, 1906, Juanita lifting glass to mouth, Delicious & Refreshing on decorative rim, 4" dia, EX, A16...**$790.00**

Coca-Cola, tip tray, 1906, Juanita lifting glass to mouth, Delicious & Refreshing on decorative rim, 4" dia, VG+, A16..**$550.00**

Coca-Cola, tip tray, 1907, Drink... above girl admiring lifted glass, Relieves Fatigue 5¢, bean & leaf rim, oval, 6x4", NM+, A16..................................$1,815.00

Coca-Cola, tip tray, 1907, Drink... above girl admiring lifted glass, Relieves Fatigue 5¢, bean & leaf rim, oval, 6x4", G-, A16...**$75.00**

Coca-Cola, tip tray, 1909, girl at table enjoying glass of Coke, St Loius Fair in the distance, oval, 6x4", VG+, A4 ....**$335.00**

Coca-Cola, tip tray, 1910, Drink Delicious Coca-Cola, girl in wide-brimmed hat, gold decorated rim, oval, 6x4", NM+, A4 ....**$995.00**

Coca-Cola, tip tray, 1910, Drink Delicious Coca-Cola, girl in wide-brimmed hat, gold decorated rim, oval, 6x4", VG+, A16...**$300.00**

Coca-Cola, tip tray, 1910, Drink Delicious Coca-Cola, girl in wide-brimmed hat, gold decorated rim, oval, 6x4", G-, A16...**$135.00**

Coca-Cola, tip tray, 1913, Drink... Delicious & Refreshing, girl in wide-brimmed hat with glass, banded rim, oval, 6x4", VG+, A13...............................**$275.00**

Coca-Cola, tip tray, 1913, Drink... Delicious & Refreshing, girl in wide-brimmed hat with glass, banded rim, oval, 6x4", EX+, A16................................**$525.00**

Coca-Cola, tip tray, 1913, Drink...Delicious & Refreshing, girl in wide-brimmed hat with glass, banded rim, oval, 6x4", NM+, A16................................**$670.00**

Coca-Cola, tip tray, 1914, Betty in a bonnet, green with gold decorative border, oval, 6x4", EX+, A13 .... **$265.00**

Coca-Cola, tip tray, 1914, Betty in a bonnet, green with gold decorative border, oval, 6x4", NM+, A16 ... **$495.00**

Coca-Cola, tip tray, 1916, Elaine leaning on hand looking over her shoulder while holding glass, oval, 6x4", EX+, A16 .... **$100.00**

Coca-Cola, tip tray, 1920, garden girl in yellow dress & floppy wide-brimmed hat holding glass, oval, 6x4", NM, A13 .... **$425.00**

Coca-Cola, tip tray, 1920, garden girl in yellow dress & floppy wide-brimmed hat holding glass, oval, 6x4", EX, A4 .... **$305.00**

Coca-Cola, toy bus, Sweetcentre, 1980s, red cardboard double-decker with contour logo front & back, M, A16 .... **$30.00**

Coca-Cola, toy car, Taiyo, 1960s, Ford Sedan, red & white tin, friction power, Refresh With Zest! lettered on sides, 9", EX+, A4 .... **$195.00**

Coca-Cola, toy car, Taiyo, 1960s, Ford Sedan, red & white tin, friction power, Refresh With Zest! lettered on sides, 9", VG, A16 .... **$95.00**

Coca-Cola, toy car, Taiyo or Dott, 1960s, Ford Taxi, red & white tin, friction power, Refresh With Zest! on sides, 9", NMIB, A13 ....$250.00

Coca-Cola, toy dispenser, image of 2 glasses above spigot, Drink... on red side panels, white flat top, 1960s, EX+, D21 .... **$45.00**

Coca-Cola, toy dispenser, plastic, Drink... contour logo on red & white tank, in original box, 1970s, VG, A16 .... **$35.00**

Coca-Cola, toy dispenser, red Drink... on white & red tank, box reads Dispenser For Coke, 1960s, NMIB, A16 .... **$50.00**

Coca-Cola, toy food stand, wood, metal & plaster, Playtown Hot Dogs Hamburgers on marquee, 1950s, complete, NMIB, A13 ....$325.00

Coca-Cola, toy shopping cart, masonite basket showing 6-pack of Coke & other grocery items, metal handle & wheels, 1950s, EX+, A16 .... **$375.00**

Coca-Cola, toy train set, Lionel, 1970s-80s, 027 gauge, cars feature Coke products, electric, NMIB, A13 .... **$250.00**

Coca-Cola, toy truck, Buddy L #420C, 1978, A16 ...... **$15.00**

Coca-Cola, toy truck, Buddy L #4969, 1970s, tractor-trailer, scarce, NM, A16 .... **$75.00**

Coca-Cola, toy truck, Buddy L #5215, 1970s, Ford, 7½", NM, A16 .... **$30.00**

Coca-Cola, toy truck, Buddy L #5215H, 1980s, pressed steel, red & white with big tires, MIB, A16 .... **$30.00**

Coca-Cola, toy truck, Buddy L #5216, 1962, A-frame, yellow plastic, holds 8 green & red plastic cases, original box, EX+, A16 .... **$425.00**

Coca-Cola, toy truck, Buddy L #5426, 1960, Ford style, steel, yellow with wrap-around bumper, whitewalls, 15", NMIB, A13 .... **$550.00**

Coca-Cola, toy truck, Buddy L #5426, 1965-69, Ford style, steel, yellow with chrome grille & bumper, whitewall tires, EX, A16 .... **$95.00**

Coca-Cola, toy truck, Buddy L #5546, 1956, International, yellow steel, 2-tier with red accents, hand trucks & cases, 14", MIB, A13 .... **$725.00**

Coca-Cola, toy truck, Buddy L #5646, 1957, GMC, yellow steel, hand trucks, loading ramp & 8 red & green cases, 14", NMIB, A13 .... **$600.00**

Coca-Cola, toy truck, Buddy L/Aiwa (Japan) #591-1350, 1980s, red steel tractor with see-through trailer, 11", rare, MIB, A16 .... **$70.00**

Coca-Cola, toy truck, Corgi Jr, 1982 World's Fair, contour logo, NM, A16 .... **$20.00**

Coca-Cola, toy truck, Goso #426-20, 1949, yellow body with Coca-Cola on red panel across open bed with bottle cases, 8", NM, A13 .... **$2,600.00**

Coca-Cola, toy truck, London, 1960s, Drink Coca-Cola decal on side of open bed, 6", M, A16 .... **$295.00**

Coca-Cola, toy truck, Marx, 1950s, Ford style, plastic, yellow with red etched logos, open bed, 6 cases, 11", scarce, NM, A13 .... **$375.00**

Coca-Cola, toy truck, Marx #1090, 1956-57, yellow tin with red trim, open bed with 5 tiers of cases, red ad panel, 17", M, D8 .... **$650.00**

Coca-Cola, toy truck, Marx #21, 1954-56, tin, yellow, red stripe on hood & trim, open divided double-decker bay, 12½", EX+, A13 .... **$200.00**

Coca-Cola, toy truck, Marx #991, 1950s, pressed steel, all yellow with Sprite boy decal on sides & back, 20", NMIB, A13 .... **$625.00**

Coca-Cola, toy truck, Marx #991, 1950s, pressed steel, gray cab, yellow stake bed, Sprite boy decal on sides & back, NMIB, A13 .... **$900.00**

Coca-Cola, toy truck, Marx #991, 1950s, pressed steel, red cab with yellow stake bed, red & green Sprite boy logo, EX+, A13 .... **$375.00**

Coca-Cola, toy truck, Marx/Canada, 1950-54, Chevy style, red plastic with wooden wheels, 6 yellow cases with bottles, 11", NM, A13 .... **$525.00**

Coca-Cola, toy truck, Matchbox, 1978, Super King, tractor-trailer, NMIB, A16 .... **$35.00**

Coca-Cola, toy truck, Maxitoys/Holland, 1980s, early van with open-sided driver's seat, yellow & black metal, 11", NM+, A13 .... **$300.00**

Coca-Cola, toy truck, Metalcraft #171, 1932, A-frame, pressed steel, red & yellow, rubber wheels, 7 glass bottles, 11", VG+, A4 ....**$575.00**

Coca-Cola, toy truck, Metalcraft #171, 1932, A-frame, pressed steel, red & yellow, rubber wheels, 10 glass bottles, 11", EX+, A16 ....**$765.00**

Coca-Cola, toy truck, Rico (Spain), 1970s, Sanson Junior, pressed steel, red with large contour logo, 13½", VG, A16 ....**$35.00**

Coca-Cola, toy truck, Sanyo/A Haddock Co, 1960s, Route Truck, yellow & white, red trim, battery-operated, original box, EX, A13 ....$275.00

Coca-Cola, toy truck, Siku Eurobuilt (W Germany), 1980s, Ford cargo, die-cast metal, red with contour logo, 7½", MIB, A16 ....**$40.00**

Coca-Cola, toy truck, Siku Eurobuilt (W Germany), 1980s, Mack tractor-trailer, die-cast metal, 12½", MIB, A16 ....**$40.00**

Coca-Cola, toy truck, Smith-Miller, 1944-45, A-frame, red wood & aluminum, wood block Coke cases, rubber tires, 14", EX+, A16 ....**$1,575.00**

Coca-Cola, toy truck, Smith-Miller, 1947-53, GMC, red metal cab with Coke bottle decals & logo on wooden open bed, 14", G, A16 ....**$495.00**

Coca-Cola, toy truck, Smith-Miller, 1979, GMC, red cast metal, 2-tier with 6 cases & bottles, only 50 made, 14", NMIB, A13 ....$1,700.00

Coca-Cola, toy truck, Uni-Plast (Mexico) #302, 1978-79, Repartidora Vanet, red plastic van with contour logo on side, NMIB, A16 ....**$35.00**

Coca-Cola, toy truck, Winross, 1994, Collector's Club, Atlanta Convention, MIB, A16 ....**$170.00**

Coca-Cola, toy truck set, Buddy L, 1980s, 4 pcs, NMIB, A16 ....**$35.00**

Coca-Cola, toy truck set, Buddy L, 1981, Brute Coca-Cola Set, 5 pcs, NMIB, A16 ....**$50.00**

Coca-Cola, toy truck set, Buddy L #4973, 1970s, 7 pcs, NMIB, A16 ....**$60.00**

Coca-Cola, toy truck set, Buddy L #666, 1980s, 15 pcs, MIB, A16 ....**$35.00**

Coca-Cola, toy van, Durham Industries (Hong Kong), 1970s-80s, Roll-Along, in blister pack, NM, A16...**$30.00**

Coca-Cola, toy van, Kennedy, 1986, Tootsie Toy copy, red die-cast metal with white Enjoy Coca-Cola lettered on side, M, A16..**$15.00**

Coca-Cola, toy van, Lemezarugyar (Hungary), 1970s, Lend-kerekes Mikrobusz (Combi-van), red plastic, friction, 7", rare, MIB, A16 ....**$200.00**

Coca-Cola, toy van, Lemezarugyar (Hungary), 1970s, Lend-kerekes Mikrobusz (Combi-van), silver plastic, friction, 7", MIB, A16 ....**$100.00**

Coca-Cola, toy van, Van Goodies (Canada), 1970s, Deni-machine, simulated wood with red & white contour logo, 12", rare, M, A16 ....**$100.00**

Coca-Cola, tray, TV, 1956, shows party food with fondue pot & bottles of Coke, decorative scalloped rim, rectangular, NM, A16.......................................**$10.00**

Coca-Cola, tray, TV, 1958, shows food cart, scalloped rim, NM, A16...**$40.00**

Coca-Cola, tray, TV, 1961, shows harvest table with fiddle & bucket of Cokes on ice, decorative scalloped rim, rectangular, NM, A16 ....**$15.00**

Coca-Cola, tray, TV, 1976, shows various sporting events, vertical rectangle, NM+, A13 ....$50.00

Coca-Cola, tray, 1901, Hilda Clark leaning over spray of roses, bean & leaf decorated rim, 9½" dia, VG+, A16 ....**$3,200.00**

Coca-Cola, tray, 1903, Hilda Clark with glass, Delicious & Refreshing, floral & gold trim, 9½" dia, VG, A13 ....**$3,200.00**

Coca-Cola, tray, 1903, Hilda Clark with glass, Delicious & Refreshing, floral & gold rim, 9½" dia, EX+, A16 ....**$5,900.00**

Coca-Cola, tray, 1903, Hilda Clark with glass, Drink, Delicious & Refreshing below, floral & gold rim, oval, 18½x15", VG+, A16.......................................**$6,270.00**

Coca-Cola, tray, 1905, Lillian Nordica with glass flanked by In Bottles 5¢ & At Fountains 5¢, decorative rim, oval, 13x11", EX, A9...**$2,050.00**

Coca-Cola, tray, 1908, lettering around topless girl holding bottle on draped lap, decorative & logoed rim, 12" dia, NM, A9...**$12,000.00**

Coca-Cola, tray, 1908, lettering around topless girl holding bottle on draped lap, decorative & logoed rim, 12" dia, G, A13..**$1,000.00**

Coca-Cola, tray, 1909, girl at table with glass, St Louis World's Fair beyond, decorative rim, oval, 13x10½", VG+, A2 ....**$745.00**

Coca-Cola, tray, 1909, girl at table with glass, St Louis World's Fair beyond, decorative rim, oval, 13x10½", NM, A16...**$2,200.00**

Coca-Cola, tray, 1910, Coca-Cola Girl, Drink Delicious Coca-Cola, Hamilton King artwork, decorative rim, 13x10½", EX+, A13 ....$2,600.00

Coca-Cola, tray, 1913, girl in wide-brimmed hat with rose holding glass, Hamilton King artwork, oval, 15x12", VG, A13 ....**$400.00**

Coca-Cola, tray, 1913, girl in wide-brimmed hat with rose holding glass, Hamilton King artwork, oval, 15x12", EX+, A13 ....$1,900.00

Coca-Cola, tray, 1914, Betty in a bonnet, plain rim, oval, 15x12", G+, A16 ....**$140.00**

Coca-Cola, tray, 1914, Betty in a bonnet, 13x10½", G+, A16...**$330.00**

Coca-Cola, tray, 1916, Elaine leaning on hand looking over her shoulder holding glass, 19x8½", G, A16 ......**$240.00**

Coca-Cola, tray, 1920, Drink... above girl in yellow & dress holding up glass, oval, 16½x13¼", EX, A16.......**$800.00**

Coca-Cola, tray, 1921, girl in blue tam holding glass against leafy background, 13x10½", VG+, A13..............**$210.00**

Coca-Cola, tray, 1922, summer girl in wide-brimmed hat looking over shoulder while holding glass, 13x10½", EX+, A16...**$635.00**

Coca-Cola, tray, 1923, close-up of girl in stole holding up glass, 13x10½", VG+, A16.....................................**$275.00**

Coca-Cola, tray, 1923, close-up of girl in stole holding up glass, 13x10½", G, A16 ....**$110.00**

Coca-Cola, tray, 1924, girl with glass looking over her shoulder against sky & trees, brown rim, 13x10½", G+, A13..**$190.00**

Coca-Cola, tray, 1925, girl in white fox stole & turban looking at glass, 13x10½", EX, A16...........................**$400.00**

Coca-Cola, tray, 1925, girl in white fox stole & turban looking at glass, 13x10½", NM+, A16.......................**$665.00**

Coca-Cola, tray, 1926, golf couple in white, he pouring her a glass of Coca-Cola, 13x10½", G+, A13 .....$210.00

Coca-Cola, tray, 1926, golf couple in white, he pouring her a glass of Coca-Cola, 13x10½", VG, A16 ....**$435.00**

Coca-Cola, tray, 1927, soda jerk serving couple in car, 10½x13", VG+, A13...**$550.00**

Coca-Cola, tray, 1928, girl with bobbed hair drinking from straw in bottle, black background, 13x10½", VG, A16........**$400.00**

Coca-Cola, tray, 1928, girl with bobbed hair drinking from straw in bottle, black background, 13x10½", EX+, A16 ....**$840.00**

Coca-Cola, tray, 1928, smiling soda jerk with 3 glasses of Coke, 13 14x10½", VG+, A13.............................**$400.00**

Coca-Cola, tray, 1929, girl wearing yellow swimsuit & draped with towl posed posed with glass, 13x10½", G+, A16..**$230.00**

Coca-Cola, tray, 1930, girl in white swimsuit & red cap with towel dra ped over shoulder posed with bottle, 13x10½", NM, A16..**$600.00**

Coca-Cola, tray, 1930, girl in white swimsuit & red cap with towel draped over shoulder posed with bottle, 13x10½", EX+, A13..**$500.00**

Coca-Cola, tray, 1930, girl in white swimsuit & red cap with towel draped over shoulder posed with bottle, 13x10½", VG, A16..**$350.00**

Coca-Cola, tray, 1930, girl in white swimsuit & red cap with towel draped over shoulder posed with bottle, 13x10½", G-, A16..**$150.00**

Coca-Cola, tray, 1930, Meet Me At The Soda Fountain, girl on phone, 13x10½", VG, A4 ....$225.00

Coca-Cola, tray, 1930, Meet Me At The Soda Fountain, girl on phone, 13x10½", EX, A16 ....$350.00

Coca-Cola, tray, 1931, fishing boy in straw hat resting under tree with Coke & sandwich while dog watches, 13x10½", VG, A13 ....$375.00

Coca-Cola, tray, 1931, fishing boy in straw hat resting under tree with Coke & sandwich while dog watches, 13x10 1/2, EX+, A16 ....$550.00

Coca-Cola, tray, 1932, girl in yellow swimsuit posing with bottle on towel-draped bench, 13x10½", EX, A4 ....$500.00

Coca-Cola, tray, 1932, girl in yellow swimsuit posing with bottle on towel-draped bench, 13x10½", VG+, A16 ....$410.00

Coca-Cola, tray, 1932, girl in yellow swimsuit posing with bottle on towel-draped bench, 13x10½", G, A16 ....$225.00

Coca-Cola, tray, 1933, Francis Dee in swimsuit seated on ledge holding bottle, 13x10½", EX+, A13 ....$475.00

Coca-Cola, tray, 1933, Francis Dee in swimsuit seated on ledge holding bottle, 13x10½", G-, A16 ....$175.00

Coca-Cola, tray, 1934, Maureen O'Sullivan & Johnny Weismuller in swimware posing back to back with bottles, 10x13", EX+, A13 ....$1,100.00

Coca-Cola, tray, 1935, party scene with Madge Evans standing with glass next to chair, bottles on table, 13x10½", EX+, A16 ....$420.00

Coca-Cola, tray, 1936, girl in white silky gown leaning back on chair with glass in hand, 13x10½", EX+, A16 ....$345.00

Coca-Cola, tray, 1937, girl in yellow swimsuit & white cape running along beach with 2 bottles, 13x10½", VG+, A16 ....$195.00

Coca-Cola, tray, 1937, girl in yellow swimsuit & white cape running along beach with 2 bottles, 13x10½", EX+, A16 ....$240.00

Coca-Cola, tray, 1938, girl in yellow dress & hat posed with bottle on her knee, 13x10½", VG+, A16...........$125.00

Coca-Cola, tray, 1938, girl in yellow dress & hat posed with bottle on her knee, 13x10½", NM, D32 ....$225.00

Coca-Cola, tray, 1939, girl in white swimsuit posed with bottle on draped diving board, 13x10½", EX, A13....$170.00

Coca-Cola, tray, 1940, fishing girl on dock enjoying a bottle of Coke, 10½x13", EX+, A16 ....$300.00

Coca-Cola, tray, 1940s, close-up of pretty girl in matador-style jacket holding bottle, Mexican, 13x10½", rare, EX+, A16.......................................$1,135.00

Coca-Cola, tray, 1940s-50s, yellow Drink above white Coca-Cola on red, yellow Delicious/Refreshing below, 12¾" dia, EX, A13 ....$325.00

Coca-Cola, tray, 1941, smiling ice skater sitting on log holding a bottle, 13x10½", NM+, A16 ....$385.00

Coca-Cola, tray, 1941, smiling ice skater sitting on log holding a bottle, 13x10½", EX+, A16.................$200.00

Coca-Cola, tray, 1942, girl with bottle leaning against open car talking to friend in car with bottle, 13x10½", EX+, A13 ....$250.00

Coca-Cola, tray, 1950, girl holding bottle with white-gloved hand against screened ground, Have A Coke on rim, 13x10½", NM+, A16 ....$125.00

Coca-Cola, tray, 1953, menu girl resting chin in hand while holding a bottle, 13x10½", EX+, A16 ....$70.00

Coca-Cola, tray, 1953, menu girl resting chin in hand while holding a bottle, 13x10½", VG+, D21 ....$35.00

Coca-Cola, tray, 1953, menu girl resting chin in hand while holding bottle, Mexican, 13x10½", NM, A16......$110.00

Coca-Cola, tray, 1957, birdhouse scene, logo on rim, 13x10½", NM+, D21 ....$100.00

Coca-Cola, tray, 1957, features umbrella girl flanked by Delicious & Refreshing, 13x10½", EX+, D21......$175.00

Coca-Cola, tray, 1957, sandwiches & bottles on individual trays with floral centerpiece, French-Canadian, 10½x13", G, A16 ....$110.00

Coca-Cola, tray, 1957, still life with Coke bottle, chicken figurine, floral arrangement & other items, 13x10½", EX+, A16 ....$165.00

Coca-Cola, tray, 1961, hand pouring from bottle into glass surrounded by pansies, logo on rim, 10½x13", NM, D21 ....$150.00

Coca-Cola, tray, 1981, pictures the Leigh Valley Bottling Co, oval, NM, A16 ....$15.00

Coca-Cola, vendor stadium dispenser, red with white Have A Coke on side, detachable strap, 1950s, 21x16x10", VG+, A13 ....$500.00

Coca-Cola, vendor's bottle carrier, rectangular carrier with shoulder straps, opener on side, Drink... on front, 1940, VG, A16 ....$150.00

Coca-Cola, Vienna art plate, girl holding rose, with original gold frame & shadow box, 1905, NM, D32........$900.00

Coca-Cola, Vienna art plate, girl wearing scarf, frontal view, beaded swag design on border, 1908-12, gold frame, NM+, A13 ....$1,350.00

Coca-Cola, Vienna art plate, girl wearing scarf, profile view, beaded swag design on decorative border, 1908-12, unframed, EX+, A16..................................**$250.00**

Coca-Cola, wallet, gold-stamped Whenever You See An Arrow Think Of Coca-Cola encircled by arrow, snap closure, rare, NM, A16 ....**$165.00**

Coca-Cola, watch fob, brass with red enamel Drink... on oval center, 4 points jutting from corners, NM+, A16...**$150.00**

Coca-Cola, watch fob, Drink... In Bottles 5¢, 1907, EX+, A16..**$80.00**

Coca-Cola, watch fob, Drink... In Bottles 5¢, 1907, G, A16..**$40.00**

Coca-Cola, water bottle, clear glass, embossed horses & riders/Compliments Of Coca-Cola Bottling Co, with lid, 9", NM, A1 ....**$310.00**

Coca-Cola, water bottle, clear glass, embossed ship/Compliments Of The Coca-Cola Bottling Co, with lid, 1940s-50s, 9", EX+, A13 ....**$210.00**

Coca-Cola, wet box, wood with zinc lining, Help Yourself Drink...Deposit In Box, with handles & hasp, 1920s, 11x15x10", G+, A13 ....$310.00

Coca-Cola, whistle, wood, cylinder shape (no smaller mouthpiece) with Pure As Sunlight & Coca-Cola logo, 1930s, M, A16 ....**$140.00**

Coca-Cola, whistle, wood, cylinder with smaller flared mouthpiece, Pure As Sunlight with Coca-Cola logo, 1930s, EX+, A16 ....**$120.00**

Coca-Cola, see also Royal Palm

Coca-Cola Chewing Gum, jar, glass, Coca-Cola Chewing Gum embossed on front, thumbnail-type lid, square with beveled corners, 1903-05, NM+, A13..........**$500.00**

Coca-Cola Chewing Gum, sign, cardboard, die-cut stand-up, Try..., The Gum That's Pure, lady's image in hand mirror, 1903-05, 11x5", EX+, A13....................**$15,500.00**

Cock of the Walk, crate label, California orange, crowing rooster on blue background, 10x11", M, D12 ......**$45.00**

Cock Tail, cigar box label, outer, 3 dice in front of container wrapped in ribbon, NM, A5 ....**$65.00**

Cockade Cut Plug, insert cards, Beautiful Women series, set of 6, all G-EX, A5..**$85.00**

Cocktail Always, pocket tin, vertical, oval, white with close-up of couple, EX, A18..............................**$600.00**

Cocomalt, tin, sample, full, 2-oz, 2¾", NM, A7..........**$45.00**

Cocomalt, tin, sample, with slot for bank, full, 1¾", NM, A7 ....**$50.00**

Cognac Cocktails, tobacco label, EX, D35 ....**$5.00**

Cognac Montangon, sign, litho hanger, elegant lady in bonnet admiring full cordial, Cognac Montangon lettered below, 16x12", NM, A8................................**$105.00**

Col Prescott Cigars, box label, salesman's sample, portrait of Col Prescott with soldiers fighting at right, 1896, EX, A5 ....**$50.00**

Cold Spring Brewing Co, mug, ceramic, souvenir, shows factory scene, dated 1905, NM+, A19 ....**$165.00**

Cold Spring Brewing Co, tray, girl leaning on tiger's head, ornate border, Kaufmann & Strauss, 13½" dia, VG+, A9...**$225.00**

Cold Spring Stock Lager/J&A Moeschlin, drinking glass, straight-sided, etched logo & lettering, 4¼", NM, A8.**$45.00**

Cole Bros Circus, poster, colorful image of tightrope performers, 1950s, 40x26", VG, A9 ....**$70.00**

Coleman's Dry Ginger Ale, sign, die-cut cardboard, The Finest Always... above smiling girl with glass, yellow & red background, 18x15", EX+, D30..................**$65.00**

Coleman's Mustard, sign, paper, polar bear sitting on iceberg, 28x18½", EX, A9..................................**$150.00**

Coles Peruvian Bark & Wild Cherry Bitters, sign, porcelain, No More Malaria...The Best Nerve Food & Blood Tonic, white on blue, late 1800s, 6x16", rare, EX, A6....$750.00

Coles Power Models, catalog, #21, 1978, 102 pgs, EX, D17 ....**$40.00**

Colfax Fruit Growers, lug box label, vignette of various fruit & mountains, Colfaz, M, D12..........................**$3.00**

Colgan's Chips, ad from Crimson Annual, Louisville Kentucky, black & white, full page, 1911, NM, A7.....**$12.00**

Colgan's Chips, ad from Saturday Evening Post, many smiling faces eating chips around center oval with text, black & white, 1911, EX, A7................................**$12.00**

Colgan's Gum, display case, oak & glass, repeated product name & various flavors in frosted letters, 17½x9x8", VG+, A9 ....**$1,100.00**

Colgan's Violet Chips, ad from The Spectator, March 1910, 4x2", EX, A7..**$30.00**

Colgan's Violet Chips, tin, 1½" dia, EX, A7..............**$20.00**

Colgate, sample set, with 2 tins, dental cream & cold cream, with contents in original shipping box, NM, A7 ....**$85.00**

Colgate, weekend set, Cashmere Bouquet, Cold Cream, Dental Cream & 2 soaps, NMIB, A7....................**$55.00**

Colgate, see also Cashmere Bouquet

Colgate's Baby Talc, tin, oval image of cute baby tin, 6x1¼", EX+, A3..**$140.00**

Colgate's Baby Talc, tin, sample, blue & gold with name & oval image of baby holding tin, gold shaker top, 2⅛x1¼x¾", NM, A3..**$155.00**

Colgate's Baby Talc, tin, sample, blue & gold with name & oval image of baby holding tin, gold shaker top, 2⅛x1¼x¾", EX+, A18......................................**$110.00**

Colgate's Baby Talc, tin, sample, blue & gold with name & oval image of baby holding tin, gold shaker top, 2⅛x1¼x¾", EX+, D37 ....$135.00
Colgate's Eclat Powder, tin, sample, with contents, 2¼", NM, A7 ....$30.00
Colgate's Fab, box, sample, with contents, NM, A7 ..$15.00
Colgate's Fab, tape measure, celluloid, pictures product box, round, EX, A11.................................$20.00
Colgate's Florient Powder, tin, sample, with contents, 2", NM, A7 ....$30.00
Colgate's Shaving Soap, sign, cardboard, name above amusing image of sailor giving another a shave, framed, 16x10", G, A21 ....$60.00

Collins Axes, sign, embossed cardboard hanger, The Axes Of The World... 'The Best Is The Cheapest,' ax over 2 globes, vertical, NM, A3.....................$100.00
Colombos Cigarettes, tin, oval image of Columbus left of product lettering, rectangular with square corners, 2x3x6", VG+, A18 ....$65.00
Columbia, tobacco box label, name arched above draped nude, bordered top & bottom, NM, A7 ....$35.00
Columbia Allspice, tin, product name above & below portrait of woman in profile, 3¾", NM, A7 ....$180.00
Columbia Belle, crate label, Washington apple, symbolic lady in stars & stripes with sword, Wenatchee, 9x11", M, D12...$5.00
Columbia Bicycles, pamphlet, colorful bicycle scene on front, ca 1917, 12 pgs, G, A6 ....$45.00
Columbia Bicycles, sign, flange, Built By Columbia bordered by Bicycles Parts-Repairs, red, white & blue, 1930s-40s, 18" dia, EX+, A13 ....$350.00

Columbia Bicycles, sign, paper, man on high wheeler passing woman on 3-wheeler, riders & cupola in background, image: 37x12", VG, A9..........................$350.00
Columbia Biscuit Co Cakes, store bin, red with glass front embossed with name, 3 sides depict name around patriotic girl in field, 10x10", EX, A2.................$990.00

Columbia Bock Beer/Columbia Brewing Co, sign, paper, Columbia above Bock Beer on red banner against blue goat on barrel, 1949, framed, 19x14", NM+, A19...$75.00
Columbia Brewing Co, tray, deep-dish, Miss Columbia with glass before eagle & barrel surrounded by wheat & hops, 12" dia, G-, A9............................$150.00

Columbia Cigarros, sign, cardboard, name & image of waiter lighting after dinner cigar for man at table, IT Co on frame, 18x12", EX, A18....................$85.00
Columbia Fine Cut, store bin, wood, round with large image of Miss Columbia, product & company name above & below, 15x15" dia, VG+, A2.................$385.00
Columbia Ice & Ice Cream Co, tray, deep-dish, 'Her Loyal Friends,' girl with dog & horse, ...Call For Nonebetter Brand on rim, oval, 16x13", G+, A9...................$200.00
Columbia Ignitor Dry Cells/National Carbon Co, poster/calendar, 1912, linen, devilish-type figure in waterfalls above boat & car, framed, 43x30", VG, D8 ..$4,300.00

Columbia Mill Co, match holder, embossed die-cut image of patriotic woman, 5½x2⅛", EX, A2 ....$880.00

Columbia Pale/Columbia Brewing Co, drinking glass, straight-sided with flat bottom, etched ribbon & leaf design encircles product name, 4", NM, A8.........$50.00

Columbia Phonograph Records, catalog, 1946, 499 pgs, EX, D17..$40.00

Columbia Records, sign, porcelain, shaped like a record, British, 24" dia, EX, D21 ....$325.00

Columbia Ribbon & Carbon Mfg Co Silk Gauze, tin, company name on banner above Silk Gauze over fancy gold & white logo, 2¼" dia, EX, D14...................$15.00

Columbia Semi-Permanent Duragold Needles, tin, flat, green with Duragold on corner band upper left of other lettering, rounded corners, ¾x1¼x1½", EX, D37 ....$40.00

Columbia 200 'De Luxe' Needles, tin, flat, 'De Luxe' Needles on banner above musical note, rounded corners, ¼x1¼x1¾", EX, D37 ....$45.00

Columbian Extra Pale Bottled Beer/Tennessee Brewing Co, sign, embossed tin, company name below bottle flanked by ribbon logos, pre-1920s, 14x10", NM, A3..$175.00

Columbian Extra Pale Bottled Beer/Tennessee Brewing Co, sign, embossed tin, company name below bottle flanked by ribbon logos, pre-1920s, 14x10", EX, A19..$135.00

Columbian Extra Pale Pilsener.../Tennessee Brewing Co, corkscrew, with wire bail cutter, wooden handle with company & product name, EX, A8...............$45.00

Columbian Pure Manila Rope, sign, cardboard stand-up with 3-D effect, circular image of ship above product & lettering, 42x40½", NM, A6..................................$150.00

Columbus Flour, rolling pin, milk glass with wood handles, light brown lettering & graphics, ...There Is No Better Flour, 18", EX+, A6 ....$875.00

Comet Cleanser, can, sample, cardboard & tin, with contents, 3", NM, A7..$15.00

Comfort Talcum Powder, tin, pictures baby on 1 side & nurse on the other, cylindrical, 3", EX, A2 ....$230.00

Comfort Talcum Powder, tin, sample, pictures baby on 1 side & nurse on the other, round, 1½", EX, A2 ..$385.00

Comic Opera Co, letter folder, tin, pictures Thos Q Seabrooke actors, Sentenne & Green, 12x3", rare, G+, A9..$175.00

Common Sense Truss, sign, reverse-painted glass & mother-of-pearl, eagle & flag logo, Adopted By The US Govt..., image: 30x22", G-, A9 ....$400.00

Commoner, cigar box label, inner lid, pilgrim dressed in brown, 1903, 6x9", M, D5 ....$7.00

Comrade Steel Cut Coffee, tin, gold product name above & below horizontal oval image of dog on white, 3-lb, EX+, A18..$255.00

Condon's Beer, label, H Condon Brewing Co, Internal Revenue Tax Paid statement, 1949-50, 12-oz, NM, A10..$30.00

Condon's Bock Beer, label, H Condon Brewing Co, Internal Revenue Tax Paid statement, 1949-50, 12-oz, NM, A10..$40.00

Condor Baking Powder, tin, green with white product name above 2-layer cake, First Always below, round with screw lid, 1-litre, 5x3", EX+, A18 ....$75.00

Conestoga, crate label, vegetable, desert scene with ox-drawn wagon, M, D3 ....$2.00

Conewango, cigar box label, inner lid, Indian in canoe, 6x9", M, D5 ....$45.00

Congress Beer/Derby Cream Ale, tray, deep-dish, orange Congress Beer on yellow above yellow Derby Cream Ale on orange, brown rim, EX, A19.....................$22.00

Congress Beer/Haberle-Congress Brewing Co, label, oval image of Capitol building above product & company name, blue background, 12-oz, EX, A19.....$10.00

Congress Light Beer, paper cup, waxed, white with Congress in script on red bands top & bottom, 1950s, NM, A19..$3.00

Congress Light Beer, paper cup, waxed, white with yellow Congress in script on black, 1950s, NM, A19..$3.00

Congress Playing Cards, sign, cardboard, shows 3 card backs with different images of children, ...Society Favorites, 18x12", NM, A9..................................$450.00

Congress Playing Cards, sign, cardboard, shows 3 card backs with oval images of different women, ...None Better, 18x12", NM, A9....................................$700.00

Congressional Seal, cigar box label, outer, gold medals on red & green background, 1909, 4½x4½", M, D5..$15.00

Conkeys First Aid Products, sign, die-cut tin flange, ugly limping bird facing product name, Poultry Service Station, 20x14", EX, A7 ....$112.00

Connecticut Mutual Life Insurance Co, sign, tin, office building on street corner with horse-drawn buggies, framed, image: 24x18", VG, A9 ....$500.00

Connermade Orange Soda, sign, orange & black with Pure & Wholesome above bottle on tilted oval flanked by In A Class By Itself, EX+, A16 ....$75.00

Connie's Root Beer, mug, clear glass with orange logo, 4x3", M, D16 ....$15.00

Conoco, display, composition & chalk, life-like man beside pump, signed Michael Garman on round base, 1980, 16", EX+, A6 ....$210.00

Conoco, lighter fluid dispenser, red & green urn shape with spigot & Conoco decal, top unscrews to fill, 9¼", EX, A1 ....$630.00

Conoco, pump sign, die-cut porcelain, product name on band across triangle, red & white, 8½x7½", NM, A6..$55.00

Conoco, salt & pepper shakers, plastic, white gas pumps with decals, 2¾", VG+, A1....................................$40.00

Conoco, sign, porcelain, logo at left of Danger High Voltage, 8x15", M, D11 ....$125.00

Conoco All Season Super Motor Oil, can, triangular logo above encircled lettering, gold, white, black & red, 5-qt, 9½x7" dia, G+, A6 ....$25.00

Conoco Gasoline & Motor Oils, sign, waxed cardboard with tin frame, minuteman & Packed With Extra Miles flank lettered oval, 21x60", rare, EX+, A1........$1,300.00

Conoco Motor Oil, can, minuteman at left of product name, blue, yellow & white, screw cap & handle, 1/2-gal, VG+, A3 ....$475.00

Conoco Pressure Gun Grease, can, minuteman left of product & company name on white, yellow background, 1-lb, scarce, lid missing otherwise VG, A1 ....$300.00

Conoco Super Motor Oil, sign, porcelain, Conoco on inverted triangle above Super Motor Oil, red, green & white, 2-sided, 30x27", VG, A6..........................$100.00

Conoco Super Motor Oil, sign, porcelain, Conoco on inverted triangle above Super Motor Oil, red, green & white, 2-sided, 30x27", G, A9 ....$65.00

Conoco Travel Bureau Service, sign, tin, road disappearing into trees with mountains beyond, red Conoco logo at top, 2-sided, 12½x23½", EX, A1 ....$600.00

Conquest Red Pepper, tin, profile of man in armour on shield, 2-oz, EX, A3...$120.00

Consolidated Tours, sign, die-cut porcelain, Member Consolidated Tours on emblem, blue, red & white, 2-sided, 19x22½", EX, A1......................................$330.00

Consols Cigarettes, sign, paper, seated man watching maid sweep floor, framed, image: 18½x13½", G, A9 ....$85.00

Consumer's Beer, sign, embossed tin, smiling man with glass at left of product name in script & Ask Father, 1940s, 10x28", EX, A13 ....$225.00

Consumer's Beer, sign, tin, smiling man with glass above product name in script & Ask Father, name & address on border, 14" dia, VG, A8 ....$85.00

Conte Equipment Corp, watch fob, pictures steam shovel & road grader, leather strap, minor wear to band, A6...$25.00

Continental Automobiles, jigsaw puzzle, Travel The Continental Line, pictures group in auto passing the Capitol building, 1933, 11x14", EX, D10 ....$125.00

Continental Cubes, pocket mirror, lady holding poker hand & sitting atop pocket tin, vertical oval, 2¾", EX, A21 ....$190.00

Continental Cubes, pocket tin, vertical, product name above scenic view with man reading paper, EX+, A19 ....$350.00

Continental Trailways Bus Station, sign, porcelain, lettering on oval in center, 2-sided, 16x36", NM+, D11 ....$250.00

Converse Cord Tires, sign, metal light-up in wood frame, ...Compression Tread, orange, white & black, 10x14½", EX, A6 ....$200.00

Cook's Goldblume Beer, sign, tin, Elwell illustration of Indians attacking stagecoach, Pioneers of Quality, framed, image: 17x25", G-, A9 ....$100.00

Cook's Goldblume Beer, tap knob, chrome with celluloid cover, white & black on red, 2" dia, EX, A8.........$35.00

Cook's Goldblume Beer & Ale, sign, debossed tin & cardboard, Now Try above product name flanked by tilted bottles, beveled edge, 8x19", VG+, A8 ....$100.00

Cook's Paints, sign, porcelain, 2-sided, 24x36", NM, D11 ....$95.00

Cookie Jar Pipe Mixture, box, cardboard, product name above & below image of cookie jar, British Blend below, NM, A7...$5.00

Cool Roasted Coffee, tin, ...Full Flavor above Coffee on center band, key-wind lid, EX, A3 ....$44.00

Coolidge Motors Inc, sign, metal, black on yellow, 10x36", G+, A6 ....$15.00

Coon Brand Guano, flue cover, celluloid, sacks of product with Safety First above & below, red, black & white, round, EX, A11..$160.00

Coon Yams, crate label, raccoon holding giant yam, Leonville, 9x9", M, D12 ....$5.00

Coon-Chicken Inn, matchbook, pictures black bellhop, 20 strike, NM, D28...$15.00

Coon-Chicken Inn, postcard, linen, ca 1940, M, A17 ....$250.00

Coon's Ice Cream, sign, waxed cardboard, soda & sundae flank product name on oval, red, white & black, framed, 23x62", VG, A1 ....$50.00

Cooney Beer, drinking glass, straight-sided with red Cooney Beer above star, Binzel Brewing Co, Oconomowoc Wis below, 4½", NM $25.00

Cooney Beer, label, Binzel Brewing Co, Internal Revenue Tax Paid statement, 1933-50, 12-oz, M, A10.........$25.00

Cooper Tires, sign, embossed tin, knight's head above product name, red, white & blue, oval, 14½x23", NM, A6 ....$45.00

Cooper Wagon, pin-back button, The Earliest Settler arched above wagon image, Better Now Than Ever below, EX, A20.......................$30.00

Cooper's Old Bohemian Beer, tray, red, white, black & gold, 12", VG, D7 ....$30.00

Coors, ashtray, white porcelain with logo, 6" dia, EX, D24 ....$4.00

Coors, salt & pepper shakers, wooden barrel shape with Coors in script, EX, A8.......................$45.00

Coors Golden Beer, mug, blue lettering on yellow, EX, A8 ....$100.00

Coors Golden Malted Milk, tin, product name above Adolph Coors Co, white, blue & silver, 4-sided, shouldered top, 14", EX, A1 ....$60.00

Coors Pure Malted Milk, container, ceramic, straight-sided with flat bottom, raised lip, no lid, EX, A8...........$45.00

Cope's Cigarettes, insert card, British Dickens Character series, 1939, set of 25, M, A5.......................$35.00

Copenhagen Castle Brand Beer, sign, light-up, reverse-painted glass, VG+, A19.......................$75.00

Copenhagen Castle Brand Beer, sign, tin on cardboard, Tired Of Ordinary Beer? above bottle & name, port city & text below, beveled edge, 10x9", EX, A8 ....$75.00

Cora, tobacco box label, cute little girl with hands clasped around her knees surrounded by flowers, image: 12x6", EX, A18 ....$50.00

Corbett's Extra Old Stock Ale, radio, Bakelite, bottle shape, 24", not original label, EX, D21.............$250.00

Corbin & Co, sign, paper, 2 women in sheer veils frolicking in woodland scene, framed, ca 1889, 40x28", VG+, A9 ....$475.00

Corbin Lock Co, salesman's sample, wooden door with lock & key, brass knob, 12½x6½", EX, A6...........$20.00

Coreco Service Station/Continental Refining Co, manual, 'How To Conduct A Service Station Successfully,' EX+, A6 ....$35.00

Corona Brewing Corp San Juan PR, tray, green, red & cream oval logo on black ground, vertical rectangle, VG, A8 ....$40.00

Cortez Cigars, tip tray, For Men Of Brains on black above red Cortex in diagonal script, Made At..., red border, rectangular, EX, A18.......................$45.00

Cortez Cigars, tip tray, For Men Of Brains on red above gold Cortex in diagonal script, Made At..., rectangular, G+, A18.......................$25.00

Corticelli Spool Silk, spool cabinet, wood with 2 glass front drawers & 1 solid drawer with product name, gold stenciled sides, 9x22", VG, A9 ....$225.00

Cote Bros & Burritt, Elevator Builders, Millwrights..., paperweight, glass, lettering below building, rectangular, M, D13.......................$65.00

Cott, sign, tin, It's Cott To Be Good! above bottle & fruit in bowl, True Fruit & Terrific! below, 23x17", NM, D30.......................$70.00

Cottolene Shortening, tip tray, image of black woman and child picking cotton, lettered rim, 4" dia, G, A21 ....$65.00

Cotton Club Syrup, bottle, clear glass with label, full, EX, A8.......................$100.00

Cottons Witch Hazel, bottle, clear glass with long neck & cork top, 7", VG, D24 ....$15.00

Count Albert, cigar box label, printer's proof, portrait flanked by fancy scroll designs, EX, A5................$30.00

Country Club Ale, label, MK Goetz Brewing Co, L-type permit number, pre-prohibition, 12-oz, EX, A10..$26.00

Country Club Beer, can, cone-top, EX, A8 ....$30.00

Country Club Crushed Plug Cut Mixture, pocket tin, vertical, red with red, gold & black lettering & trim, EX+, A18 ....$400.00

Country Club Ginger Ale, sign, porcelain, white product name on orange, 1920s-30s, 3x33", EX+, A13 ......$75.00

Country Club Quick Cook Rolled Oats/Kroger Co, container, cardboard, stalk of wheat & steaming bowl of oats above band with product lettering, 1931, 3-lb, EX+, A3 ....$25.00

Country Club Rolled Oats/Kroger Co, container, cardboard, country club scene surrounded by trees, 1920s, NM, A3 ....$145.00

Country Club Sparkling Water, bottle, shows golfer, NM, A7 ....$20.00

Country Gentleman, cigarette papers, NM, A7 ....$5.00

Country Gentleman, tobacco pouch, cloth, paper label, with contents, 1 1/2-oz, NM, A7.......................$10.00

Country Kitchen Enriched Bread, sign, tin, Serve above loaf of bread, brown background, 12x28", NM, D30 ....$95.00

County Free Library/California, sign, porcelain flange, book shelf encircled by lettering in center, orange background, 16x12", NM, A1.......................$240.00

Couture Garments, trade sign, carved wood, half-figure of lady in profile, lettered front, 1930s, 66x44", EX, A6 ....$2,600.00

Cow Brand Baking Soda, box, front pictures cow encircled by product name, 2-oz, NM, A7...................$15.00

Cow Brand Soda, sign, paper, setter in field with product box in the foreground, framed, image: 25½x17", VG, A9 ....$170.00

Cowan's Perfection Cocoa, tin, sample, product name lettered over large colorful leaf, vertical rectangle, slip lid, 1⅝x1⅜x1", EX, D37..........................$135.00

CPF Meerschum & Briar Pipes, sign, self-framed tin, man smoking pipe while reading paper with CPF advertising, C Shonk litho, 9x13½", EX, A18 ....$325.00

CPR Telegraph & Cable Office, sign, porcelain, 2-sided, EX, D21...$170.00

Crack-a-Jack Clothes Brand, sign, tin flange, I've Got My..., 'A Fit Or No Sale,' Measures Taken Here, long-legged man with box, 14x18", VG+/G-, A21......$600.00

Cracker Jack, ad, 'Golly It's Sure A Holiday,' pictures boy with box of Cracker Jack, 1920, EX, D23 ....$25.00

Cracker Jack, pin-back button, Rueckheim Bros & Eckstein above image of Cracker Jack box, Chicago Ill below, VG+, A20 ....$60.00

Cracker Jack, pocket mirror, celluloid, The More You Eat The More You Want above box, Rueckheim Bros & Eckstein below, round, EX, A11..........................$45.00

Cracker Jack, sign, cardboard, For May Days & Every Day, girl on throne watching boy with tray & dog on leash, 1920s, 20x16", NM, A13 ....$210.00

Cracker Jack, tin, Cocoanut Corn Crisp, 1940, 1-lb, 8½x5½" dia, lid missing otherwise EX, D14.........$45.00

Cracker Jack, toy train car, Lionel, O gauge, carmel & brown w/logo, doors open, ca 1973, 11", D1 ..$50.00

Cracker Jack, vending machine box wrappers, uncut sheet of 40, rare, unused, D6 ....$50.00

Crane Brand Typewriter Ribbon, tin, flat, red & gold with product name & crane logo, rounded corners, ¾x2½x2½", EX, D3, minimum value...................$25.00

Crane Co, brochure, 'The Bathroom Of Today,' 1 sheet folded to 16 pgs, 13 show modern bathrooms, 1935, 6x3", EX, D14...$5.00

Crano, cigar box label, outer, comical image of crane smoking a cigar, Kinard & Sons, VG, A5..............$35.00

Craven 'A' Virginia Cigarettes, tin, oval logo on red background, NM, D21...$12.00

Crawford Cooking Ranges, berry bowl, blue floral pattern, 1900s, 6", M, D15...$70.00

Crawford Cooking Ranges, milk pitcher, M, D15 .$130.00

Crawford Cooking Ranges, pipe holder, cast iron, M, D15..$130.00

Crawford Cooking Ranges, plate, blue floral pattern, scalloped edge, 1890s, 9" dia, M, D15.....................$135.00

Crawford Cooking Ranges, platter, blue, 1910s, 11x9", M, D15..$95.00

Crawford Cooking Ranges, recipe holder, nickel-plated cast iron, M, D15...$150.00

Crawford Cooking Ranges, vegetable bowl, blue, 1910s, 9", M, D15..$95.00

Crawford Shoe Store, paperweight, glass, If Anyone Asks Where To Find A Crawford Shoe, Tell Them...612 Olive St, St Louis, octagon, M, D13...............................$50.00

Crawford's Cherry-Fizz, syrup dispenser, ceramic, white ball shape with tall flared base, ...It's Jake-A Loo, original pump, 15", EX, A2......................................$2,860.00

Crawford's Puff Creams, sign, celluloid, product name above girl holding plate of cookies, 11x11", VG, A9...$400.00

Cream City Beer, coaster, product name & epitaph in center encircled by Famous Milwaukee & company name, green, 4¼" dia, VG+, A8.....................................$65.00

Cream City Brewing Co, foam scraper, gold on black, VG+, A8...$35.00

Cream Dove Brand Peanut Butter, pail, shows product & company name, tapered sides, bail handle, VG+, A18..$75.00

Cream Dove Brand Peanut Butter, tin, sample, product & company name with dove logo, round with pry lid, 1¾x2⅜" dia, VG+, D37..$90.00

Cream Mustard, clock, Ansonia, small drop regulator on octagonal face with brass bezel, veneered & lacquered finish, 25x17", VG, A9...$400.00

Cream of Beer, tap knob, 2-sided cream inverted trapezoid shape with rounded corners, cream & brown 1953 copyright label, EX+, A8.......................................$60.00

Cream of Malt Premium Beer, label, Hoerber Brewing Co, Internal Revenue Tax Paid statement, 1933-50, 12-oz, M, A10..$20.00

Cream of Wheat, box, sample, marked Quick, with contents, 3¼", NM, A7 ....$45.00

Cream of Wheat, sign, cardboard, black chef handing waitress a tray in front of sign, A Dainty Dish..., 1920s, framed, 8x6", NM+, A6 ....$80.00

Cream Top Old Style Beer/American Brewing Co, label, white & blue product name & blue eagle on red, 12-oz, VG+, A19...$7.00

Creme De La Creme Smoking Mixture, tin, horizontal box, name flanks oval image of queen, gold & cream, rounded corners, EX, A18 ....$215.00

Creme Oil/Peet Bros Mfg Co, pocket mirror, celluloid, For Toilet, Bath & Shampoo above product, company name below, brown & blue, round, EX, A11 ....$40.00

Cremo Cigars, display box, cardboard with dummy cigars, standard size, EX, D35 ....$85.00

Cremo Cigars, humidor trunk, tin, shows tins on sides, ...Always In Perfect Condition... on top & front, 19x19x29", G, A9...$225.00

Cremo Cigars, pocket tin, vertical, Cremo arched above farmer flanked by coins, 5¢ on red triangle in upper left corner, VG+, A18.......................$35.00

Cremo Old Stock Ale, signs, die-cut cardboard stand-ups, 1 with encircled man & 1 with woman, product name below, 16x11", NM, A19, pair...............................$40.00

Crescent Beverages, sign, embossed tin, Crescent arched above star & crescent moon flanked by Since 1893, Beverages below, 14x19", EX, A8 ....$25.00

Crescent Bread Co, pocket mirror, celluloid, Compliments Of..., blue on white, oval, EX, A11 ....$20.00

Crescent Cream Ale, label, Tarr Brewing Co, U-type permit number, Internal Revenue Tax Paid statement, 1933-36, 12-oz, M, A10.......................................$20.00

Crescent Flour, door push plate, tin, Push & Try A Sack Of above sack, Crescent Flour Sold Here below, white on black, 1920s, NM+, A13.................................$180.00

Crescent Flour, sign, wax board, 'The Flour Everybody Likes,' Voight Milling Co, Grand Rapids Mich, white on blue, 1920, 7x20", EX+, A3 ....$45.00

Crescent Pilsner Beer, label, Tarr Brewing Co, U-type permit number, Internal revenue Tax Paid statement, 12-oz, M, A10...$15.00

Crescent Resilient Mainsprings/SH Clausin & Co, tin, flat, star & crescent moon logo & lettering, decorative border, rectangular, rounded corners, ⅝x2¾x5", EX, D37...$45.00

Cretors Pop Corn, box, product name above & below girl with box against geometric background, 1936, 7¼x4¾", NM, A7...$5.00

Cretors Pop Corn, box, smiling girl with box above product name, 1929, 7x4¾", NM, A7.............................$5.00

Croft Ale, sign, tin on cardboard, product name & 3 gents tipping glasses above 'New Englands Finest Ale,' beveled edge, NM+, A19.................................$265.00

Croft Cream Ale, sign, die-cut pressed wood & foil, 3 gents (Pure, Light & Malt) drinking atop product name, It's All Malt! VG+, A19.................................$105.00

Crosley, clock, glass front with metal frame, numbers surround Time For Crosley on center dot, red, white & blue, 15" dia, EX, A6.................................$275.00

Crosley, clock, neon, Time For Crosley on face, blue & white, octagon, 21½x21½", EX, A6.....................$425.00

Crosman Bros Peerless Watermelon, sign, paper, 2 black boys carrying watermelons, framed, image: 23½x17", VG, A9.................................$1,800.00

Cross Country Motor Oil, can, Cross Country on band across US map, 100% Pure..., Sears, Roebuck & Co, orange, cream & blue, 5-qts, 13x8", EX, A6 ....$35.00

Cross Swords Plug Cut, tin, yellow with frontal image & profile image of lady flanking crossed swords, rectangular, square corners, EX+, A18.........................$70.00

Crosse & Blackwell, sign, paper, pictures chef with stew & hash, framed, EX, D34.................................$295.00

Crown Baking Powder, tin, paper label, VG, A7 ....$5.00

Crown Beer, tray, deep-dish, colorful image of cavalier raising large stein of beer, Bartles Brew Co, 12" dia, EX, A21...$105.00

Crown Gasoline/Standard Oil Co, sign, porcelain flange, large crown with lettering, red, white & blue, 26x26", EX, A15...$550.00

Crown Gasoline/Standard Oil Co, sign, porcelain flange, large crown with lettering, red, white & blue, 26x26", NM+, A6.................................$1,300.00

Crown Heads Cigars, box label, salesman's sample, 3 framed portraits, EX, A5 ....$175.00

Crown Jewel, tobacco label, EX, D35 ....$4.00

Crown Phonograph Needles, tin, flat, red with gold trim, Crown 200 Finest Needles above image of crown, rounded ends, ½x1¼x1½, EX, D37 ....$40.00

Crown Premium Motor Oil, bank, tin, can shape, 2" dia, NM, A7 ....$15.00

Crown Premium Motor Oil, can, product name on front, EX, A7 ....$10.00

Crown Ribbon & Carbon MFG Co, tin, vertical, image of crown above lettered scrolled banner, company name on banner below, 2x1⅝x1⅝", EX, D37 ....$60.00

Crubro Apple Butter, postcard, 'Our New Apple Butter Package,' shows large product jar, vertical, NM, D26 ....$50.00

Cruiser 100% Pure Pennsylvania Motor Oil, can, 2,000 Miles of Perfect Lubrication... on rectangle over diamond, yellow, black & cream, 5-gal, 15x9", VG, A6 ....$60.00

Crusader Tobacco/Watson & McGill, label, lettering around crusader standing on rock holding flag, matted & framed, image: 10x10", EX, A18 ....$105.00

Crush Carbonated Beverage, sign, porcelain, Ask For A... in white on orange above Served Ice Cold on black, pictures Crushy, 14x18", EX, D8........$260.00

Crush Carbonated Beverage, sign, tin, Ask For A...Natural Flavor! Natural Color! in yellow & white on red, 3½x26", EX+, D21 ....$95.00

Crystal Beverages, bottle topper, You Can Enjoy...Like I Do, shows boy golfer in profile, EX, A7 ....$25.00

Crystal Club Pale Dry Ginger Ale, thermometer, metal, logo & product name above bottle with dial-type thermometer in center, 27", EX, A6 ....$90.00

Crystal Lager, mug, salt-glazed stoneware, Compliments Of Crystal Spring Brewing Co, pre-1920, EX, A8......$195.00

Cub, crate label, California lemon, bear cub eating lemons on red background, yellow letters, Upland, 9x12", M, D12...$12.00

Cuban Chums, cigar box label, inner lid, 2 Cubans arm-in-arm, 6x9", EX, D5.....................................$85.00

Cuban Leaf, cigar box label, printer's proof, woman holding large leaf flanked by trees, NM, A5 ....$30.00

Cuban Pluck Cigars, box label, salesman's sample, man & woman conversing within fancy scroll design, Smoke... below, 1898, VG+, A5.....................................$50.00

Culture Crush Cut Smoking Tobacco, canister, product name on yellow emblem on green & yellow striped background, green trim, knob lid, EX, A18........$185.00

Culture Crush Cut Smoking Tobacco, canister, product name on yellow emblem on green & yellow striped background, green trim, knob lid, NM, A18 ......$255.00

Culture Crush Cut Smoking Tobacco, pack, sample, foil with paper label, product name on yellow emblem on striped ground, 1926 tax stamp, 2x1½", NM, A7..$45.00

Culture Crush Cut Smoking Tobacco, pocket tin, vertical, product name on yellow emblem on striped background, NM, A18...$95.00

Cumberland Brewing Co's Bock Beer, label, Bock Beer on blue with company name below, red border, 12-oz, VG+, A19 ....$10.00

Cumfy-Cut Vests & Union Suits, sign, die-cut cardboard, gold-framed oval image of woman posed atop sign with 2 oval images & lettering, 14x9", EX, A2 ..$245.00

Cunningham Piano, pocket mirror, celluloid, The Matchless Cunningham above multicolored piano, oval, EX, A11 ....$40.00

Cupid's Best, cigar box label, outer, woman offering cigars to cherub, 4½x4½", M, D5 ....$12.00

Curad Bandages bank, Taped Crusader figure, vinyl, 1975, 7", EX, D27 ....$35.00

Curad Bandages, bank, Taped Crusader figure, vinyl, 1975, 7", NM, A21 ....$55.00

Custom House Club Perfectos, tin, round with product name above & below large 3-story building, slip lid, Liberty Can Co, EX, A18 ....$60.00

Cutex, nail-care kit, sample, 4-pc, NMIB, A7.............$40.00

Cutex Nail White, tin, sample, name in large lettering, wavy border, ¼x7/8" dia, EX, D37 ....$6.00

Cuticura Talcum Powder, tin, product name above inset of baby flanked by lettering, For The Toilet, Bath & Nursery below, lid VG/body NM, A3...................$50.00

Cyana, cigar box, product name above image of girl in profile, Mild-Mellow below, EX+, A3...................$35.00

Cyclone Twister Cigar, sign, cardboard, Cyclone embossed in tornado with product name & Five Cents above & below, 1928, 11x9", EX+, A3.............................$75.00

Cycol Motor Oil, can, white Cycol above orange, green & yellow stripes on black, Motor Oil below, 1-qt, EX+, A1 ....$100.00

Cyrilla, cigar box, 5x9", VG, A7 ....$10.00

Cyro, cigar box label, printer's proof, bust portrait, VG, A5...$35.00

⚮ D ⚮

D&H Tobacco, cigarette papers, NM, A7 ....$6.00

D-X Lubricating Gasoline, gas globe, diamond logo above Lubricating in script, beige, red & black, plastic body, 13½" dia, NM, A6 ....$215.00

Dad's Root Beer, mug, glass barrel shape, Dad's Old Fashioned Root Beer, red & yellow rectangular logo, 5x3", NM, D16..**$15.00**

Dad's Root Beer, mug, glass barrel shape, Dad's Rootbeer in embossed lettering, M, A16.............................**$12.00**

Dad's Root Beer, mug, plastic, Dad's Old Fashioned Root Beer, red & yellow rectangular logo, 5x3", NM, A16 ..**$5.00**

Dad's Root Beer, sign, tin, die-cut, Deliciously Yours on bottle cap atop yellow panel, The Old Fashioned Root Beer, 28x20", EX+, A13 ....$200.00

Dad's Root Beer, sign, tin, die-cut bottle cap, Original Dad's Draft Root Beer, 30" dia, NM, A13............**$300.00**

Dad's Root Beer, sign, tin, Drink above Dad's Old Fashioned Root Beer on emblem, Bottles below, red & yellow on black, 19x27", EX, A6......................**$190.00**

Dad's Root Beer, sign, tin, large bottle above Also Quart 'Mama' Size & ½ Gal 'Papa' Size, red border, 1940s-50s, 27", NM, A13......................................**$290.00**

Dad's Root Beer, sign, tin, The Original Draft Root Beer at left of bottle cap, 12x32", NM, D30......................**$90.00**

Daeufers, menu board, cardboard, Daeufers in yellow script on blue with bottle, glass & food scenes above board, 23x13", EX, A19 ....**$15.00**

Daeufers, sign, cardboard, It's My Favorite...Daeufers on yellow band below lady holding glass, wood frame, 11x16", EX, A19......................................**$30.00**

Daeufers Peerless Beer, tray, logo above Daeufers in diagonal script with Since 1848 on tail of S, lettered rim, oval, VG+, A8......................................**$50.00**

Daggett's Orangeade/Fruit Syrups/Crushed Fruit, tray, 'The Invitation,' girl with pink roses holding glass against red draped background, lettered rim, 13", VG+, A21......................................**$100.00**

Dailey Beer, label, Dailey Brewing Co, U-type permit number, Internal Revenue Tax Paid statement, 1933-34, 12-oz, EX, A10......................................**$25.00**

Daily Double Beer, label, Wagner Brewing Co, Internal Revenue Tax Paid statement, 1933-50, 12-oz, M, A10...**$12.00**

Daily Double Cigars, canister, tin, red with Daily above & Double below band with horse racing scene, slip lid, 5x4" dia, NM, A18......................................**$60.00**

Dairy Brand Coffee, pail, Dairy Brand arched above cow flanked by lettering, gold highlights, wire handle with wooden grip, VG+, A3......................................**$575.00**

Dairy Made Ice Cream, sign, embossed tin, 'You're Sure It's Pure,' small child with ice-cream cone, 28x19½", G-, A9......................................**$100.00**

Dairy Made Ice Cream, tray, 'You're Sure It's Pure,' girl eating ice cream, Deco border, 1930s, 13½x10½", EX+, A13......................................**$325.00**

Dairy Maid Baking Powder, tin, paper label with product name above & below image on 2-color background, 5-oz, EX+, A7......................................**$25.00**

Dairymen's League, sign, porcelain, Dairymen's League in white on blue above Member Dairymen's League... in blue on white, 7x13", NM, D8......................................**$150.00**

Dairymen's League, sign, tin, Dairymen's League Cooperative Association below farm scene & ...League Member, yellow & green, 8x10", EX+, D8......................................**$50.00**

Daisee Cloves, tin, 3¾", NM, A7......................................**$220.00**

Daisy, crate label, California orange, large white daisy with green leaves on black background, Covina, 10x11", M, D3......................................**$2.00**

Daisy Air Rifle, display, die-cut trifold, Every Boy Wants..., image of boy & side panels designed to hold rifles, ca 1926, 50", EX, A12......................................**$875.00**

Daisy Fly Killer, tin, pictures daisies, rectangular with rounded corners, ½x3½x5", NM, A18......................................**$50.00**

Daisy Quinine Hair Tonic, sign, tin, A Daisy Tonic For Your Hair above logo, Look Your Best-It Pays below, logo in corners, 1910, 10x9", EX+, A3......................................**$255.00**

Dale Bros Coffee, tin, man in hooded sweatshirt with steaming cup of coffee flanked by Regular Grind, key-wind lid, EX+, A3......................................**$65.00**

Dallas Brewery, drinking glass, straight-sided, gold rim (slightly worn), etched lettering & elaborate 'Lone Star' logo, 3½", NM, A8......................................**$170.00**

Damascus Ice Cream, sign, die-cut porcelain, product name on emblem with red & white background, yellow border, 1920s-30s, 18x17", NM, A13......................................**$1,400.00**

Dan Patch Cut Plug Extra Good Chew-Smoke, tobacco pouch, cloth, 1910 tax stamp, EX, A7......................................**$18.00**

Dan Patch Fine Cut, tin, paper label, yellow with black name around sulky driver & horse on red circle, red slip lid, round, EX+, A18.......................$135.00

Dandy Shandy, sign, cardboard, Down Goes The Thermometer!, Down Goes The..., football player downing a glass, 1920s, 12x9", EX+, A3......................................**$45.00**

Dandy Shandy, store card, Down Goes The Thermometer! above thermometer & man drinking product, Down Goes... below, 12x9", EX, D8......................................**$130.00**

Dandy-Line Brand Typewriter Ribbon/David L Morrow, tin, flat, pictures landscape at sunset with logo, rounded corners, ¾x2½x2½", EX, D37, minimum value......................................**$50.00**

Dandy's Root Beer, syrup dispenser, ceramic, red name above black 5¢ 'The Best' on white globe, flared base, original pump, 15", EX, A2......................................**$1,595.00**

Daniel Boone Whiskey, display, plaster, Daniel Boone figure standing against fence next to space to display bottle, marked base, 14x9", EX, A8 .... **$50.00**

Daniels' Gall Cura, sign, metal, yellow on black, 6x13", G, A6 .... **$185.00**

Darby & Joan, cigar box label, outer, elderly couple at dinner table, 4½x4½", M, D5 .... **$45.00**

Dargai Cigar/Geo Kelly & Co, sign, tin, 5¢ Straight, green & gold patterned border around image of Scotsman playing bagpipes, 10x7", EX, A18 ..**$85.00**

Dark Eyes, display, ceramic, Cossack in red coat standing with hands on hips atop base with product name, 12", EX, A8 .... **$35.00**

Darlington Brewing Co, see Pittsburgh Brewing Co

Dash, tobacco box label, floral & butterfly graphics with name below, 14", NM, A7 .... **$20.00**

Daufuski Brand Oysters, tin, red product name on white above & below Indian chief in profile, blue bands top & bottom, 1-pt, NM, A18 .... **$35.00**

David Mayer, print, joyfull tavern scene, ornate gold frame, pre-1920s, 24x28", G+, A19 .... **$225.00**

Davis Baking Powder, tin, product name on paper label, 3-oz, EX, A7 .... **$15.00**

Davis Baking Powder, tin, sample, with contents, 1-oz, EX, A7 .... **$50.00**

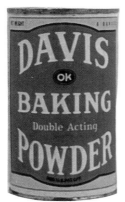

Davis OK Baking Powder, tin, product name on red emblem on yellow background, with contents, 8-oz, NM, A3 .... **$30.00**

Davison's Ice Cream, tray, colorful image of mother & 2 children eating ice cream at table, lettering on decorative rim, 10½x13", G+, A9 .... **$250.00**

Davros Cigarettes, tin, flat, holds 50 cigarettes, EX, A18 .... **$70.00**

Dawson's Ale & Beer, tray, deep-dish, 'Naturally Better' above couple at table enjoying a glass of brew, 12" dia, EX, A8 .... **$75.00**

Dawson's Ale & Beer, tray, deep-dish, 'Naturally Better' above couple at table enjoying a glass of brew, 12" dia, G+, D7 .... **$35.00**

Day & Night Tobacco, trade card, farmer loosening woman's dress from fence post, lettering on fence, 5½x3½", VG+, A5 .... **$30.00**

Daymon & Boyd Realtors, sign, porcelain diamond shape, For Sale..., 14x14", NM, D11 .... **$125.00**

Days of '49' Whiskey, sign, cowboys in wagon train stopping to trade with Indians, Meyerfeld, Mitchell & Co, framed, image: 22x34", G-, A9 .... **$1,200.00**

Dayton Brand Nuts, tin, plane & product name above seal of quality flanked by list of various kinds of nuts, blue & white, 5-lb, EX+, A15 .... **$375.00**

Dazzle Nail Polish, tin, sample, stylized leaf & floral design around product name, small squares form border, ¼x1⅝", EX, D37 .... **$20.00**

De Laval, Handy Reference Yearbook, 1947, EX, D15...**$30.00**

De Laval, oil folder, 1913, EX, D15 .... **$8.00**

De Laval, postcard, pictures the plant in Poughkeepsie NY, EX, D15 .... **$30.00**

De Laval, sign, porcelain flange, dark blue cream separator with gray buckets, Local Agency lower right, 26½x18", rare, EX, A6 .... **$550.00**

De Laval, sign, tin, We Use De Laval above logo flanked by Better Farm Living & Better Farm Income, yellow & black, NM, D15 .... **$80.00**

De Laval Brand Separator Co, can, separator & product name surrounded by star border, red with black & gold lettering, 5x6", VG, A6 .... **$65.00**

De Laval Cream Separator, sign, tin, We Use...The World's Standard, white & yellow on black, 1908-01, G-, D15 .... **$60.00**

De Laval Cream Separators, calendar, 1910, embossed cow above smaller image of farmer & wife milking cows, full pad, framed, image: 20x10", NM, A9 .... **$600.00**

De Laval Cream Separators, calendar, 1913, woman with holstein cow, M, D15 .... **$1,700.00**

De Laval Cream Separators, calendar, 1917, image of girl with dog blowing seeds from dandelions, full pad, 24x12", EX, A9 .... **$700.00**

De Laval Cream Separators, calendar, 1927, boy building dog house while mother sits on porch & watches, NM, D15 .... **$325.00**

De Laval Cream Separators, calendar top, 1908, name above oval image of milkmaid with arm around cow's neck, embellished border, 15x12", G+, A3 ....**$345.00**

De Laval Cream Separators, match holder, die-cut tin separator with embossed lettering, 1,500,000 In Use, 1913, 6½x4", EX, A9 .... **$300.00**

De Laval Cream Separators, match holder, die-cut tin separator with embossed lettering, 1,500,000 In Use, 1913, 6½x4", G, D15 .... **$225.00**

De Laval Cream Separators, match holder, die-cut tin separator with embossed lettering, 1,500,000 In Use, with original box, 1913, 6½x4", VG, A9 ....**$350.00**

De Laval Cream Separators, sign, tin, die-cut cow, brown with black lettering on front, yellow with black lettering on back, 4x5", VG, A6 .... **$85.00**

De Laval Cream Separators, sign, tin, milkmaid with cow surrounded by vignettes of cows & separators, ornate frame, 35x24", VG, A6 ....**$700.00**

De Laval Cream Separators, sign, tin, milkmaid with cow surrounded by vignettes of cows & separators, ornate frame, 35x24", NM, A15 ....$2,150.00

De Laval Cream Separators, sign, tin, The World's Standard & name on blue rim around mother using separator & child at open door, 26" dia, G+, A21 ....**$935.00**

De Laval Cream Separators, tip tray, The World's Standard, image of woman & child, ca 1907-08, 4" dia, NM+, A9 ....**$325.00**

De Laval Cream Separators, tip tray, The World's Standard, image of woman & child, ca 1907-08, 4" dia, VG+, D15 ....**$120.00**

De Laval Milker, sign, tin, We Use The arched above logo & product name, rounded top, 15x15", NM, D11 ..**$75.00**

De Voe's Makings, pocket tin, vertical, cream & red with name lettered in puff of smoke from pipe & cigarette, EX, A18 ....$285.00

De Voe's Scotch Snuff, folder of straight pins, paper, pictures snuff tin on front, US tobacco factories on back, 4½x3½", EX, D35 ....**$12.00**

De Voe's Sweet Smoke, pocket tin, vertical, product name in cloud of smoke from burning pipe & cigarette, cream & red, VG+, A18 ....**$145.00**

Dead Shot Smokeless Powder, sign, self-framed tin, wounded duck in center, 19½x15½", G-, A9 .....**$200.00**

Deans Mentholated 5¢ Cough Drops, calendar, 1914, product name above 3 Hamilton King girls in vertical row, metal strips top & bottom, 33x8", EX+, A15 ....**$300.00**

Decatur Brewing Co, mug, ceramic, barrel shape with company name around hops & leaf logo, Mettlach, 1897, EX, A8 ....**$480.00**

Decorated Shaving Cups/B Stuebner's Sons, sign, paper, ...Barber Supply Trade & logo above rows of mugs, 1905, matted & framed, 17x11", NM, A3............**$525.00**

Dee-Light Soda, sign, cardboard trifold, Drink...In Bottles... above picnic scene flanked by ball game & interior scenes, 20x30", VG, A2 ....$195.00

Deer Brand Beer/August Schell Brewing Co, label, deer head flanked by product name in red, company name below, VG+, A19..**$16.00**

Deere & Webber Co, tape measure, celluloid, large buck in center, Deere Vehicles Are All Right, round, EX+, A11 ....**$110.00**

Deere Vehicles, sign, paper, large stag pulling buggy along the Mississippi river, ...Are All Right on frame, ca 1880, rare, EX+, A3 ....**$1,265.00**

Deering Harvester Co, pin-back button, company name arched above horse-drawn plow, EX, A20 ....**$50.00**

Deering Ideal Binder, calendar, 1907, 'Deer For My Dear,' girl in floral hat before field of flowers, full pad, framed, image: 24x12", VG, A9 ....**$175.00**

Deerwood Coffee, tin, 'Super-flavor' above coffeepot & steaming cup, key-wind lid not original, EX, A3...**$20.00**

Defender Beer, label, Kewaunee Brewing Co, Internal Revenue Tax Paid statement, 1933-50, 12-oz, M, A10...**$20.00**

Defender Tomatoes, can label, product name above & below tomatoes at left of Defender Brand above sailing ship, 4x9", NM, A7..**$7.00**

Defiance Coffee, tin, steaming cup of coffee flanked by Vacuum Packed on center band, key-wind lid, NM, A3 ....**$50.00**

Dekalb, clock, crown & shield logo with rooster & The Royalty Of Poultry, Wisconsin Valley Hatchery below, 1930s, 12x12", NM, A3 ....**$105.00**

Dekalb, weathervane, die-cut metal, wings atop ear of corn, green, red, yellow & black, 24x18", EX, A6 ....**$100.00**

Dekalb Hybrid Corn, sign, embossed tin, winged ear of corn & Quality in center, cream & yellow on brick red ground, 13x19", EX, A6.....................................**$175.00**

Dekalb Profit Pullets, sign, tin, hen standing on eggs, yellow & white lettering on green with white border, 12½x28", EX+, A1...**$80.00**

Del Monte Coffee, tin, Del Monte Brand Quality on emblem flanked by lettering, key-wind lid, 1-lb, NM, A3 ....**$25.00**

Delco Batteries, sign, metal, circled battery on lined band, blue, orange & cream, marked AM 12-47, Made In USA, 2-sided, 18x24", VG, A6 ....**$40.00**

Delco Dry Charge, sign, metal, pictures a battery, blue & yellow on cream, 20x28", EX+, A6......................$125.00

Delite, crate label, Florida citrus, large yellow map of Florida with Deco designs, 9x9", M, D3 ....**$1.00**

Delmarva Beer, tray, deep-dish, oval logo above product name, 12" dia, EX+, A19......................................**$155.00**

Delta Beer, label, Delta Brewing Co, U-type permit number, Internal Revenue Tax Paid statement, 1933-36, 12-oz, NM, A10...**$20.00**

Delta Rockwell Electrical Power Tools, catalog, 1956, 76 pgs, EX, D17...**$20.00**

Dentyne Gum, jar, glass, 4-sided with decaled bust-image of girl above red sign, 9", EX, A21......................**$825.00**

Derby, pocket tin, flat, concave, fancy image of horse's head above name, white with gold trim, rounded corners, EX+, A18..**$55.00**

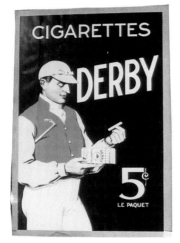

Derby Cigarettes, sign, paper, Cigarettes, Derby, 5¢ Le Paquet, jockey in orange vest & white lettering on black ground, 25x17", EX, A18.......................$60.00

Derby Gasoline, sign, porcelain, star logo with product name above & below, white, blue, red & gray, 48" dia, VG+, A6 ....$180.00

Derby's Flexgas, sign, porcelain, product name above & below Ethyl logo, 2-sided, 30" dia, VG+, D11....**$175.00**

Derby's Peter Pan Peanut Butter, tin, sample, image of Peter Pan in yelling pose, screw lid, 2¼x1¾" dia, EX, D37...**$95.00**

Desert Bloom, crate label, California grapefruit, yucca plants blooming in high desert landscape, Redlands, M, D12...**$6.00**

Desitin Nursery Powder, tin, sample, with contents, 2¼", NM, A7...**$20.00**

Despatch Oven Co, clock, cast iron, company name arched above Ovens, Minneapolis Minn below, numbered 1-12, 11½" dia, VG, A9.......................**$45.00**

Devilish Good Cigar, sign, embossed tin, open box of cigars flanked by product name, None Better lower left, 10x14", VG, A9.....................................**$150.00**

Devilish Good Cigar, sign, embossed tin, open box of cigars flanked by product name, None Better lower left, 10x14", NM+, D11 ....**$275.00**

Devoe Paints, sign, die-cut porcelain flange, hand dipping brush into paint can atop product name on rectangle, 46½x25", EX, A9..**$300.00**

Devoe Paints, sign, die-cut porcelain flange, hand dipping brush into paint can atop product name on rectangle, 46½x25", M, A1 ....$750.00

Devotion, cigar box label, outer, 2 soldiers admiring a woman, Commonwealth Cigar Co, 1918, NM, A5 ..**$70.00**

Dewar's Whiskey, charger, tin, 'The Whiskey Of His Forefathers,' Scotsman watching figures in painting coming to life, 14" dia, EX, A21..**$105.00**

DG Yuengling & Son, plate, 160th Anniversary, shows factory scene, 1 of 10,000, 1989, 10" dia, NM+, A19 ..**$35.00**

DG Yuengling & Son, see also Yuengling

DH McAlpin & Co's Plug Tobacco, sign, paper, family in tobacco field with black man promoting product, several vignettes at left, framed, 17x22", VG, A9 .**$2,400.00**

Diablita, cigar box label, printer's proof, portrait flanked by oval outdoor scenes, EX, A5.................................**$25.00**

Diablo Gold, crate label, California pear, Diablo in yellow & red on blue, Sacramento, 8x11", M, D12 ....**$2.00**

Diadem Fine Cut, pocket tin, flat, yellow with name around image of crown on tasseled pillow, rounded corners, EX, A18...**$190.00**

Diadem/TC Williams Co, tobacco label, name above crown figure with spear, company name below, matted & framed, image: 10x10", EX, A18 ....**$50.00**

Dial Smoking Tobacco, pocket tin, vertical, dial & product name in center, 'Turn To A Real Smoke' below, red & yellow, NM, A3...**$135.00**

Dial Smoking Tobacco, pocket tin, vertical, dial & product name in center, sticker reads 8¢/2 For 15¢, 100% Burley below, red & yellow, VG, A3 ....**$55.00**

Diamond 'A' Ginger Beer, bottle, stoneware vessel with diamond logo, 19", EX, A9 ....**$750.00**

Diamond Dyes, cabinet, wood, tin front, baby in framed inset surrounded by feathers & flowers, 20x16x9", G, A9...**$1,200.00**

Diamond Dyes, cabinet, wood, tin front, children playing before stairs leading to mansion, 24½x15x9", EX, A2...**$825.00**

Diamond Dyes, cabinet, wood, tin front, children playing with balloon, Standard Package Dyes Of The World, 24x16x9", VG, A9 ....$650.00

Diamond Dyes, cabinet, wood, tin front, evolution of women, Fast Colors For Domestic & Fancy Dyeing, 30x23x10", EX+, A9.............................$900.00

Diamond Dyes, cabinet, wood, tin front, evolution of women, Fast Colors For Domestic & Fancy Dyeing, 30x23x10", VG, A9.............................$450.00

Diamond Dyes, cabinet, wood, tin front, evolution of women, Fast Colors For Domestic & Fancy Dyeing, 30x23x10", G-, A9 ....$200.00

Diamond Dyes, cabinet, wood, tin front, fairy in garden with birds surrounded by lettering & vignettes, 31x24x10", VG, A9.............................$2,600.00

Diamond Dyes, cabinet, wood, tin front, lady & children dancing around maypole, It's Easy To Dye With Diamond Dyes, 30x23x10", EX, A13....$775.00

Diamond Dyes, cabinet, wood, tin front, lady & children dancing around maypole, It's Easy To Dye With Diamond Dyes, 30x23x10", G, A9 ....$350.00

Diamond Dyes, cabinet, wood, tin front, woman dyeing clothing, It's Easy To Dye With Diamond Dyes, 30x22½x10", VG+, A9.............................$925.00

Diamond Dyes, cabinet, wood, tin front, woman dyeing clothing, It's Easy To Dye With..., 30x22½x10", no back doors, G+, D21.............................$550.00

Diamond Dyes, sign, self-framed tin, 'A Busy Day In Dollville,' pictures little girl dyeing doll clothes, 1911, 11x17", VG, A9.............................$850.00

Diamond Dyes, sign, self-framed tin, 'A Busy Day In Dollville,' 1911, 11x17", G, A21 ....$385.00

Diamond F Mixture Smoking Tobacco, tin, yellow with lettering & graphics, small rectangle with square corners, EX, A18 ....$40.00

Diamond Horseshoe Calks, sign, embossed tin, team of horses pulling heavy wagon, framed, image: 35½x23½", G+, A9.............................$250.00

Diamond Match Co, pocket tin, flat, pictures fisherman with jug in pocket, 2¼x1½", EX, A18.............$165.00

Diamond Oil, can, glass with metal holder, embossed lettering, wood handle, 12", VG, A6 ....$30.00

Diamond Outboard & 2 Cycle Motor Oil, can, Diamond in curved letters over diamond shape above woman in boat, 1-qt, EX, A1.............................$270.00

Diamond Spring Ale, tray, deep-dish, elongated diamond above product name in red, 12" dia, EX, A19......$50.00

Diamond State, tap knob, round with white lettering on green insert, VG+, A19 ....$200.00

Diamond Tire Service, sign, die-cut tin flange, tire atop lettered emblem, 2-sided, 27x17½", EX, A6 ....$475.00

Diamond Wine Co Champagne, sign, paper, champagne brunch with 3 women in Victorian setting, ca 1896, framed, image: 27x19", EX, A6....$1,200.00

Diaparene, figure, Diaparene Baby, Dakin, 1980, M, D27 ....$40.00

Dick & Bros QB Co, mug, ceramic, classical lady holding garland, name below, 2-ring gold trim below lip, EX+, A8 ....$190.00

Dick Bros Pilsner, drinking glass, straight-sided with flat bottom, gold rim, etched name & graphics, worn, A8 ....$40.00

Dick Custer, cigar box label, inner lid, long-haired cowboy pointing a gun, 6x9", M, D5 ....$12.00

Dick's Beer, tray, product name in block lettering on red encircled by white band, blue rim, 12" dia, EX, A8 ....$100.00

Dick's Pilsener Beer, sign, celluloid hanger, product name on slanted rectangle in red, blue & green on gold background, 9" dia, EX, A8 ....$165.00

Dick's Quincy Beer, tray, product name on white surrounded by lettering on red rim, 11x15", VG+, A19.............$50.00

Dickinson's Big Buster Brand South American Yellow Popcorn, box, product name above & below marching drummer, 6½x4½", NM, A7 ....$8.00

Dickinson's Big Buster Brand Yellow Popcorn, tin, product name above & below marching drummer on black label, with contents, 10-oz, NM, A18.........$75.00

Dickinson's Little Buster Popcorn, tin, Brownie-type character popping popcorn on open fire, with contents, 10-oz, 5x2½" dia, EX, A3 ....$50.00

Diet-Rite Cola, lighter, aluminum flip-top, Sugar-Free in script above product name in lower-case lettering, VG, A16 ....$15.00

Diet-Rite Cola, sign, tin, Sugar-Free..., shows bottle, bordered, 18x54", EX, A6 ....$25.00

Diet-Rite Cola, sign, tin, Sugar-Free..., shows bottle, bordered, 18x54", NM, A16 ....$65.00

Dill's Best, sign, cardboard, Now It's Flavor-Cut right of man smoking pipe, That's Why...For Pipes on yellow, 21x23", EX, A18 ....$25.00

Dill's Best Smoking Tobacco, pocket tin, vertical, oval image of girl with hands on her head, A Fragrant Smooth Natural-Tasting..., EX, A3 ....$100.00

Dill's Best Smoking Tobacco, sign, cardboard, Milder above woman popping out of pocket tin, Boys...You're Going..., ⅓ More..., 26x20", EX+, A18 ....$140.00

Dilly, sign, tin, It's A Dilly For Thirst on 'explosive' background, 12x36", EX, A16 ....$60.00

Dilworth's Golden Urn Coffee, tin, sample, slip lid, 2½", VG, A7 ....$50.00

Dinah Black Enamel, sign, It's My Favorite All Round..., mammy with product & paint brush behind sign, ca 1930, 25x20", NM, D8 ....$600.00

Dinner Party Coffee, container, paper on cardboard, steaming cup of coffee surrounded by flowers, 'The Cup That Cheers,' EX+, A3 ....$85.00

Ditzler Automotive Finishes/ET Satchell Co, poster/calendar, 1953, bathing beauty & her dog seated on a rock in front of red car, full pad, 46x22", EX, D8 ....$175.00

Diving Girl, crate label, apple, girl diving into lake while friends on pier watch, M, D3 ....$10.00

Divinidad, cigar box label, printer's proof, oval bust portrait with fancy scroll design, EX, A5 ....$25.00

Dixie Beer, label, Dixie Brewing Co, red & green, 12-oz, VG, A19 ....$10.00

Dixie Boy, crate label, Florida grapefruit, black child eating grapefruit half, 9x9", M, D3 ....$3.00

Dixie Brand Peanut Butter, pail, circular Dixie logo flanked by High Grade, Peanut Butter below, press lid & bail, EX, A3 ....$85.00

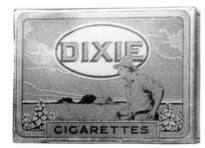

Dixie Cigarettes, tin, flat, green & gold with name on oval against sky above tobacco farmer & farm, holds 100 cigarettes, EX+, A18 ....$150.00

Dixie Cups, dispenser, 1¢, tall glass tube marked Dixie, metal base, 1910s-20s, 33", VG+, A13 ....$375.00

Dixie Queen, roly poly, inspector with cane, VG+, A18 ....$300.00

Dixie Queen Plug Cut, humidor, product name above & below encircled bust portrait of woman in fancy hat, 6x4" dia, EX, A3 ....$295.00

Dixie Queen Plug Cut Smoking Tobacco, lunch pail, circular portrait of lady in plumed hat, product name on all sides, hinged lid, bail handle, 4x8x5", EX, A1 ......$100.00

Dixie Queen Plug Cut Smoking Tobacco, lunch pail, circular portrait of lady in plumed hat, product name on all sides, hinged lid, bail handle, 4x8x5", NM, A18 ....$175.00

Dixie 390, sign, porcelain, Dixie on oval above 390, 8x12½", NM, D11 ....$150.00

Dixon's Stove Polish, sign, paper, ...Carburet Of Iron Stove Polish, girl peeking around tree, 1890s, framed, 15½x3¼", EX, A6 ....$475.00

Dixon's Ticonderoga Pencil, sign, die-cut cardboard bifold, A Fine American Name..., fort on hill above large pencil, name below, 43x15", EX, A12 ....$280.00

Dobbins' Electric Soap, sign, paper, scowling maid scrubbing child's ear while black woman watches, framed, 22x17", G+, A9 ....$700.00

Dobbs Straw Hats, miniature hat & hat box used as 3-D gift certificates to be traded in for the full-size hat, 4x5½" box, EX, A21 ....$175.00

Dobler Ale, tap knob, chrome ball shape with red & white on green enamel insert, VG+, A8 ....$20.00

Dobler Brewing Co, tray, deep-dish, profile of girl with long hair wearing red headband, 13" dia, VG+, A9 ....$65.00

Dobler Lager, label, Dobler Brewing Co, L-type permit number, pre-prohibition, NM, A10 ....$40.00

Dobyns Footwear, booklet, 1925, 16 pgs, EX, D23 ..$25.00

Doc Gordon Cigars, box label, salesman's sample, framed oval portrait flanked by logo, cigar band at right, M, A5 ....$45.00

Dodge, bobbin' head figure, 'Little Profit,' 1960s, EX, D25 ....$70.00

Dodge, tire pressure gauge, yellow with orange & black lettering, 2x3", EX+, A6 ....$65.00

Dodge Dart, bank, cardboard can with metal ends, name & emblem above America's 1st Fine Economy Car, 4x3 dia, EX, A6 ....$25.00

Dodge-Plymouth, fan, cardboard with wicker handle, steering wheel with 2 multicolored landscapes & 2 blue logos, 1936, 12x8" dia, EX, A6 ....$45.00

Dodger Beverage, sign, die-cut bottle, pressed steel, orange, cream & black with red & cream label, 65x16", EX, A6 ....$450.00

Doerschuck Bock Beer, label, North American Brewing Co, Internal Revenue Tax Paid statement, 1933-50, 12-oz, M, A10 ....$10.00

Dog 'N Suds, mug, glass with red, white & yellow sign logo, 6x3½", NM, D16 ....$8.00

Dold Food Products, pocket puzzle, celluloid, You Are Not Taking A Chance... above logo, Old Reliables Jacob Dold... below, round, EX, A11 ....$25.00

Doles' Pineapple Nectarade, see Forthoffer's Creme De Menthe

Domes of Silence, display, metal, 'Better Than Casters' above woman putting domes on chair, For All Furniture... below, 11½x11", EX, A6 ....$110.00

Dominator Tomatoes, lug box label, WWII fighter diving & shooting tracers, Watsonville, M, D12.................$2.00

Dominion Cartridge Co, fob, porcelain on metal, large red D & blue & gold-tone cartridge shells embossed on front, EX, A15 ....$525.00

Dominion Line Cigarettes, tin, flat, product lettering above & below image of a steamship bordered by flags, 3x4½", VG+, A18.........................$175.00

Domino Cane Sugar, sign, paper, Save The Fruit Crop, pictures bag of sugar, basket of grapes & jars of jelly, 1918, framed, 11x21", EX, A2...............$230.00

Domino Pure Cane Sugar, box, sample, cardboard, with contents, 2½", NM, A7 ....$12.00

Domino's Pizza/Coca-Cola, pillow, shaped like a race car, NM, A16 ....$35.00

Don Gabral Cigars, box label, salesman's sample, bust portrait with cigar band at right, Moller Kokeritz & Co, M, A5.........................$35.00

Don Nieto, cigar box label, outer, image of 17th century scholar, 1923, 4½x4½", EX, D5 ....$10.00

Don Rosa, cigar box label, printer's proof, bust portrait flanked by roses, VG, A5 ....$40.00

Don't Cry Brand Sweet Potatoes, label, shows black boy playing dice game surrounded by product name, 50-lbs Net, 9x9", NM, A7.........................$22.00

Donald Duck Bread, sign, painted tin, pictures large loaf with Donald Duck on wrapper, green backround, 18x26", NM+, A1 ....$410.00

Donald Duck Coffee, tin, sample, yellow with lettering around Donald's image, pry lid, 2¼x3" dia, EX, D37.........................$400.00

Donald Duck Cola, sign, die-cut cardboard, Tops For Flavour above Donald on bottle cap next to hand-held bottle, framed, 26x22", NM, A9 ....$180.00

Donniford Blend, pocket tin, vertical, Donniford in diagonal script & pipe image above Blend, tan background, unopened, NM, A18 ....$95.00

Dorina, cigar box label, printer's proof, oval bust portrait with fancy border, M, A5.........................$25.00

Dot Coffee, tin, sample, 5-cup size, VG, A7.............$40.00

Double Cola, door handle, name on oval above handle with Art Deco motif, 1941, VG, A16 ....$200.00

Double Cola, menu board, tin, red & white oval logo & starbursts on blue above chalkboard, 28x20", M, D30 ..$75.00

Double Cola, miniature bottle, applied color label, NM, A16 ....$15.00

Double Cola, sign, cardboard, Get More When You Pour..., kangaroo pouring babies a glass, yellow background, 10x12", NM+, D30 ....$20.00

Double Cola, sign, Drink Double Cola above bottle on yellow dot, red, black & yellow diamond shape, 1947, framed, 56x56", NM, A13 ....$400.00

Double Cola, sign, Open on large rectangle above Enjoy Double Cola on red oval with white starbursts, 28x24", NM+, D30 ....$120.00

Double Cola, sign, tin, Drink Double Cola in white on red with green & white border, oval, 24x36", EX+, D30 ....$155.00

Double Cola, sign, tin flange, Drink... in yellow outlined in red on black oval, scroll design below, 1947, 15x18", EX, A6 ....$295.00

Double Cola, soda glass, red & white logo, 4x2½", M, D16 ....$20.00

Double Cola, thermometer, dial-type, Enjoy... on center circle, EX+, A16 ....$70.00

Double Cola, thermometer, tin, Art Deco design around bulb, Drink... on oval below, 1940, EX+, A16....$244.00

Double Eagle Ale, label, National Brewing Co, U-type permit number, Internal Revenue Tax Paid statement, 1934-36, 12-oz, EX, A10 ....$22.00

Double Eagle Ale, label, New Orleans Brewing Co, Internal Revenue Tax Paid statement, 1933-50, 1-qt, M, A10 ....$12.00

Double-Orange, sign, cardboard, Truly Delightful & product name encircle portrait of girl with chin lifted, 1920s, 18" dia, NM+, A13.....................$190.00

Douglas Aviation Tested Regular Gasoline, pump sign, painted aluminum, oval shape with 2 flat sides, product lettering above & below winged heart, 18x13", NM, A1 ....$440.00

Dove Brand Ginger Ale, mug, Penn'a Bottling & Supply Co..., pictures 3 doves, brown, tan, green & white, lion head handle, 5x3", EX, D16.........................$60.00

Dower Lumber Co, calendar, 1919, 'The Call,' pictures Indian in canoe, incomplete, 2 metal strips, VG, A3 ....$40.00

Doxie Cigars, tin, tax stamp, paper label with name above oval image of horse head, round with slip lid, 1901, VG+, A18 ....$170.00

Dr AC Daniels' Horse Medicines, pocket mirror, 'Home Treatment For Dumb Animals,' woman, horse & dog viewed between lettered gate posts, 2" dia, VG, A21 ....**$65.00**

Dr AC Daniels' Animal Medicines, cabinet, wood, tin insert shows 3 horse heads on circular inset, For Home Treatment Of Horses..., 29x22", G, A9 ....**$2,700.00**

Dr AC Daniels' Dog & Cat Remedies, cabinet, tin, woman with dog & cat on front, insert of Dr Daniels on sides, product name on marquee, 20x13", VG, A9 ..**$3,200.00**

Dr AC Daniels' Horse & Dog Medicines, sign, wood, Use...For Home Treatment, Sold Here, sanded off-white lettering on blue, wood frame, 18x30½", VG, A6 ..**$400.00**

Dr AC Daniels' Veterinary Medicines, calendar, 1905, product name above young man helping young lady across creek, full pad below, 14x9", EX, A15 .....**$200.00**

Dr AC Daniels' Warranted Medicines, sign, wood, ...For Home Treatment Of Horses & Cattle Sold Here, white on blue, 12x21", EX+, A15.................................**$575.00**

Dr Belding Tooth Powder, tin, blue & white with image of smiling girl, shaker top, oval, 5", G, A2 ....**$90.00**

Dr Bell's Anti-Pain, sign, name & list of cures above boy being helped by mother under tree after stepping on nail, 38x24", EX, A2 ....$1,045.00

Dr Blumers Baking Powder, tin, paper label, with contents, EX, A7 ....**$8.00**

Dr Caldwell's Syrup Pepsin, bottle, sample, with contents, NM, A7 ....**$10.00**

Dr Caldwell's Syrup Pepsin, bottle, sample, with contents & original box, NM, A7...**$15.00**

Dr Calvin Crane's Quaker Remedies, display box, wood with slanted glass front, stork decal & lettering on 3 sides, For Man, Woman & Child..., 10x16", EX, A9 ....**$900.00**

Dr Daniels' Remedies, display figure, papier-mache dog with lettering on both sides, glass eyes, 24x26", VG+, A9 ....**$750.00**

Dr Daniels' Veterinary Medicine, sign, paper, sepia image of 3 charging horses on circular inset, matted & framed, image: 23½x20", VG, A9 ....**$750.00**

Dr Daniels' Veterinary Medicines, cabinet, wood, tin front pictures Dr Daniels with products & price list below, 27x21x7½", G, A9 ....**$950.00**

Dr Daniels' Wonder Lotion, bottle, sample, with contents, VG, A7 ....**$40.00**

Dr Davis Anti-Headache, sign, paper, After Taking... above smiling girl with arms up to head, Price 25¢ on dot below, framed, 14x10", G, A2 ....**$120.00**

Dr Drake's Glessco Cough & Croup Remedy, sign, tin, couple looking over baby in cradle, ...For Young & Old below, 14½x11½", VG, A9 ....**$375.00**

Dr Hess Healing Powder, tin, Dr Hess above woman using product flanked by Healing Powder & 4-oz 25¢, NM+, A3 ....**$25.00**

Dr Hess Instant Louse Killer, tin, black with white product lettering above & below round image, orange bands top & bottom, unopened, NM, A18........$45.00

Dr JH McLean, cabinet, wood with name frosted on curved glass front, scrolled marquee atop, hinged back door, 28x17", EX, A2...**$1,265.00**

Dr King's Life Pills, store container, glass jar with reverse-painted label, ...Always Satisfy, 13x5x5", G, A9 ..**$150.00**

Dr Koch's Pure Ground Pepper/Dr Koch Vegetable Tea Co, tin, black lettering & graphics on yellow, slip lid, 1-lb, VG+, A8 ....**$70.00**

Dr Le Gear Medicine Co, sign, tin on cardboard, 'The Giant Horse,' shows man & horse, beveled edge, copyright 1911, 14x18", EX, A6 ....**$130.00**

Dr LeGears Healing Powder, tin, sample, with contents, 1¾", EX, A7..**$65.00**

Dr Lesure's Famous Remedies, cabinet, wood, tin front pictures horse head in circular window, 28½x21x8", rare, EX, A9 ....**$3,200.00**

Dr Lynas' Hair Grower/Toilet Cream, sign, cardboard, initial logo & product names, ...Cures Scalp Diseases/...Beautifies The Complexion, 10x13", EX, A8 ....**$45.00**

Dr Lyon's Dental Cream, tin, sample, with contents, original mailer, 2¼", NM, A7..................................**$35.00**

Dr Miller's Golden Harvest Beer, keg label, lettering on red, Dr Miller Co, VG+, A19 ....**$25.00**

Dr Morse's Indian Root Pills, display, die-cut cardboard trifold, product packs & teepees flank Indian at campfire, 27x40", EX, A6...............$245.00

Dr Morse's Indian Root Pills, fan, cardboard, wooden handle, round with Indian on white horse ready to spear a bear, 8" dia, EX+, A15.....................**$275.00**

Dr P Hall's Celebrated Catarrh Remedy, sign, die-cut paper, image of box with Trade Mark portrait & lettering, 50 Cts Per Bottle, framed, 27x40", EX, A21..**$550.00**

Dr Pepper, apron, sample from manufacturer, grocer's-type with logo on bib, NM, A16 ....**$125.00**

Dr Pepper, badge, silver-plated metal with celluloid name plate, Drink Dr Pepper Good For Life & 10-2-4 logo, 1½x2½", EX+, A1 ....**$325.00**

Dr Pepper, belt buckle, chrome with red, white & black enamel inlay, EX+, A16.......................................**$160.00**

Dr Pepper, bottle opener, wall mount, embossed lettering, NM, A16 ....**$20.00**

Dr Pepper, calendar, 1945, January/February sheet shows girl in party dress & photo of soldier, complete, 22x13½", EX+, A13..**$250.00**

Dr Pepper, calendar, 1948, girl in hooded fur coat, with cover page, 22x13½", NM, A13.........................**$110.00**

Dr Pepper, calendar, 1951, shows demure girl in pearls, complete, 21x13", NM, A13 ....**$100.00**

Dr Pepper, calendar page, 1950, July, August & September page featuring close-up of beach girl with bottle, 16x13", NM, A13...**$130.00**

Dr Pepper, clock, black numbers with red 10-2-4 around red logo, green composition frame, Telechron, 1930s-40s, 15" dia, EX, A13 ....**$275.00**

Dr Pepper, clock, Drink Dr Pepper on center band encircled by numbers with enlarged 10-2-4, 14" dia, VG, A8 ....**$250.00**

Dr Pepper, clock, reverse glass, 8-sided, red, black, gold & white Deco design, Drink...Thanks Call Again below, 17x22", EX, A1 ....$850.00

Dr Pepper, drinking glass, name etched around flared top, early, 3¾", NM+, A13..**$1,150.00**

Dr Pepper, drinking glass, slightly tapered with applied ...Good For Life! label & 10-2-4 clock, M, A16...**$220.00**

Dr Pepper, match holder, Drink Dr Pepper, Good For Life! above 10-2-4 clock, Keep Dr Pepper In Your Home below, NM+, A3 ....**$110.00**

Dr Pepper, menu board, tin floor model, Drink Dr Pepper At... on checked background above board, 33½x20½", EX, A9 ....**$155.00**

Dr Pepper, radio, wood cooler-type, green & black with red, yellow & black detail, General Electric, 7½x12x7", VG, A1 ....**$600.00**

Dr Pepper, seltzer bottle, 1920s-30s, EX+, A13 ....**$180.00**

Dr Pepper, sign, cardboard, A Lift For Life! & bottle cap flank cheerleader, 1950s, 2-sided, original wood frame, 19x32", EX+, A13...**$400.00**

Dr Pepper, sign, cardboard, Drink A Bite To Eat! At..., Dr Pepper Bottling Co, hand-painted, 8x10", EX, A16 ....**$100.00**

Dr Pepper, sign, cardboard, Energy Up! Drink... on face, hands at 10-2-4, 1920s-30s, framed under glass, 13x13", EX, A13..**$3,100.00**

Dr Pepper, sign, cardboard, Fireside Fun above Dr Pepper sign left of sweater girl popping corn, 1940s-50s, 15x25", NM, A13..**$240.00**

Dr Pepper, sign, cardboard, Join Me! above Dr Pepper sign left of girl in convertible, 1940s-50s, self-framed, 15x25", NM, A13...**$425.00**

Dr Pepper, sign, cardboard, Madelon Mason left of Dr Pepper sign above bottle, 1940s-50s, self-framed, 15x25", NM, A13...**$250.00**

Dr Pepper, sign, cardboard, Shining Hours... on light rays pointing toward girl with bottle, logo at top, 15x25", VG+, D30...**$125.00**

Dr Pepper, sign, cardboard, Smart Lift above Dr Pepper sign left of fishing girl, 1940s-50s, self-framed, 15x25", NM, A13..**$200.00**

Dr Pepper, sign, cardboard, Smart Lift above Dr Pepper sign left of winter girl with dog, 1940s-40s, self-framed, 15x25", NM, A13...**$210.00**

Dr Pepper, sign, cardboard, Tops! above red logo & soldier with bottle, wood frame with calendar holder, 1940s, 15x25", EX+, A13 ....**$700.00**

Dr Pepper, sign, Glo Glass, Energy Up, Drink... above Ice Cold in 'icy' letters, 1930s, lined background, 11x14", EX, A13..**$2,500.00**

Dr Pepper, sign, paper, Comic Books Given Away..., shows boy, comics & 6-pack, red on white, 1930s-40s, 22x34", NM, A13..**$55.00**

Dr Pepper, sign, paper, Frosty Man Frosty!, The Friendly 'Pepper-Upper,' outdoor chef reaching for bottle, 1950s, 15x25", NM, A13..**$30.00**

Dr Pepper, sign, paper, Have A Picnic At The New York World's Fair, 2 bottles in picnic basket, 1964, 15x25", NM, A13..**$30.00**

Dr Pepper, sign, paper, Try A Frosty Pep..., hand pouring from bottle & hand with ice-cream scoop over glass, 15x25", NM+, D30 ....**$20.00**

Dr Pepper, sign, porcelain, Drink Dr Pepper, white on red with white border, 9x24", EX, D30 ....**$95.00**

Dr Pepper, sign, porcelain, Drink...Good For Life!, lined background with white & green border, 1930s-40s, 11x27", NM, A13...**$225.00**

Dr Pepper, sign, tin, bottle on white background, raised border, 1950s-60s, 48x14", VG+, A13..................**$190.00**

Dr Pepper, sign, tin, Dr Pepper in slanted block letters, EX, A16..**$25.00**

Dr Pepper, sign, tin, Drink Dr Pepper, Distinctively Different above can, 54x18", NM, D30......................**$185.00**

Dr Pepper, sign, tin, Drink Dr Pepper, The Distinctive Soft Drink, white on red, 12x29", NM+, D30 ....**$135.00**

Dr Pepper, sign, tin, Drink Dr Pepper, white on red elongated oval, white background, 12x30", NM+, D30..........**$135.00**

Dr Pepper, sign, tin, Enjoy above Drink Dr Pepper on oval, Distinctively Different below, 20x28", EX, D30......**$80.00**

Dr Pepper, sign, tin, Gas! above black square, While You Wait & Dr Pepper logo with 5¢ Sold Here below, 1936, 40x18", VG+, A13................**$875.00**

Dr Pepper, sign, tin, 10-2-4 clock above bottle & logo, 1930s-40s, framed, 54x18", VG+, A13................**$400.00**

Dr Pepper, thermometer, tin, Dr Pepper Hot Or Cold, canted corners, 27x8", NM, D11................**$65.00**

Dr Pepper, tray, early, Drink...At All Soda Fountains on rim around 2 ladies in garden, oval, 16½x13½", G, A16..**$605.00**

Dr Pierce's Family Medicines, sign, paper, product name on arched banner above family at table & various product boxes, framed, image: 24x30", G, A9......**$16,000.00**

Dr Pierce's Favorite Prescription for Weak Women, decal on glass, Our Delicious Soda With Fruit Will Please You, lady standing in soda glass, gold frame, VG, A13................**$2,400.00**

Dr Price's Baking Powder, tin, paper label, with contents, G, A7................**$5.00**

Dr Price's Phosphate Baking Powder, sign, tin, Dial The Price For Butter & Eggs left of product can & lettered ribbon, 1920s-30s, 9x13", EX, A13 ..$225.00

Dr Radway's 'R-R-R' Remedies, sign, paper, name & list of cures surround Uncle Sam & Miss Liberty handing out bottles to people, 26x35", VG, A2............**$1,100.00**

Dr Sayman's Toilet Powder, container, cardboard canister with tin slip lid, advertising around portrait image, floral band top & bottom, NM, A3................**$45.00**

Dr Scholl's, jar, opalescent milk glass with aluminum lid, Dr Scholl's embossed on base & lid, 2x1⅝" dia, EX, D14................**$5.00**

Dr Scholl's Foot Eazer, box, cardboard, contains used supports & instructions, copyright 1935, EX, D24......**$20.00**

Dr Scott's Safety Razor/Pall Mall Electric Assn, tin, flat, 2-tone green, rectangular with rounded corners, 1¼x1⅞x3", EX, D37, minimum value................**$495.00**

Dr Simmon's Squaw Vine Liver Medicine, calendar, 1910, advertising above dealer name & seated squaw, 11½x6", NM, A7................**$120.00**

Dr Swett's Root Beer, mug, ceramic, embossed image of Dr Swett above product name, cream, brown & blue, 6", EX, A2................**$300.00**

Dr Swett's Root Beer, sign, ...Early American Root Beer Rich In Dextrose, pilgram boy with bottle, 1940s, curved corners, 70x36", NM+, A13................**$650.00**

Dr Swett's Root Beer, sign, cardboard stand-up, lady in fitted sweater holding up full glass, product name below, 17x10", NM, A1................**$95.00**

Dr Swett's Root Beer, sign, tin, Drink...The Original Root Beer, round image of boy with glass shadowed by elderly man, 9x24", EX+, A13................**$425.00**

Dr Swett's Root Beer, syrup dispenser, ceramic, tree trunk shape with advertising & grass painted around base, original pump, 13", EX, A2..$4,180.00

Dr WB Caldwell's Syrup Pepsin, sign, cardboard, die-cut stand-up, The Dose Can Be Reduced As Need Grows Less, stacked boxes & bottles, 26x9", NM, A15................**$400.00**

Dr WB Caldwell's Syrup Pepsin, sign, cardboard, Guard Their Health With... above 2 Boy Scouts at camp with product box in open tent, 36x20", VG+, A2......**$580.00**

Dr X, matchbook, Drink...The Tempting Beverage, 20 strike, front strike, NM, D28................**$4.00**

Dragon Ale, drinking glass, straight-sided with flat bottom, green lettering over yellow dragon design, 4½", NM, A8................**$20.00**

Dream Girl Talcum Powder, tin, red with white product name lower right of woman, tall square with small round shaker top, EX+, A18................**$85.00**

Dref's Gout & Rheumatism Pills, tin, 2" dia, NM, A7...**$7.00**

Dref's Liver Pills, tin, flat, with contents, 2" dia, NM, A7................**$10.00**

Dreikorn's Bread, door push, embossed tin, Reach For Dreikorn's in script, Thanks Call Again on reverse, 3x39", EX, A1................**$45.00**

Drewrys Ale, can, flat-top, instructional, shows Canadian Mountie with horse, 12-oz, NM, A19................**$115.00**

Drewrys Beer, sign, glass with applied plastic D, Ask For Big D above name on emblem, Enjoy The Difference, wood frame, 10x12", EX, A8................**$40.00**

Driving Club Pure Rye, sign, tin, well-dressed couples in horse-drawn carriage, L Kahn & Co, 27½x19½", G, A9................**$275.00**

Droste's Cocoa, tin, Dutch woman with serving tray, 7½x4x4", VG+, D21................**$60.00**

Droste's Cocoa, tin, sample, dining car scene, product name above & below crown logo on reverse, 1⅞x1x1", EX, D37................**$190.00**

Droste's Cocoa, tin, sample, product name above Dutch couple on bench, slip lid, 3¼x1¾x1¾", EX, D37 ..**$65.00**

Droste's Cocoa, tin, sample, product name above Dutch couple on bench, 1⅞x1⅛x1⅛", EX, D37................**$75.00**

Drummond Tobacco Co, Christmas card, Good Luck & Complimets Of... in center of decorated horseshoe, 7x5", VG, A5................**$12.00**

Drummond Tobacco Co, see also Horseshoe Tobacco

Drummond's Horseshoe, sign, die-cut cardboard, girl leaning on marble-type ledge in upsidedown horseshoe, framed, 21x17", EX+, A6................**$170.00**

Dry Climate Cigars, box label, printer's proof, maps of western states on tobacco leaves above hand shake, VG+, A5 ....$60.00

DS Brown & Co, see also Satine Washing Powder

Dub-lin-Stout Malt, label, Falstaff Corp, L-type permit number, 1920-28, 12-oz, M, A10 ....$20.00

DuBarry Special Preparation For Blackheads, tin, name above pedestal bust image, round with shouldered top, 2¾x1¼", EX, D37 ....$35.00

DuBois Budweiser, sign, embossed tin, Try The Original... above bottle flanked by Truly Different, Always Good, 19x14", VG, A19 ....$60.00

Dubuque Malting Co, coin purse, tooled leather with flip-over top, metal trim, VG, A8 ....$140.00

Dubuque Malting Co, pin-back button, celluloid, company name arched above logo, round, EX, A11 ....$30.00

Duckpin Pilsener, label, Moose Brewing Co, Internal Revenue Tax Paid statement, 1933-50, 12-oz, M, A10...$15.00

Duckwall, crate label, apple, wood duck by stone wall on blue background, M, D3 ....$10.00

Duckworth's Essences & Colours, sign, cardboard, product name above 'Heart Brand' logo flanked by bottles, blue background, 12x14", NM+, D21 ....$45.00

Duffy's Pure Malt Whiskey, pocket mirror, profile of gent lifting glass, round, VG+, A8 ....$20.00

Duke of Durham Smoking Tobacco, sign, paper, colorful image of Duke of Durham slaying Bull of Durham, Smoke The Genuine..., 13½x10½", G, A9 ....$150.00

Duke of Durham Smoking Tobacco, trade card, metamorphic, lettering & circular logo above 2 crying babies, 3½x3½", EX, A5 ....$22.00

Duke's Cameo Cigarettes, tin, round, screw lid, product name above & below image of lady in plumed hat on white paper label, holds 50, EX, A18 ....$195.00

Duke's Cameo Long Cut, cigarette papers, NM, A7 ...$15.00

Duke's Cigarettes, insert booklets, Histories of Generals series, 1889, set of 10, all G-EX, A5 ....$170.00

Duke's Cigarettes, insert card, Honest Library, How To Amuse An Evening Party, 1896, VG, A5 ....$60.00

Duke's Cigarettes, insert cards, Perilous Occupations series, 1888, set of 37, all G-EX, A5 ....$375.00

Duke's Honest Long Cut, insert card, photo of New York from Brooklyn Bridge, 1885, EX, A5......................$12.00

Duke's Honest Long Cut Smoking & Chewing Tobacco, insert card, 25 Albums Of American Stars, 1886, EX, A5...$25.00

Duke's Mixture, cigarette papers, #8, white, NM, A7...$20.00

Duke's Mixture, sign, tin, pictures large product pouch with yellow label on black background, framed, 11x8", EX+, A18..$215.00

Duke's Mixture Smoking Tobacco, pouch, cloth, paper label, with contents, ⅝-oz, NM, A7.......................$10.00

Dukehart's Cream Ale, mug, ceramic, barrel shape, product name above & below deer head with hops decor, brown on cream, pre-1920s, EX+, A19 ....$80.00

Duluth Imperial Flour, sign, tin, product name above black chef with loaf of bread, Without A Rival below, beveled edge, 25x18", NM, A9 ....$2,600.00

Dunham's Cocoanut, tin, paper label showing monkeys in trees throwing coconuts at natives, round & shouldered with tapering sides, NM, A18....................$425.00

Dunham's Shred Cocoanut, tin, sample, flat, decorative encircled image of product name & cake, rounded corners,½x2¼x3½", EX, D37.................................$125.00

Dunlap's Seeds, sign, paper, Good Harvest From Good Seed, name above child holding oversized cabbage, matted & framed, EX+, A18...............................$550.00

Dunlop Tires, sign, porcelain flange, encircled hands in center, blue & white, 14x18", G+, A6 ....$375.00

Dunlop Tires, sign, porcelain in cast-iron frame, Dunlop Fort encircled above product name, yellow, red & black, 31x36", EX, A6......................................$475.00

Dunlop Tires, sign, tin, Dunlop in black on yellow flanked by Tires in yellow on black, red border, 12x54", NM+, D30..$125.00

Dunlop Tires, sign, tin, encircled D with arrow pointing to black product name on yellow with red border, 14x58", NM, D8...$95.00

Dunnsboro Mild Pipe Tobacco, pocket tin, vertical, name above & below hunt scene, VG+, A18............$1,000.00

Dunoro, cigar box label, oval portrait, TJ Dunn & Co, NM, A5 ....$30.00

Duplex Marine Engine Oil, can, product name above boat racing through water, Enterprise Oil Co below, pour spout & handle, 11x4x6", VG+, A1............$140.00

Duplex Marine Engine Oil, sign, tin, dated AM 6-48, Authorized Dealer...Use Kasson Waterproof Grease, blue & red on bluish green, 10x20", EX, A6 ......$120.00

DuPont Hunting Powders, sign, paper, hunter in woods shooting at running deer, gold logo & lettering, framed, image: 12½x16", NM, A9 ....$800.00

DuPont Life Saving Service Powder, pocket mirror, celluloid, product name arched above logo & image, round, EX, A11 ....$125.00

DuPont Paint, clock, metal with glass face, black & white with white lettering, 15" dia, EX, A6 ....$80.00

DuPont Powders, sign, self-framed tin, Shoot DuPont Powders, 2 dog's heads in profile, 22x28", G, A6 ....$200.00

DuPont Smokeless Powder, prints, paper litho, 'Buffalo Hunting'/'A Point On Woodstock,' gold ad copy on tan mat, copyright 1900, 15x34", EX, A8 ....$400.00

DuPont Smokeless Shotgun Powder, sign, paper, 'The End of a Good Day,' lettering upper right of hunter & dog coming from woods, 1911, 27x18", NM, A13 ....$650.00

DuPont Superfine Gunpowder, can, black & white paper label with oval inset & vignettes of Indians & animals, red can, VG, A6 ....$75.00

Duquense Beer, can, cone-top, 12-oz, VG+, A19......$35.00

Duquesne 'Duke'!, display, plaster bucket marked Ask For A Frosty 'Duke'!, It's Electronically Inspected, 3 glass bottles, EX, A8 ....$100.00

Duquesne Brewing Co, see also Silver Top Premium Beer

Duquesne Pilsener, ad, bottle, product name & text left of Invasion Issue Global War Map above air battle scene, framed, 11x9", VG+, A8 ....$25.00

Duquesne Pilsener, display, chalkware statue, uniformed gentleman with mug on lettered base, 11x8", EX, A19 ....$120.00

Duquesne Pilsener, sign, light-up, reverse glass, 1950s, product name on red above 'The Finest Beer In Town,' gold metal frame, EX+, A19 ....$175.00

Duquesne Pilsener Beer, banner, cloth, shows sheet music titled Have A Duke! with animated bottles top & bottom, 1960s, vertical, EX+, A19 ....$25.00

Dura Superior Motor Oil, can, Dura Superior above mountain range graphic lettered Motor Oil, white, green & red, full, 1-qt, NM+, A1 ....$100.00

Durham Smoking Tobacco, sign, cardboard, A Full Hand!, comical image of black man holding package, ca 1890, framed, image: 10x7", VG, A9 ....$650.00

Durr's Quality Foods, sign, embossed tin, name & For Health on yellow above encircled Indian camp next to products, framed, 19x27", VG+, A13 ....$250.00

Duryea's Maizena, postcard, girl behind product boxes flanked by lettering, text on back offers 12 postcards for 10 boxtops, EX+, D26 ....$30.00

Duska Toiletries, sign, die-cut cardboard stand-up, towering red & black Art Deco display advertising various products, 31", EX, A2 ....$30.00

Dutch Boy, sign, porcelain, image of the Dutch boy with paint can & brush against white background, blue border, oval, 40", EX, A21 ....$110.00

Dutch Boy Paints, display, papier-mache, standing Dutch boy figure, 15", VG, A2 ....$185.00

Dutch Boy Paints, match holder, die-cut image of boy seated with brush in hand & pail for holder, 6¼x3", EX, A2 ....$470.00

Dutch Boy Paints, see also Atlantic White Lead

Dutch Boy Products, display rack, tin, For Good Painting..., These Free Folders Give You The Facts, Dutch Boy logo, black, 22x15", EX+, A18 ....$125.00

Dutch Boy Pure White Lead, sign, porcelain flange, Dutch Boy with paint brush & can above product name, 2-sided, 21x14", G, A9 ....$500.00

Dutch Boy White Lead, see also Beymer-Bauman

Dutch Boy White-Lead, sign, black with name above image of Dutch boy, Today's Prices regulated by revolving wheels, 14x11", VG+, A2 ....$200.00

Dutch Masters Paints, sign, porcelain, Dutchman in center, red, white & black with black lettering around border, 26" dia, EX+, A6 ....$185.00

Dwinell-Wright Co Coffee, store bin, wood with colorful paper label depicting product lettering & factory scene, 29x15x15", VG, A2 ....$295.00

DX Marine Gasoline, pump sign, porcelain, DX on diamond above Marine Gasoline flanked by small boats, red, white & blue, 27x15", NM, D8 ....$525.00

Dy-O-La Improved Dye, cabinet, wood, We Sell... on tin front, 17x13½x8½", VG, A9 ....$60.00

Dybala's Spring Beverages, sign, metal, Drink above tilted bottle & bubbles, Bottled Only At The Spring below, red background, 20x9", G, A6 ....$25.00

Dyer's Cough Drops, tin, product name flanked by Indian chief & princess, horizontal rectangle, Somers, VG+, A18 ....$130.00

Dyer's Lime Juice Tablets, tin, green horizontal rectangle, Somers, VG+, A18 ....$85.00

Dynafuel, pump sign, die-cut porcelain, Dynafuel lettered over yellow die-cut diamond, 8x12¼", NM, A1 ..$130.00

❧ E ❧

E Fleckenstein Brg Co, sign, tin, company name & 2 logos above 3 men sampling brew, Ernst Bottle Beer... below, 19x14", EX+, A9 ....$450.00

E Leidy, tobacco label, die-cut arrow, EX, D35 ....$5.00

E Payne & Sons Cross Pipe Tobacco Works, sign, die-cut paper hanger, pictures girl in swing, blue mat, 11", EX, A21 ....$100.00

E Pluribus Unum Cigars, box label, salesman's sample, large eagle behind patriotic shield, 1866, EX, A5 ....$100.00

E Robinson's Sons Pilsner Beer, sign, paper, Pilsner Beer above company name, For Family Use & On Draught on 2-color background, 28x52", VG, A19 ....$50.00

E Robinson's Sons Pilsner Beer, tray, deep-dish, couples in rowboat being served by black waiter, lettering on rim, 12" dia, VG, A9 ....$250.00

E&B Special Beer, can, cone-top, NM, A8 ....$40.00

E&O Beer, label, Pittsburgh Brewing Co, U-type permit number, Internal Revenue Tax Paid statement, 1933-36, 12-oz, NM, A10 ....$20.00

E&O Bock Beer, label, Pittsburgh Brewing Co, U-type permit number, Internal Revenue Tax Paid statement, 1933-36, 12-oz, EX, A10 ....$10.00

E-Z Ball Gum, gum machine marquee, celluloid over tin, Only 5¢ Per Ball! above batter & scoreboard, red ground, 1920s, 7x10", EX+, A1 ....$425.00

EA Stephens & Co Raw Furs & Wool, whetstone, black on yellow, oval, EX, A11 ....$35.00

Eagle Ales & Lager, tray, deep-dish, eagle logo encircled by product name on blue, lettered rim, VG+, A19 ....$60.00

Eagle Beer, label, New Orleans Brewing Co, Internal Revenue Tax paid Statement, 1933-50, 12-oz, M, A10 ....$32.00

Eagle Beer, tray, deep-dish, product name arched above eagle on yellow background, Eagle Brewing Co on rim, VG+, A19 ....$85.00

Eagle Brand Coffee, tin, product name above & below eagle, round, gold screw lid, 1-lb, VG+, A18 ..$250.00

Eagle Brand Condensed Milk, sign, die-cut cardboard, baby with bottle & product cans, Gail Borden... below, 15x10", G-, A9 ....$80.00

Eagle Brand Condensed Milk/Borden's Condensed Milk Co, sign, die-cut cardboard stand-up, can atop panel reading The Milk That Saves Sugar, blue, red & white, 20x12", EX, A12 ....$190.00

Eagle Lye, pocket mirror, celluloid, pictures product can, 3¼x2¼", EX+, A11 ....$30.00

Eagle Lye Works, crumber & crumb tray, decorative red & gold graphics around product name & image, scalloped edges, 9" wide, EX, A21 ....$175.00

Early Bird Motor Oil, can, bird pulls worm from the ground before sunrise above product name on oval, blue & pink on white, 1-qt, NM+, A1 ....$330.00

Early Times Whiskey, sign, embossed tin on cardboard, exterior cabin scene in oval above Early Times & Since 1860 on ribbon, 19x17", G+, A8 ....$20.00

Early Times Whiskey, sign, 3-D altoplaster, backwoods distillery scene with ox-drawn cart, 1920s, ornate gilt & wood frame, 28x23", NM+, A3 ....$495.00

East Orange & Ampere Land Company, pocket mirror, celluloid, pictures cluster of oranges at left of The Oranges In Jersey, round, EX, A11 ....$35.00

East Side Export Beer/Los Angeles Brewing Co, can, flat-top, instructional, dated 1936, 12-oz, EX+, A19 ...$130.00

Easthampton Spinning Co, paperweight, glass, company name above factory flanked by lettering, Fine Yarns... below, rectangular, M, D13 ....$65.00

Eastside, tap knob, red Enjoy arched above Eastside lettered on shield with eagle on yellow, VG+, A19 ..$70.00

Eastside Bottled Beer, tray, eagle atop shield, 13" dia, G+, A9 ....$75.00

Eat One, crate label, California orange, large arrow pointing to juicy orange, Lindsay, 10x11", M, D3 ....$2.00

Eaton's, light bulb display, metal & glass light-up, light bulb & logo on blue & yellow front, holds 3 bulbs, 7x10x5", EX, D21 ....$100.00

Eaton's Highland Linen, display dispenser, metal, holds stationery, 26", EX, A12 ....$80.00

Eaton's Highland Linen, see also Highland Linen

Eaton's Rancho Restaurant, plate, Wallace China Desert Ware, brown, green & yellow graphics on beige, 11" dia, EX, D25 ....$75.00

EB Lamme Clothing/Bozeman, sign, embossed tin, dapper man standing at left of name, yellow on black, yellow outlined border, 6½x14", VG+, A18 ....$15.00

EB Special Beer, can, cone-top, 12-oz, NM, A19 ......$45.00

Eberhard Faber Micromatic Van Dyke Pencils, display pencil, wood with metal hanger eyelets, Authorized Agent..., 60" long, VG+, A21 ....$415.00

Eberhardt & Ober Brewing Co, sign, paper litho, aerial view of busy factory scene with company name below, 26x42", EX+, A8 ....$635.00

Eberle's Blue Star Beer, label, red & blue product & company name with blue star over rays of blue & white, 12-oz, VG+, A19 ....$20.00

Ebling's, foam scraper, gold on black, VG+, A8 ....$35.00

Ebling's Beer & Ale, tray, deep-dish, lady posed with hand on knee & holding up a glass, product name below, 2-color ground, 13" dia, VG, A8 ....$75.00

Ebling's Celebrated Beers, tray, shows factory scene with gold lettering & decoration on brown rim, VG+, A19 ....$310.00

Ebner Good Old Fashioned Lager/Carl Ebner Brewing Co, label, product name on red diagonal band across forest valley, company name below, 12-oz, EX, A19 ..$35.00

EC Simmons Fishing Tackle, sign, paper, black lettering & green fish on cream background, red border, 17¾x36", EX, A6...............................$120.00

EC Simmons Keen Kutter, see Keen Kutter

Eclipse Outfit, tin, Eclipse & Outfit flank winged creature on bike, 1806 above, For Single Tube Tires below, ½x2⅝x4½", EX, D37...............................$130.00

Economy King Separators/Sears, Roebuck & Co, postcard, product name above separator & prices, Sold By... below, NM, D26 ....$65.00

Economy Motor Oil, can, man pointing in center, United Oil Mfg Co, red, green & white, screw cap & handle, 2-gal, 11x8", EX, A6...............................$55.00

Eddy's Bread, sign, tin, Eddy's Bread on scalloped oval left of Better By Far, red, yellow & blue, raised border, 18x54", NOS, NM+, A1 ....$75.00

Eddy's Bread, sign, tin, Home Of above ribbon-type emblem & Eddy's Good Bread, red, white & yellow, 15x29", NM, A1...............................$45.00

Eddy's Bread, sign, tin, Reach For Eddy's Bread on yellow strip, 3x28", NOS, NM, A1...............................$35.00

Edel-Brau Beer, label, Mutual Brewing Co Inc, U-type permit number 1214, Internal Revenue Tax Paid statement, 1933-36, 22-oz, M, A10...............................$10.00

Edela, cigar box label, printer's proof, Edela in script across girl's back flanked by 3-leaf clovers, EX, A5........$25.00

Edelweiss Light Beer, can, cone-top, 1-qt, full, NM, A8 ..$85.00

Edelweiss Ritz Beer/Schoenhofen Edelweiss Co, label, product name over mountainous cabin scene, 64-oz, VG+, A19 ....$20.00

Edelweiss Secret Brew/Edelweiss Ritz, foam scraper, red, EX, A8 ....$60.00

Eden Cube Cut, pocket tin, vertical, red with black Eden lettered on white tobacco leaf, lettering above & below, EX+, A18...............................$275.00

Edgeworth Extra, pocket tin, sample, cut-down vertical, Edgeworth arched above Extra, blue on blue, EX, A18 ....$70.00

Edgeworth Extra High Grade Smoking Tobacco, sign, embossed tin, product name flanked by 2 gents facing each other, Ready-Rubbed Or Plug Slice, 11x27", EX, A13 ....$475.00

Edgeworth Junior Extra High Grade Tobacco, pocket tin, vertical, EX+, A18...............................$60.00

Edgeworth Junior Light Mild Burley Tobacco, pocket tin, vertical, unopened, NM, A18 ....$110.00

Edgeworth Ready-Rubbed Extra High Grade, pocket tin, vertical, EX, A18 ....$245.00

Edgeworth Ready-Rubbed Smoking Tobacco, pocket tin, sample, cut-down vertical, blue on blue, EX, A18...............................$45.00

Edinburgh Ale, label, Edinburgh on diagonal band on gold & brown, 12-oz, VG+, A19...............................$5.00

Edison Batteries, display, metal with advertising on porcelain sides, product name & E Mark logo in white on green & black, 15x14", EX, A6 ....$25.00

Edison Mazda Lamps, display, metal trifold with 2-sided posters, girl looking in mirror, So Much Depending..., 1920s, NM, D21 ....$2,800.00

Edison Mazda Lamps, display, 2-sided reversed glass panels, For Good Light..., illuminated bulb/marching soldiers, 13x21", VG, A13 ....$250.00

Edison Mazda Lamps, tape measure, celluloid, multicolored Maxfield Parrish design on front, NM, D22 ....$185.00

Edison Phonographs, sign, cardboard, ...Gold Moulded Records, black & white oval portrait of Thomas Edison, 19x12½", G+, A9 ....$220.00

Edwards Department Stores, match striker, aluminum, image of store & lettering above striking area, 5x2½", EX, A7 ....$7.00

Efficiency Gas Oil, can, man driving race car above product name on emblem, yellow, blue & cream, pour spout & handle, ½-gal, 7x8", EX, A6 ....$170.00

Egyptian Cigarettes, pocket tin, flat, name & logo with oval inset of pyramids flanked by Egyptian ladies, square, rounded corners, EX+, A18 ....$75.00

Egyptian Prettiest/Schinari Bros, sign, cardboard, The Original Egyptian Cigarette, name above lady holding burning cigarette, 14x10½", VG+, A18 ....$150.00

Egyptienne 'Straights' Cigarettes, sign, cardboard, girl's head in bonnet above product pack, name & Absolutely Pure, original frame, 31x20", G, A5 ....$125.00

Egyptienne 'Straights' Cigarettes, sign, paper, girl's head in bonnet above product pack, name & Absolutely Pure, original frame, 16x14", EX+, A18...............................$140.00

Ehret's, foam scraper, blue on white, EX, A8 ....$25.00

Ehret's, see also Geo Ehret's Extra

Ehret's Extra Beer, foam scraper holder, plastic, red cup with product name on black base, EX, A8...........$80.00

Eichler Beers, tray, deep-dish, profile image of lady in hat smelling nosegay, 12" dia, G+, A21 ....$65.00

Eichler's Beer, sign, reverse glass, Good Old Beer Since... on black above & below Eichler's on white diagonal band, 8x10", NM, A19...................$115.00

Eichler's Beer, sign, tin on cardboard, Since 1862 & Beer on black above & below Eichler's on yellow diagonal band, 9x19", EX, A19 ....$80.00

Eight Bells, tobacco label, colorful image of ocean liner flanked by rows of bells, 7x13", NM, A3 ....$30.00

Eight Brothers Long Cut Tobacco, pail, product name above & below 8 Brothers logo, EX, A3...............$65.00

Eight O'Clock Coffee, bank, tin, NM, A7 ....$15.00

Eisemann's Klondike Head Rub, sign, cardboard hanger, white with bottle at right of product name & Application 10¢..., rounded corners, 8x11", EX, A2.........$55.00

Eisenlohr's Cinco 5¢ Cigars, sign, tin, Eisenlohr's above Cinco in diagonal script, red & black on orange, 2-sided, 9x16", EX+, A3 ....$80.00

El Barco, cigar box label, outer, tropical barge full of tobacco, 1901, 4½x4½", EX, D5 ....$20.00

El Bubble, display box for 5¢ bubble gum cigars, inner lid shows image of Indian chief & advertising, EX+, A3 ....$35.00

El Carlan Cigars, box label, salesman's sample, framed portrait flanked by branches & medallions, cigar band at right, M, A5 ....$35.00

El Celibe Cigars, box label, salesman's sample, man playing guitar flanked by medallions, cigar band at right, M, A5 ....$40.00

El Dallo Cigars, tip tray, dark blue with El Dallo on red emblem above 'Each Cigar In Its Own Humidor,' rectangular, EX, A18 ....$30.00

El Juanita, cigar box label, printer's proof, cute little girl with hands to cheek, VG, A5 ....$25.00

El Mascotte Tampa, cigar box label, printer's proof, oval portrait flanked by palm trees with ship & house beyond, NM, A5 ....$45.00

El Minero, tobacco box label, image of miner with pick, name below, Giles litho, 14", NM, A7 ....$20.00

El Moriso 5¢ Guaranteed Hi-Grade Cigar, sign, cardboard, product name in black & red flanked by Cellophane Wrapped in white, yellow ground, 10x13½", EX, A6 ....$40.00

El Moro, cigar box label, printer's proof, oval portrait of woman smelling flowers, EX, A5 ....$30.00

El Paratus Havana Claro Cigar Co, box label, printer's proof, 3 portrait vignettes, EX, A5 ....$55.00

El Primo, crate label, California lemon, design of lemons & view of groves & hills, Claremont, 9x12", M, D12 ..$12.00

El Stymo, cigar box label, inner lid, Indian giving tobacco to ladies, 6x9", M, D5 ....$20.00

El Teano Cigars, tin, product name above seated lady on label against vertical cigars, vertical oblong with green lid, holds 50, EX+, A18 ....$55.00

El Tolna, cigar box label, printer's proof, portrait surrounded by fancy scroll design, For Gentlemen Who Know Quality, EX, A5 ....$65.00

El Verso Havana Cigars, tip tray, El Verso arched above man relaxing & smoking a cigar, Havana Cigars below, black with gold trim, 5x7", NM, A1 ....$65.00

Elastica Floor Finish, bookmark, celluloid, image of young boy on rocking horse at top, 6", EX, A11 ....$85.00

Elastilite Varnish, display cabinet, galvanized metal in shape of can with lithographed label, back opens to shelving, 34x20x10", EX, A21 ....$580.00

Elder Brau/Maier Brewing Co, can, flat-top, red circle on white, 12-oz, VG+, A19 ....$18.00

Electric Brand Golden Pumpkin/Electric Brand Canned Goods, can label, 2 images, name above & below pumpkin, name above & below girl emiting electricity in clouds, 4x11", NM, A7 ....$12.00

Electric City Beer, label, Electric Brewing Co, U-type permit number, Internal Revenue Tax Paid statement, 1933-36, 12-oz, EX, A10 ....$25.00

Elephant Salted Peanuts, jar, glass, ball shape with embossed name, figural peanut lid, 10" dia, EX, A2 ....$525.00

Elephant Salted Peanuts, tin, white diamond on red background with red name above & below image of red elephant, pry lid, 10-lb, VG, A2 ....$385.00

Elfenbrau Beer, label, La Crosse Brewery Co, U-type permit number, Internal Revenue Tax Paid statement, 1933-36, 64-oz, NM, A10 ....$40.00

Elgin Watches, postcard, barefoot boy in tattered overalls, My Elgin's All Right, 1914, VG+, D26 ....$40.00

Eliasso Bros & Co Mainsprings, tin, flat, fancy initial logo & lettering, decorative border, hinged lid, square corners, ¾x2⅞x3⅜", EX, D37 ....$40.00

Elite, crate label, Washington pear, stylized white script logo on 2-tone blue, 8x11", M, D12 ....$2.00

Elk Brand Prunes, lug box label, elk head in center, red background, Cupertino, M, D12 ....$6.00

Elkay Cocoa, container, cardboard & tin, product name above & below cup & saucer, vertical square, 1-lb, EX, A18 ....$10.00

Elkay's Dye, sign, cardboard, 2 women on porch looking out window at house, product bottle lower right, framed, image: 20x20", G, A9 ....$130.00

Ellen Kay Quality Coals, pocket mirror, celluloid, Logan & Kanawha Coal Co Inc arched above & below product name, brown & yellow, round, EX, A11 ....$8.00

Elsedor, cigar box label, inner lid, woman riding horse, 6x9", EX, D5 ....$35.00

Embassy Gramophone Needles, tin, flat, Extra Loud Tone, rectangular, rounded corners, ½x1¼x1¾", EX, D37 ....$40.00

Embassy Long Playing Radiogram Needles, tin, flat, Extra Loud Tone, rectangular, rounded corners, ½x1¼x1¾", EX, D37 ....$40.00

Emerald Beauty, crate label, Washington pear, Senorita with guitar & 2 green birds, 8x11", M, D12 ....$8.00

Emerson Piano Co Boston, trade card, silhouette design of 4 devilish-type figures dancing, musical notes above, EX, D23 ....$60.00

Emerson's Bromo Seltzer, postcard, Crowned Best Headache Cure, US & Canadian flags flank Uncle Sam crowning large bottle, NM+, A17 ....$115.00

Emerson's Ginger-Mint Julep, sign, paper, product name flanked by Gives Pep In Bottles & Quenches Thirst..., 4½x20¼", EX, A7 ....$20.00

Emery Mfg Co Emco Gasoline, gas globe, glass with black & red etched lettering, 1-pc, 16", rare, EX, A6 .....$750.00

Emil Sick's, tap knob, red plastic with name lettered on large red 6 on yellow background, round, EX+, A8...$110.00

Emil Sick's Select Beer & Ale, sign, plastic over cardboard, easel-back, product name on 6 left of The Famous Beer From Seattle!, EX, A8 ....$100.00

Emmetsburg Seed House, whetstone, celluloid, pictures large building in center, black & white, round, EX, A11...$20.00

Empire Beer, label, vignettes around 3 men above product name, Bechaud Brewing Co, 12-oz, VG+, A19 ....$15.00

Empire Builder, crate label, Washington apple, packing house, trucks & train in valley orchard, Cashmere, 9x11", M, D12 ....$4.00

Empire Cream Separator, pocket mirror, 'Nothing Else Will Do,' pictures milkmaid in innocent pose, vertical oval, 2¾", EX, A21 ....$100.00

Empire Mills Coffee, tin, product scene above & below Santa & reindeer, orange background, small slip lid, 1890s, 9x4", EX, A15 ....$425.00

Empire Tobacco Co, cigar cutter, cast iron, embossed lettering & gold highlights, 6½x17½", VG, A6 ....$50.00

Empress Coffee, tin, Empress Coffee in bold letters in center, crowns surround top & bottom band, key-wind lid, 2-lb, NM, A3 ....$55.00

Empress Coffee, tin, Regular Grind crown logo above product name, empress with steaming cup in lower left, key-wind lid, 1-lb, EX, A3 ....$22.00

Empress Pure Strawberry Jam, tin, Empress in bold letters above ocean liner & oval inset, pry lid, 48-oz, NM, A3 ....$22.00

En-Ar-Co Motor Oil, bank, tin, 5-gal oil can shape, also promotes En-Ar-Co Gear Compound Gun Grease & White Rose Gasoline, 4x3x3", EX+, A15............$325.00

En-Ar-Co Motor Oil, can, National... above encircled boy holding sign, cream, green & red, with contents, 1-qt, 5½x4" dia, EX+, A6 ....$20.00

En-Ar-Co National Motor Oil, can, eagle atop product name, orange, blue & cream, metal spout, 10½", scarce, VG, A6 ....$85.00

En-Ar-Co Penn Motor Oil, can, National... above encircled boy holding sign, green, red & cream, 10x7" dia, 5-qts, VG, A6 ....$30.00

Encore Beer/Monarch Brewing Co, tray, product & company name on red center, Encore repeated around rim, round, VG+, A19 ....$25.00

Enders Dollar Safety Razor, sign, tin stand-up, black with yellow lettering around image of razor, ...Blades 5 For 25¢, yellow border, 14x9", G, A2 ....$90.00

Endicott Shoes, pocket mirror/calendar, 1911, celluloid, lettering surrounded by calendar, violet & white, round, EX, A11 ....$45.00

Endicott-Johnson Shoes, clicker, tin, EX, A7............$4.00

Endicott-Johnson Shoes, whistle, tin, rectangular, 2½", NM, A7 ....$10.00

Energee Detonox Gasoline, gas globe, blue & orange lettering, blue metal body, 15" dia, rare, NM, A6...$425.00

Energizer Batteries, bunny, battery-operated, lights up, 3¾", M $10.00

Englebert Balloon Tires, postcard, elegant woman atop tire rolling across rocky terrain, signed Henry Le Monnier, French, 1925, VG+, D26 ....$45.00

English Lad Beer, label, Westminster Brewing Co, Internal Revenue Tax Paid Statement, 1933-50, 1-qt, M, A10 ....$10.00

English Ovals Cigarettes/Philip Morris & Co Limited, sign, cardboard trifold, The Choice At Ranelagh, 3 men in center oval flanked by product ovals, pre-WWI, 34x60", EX, A18...$415.00

English Pug Smoking Tobacco, tin, shows pug dog in oval left of product name, blue, gold & cream, flat with rounded corners, EX+, A15 ....$250.00

English Walnut Smoking Tobacco, pocket tin, vertical, white English Walnut on black above red & yellow lion emblem, VG+, A18 ....$390.00

Ensign Mixture, tin, product name & pennant on cream, gold trim, 2½x4x2¾", VG+, A18 ....$60.00

Enterprise Bohemian Lager, tray, jolly old fellow toasting with glass of lager, It's Aged & Mellowed on rim, 13x10½", EX, A9 ....$75.00

Epicure Shredded Plug Tobacco, pocket tin, vertical, Epicure in script above man resting in wooded area, Shredded... below, EX, A3.................................$120.00

Epicure Shredded Plug Tobacco, pocket tin, vertical, Epicure in script above man resting in wooded area, Shredded... below, with contents, NM, A18 ....$210.00

Equestrian Trails, sign, porcelain flange, horse head & lettering on bell, 2-sided, 16x14", EX, A9 ....$100.00

Erie Club Beverages, calendar, 1939, girl in see-through gown standing on swing, full pad, 20x10", EX+, A13 ....$150.00

Erie Foundry, watch fob, shield shape with embossed image of the foundry, EX, A20 ....$35.00

Erie Preserving Co's Reliable Canned Goods, sign, paper, woman in store inspecting labels, Calvert litho, 22x13", G, A9 ....$1,600.00

Erlanger DeLuxe, tap knob, chrome with celluloid cover, red & black on white, 2" dia, EX, A8 ....$30.00

Ernesta, cigar box label, outer, woman wearing large hat, 4½x4½", EX, D5 ....$10.00

Eskimo Pie, container, hard plastic, 1970s, EX, D27 ...$25.00

Eskimo Pie, sign, porcelain, product name only, 6x36", NM, D11...$140.00

Eskimo Pie, sign, tin, lettering & ice cream bar in center oval, M-m-melts In Your Mouth!, 1948, 2-sided, 24x36", scarce, VG, A6 ....$240.00

Esmeralda, tobacco box label, image of lady with bird on hand, product name below, Heppenheimer & Mauer litho, 14", NM, A7 ....$30.00

Esquire Brushless Scuff-Kote for Childrens Shoes, box, cardboard, pictures circus animals & band leader, 1950s, EX, D24...$6.50

Essavie's Complexion Powder, tin, pictures close-up of lady in bonnet, no lettering, square with rounded corners, 1⅜x3x3", EX, D37 ....$70.00

Essem Quality Cooked Meats, display, chalkware pig incised with Essem Quality, Cooked Meats Ready To Eat incised on base, 4½x7½", EX, A8 ....$100.00

Essex Mixture, pocket tin, vertical, lettering around encircled image of a poker hand against red & black checked ground, EX+, A18..............................$6,050.00

Esslinger Repeal Beer, tray, America's Finest Beer & On Draught-In Bottles on gold & blue rim around bellhop with tray, rectangular, VG+, A19.....................$55.00

Esslinger's Beer, tray, deep-dish, Good Old arched above bellhop with tray & product name, yellow background, 12" dia, EX+, A19 ....$55.00

Esso, attendant's hat, red, white & blue, VG+, A6 .....$80.00

Esso, bank, Esso Drop figure, plastic, white with blue & red logo on chest, 1960s, 7", EX, D27...................$60.00

Esso, bank, Esso Tiger figure, vinyl, 1960s, EX, D27 ..$15.00

Esso, bank, truck, plastic, red, 6¾" long, EX+, A6 .....$35.00

Esso, birthday candles, 'For Your Birthday From The Tiger & Your Humble Dealer,' boxed set of 36, EX, D14...$12.00

Esso, display figure, Esso dog, composition, brown with white patch under his neck, red Esso on tag, 44" long, scarce, EX, A6 ....$1,200.00

Esso, display figure, Esso dog, papier-mache, tan & black with silver & red collar & tag, 40" long, EX, A6..$1,200.00

Esso, drinking glasses, set of 6 in original box, 1955, EX, D6...$35.00

Esso, pocketknife, metal gas pump shape, 2½", EX, A6 ..$75.00

Esso, salt & pepper shakers, plastic gas pumps, red, white & blue, crazing to decals, EX, A6........................$40.00

Esso, sign, porcelain, Esso Credit Cards Honored, 2-sided, 14x18", NM, A6...$200.00

Esso Aviation, gas globe, red & blue lettering on white, metal body, 15" dia, lens NM/body VG, A6....$1,400.00

Esso Extra Motor Oil, sign, porcelain, Esso on oval at top, Long Mileage/Protection/Quick/Starting below, red, white & blue, EX+, A6.........................$200.00

Esso Marine Gasoline, pump plate, porcelain, white on red, 3" dia, EX+, D8 ....$65.00

Esso Touring Service, map holder, metal, slots marked Free & Take One, Happy Motoring below, red, white & blue, 23½x12½", VG, A6 ....$75.00

Essolube Motor Oil, jigsaw puzzle, family driving auto through forest inhabited by 'auto-ailing' Dr Seuss creatures, 1933, 12x17", EX, D10 ....$150.00

Estabrooks' Red Rose Coffee, sign, embossed tin, pictures large can of product on green background, 16x18", EX+, A3 ....$230.00

Ethyl, pump plate, porcelain, triangular logo & lettering on lined background, white, orange & black, 7" dia, VG+, A6...$55.00

Eugene's Secret of Beauty for the Complexion, sign, die-cut cardboard, shaped like artist's palette with colors painting picture of woman & cherub, 12", EX, A2..$110.00

Eulberg Crown Select Beer, foam scraper, blue on aluminum, EX, A8...$100.00

Eulberg's Picnic Beer, label, Eulberg Brewing Co, U-type permit number, Internal Revenue Tax Paid statement, 1933-36, 64-oz, NM, A10...........................$25.00

Eureka, crate label, Florida citrus, Indian standing by river, 9x9", M, D3 ....$2.00

Eureka Centre Draft Mower, handbill, image of children in field playing ring-around-the-rosie, 1880s, 6x10", EX, D8.......................................$100.00

Eureka Grade, tobacco label, EX, D35.....................$3.50

Eureka Harness Oil, can, product name & other lettering surrounded by fancy scroll designs, gold & black, screw lid & handle, 5-gal, VG, A6 ....**$15.00**

Eureka Harness Oil, sign, embossed tin, name above 2 encircled horses flanked by Lengthens The Life & Of Your Harness, 12x20", NM, A1 ....**$445.00**

Eureka Hoosier Kitchen Cabinet, salesman's sample, painted & stained wood, brass knobs, internal metal flour sifter, several drawers, 16", VG, A21 ....**$1,540.00**

Evangeline Motor Oil, can, product name encircles tree above Tough As The Evangeline Oak, red & green on white, 1-qt, NM, A1 ....**$185.00**

Evans Reddy Waterless Cleanser, pail, band of saluting men around bottom, red, yellow & black, press lid & bail, VG+, A6 ....**$60.00**

Eve Cube Cut, pocket tin, vertical, name at left of Eve gazing at apple tree, brown colors, EX+, A18 ....**$270.00**

Eve Cube Cut, pocket tin, vertical, name at left of Eve gazing at apple tree, green colors, VG+, A18 ....**$150.00**

Ever-Ready Radio Steel Blades, box with shaving brush, cardboard, pictures 'Trade Mark Face,' 9½x7x4", G, A6 ....**$100.00**

Ever-Ready Radio Steel Blades, sign, tin, man shaving at left of product name, 3x11", VG, A9 ....**$300.00**

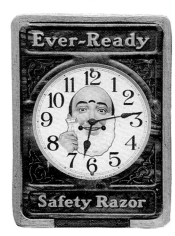

Ever-Ready Safety Razor, clock, metal, rectangular with embossed name above & below image of man shaving, 18x12½", VG, A6 ....**$850.00**

Ever-Ready Safety Razor, clock, wood, round with Roman numerals surrounding decal of man shaving, name below, with pendulum, 28x18", G, A9 ....**$675.00**

Ever-Ready Safety Razor, clock, wood, round with Roman numerals surrounding decal of man shaving, name below, with pendulum, 22x18", EX, A21 ....**$2,200.00**

Ever-Ready Safety Razor, display, tin, glass & wood, man shaving flanked by $1 Complete & 12 Radio Blades on die-cut marquee, 12x10", VG, A6 ....**$1,100.00**

Ever-Ready Safety Razor, sign, die-cut cardboard, ...De Luxe Models $1.00 flanked by open boxes showing product, 1920s, 11x27", EX+, A15 ....**$400.00**

Ever-Ready Shaving Brushes, display brush, oversized wooden handle with brush bristles, ca 1910, 19", VG, A21 ....**$140.00**

Ever-Ready Shaving Brushes, sign, die-cut cardboard stand-up, D — n It! They Won't Come Out, parrot & brush atop sign, 1920s, EX+, A15 ....**$210.00**

Ever-Ready Spotlight Torch, display, cardboard, product name on marquee above screen with man in open car shining light on road sign, 14x14", NM, A1 ....**$245.00**

Eveready, sign, porcelain, from India, little man holding oversized flashlights behind 3 batteries, blue ground, 18x12", G+, D21 ....**$225.00**

Eveready Batteries, bank, black cat figure, Save With The Cat & image of a battery on side, white eyes, nose & chest, 1981, 8½", M **$40.00**

Eveready Batteries, display case, metal & wood with plexiglass, product name on white irregular shape atop case with slanted front, EX, A18 ....**$110.00**

Eveready Energizer Batteries, flashlight, Energizer Bunny figure, squeezable vinyl, 1991, on original card, 4", M, D27 ....**$10.00**

Eveready Extra Long Life Flashlight Batteries, display case, metal, ...10¢ Each emblem on pediment atop 4-row slanted bin, ...The Date Line Is Your Guarantee, EX, A12 ....**$120.00**

Eveready Flashlight Batteries, sign, die-cut cardboard, logo atop image of man shining flashlight on family of skunks, ad panel below, 26x14", EX, D21 ....**$40.00**

Eveready Flashlight Batteries & Mazda Lamps, display case, tin & glass, Let Us Reload... above hands on oval, orange, blue, green & cream, 16x10", VG, A6 ...**$130.00**

Eveready Flashlights, sign, paper, Gosh! Terrible! What! Fine!..., 4 oval images of man pondering a Christmas gift, 1960, 8x28", EX+, A3 ....**$85.00**

Eveready Flashlights & Batteries, poster, cloth-backed paper, 'A Friend In Need,' signed Frances Hunter Tipton, little boy with flashlight, 30x19", EX, A6 .....**$500.00**

Eveready Prestone Anti-Freeze, can, pictures front of car beside thermometer, ...Does Not Boil Off, orange, blue & cream, 1-gal, 11x6½", VG+, A6 ....**$75.00**

Eveready Tungsten Batteries, display, cardboard stand-up, 5-tiered pyramid of batteries, We're Eveready With... across bottom tier, 19x16", EX, A6 ....**$65.00**

Everett Flour Mills, banner, hangs from carved wood staff with figure of Miss Liberty, black boy atop E in Everett on banner, 45", EX, A2 ....**$1,265.00**

Eversweet Perspiration Deodorant, tip tray, woman in diaphanous gown with roses, A Dainty Toilet Necessity For Refined People, ornate rim, 8x3", EX, D14 ....$65.00

Evervess Bonded Sparkling Water, tray, deep-dish, Yes! Yes!...A Product Of Pepsi-Cola on striped background, round, EX+, A16 ....**$45.00**

Evervess Sparkling Water, sign, celluloid hanger/stand-up, A Product Of Pepsi-Cola Co above mountains, Big 12-oz Bottle 5¢, 9" dia, EX+, A13 ....**$250.00**

Evinrude Motor Co, tip tray, image of girl in motorboat, lettering on rim, 4" dia, EX, A21 ....**$265.00**

Ex-Lax, door plate, reverse-painted plastic, Push above product box on yellow dot, Get Your Box Now, blue ground, 8x4", EX+, A3 ....$30.00

Ex-Lax, thermometer, porcelain, ...The Chocolated Laxative above bulb, Keep Regular With Ex-Lax below, 36", VG, A6...**$60.00**

Ex-Lax, thermometer, porcelain, ...The Chocolated Laxative above bulb, Keep Regular With Ex-Lax below, 36", EX+, D21...**$165.00**

Ex-Lax, thermometer, porcelain, Keep Regular... on zigzag ribbon, horizontal bulb in center, 21x5", EX+, A13 .....**$400.00**

Ex-Lax, thermometer, porcelain, lettering above & below dial in center, white & yellow on blue, 1920s-30s, 36x8", EX+, A13...**$300.00**

Ex-Lax, tin, sample, with contents, NM, A7.............**$15.00**

Exceloyl Oils, can, product name above Deco design with appearance of sun rising over mountains, HK Stahl at bottom, 1-qt, NM+, A1 ....**$95.00**

Excelsior Brewing Co, drinking glass, pilsener stem with embossed knight & flag, NM, A8 ....**$60.00**

Excelsior Brewing Co, tray, shows bust of girl with glass flanked by 2 bottles, lettering on wood-grain rim, oval, 16½", VG, A8...**$120.00**

Excelsior Motor Oil, can, yellow with name over black image of open touring car in country scene, 1-gal, VG+, A6...**$200.00**

Export 'Aquafuge' Cigarette Papers, dispenser, green label with product lettering on tan vertical holder, opening at bottom, EX, A18 ....**$40.00**

Express Fine Cut Tobacco, tin, product name above locomotive, Globe Tobacco Co, Detroit Mich, USA below, 2x8" dia, G-, A9 ....**$50.00**

Extra Pale Beer, label, Ambrosia Brewing Co, Internal Revenue Tax Paid statement, 1933-30, 12-oz, M, A10...**$10.00**

Extra Sugar Loaf Pineapple/Greely Burnham Grocer Co, can label, 2 images with name above & below pineapple/building & encircled buffalo head with flowers, 1880s, NM, A3...**$15.00**

Eye-Fix, tip tray, cherub putting drops into lady's eye, ...The Great Eye Remedy on rim, 4" dia, VG, A9.............**$85.00**

Eye-Fix, tip tray, cherub putting drops into lady's eye, ...The Great Eye Remedy on red rim, 4" dia, NM, A3...**$275.00**

EZ Serve Gasoline, sign, porcelain, product name on emblem in center, 18x14", NM, D11 ....**$75.00**

Eze-Orange, sign, cardboard stand-up, ...Appetizing-Refreshing above bottle & 5¢ Easy To Serve Easy To Drink, 10x5", EX+, A16 ....**$15.00**

F

F&F Cough Syrup, tin, sample, with contents, EX, A7..**$35.00**

F&S Beer & Ale/Furhmann & Schmidt Brewing Co, tray, deep-dish, We Serve... at left of bellhop with 4 full glasses on tray, 12" dia, VG+, A8 ....**$30.00**

Fab, see Colgate's Fab

Fabrica de Tabacos, cigar box label, inner lid, cute cat looking over red ruler, 6x9", M, D5 ....**$35.00**

FADA Radio Sales-Service, sign, porcelain hanger with ornate bracket, red & black Art Deco design, 8x18", scarce, NM, A1 ....$650.00

Fair Department Store, calendar top (?), die-cut, Compliments Of... PE Marcus... above lady's profile surrounded by roses, 20x14", EX+, A3 ....**$320.00**

Fairbank's Gold Dust Washing Powder, calendar, 1933, Gold Dust twins above Gold Dust in bold letters, Lever Bros Co, full pad, 12½x7½", NM, A3 .... **$55.00**

Fairbank's Gold Dust Washing Powder, product box, cardboard, product name above & below the Gold Dust twins, orange, black, white & yellow, 6 ½-oz, M, A1 .... **$55.00**

Fairbank's Gold Dust Washing Powder, sign, cardboard, Something New! Larger Packages..., product box flanked by Gold Dust twins, 21x14", G+, A9 ..... **$400.00**

Fairbank's Gold Dust Washing Powder, sign, paper, Kept Clean & Safe With... & image of twins at left of soap box, baby bottles & milk, 10x19", VG, A2 .... **$145.00**

Fairbank's Gold Dust Washing Powder, store display, die-cut tin, letters on top of boxes spelling product name, 2-sided, 7½x15½", EX, A9 .... **$8,000.00**

Fairbank's Gold Dust Washing Powder, see also Gold Dust

Fairbanks Scales, sign, porcelain, bold white lettering on blue background, 9x44", EX, A6 .... **$75.00**

Fairmont Brewing Co, mug, ceramic, barrel shape with woman riding sidesaddle above company name & Fairmont W Va, EX+, A8 .... **$155.00**

Fairway Rolled Oats, container, cardboard, bold white lettering on dark blue against yellow with images of baker & elves, 3-lb, NM+, A3 .... **$45.00**

Fairway White Label Rolled Oats, container, cardboard, shows boy & girl making an exchange, Twin City Wholesale Grocer Co, 3-lb, EX+, A3 .... **$65.00**

Fairy Soap, sign, cardboard, girl atop bar of soap flanked by lettering, Have You A Little... on back, ca 1936, framed, EX, A3 .... **$275.00**

Fairy Soap, tip tray, ca 1936, little girl seated atop bar of soap, Have You A Little Fairy In Your Home? on rim, 4" dia, EX, A6 .... **$65.00**

Fairy Wings, cigar box label, inner lid, fairy floating through floral branch above large ship, NM, A5 .. **$65.00**

Falcon Motor Oil, can, product name above & below falcon flanked by Dependable & Tenacious, 1-qt, 5½x4" dia, NM, A6 .... **$35.00**

Falk Tobacco Co Highest Grade Smoking Tobacco, tin, green with black & gold lettering, fancy gold borders, 'Smokit' paper label on side, rectangular, NM, A18 .. **$50.00**

Falk's American Mixture, pocket tin, vertical, product name on paper label, 1909 tax stamp, 4½x3½", EX, A18 .... **$75.00**

Falls City Beer, can, flat-top, instructional, 12-oz, VG, A19 .... **$8.00**

Falls City Beer, display, molded plastic, horse statue on trapezoid base, Always A Winner above product name on oval, 10x10", EX+, A19 .... **$50.00**

Falls City Beer, sign, chalk mosaic hanger, On above & Tap below on oval border, product name in center, beveled edge, 10x13", EX+, A19 .... **$40.00**

Falstaff Beer, can, flat-top, Internal Revenue Tax Paid statement, 12-oz, EX+, A19 .... **$15.00**

Falstaff Beer, charger, shows 'Old World' lady in jeweled hat & high ruffled collar tipping glass, emblem on bust, 16" dia, VG+, A8 .... **$30.00**

Falstaff Beer, charger, shows bust of 'Old World' commoner holding Falstaff tankard, 16" dia, VG+, A8 .... **$30.00**

Falstaff Beer, charger, 3 ladies & gent in brewery with case of bottles on the floor reading ...Made In The Brewery Of Kemp, VG+, A19 .... **$200.00**

Falstaff Beer, mug, barrel shape with Falstaff in large script, 3½", EX, A8 .... **$140.00**

Falstaff Beer, postcard, Easter Greetings, shows large bottle & bunny with egg that changes color with humidity, very scarce, VG, A17 .... **$125.00**

Falstaff Beer, sign, celluloid, Premium Quality above name, The Choicest... below, gold & white on red, curved corners, 8x11", EX, A8 .... **$40.00**

Famous Beverwyck Ale, can, cone-top, 12-oz, VG, A19 .. **$52.00**

Fan Tan Gum, tray, product name above Oriental woman, gum packages on rim, 10½x13¼", G+, A9 .... **$250.00**

Fanita, cigar box label, outer, woman holding feather fan, 4½x4½", VG, D5 .... **$10.00**

Farm Bureau, sign, tin, Farm Bureau in red on key design in center, Member Empire State above & below, orange ground, 8x13", NOS, A6 .... **$85.00**

Farmer Seed & Nursery Co, catalog, 1932, 84 pgs, EX, D17 .... **$40.00**

Farmers Delight, tobacco label, EX, D35 .... **$6.00**

Farmers Lager Beer, coaster, lettering on bands around standing farmer, 'As Good As Ever,' red & black, 4" dia, EX, A8 .... **$40.00**

Farmers Pride Extra Quality Food Products, sign, canvas, tilted product can at left of product & company name, ca 1920, 18x36", VG+, A3 .... **$55.00**

Farnese, cigar box label, printer's proof, portrait on shaded background flanked by flowers, EX, A5 .... **$45.00**

Fashion Cut Plug Tobacco, lunch box, tin, yellow with dapper couple in early street scene left of product name, hinged lid, wire handle, EX, A18 .... **$120.00**

Fashion Cut Plug Tobacco, lunch box, tin, yellow with dapper couple in early street scene left of product name, hinged lid, wire handle, VG, A18 ....$50.00

Fast Mail Chewing Tobacco, pail, red & black product name above & below steam engine train, wire handle, no lid, Ginna, very rare, VG, A18 ....$385.00

Fast Mail Chewing Tobacco, pocket tin, flat, product name above & below steam engine train on lid, rounded corners, 2¼x3½", EX, A7......................$275.00

Fasteeth, tin, sample, Holds Dental Plates Firmly & Comfortable In The Mouth, shouldered top, 2⅛x1¼x¾", EX, D37...$20.00

Father John's Medicine, sign, paper, blue with yellow name & The Greatest Body Builder No Drugs left of oval image of doctor, 13x22", EX, A2 ....$155.00

Fatima Turkish Blend Cigarettes, can, holds 50 cigarettes, 3" dia, NM, A7......................................$80.00

Fatima Turkish Blend Cigarettes, pack, paper, Series 122 tax stamp, 85mm, unopened, M, D35...................$20.00

Fatima Turkish Blend Cigarettes, sign, cardboard, Every Time You See..., open pack & 20 For 15¢ above The Original...A Sensible Cigarette, 34x21", EX, A7 ....$50.00

Fatima Turkish Blend Cigarettes, sign, self-framed tin, oval image of veiled woman holding pack above name & 20 For 15 Cents, 22½x16½", EX, A18 ....$330.00

Fatima Turkish Blend Cigarettes, thermometer/barometer, porcelain, yellow with bulbs on white, graphics above & below, arched top, 28", EX, A18..........$210.00

Fauerbach Brewing Co, seltzer bottle, dome-shouldered with short neck, etched lettering, VG, A8 ....$20.00

Fauerbach CB, tap knob, chrome ball shape with red, white & gold enamel insert, EX-, A8 ....$140.00

Faust Bottled Beer/Anheuser-Busch, sign, debossed tin hanger, product name & 10¢ above company name, gold on red, beveled edge, 6x15", VG+, A8.......$185.00

Faust Dining Room & Cafe, pocket mirror, celluloid, photo image of child with stuffed animals, round, EX, A11 ....$110.00

Faust St Louis, mug, ceramic, devil posed with name, miniature, EX, A8 ....$215.00

Favorite Straight Cut Cigarettes, sign, tin flange, dog's head at left of product name & open pack, Liggett & Myers Tobacco Co, 9x18", EX, A13 ....$2,100.00

Favorite Straight Cut Cigarettes, sign, tin on cardboard, dog's head above name, 10 For 5¢ & open pack below, green field, 2-sided, 19x10", EX, A13 ....$1,500.00

Fawn Beverage, sign, tin, Drink above tilted bottle & product name, Try Our Orange below, 9x18", NM, D30 ....$120.00

Federal Judge Cigars, tin, vertical, cream with product name arched above eagle atop portrait, 5¢ & Mild on red emblems below, EX+, A18...........................$110.00

Federal Sugar Refining Co, sign, paper, factory scene near a bay with tugboats in the foreground, framed, image: 22x35", G, A9 ....$250.00

Federal Tires, sign, porcelain, 2-sided, Authorized Sales Agency...Extra Service, white on blue, 18x36", EX, A6 ....$110.00

Federal Trucks, calendar, 1946, paper, woman standing in pond with fish in net, trucks beyond, full pad, EX, A6 ....$75.00

Feen-A-Mint Chewing Gum Laxative, sign, paper on wood, product name on red oval flanked by flapper girl & product box, framed, 3¾x12", EX, A21......$40.00

Feen-a-mint Laxative, display cabinet, tin, woman taking laxative above open box, oval mirror on marquee, 16x7½x5", VG+, A9..$375.00

Feen-a-Mint Laxative, sign, laminated on wood, stand-up, lady touting Feen-A-Mint The Chewing Laxative, 1920s-30s, framed, 4x12", NM+, A13 ....$325.00

Feen-a-Mint Laxative, sign, porcelain, ...The Chewing Laxative on elongated oval flanked by product, Chew It Like Gum below, 8x30", VG, A6 ....$285.00

Fehr's Beer, sign, self-framed cardboard, 'It's Always Fehr Weather,' 1954 Indy 500 race scene with list of drivers, EX, A8 ....$100.00

Fehr's Beer, sign, self-framed tin, nymph holding up large bottle in front of sleeping elderly gent, pre-1920s, 28x22", VG, A19 ....$600.00

Fehr's Beer, tip tray/coaster, jockeys on horses encircle logo, raised rim, 4" dia, VG+, A8 ....$100.00

Fehr's Beer, tray, deep-dish, product name on red around classical scene, black rim, 16" dia, VG+, A19.......$45.00

Fehr's Malt-Tonic, sign, self-framed tin, The Fountain Of Health, A & eagle logo above bottle & maidens serving cherubs, 29x22", G, A21 ....$220.00

Feigenpan's Half & Half, sign, paper litho, bottle left of product name & 'The Real Strength...,' Newark NJ below, framed, 13x10", EX+, A19.........................$80.00

Feigenspan's, see also PON

Fell Beer, Ale & Porter, sign, reverse glass, red with We Serve... above product name & bottle on white triangle, company name below, NM, A19..............................$90.00

Fell Beer, Ale & Porter, sign, reverse glass, red with We Serve... above product name & bottle on white triangle, company name below, EX, A19 ....$60.00

Fels-Naptha, trolley sign, cardboard, Cleans And Cleans lettered all over background with large wrapped product bar, 11x21", EX+, A1 .... **$50.00**

Felsenbrau, tap knob, chrome ball with red & gold on black enamel insert, VG+, A8 .... **$100.00**

Fenwick, crate label, cranberry, spray of berries & green leaves, early 1900s, 7x10", M, D3 .... **$2.00**

Ferdinand de Alba, cigar box label, inner lid, Spanish military portrait, 6x9", M, D5 .... **$6.00**

Ferguson System, sign, self-framed tin, Tractors & Implements, Fischer Tractor Sales..., tractor above, blue & white, 36x60", VG, A6 .... **$100.00**

Ferguson System, sign, tin, This Farm Uses The Ferguson System, tractor above, 12x21", EX, D8 .... **$385.00**

Fern Glen Rye, sign, self-framed tin, 'I'se In A Perdickermunt,' black gent holding chicken & watermelon, 33x23", VG, A9 .... **$1,800.00**

Ferndell Coffee, tin, Ferndell in script above Steel Cut, Our Best Grade on band at top, key-wind lid, VG+, A3 .... **$30.00**

Ferry's Seeds, sign, paper, A Word To The Wise above owl, Buy...The Best That Crow, DM Ferry & Co, framed, 36x27", VG, A6 .... **$425.00**

Festival Brand Coffee, tin, product name on emblem above McFadden Coffee & Spice Co, pry lid, 1-lb, EX, A3 .... **$75.00**

FF Adams & Co Peerless Chew or Smoke, pail, yellow with black lettering around factory image, bail handle, EX+, A18 .... **$95.00**

Fido, crate label, California lemon, cartoon image of white pup with black spot over 1 eye, Orosi, 9x12", M, D12 .... **$30.00**

Field-Craft Cigars, box label set, Field-Craft on diagonal band across fields with horse-drawn equipment, 2 pcs, NM, A5 .... **$40.00**

Fiery Grapes, lug box label, arched white & red 3-D lettering on blue background, Lodi, M, D12 .... **$2.00**

Fiesta Mustard, tin, 3¾", NM, A7 .... **$110.00**

Filtered Gasoline, gas globe lens, red lettering on white, 15" dia, EX+, A6 .... **$65.00**

Fina, pump sign, die-cut porcelain shield, product name on center circle, red, white & blue, 9x8½", EX, A6 ... **$80.00**

Finzer, tobacco label, round, EX, D35 .... **$2.50**

Fire Brigade Cigars, mirror, reverse-painted, 5¢ in upper corners, Smoke... & Geo Yerkes & Co below, ornate gold frame, 15x27", EX, A21 .... **$360.00**

Fire-Chief Gasoline, see Texaco

Firestone, puzzle, pictures world map, Diamond Service Stores Inc, 15x11", G, A6 .... **$15.00**

Firestone Auto Supplies, catalog, Spring/Summer, 1944, 53 pgs, EX, D17 .... **$25.00**

Firestone Tires, sign, die-cut porcelain, Firestone Tires above logo & The Mark Of Quality, orange on blue, 31x36", EX+, A6 .... **$450.00**

Firestone Tires, sign, die-cut porcelain, Tires flanked by Gasoline Lubricants..., logo & Mark Of Quality below, 2-sided, 31x36", G, A6 .... **$180.00**

Firestone Tires, sign, reverse-painted glass, Tires flanked by Batteries Brake Lining & Spark Plug Accessories, VG, A6 .... **$275.00**

First Aid Syrup Co, pocket puzzle, celluloid, During & After The Game Refresh Yourself With..., green & yellow, round, EX, A11 .... **$30.00**

First Grade, cigar box label, inner lid, hand holding bouquet of flowers, 6x9", EX, D5 .... **$25.00**

First Mate, cigar box label, outer, portrait of young boy with ships beyond, EX, A5 .... **$45.00**

First Premium Lager Beer/KG Schmidt Brewing Co, label, product name on banner above gentleman with tankard, company name on red band below, 12-oz, EX+, A19 .... **$3.00**

First Roman, cigar box, 6x9", EX, A7 .... **$10.00**

First Trip Cigars, box label, salesman's sample, seated man in top hat surrounded by papers, EX, A5 .. **$125.00**

Fischbach's Weiss Beer, label, Fischbach Brewing Co, U-type permit number, Internal Revenue Tax Paid statement, 1933-36, 12-oz, NM, A10 .... **$35.00**

Fish Brown Farmer/Towers' Slickers, sign, paper, The Fish Brand Farmer above man in a Towers slicker, Everybody's Satisfied..., 1890, framed, 20x13", EX, A3 .... **$35.00**

Fisher Beer, salt & pepper shakers, bottle shape, NM, A8 .... **$30.00**

Fisher Bread, end label, pictures Tom Corbett, Back To Earth, red border, EX, D29 .... **$20.00**

Fisher Bread, end label, pictures Tom Corbett, Home Again, yellow border, EX, D29 .... **$20.00**

Fisher-Price Toys, dealer catalog, 1956, 16 pgs, EX, D17 .... **$100.00**

Fisher's Salted in the Shell Peanuts, canister, For Health's Sake Eat More Peanuts above logo on peanut background, pry lid, 25-lb, EX+, A3 .... **$140.00**

Fisk Rubber Co, see French Chalk

Fisk Tires, calendar, 1927, 'Time To Re-Tire,' white embossed image of boy in pajamas with tire & candle on blue, complete, VG+, A21 .... **$60.00**

Fisk Tires, display, cardboard, circus theme backdrop with die-cut pieces, instructions & game sheets, never used, 35x62", EX, D8 .... **$185.00**

113

Fisk Tires, emblem, brushed brass metal, molded boy with tire & candle atop bar embossed Time To Re-Tire, 5x3½", NM, A6 ....$400.00

Fisk Tires, jigsaw puzzle, 'Time To Re-tire,' boy in pajamas holding tire & candle, 1933, 11x9", EX, D10 ....$65.00

Fisk Tires, sign, porcelain, little boy with candle leaning on tire, Time To Re-Tire at right, Buy Fisk below, 36x28", NM, A6...................$900.00

Fisk Tires, sign, porcelain flange, blue, yellow & white, 20x25½", VG+, A6..................$70.00

Fitger's Beer, thermometer, metal, Everybody Here Likes... above bulb on pilsener glass, white background, curved corners, 12", VG+, A8...............$50.00

Fitzgerald Bro's Brewing Co, tray, pictures 2 women & 3 bottles with factory scene beyond, Export Lager... below, oval, 15x19", rare, EX, A9 ....$1,300.00

Fitzgerald Lager Beer, can, cone-top, EX+, A8.........$40.00

Five Bros Plug Tobacco, pouch, cloth, VG, A7 ....$8.00

Five G&G Quality Auto Fuses, tin, flat, American Can Co, ¼x1¼x1¾", EX, D37 ....$15.00

Five Roses Flour, door push, porcelain, product name above bouquet of roses, red on white with red border, 12x4", EX, D21 ....$260.00

Five Roses Flour, door push, porcelain, white lettering on red, 3x30", EX, D21 ....$60.00

Five Roses Flour, sign, die-cut cardboard stand-up, little girl in chef's hat holding basket of pies overhead, 20x18", NM, D21 ....$95.00

Five Roses Flour, sign, die-cut cardboard stand-up, little girl in chef's hat sitting in chair with mixing bowl, 20x18", NM, D21 ....$95.00

Five Roses Flour, sign, tin, Five Roses in red above The All-Purpose in black script underlined in red, white ground, 8½x27", NM, D21 ....$25.00

Five Roses Flour, thermometer, porcelain, Buy... above bulb, The All-Purpose Flour below, white on red, rounded ends, 39", EX+, D21 ....$180.00

Five Sons Cafe, matchbook, photo of 1 son on each stick, 20 strike, front strike, NM, D28 ....$3.00

Flag Beauty Cigars, box label, salesman's sample, woman with flag draped on her head & shoulders, EX, A5 ....$80.00

Flanagan-Nay, tray, deep-dish, product name & It's A Man's Beer lettered around man in bib overalls looking at glass, 12" dia, EX, A19 ....$260.00

Flaroma Coffee, tin, ETA logo flanked by Choicest & Selected, Grand Union Tea Co, Brooklyn NY below, 1-lb, EX, A3 ....$55.00

Fleetwood Aero Craft Motor Oil, can, Fleetwood on band above aerial view of military-type single-engine plane, 2500 Miles of Lubrication, 1-qt, VG+, A1............$650.00

Fleischmann's Yeast, sign, cardboard, Good? Sure!!..., boy handing loaf of bread over fence to girl, 1880s, 2-sided, 15x11", EX+, A3............$450.00

Fletcher Manufacturing Co, paperweight, glass, company name & other lettering arched above aerial factory view, oval, M, D13 ....$60.00

Fletcher's Rosebud Cayenne Pepper, container, cardboard, product name above & below 2 red roses, 1 ½-oz, EX+, A3 ....$45.00

Fli-Line Dress, tin, 2½" dia, NM, A7......................$9.00

Flint's Powders for Horses & Cattle, sign, cardboard, encircled horse head at left of product name & Made Of Pure Drugs, red, yellow & black, 6x23", VG, A6 ....$300.00

Flor de Alcino Cigars, box label, salesman's sample, framed portrait of a woman surrounded by medallions & ornate design, M, A5 ....$52.00

Flor de Belar Cigars, sign, self-framed tin, product name flanked by cigars, Perfection Of Quality below, gold background, 1915, 8x10", NM, A3 ....$95.00

Flor de Dindigul, cigar box label, outer, black boy flanked by white elephants, 4½x4½", M, D5....................$25.00

Flor de F Garcia Y Hermano, cigar box label, inner lid, Cuban & bare-breasted Indian, 1887, EX, D5.......$25.00

Flor de Franklin Cigars, tin, vertical, shows Franklin flying kite, EX, A18 ....$105.00

Flor de Franklin 5¢ Cigar, sign, cardboard hanger, name above lady stepping from coach to waiting man in top hat, 5¢ Cigar below, 9x7½", G, A2......................**$145.00**

Flor de Moss Cigars, sign, cardboard, plane shining spotlight on side of hill behind 2 men on veranda, arched top, 37x28", VG, A6......................**$245.00**

Flor de Salzburg Havana Cigars/Goetz Cigar Company, sign, self-framed tin, hanger or stand-up, oval image of town with river & mountains, name above & below, 7x10", EX, A18......................**$200.00**

Florida Department of Citrus, bank, Florida Orange Bird, plastic, 1970s, 5", M......................**$30.00**

Flying A, emblem, embossed porcelain, red & white winged A embossed on black circle with wings protruding, 9x13", VG+, A1......................**$335.00**

Flying A, pump sign, porcelain, winged A in red on white oval in center, red background, 8x15", M, D11 ...**$200.00**

Flying A Aero-Type Gasoline, sign, porcelain, white winged-A logo shadowed in green, red background with green border, 2-sided, 36" dia, EX, A1....**$1,000.00**

Flying A Aero-Type Gasoline, sign, porcelain, winged-A logo in white shadowed in green, red background with green border, 2-sided, 36" dia, NM, A1..........**$1,700.00**

Flying A Gasoline, pump sign, porcelain, winged-A logo in red shadowed in black, white background, 10x10", EX+, A1......................**$180.00**

Flying A Kerosene, gas globe, winged-A logo in center, white on red, 3-pc glass with red metal bands, 13½" dia, NM, A6......................**$750.00**

Flying A Service, salt & pepper shakers, plastic gas pumps, red & green with winged-A logo, 3", scarce, EX+, A1......................**$325.00**

Flying A Service, sign, die-cut porcelain, large winged-A in center, red, white, blue & black, 55" wingspan, 42" dia, VG+, A6......................**$650.00**

Flynn & Doyle, calendar, 1909, 'A Twentieth Century Hold Up,' from a painting by Bengough, full pad, framed, 13x15", EX, A6......................**$110.00**

Folger's Coffee, jigsaw puzzle, shows coffee can with oval image of ships, original tin container, NM, A3.....**$45.00**

Folger's Ginger, tin, 3¼", NM, A7......................**$50.00**

Folger's Golden Gate Mace, tin, red with white lettering above & below circular image of ship at sea, dial top, 2-oz, EX+, A3......................**$45.00**

Fond Hearts, cigar box label, outer, man serenading woman with mandolin, 4½x4½", EX, D5 ....**$30.00**

Fontenac Brand Peanut Butter, tin, 12-oz, bail missing, EX+, A8......................**$55.00**

Fontenac White Cap Ale & Special Lager Beer, tray, deep-dish, porcelain, Fontenac on white in center, products above & below, white ground, 13" dia, VG+, A1......................**$40.00**

Foot-Schulze Shoes, shoe holder/display, wood-grained tin, product name & outstretched hand on oval in center, 18½", EX, A3......................**$80.00**

Forbes Quality Gas Roasted Coffee, tin, sample, name & logo against light blue & white line design, gold slip lid, 2¼x3" dia, EX, D37......................**$160.00**

Ford, charcoal grill, metal portable box with Use Ford Charcoal Briquets embossed on front, with 2 boxes of charcoal, EX, A6......................**$210.00**

Ford, clock, metal & glass light-up, octagon shape, oval logo above Sales & Service, Parts & Accessories, 18x18", VG+, A6......................**$750.00**

Ford, fan, cardboard, open car with passengers & mountain scene, 5 other models on handle, green text on back, 11x8", VG, A6......................**$85.00**

Ford, pin-back button, tin, 100% Ford, 1½" dia, VG, A7..**$10.00**

Ford, pin-back button, tin, 1932, ¾", NM, A7 ....**$20.00**

Ford, sign, porcelain, Ford Genuine Parts, oval, 16x24", NM, D8......................**$675.00**

Ford, sign, porcelain, Ford Genuine Parts, oval, 16x24", VG+, A1......................**$425.00**

Ford, sign, porcelain, Ford Parts Dept, white on blue, 18x24", EX, D8......................**$775.00**

Ford, tire pressure gauge, Ford Model A, green with blue & red lettering, 2x3", NM, A6......................**$120.00**

Ford Cigars, box, wood, lid with name in black script in cloud of smoke from cigar, 5¢ symbol upper right, 9x5½", VG, A6......................**$160.00**

Ford Sales & Service/Deary Garage, sign, embossed tin, lettering on sleeve of arm with hand pointing finger, black on yellow, 7x28", EX, A1......................**$425.00**

Fore 'n Aft Sliced Plug, sign, cardboard, bearded pipe-smoking fisherman tending to line in boat, open product box in foreground, 23x15", EX, A18............**$250.00**

Foremost Buttermilk, sign, embossed tin, carton shape, 30x15", NOS, D11.................................$135.00

Forest & Stream Pipe Tobacco, pocket tin, vertical, red with white product name on black bands above & below duck in flight on white oval, VG+, A18 ....$80.00

Forest & Stream Pipe Tobacco, pocket tin, vertical, red with white product name on black bands above & below duck in flight on white oval, EX+, A18...$115.00

Forest & Stream Tobacco, can, red lettering above & below 2 fishermen in canoe, 1 fisherman on reverse, key-wind (?), EX+, A18 ....$535.00

Forest & Stream Tobacco, canister, red with name above & below oval image of man fishing in stream, red & gold striped dome lid, small, EX, A18..$225.00

Forest & Stream Tobacco, pocket tin, vertical, red with white product name above & below fishermen in canoe in mountain stream, EX, A18....................$250.00

Forest & Stream Tobacco, pocket tin, vertical, red with white product name above & below fishermen in canoe in mountain stream, NM, A18 ....$385.00

Forest & Stream Tobacco, pocket tin, vertical, red with white product name above & below fisherman standing in stream, VG+, A18...$110.00

Forest Brew, label, August Schell Co, L-type permit number, 1928-33, 12-oz, M, A10 ....$18.00

Fort Bedford Peanuts, pin-back button, I Eat Fort Bedford Peanuts lettered around girl's head, 1" dia, VG, A7 ..$7.00

Fort Dearborn, cigar box label, outer, pictures Fort Dearborn, Randall-Landfield Co Makers on banner below, NM, A5 ....$80.00

Fort Dearborn Regular Rolled Oats, container, cardboard, red, yellow & blue with circular inset of fort over silhouette cityscape, 3-lb, no lid, VG+, A3..$40.00

Fort Garry Coffee, pail, Making Friends Everywhere above inset of Indians, canoers, soldiers & fort, bail handle, 5-lb, EX, A3...$200.00

Fort Pitt Beer, can, flat-top, instructional, product name above & below waiter running with full glass on tray, VG, A19 ....$400.00

Fort Pitt Beer & Ale, display, plaster, figural hand with lettered cuff positioned to hold glass, VG+, A8 ....$85.00

Fort Pitt Beer & Old Shay Ale, dinner plate, lettering & lines on rim, 10" dia, EX, A19..............................$10.00

Fort Pitt Special Beer, sign, light-up, reverse glass, Fort Pitt on black left of Special Beer, 1940s, metal frame, horizontal, EX, A19 ....$175.00

Fort Pitt Special Beer, sign, tin, round with product name on fancy shield, gold decoration on red around rim, EX+, A19 ....$65.00

Fort York Coffee, tin, 'Refreshes & Revives' above product name & image flanked by Vacuum Fresh, pry lid missing, 1-lb, EX+, A3..........................$65.00

Forthoffer's Creme De Minth Cola/Doles' Pineapple Nectarade, sign, cardboard stand-up, man with paper & pipe upside down & lady's bow string caught on his lapel, 1910, 9x7", VG+, A3...................................$85.00

Fortune Gasoline, sign, porcelain, pictures horseshoe & 4-leaf clovers in center, 11½x11½", M, D11.........$175.00

Foss Schneiser Brewing Co/Nonpareil Export Lager Beer, drinking glass, embossed stem, 6", NM, A8...$90.00

Foster Hose Supporters, sign, celluloid, The Name Is On The Buckles, woman superimposed over corset with supporters, 17x9", EX+, A9..............................$275.00

Foster Hose Supporters, sign, celluloid, The Name Is On The Buckles, woman superimposed over corset with supporters, 17x9", VG, A21 ....$110.00

Foster's Cherry Smash, see Cherry Smash

Foster's Old Fashioned Freeze, sign, die-cut porcelain, can shape, blue & white, 11½x6", NM, D11 ......$300.00

Fountain Fine Cut Tobacco, tin, product name around circular image of fountain, gold on blue, 1-lb, 2x8" dia, EX+, A18 ....$152.00

Fountain Fine Cut Tobacco, tin, product name around circular image of fountain, gold on blue, 1-lb, 2x8" dia, VG, A18...$75.00

Fountain Sand & Gravel Co, sign, porcelain, Red-E-Mix Concrete on emblem in center, Lincoln 4-5451 below, 16x24", VG+, D11..$75.00

Four Roses Smoking Tobacco, pocket tin, vertical, company name & product name above oval image of roses, VG+, A3 ....$220.00

Four Roses Smoking Tobacco, pocket tin, vertical, embossed, red & silver with product name above & below red roses, 4¼", EX+, A18 ....$450.00

Four Roses Smoking Tobacco, pocket tin, vertical, product name above & below red roses on vertically striped background, G+, A18...$115.00

Four Roses Whiskey, sign, self-framed tin, oval image of 2 men betting on cock fight, 24x20", G-, A9 ....$150.00

Four Star, crate label, Washington apple, large number 4 with 4 stars on blue background, Cashmere, 9x11", M, D12..$2.00

Fowler's Cherry Smash, see Cherry Smash

Fowler's Root Beer, syrup dispenser, ceramic potbelly shape, Drink...5¢ 'The Best,' brown on white, 15x9" dia, VG, A4 ....$440.00

Fowler's Root Beer, syrup dispenser, ceramic potbelly shape, Drink...5¢ 'The Best,' brown on white, 15x9" dia, NM, A1..$1,075.00

Fox DeLuxe Beer, can, flat-top, instructional, huntsman blowing horn above product name, 12-oz, EX, A19 ....$55.00

Fox DeLuxe Beer, can, flat-top, 12-oz, bottom cut out otherwise EX+, A19 ....$15.00

Fox DeLuxe Beer, sign, celluloid, cardboard back, huntsman blowing horn, black, gold & white on red, 9" dia, EX, A8 ....$95.00

Fox DeLuxe Beer, tap knob, chrome ball with red, black & gold on white insert, EX, A8 ....$45.00

Fox Head '400,' tap knob, chrome with brown, gold & cream celluloid insert with logo & product name, 2" dia, VG+, A8 ....$70.00

Fox Head '400' Beer, sign, tin on cardboard, encircled fox logo above product name, Brewed With... below, beveled edge, 7½x11", NM, A8 ....$35.00

Fox's Cherry, drinking glass, modified flared top, fluted, fox head above name, NM, A16 ....$95.00

Fra-Bac Mixture, pocket tin, vertical, The Better Pipe Tobacco above encircled name divided by red band, black, red & white with gold lid, NM, A18 .....$1,650.00

Fram Filter Service, thermometer, tin, red & black lettering above bulb, shows filter below, cream ground, red border, 39x8", NM, D8 ....$425.00

Frank E Davis Fish Co, pocket mirror, lettering around colorful image of hand holding fish & lobster, horizontal oval, 2¾", EX, A21 ....$190.00

Frank Mayo, cigar box label, inner lid, theatrical mask, man & flame, 6x9", M, D5 ....$6.00

Frank X Schwab Beer, label, St Marys Beverage Co, U-type permit number, Internal Revenue Tax Paid statement, 1933-36, 12-oz, M, A10 ....$28.00

Frank's Bar, sign, paper, patriotic image of Victory with flag & eagle surmounting the world, framed, image: 19½x15", VG, A9 ....$150.00

Frank's Old Fashioned Beer, label, M Frank & Son Brewery, Internal Revenue Tax Paid statement, 1933-40, 12-oz, EX, A10 ....$50.00

Frank's Pale Dry Ginger Ale, sign, tin, Frank's Is The Best on red oval above tilted bottle & other lettering, white ground, 30x12", M, D30 ....$95.00

Frank's Quality Beverages, bottle topper, shows smiling girl left of product lettering, EX, A7 ....$8.00

Frank's Quality Beverages, sign, cardboard, product name on emblem & tilted bottle above list of flavors, 28x12", NM, D30 ....$75.00

Frank's Root Beer, can, cone-top, lettered shield logo, VG+, A16 ....$25.00

Frankenmuth Beer & Ale, display, plaster, dachshund sitting on hind legs on base marked with product name, EX+, A8 ....$55.00

Frankenmuth Beer & Ale, display, plaster, dachshund sitting on hind legs on base marked with product name, VG, A8 ....$20.00

Franklin Mills Wheatlet Cereal, thermometer/barometer, wood & tin, 'Wheatlet Is Eaten & Enjoyed In All Kinds Of Weather,' 9x3", VG+, A21 ....$50.00

Franz Bartl Brewing Co, pocket mirror, celluloid, oval barrel shape with eagle & company name on end, EX, A11 ....$135.00

Fred Edgar Washburn Musical Instruments, sign, die-cut porcelain, Fred Edgar on banner above banjo, guitar & mandolin, 1900-05, 2-sided, 24x18", EX+, A13 ....$3,000.00

Fred Krug Brewing Co, mug, heavy clear glass with etched circular logo above name, 5", EX, A8 .....$100.00

Fred Krug Brewing Co, mug, miniature, ceramic, barrel shape with circular logo above name & city, EX, A8 ....$155.00

Fred Sehring Brewing Co, mug, ceramic, 1868 & 1903 flank shield above factory scene, company name & Joliet Ill below, EX+, A8 ....$85.00

Fred's 4 Crown Beer, label, Frederick's Brewing Co, Internal Revenue Tax Paid statement, 12-oz, M, A10 ..$10.00

Fredericks of Hollywood, catalog, Spring, 1976, 76 pgs, EX, D17 ....$25.00

Free Flags Cigars, box label, salesman's sample, patriotic image with eagle atop shield flanked by flags, Smoke..., VG, A5 ....$135.00

Freedom FC Motor Oil, can, bulldog atop Freedom above FC on emblem with diagonal corners flanked by stripes, Motor Oil below, 1-qt, VG, A1 ....$25.00

Freedom Perfect Motor Oil, can, bulldog atop Freedom above Perfect Motor Oil & Vacuum Process on circle with bands protruding, 1-qt, NM, A1 ....$290.00

Freedom Perfect Motor Oil, sign, porcelain, 100% Pure Pennsylvania Oil logo above product name, yellow & blue, 2-sided, 23½" dia, VG, A6 ....$125.00

Freimann's Old Lager Beer, label, encircled Indian head upper left of product lettering, 12-oz, EX, A19 ....$12.00

Fremlins Ale, sign, die-cut porcelain, elephant shape with name on red back blanket, 9x12", VG+, A8.......**$220.00**

Fremont Gas Market, whetstone, celluloid, Gas With Us, Eat At Al's Cafe, black & yellow, round, EX, A11 ..**$12.00**

French Chalk/Fisk Rubber Co, tin, green with white graphics & lettering, tall & round with domed slip lid, 7½x1½" dia, NM, A18 ....**$25.00**

French's Prepared Mustard, sign, porcelain, Cream Salad Brand, product jar left of yellow & white text on red, 1920s-30s, 15x30", VG+, A13 ....$350.00

Fresno Bohemian Export Beer, label, Fresno Brewing Co, Internal Revenue Tax Paid statememt, 1933-50, 11-oz, M, A10...**$15.00**

Friars Ale, print, paper lithograph, friar seated by fireplace drinking from stein, bread & knife atop upright keg, 23x18", EX, A8 ....**$85.00**

Frictionless Metal Co, sign, self-framed tin, 'The Metal That Never Fails' above nude boy holding up metal bar, 22x16", VG, A9...**$500.00**

Friendly Cola, soda glass, red logo, Friendly Cola on 1 side, The Only Cola Served In This Shop on the other, 5x2½", M, D16...**$20.00**

Friendship Cut Plug, alarm clock, Chew... on yellow around white numbered band encircling man's face, round footed case, 1885, EX, A2........................**$935.00**

Friendship Tobacco, pocket tin, flat, litho on 2 sides, VG, D35...**$65.00**

Frigidaire, pin-back button, image of Uncle Sam tipping his hat, Hats Off To The New Frigidaire, EX, A20 ....**$12.00**

Frigidaire Electric Refrigerating System, sign, porcelain, Equipped With above product name, white on cobalt blue, 7x24", NM, A1 ....**$150.00**

Frigidtest Anti-Freeze, can, Frigidtest on white band above plane flying over eclipse & 2 polar bears, Anti-Freeze below, round, 1-gal, EX/G, A1.................**$40.00**

Frings 3 Bros Cigars, door push, yellow with black Frings Cigars above red 3 Bros, yellow lettering on black shield below, 9x3½", NM, A18 ....**$80.00**

Frisch's Big Boy, see Big Boy

Fritzie's/Gettleman Brewing Co, sign, die-cut wood, white-bearded man running in front of billboard reading Fritzie's Going Places, 6x10", VG, A8 ....**$45.00**

Front Row Cigars, box label, salesman's sample, 3 smiling men with binoculars, EX, A5 ....**$90.00**

Frontenac Brand Peanut Butter/Gannon Grocery Co, pail, logo above Frontenac lettered diagonally, NM, A3 ....**$45.00**

Frontier, gas globe, black silhouette of man on rearing stallion, Rearin'-To-Go, red & white ground, plastic body, 14" dia, NM, A6...**$375.00**

Frontier 1846 Brand Pure Rolled White Oats, container, hunters checking their shot on large elk, Naves-McCord Mercantile Co, 54-oz, NM, A3...........................**$600.00**

Frostie Old Fashion Root Beer, bottle, full, NM, A7...**$10.00**

Frostie Root Beer, thermometer, tin, figure behind bottle cap above bulb, 6-pack carton below, 30", EX, D30 ....**$125.00**

Frostop Root Beer, mug, glass, yellow logo, Icy Cold Frostop Root Beer, 6x3", M, D16...........................**$15.00**

Fry's Cocoa, sign, embossed tin, black boy flanked by 300 Gold Medals & Pure Concentrated, framed, image: 17½x11½", G, A9 ....**$600.00**

Fry's Cocoa/Fry's Milk Chocolate, postcard, 'Cocoa, Sah!,' name above smiling black boy holding up large cocoa bean & box of candy bars, British, NM, D26...$125.00

Fry's Pure Breakfast Cocoa, tin, sample, lid shows The Largest Seller In Canada upper left of tilted can, rounded corners, ½x2x2⅜", EX, D37 ....**$70.00**

Full Dress, pocket tin, vertical, gold with red oval image of man in tuxedo & top hat, beveled edges, EX+, A18 ....**$360.00**

Full Dress, tin, horizontal box, pictures elegant couple (no lettering), rounded corners, 2x5x3¾", EX, A18 ..**$275.00**

Full Dress Pipe & Cigarette Tobacco, pocket tin, vertical, tan with name above & below 3-quarter image of man in tuxedo, Sears Roebuck & Co, EX, A18..........**$535.00**

Fuller Furniture Polish, tin, sample, with contents, 2½", NM, A7 ....**$20.00**

Fuller's Pure Prepared Paint, sign, embossed tin, Use... above Made Of Pioneer White Lead, Oxide Of Zinc..., yellow on black, 5x28", EX+, A1 ....**$10.00**

Fulmer Ice Cream, sign, porcelain, One Of The Good Things... below product name on oval, red, white & blue, 2-sided, 24x34", NM, A1 ....**$85.00**

Fulton Electric Sleet-Frost Shield, sign, cardboard, colorful image of busy street scene during a storm, red & blue lettering, 12½x21", EX+, A6 ....**$80.00**

Fun-To-Wash Washing Powder, box, product name above & below mammy's head, with contents, 3¼", NM, A7 ....**$35.00**

Funk's Hybrid, sign, tin, EX, D34 ....**$30.00**

G Biedermann & Co Port Washington Wisconsin, drinking glass, straight-sided with flat bottom, etched lettering above & below initial logo, 3½", EX, A8 .... **$70.00**

Gabriel Snubbers, sign, cardboard, car driving past scene of little boy tying bull to tree, Gabriel & Only Gabriel..., 16x26", VG+, A6 .... **$1,100.00**

Gaddis Blueberries, can label, 2 images of blueberries in cut glass bowl, Maine, 6x10", M, D3 ....**$2.00**

Gail & Ax Navy Tobacco, cigarette papers, NM, A7. **$18.00**

Gail & Ax Navy Tobacco, sign, paper, lettering at right of sailor standing with foot on product box, yellow field, 1915, framed, 42x32", EX, A13 .... **$350.00**

Gail & Ax Tobacco, trade card, paper litho, Baron Munchausen Series H764, 3x6", EX, D35 .... **$55.00**

Galena Processed Motor Boat Oil SAE No 30, can, Galena arched above topless mermaids logo, product name below, pour spout & handle, 1-gal, 10x9x3", EX, A1 .... **$300.00**

Galleon, crate label, California lemon, galleon sailing high seas, Oxnard, ca 1937, 12x9", M, D3 .... **$5.00**

Galliano Root Beer, baby mug, plastic, white logo, NM, D16 .... **$12.00**

Galveston Brewing Co, mug, miniature, ceramic, Drink 'High Grade'... with grain & hops design, EX, A8 .... **$110.00**

Gamble's De Luxe Coffee, tin, G/S logo above product name & Distributed By Gamble Stores, key-wind lid, NM, A3 .... **$45.00**

Game Fine Cut/Jno J Bagley & Co, store bin, grouse in brush flanked by lettering, rectangular, 7x12", EX+, A18 .... **$500.00**

Gamecock Cream Ale/Cumberland Brewing Co, can, pull-tab, green & red on white, 12-oz, NM, A19.. **$35.00**

Gander Brand Cooking & Salad Oil, sign, tin, woman being served by black servant, 'Makes Good Things To Eat,' framed, image: 13x19", VG, A9 .... **$950.00**

Garcia Grande Cigar, tip tray, Don't Be Fooled on yellow above Ask For Full Name... on red band, black lettering on rim, rectangular, EX, A18 .... **$25.00**

Gardenia Face Powder/Richard Hudnut, tin, sample, white floral & gold web design around lettering on light blue, ¼x1½x1½", EX, D37, minimum value **$50.00**

Garfield Manor, cigar box label, outer, cluster of houses, 1934, 4½x4½", M, D5 .... **$25.00**

Gargoyle, see also Mobiloil or Vacuum 'B' Mobiloil

Gargoyle Specialty Greases, service box, wood, white with red Gargoyle & black lettering, hinged lid with locking clasps & handle, 8x25", G+, A1 .... **$80.00**

Garland Stoves & Ranges, broom holder, product name on emblem flanked by floral garlands, EX+, A15 .... **$150.00**

Garland Stoves & Ranges, pocket mirror, celluloid, Michigan Stove Co above logo & Largest Makers Of Stoves In The World, oval, EX, A11 .... **$20.00**

Garrett & Co, tray, 'Paul & Virginia,' scantily clad couple frolicking around woods, lettering on red rim, 12" dia, G, A21 .... **$160.00**

Garrett's Snuff, tin, sample, with contents, NM, A7... **$15.00**

Garrett's XXXX Baker Rye, pocket mirror, celluloid, image of woman in transparent veil holding bow, Oldest Brand In Baltimore, oval, 3x2", G-, A9 .... **$185.00**

Garrick Smoking Mixture, canister, paper on tin, pictures a sphinx & lettering on front, shows Abel Drugger on back, 4½x3" dia, EX, A3 .... **$25.00**

Gates Fan Belts, display rack, wood with 3 rows of hooks for different size fan belts, 47x23", VG+, A6 .... **$30.00**

Gateway Motor Co Ford Service, sign, die-cut tin arm with pointing finger, lettering on sleeve, ...Wilsall, Mont, 6½x28", EX, A9 .... **$225.00**

Gay Paree, cigar box label, salesman's sample, ballerina resting on wall in front of tree, 1900, VG, A5 ...... **$55.00**

Gayrock Clothing, sign, embossed tin, pictures dapperly dressed man, FS Burberry...Kohn Brothers, framed, image: 39½x27½", VG, A6 .... **$450.00**

GB Bock Beer/Grace Bros Brewing Co, can, flat-top, 12-oz, EX, A19 .... **$35.00**

GBS Eigenbrot Brewery Schiller Beer, sign, tin, GBS on diamond flanked by filigree design above company & product name, beveled edge, pre-1920, 9x13", EX, A8 .... **$40.00**

GE, clock, white cast-metal monitor-top refrigerator with clock face on front, 8x4", EX, A21 .... **$145.00**

GE, sign, die-cut porcelain, white icebox with blue trim & large logo on door, 2-sided, 36", extremely rare, VG+, A21 .... **$4,510.00**

GE, see also General Electric

Gebhart's Gold Comet Motor Oil, can, shows product name & image of comet streaking to foreground, blue, red, white & yellow on black, 1-qt, NM, A1 ...... **$120.00**

Geissler's Shoes, pocket mirror, colorful image of woman surrounded by gold lettering, Wear..., EX+, D18 .... **$125.00**

Gem Beer, label, Walter Bros Brewing Co, Internal Revenue Tax Paid statement, 1933-50, 12-oz, EX, A10 .... **$10.00**

Gem Cafe, note pad, celluloid with metal frame, Gem Cafe, Newest & Most Modern Cafe In Alaska..., 2x1½", EX, A11 .... **$85.00**

Gem City Ice Cream, sign, embossed tin, We Sell..., carton of ice cream at left, yellow, blue & red, 9¼x20", EX, A6 .... **$20.00**

Gem Damaskeene Blade Co, mirror, die-cut tin, man, baby & product packages on wood-textured surface with beveled mirror in center, 18x10", G, A9 ..... **$300.00**

Gem of the Lake, crate label, California pear, 3-D lettering above large pear on blue background, Sacramento, 8x11", M, D12 .... **$2.00**

Gem Safety Razor, tin, vertical, name flanks man shaving, gold & brown, slip lid, 1⅜x2¼x1½", EX, D37...**$100.00**

Gemesee All Malt, can, flat-top, instructional, 12-oz, NM, A19...**$125.00**

General Electric, see also GE

General Electric, figure, jointed wood drum major, design by Maxfield Parrish, 18½", missing hat plume & belt, VG+, A1....................................$400.00

General Electric, watch fob, shaped like a stove, EX, A20 ....**$40.00**

General Electric Edison Lamps, box, natural wood with red & green Christmas graphics, 7x6x13", EX+, A18...**$115.00**

General Electric Lamps, display, metal & glass, displays 8 bulbs on top, GE logo & bulb surrounded by advertising on front, 18x27", VG, A6 ....**$210.00**

General Electric Radiotrons, sign, cardboard, lettered scroll on red background, Made In Canada on black band at bottom, 15x15", EX, D21 ....**$20.00**

General Electric Radiotrons, sign, cardboard, 7 men spelling out Service on their jackets above advertising, 17x15", EX+, D21 ....**$25.00**

General Gasoline & Lubricants, sign, porcelain, General Petroleum Corporation above General on center band, green, black & white, 30" dia, VG, A6..$275.00

General Motor Fuel, gas globe, General on diagonal band over shield with knight atop, yellow, red & black, white metal body, 15" dia, NM, A6 ....**$500.00**

General Motors, sign, embossed tin, yellow General Motors vertically lettered on blue, used on GM diesel engines, 29x3¼", NOS, EX, A1 ....**$70.00**

General Sherman, cigar box label, salesman's sample, portrait surrounded by shield, flags & vignettes, NM, A5 ....**$215.00**

General Water Heaters, sign, porcelain, 6x19", NM+, D11...**$60.00**

Genesee Beer, sign, cardboard with stand, Enjoy The Holiday above Genesee billboard & convertible, Drive Carefully! below, VG+, A19 ....**$15.00**

Genesee Beer, sign, tin on cardboard, shows couple from waist down seated back to back on cooler, beveled edge, 7x15", EX, A3...**$50.00**

Genesee Lager Beer, sign, plastic, Great Beer Then...And Now above factory scene on green background, product name below, 14x20", VG, A8 ....**$30.00**

Genesee Lager Beer, sign, tin litho, rectangular tray shape with 2 gentlemen seated at table on bow of ship, wood-grain rim, 18x26", EX, A19 ....**$60.00**

Genesee 12 Horse Ale, tray, deep-dish, product name above & below horse-drawn wagon, NM, A19..$40.00

Genesse, sign, light-up, red cut-out lettering on metal base marked On Draught with backdrop that lights up, 7x12", EX, A8..**$75.00**

Gentiane-Kola, sign, embossed tin, enthusiastic girl holding up glass, large bottle in foreground, 19½x14", EX, A9 ....**$500.00**

Genuine German Beer, label, H Clausen & Son Brewing Co, pre-prohibition, NM, A10 ....**$22.00**

Genuine Rail Road Mills Snuff, trade card, 4 monkeys in tops hats hanging on a bar, 3x5", VG+, A5 ....**$18.00**

Geo Ehret's Extra, tray, deep-dish, name surrounds initial star logo flanked by Hellgate & Brewery on scrolled banners, 12" dia, EX, A8.................................**$100.00**

Geo Ehret's Extra, tray, deep-dish, name surrounds initial star logo flanked by Draught & Beer on scrolled banners, 12" dia, VG, A19...**$40.00**

Geo Walter's Adler Brau, foam scraper, gray on white, EX, A8 ....**$55.00**

Geo Wiedemann Brewing Co, sign, cardboard, elderly gent reading paper & enjoying a glass of brew by crate, framed, 19x20", EX+, A19 ....**$65.00**

Geo Wiedemann Brewing Co, see also Wiedemann's

George Lawrence Co Dog Chains & Leads, display/sign, metal, diagonal square with holes at 2 bottom edges to display product, dog & text above, 7x7", EX, A8..**$70.00**

George Thatcher's Minstrels, sign, paper, comical baseball scene with fancy border, Darktown Brotherhood vs Blackwell League, image: 29x40", G+, A9.......**$4,500.00**

George Vanderbilt Cup/Roosevelt Raceway, sign, cardboard litho, pictures American & foreign flags above blue race car, Columbus Day, October 12th, 21x14", EX, A6 ....**$1,000.00**

George W Childs 5¢ Cigar, sign, embossed tin, bold product name with Generously Good! above 5¢, 16½x36", VG, A9 ....$70.00

George Walters Bock Beer, label, George Walter Brewing Co, Internal Revenue Tax Pid statement, 1933-50, 12-oz, M, A10..$30.00

George Washington Cut Plug, tobacco pouch, cloth, oval image of Washington with stars & product name against striped background, NM, A7....................$28.00

George Washington Instant Coffee, tin, rectangular, 3-cup size, NM, A7 ....$25.00

George Washington's Coffee, tin, G Washington's in script above Instant Coffee & steaming cup, 16-oz, VG+, A3 ....$25.00

Geraldine, cigar box label, outer, country girl in straw hat, 4½x4½", EX, D5 ....$10.00

Germania Brewing Co/Chammer's High Grade Bottled Beers, tip tray, girl holding flowers, lettered rim, 4" dia, NM, A8...$165.00

Gerst Bock Beer, label, W Gerst Brewing Co, U-type permit number, Internal Revenue Tax Paid statement, 1933-36, 12-oz, A10..$20.00

Gettelman, tap knob, chrome ball with white & gold on dark brown insert, VG+, A8 ....$55.00

Gettelman Bock Beer, label, Gettelman Brewing Co, Internal Revenue Tax Paid statement, 1933-50, 12-oz, NM, A10..$12.00

Getty, radio, pocket transistor, shaped like gas pump with hose & nozzle, red, white & chrome, 5x2", EX, A6 ..$45.00

Getty Oil Co, sign, porcelain, company name on band above Headlee Devonian Un RRC No 20084 left of Well No 57-1, 12x24", NM, A7 ....$40.00

Gettysburg, see Venable Tobacco Co

Getup, sign, tin, Drink above Getup lettered on individual ovals, striped background, It's King-Size below, 14x24", NM, D30..$65.00

Giant Brand Roasted Coffee, pail, shield logo in center, slip lid & bail, EX, A3 ....$120.00

Gibbons Beer, sign, cardboard, die-cut, If It's Gibbons... on card above hand-held glass & bottle, Best Beer In Town!, 14x9", VG, A19..$20.00

Gibbons Beer, sign, cardboard stand-up, die-cut bottle with IRTP label, Dependable Quality on base, 17x7", EX, A1 ....$25.00

Gibbons Beer, sign, cardboard stand-up, name above bust image of lady in suit & hat with glass, beveled edge, 1940s, 30x21", NM, A19 ....$75.00

Gibbons Beer, sign, tin on cardboard, Gibbons above bottle on 2-tone blue background, Enjoyed Everywhere below, embossed, VG, A19 ....$150.00

Gibbons Beer, tray, white, red & black, 13", NM, D7 ..$10.00

Gibbons Premium Quality Beer, can, cone-top, NM, A8...$65.00

Gibbs & Co, catalog, 1965, 104 pgs, EX, D17 ....$30.00

Giblin's Liniment, display case, wood with 2 glass front doors & 2 shelves, product name across top, 26x24x8", G, A9 ....$400.00

Gillett's Lye, sign, cardboard, ...'It's Flaked' above woman using product & An Old Friend In New And Improved Form, 11x21", EX, D21.....................................$70.00

Gillette, display case, wood with hinged glass top, 2x18x14", EX+, A18..$100.00

Gillette Blue Blades, matchbook, 20 strike, front strike, NM, D28..$2.00

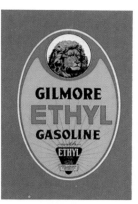

Gilmore Ethyl Gasoline, pump decal, lion's head above product name, Ethyl logo below on red-painted sheet metal, 23x16", NOS, NM+, A1 ....$275.00

Gilmore Gasoline, flag, cloth, white & black checked background with red leaping lion in center, 22x36", rare, NM, A1 ....$400.00

Gilmore Oil Co, see Golden Lion Motor Oil

Gilt Edge Lager/Ruhstaller's Brewing Co, tray, deep-dish, pictures seated lady in profile with dove on her knee, round, VG, A19 ....$85.00

Gilt Top Cream Ale, sign, cardboard, product name above elves carrying large bottle, matted & framed, 17x14", EX, A19 ....$200.00

Gilt Top-O, label, Spokane Brewing & Malting Co, L-type permit number, 11-oz, 1920-28, M, A10................$10.00

Giltedge Guaranteed Furnaces, brush, celluloid back, 50th Anniversary Of...RJ Schwab & Sons Co, 6" long, EX, A11 ....$45.00

Girard Cigar, sign, die-cut trifold, man holding oversized cigar on end flanked by repeated images of man's face, 18x21", EX, A18 ....$275.00

Girard Cigars, sign, tin, portrait insert of Steven Girard, 'We Suggest'...Cigars Of Prestige, wood-grained background, 13x9", EX+, A9 ....$135.00

Girton Dairy Equipment, ashtray, stainless steel, product name within outline of cow's head, 3¾" dia, EX, D14 ....**$10.00**

Glacier Beer, label, Kalispell Malt & Brewing Co, pre-prohibition, 8-oz, M, A10 ....**$80.00**

Gladiola, crate label, California orange, 2 large sprays of pink gladiolas on gold & tan background, Covina, 10x11", M, D3 ....**$2.00**

Gleaner Life Insurance Society, ink blotter/calendar, 1941, celluloid, Season's Greetings, little girl left of lettering & calendar, 3x8", EX, A11 ....**$10.00**

Glendale Yellow American Pasteurized Process Cheese, box, wood, green & red lettering & graphics, 11½", EX **$15.00**

Glendora Coffee, container, sample, cardboard & tin, white, gold & black, round with smaller round lid, 3¼x2" dia, EX+, A18 ....**$40.00**

Glendora Fruit, can label, fruit vine & dark blue logo, 6x10", M, D12 ....**$5.00**

Glennon's Beer, Ale & Porter, tray, Good Old... in center, Liberty Brewing Co, Pittston, Penna on rim, 13" dia, VG, A19 ....**$110.00**

Glennon's Beer, Ale & Porter, tray, pre-1920, 'St Vincent,' shows stock image of bulldog, gold lettering on black rim, 13x13", VG+, A8 ....**$210.00**

Glenwood Brand Roasted Coffee, milk can, green with red Glenwood above gold-lettered red dot, bail handle, 5-lb, 12", G-, A2 ....**$95.00**

Glenwood Brand Roasted Coffee, milk can, green with red Glenwood above gold-lettered red dot, bail handle, arched handle on lid, 5-lb, 12", EX, A2 ....**$385.00**

Glenwood Motor Oil, can, star logo above car on center band, Real Value Motor Oil below, screw cap, 2-gal, 11x8½", VG, A6 ....**$105.00**

Glidden, sign, celluloid over tin, Glidden, Everywhere on Everything... flanked by various product cans, minor scratches, A6 ....**$65.00**

Glidden, sign, die-cut porcelain, paint can shape with 3 lettered ovals, 32x27", NM+, D11 ....**$225.00**

Glidden Jap-A-Lac Varnish Stains, sign, celluloid, Japanese girl & lettering above color samples, 20x4½", EX, A6 ....**$30.00**

Globe Gasoline, gas globe, Globe on band across world globe, fired-on white ripple body with metal base, 13½" dia, NM, A6 ....**$1,900.00**

Glove A1 Products, pocket mirror, large letters superimposed over red, black & white globe, round, EX+, D18 ....**$75.00**

Gluek Picnic Beer, label, Gluek Brewing Co, Internal Revenue Tax Paid statement, 1933-50, ½-gal, NM, A10 ....**$22.00**

Gluek's Bock Beer, label, product name above & below goat's head on yellow circle, 12-oz, EX+, A19 .....**$25.00**

GMC Trucks, sign, porcelain, Sales & Service in blue on orange above GMC in white on blue circle, 42" dia, EX, D8 ....**$950.00**

GMC Trucks, sign, porcelain, yellow & white GMC on blue surrounded by General Motors Trucks in blue on yellow, round, EX, D8 ....**$850.00**

Goal Line Needles, needle card, features futuristic car & early motorcycle, folds out to show sewing needles, 2-sided, 3⅜x6½", NM, A1 ....**$75.00**

Gobblers, tin, cream with The Latest Smoke arched above red Gobblers lettered diagonally across turkey, round, rare, EX+, A18 ....**$650.00**

Goblin Candy Mint, trade stimulator, metal with faux wood finish, paper sign with nude elf-like figures on marquee, 13x15x9", rare, EX+, A1 ....**$450.00**

Goblin Soap, box, sample, cardboard, with contents, 2½", NM, A7 ....**$50.00**

Goebel Bantan Beer, can, flat-top, 8-oz, VG+, A19 ..**$12.00**

Goebel Beer, can, flat-top, instructional, 12-oz, NM, A19 ....**$35.00**

Goebel Beer, display, plaster, animated rooster tipping top hat to bottle on green beveled base with red lettering, 8x10x4", EX, A8 ....**$100.00**

Goebel Beer, tip tray, German man at table with bottle & glass encircled by name & Detroit USA on rim, 4" dia, VG+, A8 ....**$100.00**

Goebel Beer, tip tray, shows Dutch boy with basket by boat, 4¼" dia, EX, A8 ....**$65.00**

Goebel Beer, tray, deep-dish, Dutch girl on cobblestone walk by water's edge, lettered & decorated inside rim, 12" dia, VG+, A19 ....**$65.00**

Goebel Extract, match holder, metal, 2 Dutch girls on beach with basket, ...A Perfect Tonic, Ask Your Druggist on holder, G+, A8 ....$285.00

Goebel 22 Beer, mobile, die-cut cardboard, features 2 openers with product sign, bottle, can & rooster with glass, 19x15", VG+, A8........................$45.00

Goebel 22 Beer, sign, light-up, slanted sides, You'll Enjoy & From The Cypress Casks... on gold frame, name in center, 14x23", EX, A8........................$65.00

Goebel's Pure Meat Food Products, sign, porcelain, Quality First above & below product name, red, white & blue, 19" dia, M, D11 ....$175.00

Goetz Country Club Malt Liquor, can, flat-top, 8-oz, EX, A19........................$10.00

Goetz Country Club Malt Lager, can, flat-top, 8-oz, VG, A19........................$5.00

Goff's Braid, spool cabinet, walnut, 2-drawer with original gutta-percha knobs, 7½x17¼x17¼", EX, A12 ....$380.00

Gold Bond A1 Coffee, tin, Jewett & Sherman Co, slip lid, VG+, A3 ....$45.00

Gold Bond Coffee, store dispenser, pressed metal & glass light-up, Good Coffee on top panel, small door & scoop at bottom, 27x14", G, A9 ....$50.00

Gold Bond Metal Lath Products, display rack, metal, Gold Bond man standing in lettered arch surrounded by various types of lath, 23x28", EX, A6 ....$45.00

Gold Bond Old Reliable Cross Cut Plug Smoking Tobacco, pocket tin, short vertical, white with gold lettering on blue bow, Pipe or Cigarette on band below, EX, A18 ....$200.00

Gold Bond Old Reliable Cross Cut Plug Smoking Tobacco, pocket tin, tall vertical, white with gold lettering on blue bow, Pipe Or Cigarette on band below, EX+, A18 ....$220.00

Gold Bond Stamps, sign, tin flange, We Give...100 Free If We Forget To Give You Your Stamps, black on orange, 28x17", EX+, D21 ....$75.00

Gold Brand Bartlett Pears, can label, product name above & below pear/Mt St Helen, 4½x13", NM, A7........$2.00

Gold Coin Stoves & Ranges, see Chicago Stove Works

Gold Crown, tap knob, black ball with gold on blue enamel insert, EX, A8........................$65.00

Gold Crown, tap knob, chrome ball with gold on blue enamel insert, VG+, A8........................$25.00

Gold Crown Beer, sign, embossed tin on cardboard, crown emblem on red vertical field left of gold product name on black, 7x15", EX+, A19........................$110.00

Gold Dust Tobacco, pocket tin, vertical, Worth Its Weight In Gold at bottom of image of 2 men looking at miner's pan, VG+, A18 ....$975.00

Gold Dust Washing Powder, trade card, die-cut cardboard, pictures the twins in wash tub, EX+, A3...$65.00

Gold Dust Washing Powder, see also Fairbank's

Gold Label, tap knob, gray ball shape with gold lettering on black insert, VG+, A8 ....$40.00

Gold Label Baking Powder, tin, paper label, with contents, 6-oz, EX, A7........................$20.00

Gold Label Beer, label, Walter Bros Brewing Co, pre-prohibition, EX, A10 ....$15.00

Gold Label Imperial Beer/Beadleston & Woerz, tray, 'The Finishing Touch,' image of lady adding product bottle to dinner table, lettering on red rim, 13x13", NM, A8 ..$350.00

Gold Label Imperial Beer/Beadleston & Woerz, tray, 'The Finishing Touch,' image of lady adding product bottle to dinner table, lettering on red rim, 13x13", VG+, A21 ....$160.00

Gold Medal Beer, can, cone-top, 12-oz, EX+, A19....$35.00

Gold Medal Brand Apricots, can label, 2 images with product name above & below 2 apricots & double gold medals, 4¼x13", NM, A7........................$2.00

Gold Medal Brand Corn Flakes, container, Indian head nickel logo on ribbon in center, 10-oz, EX+, A3..$45.00

Gold Medal Oats, container, table setting on octagon in center, ...With Assorted Glassware, Northern Illinois Cereal Co, 14-oz, NM, A3 ....$25.00

Gold Seal Champagne/Urbana Wine Co, tip tray, colorful image of bottle & grapes, product & company name in cream & black on gold rim, 6½x4½", EX, A6 ......$40.00

Gold Seal Wine/Urbana Wine Co, sign, tin, colonial man lifting glass at elegant dining table, C Shonk litho, framed, G+, A19 ....$85.00

Gold Wing, crate label, California pear, gold winged pears & white lettering on black background, Sonoma, 8x11", M, D12........................$5.00

Gold Y Rock Draught Birch Beer/Clifton Bottling Works, sign, tin, yellow Gold Y Rock on black above yellow Birch Beer on black, black company name on yellow, 9x20", EX+, A8 ....$20.00

Gold-en Cola, sign, flange, Refreshing As A Cup Of Coffee, die-cut cup & saucer, 1950s, 15x22", NM, A13...$300.00

Goldcrest Beer/Tennessee Brewing Co, sign, paper, Louise Franklin Says 'You'll Go For My Beer Too,' Louise on diving board with glass, 20x16", VG+, A8........$65.00

Golden Ale, label, U-type permit number, Internal Revenue Tax Paid statement, 1933-36, 12-oz, M, A10........$18.00

Golden Bridge Root Beer, sign, embossed tin, Remember above ribbed bottle, 12x4", NM, D11................$50.00

Golden Circle, crate label, California orange, large circle of oranges around RCFA monogram, Redlands, 10x11", M, D12........................$6.00

123

Golden Creme Bock Beer, label, Vernon Brewing Co, U-type permit number, Internal Revenue Tax Paid statement, 1933-36, 11-oz, M, A10 .... **$20.00**

Golden Creme Extra Pale Beer, label, backside of sexy lady standing left of ...The Beer Supreme, Vernon Brewing Co, light blue border, 11-oz, VG+, A19 .... **$12.00**

Golden Crown Table Syrup, tin, paper label, pry lid, with contents, 2", NM, A7 .... **$25.00**

Golden Drops Lager Beer/Two Rivers Beverage Co, tray, name on green rim bordering 'Decidedly Different' on red above drinking cavaliers, 10x13", EX+, A19 ..**$155.00**

Golden Eagle, crate label, California orange, fierce eagle guarding cluster of oranges, gilt highlights, Fullerton, 10x11", M, D3 .... **$4.00**

Golden Eagle, pump sign, porcelain, yellow eagle on black above Golden Eagle in black on orange, white border, 13x13", NM, D8 .... **$500.00**

Golden Eagle, tobacco box label, product name below eagle & flag, Hone litho, 14", D8 .... **$20.00**

Golden Eagle Motor Oil, can, product name on band encircling soaring eagle, Parafin Base below, red, cream & blue, 1-qt, EX, A1 .... **$330.00**

Golden Eagle Motor Oil, can, product name on band encircling soaring eagle, screw cap & handle, 2-gal, 11x8½", NM, A6 .... **$110.00**

Golden Glow Beer, label, Blumer Products Co, U-type permit number, Internal Revenue Tax Paid statement, 1933-36, 12-oz, M, A10 .... **$30.00**

Golden Glow XXX Ale, beer can, cone-top, oval logo, marked One Full Quart, EX, A8 .... **$100.00**

Golden Grain Smoking Tobacco, cigarette papers, gummed, NM, A7 .... **$5.00**

Golden Grain Smoking Tobacco, cigarette papers, not gummed, NM, A7 .... **$6.00**

Golden Grain Smoking Tobacco, pouch, cloth, paper label, ⅞-oz, NM, A7 .... **$15.00**

Golden Harp, cigar box label, outer, die-cut harp with portrait in center, NM, A5 .... **$20.00**

Golden Leaf Motor Oil, can, product name above & below leaf, 1-qt, 5½x4" dia, NM, A6 .... **$35.00**

Golden Lion Motor Oil, can, product name above & below image of leaping lion, metallic gold & red on black, 1-qt, NM, A1 .... **$330.00**

Golden Rod Coffee, milk can, green with cream label lettered in gold, red & green above & below round logo, bail handle, 5-lb, 12", A2 .... **$295.00**

Golden Rod Coffee, postcard, 'Camping Out,' camping scene, Milliken Tomlinson Co... on fancy emblem below, EX, D26 .... **$65.00**

Golden Rule Blend Roasted Coffee, store bin, black with gold product lettering above & below white outlined shield, flat top, 16x12", EX, A2 .... **$285.00**

Golden Rule Tea, tin, red with gold lettering & graphics, tall square shape with round screw lid, EX+, A18 .... **$30.00**

Golden Shell, bank, tin, image of hippo & leopard with poem on yellow ground, Save With Shell in red on top, 3x2" dia, rare, EX, A6 .... **$375.00**

Golden Shell Motor Oil, can, Golden Shell lettered on large shell with Motor Oil below, red, yellow & white, 1-qt, EX+, A1 .... **$65.00**

Golden Shell Oil, watch fob, 'So Pure It Lubricates This Watch,' product name in center, 1¼" dia, EX, A7 ...**$65.00**

Golden Spur, crate label, Washington apple, brand name coiled in cowboy rope around large spur, Yakima, 9x11", M, D12 .... **$2.00**

Golden Spur Premium Motor Oil, can, silhouette of western-type boot with spur in oval above product name, red & white on metallic gold, 1-qt, G, A1 .... **$90.00**

Golden State Beer/San Francisco Brewing Co, label, red Golden State above eagle & initial logo flanked by Quality & Satisfies, Beer below on yellow, 32-oz, EX, A19 .... **$4.00**

Golden Sun Coffee/Woolson Spice Co, pocket mirror, celluloid, product name on sunrise scene, Changeless As Its Namesake & company name below, oval, EX+, A11 .... **$75.00**

Golden Voice Needles, tin, flat, Extra Loud, red with gold trim, rounded ends, ½x1¼x1½", EX, D37 .... **$40.00**

Golden Wedding Coffee, tin, sample, gold & pink lettering on cream with oval silhouette image of couple drinking coffee, 2x3" dia, EX, D37 .... **$120.00**

Golden Wedding Coffee, matchbox holder, product name in diagonal script, Make It Your Own Way... on rose-colored ground, 1½x2", EX+, A3 .... **$75.00**

Golden Wedding Coffee, tin, Golden Wedding in bold diagonal letters above Coffee, key-wind lid, NM, A3 .... **$30.00**

Golden Wedding Coffee, tin, sample, gold & pink lettering on white with oval image of couple drinking coffee, pry lid, 2x3" dia, EX, D37 .... **$120.00**

Golden Wedding Extra Fine Flake Cut, tin, blue lettering over yellow bell, rectangular, square corners, EX+, A18 .... **$85.00**

Golden Wedding Ginger, container, cardboard with tin dial lid, red with white script name, EX, A3 .... **$22.00**

Golden West Coffee, tin, cowgirl flanked by Vacuum & Packed, Golden West on red above, Coffee on black band below, 3-lb, rare, EX+, A3 .... **$200.00**

Golden West Coffee, tin, name at left of 3-quarter length cowgirl ready to sip from cup, key-wind, 2-lb, NM, A3 .... **$135.00**

Golden West Oil Co, pump plate, porcelain, mountain & lake scene with product name on large sunset, blue, gold & white, 10" dia, NM, A1 .... **$425.00**

Goldenmoon/Buckeye Root Beer Flavoring Sirup (sic), can, Goldenmoon on blue above Fruits & Sirups on white above laughing moon, Cleveland Fruit Juice Co, 1-gal, VG+, A15 .... **$190.00**

124

Goldenrod Beer, Porter & Ale, tray, deep-dish, The Home Of... above panoramic factory scene, oval, NM+, A19 ....**$165.00**

Gollam's Lebanon Ice Cream, sign, tin, We Serve & boy with huge cone above product name, 2-sided sidewalk, 1941, NM+, A13 ....**$250.00**

Gonseth Garage, calendar, couple in open car looking at girl behind them, full pad, 1932, 16x16", VG+, A6 ....**$110.00**

Gonzalez & Sanchez Havana Cigars, watch fob, colorful bust portrait of girl on celluloid center, oval, EX, A20 ....**$100.00**

Good Cheer Cigars, container, stein shape, dome lid, EX+, A18 ....**$140.00**

Good Company Cigars, box label set, pictures open box of cigars, checkerboard, poker chips, deck of cards, etc, 2 pcs, EX, A5 ....**$140.00**

Good Grape, sign, tin, Drink above Good Grape on red scroll, ...That Good Grape Drink below, yellow background, 8x24", EX+, D30 ....**$135.00**

Good Gulf, pump sign, porcelain, Good Gulf in blue & orange with intertwined G's, white ground, 10½" dia, VG, A6 ....**$55.00**

Good Gulf Gasoline, gas globe, That Good Gulf Gasoline in black with orange center circle, black metal body, 15" dia, EX+, A3 ....**$500.00**

Good Gulf Gasoline, pump sign, porcelain, That above Good Gulf in shadowed letters, blue, white & orange, 10½" dia, EX+, A6 ....**$160.00**

Good Housekeeping Magazine, restroom sign, porcelain, plus sign logo in center, A Home-Clean Restroom..., blue, orange & white, 7" dia, EX, A6 ....**$195.00**

Good Humor, sign, porcelain, 2-pc panel with small red truck left of blue lettering, white ground, blue border, 16x54", NM, A1 ....**$60.00**

Good Humor Ice Cream, sign, porcelain, product name above & below ice-cream bar with bite missing, white background, 18x44", EX+, A1......$710.00

Good Joke, cigar box label, inner lid, woman laughing at dog smoking, 6x9", EX, D5..................................**$75.00**

Good Luck Ale, sign, tin on cardboard, debossed product name above & below horse head in horseshoe, beveled rim, 6x9", VG+, A8 ....**$165.00**

Good Luck Baking Powder, tin, Pat 1901, with contents, VG, A7 ....**$10.00**

Good Luck Drummond Tobacco Co, sign, paper, girl holding winged fairy & 4-leaf clover, framed, image: 15x15½", NM, A9 ....**$400.00**

Good Luck Smoke, tobacco label, EX, D35.............**$6.00**

Goodrich Rubber Footwear, sign, porcelain flange, red logo above product name in white, blue background with green border, oval, 19x22", VG, A6..........**$120.00**

Goodrich Silvertown Safety League, license plate attachment, stainless steel, custom mounted, impressed lettering with red beaded center, 5½", EX, A6 ....**$15.00**

Goodrich Silvertown Tires, clock, glass front with wood frame, ...With The Life Saver Golden Ply in squared border, numbered 1-12, 15x15", EX, A6 ....**$325.00**

Goodrich Sport Shoes, sign, die-cut cardboard, Indian with tomahawk checking out footprints in the sand, framed, 41x26", VG, A6 ....**$260.00**

Goodrich Tires, sign, embossed tin, Cruikshank & Kollin, Pleasanton on band above ...Best In The Long Run, 12x36", M, D11 ....**$145.00**

Goodrich Tires, see also BF Goodrich

Goodrich Zippers, sign, die-cut cardboard stand-up, 2 ladies talking to doorman above New Goodrich...In Colors! & 2 boots, 1929, VG+, A3 ....$50.00

Goodyear, pocketknife, opalescent pearl over metal, blue lettering & logo, NM, A6......................................**$20.00**

Goodyear Automotive Belts, belt rack, winged foot logo in yellow on blue elongated diamond at left of Automotive Belts in red, 8x24", NM, D8..................**$65.00**

Goodyear Balloon Tires, sign, porcelain, image of tire encircling world globe on blue ground with white border, 40x46", NM, D8 ....**$1,400.00**

Goodyear Rubber Heels, sign, porcelain, Goodyear Rubber Heels Applied Here, yellow & white on blue, 10x20", EX+, D21 ....**$60.00**

Goodyear Tires, pin-back button, trademark name above crescent moon shining on Earth encircled by tire, EX, A20..**$25.00**

Goodyear Tires, pocketknife, tire shape, VG+, A6..**$115.00**

Goodyear Tires, sign, paper, They All Roll Best..., elegant girl in tires encircled by vehicles, copyright 1899, 37½x31", EX, A6..................................**$550.00**

Goodyear Tires, sign, posterboard, baby's face poking through tire above My Daddy Insures My Safety By Using..., 40x27", VG, A6....................................**$50.00**

Goodyear Tires Agency, sign, self-framed tin, winged foot flanked by Goodyear, Akron, Ohio, Agency Tires above & below, 10x16½", EX, A6 ....**$1,400.00**

Goodyear Tractor Tires, watch fob, logo & lettering on emblem atop tire, EX, A20...............................**$20.00**

Goose Root Beer, mug, pictures a goose & Root Beer in red, straight-sided, 5x3", EX, D16.......................**$65.00**

Gordon Hats, pocket mirror, crown logo in center, If You Wear...You Needn't Be Afraid To Look At Yourself, round, EX, A20 ....$25.00

Gordon's Fresh Foods, jar, clear glass, 'Trucks Serving The Best,' applied red truck, with lid, 10x7" dia, EX, A6 ....$80.00

Gorton's Fish, figure, Gorton Fisherman, 1970s, NM, D27 ....$125.00

Goshen Buggy Top Co, catalog, 1916, 160 pgs, EX, D17 ....$100.00

Gosling, crate label, Oregon apple, fluffy yellow gosling on red background, M, D3 ....$15.00

Gossiper Cigars, box label, salesman's sample, product name above parakeet, A Cigar That Talks For Itself below, 2 holes at left, A5 ....$45.00

Gottignies, sign, cardboard hanger, La Qualite left of man in suit rolling cigarette, name & products below, 17½x12", EX+, A18 ....$10.00

Gould's Beer, label, 1936-38, Gould Brewing Co, Internal Revenue Tax Paid statement, 12-oz, M, A10 ....$30.00

Gowans & Stover Soap, sign, cardboard, boy leaning over bowl washing his face, Buffalo NY below, framed, image: 26½x21", G-, A9 ....$175.00

Grace Graham Co Custom Corsetiere, sign, reverse-painted glass with gold leaf lettering, 15x39", G, A9 ....$45.00

Graham's Ale, label, Burton Products Inc, U-type permit number, Internal revenue Tax Paid statement, 1933-36, ½-gal, M, A10 ....$10.00

Graham's Beer, label, Burton Products Inc, U-type permit number, Internal Revenue Tax Paid statement, ½-gal, M, A10 ....$10.00

Graham's Ice Cream, product box, shows Graham's Ice Cream delivery truck on city street, 1 of 4 images, 1-pt, EX, A3 ....$18.00

Graham's XXX Ale, tap knob, green speckled ball shape with white & gold lettering on green enamel insert, VG+, A8 ....$95.00

Grain Belt, register sign, light-up, Have A Cool & Now! flank name on red diamond against blue & white snow scene, 1950s, NM, A19 ....$30.00

Grain Belt Beer, sign, reverse-painted glass, bottle cap left of diagonal Grain Belt, black, red, white & silver on yellow, VG, A8 ....$50.00

Grain Plug Cut, pocket tin, yellow with product lettering above company name on tag, EX, A18 ....$150.00

Gran Fabrica de Tabacos Flor Fina, cigar box label, inner lid, winged goddess seated on edge of fancy tub, EX, A5 ....$62.00

Grand Army, cigar box label, inner lid, US flags, cannons & medal, 6x9", EX, D5 ....$30.00

Grand Knight, cigar box label, outer, knight wearing gold armor, 1896, 4½x4½", M, D5 ....$15.00

Grand Prize Beer, display, plaster, Pale Dry Pete figure looking at bottle sitting on base, rare, G+, A8 ...$260.00

Grand Rapids Brewing Co, tray, family scene with mother entertaining children & dad reading the paper, ...Silver Foam, oval, 13x16", rare, G+, A9 ....$1,000.00

Grand Rapids Cabinet Co, pocket mirror, celluloid, company name above 'Tray-Pack' The 100%... & man in front of cabinet, round, EX+, A11 ....$80.00

Grand Union Tea Co Baking Powder, tin, paper label, slip lid, 5x3¼" dia, VG+, A18 ....$35.00

Grandma's Borax Powdered Soap, box, image of smiling grandma doing dishes, Globe Soap Co, red, black & cream, with contents, 2-lb, EX, A6 ....$60.00

Grandma's Cookies, bank, hard plastic, 1970s, M, D27 ....$35.00

Granger Pipe Tobacco, sign, paper, baseball star Ducky Medwick seated in grass with pipe, Keeps The Pipe Bowl Cool..., 19x13", G, A2 ....$165.00

Granger Rough Cut, sign, paper, product name & The Tobacco That's Made For Pipes left of tilted pack & 10¢ on white label, 8x20", NM, A7 ....$10.00

Granger Rough Cut Pipe Tobacco, canister, Rough Cut lettered on leaf in center, NM, A3 ....$40.00

Granger Rough Cut Pipe Tobacco, pocket tin, vertical, orange product lettering on black above & below Rough Cut lettered on tobacco leaf, EX+, A18...$375.00

Granger Twist, container, cardboard, product name above tobacco leaf bursting through label, King Of It's Kind, unopened, EX, A18 ....$50.00

Grant Battery Service, metal, Grant lettered vertically above Battery Service on battery, black, orange & yellow, 38½x12½", EX, A6 ....**$80.00**

Granulated 54 Sliced Plug (no Tobacco), pocket tin, vertical, yellow & blue with name above yellow 54 on tobacco leaf, John Weisert Tob Co below, EX, A18 ....**$100.00**

Granulated 54 Sliced Plug Tobacco, pocket tin, vertical, yellow & blue with name above & below yellow 54 on tobacco leaf, John Weisert Tob Co, EX+, A18....**$140.00**

Grape Dee-Light, sign, cardboard hanger, Gee, But It's Good!, young girl looking at full glass & bottle, 1920s, 14x10½", VG+, A13 ....**$45.00**

Grape Smack, sign, cardboard, Drink in script & Grape Smack above bottle flanked by Always & Good, Ice Cold..., vertical, EX, A16 ....**$125.00**

Grape Smash, sign, tin, Better Than Straight... above grape cluster & product name, 5¢ Carbonated-In Bottles 5¢, 10x14", EX, A13 ....**$325.00**

Grape-Julep, syrup dispenser, ceramic potbelly shape, Drink Grape-Julep, gold trim on base, original pump, 14x9", VG, A9 ....**$750.00**

Grape-Julep, see also Howel's

Grape-Nuts, sign, self-framed tin, 'There's A Reason,' classic image of girl & St Bernard, To School Well Fed..., 30x20", EX+, A12 ....**$3,300.00**

Grape-Nuts, sign, self-framed tin, 'There's A Reason,' classic image of girl & St Bernard, To School Well Fed..., 30x20", G, A9 ....**$875.00**

Grapette, calendar, 1949, bust image of pretty blonde & bottle, full pad below, Pearl Frush artwork, 14x7½", NM+, A13 ....**$550.00**

Grapette, sign, cardboard, Enjoy Grapette Soda on oval at left of bottle in lower right, pictures tennis girl, 24x18", EX+, D30 ....**$125.00**

Grapette, sign, cardboard, Thirsty Or Not! in upper left, girl with bottle & flowers, 28x24", NM+, D30 ....**$140.00**

Grapette, sign, neon, counter-top, blue Grapette oval on encased yellow panel surrounded by white tube, 1930s-40s, 13x22", VG, A13 ....**$500.00**

Grapette, sign, porcelain, Grapette Soda in white on dark blue oval plaque with white & red border, 1930s-40s, 10x17", NM+, A13 ....**$550.00**

Grapette, sign, tin, Thirsty Or Not & hand-held bottle on yellow above blue oval, curved corners, 28x20", EX+, A13...$280.00

Grapette, thermometer, tin, Remember To Buy Grapette above large bottle & bulb, 15", EX, D30 ....**$95.00**

Graphinoil, sign, metal flange, We Sell Graphinoil, The Quality Lubricant, orange on black with orange border, 9x18½", EX, A6..**$65.00**

Grauley Hand-Made Cigars, trade card, product name on banner & Trade Mark logo surrounded by flowers & butterflies, QA Robinson..., 3x5", EX, A5.............**$12.00**

Grayson-McLeod Lumber Co St Louis, paperweight, glass, company name arched above & below Yellow Pine in bold red letters, oval, M, D13 ....**$50.00**

Gre-Solvent, tin, sample, with contents, 2" dia, NM, A7..**$12.00**

Great American Hand Made Cigar, canister, Great American above Hand Made flanked by 5¢, Genuine Imported Sumatra Wrapper... below, EX, A3 ....**$60.00**

Great Atlantic & Pacific Tea Co, sign, cardboard, profile of a woman with demitasse cup & sauser, copyright 1888, 9x7½", VG, A6 ....**$75.00**

Great Auk Cigarettes, tin, pictures auk at left of name, decorative border, rectangular, slightly rounded corners, 2x3x5½", rare, EX, A18 ....**$365.00**

Great Christopher, cigar box label, outer, portrait of Christopher Columbus, EX, A5.........................**$120.00**

Great Heart Coal, thermometer, porcelain, product name on red heart & Satisfaction... above, Less Than A Bushel..., 1915, 39", NM, A3 ....**$250.00**

Great Puff, cigarette papers, NM, A7 ....**$20.00**

Great Slice Plug/Brunoff Mfg Co, tobacco cutter, metal on wood base, 6x16x6", EX, A12 ....**$180.00**

Great West Cut Plug, lunch box, red with black & gold product lettering with encircled product image, rectangular, wire handle, EX, A18..............................**$185.00**

Great West Cut Plug, sign, porcelain, white product name on navy, 3x24", EX, A15 ....**$325.00**

Greek Slave Smoking Tobacco, label, Greek Goddess statue & 2 inserts promoting Buck & Cupid's Delight, WN Woodson & Co, 12½x10", G, A9 ....**$175.00**

Green Giant, figure, Little Sprout, molded vinyl, movable head, 1970s, 6½", M **$15.00**

Green River, mirror sign, 1940s, EX+, D32.............**$175.00**

Green River, sign, cardboard & tin, product name over oval sunrise scene in bright colors, red background, 18x54", NM+, D30 ....**$300.00**

Green River Beer, label, Sweetwater Brewery Inc, U-type permit number, Internal Revenue Tax Paid statement, 1933-36, 12-oz, EX, A10 ....**$50.00**

Green Seal Shoes, pocket mirror, celluloid, Southern Shoes For Southern People above & below logo, red & green, oval, EX, A11..$40.00

Green Spot, menu board, tin, Green Spot on circle & tilted bottle above chalkboard, 35x22", NM, D30........$125.00

Green Spot, sign, tin, product name on circle above tilted bottle, 42x12", M, D30 ....$135.00

Green Spot Orange-Ade, sign, tin, embossed, Ice Cold above Green Spot dot & tilted bottle, Orange-Ade 5¢ below, 1940s-50s, 12x20", NM+, A13 ....$70.00

Green Turtle, tobacco label, EX, D35 ....$6.00

Green Turtle Cigars, lunch pail, green & white graphics on green, wire handle, EX+, A18 ....$400.00

Green's Seed Corn, sign, tin, proud farmer with ribbon on his chest at right of product name, 12x36", NM+, D30 ....$75.00

Greenback Smoking Tobacco, cigarette papers, NM, A7...$45.00

Greenback Tobacco, sign, celluloid, marsh scene with frog spying through the cattails at 2 courting frogs, framed, image: 11x6", EX, A21 ....$155.00

Greenback Tobacco, sign, paper, 'The Tug Of War,' pictures 2 ducklings playing tug of war with frog, framed, 14x18", EX+, A18 ....$500.00

Greenback Tobacco, sign, paper, 'The Victory,' Smoke... arched above frog on rock watching ducks & ducklings, framed, 14x18", EX+, A18 ....$500.00

Greenback Tobacco, see also Seal of North Carolina

Greensmith's Derby Dog Biscuits, sign, cardboard, Dalmation jumping through clown's hoop, Manufactory Hilton Mills & Derby, 18½x23½", VG, A9 ....$200.00

Gretz Beer, can, crown-top, 12-oz, EX+, A19 ....$160.00

Gretz Beer, tray, blue, yellow & white, 12", EX+, D7..$30.00

Greyhound, clock, glass lens, metal frame, Greyhound Lines, black numbers on white around dog & name on blue, 15" dia, EX, A15 ....$350.00

Greyhound, flier, ...Havana Tours, 1941, EX, D23 ....$22.00

Greyhound, sign, porcelain, dog on white above Greyhound on blue, rounded corners, 1940s-50s, 2-sided, 24x40", EX+, A13 ....$375.00

Greyhound, sign, tin, Greyhound Package Express, dog above lettering, blue on off-white with blue border, 2-sided, 18x28", NM, A1..............................$145.00

Griesedieck Bros Beer, sign, tin on cardboard, No Finer Beer..., library scene with tankard & product, beveled edge, 1945, 10x12", EX+, A8 ....$210.00

Griesedieck Bros Light Lager Beer, sign, cardboard hanger, 'Brook Trout,' shows large fish with bamboo border & red receding sign, 1930s, 13x20", VG+, A3 ....$60.00

Griesedieck Bros Premium Light Lager Beer, matchbook, St Louis, Mo, 20 strike, front strike, NM, D28........$12.00

Griesedieck Bros Premium Light Lager Beer, sign, embossed tin, Drink Naturally Smoother..., It's De-Bitterized below, 42", VG+, D11..............................$140.00

Griffith's Home Farm Butter, sign, tin, Oh Boy It's Good & image of little boy eating stick of butter at left of box, 11x35", EX, D8..............................$395.00

Grimes 5 Cent Cigar, box label, outer, eagle & banner, 4½x4½", M, D5..$7.00

Griz H Hoklas & Sons, cigar box label, inner lid, bear flanked by fancy design with various weapons & portrait, EX, A5 ....$185.00

Grizzly Full Moulded Brake Lock Lining, sign, embossed tin, 'A Bear For Wear' & image of bear at right, For Safety, Dependability & Economy..., 20x27", VG+, A11..$140.00

Grossvater Beer, tray, deep-dish, Grossvater Beer It's Extra Good, hand holding full glass above lettered ribbon, 14" dia, VG, A8..$45.00

Guarda Costa, cigar box label, salesman's sample, coastal scene with large ship flanked by open cigar box & palm trees, EX, A5..$90.00

Guelph Motor Car Co, match holder, metal, Nothing Matches The Cars Sold By The... above group in touring car, 6x4x4", VG, A6..$325.00

Guide Pipe & Cigarette Tobacco, pocket tin, vertical, product name above & below man standing before canoe, shaded brown & cream, NM, A18..........$200.00

Gulf, attendant's cap, tan & black, EX, A6..............$110.00

Gulf, doll, Buddy Lee, gray & black uniform, black hat with emblem, VG+, A13..$350.00

Gulf, gas globe, plastic with logo in center, orange & blue, 14½" dia, EX, A6..$140.00

Gulf, paper cup dispenser, orange metal with blue & cream logo, Ajax Drinking Cups on plate at top, 15x3½", EX A6..$70.00

Gulf, sign, cardboard, 3-D plastic image of Gulf man in center, Thank You..., We Appreciate Your Business, 32x25", EX, A6..$300.00

Gulf, sign, porcelain, Authorized Dealer flanked by round Gulf logos, 1930s, 9x40", EX+, A13....................$130.00

Gulf, toy truck, orange Walt Reach friction tanker with Gulf emblem on doors & lettering on tanker, 2-pc, 13", EX+, A1..$360.00

Gulf Coast, gas globe, white lettering, red metal body, 15" dia, NM+, A6 ....$700.00

Gulf Diesel Fuel, gas globe, encircled Gulf above Diesel Fuel on large band, blue & orange, 3-pc Gill body 12½" dia, NM, A6..$525.00

Gulf Gasoline, see also Good Gulf Gasoline

Gulf High Pressure Grease, can, large Gulf logo in center, product name around top band, orange, blue & cream, 4½x3½" dia, VG+, A6 ....**$25.00**

Gulf Marine, pump sign, porcelain, Gulf logo above Marine in bold letters, blue, orange & white, 8½x11", EX+, A6 ....**$80.00**

Gulf Marine White, pump sign, porcelain, red on white with black border, 8x10", NM, D8 ......**$165.00**

Gulf No-Nox, pump sign, porcelain, white on blue, 8½x10½", VG+, A6...**$30.00**

Gulf No-Nox Motor Fuel, sign, porcelain flange, encircled product name in center, Gulf Refining Co below, blue, orange & white, 18x18", EX, A6...........................**$150.00**

Gulf Oil, belt buckle, brass with blue, white & orange enameled logo, EX, D22 ....**$65.00**

Gulf Supreme Motor Oil, pump plate, enamel on steel, Gulf on orange circle surrounded by Supreme Motor Oil in black on cream, 7" dia, EX, D8 ....**$450.00**

Gulflex, sign, metal with reverse-painted glass front, Your Car Needs..., Registered Lubrication & Gulf logo below, 9x19", VG, A6 ....**$310.00**

Gulflube Motor Oil, can, product name above encircled Gulf, cream, blue & orange, 1-gal, 11x8", VG, A6...........**$110.00**

Gulfpride, sign, plastic light-up with metal frame, Use...Gulfpride, The World's Finest Motor Oil, 9x26", EX, A6 ....**$360.00**

Gulfpride, sign, porcelain, Gulfpride in script above Gulf logo & The World's Finest Motor Oil..., 11x21", VG+, A11 ....**$125.00**

Gulfpride HD Select Motor Oil, bank, tin, can shape, 3", EX, D25 ....**$20.00**

Gulfpride Oil, can, product name above circular Gulf logo, screw lid & handle, 5-gal, 15x9", EX, A6 ....**$55.00**

Gunther's Beer, can, flat-top, brown lettering on orange, Internal Revenue Tax Paid statement, 12-oz, EX+, A19 ....**$18.00**

Gunther's Beer, tap knob, black ball shape with brown & gold lettering & logo on cream enamel insert, EX, A8 ....**$70.00**

Gunther's Beer, tap knob, gold-speckled ball shape with brown lettering & logo on cream enamel insert, VG, A8 ....**$20.00**

Gunther's Premium Dry Beer, sign, tin, lion & G logo above product name, yellow & black on off-brown, raised border, 13x19", VG, A8 ....**$40.00**

Gus' Topper Beer, sign, embossed tin, Gus' above Topper Beer on diagonal field, The Premium Beer below, blue & yellow, 18x24", EX+, A8 ....**$100.00**

Gutsch Brewing Co, plate, porcelain, scalloped gold rim & swag design around 2-tone grape cluster, gold script ad on back, 9" dia, EX, A8...**$70.00**

Guyler Brand Gasoline & Motor Oils, gas globe, Guyler Brand on elongated diamond in center, blue & red on white, 3-pc Gill body, 15" dia, rare, NM, A6...**$1,200.00**

GW McNess Breakfast Cocoa, tin, sample, product name & other lettering above maid with serving tray, slip lid, 2¼x1¾x1¼", EX, D37 ....**$50.00**

Gypsy, tobacco box label, name above dancing gypsy girl, Hone litho, 14", NM, D8 ....**$40.00**

Gypsy Salmon, can label, dancing gypsy lady on red background, Chinook, M, D3 ....**$3.00**

❧ H ❧

H Berghoff Brewing Co/Salvator, drinking glass, embossed stem, 6¾", NM, A8................................**$90.00**

H Clausen & Son, calendar, 1991, EX, A19 ....**$25.00**

H Weinhard, mug, ceramic, embossed name above circular eagle logo, Portland Ore below, German-made, Diesinger design, .03 L, EX+, A8.........................**$105.00**

H&H Tender & Tasty Popped Corn, box, 6¾x4¼", NM, A7 ....**$18.00**

H&K Vacuum Packed Coffee, tin, encircled Arab with coffee tray above product name, key-wind lid, EX, A3 ......**$70.00**

H&N 'Nick Chick' Leghorns, sign, embossed painted tin, H&N above chick on lettered platform, dealer name below, rounded corners, 17x17", NM, A1.............**$95.00**

H-O Tobacco, lunch box, gold on red with clasp closure on lid, EX, A18 ....**$70.00**

HA Kamps Co Diamond Jewelers & Opticians, pocket mirror, celluloid, jemstone & lettering surrounded by birthstones, round, EX+, A11...............................**$30.00**

HA Rogers Co, pocket mirror, celluloid, Supplies & Equipment For Engineers, Architects & Artists..., blue & white, round, EX+, A11...**$20.00**

Haig Ale, sign, tin flange, Refreshing above Haig Ale, Sold Here on scrolled banner on oval, yellow on black, EX, A1 ....**$50.00**

Haines Dairy Farm, thermometer, metal, bulb & product lettering on bottle of milk, 6", NM, A7...................**$25.00**

Half & Half, cigarette papers, A Cargo, NM, A7...........**$4.00**

Half & Half, cigarette papers, Burley Bright, NM, A7..**$3.00**

Half & Half, cigarette papers, Lucky Strike, NM, A7..**$10.00**

Half & Half, pocket tin, sample, cut-down vertical, shows red circular Burley Bright logo, EX, A18 ....**$60.00**

Half & Half, pocket tin, sample, vertical, Half & Half on diagonal white band dividing Burley Bright from Buckingham Bright, EX, A18 ....$100.00

Hall Co's Quality Ice Cream, tray, mother with tray serving anxious children, decorative border, 13¼x10½", VG+, A9 ....$400.00

Hall's Ice Cream, tray, children gathered around lady with tray of ice cream, lettered & decorative rim, vertical rectangle, 13", EX, A21 ....$550.00

Hallmark Umbrellas, sign, porcelain, Hallmark on oval with Guaranteed For 1 Year on tail of K above Umbrellas, 3½x20", EX, A6 ....$140.00

Halls Beer, shoes, plaster, pair of simulated wood or yellow Dutch clogs with advertising on tops, wire hangers, 7", EX, each pair $30.00

Hambone Smoking Tobacco, pouch, cloth, paper label, 1-oz, VG, A7 ....$105.00

Hamburg-American Line, sign, tin, pictures large passenger ship & 2 smaller sailing ships on choppy seas, artist signed, 36x46", VG, A2 ....$745.00

Hamburg-American Packet Co, sign, paper, sailing steamship surrounded by lettered vignettes, Chas Shields' litho, framed, 20x25½", G-, A9 ....$200.00

Hamburger Helper, radio, Helping Hand figure, plastic, General Mills/Hong Kong, 1980s, 7", M................$40.00

Hamilton Watch, sign, self-framed tin, product name above angelic little girl, America's Standard Railroad Keeper below, 19x13", EX, A9 ....$300.00

Hamilton Watches, tin, flat, green with lettering surrounded by decorative border, hinged lid, rounded corners, ⅝x2¾x5⅛", EX, D37 ....$55.00

Hamm St Paul Velvet-Excelsior-Old Lager-Export..., tray, Hamm St Paul in gold script & gold stars on blue around eagle & H logo, product names on rim, round, VG+, A19 ....$75.00

Hamm's, decanter, Hamm's bear as a bartender holding frothy mug, 1973, EX+, A8 ....$135.00

Hamm's, decanter, Hamm's bear holding Hamm's sign, with origial tag, 1973, EX, A8 ....$100.00

Hamm's Beer, bank, ceramic, Hamm's bear with hands behind back expressing a goofy grin, VG, A8 .....$65.00

Hamm's Beer, bank, ceramic, Hamm's bear with head in profile holding Hamm's Beer sign, From The Land Of..., NM, A8..$355.00

Hamm's Beer, display, light-up, bear by building showing 5 bottles dancing in single file in landscape, brick-type base, VG+, A8..$85.00

Hamm's Beer, display, light-up, product name on starry sky over lake scene, The Refreshingest! below, slant top, 17x30", NM, A19 ....$115.00

Hamm's Beer, display, light-up barrel shape with scenes on flipping cards, Hamm's Beer label on front, EX, A8 ....$75.00

Hamm's Beer, display, light-up building with pitched roof showing lake scene, 4 frosty glasses above Hamm's sign, EX, A8 ....$75.00

Hamm's Beer, display, light-up building with slanted roof showing moonlit lake & perforated frosty glasses in sky, EX, A8 ....$180.00

Hamm's Beer, display, light-up roofed panel with picture that changes from waterfalls to camping scenes, 18x31", EX, D21..$395.00

Hamm's Beer, display, plastic, Hamm's bear holding Good Friends Meet Here sign on base, ...Big Bear Drinking Brotherhood, 16", EX, A8.......................................$90.00

Hamm's Beer, paper cup, waxed, Hamm's bear on log in water, red & blue on white, 1960s, NM, A19 ....$5.00

Hamm's Beer, sign, die-cut cardboard, Hamm's Beer In Cans on yellow circle & tilted can on red base, Keglined Cans..., VG+, A19 ....$70.00

Hamm's Beer, sign, neon, Hamm's in blue lettering, 8x26", EX+, A19 ....$90.00

Hamm's Beer, tap knob, chrome ball shape with red, white & gold enamel insert, G+, A8 ....$50.00

Hamm's Krug Klub, mug, embossed with Hamm's bear, beaver, owls & ducks, Red Wing Pottery, 5", NM+, A3...$55.00

Hammond Brewing Co, see Muhlhauser

Hammond Superior Typewriter Ribbon, tin, flat, blue with lettering above & below image of early typewriter, rounded corners, ¾x2½x2½", EX, D37 ....$95.00

Hammond Typewriter Non Filling Ribbon, tin, flat, blue with image of world map encircled by lettering, square, rounded corners, ⅞x2½x2½", EX, D37 ....$75.00

Hampden Ale, tap knob, chrome with celluloid cover, red & black on cream, 2" dia, EX, A8.........................$65.00

Hampden Mild Ale, can, flat-top, gold oval on green, 12-oz, VG+, A19 ....$28.00

Hampden Mild Ale, tray, So Mild But Sturdy!, product name above & below animated waiter with oversized tray & 2 glasses, round, VG+, A19 ....$30.00

Hampden On Tap, coaster, bust of waiter with glasses on tray encircled by name & Lager, Porter, Ale & Mild Ale decorative rim, EX+, A8...$85.00

Hampden Porter, tap knob, red with green enameled insert, round, EX+, A8 ....$100.00

Hand Bag Cut Plug, lunch box, shaped like leather purse with product name on image of tag on hinged lid, with handle, EX, A18 ....$50.00

Hand Made Flake Cut/Globe Tobacco Co, pocket tin, vertical, Hand Made above hand on globe, company name below, VG+, A3 ....$110.00

Handsome Dan Mixture, tin, blue with blue lettering on gold graphics with image of dog, rectangular, square corners, EX+, A18...........................$215.00

Handy Package Dyes, sign, paper, cherubs hanging clothes on line & laying fabric in yard to spell Handy Package Dyes, 13x17", EX, D8............$60.00

Hanford's Ice Cream, tray, colorful image of 3 girls eating sundaes & cones, 10½x13", G+, A9 ....$225.00

Hanley Brewing Co, print, paper, bulldog on back of sofa admiring his portrait, 1943, 12x10", EX, A8.......$100.00

Hanley Export Lager Beer, can, flat-top, blue oval on gold, 12-oz, G+, A19 ....$65.00

Hanley's Peerles Ale, tray, deep-dish, shows bulldog resting atop Hanley's lettering, Peerless lettered on Ale below, 12" dia, VG+, A8 ....$75.00

Hanna's Green Seal Paints, sign, die-cut cardboard stand-up, full-figure man in painter's clothes & lettered hat holding up paint brush, VG+, A2.....................$285.00

Happy Days, cigar box label, salesman's sample, elegant woman with glass above ribbon banner, M, A5 ..$165.00

Happy Family Baking Powder, tin, with contents, 6-oz, EX, A7 ....$15.00

Happy Home Peanut Butter, pail, product name above & below oval image of peanuts, bail handle, VG+, A18 ....$150.00

Happy Thought Tobacco, sign, paper roll-down, oval portrait & product name above sailor & ship, framed, image: 29x12", EX, A9 ....$1,100.00

Hare Truck Lines, pocket mirror, celluloid, smiling man flanked by The One We Want To Serve Is On The Other Side, round, EX+, A11 ....$85.00

Harley-Davidson, booklet, 'Instruction Book For Harley-Davidson Big Twins Sidecars & Parcelcars,' 1920, 7x4½", VG, D8...........................$45.00

Harley-Davidson, brochure, 'Harley-Davidson for 1939,' photo images on front, EX, D8 ....$65.00

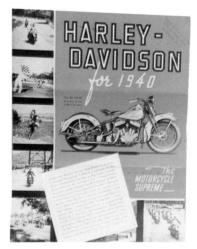

Harley-Davidson, handbill, 'Harley-Davidson for 1940,' photo images & motorcycle on front, EX, D8 ..$65.00

Harley-Davidson, pin, winged emblem, red on gold, 2" long, EX+, A6 ....$55.00

Harley-Davidson, plate holder, brass, eagle atop company name, Made In USA at bottom, EX, A6.................$20.00

Harley-Davidson, police lamp, red rotating 12-volt, with original box, 7" long, NM, A6...........................$225.00

Harley-Davidson, sign, embossed metal, Authorized Dealer above emblem, ...Sales & Service, address & phone number below, 23x30", EX+, A15........$1,650.00

Harley-Davidson, sign, neon, eagle atop emblem, yellow & white, new, 24x34", NM+, A6...........................$300.00

Harley-Davidson, sign, porcelain, pictures trademark image on black, hooded top, 2-sided, 36x60", VG+/VG, A13...........................$3,000.00

Harley-Davidson, sign, self-framed tin, Insist On Genuine Parts & Accessories above & below black & gold logo, red ground, 29x16", NM, D8 ....$200.00

Harley-Davidson, siren cover, stainless steel, 1958, 5½" dia, NM, A6...........................$60.00

Harley-Davidson Chain Saver Lubricant, can, bar & shield logo above text on white emblem, orange ground, rectangular with screw cap, 1950s, 8-oz, NM, A1...........................$150.00

Harley-Davidson Cigarettes, sign, tin, smiling couple on motorcycle behind product name, 1984, 17x21", M, D11 ....$55.00

Harley-Davidson Drop-Forged Forks, banner, paper, Drop-Forged Forks on red emblem at left of 1930 Harley-Davidson in black, EX, D8 ....$525.00

Harley-Davidson Leather Lacquer, can, orange & black paper label, pry lid, 1940s, ¼-pt, 2" dia, EX+, A1 ..$25.00

Harley-Davidson Pre-Luxe Motorcycle Oil, can, logo above product name, black & orange on white, 1-qt, 5½x4" dia, EX+, A6...........................$65.00

Harley-Davidson Racing Motorcycle Oil, can, logo above product name, black & orange on white, 1-qt, full, NM, A1...........................$100.00

Harmony Pure Cocoa Butter, tin, tubular with slip lid, 1x2⅞", EX, D37 ....$25.00

Harold's Club, license plate attachment, die-cut tin, Harold's Club Or Bust! on Conestoga wagon, Reno Nevada below, 8x14", EX+, A1 ....$90.00

Harp Plug Cut, pouch, cloth, NM, A7 ....$8.00

Harper Whiskey, display statue, painted plaster, draped nude with harp points to writing on stone wall, boy watches, 30", EX, A21 ....$605.00

Harper Whisky, display statue, painted plaster, ferocious tiger seated on lettered base holding glass bottle, 30", EX+, A21 ....$745.00

Harrington & Richardson Arms Co, calendar, 1906, company name above pheasant hanging upside-down, full pad, framed, image: 23½x11½", NM, A9 ....$400.00

Harrington & Richardson Arms Co, calendar, 1927, company name above setter dog, incomplete pad, framed, image: 16x9", NM, A9 ....$450.00

Harris Bros, pocket mirror, celluloid, Harris Bros arched above Harness, Horse Furnishings, Blankets, Robes, etc, round, EX, A11 ....$15.00

Harris Radio Co, catalog, 1958, 167 pgs, EX, D17....$60.00

Harrison & Reid, cigar box label, salesman's sample, oval portraits flanked by flags, sailor & soldier, EX, A5..$395.00

Harrison's Heart O' Orange, sign, tin, ...Sold Here, 2 orange fruit faces sipping from straws, bluish green, cream & black, 14" dia, VG, A6 ....$100.00

Harry F Bowler Brewer, tray, shows close-up profile image of lady with pink rose & boa, lettered rim, 13" dia, VG+, A21 ....$145.00

Harry Mitchell's Quality Lager Beer, matchbook, Drink..., 20 strike, front strike, NM, D28.................$3.50

Hartford Accident & Indemnity Co, matchbook, 20 strike, front strike, NM, D28 ....$2.50

Hartford Fire Insurance Co, sign, tin, 'The Monarch of the Glen,' statuesque image of an elk, wood-look self-frame, oval, VG, A8..........................$138.00

Hartford Fire Insurance Co, sign, tin, Live Stock Shipped To Market In This Truck Is..., pictures an elk in upper left corner, 11x19", EX+, D21 ....$55.00

Hartford Time Tested Insurance, clock, light-up, blue numbers surround yellow dot with blue elk & name, metal frame, 15" dia, EX+, A18 ....$165.00

Hartford Tires, sign, die-cut metal flange, orange & blue sign in center of tire, ...Give Tire Insurance, 19½x12½", EX, A6..........................$1,300.00

Hartig's Select Beer, label, Hartig Co, Internal Revenue Tax Paid statement, 1933-50, 12-oz, M, A10........$20.00

Hartl's-87-Certified, label, Marshfield Brewing Co, 12-oz, NM, A10 ....$25.00

Hartshorns Root Beer Extract, sign, paper litho, product name above girl, Extract below, framed, 13x9", VG+, A8 ....$105.00

Hartz DeLuxe Quick Cooking Rolled Oats, container, cardboard, yellow with blue lettering above & below harvest scene, 3-lb, EX, A3 ....$45.00

Hartz Mountain, figure, Hartz cat or dog, plastic, 1974, M, D27...$30.00

Harvard Ale, can, flat-top, instructional, 12-oz, NM, A19 ....$55.00

Harvard Ale, tap knob, chrome with celluloid cover, white on red, EX, A8 ....$75.00

Harvard Ale-Beer, tray, deep-dish, red product lettering on gray background, 12" dia, NM, A19 ....$115.00

Harvard Ales-Beer-Porter, tray, deep-dish, Fully Aged, Tastes Better, girl in black swimsuit posed with glass on knee, 12" dia, NM, A19 ....$120.00

Harvard Beer, sign, embossed die-cut tin hanger, red-lipped black man in straw hat seated with sign reading ...Is Pure, 52", VG, A2 ....$6,700.00

Harvard Pure Malt Beverages, ad, 1901 Pan Am Expo, tower flanked by 2 bottles connected by ...$1000 Pure Beer banner, lettering below, 13x9", EX, A8......$100.00

Harvard Pure Rye, sign, tin, 2 college boys partying with 2 fun-loving ladies, framed, 22x30", G, A21 ....$385.00

Harvester Cigar, sign, self-framed tin, girl in heart-shaped inset, Heart Of Havana..., yellow with black border, oval, 13x9", EX, A6 ....$140.00

Hauswald's Bread, end label, pictures a flamingo, Color For Fun, white border, EX, D29 ....$3.00

Hav-A-Tampa, cigar box, pressed paper, 4¾x8½", EX, A7 ....$10.00

Havacup Coffee, bill hook, product can on oval plaque above hook, EX, A7 ....$75.00

Havana Cadet, tin, light blue with name & image of pipe-smoking cadet on fancy red, yellow & green emblem, round, slip lid, EX, A18..........................$70.00

Havana Inn, cigar box label, inner lid, old car parked next to inn, 6x9", M, D5 ....$20.00

Havana Post, cigar box label, inner lid, Cuban newspaper of Morro Castle, 1904, 6x9", M, D5 ....$9.00

Have One, crate label, California orange, hand holding partially peeled orange on royal blue ground, Lemon Cove, 10x11", M, D3................................$2.00

Havelock Brand/Jesse Brown, Cameron & Crawford, tobacco label, name on banner above oval image of commander directing baracaded soldiers, text below, 12x6", EX, A18 ....$55.00

Havoline, bank, tin, can shape, Custom-Made lettered diagonally above bull's-eye logo, NM, A7 ....$25.00

Havoline, bank, tin, can shape, Custom-Made lettered diagonally above bull's-eye logo, VG+, A7 ....$12.00

Havoline, sign, die-cut porcelain flange, plain bordered circle atop ...The Power Oil, Indian Refining Co Inc, 19x24", EX, A6................................$600.00

Havoline, sign, porcelain, bull's-eye logo flanked by Refinery Sealed above ...Wax Free, 2-sided 11x22", NM, A6..$275.00

Havoline Motor Grease, can, product name & 'It Makes A Difference' above winged logo, blue & cream, press lid & bail, 5-lb, 6" dia, VG+, A6 ....$75.00

Havoline Oil, booklet, 'Concise Atlas of the World War,' Indian Refining Co, 7x6", VG, A6........................$105.00

Hawkeye Incubator Co, tray, woman seated by fireplace holding up glass of beer, lettered rim, vertical rectangle, 17¼", G, A21 ....$60.00

Hayes Fashions for Ladies, catalog, Spring/Summer, 1968, 76 pgs, EX, D17..$15.00

Hayes Half-Size Fashions for Ladies, catalog, Spring/Summer, 1954, 50 pgs, EX, D17 ....$15.00

Haynes Auto Co & Kokomo Rubber Co, watch fob, red & blue porcelain, Chief Kokomo embossed on front, embossed buggy on back, NM, A20 ....$90.00

Haynie's Special, cigar box label, outer, boy flanked by trees, 4½x4½", M, D5..............................$4.00

Hazard Smokeless Powder, calendar, 1910, 'Return of the Hunters,' boy & his dog with game bird, incomplete pad, framed, image: 17x12", VG, A9..................$150.00

Hazard Smokeless Powder, tin, crossed shotguns above duck-hunting scene encircled with product & company name, dated 1893, no cap, NM, A15..................$425.00

Hazard Table Specialties, sign, paper, political satires picturing people with various products, 22x13½", G-, A9..$160.00

Hazle Club Cream Soda, sign, tin over cardboard, frothy mug with On Tap label in center, 9" dia, NM, A3..................................$140.00

Hazle Club Sparkling Beverage, push plate, embossed tin, Finer Flavor Drink above tilted bottle, 1950s, vertical, NM+, A13 ....$90.00

Hazle Club Sparkling Tru-Orange, sign, tin flange, Sparkling & bubbles on center band, Enjoyment Guaranteed..., orange background, 20x14", EX, A6...$130.00

Head Pin, cigar box label, outer, large man with bowling ball, EX, A5 ....$160.00

Headlight Shrunk Overalls, sign, cardboard, name on light beam from locomotive, A New Pair Free If They Shrink below, 1930s, 10x21", EX+, A13..............$150.00

Headlight Union Made Overalls, sign, neon, train reflects Headlight in receding letters above Overalls, 1930s, 14x26", EX, A13....................................$2,000.00

Headlight Union Made Overalls, sign, porcelain, Headlight Union Made on light beam from locomotive, Agency For above, Overalls below, 10x32", VG, A13....................................$450.00

Health Beverage Co Famous Reading Beer, tray, company name arched above factory scene, product name & city below, decorative rim, 1933-34, round, VG+, A8..$60.00

Hearts Delite, crate label, Florida citrus, couple dancing in front of red heart, Weirsdale, 1950s, M, D12.........$5.00

Hech's Liver Pills, pouch, paper, 50 Pills For 25 Cents, NM, A7 ....$7.00

Hecker's Cream Farina, sign, die-cut cardboard standup, ...Quick Energy Cereal, child with mixing bowl & product box, 1920s, 28x19", EX, D8 ....$375.00

Heidel-Brau Beer, label, Sioux City Brewing Co, Internal Revenue Tax Paid statement, 1933-50, 12-oz, M, A10..$15.00

Heidelberg Beer, display, plaster, Lets Have A Heidelberg sign behind 3-D bar with bartender & customer conversing, 9x13", VG+, A8................................$60.00

Heidleberg Beer, display, plaster, princely fellow in cape holding up mug of brew on base marked with product name, 13", EX, A8 ....$100.00

Heileman's Old Style Lager, coaster, 'Paul Revere' on horse yelling 'I'm Asking For...The Beer With A Snap To It,' black on orange, round, EX, A8................$30.00

Heileman's Old Style Lager, coaster, man screaming into microphone 'I'm Asking For...The Beer With A Snap To It,' black on orange, round, EX, A8 ....$30.00

Heileman's Old Style Lager, print on canvas, cavalier standing with bottle & glass, product name on vest, framed, 34x23", EX, A8 ....$60.00

Heileman's Old Style Lager, tap knob, black ball with white, maroon & black on gold enameled insert, EX+, A8 ....$55.00

Heineken Holland Beer, sign, tin/cardboard, Imported... & Since 1620, World's Finest Lager on decorative scalloped field, 1950s, 11x14", EX, A8 ....$20.00

Heinz, alarm clock, Aristocrat Tomato figure behind logo-shaped clock on round base, 1990, 9½", MIB, D27..$150.00

Heinz, see also HJ Heinz Co

Heinz Apple Butter, jar, pottery, paper label, lid & bail handle, 8", VG, A2 ....$132.00

Heinz Baked Beans, postcard, We Make Baked Beans By Hundreds... at right of people conversing, EX+, D26 ....$35.00

Heinz Cereal Food, box, 7x5", EX, A7 ....$8.00

Heinz Pickles, pin, plastic pickle with embossed Heinz, EX, D6 ....$6.00

Heinz Pure Foods/57 Varieties, string holder, tin, pickle chained to 2-sided panel, 17x14", VG, A2.......$3,400.00

Heinz Salad Cream, display bottle, molded plastic, 19", G, A21 ....$55.00

Heinz Vinegar, dispenser, etched glass barrel shape on square base, 13½x6½x6½", EX, A9 ....$100.00

Heinz Vinegars, sign, paper, Four Kinds..., Pints, Quarts..., 57 upper left of product bottle & plate of salad, 1920, 12x22", EX, A2..$155.00

Heinz 57 Ideal Steak Sauce, display bottle, molded plastic with paper labels, 20½", G, A21 ....$35.00

Heinz 57 Varieties, jigsaw puzzle, children playing grocery store with a variety of Heinz products on shelves, 1932, 12x10", EX, D10 ....$65.00

Heinz 57 Varieties Pure Food Products, label, circular with Pure Food Products around Estb 57 1869, image of Heinz pickle & Varieties, framed, 14" dia, EX, A21..........$120.00

Heinz's Aromatic Malt Vinegar, jug, pottery, paper label, short neck, molded ring handle, 10", VG+, A2 ..$550.00

Heinz's Octagon Ketchup, jug, pottery, paper label, short neck, bail handle, 10", VG+, A2......................$550.00

Heinz's Preserved Black Raspberries, crock, pottery, paper label, recessed lid, bail handle, 10x10" dia, EX, A2..$635.00

Heinz's Sweet Picklette, bucket, wood, paper label, lid & bail handle, 11x10" dia, G-, A2 ....$155.00

Heinz's Tomato Preserves, crock, stone litho label, bail handle with wood grip, dated 1883, NM, A15 ...$550.00

Helena Grapes, lug box label, view of Napa Valley, geyser, mountain & grapes, Stockton, M, D12 ....$3.00

Hellman Brewing Co's Bock, print, paper litho, Just Out..., shows ram bursting through end of barrel, 24x18", EX, A8..$25.00

Helmar All-Turkish Cigarettes, sign, cardboard, white product name above black silhoutted Turkish city against red sky, blue border, 28x19", EX, A18 .....$85.00

Helmar Turkish Cigarettes, matchbook, very colorful, 20 strike (few sticks broken), front strike, EX, D28 ..$12.00

Helmar Turkish Cigarettes, sign, paper, name above & below profile image of Egyptian queen on green draped background, framed, 30x20", VG+, A18 ....$100.00

Helmar Turkish Cigarettes, sign, porcelain, red with smiling lady at left of white oval with product lettering & 10¢ pack, 10x28", VG, A18..............................$110.00

Helmar Turkish Cigarettes, sign, porcelain flange, die-cut girl in straw hat behind sign, ...Quality Superb, 2-sided, 23x16", VG, A6..................................$700.00

Helmar Turkish Cigarettes, sign, tin, girl in straw hat holding box of cigarettes flanked by lettering, product name above & below, 14" dia, G+, A9 ....$350.00

Helmar Turkish Cigarettes, sign, tin, Quality Superb above girl in straw hat with box of cigarettes, self-framed, 28½x22", VG, A9 ....$350.00

Hemmer's Ice Cream, tray, Quality Hemmer's above oval showing product with Ice Cream on ribbon banner, lettered rim, 1920s, 13x13", VG+, A13 ....$170.00

Hennepin Brau, label, 13-oz, VG+, A19..................$25.00

Henry Clay Habana, sign, paper, name above Juan Alvarez & fort surrounded by wreath of cigars & boxes, flowers & shields, 24x18", EX, A2 ....$155.00

Henry Clay Habana Cigarrillos, album with photo cards, 153 cards with scenes from around the world, 1910, M cards/VG cover, A5..$140.00

Henry George 5¢ Cigar, sign, embossed tin, oval portrait with stars & scrolled border, Hirschhorn Mack & Co Makers, NY, image: 20x14", EX+, A9..............$1,750.00

Henry W Price, sign, cardboard, interior scene with woman painting at easel surrounded by children at play, 12x8", VG+, A2..$66.00

Hensler Draught Beer, tap knob, chrome with celluloid cover, red, gold & blue on white, 2" dia, VG+, A8..$35.00

Hensler Light Beer, display, plastic, Since 1860 & Light Beer flank Hensler on red base that holds 3 drinking glasses, NM, A19 ....$60.00

Hensler Private Label, tap knob, chrome with celluloid cover, gold, white & red lettering on black, 2", VG+, A8 ....$65.00

Hep, sign, flange, Get Hep For Yourself at right of tilted bottle on oval, red & green on cream, 13x17½", EX, A8 ....$220.00

Herbert Tareyton Cigarettes, sign, die-cut cardboard stand-up, dapper man in top hat & monocle with open pack, lettering below, 20x13", NM A18.................$60.00

Hercules EC & Infallible...L&R Orange Extra, sign, 'Dah He Goes,' snow scene with 2 black men looking frightened while reloading, 24x15½", NM, D8...........$675.00

Hercules Powder, sign, tin on cardboard, image of Hercules on red with black scalloped border, 13x9", A15 ....$325.00

Hercules Powder Co, banner, features Grand Prize ribbon from the Panama Pacific International Exposition, San Francisco 1915, 19x13", EX, A9 ....$200.00

Hercules Powder Co, calendar, 1936, 'Days End,' signed Frederic Stanley, girl & dog watching birds, 1-sheet calendar below, 30x13", EX, A6 ....$70.00

Hercules Powder Co, calendar, 1941, Norman Rockwell print of farmer boy & dog at top, 29½x13", EX, A6.........$75.00

Hercules Powder Co, sign, paper, 'Stowaways,' boy in trunk trying to keep puppy silent, matted & framed, image: 19x12", G+, A9 ....$200.00

Hercules Powder Co Infallible Smokeless Shotgun Powder, sign, paper with metal strips, product name above back view of man with rifle, company name below, 1914, 31x20", G, A9 ....$350.00

Hercules Spark Plugs, spark plug tester, wood, 4x8½", EX, A6 ....$20.00

Hercules Spring, sign, self-framed tin, Real Restful Rest below oval inset of woman resting on box springs, 9x19", G-, A9 ....$175.00

Herold Smoked Sardines, tin, book form opens to show red product lettering & image of open can of sardines, 4x10x10", G, A21 ....$50.00

Hershey's Ice Cream, sign, cardboard, Peaches 'N Cream Peach Sundae Supreme on banner above large sundae, 20x13", EX, A6 ....$60.00

Hershey's Milk Chocolate, dispenser, 1¢, metal with glass front, Hershey's on diagonal band, 2 slots, brown, yellow & green, 19x9", VG, A6 ....$70.00

Hershey's Mr Goodbar, pillow, candy bar shape, 1989, 4x6", NM, D24 ....$8.00

Herters Hunting & Fishing Equipment, catalog, 1971, 628 pgs, EX, D17.....................................$30.00

Herzkafer, cigar box label, outer, woman with parasol walking in park, 4½x4½", M, D5 ....$8.00

Hesperian, crate label, Washington apple, outline drawing of lady on orange background, Wenatchee, 1930s, 9x11", M, D12 ....$2.00

Hi Hat Hair Dressing, tin, product name left of tap-dancing couple, ¼x1¼" dia, EX, D37 ....$25.00

Hi-Cliff Beer, label, Clyffside Brewing Co, Internal Revenue Tax Paid statement, 1933-50, 12-oz, NM, A10 ....$45.00

Hi-Plane Smooth Cut Tobacco for Pipe & Cigarettes, calendar, 1937, paper, Indians on horseback with tobacco tin in the foreground, full pad, framed, image: 30x18", EX, A9...$100.00

Hi-Plane Smooth Cut Tobacco for Pipe & Cigarettes, cigarette papers, NM, A7...................................$20.00

Hi-Plane Smooth Cut Tobacco for Pipe & Cigarettes, pocket container, cardboard, vertical, red with white product name above & below single-engine plane, rare, NM, A18.$450.00

Hi-Plane Smooth Cut Tobacco for Pipe & Cigarettes, pocket tin, vertical, red with name above & below single-engine plane, VG+, A18 ....$65.00

Hi-Plane Smooth Cut Tobacco for Pipe & Cigarettes, pocket tin, vertical, red with name above & below 4-engine plane, EX+, A18 ....$720.00

Hi-Plane Smooth Cut Tobacco for Pipe & Cigarettes, pocket tin, vertical, red with name above twin-engine plane, EX+, A18...$150.00

Hi-Plane Smooth Cut Tobacco for Pipe & Cigarettes, sign, embossed tin, image of pocket tin & 10¢ left of product name, black & white on red, 12x35", VG, A8.........$35.00

Hi-Speed Cream Separator & Household Oil, tin, image of cream separator in center, black & red lettering on white background, 8x4½", EX+, D21...................$35.00

Hiawatha, tobacco label, die-cut, red, EX, D35...........$6.00

Hiawatha Dark Fine Cut, tin, orange with brown & gold lettering & trim, pictures Indian, Norton Bros, round 2x8" dia, EX, A18 ....$150.00

Hiawatha Granulated Mixture Tobacco, tin, yellow with black & red name right of Indian, red decorative border, rectangular, rounded corners, EX+, A18.....$100.00

Hiawatha Light Fine Cut, tin, yellow with red & black lettering & trim, pictures Indian, Spaulding, round, 2x8" dia, EX+, A18...$220.00

Hick's Capudine Liquid, tray, ...10-25 & 50 Cts A Bottle on band around image of 3 cherubs flying around product box, 9¾" dia, G+, A21 ....$95.00

Hickey & Nicholson, tin, horizontal, EX, D35.........$35.00

Hickory Extremely Mild Pipe Mixture, pocket tin, vertical, red with white lettering above & below white image of crossed pistols, NM, A18.....................$75.00

High Grade Smoking Tobacco/Cameron & Cameron, pocket tin, vertical, green, red & black lettering around circular graphics, Ilsley, EX+, A18.....................$625.00

High Grade Smoking Tobacco/Cameron & Cameron, pocket tin, vertical, silver, red & black lettering around circular graphics, Hasker & Marcuse, EX, A18 ...**$585.00**

Highland Linen, see also Eaton's Highland Linen

Highland Linen Writing Paper/Eaton Crane & Pike Co, sign, cardboard trifold, woman at window seat, postman beyond, envelope examples on outer panels, ca 1916, EX, A12 ....**$230.00**

Highlander Beer, sign, die-cut porcelain, Famous...Beer On Tap on emblem with diamond designs, red ground, 2-sided, 22x36", EX, A8.......................................**$950.00**

Highlander Beer, sign, tin on cardboard, product name in script & eagle above None Finer..., red & silver rim, 8x12", EX+, A19...**$145.00**

Highlander Pilsener Brew, sign, Highlander in diagonal script above 2 bottles & glass of beer, Quality Beer upper left, 14x19", EX+, D21 ....**$260.00**

Hignett's Golden Butterfly Cigarettes, tin, embossed image of butterfly with product lettering, rectangular with slightly rounded corners, VG, A18 ....**$100.00**

Hill & Hill Kentucky Bourbon Whiskey, clock sign, reverse-painted glass, clock & advertising on red rectangle, curved corners, metal frame, 10x17", EX, A8 ..**$75.00**

Hill Bicycle Store, pocket mirror, celluloid, smiling man above I Bought My Sporting Goods, Stoves, Gas Supplies..., round, EX, A11 ....**$20.00**

Hill's Standard, cigar box label, inner lid, US map, 1914, 6x9", EX, D5 ....**$75.00**

Hills Bros Coffee, thermometer, porcelain, man in turban & gown drinking coffee beside bulb above product name, 21", EX, A13 ....$325.00

Hills Bros Coffee, thermometer, porcelain, man in turban & gown drinking coffee beside bulb above product name, 21", NM, A1 ....**$450.00**

Hills Bros Vending Special Coffee, tin, silver lettering on red, key-wind lid, 2-lb, NM+, A3............................**$35.00**

Hillsboro Pale Beer, drinking glass, straight-sided with red logo above product name, Hillsboro Wisconsin, 4", NM, A8 ....**$55.00**

Hillside Regular Grind Coffee, tin, black & silver with silver silhouette of man & horse-drawn cart, key-wind lid, 2-lb, EX+, A18..**$25.00**

Himyar, cigarette papers, NM, A7..............................**$15.00**

Hinz's Pride of Queen City Coffee, tin, blue with name above & below oval image of city skyline, yellow Coffee on red band below, key-wind, 1-lb, EX+, A18.......**$45.00**

Hiolube, can, lettered monument before rising sun in circle above Hiolube in script, yellow & black on white, 1-qt, VG+, A1 ....**$160.00**

Hippo Permanent Pliable Oil, can, product name above bucket of water being poured on hippo's back, Canadian cities below, screw cap, 11", VG+, A1..........**$30.00**

Hippo Washing Powder, product box, pictures monkey scrubbing a hippo, Iowa Soap Co, full, VG, A3...**$25.00**

Hiram Sibley & Co's Celebrated Melon Seeds, sign, paper, comical image of black boy laying beside melons & holding large slice, framed, image: 25x17", G+, A9...**$1,550.00**

Hirch's Goodies, jar, glass, fish bowl type, product name embossed on lid, 11" dia, EX, A2.......................**$470.00**

Hires, ad from Literary Digest, soda jerk at counter, 1919, VG, D31 ....**$8.00**

Hires, ad from National Weekly, 'There Is No Other Drink Like Hires,' 1919, VG, D31.............................**$4.00**

Hires, ad from Pictorial Review, 'This Liberal Trial At Hires Expense,' 1928, EX, D31......................................**$10.00**

Hires, ad from Saturday Evening Post, 'Three Ways To Get Hires,' EX, D31 ....**$8.00**

Hires, ashtray, glass bottle shape, EX+, D31 ....**$12.00**

Hires, booklet, 'Hires Extracts', pictures seated boy with glass looking up at sign, EX, D31 ....**$15.00**

Hires, booklet, 'How To Make Hires Root Beer At Home,' EX, D31..**$10.00**

Hires, booklet, 'Legend of the Golden Chair,' early, EX+, A16 ....**$15.00**

Hires, booklet, pictures owl & parrot on a branch & hands holding bottle, 1896, rare, EX, D31 ....**$45.00**

Hires, bookmark, pictures ducks, rare, EX, D31........**$28.00**

Hires, calendar, 1893, pictures 2 little girls with kitten, full pad, rare, NM+, D4 ....**$650.00**

Hires, calendar, 1893, top only, pictures 2 little girls with kitten, rare, EX, D31..**$175.00**

Hires, calendar, 1957, hand holding frothy mug in front of 8-pack carton, Number One In More Ways..., full pad, M, D31 ....**$25.00**

Hires, calendar & note pad, 1890, Compliments Of Charles E Hires, Philadelphia on front, rare, EX, D31.......**$45.00**

Hires, checkerboard, Drank All The Year Round above Hires boy on front, 1892, 12x12" (open), rare, VG, A6...**$185.00**

Hires, decal, Drink Hires in gold on black emblem, blue & white striped background, EX, D31 ....**$8.00**

Hires, decal, Drink Hires Root Beer on bottle cap, EX, D31 ....**$15.00**

Hires, door push, porcelain, Buvez Hires Naturellement Bon!, blue & red on turquoise, 3x30", EX, D21 ..**$160.00**

Hires, door push, tin, Finer Flavor Because Of Real Root Juices & tilted bottle, Ice Cold below, 11½x3½", NM, A13 ....**$150.00**

Hires, door push, tin, It's High Time For Hires Root Beer, bottle cap at left, white background, chrome frame, 4x30", G+, A1 ....**$35.00**

Hires, door push insert, tin, ...Ask For above Hires on diagonal panel & tilted bottle, 1940s-50s, NM+, A13 ..**$60.00**

Hires, ice-cream scoop, plastic, Only One Taste Says Hires To You lettered on handle, EX, D31....................**$10.00**

Hires, invitation, Got A Minute, Have A Hires, pictures glass of root beer, G-, D31 ....**$3.00**

Hires, menu board, tin, Hires R-J Root Beer With Real Root Juices Ice Cold 5¢ Bottles above board, EX+, A16...**$195.00**

Hires, menu board, tin, Hires Root Beer in red on white above board, 27x19", EX+, D21 ....**$70.00**

Hires, milkshake mixer, white porcelain over iron, embossed Hires The Flavor For Milk Drinks, 1890s, very rare, EX, A15.....................**$1,050.00**

Hires, mug, ceramic, barrel shape with pointing Hires boy, Drink Hires Rootbeer, handled, NM, A16..........**$220.00**

Hires, mug, ceramic, Drink Hires It Is Pure on red diamond, 5½x4", EX, D16 ....**$35.00**

Hires, mug, ceramic, Hires in red, multicolored image of Hires boy in robe, English Cauldonware, M, D16............**$125.00**

Hires, mug, ceramic, hourglass shape, white with multicolored image of pointing Hires boy, handled, Mettlach, scarce, NM, D21 ....**$175.00**

Hires, mug, ceramic, tapered, Join Health & Cheer above Hires boy in tuxedo, Drink... below, handled, Mettlach, 5", EX+, A13 ....**$210.00**

Hires, mug, ceramic, multicolored image of pointing Hires boy in robe, marked Villeroy & Bock..., handle reglued, 4x3", D16 ....**$140.00**

Hires, mug, glass, applied label with Drink in script above Hires on slanted band, Root Beer below, handled, M, A16 ....**$35.00**

Hires, mug, plastic, brown & red logo, Hires Root Beer, 5x3", NM, D16 ....**$5.00**

Hires, pencil clip, celluloid, round head, blue, gold & black, rare, EX, A16.....................**$75.00**

Hires, pocket mirror, celluloid, Put Roses In Your Cheeks..., woman holding roses & mug, oval, ca 1908, rare, EX, D31 ....**$290.00**

Hires, pocketknife, features Josh Slinger in white jacket & tie, 1915, rare, EX+, D31.....................**$245.00**

Hires, puzzle book, elephant pictured on front, EX, D31.....................**$35.00**

Hires, recipe booklet, 'Hires Food & Drink Recipes,' soda fountain scene with large frothy mug in the foreground, EX, D31 ....**$15.00**

Hires, sign, cardboard, die-cut, Enjoy...Take Home A Carton! on emblem across girl with glass on striped circle, 13x9", EX, D21.....................**$30.00**

Hires, sign, cardboard, die-cut, Hires RJ Root Beer on circle above bottles, glass & sandwich tray, 10x9½", VG+, D21.....................**$25.00**

Hires, sign, cardboard, die-cut, R-J bottle & foaming glass on tab reading With Lunch, 11x10", NM+, A3 ....$50.00

Hires, sign, cardboard, Drink above Hires flanked by 5¢ symbols, framed, 11x25", EX, A7 ....**$50.00**

Hires, sign, cardboard, Enjoy in script at left of girl with glass & Hires Delicious... sign, 1950s, 13" dia, EX, A4.....................**$125.00**

Hires, sign, cardboard, Got A Minute Have A Hires above bottle & Your Invitation To Refresh, 30x24", NM+, D30.....................**$175.00**

Hires, sign, cardboard, Say Hires above & below pointing Hires boy with frothy mug, 1880-90, oval, 24x20", VG+, D21 ....**$1,000.00**

Hires, sign, cardboard trolley, Thirsts Gently Suffocated By...5¢ Per Snuff left of smiling man, framed, image: 6x10", EX, A9.....................**$275.00**

Hires, sign, flange, Hires on dot above check mark & Made With Roots*Barks*Herbs, So Refreshing below, EX+, A13.....................**$200.00**

Hires, sign, from dispenser, steel, die-cut, Hires over circular panel, Since 1876, Root Beer With Roots* Barks*Herbs, NM, A13.....................**$95.00**

Hires, sign, from dispenser, tin, Hires R-J Root Beer With Real Root Juices, embossed, 12" dia, EX+, A13..**$150.00**

Hires, sign, paper, die-cut, Hires across front of large foamy glass, NM, A16 ....**$175.00**

Hires, sign, paper, Drink Hires In Bottles, oval image of Haskell Coffin girl, bottle in the foreground, framed, G, D31.....................**$420.00**

Hires, sign, reverse-painted glass, Drink Hires Rootbeer below pointing Hires boy with mug, chain frame, 8x7", rare, NM, A6.....................**$1,700.00**

Hires, sign, reverse-painted glass, Hires Rootbeer Is Very Refreshing...5¢, white on blue, beveled edge, 12x16", EX, A13 ....**$650.00**

Hires, sign, tin, -And It's Always Pure at left of sneaky girl with book & glass, ...In Bottles, framed, image: 14x20", G+, A9.....................**$300.00**

Hires, sign, tin, Ask For Hires In Bottles in cream outlined in white on brown, embossed, 1920s, 10x28", NOS, EX+, A1 ....**$150.00**

Hires, sign, tin, die-cut bottle, 1950s, 58x16", NM, A13..**$425.00**

Hires, sign, tin, die-cut bottle, 78x22", EX, A13...$400.00

Hires, sign, tin, Drink Hires In Bottles, pictures elegant woman, hanger with cardboard back, 9x6½", EX, A1 ....**$310.00**

Hires, sign, tin, Drink Hires In Bottles, yellow & blue background outlined in red, embossed, 1930s, 5x14", NM, A13.....................**$110.00**

Hires, sign, tin, Drink Hires In Bottles lower left of smiling girl, 9x6", G+, A9 ....$320.00

Hires, sign, tin, Drink Hires In Bottles on yellow diamond against red, black border, embossed, 10x27", VG+, A16 ....$300.00

Hires, sign, tin, Drink Hires in red on yellow emblem & tilted bottle, striped background, 9½x27", EX, D21..........$70.00

Hires, sign, tin, Drink on oval left of Hires, The Genuine Root Beer below, embossed, 5½x20", EX+, A16 ....$650.00

Hires, sign, tin, Drink...It Hits The Spot, Try A Bottle..., Josh Slinger with bottle, embossed, 1915, 10x16", EX+, A1 ....$370.00

Hires, sign, tin, Drink...It Hits The Spot, Try A Bottle..., Josh Slinger with bottle, embossed, 1915, 10x16", VG, A13 ....$225.00

Hires, sign, tin, Enjoy Hires It's Always Pure left of girl in red hat ready to sip from straw, embossed, 10x28", NM, A13 ....$650.00

Hires, sign, tin, Hires In Bottles over tilted bottle, tan & orange on dark brown, embossed, 10x28", EX, A1 ....$160.00

Hires, sign, tin, Hires R-J Root Beer in white on blue & red circle, With Real Root Juices on red band, 8x12", EX, D30..$70.00

Hires, sign, tin, Hires R-J Root Beer in white on blue & red circle, With Real Root Juices on red band, 12" dia, NM, D30..$90.00

Hires, sign, tin, Hires... & For Pleasure & Thirst flank tilted bottle against burst of white on blue, 1950s, 18x56", NM, A13 ....$725.00

Hires, sign, tin, It Tastes So Good, Real Root Juices, R-J logo on blue above tilted bottle on white, 1940s, 48x14", EX+, A13..$575.00

Hires, sign, tin, Say Hires above & below pointing Hires boy with frothy mug, 1907-08, self-framed oval, 24x20", G+, A13 ....$600.00

Hires, sign, tin, Say Hires above & below pointing Hires boy with frothy mug, 1907-08, self-framed oval, 24x20", EX, A2 ....$990.00

Hires, sign, tin, Say! Drink Hires It's Pure, fancy corner borders, 8x18½", rare, G, A16..$650.00

Hires, sticker, shows pointing Hires boy, NM, A16 ...$50.00

Hires, straw dispenser, Hires flanked by lettering on top panel, 5¢ Hires For Thirst on side panels, rare, EX, D31 ....$1,195.00

Hires, syrup bottle, For Malted Milk Flavored With Hires on label, metal cap, EX, A16..$660.00

Hires, syrup bottle, Hires in red on white label under glass, metal cap, VG, A13 ....$230.00

Hires, syrup dispenser, ceramic hourglass shape, Drink Hires It Is Pure, rare spigot at bottom, 12x7½", VG, A9 ....$700.00

Hires, syrup dispenser, ceramic hourglass shape, Drink Hires It Is Pure, original pump, 14½x7½", VG, A9.........$450.00

Hires, syrup dispenser, ceramic hourglass shape, Drink Hires It Is Pure, original pump, 14½x7½", NM, A4 ....$700.00

Hires, syrup dispenser, Drink Hires It Is Pure on milk glass globe atop brass spigot, marble base, 1910, 36x16x16", EX, A9..$7,500.00

Hires, thermometer, die-cut tin bottle, 27x8", NM, D11 ..$125.00

Hires, toy dispenser, barrel shape, in original box, EX, A16..$28.00

Hires, trade card, bust portrait of girl with roses, Put Roses In Your cheeks, EX, D31 ....$30.00

Hires, trade card, die-cut, girl in bonnet with glass, VG, D31..$16.00

Hires, trade card, dog drinking from glass in front of angry child, EX, D31..$16.00

Hires, trade card, features Hires girl, 1890, EX, rare, D31..$30.00

Hires, trade card, Hires Extract, side-view of girl in bonnet holding bottle of extract, 1891, G, D31 ....$15.00

Hires, trade card, Hires girl seated, 1888, rare, EX, D31 ..$24.00

Hires, trade card, It Cured My Cold, little girl standing on hillside, 1888, rare, EX, D31 ....$20.00

Hires, trade card, It's Time To Drink Hires Rootbeer, little girl atop ladder changing time on clock, EX, D31.........$18.00

Hires, trade card, pictures lady in black dress, 1890, EX, D31..$20.00

Hires, tray, 'Things Is Getting Higher But Hires Is Still A Nickel A Trickel,' features Josh Slinger, 1915, rare, EX, D31..$425.00

Hires, tray, shows white oval bust image of young woman against wood-grain background, lettered rim, vertical, 13", VG+, A21..$250.00

Hires Condensed Milk, booklet, pictures product can on front, 1898, EX, D31..$25.00

Hires Home Recipe, full bottle of extract with box, EX+, A16 ....$15.00

Hires/McKesson Drug Store, clock, green & red neon surrounds clock with moving ad panel, Drink Hires 5¢ on reverse clock face, 20x26", EX, A1 ....$2,200.00

HJ Heinz Co, postcard, exterior & interior views of the new Administration Building, NM, D26................$40.00

Hoagland Jeweler & Optician, sign, stenciled wood, Perfect lettered above middle view of man pulling watch from pocket, name below, 36", VG+, A2............$300.00

Hoberg Tissue Paper, watch fob, black & flesh-tone porcelain, 2 cherubs with roll of toilet paper flanked by Trademark Registered, EX, A20..$128.00

Hochgreve Bavarian Style Beer, coaster, red & blue, 4" dia, EX, A8 ....$30.00

Hochgreve Special, tap knob, black ball shape with gold on black enamel insert, VG+, A8 ....$90.00

Hodell Anti-Freeze, sign, cardboard, B-R-R-R Get That Anti-Freeze Now above car stuck in the snow, ...Lasts All Winter Long, 28x17", NM, A6 ....$70.00

Hoff-Brau, tap knob, red plastic with white plastic insert, oval, EX, A8 ....$30.00

Hoffman Beer, tap knob, name on red oblong insert on white porcelain, EX, A8 ....$100.00

Hoffman Beer, tap knob, plastic, name on red loop chain-linked around yellow loop, VG+, A8 ....$25.00

Hohenadel Beer, sign, tin, image of famous boxer John L Sullivan, Well Earned Supremacy..., G+, A19 .....$160.00

Hohenadel Beer, sign, tin, image of famous boxer John L Sullivan, Well Earned Supremacy..., 23x17", EX, A9 ....$275.00

Hohenadel Beer, tray, deep-dish, shows 3 religious figures at table watching a dog smoking a cigar, 13" dia, NM, A8 ....$40.00

Hohenadel Beer, tray, deep-dish, 2 glasses & bottle on table with place card reading When The 2nd Tastes As Good..., 12" dia, EX, A8 ....$30.00

Hohenadel Beer, tray, lettering on rim around food scene & pilsener glass, product name above, oval, 13x16", EX+, A19 ....$70.00

Hohenadel Light Beer, can, cone-top, Internal Revenue Tax Paid statement, 12-oz, EX+, A19 ....$105.00

Holiday Pipe Mixture, pocket tin, palm trees above large ship, Aromatic In The Pack, Aromatic In The Pipe, vertical, NM, A3 ....$35.00

Holiday Special Beer, label, George Walter Brewing Co, Internal Revenue Tax Paid statement, 1933-50, 12-oz, M, A10 ....$12.00

Holihan's Ale/Diamond Spring Brewing Co, sign, die-cut cardboard, Good & Taste... flank lady with glass atop Holihan's Ale on base, 1945, 11x10", EX, A19 ....$65.00

Holihan's Ale/Diamond Spring Brewing Co, sign, die-cut cardboard, shows girl emerging from pool with glass atop Cooling... on base, 1945, VG, 11x10", EX, A19 ....$35.00

Holihan's Ale/Diamond Spring Brewing Co, sign, paper, Refreshing & product name on sign above girl with glass encircled by rope, 22x25", EX, A19 .....$25.00

Holihan's Light Stock Ale, tray, deep-dish, lion logo above product name, 'Pride Of The Valley' below on red, NM, A19 ....$60.00

Hollyhock Brand Non-Drying Ribbon, tin, flat, image of sun setting behind house, lettering below square, rounded corners, ¾x2½x2½", EX, D37 ....$25.00

Hollywood Bread, end label, black & white photo image of Mamie Van Doren, blue border, EX, D29 ....$12.00

Hollywood Bread, sign, cardboard, Jan Sterling Says above product name & text with Jan Sterling posed against a tree, 31x22", EX, A1 ....$35.00

Holsum Bread, door push bar, metal, loaf of bread in center, red, yellow, blue & white, 41½" long, NOS, A6....$185.00

Home Brand Coffee, tin, small circular image of a mansion in center, key-wind lid, EX, A3 ....$55.00

Home Brand Coffees/Home Tea Co, bean pot, stoneware, brown-glazed top half, natural bottom half with stamped advertising, double handled, NM+, A3 ...$65.00

Home Brand Quick Cooking Rolled Oats, container, cardboard, yellow with lettering above & below circular image of house, earlier version, 3-lb, no lid, VG, A3 ....$40.00

Home Brand Regular Cooking Rolled Oats, container, cardboard, yellow with lettering above bowl of oats on red dot, 3-lb, no lid, EX+, A3 ....$35.00

Home Brewing Co, mug, blue on tan, Compliments Of above company name in black stamped lettering, VG+, A8 ....$110.00

Home Comfort Wrought Steel Ranges & Furnaces, sign, porcelain, factory scene with company name & ad text above & below, ca 1895, 4¼x6", EX+, A13 ....$250.00

Home Grown Apples, can label, product name above & below apple/lily pond, 4½x14", NM, A7 ....$2.00

Home Life Insurance Co, wheel card, 'Army-Navy Insignia Guide,' rotating wheel shows various insignias, 1942, 5x4", EX+, D14 ....$12.00

Home Mutual Insurance Co California, sign, paper, horse-drawn wagons passing buildings, firefighting equipment on side panels, framed, image: 25x31", G, A9 ....$1,900.00

Homer's Ginger & Brandy, sign, reverse-painted glass, ...Quickly Relieves Cramps & Diarrhea, 6x10", EX, A9 ....$475.00

Homestead Brand Coffee, pail, vertical black & red stripes with gold plantation scene above name on black band, bail handle, 5-lb, VG+, A18 ....$125.00

Honest Labor Cut Plug, pocket tin, flat, product name above arm & hammer logo & other lettering, EX, A3 ....$45.00

Honest Long Cut, cigarette papers, NM, A7 ....$30.00

Honest Long Cut Tobacco, calendar, 1896, pictures Papa Bear bringing armfuls of tobacco packets, complete, 10x5", EX, A21 ....$75.00

Honest Long Cut Tobacco, sign, cardboard, name above man smoking pipe, Smoking & Chewing below, framed, 24x17", G, A21 ....$155.00

Honest Scrap, store bin, tin, product name on red slanted lid, front shows product flanked by dog & cat, EX+, A15..$1,250.00

Honey & Sonny Bread, pin-back button, pictures boy & girl, 1" dia, NM, A7............................$10.00

Honey Moon Rum-Flavored Tobacco, pocket tin, vertical, red with product name above & below encircled image of man on crescent moon & large 10¢, EX+, A18......$315.00

Honey Moon Rum-Flavored Tobacco, pocket tin, vertical, red with product name above & below encircled image of man on crescent moon (no 10¢), EX, A18......$150.00

Honey Moon Rum-Flavored Tobacco, pocket tin, vertical, red with product name above & below encircled image of man on crescent moon (no 10¢), VG+, A18...$110.00

Honey Moon Tobacco/Penn Tobacco Co, pocket tin, vertical, red with product & company name above & below encircled image of man on crescent moon, EX+, A18..$100.00

Honey Moon Tobacco/Penn Tobacco Co, sign, embossed tin, pictures product with romantic couple seated on crescent moon, 10x7", NM+, A13.......$300.00

Honey-Fruit Gum, sign, tin over cardboard, Nothing Like It upper left of gum pack, Delightful Flavoring lower right, 6x9", EX, A13............................$1,300.00

Honey-Fruit Gum, whistle, paper, shows 5¢ pack of gum with Blow For above & 'The Tastiest Chewing Gum' below, rare, EX+, A16.......................$375.00

Honeymoon Breakfast Coffee, container, paper on cardboard, Keen Cut & romantic couple on crescent moon flanked by lettering, rare, VG+, A3.....................$120.00

Honeymoon Breakfast Coffee, tin, Keen Cut & romantic couple on crescent moon flanked by lettering, pry lid, VG+, A3 ....$170.00

Honor Brand Quick Cooking Rolled Oats, container, cardboard, lettering & portrait of Geo Washington on white & blue with gold trim, 3-lb, no lid, rare, VG+, A3 ....$95.00

Hood Canvas Footwear, sign, die-cut cardboard stand-up, Hood on arrow above split image of beach scene & mountain scene, 8x17½", EX, A6 ....$90.00

Hood Dairy, squeeze toy, Hood Dairyman figure, vinyl, 1981, M, D27...$60.00

Hood Finest Linen Thread, tin, arrow logo above Hood tire man & product name on green, slip lid, 1-lb, 4x4" dia, NM, A1...$160.00

Hood River, crate label, Oregon pear, Mount Hood across valley, dark blue diamond logo, Hood River, 8x11", M, D12..$4.00

Hood River Spitzenburgs, trolley sign, cardboard, apple pointing to ...The Apple Center Of The World on map, Blue Diamond Brand, 11x21", G+, A1 ....$10.00

Hood Rubbers, pocket mirror/calendar, 1912-13, celluloid, We Sell... above shoe & lettering surrounded by calendar, round, VG+, A11.............................$30.00

Hood Tires, sign, porcelain, Hood Tire man signaling to stop at left, white, black & red, 22x28", G+, A6..$425.00

Hood Tires, thermometer, wood, Hood Tire man with flag above bulb, round logo below, curved top, 15x4", A1..$215.00

Hood's French-American Ice Cream, sign, reverse-painted glass, stemmed dish of ice cream left of ...Ice Cream Always Delicious on blue, 10x16", NM, A2..$360.00

Hood's Ice Cream, sign, embossed tin, It's Hoods Ice Cream on red sign above ice-cream cone & encircled cow, 32x24", EX, A6 ....$375.00

Hood's Royal Oak Rubber Boots, sign, embossed die-cut tin, Resists Hard Wear, lettering around large boot on yellow & green background, 12x9", EX+, A21...$340.00

Hood's Sarsaparilla & Pills, jigsaw puzzle, 'A Wedding In Catland,' wedding party exiting church, bridge on reverse, 1890s, 10x15", EX, A10 ....$175.00

Hood's Sarsaparilla, calendar, 1886, profile of blond-haired little girl in white bonnet with pink flowers, incomplete pad, 7x5", G, A6 ....$40.00

Hood's Sarsaparilla, calendar, 1892, images of children sewing, original top sheet, round, NM, A18........$80.00

Hood's Sarsaparilla, calendar, 1894, 'Sweet Sixteen,' oval image of girl in bonnet & pearl-colored blouse, incomplete pad, 9x6", G, A6....................$50.00

Hood's Sarsaparilla, calendar, 1897, die-cut image of girl's head, Coupon..., original top sheet, NM, A18......$80.00

Hood's Sarsaparilla, calendar, 1898, encircled portrait of small girl surrounded by flowers, Coupon..., original top sheet, NM, A18..................$80.00

Hood's Sarsaparilla, calendar, 1899, 'The American Girl,' girl in profile on American flag background, full pad, 9½x6½", NM+, A3 ....$100.00

Hood's Sarsaparilla, calendar, 1913, 'The Dinner Bell,' girl pouring milk for kittens while small child rings bell, full pad, 8x7", EX+, A3 ....$80.00

Hood's Sarsaparilla, jigsaw puzzle, man in horse-drawn wagon, factory scene beyond, original box, 2-sided, framed, 10x15", EX, A21 ....$145.00

Hood's Sarsaparilla, paper dolls & costumes, 2 dolls with 1 pink & white & 1 blue & white sailor suit, 1894, VG, D14.........................$12.00

Hoody's Peanut Butter, pail, red with white product name above & below 2 kids on seesaw, bail handle, VG+, A18..........................$150.00

Hoosier Beer, label, South Bend Beverage & Ice Co, U-type permit number, Internal Revenue Tax Paid statement, 1933-36, 12-oz, M, A10 ....$10.00

Hoosier Beer, sign, tin, Good Old Hoosier Beer above fisherman in boat with dog, The Quality Beer, beveled edge, 1930s, 15x13", EX, A8 ....$510.00

Hoosier Maid Cloves, tin, paper label, 2½", NM, A7..$22.00

Hoosier Poet Allspice, tin, paper label, 2¾", NM, A7 ..$45.00

Hoosier Stove Co, catalog, 1908, 64 pgs, EX, D16....$90.00

Hooton's Amazon Cocoa, tin, sample, product name encircles 2 girls sharing a steaming cup of cocoa, slip lid, 2x1¾x1¼", EX, D37.....................$95.00

Horlacher, sign, paper litho, pictures Betsy Ross making flag, text below, framed, image: 28x21", EX+, A8 ..$385.00

Horlacher Brewing Co, calendar, 1962, 'Beach Party,' girl on beach above 12-month calendar flanked by penguins, 33x16", EX, A7 ....$35.00

Horlacher's Genuine Bock Beer, sign, die-cut cardboard stand-up, ram holding frothy glass standing behind fence with sign & tulips, 21x21", VG, A8.............$20.00

Horlacher's Perfection Beer, art plate, decorative gold & green rim around bare-breasted beauty with draped shoulders, ad text on back, EX, A8.....................$90.00

Horlick's Malted Milk, bottle, sample, sealed in paper wrapper with product advertising, 3½", NM, A7..$45.00

Horlick's Malted Milk, pocket mirror, milkmaid & cow encircled by lettering on gold border, round, M, D18................................$95.00

Horlick's Malted Milk, store jar, clear glass with black enameled lettering, ground stopper lid, 8x4" dia, NM+, A3 ....$35.00

Horlick's Malted Milk, tin, Horlick's arched above dairy cow, embossed screw lid, EX, A3.....................$170.00

Horlick's Malted Milk, tin, sample, paper label, pry lid, with contents, 1½", NM, A7.....................$50.00

Horlicks, mixer, Staffordshire China, image of winged lady on center cameo, original metal plunger inside, handled, 8", NM, A3..........................$115.00

Horner's Snag Proof Boots, sign, tin under glass in wood frame, boot in shield flanked by Rubber Duck Gum Boot, E Stout's Patent below, 15", G, A6 ....$160.00

Horniman's Pure Cocoa, tin, sample, vertical rectangle, slip lid, 1½x1x1½", EX, D37, minimum value $100.00

Hornung's Beer, tray, deep-dish, Taste Why! Crowds Buy! above cartoon man drinking, product name below, yellow ground, 12" dia, EX+, A19 ....$85.00

Hornung's White Bock, sign, cardboard, Hornung's upper left of White Bock in red script, In Bottles below, bottle at left, framed, EX, A19 ....$60.00

Horrocks-Ibbotson Co Makers of Fishing Tackle, sign, tin, large trout in pond with lily pads above elongated diamond flanked by Best By Test, 10x14", NOS, A6....................................$850.00

Horse Shoe Plug, tobacco pouch, leather, EX, A7....$15.00

Horse Shoe Tobacco, trade card, Chew... above man & dog within horseshoe, Manufactured By Drummond Tobacco Co..., 5x3", VG, A5 ....$15.00

Horsford's Acid Phosphate, sign, paper, product name & other lettering above little girl with banana curls & red cap, 15x11", G, A9 ....$100.00

Horton Beer, sign, die-cut cardboard, image of girl emerging from pool with glass atop Horton Beer on base, 1945, 11x10", NM, A19............................$55.00

Horton Old Stock Ale, can, cone-top, 32-oz, EX+, A19................................$125.00

Horton Pilsener Beer, tray, deep-dish, America's Finest above Horton, 2 hands toasting on center oval, Beer below, 12" dia, EX, A19...........................$45.00

Hoster's, mug, ceramic, name in brown diagonal script, brown lip, 5", EX+, A8.......................$435.00

Hostess Brand Coffee, tin, product name above In A Class By Itself on emblem, slip lid, EX+, A3.................$55.00

Hostess Ginger Ale, sign, porcelain, lady's silhouette on oval left of black & green product name on white, 1930s, 8x22", NM+, A13.......................$275.00

Hostess Paprika, tin, 4", NM, A7............................$82.00

Hot Cale Panetelas, cigar box, 5½x8", VG, A7 ....$15.00

Hot Popcorn, sign, porcelain, 1930s-40s, Hot Popcorn on diamond over Deco design flanked by 5¢, red, white & blue, NM+, A13 ....$425.00

Hotel Statler, pocket mirror, colorful image of hotel being built in 1906, vertical oval, 2¾", EX, A21 ....$88.00

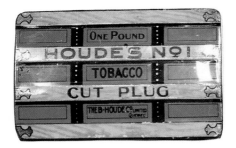

Houde's No 1 Cut Plug Tobacco, tin, red trunk shape with wood-look bands, 1-lb, VG+, A18 ....$35.00

Household Lubricant, see Standard Oil Co Household Lubricant

Howard Johnson's Restaurant, cigar box, wood with blue, gold & black label, NM, D25......................$75.00

Howard Johnson's Restaurant, grill plate, marked Syracuse China 90-C, 9½" dia, EX, D25.....................$38.00

Howard Stove & Furnace Co, whetstone, celluloid, More Heat With Less Fuel above Howard Overdraft on wavy band, blue & white, oval, EX+, A11......................$22.00

Howdy, sign, tin hanger, ...The Orange Flavored Sugar Drink, receding bottles, white, black & orange, 1930s, 9x6", NM, A13..$90.00

Howel's, see also Cherry Julep, Grape Julep or Orange Julep

Howel's Cherry-Julep, syrup dispenser, ceramic potbelly, Drink...5¢ in white on red, white flared base, original pump, 1920, 15", EX, A2 ....$1,650.00

Howel's Cherry-Julep, syrup dispenser, ceramic potbelly, white Drink... on red, white flared base, gold trim, original pump, 15", G, A9 ....$650.00

Howel's Grape-Julep, syrup dispenser, ceramic potbelly, white Drink... on purple, white flared base, original pump, 1920, 15", EX, A2 ....$1,650.00

Howel's Julep, dispenser, cast aluminum, spigot slides up from front slot to replace bottles, 12", NM, A3.....$65.00

Howel's Orange-Julep, drinking glass, Howel's in script above Orange-Julep receding from large to small & small to large, stemmed, NM, A13 ....$120.00

Howel's Orange-Julep, drinking glass, milk glass with applied orange lettering, flared top, NM+, A16..$140.00

Howel's Orange-Julep, sign, reverse glass, Drink... over image of orange above Made From Fresh Ripe Fruit, 5¢ each corner, 6x10", EX+, A16............................$755.00

Howel's Orange-Julep, syrup dispenser, ceramic, white Drink... on orange ball shape, white flared base, original pump, ca 1920, 15", EX, A2 ....$1,210.00

Howel's Root Beer, mug, glass, embossed script lettering on oval, fluted sides, 5x3", NM, D16....................$35.00

Howel's Root Beer, sign, tin, Drink...With That Good Old Fashioned Flavor in red & black on yellow, 24" dia, NM+, D30 ....$195.00

Howel's Root Beer, sign, tin, embossed die-cut bottle, VG, A21 ....$165.00

Hoyt's German Cologne, sign, paper, young girl watches boy scribble, ...Is The Best on brick wall next to bottle & flowers, 29x20", EX, A2 ....$1,375.00

Hrobak's Beverages, sign, embossed tin, Drink... above Triple Action Lithiated Lemon & Falcon Pale Dry, red & black on white, 9x20", VG, A8 ....$20.00

Hub, tobacco label, die-cut, yellow, large, EX, D35.....$6.00

Hubbard Fertilizer Co, pocket mirror, celluloid, elegant woman surrounded by lettering, Use Hubbard's Bone & Blood Fertilizers, round, EX+, A11......................$180.00

Hubers, tap knob, red plastic with red & white insert, round, VG+, A8 ....$95.00

Hudepohl Beer, sign, self-framed tin, oval image of man with corncob pipe displaying bottle & full glass, product name below, VG+, A19 ....$200.00

Hudepohl Brewing Co, paperweight, clear lucite with stein inside, EX, A8 ....$20.00

Hudepohl Cincinnati Fine Beers, tray, product lettering on wood-grain background, 'Decidedly The Best' below, 15" dia, EX+, A19..$40.00

Hudepohl Golden Beer, can, flat-top, horizontal oval logo, M, A8 ....$20.00

Hudepohl Pure Grain Beer, plaque, embossed plaster plate, product name encircling horse-drawn wagon, hops design on rim, 22" dia, EX+, A1 ....$45.00

Hudson Authorized Service, sign, porcelain, Hudson Built Cars... on triangle, red & blue on white with blue border, 36" dia, NM, D8................................$350.00

Hudson Cream Ale, sign, coated stock paper, product name above pitcher, barrel, wheat & hops, etc, On Draught below, 22x18", G-, A9 ....$175.00

Hudson Essex Service, sign, porcelain, Hudson Essex above & below Service on center band, 16x30", VG+, D11..$250.00

Hudson Parts & Service, sign, porcelain, Hudson on red emblem flanked by Parts & Service, white lettering on blue, 26x42", EX, D8....................$575.00

Hugh Campbell's Shag Smoking Tobacco for Pipe & Cigarette, pocket tin, vertical, 2-oz & 10¢ upper corners above name on shadow of man smoking pipe, tan background, EX+, A18..$335.00

Hugo Meyer Photographic Lens Supplies, catalog, 1929, 32 pgs, EX, D17..$20.00

Hula, crate label, Washington apple, topless Hawaiian girl under palm tree holding apple, Seattle, 9x11", M, D12..$5.00

Hull's, sign, molded composition, Hull's On Draught, Worth Stopping For, 1950s, 9x13", NM, A19 ....$55.00

Hull's Bock Beer, can, flat-top, brown oval on yellow, 12-oz, VG+, A19 ....$20.00

Hull's Cream Ale, can, flat-top, 12-oz, EX+, A19 ......$30.00

Hull's Export Beer, sign, cardboard with stand, shows bathing beauty & pilsner glass, Connecticuts Only Brewery!..., 19x15", NM+, A19 ....$35.00

Hulman's Quality Roasted Coffee, store bin, gold lettering & border on blue, 16x18x18", EX, A18 ....$125.00

Humble, sign, porcelain, For Your Safety We Don't Smoke... at right of Humble service man, green & white, 11x14", NM, A6 ....$400.00

Hummer Hammer Mills & Economy Hog Self Feeders, whetstone, celluloid, Omaha Western Sales Co..., blue & white, oval, EX+, A11...........................$20.00

Humphery's Veterinary Specifics, cabinet, oak, tin front pictures farm animals & list of cures, 28x22x9", VG+, A2...........................$4,070.00

Humphrey's Veterinary Remedies, cabinet, oak, tin front pictures farm animals & list of cures, ...Specific Remedies on marquee, 33x21x10", G, A9 ....$3,350.00

Humphrey's Witch Hazel Oil, trade card, barefoot girl with long hair running along stream, EX, D23.....$15.00

Hunter, display, cast metal, huntsman on horse leaping over fence on lettered base, Hunter First..., 15x14x8", EX, A8 ....$125.00

Hunter, tin, product name above painted image of huntsman on horse leaping over fence, gold slip lid, vertical oval, VG, A18 ....$75.00

Hunter's Prize, cigar box label, inner lid, 1899, deer hunting scenes, 6x9", M, D5 ....$35.00

Hunters Tap Beer, label, product name over cabin scene with hunter & dog, 12-oz, EX, A19 ....$10.00

Huntley & Palmers Biscuits, tin, sample, square with Miniatures encircled by product name, decorative border, slip lid, 1¾x1½x1½", EX, D37 ....$75.00

Huntsman, crate label, Florida citrus, Indian drawing bow toward flying cranes, 9x9", M, D3 ....$2.00

Hupmobile Service, sign, porcelain, 2-sided, H on circle in lower left, blue on white with blue border, copyright 1915, 16x30", VG, A1 ....$375.00

Hurley Burley Smoking Tobacco, canister, PL Co logo in center, EX+, A3...........................$65.00

Husemann's Soda, sign, embossed tin, Drink above product name, Clear & Sparkling, Guaranteed 100% Pure..., horizontal, EX+, A16 ....$55.00

Husky, globe, 3-pc painted milk-glass Gill body, colorful trademark image of dog above name, 13½" dia, NM+, A6...........................$2,750.00

Husky Heavy Duty Motor Oil, can, full image of husky dog & northern lights logo on orange background, product name above, 1-qt, NM, A1...........................$550.00

Husky Heavy Duty Motor Oil, can, head image of husky dog & northern lights logo on yellow background, product name below, 1-qt, EX, A1...........................$380.00

Husky Hi Power, pump plate, porcelain, husky dog standing atop Husky emblem, Hi Power on band below, red, white & blue, 12x12", NM, A1...........................$450.00

Hustings Beverages, sign, Drink above Hustings in script on oval above Beverages & For Thirst-Sake!, EX+, A16.$55.00

Huyler's Cocoa, tin, sample, Huyler's in script above square graphic with lettering, slip lid, 1⅝x1⅜x1⅛", EX, D37.$70.00

Hy Flash Motor Oil, can, Hy Flash on diagonal band with plane above, Motor Oil & 1930s car below, red, black & yellow, 1-qt, VG+, A1 ....$350.00

Hy Flash Motor Oil, can, product name between 100% Pure... & airplane above car & SAE 30, red, blue & yellow, 2-gal, rare, EX+, A1...........................$120.00

Hyde Park, lighter, metal bottle shape, miniature, EX+, A8 ....$25.00

Hyde Propellers Sales & Service, sign, porcelain, propeller & Hywinco Trade Mark in center, yellow on black with yellow border, 26x17", NM, D8 ..$875.00

Hydro-Pura Modern Washing Powder, sign, embossed tin, 3x20", NOS, D11 ....$45.00

Hyklas Beverages, tip tray, 'High Class,' shows girl with glass & bottle against striped ground, name on rim, vertical rectangle, G, A21 ....$45.00

Iced Brilliant Ale, label, Clausen-Flanagan, pre-prohibition, NM, A10 ....$18.00

I

Icee, bank, Icee Bear figure, plastic, 1974, 8", EX, D27..$25.00

Icy-Brook Beverages, bottle, EX, A7 ....$15.00

Ideal Beer, label, Cape Brewing Co, Internal Revenue Tax Paid statement, 1933-50, 12-oz, M, A10 ....$15.00

Idle Hour Cut Plug, pocket tin, flat, dark green with name above & below winged product package, gold trim, rounded corners, EX+, A18 ....$42.00

IGA, sign, die-cut porcelain shield, IGA emblem over eagle, yellow, blue, black & red, 12½x12½", EX, A6 .....$20.00

IGA Deluxe Coffee, tin, eagle logo at top, Vacuum Packed Coffee below, key-wind lid, EX, A3 .....$40.00

IGA Quick Cook Rolled Oats, container, cardboard, images of children in various seasons above lettering on yellow, 3-lb, no lid, VG+, A3 .....$45.00

IGA Quick Cook Rolled Oats, container, cardboard, children playing around top, product name on yellow below, months surround lid, 18-oz, NM, A3 .....$28.00

IGA Rolled Oats, container, cardboard, children playing around top, product name on red below, 42-oz, EX+, A3 .....$40.00

Imperial Ale, label, Imperial Brewing Co, Internal Revenue Tax Paid statement, 1933-50, 12-oz, M, A10 .....$10.00

Imperial Ale, label, Imperial Brewing Co, U-type permit number, Internal Revenue Tax Paid statement, 1933-36, 11-oz, NM, A10 .....$18.00

Imperial Bock Beer, label, Trenton Brewing Co, Internal Revenue Tax Paid statement, 1933-50, 12-oz, M, A10 .....$15.00

Imperial Cabinet Bourbon, sign, tin, bust portrait of girl with head slightly tilted, octagon, 15x15", G+, A9 .....$450.00

Imperial Club 5cts Cigar, sign, embossed tin, Smoke The...Best For The Money at left of open box of cigars, 10x14", G, A9 .....$25.00

Imperial Club 5cts Cigar, sign, embossed tin, Smoke The...Best For The Money at left of open cigar box, 10x13½", EX, A6 .....$60.00

Imperial Ethyl Refineries, gas globe, Ethyl logo in center, red, yellow & black lettering on beige & white ground, plastic body, 14" dia, NM, A6 .....$160.00

Imperial Garage, sign, embossed tin, Automobiles in bold letters at left of early car, Supplies, Repairs, Chilton Wis, 13x20", NM, D11 .....$250.00

Imperial Ice Cream, tray, little boy & girl eating ice cream with glass of water, lettering inside rim, 13" dia, G, A9 .....$50.00

Imperial Marvelube Motor Oil, case, porcelain & wood, Authorized Quart Service above Imperial on circle, Marvelube... below, footed, 23x20x20", VG, A6 .....$80.00

Imperial Polarine, can, Polarine above polar bear on ice flanked by lettering on emblem, red & blue lettering, pour spout, 1-gal, VG, A1 .....$230.00

Imperial Roll Film, sign, porcelain, Imperial in diagonal script above Roll Films & box of film, 2-sided, 10x14", EX, D21 .....$195.00

Imperiales' Cigarettes, sign, product name above man in top hat with cane, John Bollman Co & logo in lower left, 20x16", NM+, A6 .....$200.00

Imported, cigar box label, inner lid, woman pointing to banner & cherub, 6x9", EX, D5 .....$12.00

Imps, container, celluloid, For All Who Breath above image flanked by Throat Ease & Breath Perfume, 5¢ below, round, EX+, A11 .....$25.00

INB Bank, bank, Barnaby Bee, ceramic, 6¾", M $18.00

Incandescent Light & Stove Co, tip tray, Home Lighting & Cooking Plant lettered above mother & child in kitchen, lettered rim, 4" dia, VG+, A8 .....$65.00

Independent, cigar box label, outer, 1896, Washington taking oath of office, 4½x4½", M, D5 .....$75.00

Independent Brewing Association, stein, blue & gray salt-glazed stoneware, 3 embossed images of Iulius (sic) Cesar, Prima & Alexander, with lid, EX+, A8 .....$220.00

Independent Brewing Co, tray, German girl in clogs on simulated wood background, Old German Lager on rim, 13¼x10½", EX+, A1 .....$85.00

Independent Burg Brau, mug, product name above & below logo with leaf & hops motif, maroon & gold on tan, white interior, VG+, A8 .....$45.00

Independent Rienzi Brau, mug, ceramic, product name above & below logo with leaf & hops motif, gold trim, handled, 6", VG+, A8 .....$210.00

Index, crate label, California lemon, large hand in upper right with index finger pointing at crate, 1933, 9x12", M, D12 .....$10.00

India Pale Ale, label, William Peter Brewing Co, Internal Revenue Tax Paid statement, 1933-50, 12-oz, M, A10 .....$10.00

Indian Commercial Motorcycles, brochure, More Business At Less Expense above encircled image of 2 men on front, 1930s, EX, D8 .....$60.00

Indian Corn Cigars, box label set, Indian in full headdress with teepees & field beyond, 2 pcs, NM, A5 .....$440.00

Indian Deer, crate label, citrus, Indian in profile & deer face, 9x9", M, D3 .....$3.00

Indian Gas, gas globe, glass, product name in blue arched above red dot, Havoline down side, 1-pc, 15½" dia, rare, EX, A6 .....$950.00

Indian Gasoline, pump plate, curved porcelain, multicolored symbols on green above product name in white & green on blue, 18x12", NM, A1 .....$275.00

Indian Head Gasket Shellac Compound, container, glass with cork stopper, lettering & Indian in profile on paper label, 4¼", VG, A6............$20.00

Indian Head Hydraulic Brake Fluid, can, profile of 'Chief Permatex' in full headdress, cone-top with screw lid, 6x3½" dia, EX, A6 ....$25.00

Indian Motocycle (sic), match holder, embossed brass, encircled Indian & product name on front, Powerplus logo on back, 2¼x1½", EX+, A6............$300.00

Indian Motocycle (sic) Co, booklet, 'Indian Riders' Instruction Book,' 1934, 7x5", VG, D8............$65.00

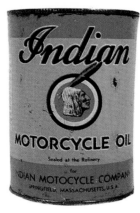

Indian Motorcycle Oil, can, encircled Indian in center, red, orange, black & cream, 5½x4" dia, 1-qt, VG+, A6............$300.00

Indian Motorcycles, brochure, 40th Anniversary, 1941, EX, D8............$90.00

Indian Motorcycles, clock, metal & glass, red lettering & black numbers on white, 18½" dia, NM+, A6..$1,700.00

Indian Plug, tobacco label, yellow, EX, D35............$8.00

Indian Refining Co Handy Lubricant, can, early, green product lettering & detail on orange, Indian chief's head depicted on arrowhead logo, 4-oz, EX, A1............$170.00

Indian Rifle Gunpowder, tin, oval image of Indian with rifle on red, EJ Dupont De Nemours & Co, screw lid, Pat Nov 12, 1908, 4", NM, D14......$195.00

Indian Rock Ginger Ale, syrup dispenser, ceramic, white urn, flared base, red name & 5¢ above & below image of Indian, original pump, EX, A2............$2,035.00

Indian Spring Frame Motorcycles, brochure, pictures a motorcycle, 1940, NM, D8............$80.00

Indianapolis Brewing Co Beer, sign, porcelain, exotic girl flanked by Brewing Co, Indianapolis Beer arched above & below, 17½" dia, VG+, D11............$385.00

Indianapolis Glove Co, display rack, triangular wire hanger with Indian Apple Us sign, includes 10 pairs of original gloves, 22x16", EX, A2............$1,210.00

Indianapolis Glove Co, thermometer, wood, keyhole shape with company name around Indian Apple Us logo, bulb below, VG+, A2............$60.00

Indianapolis Motor Speedway, ashtray, race car #2 in center, 5x6½", tarnished, A6............$20.00

Indy Racing Oil, can, pictures a race car & checkered flags, gold, red, white & black, 1-qt, 5½x4" dia, EX, A6.$260.00

Ingersoll, display, tin, ...Reliable Watches At Low Prices above display space for 9 different pocket watches, 16x10", G+, A8............$120.00

Ingersoll, sign, porcelain, Ingersoll in diagonal script above pocket watch, The Watch That Made The Dollar Famous, 48x48", NM, A11............$475.00

Inland Green Top Tube Repairs, display rack, metal, 'The 3-Ply Patch With The Green Top'..., 12½x12", VG+, A6............$30.00

Inland Tires & Tubes, sign, embossed metal, Inland on vertical oval, Tires & Tubes above & below, green, yellow, red & white, 53x16", EX+, A6............$50.00

Instant Postum, see Postum

Inter-State Common Motor Carriers System, sign, electric, wood with revolving circles, red, white & blue, 13x18½", VG, A6............$125.00

Interlux Marine Finishes, sign, embossed tin, men hard at work painting boats, International paints logo upper right, 32x56", VG+, A9............$250.00

International Fertilizers, sign, porcelain, sack of fertilizer at left, ...Sales Agency, 7x13", NM, D22............$200.00

International Franken Muth Beer, can, flat-top, circular logo within rectangular logo, NM, A8............$20.00

International Harness Soap & Ebony Oil Dressing, tin, pictures black stable boy polishing horse collar, M, D6............$100.00

International Harvester Co of America Cream Harvester, sign, paper, name above farm scene with farmer & dog watching lady operating red separator on porch, 24x17", VG+, A21............$175.00

International Harvester Motor Trucks, gas globe, International on emblem over 3 diamonds surrounded by product name, Hull body, 13½" dia, NM, A6..$2,100.00

International Louse Killer, sign, paper, large can surrounded by lettering, Hens With Lice Lay Few Eggs..., framed, image: 28x21", EX, A9............$175.00

145

International Shirt & Collar Co, pin-back button, celluloid, multicolored image of man with rifle in front of camel, round, EX, A11 ....$40.00

International Stock Food Tonic, thermometer, wood, 3 Feeds For One Cent arched above product box & animals, horses below, white ground, 46x9", EX+, A15.....$4,000.00

International Tailoring Co, thermometer, wood, circular King of Tailors & lion logo, company name below, 23x7", not working, G, A9 ....$135.00

Invader Motor Oil, sign, tin, knight on horse & product name above Perfected Lubrication, black, yellow & red, 12x23", VG, A6 ....$140.00

Invader Motor Oil, sign, tin, Use... & 100% Pure logo left of knight on horse & lasts Longer, Serves Better, 1930s, 9x36", EX+, A1 ....$195.00

Invader Oil, sign, metal, 2-sided, knight on horse above product name, marked AM 4-59, red, yellow, black & cream, 24" dia, NM, A6 ....$400.00

Invincible, cigar box label, outer, large image of lion's face, EX, A5 ....$55.00

Invincible Motor Insurance, sign, tin, beam of light shining on car, ...Invincible Policies Limited, 9½x20", EX, A6 ....$210.00

Invincible Schley Cigars, box label, salesman's sample, portrait surrounded by patriotic images, Smoke... below, 1898, EX, A5 ....$150.00

Iodent Tooth Paste, clock, Correct Time To Buy... on textured dial, numbered 1-12, 15½x15½", VG, A9 ...$75.00

Iodent Tooth Paste, trolley sign, cardboard, Two Tubes For The Two Kinds Of Teeth, arrows pointing toward tubes, framed, 13x23", EX, A6 ....$85.00

Iona Peas, can label, product name above & below pea pods/product name above & below emblem, 4x11", NM, A7 ....$15.00

Iowa Stock Food Co, pocket mirror, celluloid, Iowa lettered over trademark flower, round, EX, A11 ......$25.00

Iron City Beer, sign, metal, Enjoy... in cream outlined in black, red background, oval, 36x54", EX, A6 .....$120.00

Iron City Bock Beer, label, Pittsburgh Brewing Co, Internal Revenue Tax Paid statement, 1933-50, 12-oz, M, A10 ....$10.00

Iron City Stout, label, Pittsburgh Brewing Co, pre-prohibition, 12-oz, M, A10 ....$30.00

Iron Clad Specialties/Enameled Iron Ware, sign, paper, 2 chefs looking out kitchen porthole, product names on wall above, framed, 25x15", EX, A8 ....$660.00

Iron Fireman, playing cards, double-deck, 1 orange image & 1 blue, NMIB, D21 ....$35.00

Iron Fireman Automatic Coal Burner, sign, porcelain, iron fireman with shovel on red circle surrounded by red lettering on white, 12" dia, NM, D8..............$500.00

Iron Horse, cigar box, 1901 stamp, 5x8¼", G, A7 ....$30.00

Iroquois, cigar box label, salesman's sample, jockey on running horse, EX, A5...$55.00

Iroquois Brewing Co, mug, ceramic, Indian head in profile with company name & Buffalo NY below, 'Dutch Kitchens' on back by handle, EX, A8 ....$165.00

Iroquois Brewing Co, mug, salt-glazed stoneware, incised Indian head in profile flanked by Iroquois Brewery in script, Buffalo NY, EX+, A8 ....$165.00

Iroquois Chief, gas globe, red product name surrounds encircled Indian in profile with red, white & blue headdress, 3-pc, 14", NM, A1 ....$2,400.00

Iroquois Club, cigar box label, outer, bust of Indian chief, 4½x4½", VG, D5 ....$45.00

Iroquois Indian Head Beer & Ale, sign, embossed composition, Indian chief's head above product name in gold on wood-grain background, 17x14", EX, A8 ....$75.00

Iroquois Indian Head Beer & Ale, tray, deep-dish, Since & 1842 flank Indian head in profile, red product name below, white background, 14" dia, EX, A19.........$45.00

Isaac Walker Hardware Co, catalog, 1953, 892 pgs, EX, D17 ....$75.00

Isengart Brewing Co, tray, deep-dish, girl in feather boa, Troy's Best Beer... inside rim, VG+, A9 ....$500.00

Island Brand, crate label, California pear, stone litho of wooded isle & birds, Grand Island, 8x11", M, D12...$30.00

Italian Swiss Colony, display, plaster, seated couple with bottle on lettered base, 6x9", EX, A8 ....$70.00

Ithaca Brand Cigar, box label, inner lid, photo of early American orchestra, 6x9", VG, D5........................$20.00

Ithaca Guns, sign, paper, promotes Nitro Powder, 2 pheasants among leaves looking toward water, metal strips, ca 1913, 27x16", G, A9 ....$600.00

Ivanhoe Grapes, lug box label, big tomatoes tied to yellow Ivanhoe tag, black background, M, D12 ....$2.00

Ivory Gloss Starch, tin, embossed gold lettering on black emblem, 6-lbs, EX+, A18 ....$55.00

Ivory Soap, sign, cardboard, product name above girl in bonnet, original frame, 33½x26", G, A9 ....$275.00

Ivory Soap, trolley sign, cardboard, pictures Ivory baby No Soap Can Make Your Skin..., signed Dorothy Hope Smith, 13x23", EX, A6 ....$30.00

IW Harper's Whiskey, sign, Vitrolite, interior cabin scene with bear skin, guns, dog & other items, ca 1910 framed, image: 24x18", NM, A9....................$700.00

IW McNess Breakfast Cocoa, tin, 2½", NM, A7........$25.00

J Friedman & Co, pocket mirror, tin with paper insert, company name arched above image, Chicago, Ill below, round, EX, A11 .... $20.00

J P Palley's 5¢ Hambone Sweets Cigars, sign, cardboard, advertising surrounds cartoon image of pilot in plane, gold border, 2-sided, 1915, 7" dia, NM, A3 .... $45.00

J&P Coats, spool cabinet, wood, 6 black & gold labeled drawers, VG, A12 .... $800.00

J&P Coats Spool Cotton, sign, paper over plaster, fisherman catching trout while girlfriend sews, ...Is Strong, framed, image: 16x20", G, A9 .... $150.00

J&P Coats Thread, trade card/calendar, 1879, pictures woman sewing & man reading newspaper, calendar on back, VG, D23 .... $25.00

J&W Nicholson & Co Ltd London Gin, sign, tin, elegant woman pouring glass for seated gentleman, framed, image: 23x18", G+, A9 .... $200.00

Jack & Jill Gelatin Dessert, whistle, tin, 1¼", EX, A7 ... $18.00

Jack Daniel's Old No 7 Whiskey, mirror, with logos, framed, 4x4", VG+, D24 .... $5.00

Jack Frost Cinnamon & Sugar, tin, paper label, 4", NM, A7 .... $40.00

Jack Frost Confectioners Sugar, box, sample, with contents, 2¾", NM, A7 .... $28.00

Jack Frost Granulated Sugar, box, sample, with contents, 2¾", EX, A7 .... $15.00

Jack Sprat Celery Salt, container, cardboard, tin top & bottom, yellow with name & Jack's image, white band at top, 2-oz, EX, A3 .... $25.00

Jack Sprat Ginger, tin, paper label, 3", NM, A7 .... $18.00

Jack Sprat Quick Cooking Rolled Oats, container, cardboard, yellow with name & Jack's image above bowl of oats, blue band at bottom, 3-lb, EX+, A3 ...... $50.00

Jackson Beer, label, Jackson Brewing Co, Internal Revenue Tax Paid statement, 1933-50, 12-oz, M, A10 .... $30.00

Jackson's Best, tobacco label, hexagonal, EX, D35 .... $5.00

Jacob & Co's Biscuits, display cabinet, oak with multi-tiered glass front & marble top, 38x42x19", VG+, A9 ..... $600.00

Jacob Conrad Keystone State Brewery, calendar, 1897, company name above elderly gent with glass mug, pad below, matted & framed, 27x22", EX+, A19 .... $650.00

Jacob Conrad Keystone State Brewery, sign, cardboard hanger, fancy patriotic logo & company name above distant factory scene, address below, 12x11", VG+, A8 .... $220.00

Jacob Hoffmann Brewing Co, sign, paper, company name above urn of flowers, foaming glass & cigar, J Ottman litho, framed, 31x21½", EX, A9 .... $70.00

Jacob Hoffmann Brewing Co, sign, paper, company name above urn of flowers, foaming glass & cigar, J Ottman litho, framed, 31x21½", NM, A9 .... $100.00

Jacob Ruppert Beer-Ale, tray, product name above 2 hands toasting with full mugs against wood-grain background, 1930s-40s, oval, 15", EX, A8 .... $35.00

Jacob Ruppert Extra Pale/Ruppiner Beer, tray, name on red band around patriotic symbol against blue sky, lettered & decorative rim, 12" dia, G+, A21 .... $145.00

Jacob Ruppert Knickerbocker Beer, can, flat-top, instructional, 12-oz, EX, A19 .... $45.00

Jacob Ruppert's Beer, sign, reverse-painted glass, black with white & silver lettering, oval, framed, 12½x18", EX, A6 .... $130.00

Jacob Ruppert's Beer, see also Ruppert Beer & Ale

Jacob Ruppert's Rose Bud, tray, product name below bunch of roses with inset of enlarged rose, early 1900s, horizontal oval, EX, A16 .... $240.00

Jacob Schmidt Brewing Co, sign, tin, aerial factory scene, logo & company name at bottom, 27½x39½", G+, A9 .... $1,250.00

Jacob Stahl Jr & Co's Nip 5¢ Cigar, tray, dog having a nip from tobacco bail, 12" dia, VG+, A9 .... $350.00

Jacob Widman & Co, calendar, 1912, matted image of cherubs & nymphs in classical garden setting, incomplete pad below, EX, A19 .... $175.00

Jaguar Beer, can, pull-tab, 12-oz, EX+, A19 .... $45.00

James Hanley Brewing Co, print, 'I Dood It,' shows bulldog climbing red-carpeted stairs, dated 1943, 12x10", EX, A8 .... $75.00

James Lutted Cough Drops, tin, yellow with black graphics & lettering, vertical square with smaller round lid, Ginna, 5-lb, VG, A18 .... $85.00

James Pepper Whiskey, tray, large bottle image with Revolutionary War soldiers, patriotic border, oval, 14x17", EX+, A15 .... $275.00

Jap Cultivator/Lehr Agricultural Co, pocket mirror, celluloid, product name arched above cultivator, company name below, round, EX+, A11 .... $135.00

Jap Rose Soap, sign, cardboard, 2 children in Japanese attire bathing doll in tub, framed, image: 24½x30½", G, A9...**$400.00**

Jap Tooth Silk Dental Floss/Bauer & Black, tin,¼x1⅛" dia, EX, D37...**$25.00**

Japp's Hair Rejuvenator, sign, tin over cardboard, hair samples surrounded by oval portraits & advertising, ca 1910, 10x13", NM, A6.......................................**$300.00**

Jas E Pepper Whiskey, watch fob, celluloid & nickel, multicolored image of soldier on oval center, 2x1¼", EX+, A11 ....**$100.00**

Jas E Pepper Whiskey/Joseph Spang Distributor, watch fob, ornate frame shape with celluloid profile image of sentry flanked by '17 & 80,' EX, A20 ....**$85.00**

Jas Hubbard & Son Oysters, sign, paper, King Neptune offering an oyster to maiden in diaphanous gown, ships beyond, framed, image: 24x15", EX, A9.$1,750.00

Jas E Pepper Whiskey, tray, continental soldiers sampling whiskey with large bottle in the foreground, patriotic border, oval, 14x17", G-, A9...............................**$125.00**

Java & Arabian Mocha Fresh Roasted Coffee, canister, product name above lettered emblem, Montgomery Ward & Co Coffee Importers below, screw lid, 9x7x7", EX, A3...**$100.00**

Java Coffee Mills, pocket mirror, celluloid, For Quality Coffee..., black & white with opalescent lettering, oval, EX, A11 ....**$15.00**

Jax Beer, pocket lighter, logo on front, Smooth Yellow Jax on reverse, red, blue & yellow, unused, MIB, A8..**$35.00**

Jax Beer, tray, 'Texas Brags' And Texans Drink... on map of Texas, with other lettering & graphics, red on cream, 11x13", EX, A8...**$30.00**

Jayne's Expectorant, dexterity puzzle, die-cut tin & string, medicine bottle with puzzle instructions on reverse, VG, A21...**$55.00**

JB Pace Tobacco Co's Scroll Cut Twist, tin, flat, yellow & light blue, rectangular, rounded corners, 4x6", EX, A18 ....**$55.00**

JC Penney, catalog, Christmas, 1950, EX, D17.........**$100.00**
JC Stevens, see Old Judson

JC Tessin & Son, pocket mirror, celluloid, Seeing Is Believing, If It's Hardware See...Courtesy, Quality & Service, round, EX, A11 ....**$15.00**

JD Iler Rochester Brewery, mug, stoneware, name above Kansas City in script, pre-1895, very rare, VG+, A8..**$165.00**

Jefferson Br'g & Malt'g Co Lager Beer, sign, tin on cardboard, company name above 3 gents in tavern, Lager Beer & Jefferson Wis below, 19x14", EX, A8....$450.00

Jell-O, matchbook, Jell-O Recipe series, pictures man on scale, 20 strike, front strike, NM, D28....................**$2.00**

Jell-O, sign, die-cut cardboard, little girl holding box on center panel flanked by strawberry & lemon flavors, 34x48", VG, A9...**$675.00**

Jenner Beer, mug, There Is Good Cheer In Jenner Beer, tan with black lettering, white interior, pre-1920, EX, A8 ....**$150.00**

Jenney Aero, pump sign, porcelain, Jenny above large Aero, horizontal rectangle with bowed top & bottom, bordered, 9x12", EX+, A1....................................**$100.00**

Jenney Aero Gasoline, tip tray, Aero lettered over airplane on band in center surrounded by lettering, cars on rim, 4" dia, EX+, A6..**$150.00**

Jenney Aero Solvenized, pump sign, porcelain, Aero superimposed over airplane in center, yellow, white, blue & black, 9" dia, rare, NM, A6 ..$2,750.00

Jenney Manufacturing Co, pump sign, porcelain, product name on center band over factory scene, Solvenized Hy-Power above & below, 12" dia, M, A6......**$1,500.00**

Jenny Wren Brand Coffee, tin, product name above & below image of 2 kids on sidewalk watching wren, paper label, pry lid, 1-lb, rare, EX+, A15............**$425.00**

Jergens Miss Dainty Talcum Powder, tin, lettered oval flanked by 4 girls, cream background, gold shaker top, oval, 5", EX, A2 ....**$300.00**

Jergens/John Woodbury's One Week Treatment, set with facial cream, powder & soap, NMIB, A7......**$65.00**

Jergens/John Woodbury's 10-Day Treatment, set with facial cream, cold cream, powder & soap, NMIB, A7 ....**$55.00**

Jeris Hair Tonic, sign, die-cut stand-up, Look Your Best!..We Recommend Jeris..., close-up of couple & bottle on diamond, 27x21", NM, A3....................**$95.00**

Jersey-Creme, tray, girl in feather boa & hat with glass on table, ...The Perfect Drink on rim, 12" dia, VG, A9..**$150.00**

Jersey-Creme, tray, profile image of lady in bonnet & banana curls, red background, lettered rim, 12" dia, EX, A8..**$200.00**

Jersey-Creme, tray, profile image of lady in bonnet & banana curls, red background, lettered rim, 12" dia, G+, A21..**$75.00**

Jet Malt Liquor, can, flat-top, 12-oz, VG+, A19.........**$10.00**

Jevne's Bread, sign, embossed tin, 13½x16", NM+, D11 ..**$50.00**

Jewels, cigar box label, outer, diamond ring on cigar, 4½x4½", EX, D5 ....**$12.00**

JG Dill's, see also Dill's

JG Dill's Look Out Cut Plug, pocket tin, flat, rectangular with rounded corners, VG, A18 ....**$175.00**

JG Hutchinson & Co's Wholesale Grocer, cigar cutter, cast iron with embossed lettering, 8½x15x4", G, A9...**$150.00**

JH Cutter Whiskey, sign, reverse-painted glass in black & gold, 7x12", G+, A9 ....**$200.00**

JI Case Plow Works, pin-back button, celluloid, multicolored image of eagle on tractor, round, EX+, A11 ....**$100.00**

JI Case Threshing Machine Co, pin-back button, celluloid, eagle atop globe, round, EX, A11.................**$35.00**

JI Case Threshing Machine Co, pocket mirror, celluloid, shows eagle atop globe, vertical oval, NM, A15 ..**$110.00**

JI Case Threshing Machine Co, screwdriver, Racine, Wis, G, A20 ....**$18.00**

Jiggs Electric, sign, porcelain, smiling light bulb in center, blue on white, 24x17", EX, D11 ....**$275.00**

Jim Beam Kentucky Straight Bourbon Whiskey, display (made for Jim Beam Club), china, cowgirl seated next to space for bottle on lettered base, EX, A8.........**$65.00**

Jim Beam Kentucky Straight Bourbon Whiskey, display (made for Jim Beam Club), china, crosslegged cowboy standing next to space for bottle on lettered base, EX, A8..**$65.00**

Jim Dandies Peanuts, can, baseball scene on 1 side, kids by bulletin board on reverse, checked border, pry lid, 10-lb, 11x7½" dia, G, A9.................................**$400.00**

Jim Hogg Cigars, sign, paper, New Governor Size...Back To 5¢, Corona Size 3 For 20¢ & portrait, Schlegal Litho, framed, 11x23", EX, A19 ....**$80.00**

Jim Hogg Cigars, sign, paper, New Governor Size...Back To 5¢, Corona Size 3 For 20¢ & portrait, Schlegal Litho, framed, 11x23", NM, A18...............................**$145.00**

Jipco Brand Pumpkin, can label, product name above & below buffalo/product name above & below pumpkin, 4½x14", NM, A7..**$10.00**

JK Souther & Sons Burton Musty Ale, mug, salt-glazed stoneware, incised lettering, pre-1898, EX+, A8..**$358.00**

JL Stifel & Sons, clip, brass, embossed boot & lettering, ...Indigo, Drills, Prints, Denims, Established 1835, EX, A3..**$30.00**

JL Taylor & Co, thermometer, painted wood, Custom Made Clothes, Let Taylor Do Your Tailoring, image top & bottom, 24", VG, A2..**$220.00**

Jo Sole Grape Juice, can label, 2 images of little black boy, 'So Soul Tasty,' 1969, 13x6", M, D3 ....**$2.00**

Jockeys, cigar box label, outer, jockey on horse next to 2 circular portraits, EX, A5.................................**$35.00**

Joe Sammy's Yams, crate label, black youngster holding crate of yams, Sunset, 9x9", M, D12....................**$4.00**

John A Salzer Seed Co, catalog, 1951, 78 pgs, EX, D17..**$15.00**

John Bremond High Grade Coffees, pail, sample, gold lettering on red, slip lid, bail handle, 2½x2½" dia, EX, D37..**$230.00**

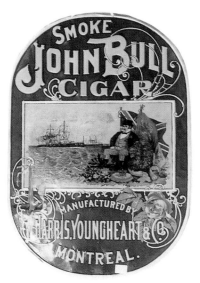

John Bull Cigar/Harris Youngheart & Co, sign, embossed tin, gold embellished lettering above & below man & lion watching ships at sea, oval, 20x14", EX, A18 ....**$550.00**

John Deere, calendar, 1944, pictures young boy & girl looking in store window, complete, 16x11", NM, D21 ....**$90.00**

John Deere, tape measure, celluloid, pictures cameo of John Deere on 1 side, running deer logo on the other, NM, D22..**$80.00**

John Deere, watch fob, bright blue porcelain with embossed deer, oval, EX, A20............................**$160.00**

John Deere, watch fob, ivory shield shape with raised image of deer & plow, band slightly faded, A6 ...**$70.00**

John Deere Farm Implements, sign, tin, pictures deer jumping over log, EX, D34.................................**$225.00**

John Eichler Brewing Co, calendar, 1944, eagle logo & company name above pad, 11x9", VG+, A19.......**$85.00**

John Finzer & Bro's, clock, Baird, figure-8 with Roman numerals, advertises Jolly Tar, Pastime, Old Honesty & Plank Road tobaccos, VG, A13.........................**$750.00**

John Gessert Watertown Shoes, Rubber & Leather Goods Store, sign, embossed tin, lettering above & left of man holding shoe & pipe, blue & white background, 14x20", EX, A1...**$30.00**

John Gund Brewing Co, drinking glass, stemmed goblet with embossed Gambrinus logo, 7", NM, A8 .....**$115.00**

John Hauck Brewing Co, drinking glass, stemmed with embossed logo, NM, A8...................................**$50.00**

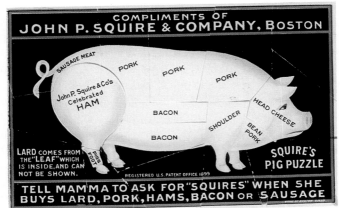

COMPLIMENTS OF
JOHN P. SQUIRE & COMPANY, BOSTON

SQUIRE'S PIG PUZZLE

TELL MAMMA TO ASK FOR "SQUIRES" WHEN SHE
BUYS LARD, PORK, HAMS, BACON OR SAUSAGE

John P Squire & Co, jigsaw puzzle, 'Squire's Pig Puzzle,' image of pig showing the different cuts of meat, 1899, 9x12", EX, D10 ....$100.00

John P Squire & Co, sign, self-framed tin, trademark pig with human eyes on blue ground, I Make Squire's Pure Food Products, oval, G, A9 ....$285.00

John P Squire & Co, see also Squire's

John Weisert's 54 Smoking Tobacco, pack, cardboard, John Weisert's in script above 54 on tobacco leaf, ...For Pipe & Cigarette below, full, M, A3 ....$25.00

Johnnie Walker Red Label, wall plaque, Meet Scotland's Favourite Son..., Born 1820, Still Going Strong!, shows man in top hat, round, EX+, A11 ....$50.00

Johnson & Johnson, sign, self-framed cardboard, 'From Start To Finish,' pictures image of cotton pickers at work, 29x41", VG, A2 ....$525.00

Johnson Halter, display, papier-mache horse head with red name embossed on neck, 19x20", VG+, D38....$1,400.00

Johnson Outboard Motors/Zimmerman Garage, sign, tin, winged horse beside speedboat, ...Sales & Service & Parts, black, white & red, 14x20", NM, D8 .....$385.00

Johnson Smith Co, catalog, 1940, 600 pgs, EX, D17..$75.00

Johnson's Baby Powder, tin, with contents, 3", NM, A7.....................$30.00

Johnson's Baby Powder, Cream & Soap, sample products in original mailer, NM, A7.....................$40.00

Johnson's Dental Floss, tin, lettering on lid, 10 Yds, ¼x1¼" dia, EX, D37 ....$6.00

Johnson's Prepared Wax, tin, pry lid, with contents, 1¼", NM, A7 ....$65.00

Johnson's Steam Fire Engine, sign, paper, fire engine with etched glass lantern & intricate fire apparatus, ca 1865, framed, image: 16x21", G, A9.....................$400.00

SAMPLE
Johnston's
BREAKFAST COCOA

Johnston's Breakfast Cocoa, tin, sample, Johnston's in script above steaming cup, Breakfast Cocoa below, 2¼x1⅝x½", EX, D37, minimum value $130.00

Johnston's Hot Chocolate, display cup & saucer, product name lettered on white cup with black serrated design, 8x11", EX, A13.....................$275.00

Johnston's Instant Hot Fudge, store container, aluminum with porcelain liner, original cord, EX+, A3.......$165.00

Joliet Citizens Brewing Co, mug, miniature, ceramic, pictures factory scene, 2½", EX, A8 ....$25.00

Jolly Roger Restaurant, plate, Shenango China, colorful pirate graphic, 10" dia, EX, D25 ....$35.00

Jolly Time Brand Pop Corn, box, Pop Corn above 3 kids on oval encircled by product & company name, The World's Choicest below, 1918, 10x7", NM, A7 .....$10.00

Jolly Time Giant Yellow Pop Corn, can, Jolly Time on flag & popped corn at top, Guaranteed To Pop on band below, full, 10-oz, NM+, A3 ....$55.00

Jolly Time White Pop Corn, can, dark blue with red Jolly Time on white flag above white lettering & images of popped kernals, 10-oz, full, NM, A3 ....$50.00

Jones, McDuffee & Stratton, Cor Federal & Franklin..., paperweight, glass, pictures Chicago office, 203 & 204 Masonic Building 2nd Floor below, rectangular, M, D13 ....$50.00

Jones Electric, sign, tin over cardboard, arched lettering above yellow horn, It Clears The Road... below, 9½x13½", G+, A6.....................$140.00

Joop Julepped Oranges, sherbet dishes, glass, yellow stemmed tulip shape, 1920s, 4", NM, A13, pair..$160.00

Jorgensen Steel, sign, porcelain, product name on back of large truck on center circle, 14½x14½", NM, D11 ..$115.00

Josh Giddings, cigar box label, inner lid, 1908, 6x9", M, D5 ....$22.00

JP Palley's Hambone Sweets, sign, cardboard, comical black man in plane lettered 'Going Over' flanked by 5¢, ...Finest Quality below, 7" dia, EX, A6.....................$155.00

JP Palley's Hambone Sweets, thermometer, metal, product name above bulb, Smoke Melo-Crowns below, cream, yellow & blue, dated 8-42, 38½", EX, A6 ....$120.00

Ju'cy Orange, door push plate, porcelain, Keep Healthy...Drink... on orange drop, Non-Carbonated below, 1950s, NM, A13 ....$110.00

Juicy Fruit, see also Wrigley's

Juicy Fruit Gum, art plate, Chew Juicy Fruit Gum above girl hugging dog & mule, fancy gold-trimmed border, 10" dia, VG+, A1 ....$1,025.00

Juicy Fruit Gum, match holder, tin, The Man Juicy Fruit Made Famous, shows lettering & circular portrait on red, 5x3¼", VG+, A21 ....$245.00

Juicy Gems, crate label, Washington apple, red apple & lettering on ribbon, diamond in upper left, 9x11", D12 ....$25.00

Jule Carrs Choice Cut Plug, tin, shows train caboose going through tunnel & product name around, rectangular with square corners, VG+, A18.....................$100.00

Julep, sign, embossed tin, Drink Julep Six Delicious Flavors at right of straight-sided bottle, G, A16.....................$60.00

Julep, soda glass, yellow logo & band around top, modified flared shape with syrup line, 4x2½", NM, D16.....$25.00

Julian Eltinge, cigar box label, outer, portrait of a young man, 4½x4½", M, D5 ....$4.00

Jumbo, tobacco label, die-cut elephant, EX, D35 ....$6.00

Jumbo Brand Peanut Butter, jar, glass with diagonal ribs & embossed elephant, red, black & white tin lid with product name & graphics, 7", EX, A1 ....$30.00

Jumbo Cola, sign, tin, Drink Jumbo A Super Cola above bottle on yellow background, 1940s, 35x14", EX, A13...$240.00

June Kola, sign, tin, tilted bottle at right of Now In Quarts!, 6 Full Glasses, 30x20", NM+, D30 ....$175.00

Jung, tap knob, chrome ball with red & white enamel insert, EX, A8..$90.00

Jung Beer, tap knob, olive-drab ball with off-yellow & silver on black insert, EX, A8...........................$150.00

Jungleland Pop Corn, see Coca-Cola (popcorn bag)

Junket, pin-back button, 'Little Miss Junket,' image in chef's hat, 1" dia, NM, A7 ....$8.00

Juno Mustard, tin, 3¼", NM, A7 ....$50.00

Juno/TC Williams Co, tobacco label, name above queen of the gods, company name below, image: 12x6", EX, A18 ....$50.00

Just It, cigar box, 4x8", EX, A7 ....$15.00

Just Right Coffee, tin, paper label with product name above & below plantation scene, round, 1-lb, VG+, A18..$55.00

Just Suits Cut Plug, cigarette papers, NM, A7 ....$20.00

Just Suits Cut Plug, lunch pail, tin, red with gold lettering right of gold & black circular logo, wire handle on hinged lid, EX+, A18.....................................$80.00

Justice, crate label, Florida citrus, Lady Justice holding scales, 9x9", M, D3 ....$2.00

∽ K ∽

K-N Root Beer, baby mug, glass, orange logo on circle, M, D16..$20.00

K-O-K-O Tulu Chewing Gum, trade card, pictures 3 small girls in sitting room, 6½x4", NM, A7.....................$45.00

Kaeser & Blair Inc, saleman's sample book, shows all products made, 1946-47, 26 pgs, EX, A2............$105.00

Kaffo/Anheuser-Busch, pocket mirror, ...A Carbonated Coffee Beverage..., pictures mounted huntsman, American Art Works, oval, NM, A8.............................$115.00

Kahn's Hot Dogs, figure, Kahn's Hot Dog, plastic, 1980s, EX, D27 ....$15.00

Kaier's Beer-Ale, sign, light-up, reverse glass on metal stand, Kaier's above logo, Beer-Ale below, bordered, 10x10", EX+, A19.....................................$45.00

Kaier's Old Time Bock Beer, sign, paper hanger, It's Here! & Kaier's above ram's head flanked by Old & Time, Bock Beer Below, 16x13", EX, A8........................$20.00

Kake Kan Koffee, tin, product name lettered vertically with oversized K, slip lid, EX, A3.........................$35.00

Kalamazoo Bats, insert card, features actress Annie Leslie, EX, A5 ....$20.00

Kamm's Light Beer, display, plaster, Drink...None Better on beveled base with cuffed hand holding full glass next to bottle, 9x9x5", EX, A8.............................$220.00

Kanotex, gas globe, Kanotex in red on white star & yellow sunflower, Gill lens & orange rippled body, 14" dia, NM, A6...$1,500.00

Kansas Calf & Cattle Co, whetstone, celluloid, We Specialize In Calves & Yearlings, See Us First..., blue & white, oval, EX, A11 ....$18.00

Kansas City Breweries Co/Old Fashioned Lager Beer, hand mirror, beveled glass with back showing Asti girl, thick wire handle & frame, 4" dia with 4" handle, VG, A8 .$65.00

Kansas Cleansing Powder, container, sample, cardboard & tin, 2¾", NM, A7...$35.00

Kar-A-Van Coffee, tin, oval image of camel above product & company name, pry lid, EX, A3 ....$105.00

Kaukauna Lager, label, Electric Brewing Co, Internal Revenue Tax Paid statement, 1933-50, 12-oz, M, A10...$20.00

Kaweah Maid, crate label, California lemon, pretty Indian girl wearing turquoise beads, brown background, Lemon Cove, 12x9", M, D3 ....$5.00

Kayo Chocolate Drink, sign, tin, Kayo boy with bottle on yellow says 'Tops In Taste Kayo,' It's Real Chocolate Flavor on blue, 27x14", G, A21 ....$60.00

Kayo Chocolate Drink, thermometer, tin, Kayo Chocolate on horizontal oval above tube & bottle, vertical, rounded corners, EX+, A16 ....$120.00

KC Baking Powder, tin, with contents, 5-oz, EX, A7..$5.00

Keds, display, die-cut cardboard, ...Comfortable Shoes For Warm Days, 2 men in suits & hats on lettered base, 17x7", EX, A6..$90.00

Keds, sign, cardboard stand-up, At Work & At Play, boy with groceries on bicycle waving at boys playing ball, 11x6", NM, D8 ....$185.00

Keds Perfected Rubber-Soled Canvas Shoe, sign, die-cut cardboard trifold, boy & girl flank banner before group of people, For Men, Women..., 20x41", EX, A12 ..$750.00

Keebler, figure, Keebler Elf, vinyl, 1974, EX, D27 .....$20.00

Keen Kutter, clock, glass front with metal frame, EC Simmons Keen Kutter logo in center, 14½x14½", EX, A $425.00

Keen Kutter Store, postcard, Pleased To Meet You!, Our Daddy Runs The Keen Kutter Store..., Thaddeus Wilkerson photo of 3 girls, M, A16 ....$115.00

Keen's Mustard, tin, 8-sided, shows waring armies with Rear Admiral Sir Horatio Nelson, 6x7¾x5½", VG+, A18 ....**$150.00**

Kego Beer/Superior Brewing Co, label, red, blue & white logo on light brown, 12-oz, VG+, A19 ....**$8.00**

Kellogg's, doll kit, Dandy the Duck, uncut cloth pattern with instructions lettered on the cloth, 1935, NM+, A3 ....**$135.00**

Kellogg's, doll kit, Dinky the Dog, uncut cloth pattern with instructions lettered on the cloth, 1935, VG+, A3 ..**$95.00**

Kellogg's, doll kit, Little Bo Peep, uncut cloth pattern with instructions lettered on the cloth, 1928, EX+, A3 ..**$135.00**

Kellogg's All-Bran/Pep Whole Wheat Flakes, display, white oversized cereal box with All-Bran advertising on 1 side & Wheat Flakes on reverse, 20x6x6", NM, A1 ....**$20.00**

Kellogg's Corn Flakes, cereal box, sample, 2x1¼", NM, A7 ....**$25.00**

Kellogg's Corn Flakes, postcard, 'Circumstances Alter Faces,' shows sad face & happy face above product box & WK Kellogg signature, NM, D26 ....**$35.00**

Kellogg's Corn Flakes, see also Ball Fruit Jars

Kellogg's Cream of Tarter, tin, 3¾", NM, A7 ....**$18.00**

Kellogg's Drinket, tin, sample, A Coffee-Like Beverage..., no graphics, 2⅛x1½x¾", EX, D37 ....**$75.00**

Kellogg's Drinket, tin, sample, A Delicious Beverage, pictures encircled image of girl ready to drink from cup, 2⅛x1½x¾", G, A7 ....**$25.00**

Kellogg's Drinket, tin, sample, A Delicious Beverage, pictures encircled image of girl ready to drink from cup, 2⅛x1½x¾", EX, D37 ....**$90.00**

Kellogg's Drinket, tin, sample, Instead Of Coffee, pictures steaming cup, 2⅛x1½x¾", EX, D37 ....**$80.00**

Kellogg's Frosted Mini Wheats, Friendly Folk figures, Snap!, Crackle! & Pop!, wood with labeled hats, 3 from set of 5, 1972, scarce, M, D6 ....**$120.00**

Kellogg's Kaffee Hag Coffee, sign, paper, ...Is Real Coffee Minus Caffeine with can & 2 rows of encircled coffee beans, 25x19½", G+, A1..**$10.00**

Kellogg's Kaffee Hag Coffee, tin, Kellogg's above Kaffee Hag lettered on dot flanked by 97% Caffeine Free, keywind, 1-lb, EX, A7 ....**$12.00**

Kellogg's Krumbled Bran, display box, 12x9x5", NM, A7 ....**$40.00**

Kellogg's Krumbles Shredded Whole Wheat, cereal box, 13½x10", NM, A7..**$40.00**

Kellogg's Rice Krispies, figures, Snap!, Crackle! & Pop!, vinyl, movable arms, 1975, EX, D27 ....**$105.00**

Kellogg's Tasteless Castor Oil, banner, cloth, encircled baby with teething ring above name left of product on table, 31x39", G-, A9 ....**$200.00**

Kellogg's Toasted Corn Flakes, sign, cardboard, A Hit & A Miss, shows girl eating, Don't Forget... on reverse, 2-sided hanger, 1915, 16x11", EX+, A13 ....**$250.00**

Kellogg's Toasted Corn Flakes, sign, cardboard, 36 One-Half Pound Packages...Corn Flake Co, Battle Creek, Mich, red & green, 17x11", G, A6 ....**$30.00**

Kellogg's Toasted Corn Flakes, sign, die-cut tin flange, baby in carriage looking down at product box, Oh! Look Who's Here, 19¼x13½", G, A1................**$825.00**

Kellogg's Toasted Corn Flakes, sign, paper hanger, Fine With Berries above full bowl & milk pitcher, box at right, ca 1920, 15x20", EX, A12 ....**$200.00**

Kelly Bar/Kelly Handle Bar Co, sign, paper litho, Simple Safe Strong..., draped nude fairy & handlebar images in bubbles, framed, 24x16", EX, A8........................**$825.00**

Kelly Tires, tire insert, die-cut cardboard, frontal view of waving lady motorist, copyright 1915, 33x23", EX+, A6..**$1,200.00**

Kelly-Springfield Tires/Consolidated Rubber Tire Co, pocket mirror, celluloid, He Is A Happy Man..., product & company name encircle devilish-looking man, round, NM, A15 ....**$600.00**

Kemp St Louis, drinking glass, straight-sided with shield logo encircled by etched lettering, 4", NM, A8.....**$50.00**

Kemp's Balsam, bottle, sample, with contents, NMIB, A7 ....**$50.00**

Kemp's Balsam, sign, die-cut cardboard, ...For That Cough, keyhole-shaped image of girl ready to take medicine, framed, 14½", EX, A2 ....**$75.00**

Ken-L-Ration/Ken-L-Biskit/Ken-L-Meal, sign, metal, die-cut dog's head above Feed Your Dog... above list of products, yellow & white on blue, 21x14", NM, A8........**$65.00**

Kendall DeLuxe, pump sign, painted metal, ...Aristocrat Of Motor Fuels above Ethyl logo, marked AM-50, 11" dia, G+, A6..**$75.00**

Kendall GT-1 Racing Oil, clock, metal & glass light-up, product name & checkered flags in center, red & black, 15" dia, VG, A6..**$100.00**

Kendall Motor Oil, clock, metal & glass, Superb Kendall Motor Oil in center, red, black & white, 15" dia, NM, A6 ....**$350.00**

Kendall Motor Oils, sign, porcelain, 2-sided, Ask For above product name & 100% Pure logo, red, white & blue, oval, 16x24", G, A6 .... **$130.00**

Kendall Motor Oils, sign, tin, The Dealer Sign Of Quality & logo above Kendall lettered vertically, 72x12", NOS, NM, A6 .... **$70.00**

Kendall Penzbest Motor Oils, can, product name & 100% Pure Pennsylvania logo, easy pour spout, 5-gal, 16" dia, VG, A6 .... **$100.00**

Kendall 2000 Mile Oil, can, 2-finger logo & product name on circle in center, cars surround bottom, red, cream & black, 1-qt, G+, A6 .... **$20.00**

Kendall 2000 Mile Oil, clock, metal & glass, 2-finger logo above product name, red, black & white, 15" dia, NM, A6 .... **$275.00**

Kendall 2000 Mile Oil, clock, reverse-painted glass, Time For Kendall on face flanked by product cans, 2000 Mile Oil below, 16x25", EX, A6 .... **$750.00**

Kendall 2000 Mile Oil, curb sign, porcelain with cast iron frame, Sold Here In Sealed Cans above 2-finger logo & lettering, 50x24" dia, EX+, A6 .... **$525.00**

Kendall 2000 Mile Oil, sign, porcelain, can shape, 2-finger logo & product name above band of cars, red, white & black, 20x12", NM, D8 .... $400.00

Kendall's Spavin Cure, sign, paper, woman beside horse with beagles & child looking on, framed, image: 28x22", EX+, A9 .... **$650.00**

Kendel Kind Parlor Bed, sign, self-framed paper-on-cardboard hanger, lettering around 3 images of girl showing uses, 1907, 8x12", EX+, A3 .... **$25.00**

Kennedy's Fruit Cake/Somers Bros, tin, name upper left of Fruit Cake on arched band over cornucopia of fruit, rectangle, rounded corners, 2x4x6", EX, A18 .... **$65.00**

Kent Cigarettes, door push plate, tin, product name on white above open pack on red, Micronite Filter on white below, 1950s-60s, EX, A13 .... **$60.00**

Kent Club Beverages, window display, die-cut, They Surpass left of bottle, glass & mask on tray below girl holding glass, 32x20", G+, A16 .... **$75.00**

Kentucky Belle of Bourbon, sign, painted glass, horse head & Kentucky above product name on diagonal band, Is Here below, framed, 6x12", EX, A8 .... **$60.00**

Kentucky Club Pipe Tobacco, thermometer, tin, blue & white, shows product at bottom, rounded top & bottom, EX+, A18 .... **$200.00**

Kentucky Derby/Churchill Downs, drinking glass, frosted with green graphics, 1948, 5½", NM, A8 .. **$75.00**

Kentucky Fried Chicken, nodder, Colonel Sanders figure, plastic, 1964, EX, D27 .... **$75.00**

Kentucky Tavern, print, paper, 'Old Friends,' distinguished man at tavern table, bartender & black waiter beyond, framed, 27x21", VG+, A8 .... **$125.00**

Kentucky Twist, tobacco label, EX, D35 .... **$4.00**

Kentucky Winners, cigarette tin, flat, name on sky above 3 racing horses with jockeys, square corners, holds 50 cigarettes, EX+, A18 .... **$110.00**

Kessler, display, plaster, early bowling figure next to space to display bottle on marked base, Smooth As Silk..., EX, A8 .... **$55.00**

Kessler Lorelei, tray, deep-dish, emblem logo on circle above product name, Kessler Brewing Co, wood-grain background, 13" dia, VG, A8 .... **$380.00**

Ketch-Em Brand Salmon Eggs, crate label, name above image of product & man fishing in stream, company name below, 1930s, framed, 9x8", NM, A13 ... **$175.00**

Kewpie Pie, sign, cardboard, ice-cream sandwich & kewpie with banner above Ice Cream...10¢, Hendlers Ice Cream, 19x10", NM, A6 .... **$85.00**

Key West Havanas, cigar box label, outer, tropical river scene & fields, 4½x4½", EX, D5 .... **$20.00**

Key-Penn Motor Oil, can, product name on key above 100% Pure Pennsylvania Motor Oil, 1-qt, 5½x4" dia, NM, A6 .... **$65.00**

Keynoil/White Eagle Motor Oil, sign, embossed tin, Keynoil Lubricates & Lasts at left of octagon shaped White Eagle Motor Oil logo, 4x14", EX+, A1 ...... **$575.00**

Keystone, gas globe, red keystone with blue lettering, 3-pc Gill body, 13½" dia, EX+, A6 .... **$170.00**

Keystone Automobile Club, sign, porcelain, Official Garage above logo & Largest In The East on keystone, 2-sided, oval, 29½x24", EX+, A6 .... **$210.00**

Keystone Beverages, drinking glass, straight-sided, gold trim, NM+, A16 .... **$68.00**

Keystone Manufacturing Co, trade card, mechanical, image of Uncle Sam in front of crowd of people from all nations, EX, D8 .... **$60.00**

Keystone Marble Works, sign, paper, multiple vignettes of interior & exterior factory scenes, ca 1865, 19x16", VG+, A9 .... **$200.00**

Keystone State Brewery, see Jacob Conrad

Kickapoo Joy Juice, sign, cardboard hanger, Explosives Permit!, This Here Establishment Is Hereby Licensed..., 1965, 11x9", NM, A16 .... **$25.00**

Kickapoo Joy Juice, soda glass, pictures Li'l Abner & Daisy Mae, red, white & black logo, tapered, 5x3", M, D16 .... **$20.00**

Kik Cola, sign, tin, product name in red above 'Le Cola Des Familles' in black, white background, rounded ends, 3x10", EX, D21..................................**$50.00**

Kim-Bo Cut Plug Tobacco, pocket tin, tall vertical, product name & 5¢ The Can above & below maiden on green background, unopened, NM, A18 ....**$330.00**

King Coal, cigar box label, outer, king on throne with rays of light coming from his crown, 1905, EX, A5 .....**$35.00**

King Cole Coffee, tin, encircled image of King Cole left of product name, Vacuum Packed below, key-wind lid, 1-lb, EX, A18...**$65.00**

King Cole Coffee, tin, red name above & below image of servant with tray offering coffee to King Cole, tall, 1-lb, EX, A18...$315.00

King Cole Coffee, tin, red name above & below image of servant with tray offering coffee to King Cole, short, ½-lb, VG+, A18....................................$265.00

King Cole Tea, door push, porcelain, product name in white above You'll Like The Flavor in yellow, black background, 11x3", NM, D21 ....**$160.00**

King Cole Tea & Coffee, door push, porcelain, oval image of King Cole in red & white above product name in yellow & white, 8x3", rare, VG, A6.....................**$300.00**

King Cole Tea & Coffee, door push, porcelain, The Cafe & Tea & Coffee flank 'King Cole,' EX, A13 ....**$95.00**

King Cole Tea & Coffee, sign, porcelain, keyhole shape with king & steaming cup above product name, blue background, 1920s-30s, 15x9", EX+, A13 ....**$1,050.00**

King David, crate label, California orange, king with white beard & crown, Placentia, 10x11", M, D3 ....**$5.00**

King Edward Crimp Cut Smoking Tobacco, pocket tin, vertical, red with product name above & below profile image, EX, A18...**$500.00**

King George Cross Cut, pocket tin, vertical, cream with red product name above red & cream oval image, company name below, EX+, A18..............................**$425.00**

King Jack Mustard, tin, paper label, 3", NM, A7.......**$36.00**

King Syrup, can, product name above & below lion's head on paper label, multicolored, pry lid, 2-lb 8-oz, EX, A1..**$10.00**

King Tut, crate label, California lemon, pictures lemons, blossoms, lemonade & sugar bowl, Santa Barbara, 9x12", M, D12 ....**$8.00**

King's Pure Malt, tip tray, early barmaid holding tray with bottle, Panama Pacific International Expo emblem below, oval, 6", EX, A21 ....**$88.00**

Kingfish Asparagus, crate label, jumping large-mouth bass wearing crown, Sacramento, M, D12....................**$4.00**

Kings Beer, coasters, name above crown logo flanked by Wurtzburger & Pilsner ribbons with 3 different verses below, 4", EX, A8, each **$60.00**

Kings Beer, label, Kings Brewery, U-type permit number, Internal Revenue Tax Paid statement, 1933-36, 12-oz, M, A10..**$22.00**

Kings County Truck Lines, sign, porcelain, Refrigerated General Commodities... surrounded by cities of California, cream on red, 20" dia, NM, D11 ....**$275.00**

Kingsbury Beer, sign, self-framed tin, celluloid cover, Kingsbury above Aristocrat Of Beer, incised gold letters on red, 6x15", EX, A8.....................................**$100.00**

Kingsbury Beer, tap knob, black ball with white & gold on blue enamel insert, VG+, A8..........................**$50.00**

Kingsbury Beer, tap knob, chrome ball with red & black on white insert, VG+, A8.....................................**$75.00**

Kingsbury Mixture, pocket tin, vertical, Christian Pepper Tobacco Co shield logo in center, rare, VG+, A3 .**$250.00**

Kingsbury Pale Beer, sign, wooden hanger, fish-bowl shape with lion logo above Kingsbury in diagonal script, Pale Beer below, 11x13", EX, A8 ....**$20.00**

Kingsbury Pale Beer, tap knob, chrome ball with blue & gold on white insert, VG+, A8...............................**$50.00**

Kingsbury Picnic Beer, sign, cardboard, Enjoy above product name over bottle with original label, Take One Home, Save On Metal, 17x11", EX, A8 ....**$30.00**

Kingston Roller Skates, sign, embossed tin, name & Proved Best... on scrolled banner above company name, diagonal top corners, 6x15", EX, A8 ....**$55.00**

Kinney Bros High Class Cigarettes, cabinet card, features 1862 derby winner Caractacus, 1890, 8x10", G, A5..**$65.00**

Kirk's Pancake Flour, sign, embossed tin, Kirk's above silhouetted chef at right of Pancake Flour, 1930s-40s, 14x20", NM+, A13 ....$225.00

Kirkland Garage, sign, die-cut tin, lettering on man's arm with pointing finger, ...24 Hour Service, green & white, 7x29", VG+, A6.....................................**$325.00**

Kirster's Half Shell High Grade Havana Cigars, box label, outer, open shell with product name above & below, NM, A5..**$25.00**

Kis-Me Gum, calendar, 1911, embossed die-cut cardboard, oval rowboat scene above They All Chew..., pad below, framed, 16x12", NM, A7 ....**$1,075.00**

Kis-Me Gum, cutouts, Blind Man's Bluff, 6x9", NM, A7 ..**$10.00**

Kis-Me Gum, cutouts, In Fancy Dress, 6x9", NM, A7 ..**$10.00**

Kis-Me Gum, fan, fold-out type, 10", VG, A7............**$85.00**

Kis-Me Gum, jar, embossed glass with paper label picturing 2 children kissing, 2 neck labels, glass stopper, 11x4½", EX, A9...**$350.00**

Kis-Me Gum, sign, cardboard, 'Kis-Me' & Gum- diagonally above oval portrait of girl in filigree frame, framed, 16x10", EX, A7 ....$850.00

Kis-Me Gum, sign, cardboard, child's head pops up with 'Kis-Me' below within framed border, framed, 8½x6½", EX, A7 ....$700.00

Kis-Me Gum, sign, cardboard, lady standing with hand on hip in oval with ornate border, copyright 1896, framed, 19½x14", EX, A7 ....$2,340.00

Kis-Me Gum, sign, cardboard, pictures child resting on 'Kis-Me' pillow, framed, 5x7½", EX, A7 ....$425.00

Kist, door push bar, porcelain, Toujours left of Kist within eccentric circles, ...Pour Vous Rafraichir! at right, VG, A16 ....$65.00

Kist Beverages, calendar, 1930, girl with bottle leaning on fence, Kansas City Kist Bottling Co, full pad, 27x12", NM, D30 ....$95.00

Kist Beverages, calendar, 1946, girl sitting in flower garden, complete, NM, A16 ....$130.00

Kist Beverages, sign, cardboard, I Want To Get Kist..., Kist lips above bottle & girl with lips puckered, 18x12", EX+, D30 ....$45.00

Kist Beverages, sign, cardboard, Kist For A Nickel & tilted bottle at right of teacher & student, 10x24", VG+, D30 ....$45.00

Kist Beverages, sign, cardboard stand-up, die-cut boy holding grocery sack & drinking from bottle, 1940s, 50x19", NM, A1 ....$460.00

Kist Beverages, sign, porcelain, Drink..., red lips on white with black & white lettering, red border, 1950s, 17x23", NM+, A13 ....$140.00

Kist Beverages, sign, tin, die-cut bottle, Enjoy Kist Beverages label on orange bottle, 1940s, 55x15", NM+, A13 ....$450.00

Kist Beverages, sign, tin flange, Enjoy...Take Home A Carton on red with black & white lined border, Art Deco style, 14x18", EX+, A1 ....$180.00

Kist Beverages, sign, tin on cardboard, hanger, orange Drink above bottle, Kist Beverages below on black, beveled edge, 13x6", EX+, A19 ....$75.00

Kist Beverages, soda glass, red logo, Enjoy Kist Beverages, tapered, 4x2½", M, D16 ....$20.00

Kist Beverages, thermometer, tin, Did You Get Kist Today? above bottle & bulb, lady's head below, vertical, rounded corners, EX, A16 ....$190.00

Kist Beverages, see also Orange Kist

Kist Root Beer, sign, paper, Kist on diagonal band across barrel lettered Drink above & Root Beer below, 13½" dia, NM, A7 ....$25.00

Kist Root Beer/Kist Orange, sign, paper, For 5¢ Only! above bottle, 6-pack & lettering, 19x28", NM+, D30 ....$25.00

Kite Mentholated Cigarette Tobacco, sign, paper, 5¢ product box left of New!! above diagonal Mentholated Cigarette Tobacco & 5¢, 12x18", NM, A7 ....$15.00

Kitty Grey, cigar box label, inner lid, woman & black cat, 6x9", M, D5 ....$35.00

Kiwi Polishes, cabinet, painted tin with cast aluminum foot rest atop, blue with white product name on all sides, 12x15x16", VG+, A1 ....$20.00

KK (Krispy Kreme Donuts), sign, porcelain, 2 Ks with faces wearing crowns & holding up donuts on oval surface, 15x24", NM, A7 ....$85.00

Klaxon, display, metal, Danger Sound Klaxon above colorful scene with 2 early cars, 13x15x8", VG, A6 ....$650.00

Klean Kold Ice Box, salesman's sample, wood, metal hardware, 3 opening insulated doors, hinged drip pan cover, original decal, 12", VG, A3 ....$1,265.00

Kleckner's Saffron, tin, oval photo image at left of product name, Beware Of Imitations below, red, white & blue, 1½x2½", EX, D14 ....$18.00

Klein's Breakfast Cocoa, tin, sample, green with product name above & below circular image of parrot, slip lid, 1¾x1½x1¼", EX, D37 ....$115.00

Kloster Brau, label, Conrad Eurich's Brewing Co, pre-prohibition, EX, A10 ....$15.00

Knapstein Brewing Co Special Brew, tip tray, bust portrait of girl in profile, lettering on rim, copyright 1907, Meek Co lithograph, 4" dia, EX, A8 ....$195.00

Knapstein Brewing Co Special Brew, tip tray, elk head in center, lettering on rim, EX, A8 ....$180.00

Knapstein's Beer, drinking glass, straight-sided with inside fluting, red lettering, 4¼", NM, A8 ....$45.00

Knapstein's Draught Beer, label, Knapstein Brewing Co, Internal Revenue Tax Paid statement, 1933-50, ½-gal, EX, A10 ....$14.00

Knapstein's Red Band Beer, label, Knapstein Brewing Co, Internal Revenue Tax Paid statement, 1933-50, 12-oz, M, A10 ....$10.00

Knapsteins Bottled Beer, tray, 'Good Friends,' girl in early red riding habit posed with horse, lettered rim, vertical rectangle, 17", VG+, A8 ....$255.00

Knicker-Bocker Mustard, tin, 3½", NM, A7 ....$60.00

Knickerbocker Beer, display, man with cardboard body & rubber head touting the New! Flip Cap..., No Opener Needed on sidewalk sign, NM, A19 ....$50.00

Knickerbocker Beer, sign, die-cut tin, Take Home! on house with products, Today's Special & product name below, 15x8", NM, A8 ....$55.00

Knickerbocker Beer, sign, tin on cardboard, New York's Famous... above colonial man, gold rim, VG+, A19 ....$40.00

Knickerbocker Brace, sign, paper, **No More Round Shoulders above oval image of lady in brace, The Improved... & flowers below, 26x19", EX, A2...$880.00**

Knickerbocker 100% Pure Pennsylvania Motor Oil, can, Knickerbocker arched above lettered shield flanked by Quaker men, screw lid & handle, 2-gal, 9½x9½", G+, A6 ....$70.00

Knight Hood Cloves, tin, paper label, 2½", NM, A7 ..$22.00

Knorr's Chicken Bouillon Cubes, tin, name above & below Knorr man with banner, National Can Co, slip lid, 3½x1" dia, EX, D37 ....$15.00

Knox New York, salesman's sample, cardboard hat box with sample cloth hat, used as trade-in for full size, EX+, A18 ....$45.00

Koch's Beer, tray, deep-dish, red Drink above Koch's on white oval within red diamond, Beer below, lettered rim, EX+, A19 ....$40.00

Kochs' Toilet Requisites, wall cabinet, oak with etched glass door front, 3 shelves, 36x23½", EX, A21 ...$495.00

Kodak Cameras & Film, sign, tin, Kodak on orange bar over black square, Cameras & Film above & below, 2-sided, 18x24", NM, A1 ....$20.00

Kodak Film, sign, light-up, Buy Kodak Film, Order Prints Here, red & yellow, 12" dia, NM+, D30 ....$95.00

Kodak Instamatic Cameras, display camera, cardboard & plastic with electrified flash, 22x21x11", G, A21 ..$145.00

Kodak Verichrome, sign, metal with wrought iron hanger, box of film on inverted triangle, Developing, Printing..., 17x17", EX, A6 ....$280.00

Koehler's Beer, tray, deep-dish, cartoon image of 3 singing gents above product name & There Is No Better Beer!, 12" dia, EX+, A19 ....$35.00

Koening Brand Fresh Roasted Coffee, store bin, tin, black with gold & white lettering, gold trim, slant top, 20x16", scarce, EX, A2 ....$385.00

Koken Shop, sign, porcelain, lettering & barber pole surrounded by holes for light bulbs, red, white & blue, 31" dia, rare, VG, A6 ....$1,800.00

Koko Kooler, sign, paper litho, 25¢ To A Dollar, Sunshades-Koko Koolers..., 14 heads modeling different hats, 21x14", EX, A12 ....$160.00

Kokomo Rubber Co, see Haynes Auto Co

Kola-Ade, syrup bottle, Drink Kola-Ade label, metal cap, EX, A16 ....$95.00

Kolb's Dandy Bread, sign, tin over cardboard, pictures loaf of bread on light yellow background, EX+, D30 ...$75.00

Komo Paste, sign, porcelain, trademark image of elf-like boy carrying large can, 'Komo For Metals' below, 30x24", G+, A9 ....$525.00

Komo Paste, sign, porcelain, trademark image of elf-like boy carrying large can, 'Komo For Metals' below, 30x24", EX, A1 ....$750.00

Kooba, screen door signs, We Serve Kooba A Cola Drink 5¢ on triangular shape, set of 2, EX+, A16 ....$60.00

Kool Cigarettes, display cigarette carton, Cork Tipped..., green, white & black with penguin, EX, A18 ....$60.00

Kool Cigarettes, fan, vertical rectangle with image of open pack & penguins on iceberg, wooden stick handle, EX, A18 ....$15.00

Kool Cigarettes, Scatter Pins on cardboard card, Here We Are, Your Willie & Millie Scatter Pins, NM, A7....$30.00

Kool Cigarettes, sign, paper, Mr Kool Will Broadcast..., Derby Day May 4th, penguins at microphone, horse & jockey, 1934, 22x14", EX, A12 ....$220.00

Kool Cigarettes, sign, tin, We Sell Cigarettes, Smoke... flanked by penguin & cigarette pack, 12x34", NOS, D11 ....$65.00

Kool Cigarettes, tin, flat, white with black border, green & white Kool logo, VG+, A18 ....$105.00

Kool-Aid, figure, Kool-Aid Dancing Man, 1991, EX, D27...$40.00

Koolmotor Gasolene (sic), gas globe, High Test Anti Knock arched above, green & white with black lettering, green metal body, 15" dia, NM, A6 ....$425.00

156

Kopper King Spark Plugs, tin, name in receding letters, tall square, slip lid, 4⅝x1⅜x1⅜", EX, D37 .... **$95.00**

Koppitz Victory Beer, label, Koppitz-Melcher's Inc, Internal Revenue Tax Paid statement #36, 1933-50, 12-oz, M, A10 .... **$25.00**

Koppitz-Melchers Brewing Co, tip tray, intertwined initials on star burst in center with company name on rim, 4" dia, VG+, A8 .... **$45.00**

Koppitz-Melchers Brewing Co Pale Select, drinking glass, straight-sided with flat bottom, Pale Select logo with hops above diagonal name, 3½", NM, A8 .... **$35.00**

Korbel Sec California Champagne, sign, tin over cardboard, classical lady admiring cluster of grapes on vine left of bottle, 13x19", EX, A9 .... **$100.00**

Korbel Sec California Champagne, sign, tin over cardboard, classical lady admiring cluster of grapes on vine left of bottle, 13x19", M, D11 .... **$250.00**

Korn Krisp, sign, paper hanger, Free Doll! This Life Size Rag Doll Given Free With 2 P'k'g's... next to doll, 16x20", EX, A2 .... **$230.00**

Kotex, sign, tin, name above 3-quarter image of a nurse with product box, light blue background, framed, 19x12", VG, A21 .... **$340.00**

Kraft Kraylets, sign, die-cut tin pig with lettering, I Get The Milk Bank Boost From Kraylets, Kraft logo below, 12x19", M, D11 .... **$125.00**

Kraft Macaroni & Cheese, figure, Cheesasaurus Rex Surfer, hard vinyl, 1991, 5", M **$8.00**

Kramer's, door plate, All Flavors, 2-color background with name above tilted bottle, vertical, EX, A16 .... **$25.00**

Kreemee Root/Gluek Brewing Co, label, yellow name & A Delicious Root Beer flanked by illustrated product images, company name below, 12-oz, EX, A19 ... **$10.00**

Krueger, tap knob, black ball shape, Krueger in white & gold with white band above & below on red enamel insert, VG+, A8 .... **$35.00**

Krueger Ale, tap knob, black ball with cream on green insert, EX, A8 .... **$45.00**

Krueger Beer, can, cone-top, 12-oz, VG, A19 .... **$45.00**

Krueger Beer, can, flat-top, instructional, 12-oz, EX+, A19 .... **$125.00**

Krueger Cream Ale, can, cone-top, Internal Revenue Tax Paid statement, 32-oz, EX+, A19 .... $200.00

Krueger Cream Ale, sign, molded plastic, green & white tankard with gold lid, 16x6x3", NM, A19 .... **$40.00**

Krueger Cream Ale, tap knob, green ball shape with red & cream on green insert, 2-sided, EX, A8 .... **$85.00**

Krueger Extra Light Cream Ale, tap knob, green & white enamel with gold border, EX+, A8 .... **$35.00**

Krueger Extra Light Dry Beer, tap knob, red & white enamel with gold border, VG+, A8 .... **$20.00**

Krueger Finest Beer, tap knob, red ball shape with cream & black on red insert, 2-sided, EX, A8 .... **$30.00**

Krueger Kooler-Keg, tap knob, black ball shape with white Kooler-Keg above band with white Krueger below on red celluloid insert, EX, A8 .... **$70.00**

Krug Luxus Beer, label, Fred Krug Brewing Co, U-type permit number, Internal Revenue Tax Paid statement, 1933-36, 12-oz, NM, A10 .... **$14.00**

Kuco Toilet Powder, container, cardboard with tin base & push-tab lid, oval inset with small child reaching for can on table, 5", NM, A3 .... $160.00

Kuebeler-Stang Brewing Co, mug, ceramic, straight-sided, shield with hops & leaves above company name, multicolored, 4½", EX, A8 .... **$95.00**

Kuebler Beer, sign, cardboard, Old Timers Say 'It's The Beer That Tastes The Best,' shows elderly gent pouring & 1852, 15x10", EX, A19 .... **$85.00**

Kuebler Beer, sign, porcelain neon, red product name on blue, 2-sided hanger, 16x30x10", EX+, A19 .... **$360.00**

Kuebler Beer, tap knob, black ball with multicolored image of man in top hat on red metal insert, EX, A8 ...... **$65.00**

Kuebler Beer/Ale, sign, tin hanger, Kuebler above man pouring from bottle into glass flanked by Beer & Ale Since 1852, 6x11", EX, A19 .... **$110.00**

Kulmbacher Beer, label, Effinger Co, U-type permit number, Internal Revenue Tax Paid statement, 1933-36, 12-oz, NM, A10 .... **$15.00**

KunZoil, can, product name above large oil drop flanked by tropical scene at left & arctic scene at right, 1-qt, EX+, A1 .... **$240.00**

Kupferberg Champagne, postcard, range rider leaning against rock with bottle & holding up glass, horse beyond, H Eichrodt/Germany, M, A16 .... **$75.00**

Kupferberg Gold Champagne, postcard, German, elegant table setting with Zum Geburtstag on banner, EX, D26 .... **$65.00**

Kurth's Beer, sign, porcelain, product name & logo above 'The Old Favorite,' company name below, red & black on cream, 14x20", VG+, A8 .... **$60.00**

Kurth's Beer, sign, self-framed tin on cardboard, Drink... The Old Favorite, Kurth Co & Columbus Wis in lower corners, 6x9", EX+, A8 .... **$35.00**

Kwickwork Enamel, sample display, celluloid over metal, 12 samples picturing cars, 11x6", VG, A6 .... **$400.00**

KY Tobacco, label, black man winning derby on broken down pony, Holbrook Bros & Co, Louisville KY, framed, image: 11x11", EX, A9 .... **$450.00**

Kyra, cigar box label, inner lid, exotic woman dancer, 6x9", M, D5 ....$14.00

Kyra, cigar box label, outer, exotic woman dancer, 4½x4½", M, D5 ....$8.00

L

L Lamb Lumber Co, match safe, product name arched above logo & Minneapolis, Minn, red, white & blue, 2¾x1½", EX, A11 ....$85.00

L&C Mayer Jewelry, catalog, 1955, 496 pgs, EX, D17 ..$75.00

L&H Electric Iron, ad flier, 2 smiling women, 1 ironing, 4 pgs, G-, D23 ....$8.00

L&M Cigarettes, sign, tin, pictures pack of cigarettes, EX, D34 ....$55.00

La Azora Cigars, charger, ...Cigar Of Cigars, Turkish princess with Nubian slaves in fancy vessel, 24" dia, VG, A9 ....$375.00

La Belle Creole, pocket tin, flat, woman's portrait encircled by coins with banner above, rounded corners, Ginna, pre-1901, EX+, A18 ....$250.00

La Britanica, cigar box label, outer, bright sunrise scene & woman with gold harp, 4½x4½", M, D5 ....$18.00

La Britanica, cigar box label, outer, oval portrait with crown atop flanked by Fadrica & Tabacos, 1903, EX, A5 ....$50.00

La Cavalerie, cigar box label, printer's proof, cavalier drawing weapon at right of lettering & shield logo, EX, A5 ....$25.00

La Coqueta, cigar box label, salesman's sample, elegant couple in front of mirror, VG+, A5 ....$55.00

La Corona, tin, classical scene with draped lady holding globe, holds 50, oval, A18 ....$45.00

La Corona de Laurel, cigar box label, salesman's sample, outdoor scene with children & adults, M, A5.......$85.00

La Fendrich Cigar, thermometer, tin, Ask For... on red above Always A Cool Smoke on yellow left of bulb on cigar image, EX+, A18................................$220.00

La Festa, cigar box label, inner lid, scene of ancient Greece & man dressed in red, 1911, 6x9", M, D5 ....$12.00

La Festa, cigar box label, outer, Roman dressed in red toga, 1911, 4½x4½", M, D5..................................$5.00

La Flor de Erb 10¢ Cigar, sign, tin over cardboard, bust portrait of man in center, DS Erb & Co Makers, yellow & white on blue, 6x13½", EX, A6 ....$70.00

La Flor de John Adams Cigars, box label set, portrait of John Adams flanked by medallions, 2 pcs, EX/M, A5..$85.00

La Floridan, cigar box label, outer, nude woman hidden by daisies, 1909, 4½x4½", M, D5 ....$22.00

La Fotesca Clear Havana Cigars, box label, printer's proof, 2 foxes in front of fountain with nude woman in center, EX, A5................................$50.00

La Indiana, cigar box label, salesman's sample, oval bust portrait of woman flanked by Indians, EX, A5.....$90.00

La Mia Cigars, sign, paper, cigar box label with elegant girl, Lozano, Pendas & Co..., scroll design in each corner, 18x14", VG, A9 ....$100.00

La Palina Cigars, box, circular portrait of woman flanked by Mild & Made Good, EX, A3........................$35.00

La Palina Cigars, canister, brass, VG+, D35 ....$30.00

La Penserosa, cigar box label, printer's proof, girl in feathered hat surrounded by flowers, EX, A5 ....$60.00

La Preferencia Seconds, sign, paper, My! This Is A Mild Cigar, 5¢ Straight, man in dark gray coat & hat lighting a cigar, framed, 19x23", EX, A6 ....$30.00

La Relacion, cigar box label, product name & medallions above outdoor scene with soldier conversing with 3 women, M, A5..$50.00

La Romancia, cigar box label, inner lid, 17th century couple dancing within heart shape, 6x9", EX, D5......$30.00

La Salle Lager, label, McGovern Brewing Co, Internal Revenue Tax Paid statement, 1933-50, 12-oz, M, A10...$10.00

La Turbana, cigar box label, outer, woman in blue & red turban, 1887, 4½x4½", M, D5............................$15.00

La Zoos, cigar box label, inner lid, swan beside 5 ladies in a boat, 6x9", EX, D5..............................$25.00

Labatt's, tray, porcelain, Labatt's in script above trademark logo flanked by Union Made, red on cream, 12x16", EX, A6 ....$60.00

Labor King, cigar box label, salesman's sample, smiling man seated in front of table flanked by logos & vignettes, M, A5...$165.00

Laco Olive Oil, bottle, clear glass with metal cap, 4", EX, D24 ....$6.50

Lacquerwax, sign, tin, Motorists Relax With... above can in front of car & other lettering, yellow, blue & red, 14x20", VG, A6 ....$170.00

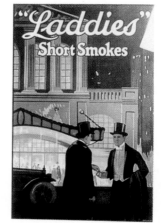

Laddies Short Smokes, sign, cardboard, name above 2 gentlemen in top hats sharing a Laddie across from opera house, 33x21", EX, A2................$175.00

Ladies & Childrens Hair Bobbing, sign, porcelain flange, ...Our Specialty on geometric background, red, white & blue, 12x24", EX, A6 ....$350.00

Ladies Friend Baking Powder, tin, paper label, 4-oz, VG, A7 ....$20.00

Lady Churchill, cigar box, product name arched above ornate design with fan, NM, A3 ....$35.00

Lady Hellen Coffee, container, cardboard with metal lid & bottom, product name above & below lady's portrait, pry lid, 1-lb, EX, A3 ....$75.00

Lady Macbeth, cigar box label, outer, woman in red robe, 4½x4½", EX, D5 ....$28.00

Laflin & Rand Powder Co, sign, Orange Rifle Powder above family of quail & sprigs of real grass, gold leaf letters, framed, image: 14x18", EX, A9 ....$650.00

Laflin & Rand Smokeless Powder, sign, paper, rough rider in uniform holding revolver, ca 1899, framed, image: 13x8½", NM, A9 ....$200.00

Lagoon, crate label, California orange, SF Expo buildings & lagoon, E Highland, 10x11", NM, D3 ....$10.00

Lake Ridge, crate label, California pear, mountain view with lake & orchard, red logo, Kelseyville, 8x11", M, D12 ....$5.00

Lake Shore Ice Cream Co, tray, image of lady in white with red band around hat & red collar holding product, lettered rim, oval, 16", VG, A21 ....$75.00

Lake Wenatchee, crate label, Washington apple, lake & cabin scene with pines, mountains & apples, 9x11", M, D12 ....$3.00

Lakeland Quick Cooking Rolled Oats, container, cardboard, red with name above & below silhouette image of moon shining on lake, 3-lb, EX+, A3 ....$55.00

Lakeland Rolled Oats, container, cardboard, red with name above & below silhouette image of moon shining on lake, 3-lb, EX, A3 ....$45.00

Lakeside Club Bouquet, sign, Vitrolite, product name above filigree oval with lady & 2 gentlemen, ca 1905, shadow-box frame, 26x30", EX+, A13 ....$2,000.00

Lamb Knit Sweaters, display, papier-mache, figural lamb with raised black lettering on sides, black ears & feet, 15", VG+, A2 ....$465.00

Lambertville 'Snag-Proof' Rubber Boots & Shoes, sign, flange, yellow with red product lettering & brownies inspecting a boot & shoe, red border, 13x18", EX, A2 ....$3,850.00

Lambertville Rubber Co, calendar, 1901, 'Snag-Proof' above brownies working on boot, calendar flanked by boots below, 10x7", VG+, A2 ....$120.00

Lambertville Rubber Co, calendar, 1902, 'Snag-Proof' above 3 brownies high-stepping in boots, calendar flanked by boots below, 10x7", VG, A2 ....$75.00

Lambertville Rubber Co 'Snag-Proof' Boots, calendar, 1906, 'The Lambertville Girl,' complete, 14x12", EX, A6 ....$200.00

Lambertville Rubber Co, sign, paper roll-down, 'Snag-Proof' above image of brownies working on large boot, company name below, 22x15", VG+, A2 .$900.00

Land O' Lakes, thermometer, dial-type, chickens & Amprotection above Indian princess & product name, 1968, 10" dia, EX, A6 ....$40.00

Lane Bryant, catalog, Spring/Summer, 1969, 166 pgs, EX, D17 ....$20.00

Lane Bryant Apparel for Expectant Mothers, catalog, Spring/Summer, 1925, 36 pgs, EX, D17 ....$40.00

Lane Bryant Baby Fashions, catalog, Fall/Winter, 1926, 44 pgs, EX, D17 ....$40.00

Lane's Cold Tablets, sign, die-cut cardboard, keyhole-shaped image of lady holding small pill with open box, name below, framed, 14", EX, A2 ....$75.00

Lang's Highest Quality Beer & Ale, tray, deep-dish, product name on red encircled by red & black diamond band, round, NM, A19 ....$35.00

Langendorf Bread, sign, tin, product name above loaf of bread, America's Finest Bread below, 16x26", VG+, D11 ....$60.00

Laquerwax, sign, die-cut cardboard stand-up, arched top with clouds blowing different weather conditions at car, 30x22", VG+, A1 ....$170.00

Larco Gasoline, gas globe, logo & product name on shield, blue, gray & white, blue metal body, copyright 1935, 15" dia, EX+, A6 ....$1,000.00

Larkin Orange Blossom Powder, tin, with contents, 2", NM, A7 ....**$55.00**

Larro Sure Raise & Larro Sure Calf, sign, porcelain flange, cow's face & Raise Better Calves, New... in white on blue, orange & white border, 20x22", NM, D8 ....**$350.00**

Lash's Bitters, cribbage board, wood with stenciled lettering, For Headache, Malaria..., orange & black, 4½x13", rare, EX+, A3 ....**$75.00**

Lash's Root Beer, mug, black logo, L forms curved tail, footed, 6x4", M, D16 ....**$65.00**

Last Edition/Hunsicker & Co, cigar box, wood, shaped like a book, 1883 tax stamp, EX+, A18 ....**$30.00**

Laughing Eyes, cigar box label, salesman's sample, ...Manufactured From Finest Selected Tobacco above girl with hand to chin, NM, A5...**$60.00**

Laurel, crate label, California orange, 3 oranges surrounded by laurel wreath, Corona, 10x11", M, D12..............**$5.00**

Laurier Premier 10¢ Cigar/Rock City Cigar Co, sign, self-framed tin horseshoe shape with bust image of somber-looking man, gold frame, 24x19", VG+, A18 ....**$220.00**

Lautz Bro's & Co's Soaps, sign, paper, company name above & below white man washing black boy until he turns white, 27x21", G, A2 ....**$630.00**

Lava Soap, sample bar in box, EX, A7......................**$10.00**

Lawrence Barrett Cigar, sign, die-cut porcelain, bust of man atop sign with lettering on faux wood-grain, stamped BS Co..., 20x18", NM, A1 ....**$2,400.00**

Lax-ets, match holder, Only 5¢ Per Box, product pack & ad text on plate above holder, NM, A7..................**$140.00**

Lazell's Massatta Talcum Powder, tin, sample, shows oriental lady & child on orange background, blue trim, shaker top, 2x1⅛x¾", EX, D37 ....**$115.00**

LC Smith Typewriter Ribbon, tin, vertical, green with early typewriter in horseshoe & horse head logo, slip lid, 2x1¾x1¾", EX, D37....................................**$30.00**

Le Nil Cigarettes, sign, cardboard, Je Ne Fume Oue Le Mil in receding letters before prancing elephant with red blanket, 12x8½", EX, A18 ....**$50.00**

Le Roy All Tobacco Cigarettes/L Miller & Sons, sign, tin, Society Smoke upper left of sealed pack, All Tobacco Cigarettes lower right on dark green, 10x14", EX+, A18 ....**$250.00**

Le Roy Cigarettes All Tobacco/L Miller & Sons, sign, paper, Smoke The Le Roy above 2 cherubs in thoughtful pose, All Tobacco...Ten Cents, framed, VG, A18...**$70.00**

Leadership Grapes, lug box label, white 3-D script logo with blue shading on red background, Lodi, M, D12.........**$2.00**

Lee Wards Mills Crafts & Supplies, catalog, Fall/Winter, 1954, 44 pgs, EX, D17..**$25.00**

Lefevre-Utile Biscuits, sign, paper, woman in elegant dress surrounded by dogwood flowers, 1907, framed, 27x20", VG, A9 ....**$300.00**

Legal Tender, crate label, California orange, $250 bundle of currency on blue & black background, Fillmore, 10x11", M, D3 ....**$3.00**

Lehnert's Beer, tip tray, dog smoking cigar, lettered rim, 4" dia, VG+, A8..**$130.00**

Leinenkugel Chippewa Pride Beer, display, hand holding bottle, Here's The Best In The House... on sleeve, 1940, 10", NM, A3..**$60.00**

Leinenkugel High Grade Beers, tray, Leinenkugel on scrolled banner with floral & hops logo above, Ruby Malt... on rim, pre-1920, 13" dia, VG+, A8 ....**$550.00**

Leinenkugel's, clock, light-up, Indian girl in profile above name on diagonal band, Made With Chippewa Water..., 1950s, round, EX, A8 ....**$190.00**

Leisy Beer, drinking glass, pilsner style featuring 90th Anniversary in yellow & blue, 1952, 8½", NM, A8 ..**$25.00**

Leisy Brewing Co Premium Lager, sign, paper, 'Worth Shouting About,' girl in red dress bursting through circle, ca 1898, framed, image: 18x14", EX, A9 ...**$1,000.00**

Lembeck & Betz, tray, 'Introduction,' 2 children showing kitten to pup in yard, lettered rim, American Art Works, 1910, square, EX+, A8 ....**$775.00**

Lemon-Julep, sign, tin, Drink Lemon-Julep In Bottles in yellow & white on blue, 10x32", NM+, D30 ....**$155.00**

Lemon-Kola, sign, tin over cardboard, product name & 5¢ below lady in hat & draped shawl holding glass, 9x6", VG+, A13 ....**$400.00**

Lemp Brewing Co, drinking glass, straight-sided with company name etched above man in top hat having a brew, 3½", NM, A8 ....**$35.00**

Lemp Extra Pale Beer, label, Wm J Lemp Brewing Co, Internal Revenue Tax Paid statement, 1933-50, 12-oz, M, A10 ....**$12.00**

Lennox Furnace Co, salt & pepper shakers, matte glaze Lennie Lenox figures, full-color, incised lettering, 4½", EX, D25 ....**$175.00**

Lennox Torrid Zone All Steel Furnace, pocket mirror, celluloid, product name arched above furnace, Lennox Furnace Co below, black & white, round, EX, A11 .....**$22.00**

Lenox Soap, sign, porcelain, lined border with inverted corners around product name, 6x10", EX+, A13 ......**$120.00**

Lenox Tobacco, pocket tin, metallic blue with gold name above red image of early open car, red & gold emblem below, VG+, A18 ....**$850.00**

Leonard Karn Bottler, tray, patriotic allegory scene with lettering & hops design on rim, oval, 16", VG+, A8 ..**$500.00**

Leopard Skins, cigarette papers, NM, A7 ....**$10.00**

Lester & Co Boots & Shoes, sign, plaster, embossed lettering above company seal & high-top shoe, ornate border, 20½x24½", EX, A9 ....**$750.00**

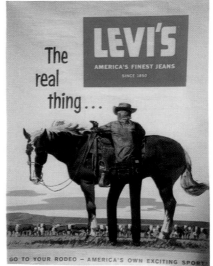

Levi's, sign, paper, The Real Thing..., shows backside of cowboy ready to mount horse, cow herd beyond, 36x24", EX, D38 ....**$200.00**

Lewie's Refreshing Beverages, sign, tin over cardboard, Cheerio It's...I Want & Invigorating right of man with bottles, beveled edge, 8x11", EX, A13 ....**$35.00**

Lewis 66 Whiskey, tip tray, close-up image of girl in red plumed hat, red decorative border, 4" dia, EX, A21 .**$100.00**

Libby, McNeill & Libby Corned Beef, tin, sample, trapezoid shape with Corned Beef above & company name below oval image of factory, 1¼x2x1½", EX, D37 ....**$80.00**

Libby's California Asparagus, tin, sample, pictures circular image of asparagus, 2⅝x1⅜x1⅝", EX, D37 ....**$35.00**

Libby's Fancy Red Alaska Salmon, tin, sample, product name above image of salmon marked Red, Packed In Alaska below, 2x1⅜" dia, EX, D37......................**$40.00**

Libby's Kraut, tin, sample, pictures head of cabbage, pry lid, 2x1¾" dia, EX, D37..............................**$35.00**

Liberty Bond, cigar box label, outer, document promoting American bonds, 4½x4½", M, D5 ....**$6.00**

Lieber Lager Beer, label, Lieber Brewing Co, U-type permit number, Internal Revenue Tax Paid statement, 1933-36, 12-oz, NM, A10..............................**$15.00**

Liebert & Obert, see Manayunk Bock Beer

Life Belt, cigar box label, salesman's sample, young sailor surrounded by nude women swimming, EX, A5 ..**$400.00**

Lifebuoy Soap, tin, sample, rectangular with name in shadowed lettering on lid, square corners, ⅝x1¼x1½", EX, D37 ....**$60.00**

Lifesavers, display, tin box sectioned off by flavors, fold-down lid, 4½x15¾x9⅛", rare, NM, A2 ....**$2,530.00**

Lifesavers, figure, bendable, 1967, VG, D27 ....**$150.00**

Lifesavers, pin, 3-D metal, Five Flavor pack of Lifesavers with foil, 1¼" long, NM, D24....................................**$8.50**

Lifesavers, sign, tin, Real Lifesavers, Always Good Taste, arrow points to pack, black ground, metal frame, 1920s, 60x27", NM, A21 ....**$1,900.00**

Lift Beverage, mirror, features bottle, 3-sided arched top, 18x10", A13 ....**$20.00**

Lift Beverage, sign, tin, Drink above bottle with airplane on label, It's Good For You below, cream background, 24x12", VG, A6 ....$185.00

Lily Cigarettes, box, cardboard, yellow & white with product name above & below encircled lily, full (16 cigarettes), EX+, A18 ....$45.00

Lily Gloss & Corn Starch, sign, paper roll-down, pictures babies from various ethnic backgrounds surrounded by fairies & gnomes, 28x12", VG, A9 ....$1,400.00

Lime Cola, sign, celluloid, Drink Lime Cola (Trade-Mark Registered on L) lettered over bottle, 1950s, 9" dia, NM+, A13..$130.00

Lime Cola, sign, die-cut bottle, 1940s-50s, 45x12", NM, A13 ....$350.00

Lime Cola, sign, tin on cardboard, Drink... above In Bottles on yellow, beveled edge, 1940s, 6x13", NM+, A13 ..$70.00

Lime Kiln Club, tobacco box label, depicts gathering of black men, product name below, 6x7¾", NM, A18 ....$35.00

Lime-Crush, sign, cardboard hanger, — Like Limes? Drink... below Rockwell lady in sun hat sipping from bottle, 12x9", rare, VG, A16 ....$535.00

Limoneira Co, crate label, Sunkist lemon on open wrapper, red background, Santa Paula, 12x9", M, D3....$1.00

Lincoln Loan Service, matchbook, pictures 2 black folks throwing dice, Harrisburg, PA, NM, D28 ....$12.00

Lion, gas globe, roaring lion above product name, orange, black & white, glass body, 13½", NM+, A6 ....$900.00

Lion Ale, can, flat-top, Internal Revenue Tax Paid statement, 12-oz, EX+, A19 ....$62.00

Lion Beer, tray, blue, silver & gold, 13", VG, D7.......$20.00

Lion Brew, label, circular lion logo upper left of product name on red diagonal band, company name lower right, 11-oz, VG+, A19 ....$45.00

Lion Coffee, card set, pictures black workers picking coffee beans, late 1800s, EX, D6 ....$45.00

Lion Coffee, paper dolls, 'Little Boy Blue,' Woolson Spice Co, ca 1900, 4 pcs, cut but unused, NM, D14 ......$65.00

Lion Coffee, paper dolls, 'Little Jack Horner,' Woolson Spice Co, ca 1900, 4 pcs, cut but unused, NM, D14 ....$60.00

Lion Coffee, paper dolls, 'Mary Had A Little Lamb,' Woolson Spice Co, ca 1900, 4 pcs, cut but unused, NM D14 ....$60.00

Lion Coffee, sign, cardboard, product name above lion in blue uniform & hat smoking pipe, product in foreground, 31x20", rare, VG, A6 ....$400.00

Lion Coffee, tin, encircled lion in center, key-wind lid, 1 lb, EX+, A3..$28.00

Lion Heat Resistant Lubricant, can, product name above lion logo, orange, black & white, 1-lb, NM+, A1 .$95.00

Lion Naturalube, license plate attachment, metal, roaring lion atop lettering, New Type Motor Oil..., orange black & cream, 6", VG, A6 ....$70.00

Lipton's Tea, sign, porcelain, product name above None Genuine Without This Signature at left of signature 12x60", EX, D11 ....$175.00

Lipton's Teas, sign, cardboard, name above Ceylonese woman with red parasol, framed, 16½x13", G, A21 ....$120.00

Lipton's Teas & Coffees, sign, cardboard, name around lady in thoughtful pose over table with tea service & open tin, framed, 20x14", VG, A21...........$395.00

Lipton's Yellow Label Coffee, tin, yellow with product name on red bands above & below logo, round with screw lid, 1-lb, EX+, A18 ....$95.00

Listerine Toothpaste, full tube with box, NM, A7 ...$20.00

Lithia Beer, tap knob, black plastic with red & cream insert, round, EX+, A8..$90.00

Litholin Waterproofed Linen, pocket mirror, pictures collar with lettering & red bow tie on deep blue background, oval, 2¾", EX, A21 ....$55.00

Litholin Waterproofed Linen, trolley sign, A Summer Necessity above man & large collar flanked by other lettering, 11x21", EX, D8 ....$195.00

Little Caesars Pizza, figure, Pizza-Pizza Man, plush, 1990 EX, D24 ....$5.00

Little Caesars Pizza, picnic jug, pictures Pizza-Pizza Man & Coke emblems, 1991, EX+, D24 ....$5.00

Little Dutchman Beer, label, Vienna Brewing Co, Internal Revenue Tax Paid statement, 1933-50, 12-oz, NM, A10 ....$22.00

Little Fairies Baking Powder, can label, product name above & below man's portrait in heart flanked by fairies, 5x11", NM, A7..$12.00

Little Fairies Baking Powder, container, cardboard, round with product name above & below heart-shaped portrait of a man on yellow, 4x2¼", EX, A18 ....$70.00

Little Mozart, cigar tin, oval with name next to oval profile portrait & 5¢, name repeated around slip lid, EX, A18..$60.00

Little Rhody Cut Plug, insert card, features actress Edith Chester, VG, A5 ....$20.00

Little Rock Board of Trade, pin-back button, celluloid, pictures Board of Trade building, black & white, 44mm, EX, A11 ....$10.00

LM Crane & Co Oil Merchants, calendar holder, aluminum, early open car & lettering in black, EX+, A6 ....$10.00

Lodge & Davis Machine Tool Co, sign, paper, name around colorful bust image of girl, machine below, framed, 30x14½", G, A21 ....$275.00

Loewer's Gambrinus Brewery Co, sign, embossed tin, barrel shape with impressed image of King Gambrinus toasting frothy mug, 26x20", G, A9.....................$300.00

Loewer's Lager Beer & Ale/Gambrinus Brewing Co, tray, black with red & yellow product & company lettering, red Lager Beer & Ale on white ribbon, round, EX+, A19 ....$60.00

Log Cabin Syrup, see Towel's Log Cabin Syrup

Log Cabin Tobacco, sign, paper, Smoke... above pioneer in front of cabin, Manufactured By Lambert & Butler, framed, image: 22x18", G, A9...........................$300.00

Logan Brew/Columbia Brewing Co, label, diagonal product name above B logo & company name, 22-oz, VG+, A19 ....$15.00

London Bobby Beer, label, Miami Valley Brewing Co, Internal Revenue Tax Paid statement, 1933-50, 12-oz, M, A10 ....$10.00

London Life Cigarettes, sign, self-framed tin, cricket players & spectators gathered under lettered awning, 39x28", EX, A9 ....$550.00

Lone Jack Tobacco, tin, horizontal, VG+, D35..........$75.00

Long Chew Gum, trade stimulator, clown with sign showing clown giving giraffe gum, round base, yellow & blue, electric, 20", EX, A2..............................$5,400.00

Long Tom Smoking Tobacco, tin, yellow with image of tall black man at left of name, bordered, gold trim, rectangular, rounded corners, VG+, A18 ....$240.00

Longfellow, cigar box label, outer, white-bearded man flanked by Indian & maiden, 1903, EX, A5 ....$45.00

Longman & Martinez Paints, color card & sample book, ca 1914, EX, A12 ....$50.00

Longware Laces, display dispenser, metal, octagonal shape turns on round pedestal, knob finial, 10¢ advertising, 14", EX, A12 ....$100.00

Look Out Cut Plug, see JG Dill's Look Out Cut Plug

Lord Baltimore Cigar, sign, cardboard, product name above half-burnt cigar, Try Them, 'Tastes Good,' yellow ground, 7x13", EX, A8..$45.00

Lord Delaware, cigar box label, inner lid, man flanked by shipyard & seashore, 6x9", EX, D5 ....$45.00

Lord Kenyon Blend Super-Mild Tobacco, pocket tin, vertical, cream & blue lettering & graphics, short, EX+, A18 ....$485.00

Lord Maxwell Ginger Ale, thermometer, tin, America's Finest on red arrow pointing to large bottle, 15", NM, D30..$65.00

Lord Needles, tin, flat, trapezoid shape with trademark image, rounded corners, ½x1½x2¾", EX, D37 ....$50.00

Lord Salisbury Turkish Cigarettes, tin, flat, gold lettering on dark blue background, gold border, holds 50 cigarettes, EX+, A18 ....$65.00

Lord Tennyson Puritanos, tin, lime green & yellow stripe with name on fancy red bands above & below oval bust image & nymphs, EX+, A18 ....$110.00

Lorelei Beer/Kessler Brewing Co, sign, paper, name upper right, draped nude seated on cliff looking down at boat, castle beyond, framed, 24x19", EX, A8..$1,220.00

Lorillard Indian Snuff, bottle, with contents, unbroken tax stamp, 1898, M, D6 ....$50.00

Lorillard's Redicut Tobacco, lunch box, vertical with product name above hand-held open pack, Just Break Off A Piece To Fit lettered below, EX, A18.........$80.00

Lorillard's Stripped Smoking Tobacco, lunch box, lid shows product pack on woven background, EX+, A18 .... **$15.00**

Los Angeles Brewing Co, beer jug, ceramic with nap top, marked with company name & 738 on cream background, EX, A19 .... **$260.00**

Lotos, beer label, Adam Scheidt Brewing Co, L-type permit number, 1928-33, 12-oz, M, A10 .... **$30.00**

Lotos Export, see Adam Scheidt

Lotta Cola, lighter, rows of repeated Lotta Cola divided by rows of repeated 16-oz, M, A16 .... **$25.00**

Louis Bergdoll Brewing Co, cigar cutter/ashtray/match holder, ceramic, black lettering & graphics on white, gold bands, EX+, A19 .... **$125.00**

Louis F Dow Co, calendar, 1927, Goodwill Advertising above Earl Christy girl, full pad, 46x22", EX, D8 ..**$80.00**

Louis Oberts Famous Lager Beer, drinking glass, stemmed, embossed logo, NM, A8 .... **$65.00**

Louisville Tin & Stove Co, catalog, Fall, 1938, 80 pgs, EX, D17 .... **$50.00**

Lounsberry & Harris Lumber Dealers, sign, embossed tin, Lumber Furnished By...Los Angeles, 19x27", M, D11 .... **$65.00**

Loving Cup Coffee, tin, Loving Cup in red on white above Coffee in white on red, key-wind lid, 1-lb, NM+, A3 .... **$45.00**

Lowe Brothers Paints, sign, porcelain, ...For All Purposes in blue outlined in white on yellow ground, 20x28", VG, A6 .... **$45.00**

Lowney's Breakfast Cocoa, tin, sample, 1⅝x1⅜x1", EX, D37 .... **$95.00**

Lowney's Chocolates, sign, tin, Bon Voyage With Lowney's Chocolates in brown on bright yellow, 12x½x16", VG+, D21 .... **$55.00**

Lowney's Cocoa, sign, cardboard, pictures 6 cups of steaming cocoa in front of boxes, 11x21", G+, A9 .... **$175.00**

Lowney's Cocoa, string holder, tin, red lettering & graphics on black with arched cutout for string, no chain, 24", G-, A9 .... **$350.00**

Lowney's Cocoa, string holder, tin, red lettering & graphics on black with arched cutout for string, chain hanger, 24", EX+, A2 .... **$3,630.00**

Loyl Coffee, tin, blue with red product name above & below eagle, round with screw lid, 1-lb, EX+, A18 .... **$200.00**

Lubeck Beer, can, flat-top, green & yellow on gold, 12-oz, A19 .... **$30.00**

Lubri-Loy Additives, sign, painted tin, station attendant telling about product at left of large can, orange & black on white, 14x20", NM, A1 .... **$80.00**

Lubrite, gas globe, Lubrite in bold red letters, metal body, 15" dia, EX+, A6 .... **$550.00**

Lubrite Sky-Hy, gas globe, Lubrite in red above line design over Sky-Hy in blue, metal body, 15" dia, rare, EX+, A6 .... **$700.00**

Lucky Bill, cigar box label, inner lid, boy leaning on banister, 6x9", M, D5 .... **$8.00**

Lucky Club Cola, sign, die-cut cardboard, comical image of cowboy with horseshoe-shaped arms & legs, Ace For Thirst, 24x12", EX, D30 .... **$95.00**

Lucky Heart Hair Dressing Pomade With Olive Oil, tin, sample, lettering around heart-shaped image of black couple, scalloped border, ⅜x1⅛" dia, EX, D37 ...**$25.00**

Lucky Heart Jockey Club Frozen Perfume, tin, Lucky Heart above product name on heart, Triple Strength, Sweet & Charming, ¼x1½" dia, EX, D37 .... **$20.00**

Lucky Hit, tobacco label, name above girl in thoughtful pose & bird with arrow in heart, matted & framed, image: 12x6", EX, A18 .... **$55.00**

Lucky Lager, display, plaster, bearded elf holding up barrel with X logo on base next to opened bottle, 11x7x5", VG, A8 .... **$170.00**

Lucky Lager, display, sign atop revolving globe on etched base, 12", EX, A8 .... **$300.00**

Lucky Lager, keg, salesman's sample, wood with metal bands, used to show new tapping system, removable bung, VG, A8 .... **$50.00**

Lucky Lager, sign, cardboard, It's Lucky... above girl with poppies, bottle & Age-Dated Beer below, self-framed, 14x28", EX, A8 .... **$45.00**

Lucky Lager, sign, composition, X logo on emblem above We Serve...Direct From Keg in script, 10x14", rare, EX, A8 .... **$70.00**

Lucky Lager, sign, flange, X logo above Age-Dated Beer on panel, red, yellow, blue & white, 15x12", VG, A8 .... **$75.00**

Lucky Lager, sign, glass, X logo flanked by product name above deer crossing & It's Lucky When You Live In America, 9x12", EX, A8 .... **$55.00**

Lucky Lager, sign, light-up, plastic in metal holder, X logo flanked by product name, beveled edge, 3x15", VG+, A8 ....$35.00

Lucky Lager, sign, paper, A Real Buy In Glass Cans, name above bottle pouring into goblet nestled in snow, framed, 14x27", EX, A8 ....$35.00

Lucky Lager, sign, paper, Always In Finest Taste Says Kim Hamilton..., she in gold gown & fur with product, 1950s, 24x17", VG+, A8 ....$35.00

Lucky Lager, sign, paper, Happy Holidays, chef displaying cooked turkey & tray of Lucky Lager on red, framed, 13½x27", EX, A8.................................$20.00

Lucky Lager, sign, paper, It's Lucky When You Live In America, couple on floor with model home & product, 1953, 14x27", VG+, A8 ....$30.00

Lucky Lager, sign, paper, Lucky Lager Age-Dated Beer in lower right, black lady at piano with bottle & glass, 1953, 21x25", VG+, A8 ....$25.00

Lucky Lager, sign, tin, X logo above product name & Dated Beer on red seal, One Of The World's... below, 31x21", VG+, A8 ....$110.00

Lucky Lager, sign, tin on cardboard, die-cut X logo above ...One Of The World's Finest Beers, beveled sides & bottom, 7x14", EX, A8...........................$130.00

Lucky Lager, tap knob, black ball shape with X logo insert under clear plastic, VG+, A8...........................$50.00

Lucky Lager, tray, deep-dish, One Of The World's Finest Beers, Lucky Lager ribbon with bottle & glass against map, 13" dia, NM, A8 ....$25.00

Lucky Penn Motor Oil, can, 100% Pure Pennsylvania above Lucky Penn on circle, United Refining Co, yellow & red, 1-qt, 5½x4" dia, EX, A6 ....$35.00

Lucky Scratch, cigar box label, outer, backside of woman jockey in front of horseshoe, oval, M, A5............$75.00

Lucky Star Ginger Ale, sign, tin, pictures large bottle, 24x12", NM, D30 ....$100.00

Lucky Strike, ad, features Carole Lombard in pink gown, 'Her Singing Coach Advised A Light Smoke,' 1937, VG, D23..$20.00

Lucky Strike, cigarette carton, unformed, top shows man smoking & reading paper & tilted pack, other figures beyond, EX+, A18 ....$55.00

Lucky Strike, display box, cardboard, Merry Christmas in red below logo, white background, 2x10x12½", EX+, A18 ....$105.00

Lucky Strike, fan, die-cut cardboard, tobacco leaf shape with product lettering & open pack around image of Frank Sinatra, EX+, A18 ....$250.00

Lucky Strike, pocket tin, flat, rounded corners, red logo on green with decorative gold border, NM+, A18.....$50.00

Lucky Strike, pocket tin, vertical, green, Genuine above red logo, 'It's Toasted', Roll Cut Tobacco below, EX, A18 ....$95.00

Lucky Strike, pocket tin, vertical, green, Genuine above red logo, Roll Cut & For Pipe Or Cigarette below, NM, A18 ....$95.00

Lucky Strike, pocket tin, vertical, green, Genuine above red logo, Roll Cut & For Pipe Or Cigarettes below, VG, A18 ....$50.00

Lucky Strike, pocket tin, vertical, sample, green, Genuine above red logo, Roll Cut & For Pipe Or Cigarettes below, VG, A18 ....$60.00

Lucky Strike, pocket tin, vertical, white, Genuine above red logo, Roll Cut Tobacco below, 4", NM, A18 ....$645.00

Lucky Strike, sign, cardboard, Luckies A Light Smoke..., 2 men offer lady a Lucky as she boards a TWA plane, 21x13", NM, A3.................................$65.00

Lucky Strike, sign, cardboard stand-up, Christmas scene on carton above Give A Christmas Carton... & open pack, 1936, 30x20", EX, D8 ....$230.00

Lucky Strike, sign, tin, Lucky Strike above product pack & lady in circle, embossed, 1950s-60s, 24x17", EX+, A13...$300.00

Lucky Strike, sign, tin, product pack upper right of sexy lady with cigarette in hand, 1950s, 21x15", NM+, A13 ....$250.00

Lucky Strike, tin, flat, Merry Christmas above red logo surrounded by holly, green with gold trim, ¾x5¾x4½", VG+, A18 ....$110.00

Lucky Strike, tin, rectangular with rounded corners, red logo on green, Hasker & Marcus, 2x3x5", EX+, A18........**$55.00**

Lucky Strike, tin, rectangular with squared corners, red logo on green, Somers Bros, 4½", EX+, A18........**$70.00**

Lucky Strike, tin, round, green, red logo above Cigarettes in gold, holds 100 cigarettes, 4", EX+, A18..........**$85.00**

Lucky Strike, tobacco tag, round, EX, D30.................**$8.00**

Lucky Strike Apples, crate label, California apple, lakeside scene with hunter taking aim at deer, Watsonville, 9x12", M, D12 ....**$6.00**

Luden's Chewing Gum, change receiver, felt, 3 packs of gum surrounded by product name, serrated edge, 1920s, 11" dia, NM, A13......................................**$180.00**

Ludwig Pianos, tip tray, close-up profile image of girl with pink rose in her hair, lettering around rim, 4" dia, EX, A21 ....**$30.00**

Luis Martinez, cigar box label, outer, woman offering cigars to children, 4½x4½", M, D5 ....**$8.00**

Lula, cigar box label, salesman's sample, horse with jockey in sulky, EX, A5.....................................**$200.00**

Luntin Cigar Factory/TJ Winship & Co Montreal, sign, paper, Canadian, Luntin above portrait vignettes & flowers, company name below, oak frame, 20x26", rare, EX, D21 ....**$1,000.00**

Lush-Us Allspice, tin, paper label, 3", NM, A7 ....**$65.00**

Lusterlite Kerosene, sign, cardboard, Gulf Refining Co logo flanked by Highest Quality For Lighting..., For Sale Here below, 14x22", EX, A6 ....**$55.00**

Lutona Natural Cocoa, tin, sample, oval image of name with steaming cup & pot on rectangular lid, Pin Box lettered below, ½x2x1¼", EX, D37 ....**$115.00**

Luzianne Coffee & Chicory, tin, paper label pictures mammy pouring coffee, screw lid, 1-lb, EX+, A3 ..**$85.00**

Luzianne Coffee & Chicory, tin, pictures mammy pouring coffee, pry lid, with contents, 1-lb, EX, A3...........**$60.00**

Luzianne Coffee & Chicory, tin, sample, pictures mammy pouring coffee, white with red & blue lettering, round, screw lid, 3", EX, D37 ....**$150.00**

Luzianne Coffee & Chicory, tin, sample, pictures mammy with serving tray, red with white lettering, round, screw lid, 3", EX+, D37..............$175.00

Lydia E Pinkham's Vegetable Compound, trade card, floral design on front, EX, D23 ....**$10.00**

Lyons Root Beer, mug, glass, white rectangular logo with 2 lions, Since 1893 Lyons Root Beer, 5x3", EX, D16 ..**$25.00**

Lysol, booklet, 'The Country Doctor Talks To Women,' features Dionne Quints, 1937, 32 pgs, VG, D14 ....**$18.00**

M

M&M's Candy, Christmas ornament/candy container, cardboard tube with plastic M&M figure on sled, 1993, NM, D24..**$5.00**

M&S Beverages, sign, porcelain, Michigan's Supreme above emblem with product name flanked by bottles, 12x30", NM, A13................................**$190.00**

M&S Beverages, sign, porcelain, Michigan's Supreme above emblem with product name flanked by bottles, 12x30", EX, D11 ....**$145.00**

Ma's Old Fashion Root Beer, bottle topper, die-cut cardboard, Demand The Best on blue arrow circling Ma & pointing to sign, 9x9", EX+, A19 ....**$10.00**

Ma's Old Fashion Root Beer, sign, tin, Drink above lettering & portrait on oval at left of bottle, Ma Know's Best! below, 24x32", NM+, D30.................................**$135.00**

Ma's Old Fashion Root Beer, sign, tin, It's Always A Pleasure To Serve You on white at right of bottle cap on yellow, 14x28", NM+, D30...............................**$100.00**

Ma's Old Fashion Root Beer, sign, tin, Old Fashion arched above bottle flanked by mug & 5¢, The Kind That Mother Used To Make, 24x28", VG+, D30 ....**$125.00**

Ma's Old Fashion Root Beer, thermometer, Ma's on red oval above bottle with dial-type bulb, Ma Knows Best below, yellow ground, 24x6", NM+, D30 ....**$130.00**

MacArthur Cigar, box, 'Every Puff A Jap Rebuff,' 5x9", EX, A7 ....**$15.00**

Mach's Pilsen Brewery, tray, stock image of roses lying around empty vase, 1903-14, oval, 16½", EX, A8 ....**$175.00**

Machwitz Coffee, canister, tin, pictures 3 golliwog-type black boys, EX, D6....................................**$225.00**

MacX Quality Feeds, whetstone, celluloid, More Fat Less Cost arched above logo, black, white & red, round, EX, A11 ....**$20.00**

Macy's Lily White Coffee/RH Macy & Co, tin, product name & text with red star on white field with decorative border, 1930 (?), 1-lb, EX+, A15...................**$145.00**

Madie, cigar box label, inner lid, peasant girl, 6x9", VG, D5 ....**$15.00**

Magic Yeast, sign, Use... above young girl lecturing squirrel, product & For Making Bread... below, framed, 15x10", EX, A3..**$185.00**

Magnolia, crate label, California orange, white magnolia blossom on navy blue background, Porterville, 10x11", M, D3 ....**$10.00**

Magnolia Petroleum Co, sign, porcelain, company name surrounds magnolia encircled above ...Gasoline For Sale Here, 2-sided, 30" dia, VG+, A1 ....**$390.00**

Magnus Beck Brewing Co, see Beck's Bottled Beer

Mahnrosa, cigar box label, printer's proof, girl wearing jeweled crown flanked by palm trees, Godfrey S Mahn Co, EX, A5 ....**$45.00**

Maier & Zobelein Brewery, corkscrew, wooden handle lettered with company name, address & phone number, VG+, A8..**$25.00**

Maier & Zobelein Brewery, tray, aerial factory scene with busy street, Kaufmann & Strauss, 13" dia, VG+, A9 ....**$300.00**

Mail Pouch, sign, porcelain, Chew & Smoke... above Treat Yourself To The Best, white & yellow on blue, white border, 12x40", EX, D8 ....$250.00

Mail Pouch, sign, porcelain, white Chew & Smoke above yellow Mail Pouch on blue, 1920s-30s, 3x12", NM, A13 ....$180.00

Mail Pouch Tobacco, sign, cardboard, 'Seeing Through Stones,' 2 sailors looking at first piece of glass, story below, 21x14", EX+, A18 ....$100.00

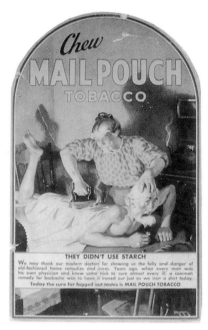

Mail Pouch Tobacco, sign, cardboard, 'They Didn't Use Starch,' woman ironing man's back, story below, arched top, 34x22", EX, A18..........................$275.00

Mail Pouch Tobacco, store bin, dark blue with yellow & white lettering, Always Fresh, Chew..., 10x3½x11", VG+, A18 ....$220.00

Mail Pouch Tobacco, string holder, tin, Chew & Smoke... on yellow & blue panel chained to Mail Pouch panel, 2-sided, 31", VG+, A2 ....$7,700.00

Mail Pouch Tobacco, thermometer, porcelain, Treat Yourself To The Best above bulb, Chew... below, white, blue & yellow, 8", VG, A6 ....$70.00

Mail Pouch Tobacco, thermometer, tin, Chew... on circle above bulb, Treat Yourself... on band below, yellow & white on blue, 9x3", NM, A13 ....$350.00

Maine Spring/WW Mansfield & Co, tin, flat, lettering above & below oval image of port city, decorative border, square corners, ¾x3¼x3⅛", EX, D37............$60.00

Majestic Co, replica of garbage can, cast aluminum, foot lever opens lid, 8", EX+, A21..............................$415.00

Major Cola, soda glass, white logo, Drink Major Cola, modified bell shape, 4x2½", M, D16....................$15.00

Majorette, crate label, California orange, vivacious majorette in red & white on maroon & green, Woodlake, 10x11", M, D3 ....$2.00

Majorette Selected Popcorn, box, shows majorette marching & product name, 8½x5¾", VG, A7 ....$8.00

Majors Cement, door push, Majors Cement Is Good For Repairing China, Glassware, Furniture, Etc, blue & white, 7½x3", EX, A6..$130.00

Makin's Golden Grain Granulated Smoking Tobacco, sign, cardboard, Some Real Makin's above product pack, Union Made & encircled 5¢ below, 18x12", G, A8 ....$40.00

Mal-Kah Cigarettes, pocket tin, flat, holds 50 cigarettes, EX+, A18 ....$45.00

Malibu Caribbean Coconut Rum, sipping cup, plastic witch with green face, black hat & glasses with orange lettering, orange straw, 7½", M............$6.00

Mallard Cigarette Tobacco, tin, round with mallard in flight on white oval with product name, screw lid, 4½x4", dia, EX, A18 ....$30.00

Malta, crate label, California orange, image of white Maltese cross, Porterville, 10x11", M, D12....................$5.00

Malvaz, drinking glass, straight-sided, etched logo & lettering, Monarch Brewery, 3½", NM, A8 ....$50.00

Malvaz, sign, die-cut cardboard, nurse serving bottle & glass on a tray above Malvaz Brings You Health sign, 13x10", EX, A8..$65.00

Malvaz & Bull Frog, drinking glass, straight-sided, applied raised white logo & lettering, Monarch Brewery, 3½", NM, A8..$60.00

Mammoth Jumbo Halves Blanched Salted Peanuts, tin, white with ring of peanuts & lettering around frontal view of elephant with large tusks, pry lid, 10-lb, EX, A2 ....$525.00

Mammoth Salted Peanuts, tin, white with ring of peanuts & lettering around frontal view of elephant with large tusks, pry lid, 5-lb, EX, A2......................$285.00

Mammy Brand Oranges, crate label, name left of mammy eating half-peeled orange, diagonal corners, 3½x9", NM, A7..$5.00

Mammy's Favorite Brand Coffee/CD Kenny Co, tin, product name on orange above & below image of mammy with tray, gold slip lid & bail handle, 4-lb, NM, A18..$500.00

Mammy's Favorite Brand Coffee/CD Kenny Co, tin, product name on orange above & below image of mammy with tray, gold slip lid & bail handle, 4-lb, VG, A2..$295.00

Mammy's Shanty, pocket mirror, celluloid, smiling mammy, ...Home Of The Best Pecan Pie, red & black on yellow, round, EX+, A11 ....$25.00

Manayunk Bock Beer/Liebert & Obert, sign, cardboard, Famous... above ram's head flanked by Bock Beer, company name below, black, tan & red, 1943, VG+, A19 ....$65.00

Manco Sliced Plug, pocket tin, flat, red with product name above & below emblem, On Edge below, rounded corners, EX, A18 ....$45.00

Manhattan Baking Powder, tin, paper label, 4-oz, EX, A7...$15.00

Manhattan Cocktails, sign, tin, man in tuxedo in wicker chair with cocktail & cigar, framed, image: 21½x27½", G, A9...$150.00

Manhattan Coffee, tin, product name lettered over mountains, key-wind lid, EX, A3 ....$25.00

Manhattan Fire & Marine Insurance Co, sign, reverse-painted glass, oval image of Indians & Americans making a trade, framed, image: 24x18", EX+, A9......$750.00

Manhattan Oil Co, pocket mirror, celluloid, black & green barrel shape, Ideal Auto Strictly Pure Pennsylvania Oil..., EX, A11 ....$30.00

Manhattan's White Soda/Ginger Ale, salt & pepper shakers, green miniature bottles, EX, A8.....................$25.00

Manley's Best Jumbo Popcorn, tin, elephant & lettered shield against popcorn graphics, red band above & blue band below, round, EX+, A18 ....$160.00

Manners Reiner Cacao, tin, pictures Chocolade Manner, knobbed slip lid, EX+, A3.................................$65.00

Manru Beer & Ale, tray, yellow, black & silver, 13", NM, D7...$35.00

Manru Coffee, tin, sample, slip lid, NM, A7 ....$45.00

Mansfield's Choice Pepsin Gum, vending case, new acid-etched celluloid sign atop case with replaced lettered glass front, 11x6x6", EX+, A13 ....$400.00

Mansfield's Choice Pepsin Gum, vendor, metal with etched glass panels, Automatic Clerk, Wintergreen & Blood Orange 5¢ at top, Pat'd 1902, 17", EX, A12.........$1,000.00

Mansfield's Pepsin Gum, display cabinet, counter-top, glass on oak base, reverse decal at top shows elegant woman at counter, 11", NM+, A1.....................$1,500.00

Mapacuba, tin, Blunt 10¢ in upper corners with name in red arched above 2 figures in boat, vertical square, EX+, A18 ....$40.00

Maple Bay Hotel, postcard, bear family painting sign, Bear In Mind..., 1910, VG, D26 ....$40.00

Maple Leaf Brand Coach Varnish/Imperial Varnish & Color Co, sign, embossed tin, gold & red product & company lettering over image of large maple leaf, gold border, 18x18", VG, A18 ....$70.00

Marathon, screwdriver, company name arched above runner & other lettering on handle, 5¼", VG, A6......$35.00

Marathon Endurance Motor Oil, can, product name & runner on oval with geometric center band, orange, green & cream, 1-qt, EX, A1.................................$155.00

Marathon Endurance Motor Oil, can, product name & runner on oval with geometric center band, orange, green & cream, 5-qts, VG, A6.................................$75.00

Marathon Ethyl, sign, porcelain, product name & Marathon man above triangular logo, 2-sided, 30" dia, VG, A6...$335.00

Marathon Lager Beer, label, Marathon City Brewing Co, Internal Revenue Tax Paid statement, 1933-50, 12-oz, M, A10...$15.00

Marathon Lager Beer, sign, blue felt-covered cardboard with gold inlay, One Of The Finer Things In Life above girl & dog, 14x22", EX+, A19.................................$115.00

Marathon Oil, sign, porcelain, trademark image of marathon runner & Best In The Long Run banner, red, white & blue, 72" dia, EX+, A9 ....$850.00

Marble City Garage, calendar, 1913, colorful image of woman with flowers climbing into car, full pad, framed, 23½x18½", EX+, A6..........................$500.00

Marcella Cigars, container, pictures line of marching soldiers in red coats, name below, round, slip lid, EX+, A18...$120.00

Marconi Wireless Telegraph Co of America, sign, porcelain, ...Commercial Messages Received Here, white on blue, 2½x17", EX+, A6.................................$700.00

Marfak Lubrication, letters, porcelain, green, each 6x4", EX+, A6...$350.00

Marfak Lubrication, see also Texaco Marfak Lubrication

Margo Bonded Root Beer, soda glass, red logo, Margo Bonded Root Beer Aged In Wood, tapered, with syrup line, 4x2½", M, D16...$25.00

Margona, cigar box label, outer, 2 women & a child holding cigars, 1917, 4½x4½", M, D5..........................$5.00

Marietta & Cincinnati Railroad Via Parkersburg, sign, paper, name on black above image of passenger coach, colorful ticket information below, framed, 22x13½", EX, A2...$745.00

Marine Products, pump sign, porcelain shield, Pegasus above product name & Socony-Vacuum, marked AM 5-51, 2-sided, 12x11", EX, A6.................................$400.00

Marinoff Beer, label, Red Bluff Brewing Co, Internal Revenue Tax Paid statement, 1933-50, 11-oz, M, A10...$15.00

Marklin, catalog, 1966, 72 pgs, EX, D17 ....$40.00

Marland Oils, atlas, open car traveling down country road above logo & text on front, 1927, VG, D8...........$35.00

Marlboro Cigarettes, sign, embossed metal, cowboy riding horse, full-color, 18x24", VG+, D24 ....$20.00

Marlborough-Bleuheim, cigar box label, outer, view of buildings with figures in the foreground, Atlantic City, NJ, NM, A5 ....$75.00

Marquette Club Ginger Ale, sign, die-cut cardboard stand-up, Mixes Best For Your Guests, bug-eyed man with bottle, 11x8", NM, A13 ....$140.00

Marshfield Lager Beer/Marshfield Brewing Co, sign, porcelain, initial logo upper left of product name, company name below, red, black, green & white, 14x20", VG+, A8 ....$125.00

Marshmallow Drops, tin, red with star logo, rectangular with rounded corners, 2x6", EX, A2.....................$85.00

Martha Washington Candies, box, cardboard, white with image of George & Martha, Mother Of American Candies, Baltimore, MD, 2x7x4", VG+, D24...............$15.00

Martin's Ice Cream, sign, tin, name above girl enjoying dish of ice cream, 'The Cream Supreme' below, blue ground, framed, 28x20", VG+, A13 ....$450.00

Martz Bus Lines, sign, porcelain, green lettering on white background with orange border, 2-sided, 18x24", EX, A6..$650.00

Marvels Cigarettes, thermometer, tin, blue, rooster & open pack above bulb flanked by Marvels, The Cigarette of Quality, 12x4", NM, A18 ....$100.00

Marvels Cigarettes, thermometer, tin, white, rooster & open pack above bulb flanked by Marvels, Quality Cigarettes below, 12x4", EX, A18 ....$55.00

Marvin's Biscuits, tin, 8-sided with horse racing scenes all around, top has a spinner for a game, 6½x4½", EX, A18..$75.00

Mary Agnes Yams, crate label, little blond girl in pigtails holding straw hat full of yams, M, D3.....................$2.00

Mary Anderson, cigar box label, inner lid, woman & theatrical scenes, 1907, 6x9", EX, D5 ....$65.00

Mary Jane Bread, end label, black & white photo image of Hopalong Cassidy on Topper, red border, EX, D29 ..$14.00

Maryland Club Coffee, tin, Maryland in script, key-wind lid, NM, A3..$24.00

Maryland Club Mixture, pocket tin, vertical, orange with product name above & below encircled mansion, EX+, A18..$255.00

Maryland Club Mixture, pouch, cloth, 1902 tax stamp, 1-oz, NM, A7..$20.00

Mas-Quo-Ta Cuban Style Cigars, box, paper on wood, pictures natives with cigars waiting for incoming ship, NM, A3 ....$35.00

Masback Hardware, catalog, #34, 1934, 806 pgs, EX, D17..$100.00

Mascot Baking Powder, tin, paper label, EX, A7 .....$12.00

Mascot Cereal, pin-back button, Rin-Tin-Tin in 'The Lightning Warrior' lettered around portrait, 1", NM, A7..$15.00

Mascot Crushed Cut Tobacco, pocket mirror, dog surrounded by product name & 5¢ In A Pouch, In Tins It Would Cost You Double, 2" dia, EX+, A3 ....$55.00

Mason's Root Beer, bottle, brown, full, NM, A7 ....$12.00

Mason's Root Beer, paper cup, pictures a bottle cap, red, yellow & blue on white, sample-size, D16.............$2.00

Massachusettes Boot & Shoe Co, sign, paper litho, company name arched above boy with felt hat, ca 1890, framed, 10x8", EX, A3 ....$75.00

Massachusetts Electric, sign, porcelain, New England Electric System on oval at right of Reddy Kilowatt, yellow background, 24x48", NM, D8.....................$275.00

Massey-Harris, calendar, 1941, pictures men playing checkers & women knitting, incomplete pad, 25½x13½", VG, D21..............................$28.00

Massey's Quality Root Beer, syrup dispenser, ceramic barrel shape, Drink flanked by 5¢ above product name, gold highlights, 15x8", VG, A9.....................$1,200.00

Massillon Agricultural Works, sign, paper, oval inset with horse-drawn machinery, factory vignette & other implements below, image: 22x18", G-, A9 ....$350.00

Master Big Loaf, sign, embossed porcelain, Really Big! upper left of loaf of bread, Really Good! lower right, on blue, 22x44", NM, A1 ....$270.00

Master Feeds, sign, porcelain, We Sell..., Master on large red center band, other lettering is blue on yellow, oval, 16x27", EX, A6..$75.00

Master Mason Ready Rubbed Smoking Tobacco, pocket tin, vertical, A Square Deal, blue with white lettering above & below oval image of man smoking pipe, VG, A18..$425.00

Master Outboard Motor Oil, can, product name above & below circle showing woman in boat with man piloting, red, white, blue & brown, 1-qt, EX, A1.......$300.00

Masterguard Stogies, pail, lid missing otherwise VG, D35..$180.00

Masury Paint Store, sign, porcelain flange, soldier standing guard left of product text, red, white & black, 1930s-40s, 16x24", NM+, A13 ....$300.00

Matz Bock Beer, label, Matz Brewing Co, Internal Revenue Tax Paid statement, 1933-50, 12-oz, NM, A10 ......**$42.00**

Max-I-Mum Coffee, tin, oval image with Arabs & camels, key-wind lid not original, 1-lb, NM, A3 ....**$60.00**

Max-I-Mum Coffee, tin, oval image with Arabs & camels, red background, gold trim, key-wind lid, 4-lb, EX, A18 ....**$100.00**

Maxitone Gramophones, sign, porcelain, Maxitone in bold diagonal script, British & Best upper left, Authorized Dealers below, 18x24", VG, D21 ....**$225.00**

Maxol-X Double Film Motor Oil, can, Double Film & Motor Oil flank car racing toward rising sun design with Maxol-X above, green & yellow, 1-qt, EX, A1 .....**$360.00**

Maxon, pocket mirror, celluloid, bust portrait of girl in profile, Maxon Sells The Best Clothes, round, EX+, A11 ....**$45.00**

Maxwell House Coffee, container, cardboard miniature of 1-lb tin, NM, A7 ....**$25.00**

Maxwell House Coffee, tin, sealed (no contents), 4-oz, NM, A7 ....**$40.00**

Maxwell Steel Vault Co, tape measure, celluloid, pictures open burial vault, It's Copper Alloy, black, blue & gold, round, EX+, A11 ....**$62.00**

Mayer Honorbilt Shoes, sign, tin flange, black & orange product name at left of black high-button shoe, orange border, 13x18", VG, A2 ....**$85.00**

Mayfair Beer, label, Eastern Brewing Corporation, Internal Revenue Tax Paid Statement, 1936-38, 12-oz, M, A10 ....**$16.00**

Mayflower, cigar box label, outer, lady stepping out of the Mayflower, 1904, EX, A5 ....**$80.00**

Mayflower Cranberries, crate label, Mayflower in full sail on crashing wave, blue background, Cape Cod, 10x7", M, D12 ....**$10.00**

Mayo's Cut Plug, insert card, 1888, features Andrew Jackson, VG, A5 ....**$35.00**

Mayo's Cut Plug, roly poly, Mammy smoking corncob pipe, 7½x7" dia, G, A9 ....**$225.00**

Mayo's Cut Plug, roly poly, Storekeeper, EX, D35..**$450.00**

Mayo's Cut Plug, tobacco pouch, cloth, 1926 tax stamp, with contents, 2 ¼-oz, EX, A7 ....**$30.00**

Maypo Cereal, doll, Marky Maypo, vinyl, red hat & neckerchief, blue shirt & pants, brown gloves & boots, 1960s, 10", VG, A21 ....**$55.00**

Maytag Multi-Motor Oil, can, product name above logo & text on cream rectangle, blue background, screw cap, 1-pt, EX+, D33 ....**$40.00**

Maytag Multi-Motor Oil, jar, clear glass with paper label, 1-qt, EX, D33 ....**$50.00**

Maytag Multi-Motor Oil, mixing can with measuring cup, 1-qt, EX, D33 ....**$75.00**

McAvoy's Malt Marrow, tray, image of dog & boy with pipe & bottle flanked by Malt & Marrow, lettering around rim, 12" dia, G-, A21 ....**$60.00**

McCabe Bros Co, whetstone, celluloid, Ship Your Grain To...Grain Exchange Winnipeg, black & white, round, EX, A11 ....**$60.00**

McCoard Airliner Gasoline, gas globe, white ripple body, single lens with plane in clouds, lettering above & below, 14" dia, NM lens/VG+ body, A1 ....**$2,400.00**

McCord Motor Gaskets, clock, metal & glass, Time To Buy... on octagon in center, blue, white & yellow with brown case, 14½x14½", EX, A6 ....**$70.00**

McCormack, crate label, California pear, McCormack in yellow on red & black checked background, 8x11", M, D12 ....**$4.00**

McCormick, calendar top, 1880s, maid & mistress playing cards in the maid's quarters, matted & framed, 16x13", NM, A3 ....**$60.00**

McCormick Bee Brand Bug Killer, tin, 1940s, unopened, M, D6 ....**$10.00**

McCormick Dairy Equipment, sign, embossed tin, red & black lettering on yellow & black, Used On This Farm...Meshoppen PA, 14x23", EX, A6 ....**$70.00**

McCormick Farm Machinery, sign, paper, pictures farmers & black workers testing horse-drawn grain cutter, framed, image: 24x35", G+, A9 ....**$475.00**

McCormick Ltd London & Canada, biscuit tin, figural golf bag with protruding clubs & embosssed image of lady ready to hit the ball, 11", EX, A2 ....**$1,540.00**

McCormick Reaper, sign, paper, 'Back From The War,' harvest scene with man, little girl & dog greeting soldier, ca 1899, 18x24", A3 ....**$230.00**

McCormick-Deering Machines, sign, embossed tin, Notice We Use Only Genuine Parts In Reconditioning..., yellow on blue, 12x16", EX, A6 ....**$80.00**

McCormick-Deering Thrashers, sign, paper, product name above farm scene & machinery vignettes, International Harvester Co, framed, 32x22", NM, A9.....**$300.00**

McCormick-Deering Triple Power Tractors, sign, paper, 1831 McCormick Reaper Centennial 1931 in upper left, features 10-20 Tractor, framed, 23x33", VG, A6..**$185.00**

McCormick's Bee Brand Mixed Pickle Spice, tin, 3¾", NM, A7 ....**$12.00**

McCray Refrigerator Co, pocket mirror, celluloid, company name arched above image, Kendallville, Ind below, round, EX, A11......................................**$60.00**

McDonald's, bank, waving Ronald McDonald figure seated on round base embossed with his name, plastic, Hong Kong, 7", M..**$18.00**

McDonald's, inflatable figure, Grimace, purple plastic, 1978, 8", M **$25.00**

McDonald's Dontboil Cocoa, tin, sample, product name above & below circular portrait of man with mustache, 1¾x1⅛" dia, EX, D37.............................**$125.00**

McDougall-Butler Paints, sign, metal, white, black & orange paint can on white ground, 30x24", EX, A6.............**$35.00**

McFadden's Electric Brand Coffee, container, paper on cardboard, ...McFadden's Coffee & Spice Co, VG+, A3 ....**$20.00**

McGovern Pilsener, label, McGovern Brewing Co, U-type permit number, Internal Revenue Tax Paid statement, 1933-36, 12-oz, M, A10.............................**$15.00**

McGowan's Blue Ribbon Salmon, can label, image of fish, tiny sailboats & couple on horseback, Illwaco, 2x11", M, D3 ....**$2.00**

McGowan's Salmon Steak, crate label, fish on scallop shell on keystone, white background, McGowan, 7x9", D3...**$6.00**

McGuigan's Shoe Store, fan, cardboard with wood handle, men watching woman's feet dangle from car, white, blue, red & brown, VG+, A6...................**$160.00**

McKay Tire Chains, display, tin, product name on top panel, Live Long Travel Far on base, red, black & cream, 25x17", EX, A1.................................**$105.00**

McKinley & Roosevelt Cigars, box label set, oval portraits with fancy scroll design, 2 pcs, EX, A5..............**$360.00**

McKinney Bread Co, calendar, 1903, die-cut cardboard, bowl of lilacs indicating each month, EX, A18 ....**$50.00**

McKinney Mfg Co, catalog, 1923, 780 pgs, EX, D17...**$50.00**

McLaughlin's Kept-Fresh Coffee, tin, product name surrounded by line design, key-wind lid, VG, A3.....**$65.00**

McNess' Humpty-Dumpty Borated Talc & Baby Powder, tin, pictures Humpty Dumpty on the brick wall, with contents, 7½x3x2", NM, A3 ....**$45.00**

McReynold's Grocery, flier, features Hawaii contest, surfer motif, 1880s, VG, D23 ....**$20.00**

McSorley Lager Beer, tap knob, red plastic with enameled insert, brown & gold on cream , EX+, A8 ....**$170.00**

McVitie & Price's Biscuits, tin, sample, boy sitting on box surrounded by The Premier Biscuit Of Britian, 3¼" dia, EX+, A3 ....**$85.00**

Meadow Gold, fountain display, ice-cream soda glass on light-up stand, heat-activated rotary interior, 30x12x12", VG, A9 ....**$525.00**

Meadow Gold, pin-back button, Safety Club lettered around Meadow Gold emblem, 1¼" dia, NM, A7 ..**$4.00**

Meadow Gold Ice Cream, sign, die-cut masonite, product name on emblem above Please Pay When Served, Kay Displays, 16x11", NM, A13...................................**$110.00**

Meadow Gold Ice Cream, sign, porcelain, Serving... in black on cream with black border, 30x20", NM, D8..$400.00

Meadow Gold Milk, sign, die-cut masonite, product name on emblem above Please Pay When Served, Kay Displays, 16x11", NM, A13.............................**$120.00**

Mecca Cigarettes, sign, cardboard, Earl Christy girl in large hat peering over her shoulder with hands on hips, framed, 18x10", VG+, A21 ....**$100.00**

Mechanics Delight, tobacco label, pictures man with tie, oval, EX, D35..**$3.50**

Medaglia D'oro Espresso Coffee, tin, product name on large label in center, little boy with cup in lower left, with contents, EX+, A3 ....**$45.00**

Medusa Mortar Cements, note pad, metal, ...Brikset Gray, Stoneset White flanked by product image at top, Over 65 Years... below, 9x6", EX, A6 ....**$5.00**

Meigs Meadow Tomatoes, can label, front shows name above & below tomato, back shows Meigs Meadow Brand above farm scene, 4½x13½", NM, A7.........**$2.00**

Meilink Mfg Co, safe, stenciled lettering on door, ...Specialty Manufacturers, Toledo Ohio, Guaranteed Fire & Water Proof, 14x10", G, A9 ....**$550.00**

Meister-Brau Beer, can, flat-top, shows couple, 12-oz, A19...**$40.00**

Meister-Brau Beer, label, Cleveland Home Brewing Co, U-type permit number, Internal Revenue Tax Paid statement, 1933-36, 12-oz, NM, A10 ....**$18.00**

Melachrino Cigarettes, display, tin trifold, product name on center panel above nighttime Arab scene flanked by product boxes, EX, A18 ....**$125.00**

Melachrino Cigarettes, display box, cardboard with glass-covered dummy cigarettes, 2½", NM, D30 ....**$25.00**

Mellin's Biscuits, tin, sample, gold round shape with screw lid, EX+, A18...**$55.00**

Mellor & Rittenhouse Licorice Lozenges, tin, gold & black square shape with arched glass window front, slip lid, EX, A18...**$175.00**

Mellow Ice Cream, sign, tin, For Goodness' Sake! Eat Mello Ice Cream, ice-cream cone man with top hat at left, 12x18", NM, A7 ....$160.00

Mellow Sweet Fine Cut Tobacco, tin, ...Manufactured Only By Myers Cox & Co, Dubuque, Iowa, 8¼" dia, G, A9 ....$190.00

Melrose, cigarette papers, NM, A7 ....$50.00

Menk's Bottle Beer, tray, Try A Bottle Of... above & below disheveled man holding a glass & bottle, red decorative rim, oval, 17", VG+, A21 ....$605.00

Mennen's Borated Sen-Yang Toilet Powder, tin, sample, Japanese lady with parasol, blue & gold decorated background, 2⅛x1¼x¾", EX, D37, minimum value....$125.00

Mennen's Borated Talcum, trolley sign, cardboard, ...For Mine!, image of baby on stomach reaching for product, framed, 11x21", VG, A21 ....$230.00

Mennen's Borated Talcum Toilet Powder, tin, sample, lettering & oval image of baby against blue with red flowers, round, 1⅝", EX, D37, minimum value .$150.00

Mennen's Borated Talcum Toilet Powder, tin, sample, lettering around oval image of baby on white inset against blue with red flowers, 2¼x1¼x¾", EX, D37 ....$95.00

Mennen's Violet Talcum, pocket mirror, pictures bouquet of lilacs & small portrait of Mr Mennen, vertical oval, 2¾", EX, A21 ....$35.00

Meow Mix, squeak toy, cat figure, 1975, 5", VG, D27 ..$40.00

Merchant's Mills Roasted Special Coffee, store bin, wooden bucket with bail handles, stenciled lettering on inside of hinged lid, 21x16", EX, A18 ....$105.00

Merchants Association, paperweight, glass, image of the New York Life Insurance Building, rectangular, M, D13 ....$25.00

Merchants Trust Co, paperweight, cast-iron turtle, Safe, Solid, Sound & Sure logo on celluloid shell, 2x1½", EX, D14..$50.00

Merita Bread, end label, shows the Lone Ranger on Silver, red border, EX, D29 ....$25.00

Merita Bread, sign, cardboard, It's Enriched, Buy Merita Bread, shows the Lone Ranger on Silver above see-through loaf, 23x15", VG, A6 ....$55.00

Merkle's Blu-J Brooms, sign, embossed tin, advertising around image of blue jay perched on broom, red, blue & black on white, 16x10", EX, A3 ....$145.00

Merrick's Spool Cotton, spool cabinet, oak, side cylinders with lettered curved glass fronts, mirrored center, 3 drawers, 26x31x16", EX, A12 ....$1,450.00

Merry Dance, cigar box label, inner lid, 1886, dancing gypsy, clown & musicians, 6x9", EX, D5 ....$35.00

Merry War Lye Soap, match holder, metal, shows girl bending over washtub that serves as holder, 5½x3¾", EX, A13 ....$230.00

Messmate Plug, sign, cardboard, 5 sailors chewing on large plug of tobacco against black & red diagonal background, 11x11", VG+, A2 ....$275.00

Meteor, crate label, California lemon, red meteor curving across night sky full of stars, San Fernando, 9x12", M, D12 ....$6.00

Metro, gas globe, red, white & green lens with name on wide center band, red metal body, 15" dia, NM, A6 ....$300.00

Metro, pump sign, porcelain, red Pegasus above Metro in green on white 5-point emblem with green outline, 13x11", NM, A1 ....$750.00

Metropolitan Life Insurance Co, calendar, 1903, shows children sitting on trunk with 6 months above & 6 months below, framed, 15x11", EX, A8 ....$235.00

Metropolitan Petroleum, bank, oil can shape, 4", VG+, D24 ....$5.00

Metz Beer, mug, ceramic, gold lip (worn), Metz & Beer flank bust portrait with Omaha's Favorite below, A8 ...$155.00

Metz Beer, newspaper ad, Swing To Metz on oval between western couple dancing, bottle & ...Since 1864 below, 1952, 11x17", EX, A8..$100.00

Metz Beer, radio, brown bottle shape with red labels, non-working, 1940s-50s, VG+, A13 ....$210.00

Metz Beer, tray, deep-dish, red M logo above product name, 12" dia, NM+, A19 ....$120.00

Mexene Chile Powder, tin, sample, product name above & Walker's Austin Texas below embellished image of a devil, round, slip lid, 1", EX, D37..........................$40.00

Mexican Java Coffee/Sherer Bros Co, pail, sample, red, slip lid & bail handle, 2½x2½" dia, VG+, D37...$215.00

Mexican Maid, cigar box label, outer, Spanish senorita, 1900, 4½x4½", VG, D5 ....$15.00

Meyer Maid Dairy Ice Cream, tray, cute little girl in nightie eating ice cream, Made Delicious, Not A Fad... on rim, 13½" dia, EX, A9 ....$250.00

Meyer-Wilms Co Dry Goods, pocket mirror, portrait of an elegant woman, oval, VG, A20..........................$235.00

MFA Sho-Me Non-Detergent Motor Oil, can, MFA 3-star emblem above product name, brown, silver, red & blue, 1-qt, NM+, A1..$32.00

MGM Records, sign, light-up, reverse-painted glass, MGM Records above lion's head & The Greatest Name In Entertainment, 6x24", EX, A1 ....$575.00

Miami Special Beer, label, Miami Valley Brewing Co, Internal Revenue Tax Paid statement, 1933-50, 12-oz, EX, A10 ....$20.00

Mich-I-Penn Oil & Grease Co Inc/Penn-Master Motor Oil, calendar, 1938, lady in hat & dress with exposed leg walking Scotty dog, Elvgren art, VG+, A8 ......$30.00

Michelin, display figure, Michelin man, plastic, white with black lettering on banner, metal mounting bracket, 18½x11", EX, A6...$110.00

Michelin, display figure, Michelin man, plastic, white with lettering on banner (no paint), 13", NM, A6.........**$55.00**

Michelin, sign, die-cut porcelain, Michelin in yellow above Michelin man on stylized bicycle, red ground, 2-sided, 18x15", NM, A1...................$450.00

Michelin, sign, die-cut porcelain, Michelin in yellow above Michelin man running beside tire, blue background, 18x15", NM, A1......................$275.00

Michelin, tire rack, contains 2 signs picturing Michelin man running with tire left of Michelin in yellow on blue, 7x12", NM, D8 ....**$95.00**

Michelin, truck cab topper, plastic Michelin man wearing yellow banner with blue Michelin, 19", M, NOS, A1...**$125.00**

Michelin Pneus Tracteurs, sign, die-cut porcelain, Michelin man on tractor on green circle, yellow background, French 1950s, 30x20", M, D8............**$650.00**

Michelin Tyres, sign, porcelain, running Michelin man at right of lettering, ...Made In England in blue on yellow, 16x58", EX+, A1.......................$750.00

Michelin/Meredith Stock, sign, wood, pointing Michelan man at left of yellow arrow & product name in white, 12½x36", G+, A6 ....**$450.00**

Michelob, display, light-up, 'Our Draught Beer,' horn in clear plastic dome with mirrored back, EX, A8....**$30.00**

Michelob, mug, miniature, Ceramarte, small logo, NM, A8 ....**$20.00**

Michelob, vase, clear crystal horn shape with 90th Anniversary logo, NM, A8................................**$30.00**

Michigan Plumbing & Heating Supply Co, mirror, seated nude & company advertising lower right corner, 9x8", VG+, A8 ....**$100.00**

Mid-Channel Mixture, pocket tin, vertical, yellow with yellow lettering on red graphics, gold lid, EX, A18 ..**$480.00**

Middleby Root Beer, dispenser, ceramic, oversized mug shape, 1920s, missing lid & base otherwise EX, A4 ....**$375.00**

Midland Co-op, gas globe, single Gill lens with Midland & Wholesale on orange band, Co-op & shaking hands across middle, 1930s, NM, A1 ....**$270.00**

Midnight Sun Beer, label, Pioneer Brewing Co, U-type permit number, Internal Revenue Tax Paid statement, 1933-36, 22-oz, M, A10......................................**$25.00**

Midway Superior, pump sign, porcelain, ...No Equal At It's Price, red & blue on white with lined border, 11x11", NM, D8 ....**$200.00**

Midwest Export Beer, label, Midwest Brewing Co, Internal Revenue Tax Paid statement, 1934-38, 12-oz, EX, A10...**$20.00**

Mil Botl, sign, embossed, Drink above large K on windmill flanked by Mil Botl, Demand... below, black & orange, 14x20", VG+, A8 ....**$40.00**

Milburn Wagon Co, sign, paper, pictures couple in wagon waving to friend on bike as they pass tree-lined estate, 20x26", G, A2.............................$340.00

Milcor Steel Co, sign, cardboard, several vignettes advertising metal roofs & embossed metal ceilings, 1931, framed, 28x21", NM, A3 ....**$75.00**

Military Foot Powder, tin, red, white & blue with advertising on white emblem between soldier & sailor shaking hands, oval, shaker top, EX+, A18.....................**$115.00**

Millar's Home Blend Coffee, tin, white & black lettering on red, key-wind lid, 1-lb, NM+, A3 ....**$75.00**

Millar's May-Day Coffee, tin, Regular Grind on band at bottom, key-wind lid, NM, A3...............................**$60.00**

Millbank Virginia Cigarettes, sign, porcelain, red & yellow, 16x28", G, D21..**$75.00**

Miller, tap knob, red plastic with red & white enameled insert, round, VG+, A8..**$55.00**

Miller High Life, display, molded plastic, 3 light-up bottles in ice bucket on rotating base, 1950s, EX, A19....**$65.00**

Miller High Life, light globe, gas-globe style with 2 glass inserts in plastic frame, girl on crescent moon logo, 17", EX, A8 ....**$50.00**

Miller High Life, sign, porcelain shield, Miller High Life On Tap in white outlined in black on red background, 34x45½", EX, A6...**$320.00**

Miller High Life Beer, charger, tin, girl on crescent moon above product name, ca 1907, 24" dia, G-, A9...**$200.00**

Miller High Life Beer, sign, porcelain, Miller in white script above High Life & The Best Milwaukee Beer on red, white border, round, EX, A19.....................**$300.00**

Miller High Life Beer, tray, deep-dish, girl seated on crescent moon, red product lettering below, gold rim, 1920s, NM, A13 ....**$275.00**

Miller High Life Milwaukee, tap knob, maroon ball shape with silver & yellow on red enamel insert, EX, A8 ..**$70.00**

Miller Special Christmas Beer, label, Internal Revenue Tax Paid statement, shows Christmas scene, 1940, EX, A8 ....**$20.00**

Miller Tires, sign, cardboard stand-up, Geared-To-The-Road, pictures large tire behind row of cars, 36x52", EX, D8...**$175.00**

Miller's Breakfast Cocoa, tin, sample, shows product name in decorative lettering, slip lid, 2x1¾x1⅛", EX, D37...**$115.00**

Millhead, cigar box label, inner lid, mill scene, Harlem Eagle Cigar Factory Product, Gus Muehlenhaupt Maker, 1913, NM, A5...**$85.00**

Millor & Rittenhouse Licorice Lozenges, tin, tan with black graphics & lettering, vertical square with flat top, Somers, 5-lb, VG+, A18...**$95.00**

Milwaukee Harvesting Machines, match holder, tin, farmer carrying basket (holder) with logo flanked by Always & Reliable, Light Draft, 6x5", VG+, A8...**$150.00**

Miners & Puddlers Smoking Tobacco/B Leidersdorf Co, pail, red with white & black lettering above & below image of 3 men, slip lid, bail handle, EX+, A18..**$250.00**

Minneapolis Brewing Co, mug, ceramic, barrel shape, circular logo with hops motif, EX+, A8.....................**$65.00**

Minneapolis Brewing Co's Golden Grain Belt Beers, mug, ceramic, circular M logo & company name above product name, gold trim, EX+, A8.........................**$45.00**

Minneopa Brand Steel Cut Coffee, tin, paper label with encircled image flanked by Steel Cut, slip lid, rare, EX, A3...**$60.00**

Minter's Candies, display case, metal & glass, 1¢ Each 5 For 5¢ encircled at right of product name & Tickle The Taste, 11x12x14", VG, A6...**$65.00**

Minute Man Motor Oil, can, pictures service man behind gas pump, red, white & blue, screw lid & handle, 2-gal, 11½x8½", VG, A6...**$50.00**

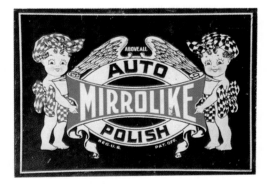

Mirrolike Auto Polish, sign, tin, 2 animated girls in checked outfits flank lettered logo, red, white & blue, 10x14", EX, A6......................................$185.00

Miss America Coffee, tin, bust portrait above product name & Regular Grind & Vacuum Packed, key-wind lid, EX+, A3...**$45.00**

Miss MD White Ladies Furnishings & Fancy Goods, trade card, floral design, 1880, EX, D23 ....**$20.00**

Mission, tray, deep-dish, ¡Hay Naranjaas! above Mission bottle cap, Es Natural! below, round, EX+, A16...**$25.00**

Mission of California, display, die-cut cardboard stand-up, elegant girl holding sign & tray, 5-ft, VG+, D21 ....**$200.00**

Mission of California, sign, cardboard, party girl ringing bell at left of ice bucket with bottles, Naturally Good... above, 20x30", EX+, D30 ....**$165.00**

Mission Orange, calendar, 1942, complete, NM, A16..**$145.00**

Mission Orange, door push, tin, Drink & bottle cap above bottle, Naturally Good! below, orange on blue, 1950s, NM+, A13...**$150.00**

Mission Orange, sign, tin, Drink Mission Orange, California Sunshine Flavor!, smiling sun & Mission pennant, 24x24", NM, A13...**$160.00**

Mission Orange, sign, tin, Drink Mission Orange on emblem at left of tilted bottle, bright yellow background, 11x28", EX+, D30 ....**$85.00**

Mission Orange, sign, tin, Mission Orange Of California on blue emblem above bottle & Naturally Good, yellow ground, 28x28", NM+, D30 ....**$125.00**

Missouri & Kansas Telephone Co, paperweight, blue glass in shape of a telephone bell, 3x¾", NM, D22......**$160.00**

Missouri Pacific Lines, perpetual calendar, metal over cardboard, calendar cards intact, 19x13", EX, A6........**$350.00**

Missouri State Life Insurance Co, paperweight, glass, pictures home office in St Louis, dollar figures & company seal below, oval, M, D13...**$50.00**

Mista Joe Vegetables, crate label, black dining car steward, 'We Serve The Best,' Salinas, 7x9", M, D12 ....**$5.00**

Mitchell's Premium Beer, drinking glass, barrel shape with applied red oval logo, 3", NM, A8................**$20.00**

MJB Co's Aladdin Coffee, pail, orange with product name above man looking up & holding lamp, 2-lb, no lid, EX+, A18...**$50.00**

MK Goetz Brewing, mug, ceramic, Prosit 1900 above seated cavalier & company name, brown, blue & gold on cream, VG+, A19...**$100.00**

MM Corsets, trade card, die-cut corset with angel, ca 1880, EX, D23...**$20.00**

Mobil, cap pin, porcelain inlay, features Pegasus on maritime flag shape, ⅝x1", NM, A15.........................**$425.00**

Mobil, clock, red Pegasus in center, no lettering, 14½" dia, EX, A6...**$500.00**

Mobil, plate, Shenago china, white with single Pegasus logo on blue-banded rim, 6" dia, EX+, A1 ....**$90.00**

Mobil, salt & pepper shakers, ceramic, barnyard scene with Pegasus on barn's weathervane, 3¼x2" dia, EX, A6..**$45.00**

Mobil, tie clasp, metal Pegasas with red enamel inlay on chain attached to bar, in box, EX, A6.................**$75.00**

Mobil Fan Belts, sign, metal, red Pegasus logo between Mobil & Fan Belts in white, blue background, 6x33", EX+, A6...**$140.00**

Mobil Premium, pump sign, porcelain, Mobil & Pegasus logo on emblem above Premium, 12x14", M, D11...**$100.00**

Mobil-flame, sign, die-cut porcelain with iron frame, Pegasus & Socony logo atop sign, ...Socony-Vacuum's Bottled Gas, 44x33", NM, A6.................................**$3,500.00**

Mobilgas, banner, cloth, image of lamb in front of sign, New Spring..., blue, green & yellow ground, 42x57", VG, A6...**$35.00**

Mobilgas, gas globe, green Mobilgas on white with red stripe above & below, high-profile metal body, 15" dia, NM, A1...**$440.00**

Mobilgas, pump sign, porcelain, Pegasus logo above lettering on white 5-point emblem, blue outline, dated 1954, 12x12", NM, A1...**$165.00**

Mobilgas, pump sign, porcelain, Pegasus logo above lettering on white 5-point emblem, blue outline, dated IR47, 12x12", EX, A1.....................................$120.00

Mobilgas, sign, die-cut cardboard, ribbon shape with Socony Presents above Pegasus logo, America's Largest Selling..., 30x16", VG, A6.....................$90.00

Mobilgas, sign, die-cut porcelain shield, Pegasus logo above lettering, I Have Pledged My Cooperation..., 7½x8", NM, A6.....................................$450.00

Mobilgas, sign, porcelain, red Pegasus logo above product name, 11½" dia, NM, A6.....................................$170.00

Mobilgas, toy truck, Japan, red friction tanker with Pegasus logos on doors, Mobilgas lettered on tanker, 9", EX+, A1.....................................$120.00

Mobilgas, toy truck, Smith-Miller, red GMC tanker truck with white Mobilgas & Pegasus logo on sides of tanker, 2-pc, 22", EX+, A1.........................$870.00

Mobilgas, uniform & hat, white with black pinstripes, red & black patch with Pegasus logo, white hat with logo & black bill, EX, A6.....................$400.00

Mobilgas Ethyl, gas globe, red Pegasus logo above blue Mobilgas, Ethyl in red below, red metal high-profile body, 15" dia, NOS, NM+, A1.....................$500.00

Mobilgas Marine, pump insert, porcelain, white lettering on red, 5¾x15", G+, A6.....................................$45.00

Mobilgas Special, gas globe, red Pegasus logo above blue & red lettering, black metal body, 15" dia, EX, A6.....................................$200.00

Mobilgas Special, gas globe lens, red Pegasus logo above blue & red lettering, 15½" dia, EX, A6.............$130.00

Mobilgas Special, pump sign, porcelain, Pegasus logo above lettering on white 5-point emblem, blue outline, dated 1958, 12x12", EX, A1.....................$110.00

Mobilgrease FS, can, tin, Gargoyle logo above product name lettered sideways on can, black, red & white, 2-lb, EX+, A1.....................................$55.00

Mobilgrease No 4, can, Gargoyle logo above product lettering, Socony-Vacuum Co lettered below, pry lid, full, 1-pt, EX, NOS, A1.....................................$20.00

Mobiloil, bottle, glass, 4-sided, metal spout & sides of bottle embossed with Gargoyle logo, 1-qt, NM, A1......$125.00

Mobiloil, can, Gargoyle logo above Mobiloil, Pegasus logo & Socony Vacuum Oil Co below, red, white & black, 1-qt, EX, A1.....................................$80.00

Mobiloil, can, Gargoyle logo above product name, small Pegasus logo on emblem & Socony-Vacuum Oil Co Inc below, 5-qts, VG, A6.....................................$60.00

Mobiloil, can, Pegasus logo above product name, Socony-Vacuum Oil Co Inc below, red, white & blue, 5-qt, 10x7" dia, VG+, A6.....................................$15.00

Mobiloil, compact, red & silver Pegasus on cover, velvet case, mirror cracked otherwise VG, 2½x3", A6....$80.00

Mobiloil, gas globe, Gargoyle logo above Mobiloil, red & black, 1-pc with metal base, oval, 13x15½", NM+, A6.....................................$2,000.00

Mobiloil, key holder, wood diamond shape with metal hook, red, white & blue Pegasus logo at top, 7x3", VG+, A6.....................................$50.00

Mobiloil, Lubrication Chart, oval Gargoyle logo at top, Socony-Vacuum Co, red, cream & blue, 1932, 19x11½", EX+, A6.....................................$95.00

Mobiloil, rack, metal with 8 glass bottles, metal tops have Gargoyle logo with various grades of oil, VG, A6........$180.00

Mobiloil, sign, porcelain flange, Gargoyle logo above product & company name, black on white, 2-sided, 15½x24", VG+, A6.....................................$250.00

Mobiloil, sign, tin, Gargoyle logo above Mobiloil advertising 30¢ & 35¢ Oils, Vacuum Oil Co below, 18x14", NOS, NM, A1.....................................$310.00

Mobiloil, sign, tin, Gargoyle logo above Mobiloil lettered vertically in white outlined in black, red background, 60x15", NM, D8 ....$850.00

Mobiloil, thermometer, porcelain, Pegasus logo & product name on emblem above bulb, Vacuum Oil Co below, 23x8", VG+, A6.....................................$200.00

Mobiloil, see also Socony Vacuum & Vacuum 'B' Mobiloil

Mobiloil 'A,' bulk tank tag, porcelain, Make The Chart Your Guide & Gargoyle logo above Mobiloil 'A,' 2-sided, 8¾" dia, NM+, A1.....................................$440.00

Mobiloil 'E,' can, tall round shape with Gargoyle logo, Ford Cars on band below, off-center spout, small screw lid, 1-qt, G-, A1.....................................$40.00

Mobiloil 'E,' crate, red Gargoyle logo above product & company name in black, 16x10½x21", G, A6......$85.00

Mobiloil Arctic, bottle holder, wire rack with 4 red tin signs, contains 8 1-qt Filpruf bottles with repro caps, NM bottles/EX signs, A1.....................................$850.00

Mobiloil Arctic, bottle rack, footed box-type holder for 8 bottles, white lettering on red panels, wire feet, 22x18", EX, A6 ....$550.00

Mobiloil Arctic, can, Pegasus logo above product name, Gargoyle logo embossed on top, blue & red on white, flat-sided, 1-gal, 10", VG, A1..................................$50.00

Mobiloil Arctic, pin-back button, celluloid over metal, Quick Starting Below Zero..., black, cream & red, 3½" dia, EX, A6 ....$160.00

Mobiloil Certified Service, sign, porcelain, red Gargoyle logo & lettering on circle with red & black wavy border, white background, 20x20", EX+, A1............$200.00

Mobiloil Marine (Light Heavy), can, Gargoyle logo above product name, black & red on cream, pour spout with screw cap & handle, 10x5x5", NOS, NM, A1 ....$160.00

Mobiloil Marine No 4 SAE 40, can, Pegasus logo above product name, red & blue on white, flat-sided with handle & screw cap, full, 1-gal, NM, A1 ....$45.00

Mobiloil-Mobilgas, ashtray/cigarette holder, plated metal, holder shaped like General Petroleum Building, shield-shaped ashtray, 6", NM, A1 ....$170.00

Mobilubrication, letter set, black porcelain, 'M' in upper case with other letters in lower case, 12" to 8", NM, A1 ....$240.00

Mocha & Java Coffee, tin, red, vertical square with flat slip lid, Ginna, 2-lb, VG+, A18 ....$75.00

Model Ethyl Gasoline, pump sign, porcelain, Model on scroll above Gasoline on emblem, red, white & black, 9x13", NM, D11 ....$200.00

Model Smoking Tobacco, pocket tin, vertical, silver with white product name on red band, 15¢ on red circle below, NM, A18....................................$55.00

Model Smoking Tobacco, pocket tin, vertical, white with red & black lettering above & below pipe & cigarette, gold stripe, EX+, A18............................$550.00

Model Smoking Tobacco, sign, porcelain, Yes, I Said 10¢..., comical image of man with large mustache, 11x34", EX, A9.................................$145.00

Model Smoking Tobacco, sign, porcelain, Yes, I Said 10¢..., comical image of man with large mustache, 11x34", VG, A6 ....$85.00

Model Smoking Tobacco, sign, porcelain, Yes, I Said Model Smoking Tobacco (no 10¢), comical image of man with large mustache, 12x24", EX, A18........$135.00

Modern Service, sign, porcelain flange, barber pole shape with stars at top, 1930s, 48", NM, A3 ....$185.00

Modox, tip tray, die-cut image of Indian head with Drink Modox on full headdress, Made From Indian Herbs, 5" dia, EX, A21 ....$550.00

Moet & Chandon White Seal Champagne, fan, paper, folds out to show circles picturing bathing beauties & product name, 10x18½", G, A21 ....$90.00

Mohawk, crate label, California orange, Indian aiming bow & arrow toward mountain scene, 10x11", M, D12 ......$50.00

Mohawk Chieftain Motor Oil, can, product name above encircled Indian, blue, orange & white, screw lid & handle, 1-gal, 10x6", VG+, A6 ....$70.00

Mohawk Chieftain Motor Oil, can, product name above encircled Indian, blue, orange & white, round, 1-qt, EX+, A1...$130.00

Mohawk Power Packed Motor Oil, can, product name above & below encircled Indian, divided 2-color background, pour top & handle, 2-gal, EX+, A1 ....$160.00

Mohican Pure Spice, tin, 3¾", NM, A7.....................$85.00

Mona Motor Oil, can, blue with white name above image of various vehicles, 1-gal, EX/VG, A6.................$325.00

Monamobile Oil, can, pitcher-type with product name above early car with passengers, blue & silver, 8", VG+, A6 ....$170.00

Monarch Ale, tray, deep-dish, shows bottle on wood-grain background, gold trim, 12" dia, EX, A21 ....$110.00

Monarch Cocoa, tin, Monarch arched above circular image of lion, slip lid, 16-oz, 6x3", EX, A3 ....$28.00

Monarch Cocoa, tin, sample, product name above & below circular image of lion, slip lid, 3x1¾x1¾", EX, D37...$120.00

Monarch Malleable Range, sign, cardboard, Make Your Cooking A Daily Pleasure above woman preparing meal, ...Will Help You Do It, 10x20", EX, A3.......$85.00

Monarch Mocha-Rich Coffee, tin, product name on square on lined background, key-wind lid, NM, A3.........$25.00

Monarch Paint, toy spinner, tin, 1½" dia, NM, A7....$35.00

Monarch Peanut Butter, pail, straight-sided, bail handle, ca 1926, EX, A18 ....$300.00

Monarch Soap, display box, shows woman using product on top panel, complete with 12 bars of soap, unused, NM, D21...$70.00

Monarch Tea, tin, lion logo above field, Green lettered on hinged lid, 4x2½x2½", EX+, A3 ....$45.00

Monarch Teenie Weenie Toffies, store tin, product name above & below circular trademark image flanked by elves, 14½x12½" dia, EX, A2 ......$630.00

Monarch Teenie Weenie Toffies, tin, product name & lion's head on emblem flanked by elves, key-wind, 1-lb, EX, A18...$95.00

Monarch Tobacco Works Kickapoo Plug, insert card, features Red Cloud, EX, A5 .... **$75.00**

Monmouth Gravel Co, match safe, celluloid, colorful image of reclining nude, 3x2", VG+, A9 .... **$325.00**

Monogram Brand High Grade Coffee, can label, product name around shield, 6x18", A7 .... **$3.00**

Monogram Motor Oil, can, Stands Up! above soldiers in a descending line & product name below on oval, red, white & blue, 1-qt, NM+, A1 .... **$110.00**

Monopol Turkish Tobacco & Cigarette, pocket tin, flat, rounded corners, ¾x3x1¾", scarce, EX+, A18 ...**$220.00**

Monroe Brewing Co, tip tray, shows King Gambrinus with mug of beer, lettered rim, King Of Rochester Beers, 4" dia, EX+, A8 .... **$110.00**

Mont-Pilat Mineral Water, postcard, French, caricatures of famous women performers with large bottle at left, NM, D26 .... **$40.00**

Montana Sport, cigar box label, inner lid, hunting dog & scenic view of Montana, 1900, 6x9", M, D5 ....**$25.00**

Montauk Salt Water Oysters, tin, white & green with red, white & green lettering & Indian graphics, 1-gal, NM, A3 .... **$35.00**

Monte Cuba, cigar box label, outer, medieval man & castle, 4½x4½", EX, D5 ....**$12.00**

Montero Cigar Factory/Pennington Runk & Co Montreal, sign, paper, Smoke Montero & Kennel Cigars, royal couple observing fox hunters & dogs, gold frame, 22x28", EX+, A18 .... $650.00

Montgomery Ward, catalog, Christmas, 1940, EX, D17.**$125.00**

Montgomery Ward, catalog, Christmas, 1950, EX, D17 ..**$100.00**

Montgomery Ward, catalog, features ladies, mens & childrens fashions, 272 pgs, 1914, EX, D17 ....**$100.00**

Montgomery Ward, catalog, Summer Sale, 1970, EX, D17 .... **$20.00**

Montgomery Ward & Co Tea, store bin, cardboard & tin, square with oriental motif, 5-lb, square slip lid, EX, A18 .... **$35.00**

Montgomery Ward Power Tools, catalog, 1937, 30 pgs, EX, D17 .... **$25.00**

Monticello Coffee, tin, name above Monticello estate on oval, key-wind, 1-lb, VG, A7 ....**$20.00**

Monticello Whiskey, tip tray, fox hunt scene on Monticello lawn, pre-1920, oval, 6", EX+, A8 ....**$165.00**

Montmorency Baking Powder, tin, round with waterfall scene on paper label, with contents, unopened, Canadian, 5¼x3" dia, NM, A18 ....**$70.00**

Moonbeam, crate label, citrus, full moon shining over groves & swamp scene, M, D3 ....**$2.00**

Moonlight Grapes, lug box label, couple in canoe on moonlit lake, Sanger, M, D12 ....**$3.00**

Moonlight Mellos/Batterson Chocolates, tin, red, white & blue graphics & white lettering on blue, slip lid, Canadian, 5x10½" dia, VG+, A18 ....**$20.00**

Moore Push-Pins, turntable display, metal, shows various pins & what they hold & woman hanging picture, 1930s-40s, 15x7x7", EX, A6 ....**$140.00**

Moore's Ice Cream, sign, metal, We Serve...Guarded Quality..., Famous For Over 60 Years, red & black on yellow, 1950s, 24x36", NM, A13 ....**$190.00**

Moores & Ross Ice Cream, tray, wood-grain with child's face above & dish of ice cream below name & The Cream Of All Creams, square, EX, A16 ....**$55.00**

Moose Bock Beer, label, Moose Brewing Co, Internal Revenue Tax Paid statement, 1933-50, 12-oz, EX, A10 ..**$14.00**

Moosehead, tobacco label, MC Tobacco Co, EX, D35 ..**$4.00**

MoPar Parts, sign, tin flange, product name in red on yellow surrounded by Plymouth, Dodge... in yellow on blue, 15x24", EX, D8 .... $250.00

MoPar Parts & Accessories, sign, die-cut cardboard, Factory Inspected banner above man with a micrometer, late 1940s, matted, 28x20½", NM, A1 ....**$150.00**

Morell's French Lotion, trade card, fairy with blue wings & butterfly in the sky, ca 1880, EX, D23 ....**$25.00**

Morlein/Burton Brewing Co, tap knob, ball shape with white & gold on red insert, EX+, A8 ....**$30.00**

Morning Glory Quick Oats, container, cardboard, blue with image of 2 morning-glories above yellow & white product lettering, 3-lb, NM, A3 ....**$35.00**

Morning Sip Coffee, sign, paper, Drink... The Better Coffee in yellow & white on red, can on black lower left, 1920s, 12x21", EX+, A3 ....**$140.00**

Morrell's, bookmark, heart shape with Morrell's in script above image & Iowa's Pride Meats on heart, 2x2¼", EX+, A11 ....**$20.00**

Morrell's Hams & Bacon, sign, cardboard, product lettering on red heart-shaped image of boy in butcher's garb flanked by 2 cans, 20x18", G, A2 ....**$75.00**

Morrell's Pride Meats, pocket mirror, celluloid, John Morrell & Co arched above delivery man & product name on heart, round, EX, A11 ....$25.00

Morris' Supreme Bacon, sign, die-cut cardboard stand-up, truck with oversized package in back, 16x14", VG, A6 ....$80.00

Morris' Supreme Peanut Butter, pail, straight-sided with horizontal oval emblem over beach scene with children, bail handle, 12-oz, EX, A18 ....$185.00

Morrison Bros Oil Equipment, catalog, 1930, 104 pgs, EX, D17 ....$60.00

Morrison Hotel & Terrace Garden, calendar, 1924, multi-colored image of the hotel & garden above full calendar, 6x4", EX+, A11 ....$25.00

Morton Salt, sign, cardboard, Morton girl with umbrella flanked by When It Rains It Pours in yellow on blue, 14x35", EX, D30 ....$45.00

Moses' Cough Drops, store bin, red with Try Moses' above portrait flanked by Cough Drops, square with round lid, pre-1901, VG+, A18 ....$285.00

Moses' Cough Drops, tin, gray, round, slip lid, 1-lb, rare, G-, A18 ....$45.00

Moth-Ene, display, die-cut cardboard, Kills Moths...Positively Guaranteed with moth looking down on 3 product tins, NM, A7 ....$45.00

Mother Goose Shoes, sign, light-up, plastic, A Happy Step In Growing Up & logo above multicolored product name, curved corners, EX, A8 ....$40.00

Mother Hubbard Cake Flour, container, encircled image of Mother Hubbard with mixing bowl, 5-lb, EX+, A3 ....$40.00

Mother Penn All Pennsylvania Motor Oil, sign, die-cut porcelain, circular portrait image flanked by 1879 above name, red, white & black, 2-sided, 6x9", NM, A6 ....$750.00

Mother Penn Motor Oil, can, portrait flanked by dates & product name on center emblem, red, white & blue, full, 1-qt, NOS, NM+, A1 ....$30.00

Mother's Carnival Oats, product box, With Quality Colored Chinaware on curved field dividing product name & cups & saucers, 10", EX+/G+, A1 ....$20.00

Mother's Complexion Powder, tin, light blue with product lettering around Trade Mark image of Mother, Flesh lettered below, 1¼x2¾", EX, D37 ....$35.00

Mother's Joy Coffee, tin, Breakfast, Luncheon, Supper above steaming cups, ...Ground To Suit above, slip lid, EX+, A3 ....$45.00

Mother's Malt/Claussen Brewing Ass'n, drinking glass, straight-sided with gold rim (worn), etched logo above name, Seattle's Best Tonic, 3", EX, A8 ....$60.00

Mother's Mustard Plasters/Bauer & Black, tin, name above oval image of Mother flanked by mustard leaves, rectangular, hinged lid, ½x3¾x4⅞", EX, D37 ......$60.00

Mother's Oats, cereal box, Quick above image of mother & child, product name & With China below, 10x6½", VG, A7 ....$10.00

Mother's Oats, container, image of mother & son with bowl of oatmeal, Quaker Oats Co, 20-oz, VG+, A3 ....$40.00

Mother's Oats, sign, 'Mother's Boy,' little nude boy wrapped in leopard skin, copyright 1901, framed, 23x16", EX, A5 ....$200.00

Mother's Oats, sign, 'The Naughty Boy,' boy in oversized pants held up by suspenders, copyright 1903, framed, 28x22", VG, A8 ....$135.00

Mother's Toy Oats, container, cardboard, red, white & blue vertical box promoting A Toy In Every Box, 2-lb, EX, A3 ....$60.00

Motor Stop, sign, porcelain, white arrow pointing left on green ground above Motor Stop in black on white ground, 6½x14", EX+, A1 ....$100.00

Motorite, sign, die-cut porcelain flange, red, white & blue shield with Motorite on diagonal center band, 20x20", rare, VG, A1 ....$425.00

Motorola, display, cardboard stand-up, girl in nightgown holding radio with bow, tag reads Motorola For Sister, 34", G+, A1 ....$40.00

Motorola Radio, clock, neon, glass front with metal frame, Motorola Radio For Home & Car, red, white & blue, 21½" dia, EX, A6 ....$650.00

Mount Kineo Ginger Ale-Beverages, sign, tin, Drink above Mount Kineo 'Mountain High In Quality' on elongated oval, Ginger Ale... below, 12x20", NM+, D30 ....$80.00

Mountain, crate label, Oregon apple, scenic view of mountains, canyon & redwoods, Portland, 9x11", M, D12...$10.00

Mountain Belle, tobacco label, EX, D35.....................$6.00

Mountain Dew, sign, tin, Drink... It'll Tickle Your Innards!, cartoon image of hillbilly with jug, 1964, 18x30", NM+, A13...$450.00

Mountain Dew, sign, tin, Ya-hooo! Mountain Dew, It'll Tickle Yore Innards! on white sign above hillbilly with a jug, 36x60", EX+, A13 ....$225.00

Mountain Dew, sign, tin, Ya-hooo!..., It'll Tickle Yore Innards!, hillbilly popping cork on jug, 1966, 17x35", NM, A13 ....$200.00

Mountain Dew Whisky, sign, cardboard, Real Mountain Dew... above man with bottle & glass before silhouette of London skyline, 23x18", EX, A2.....................$135.00

Mountain Gold Butter, sign, embossed tin, product at left of Use...Made From Pure Mountain Cream, Sold By All Dealers, 10x28", NM, D11 ....$95.00

Mountain States Telephone & Telegraph Co, ashtray, porcelain, black with name & Directory Dept on rim around saluting Yellow-Page man, round with 3 rests, NM, A18 ....$40.00

Mouquin Chicken Bouillon Tablets, tin, name on banners above & below oval image of servers with tray, square corners, ½x1⅞x2¼", EX, D37 ....$15.00

Movie Hour Supreme Popcorn, tin, product name on marquee above movie goers, 10-lb, 9½", no top, VG, A7 ....$75.00

Moxie, ashtray holder, carved wood butler figure (referred to as Hitchy Koo), 35", rare, EX, A9 .$375.00

Moxie, ashtray holders, carved wood Moxie maid & butler figures (referred to as Hitchy Koos), 28½", G, A9...$275.00

Moxie, banner, 'Mad About Moxie For Thanksgiving' says pilgram holding carton at left, Indian with carton at right, NM, A16 ....$35.00

Moxie, bottle, clear glass with reverse-painted label, 13x2", crack in label from top to bottom, G, A9..........$250.00

Moxie, bottle carrier, cardboard, 6-12oz Bottles (12 Glasses) lettered above No Deposit No Return...See What You Drink, NM, A16....................................$12.00

Moxie, bottle crate, wood, tall box with pointing Moxie man stamped on side, rare, VG, A16.................$105.00

Moxie, bottle opener, slides in & out of handle lettered Drink Moxie..., M, A16...$65.00

Moxie, bottle opener with tag, Moxie embossed on key opener, tag features pointing Moxie man & Drink Moxie, G, A16...$25.00

Moxie, bottle opener/ice pick, metal, The Best In The World, NM, A16...$35.00

Moxie, candy box, The Moxie Candy Man on oval center, decorative border, rectangular, 4 ½-oz, EX+, A16.$80.00

Moxie, cane/yardstick, Moxie in repeated pattern, 36", VG, A9..$125.00

Moxie, cigar box, wood with embossed lettering on paper labels, Moxie — Food For The Brain, 2¼x5½x8", G+, A21...$415.00

Moxie, clock, Baird regulator, ...Compound For The Nervous System surrounds face, Also A Delicious... on pendulum, 31", VG, A9......................................$7,000.00

Moxie, cooler, bottle shape, Ice Cold at top of label, Moxie below, pre-1910s, 36x12", rare, VG, A4.............$550.00

Moxie, dispenser, glass, Drink Moxie on red oval on base, EX+, D30...$350.00

Moxie, drinking glass, modified flared top, syrup line, Drink Moxie, M, A16.......................................$100.00

Moxie, drinking glass, straight-sided, Drink Moxie Nerve Food, M, A16...$100.00

Moxie, fan, die-cut cardboard, 'Peggy,' Moxie stand in park on reverse, 1916, 9", G+, A21..............................$45.00

Moxie, fan, die-cut cardboard, Frances Pritchard with glass, giant Moxie bottle at fair on reverse, 1916, 10", VG, A21..$40.00

Moxie, fan, die-cut cardboard, Lillian MacKenzie, Star Spangled Banner music graphics on back, 1918, 10", EX, A9..$60.00

Moxie, fan, die-cut cardboard, Moxie girl with compact, 1925, 8", NM+, D30..$55.00

Moxie, fan, die-cut cardboard, Moxie girl with glass, Moxie man on reverse, 1924, 8", EX, A21.......................$35.00

Moxie, fan, die-cut cardboard, Muriel Ostriche in red hat, Moxie man on reverse, 1919, 8", NM+, D30.........$75.00

Moxie, fan, die-cut cardboard, Muriel Ostriche in red hat, Moxie man on reverse, 1919, 8", VG, A21............$35.00

Moxie, fan, die-cut cardboard, Muriel Ostriche with glass, touring car at roadside Moxie stand on reverse, 1916, 9", EX, A21...$35.00

Moxie, fan, die-cut cardboard, Muriel Ostriche, Bring Back My Daddy To Me music graphics on reverse, 1918, 10", NM+, D30...$75.00

Moxie, fan, die-cut cardboard, pointing Moxie man, TNT cowboy & Moxie horse car on reverse, 1922, 8", EX, A21..$65.00

Moxie, lamp shade, leaded glass (Tiffany-type), 1930s, NM+, D4 ....$6,500.00

Moxie, match holder, die-cut tin, straight-sided bottle above bottle crate, Learn To Drink Moxie Very Healthful, EX+, A16 ....$300.00

Moxie, photograph, numerous people standing in front of various vans & the Moxiemobile, framed, image: 7½x41", A9..$95.00

Moxie, plate, china, logo & pointing Moxie man in center, gold banded rim, 6", M, A16 ....$45.00

Moxie, sign, cardboard, die-cut, ...Never Sticky Sweet on red circle at right of pointing Moxie man, 8x12", NM+, D30..$65.00

Moxie, sign, cardboard, die-cut, boy with dog carrying a 3-pack of Moxie Teers, 1928, 21x12½", VG+, A9 ..$325.00

Moxie, sign, cardboard, die-cut, Drink Moxie on carton with girl peaking over the top, 24x20", VG+, D30 ......$140.00

Moxie, sign, cardboard, die-cut, Drink Moxie 100%, girl holding glass & large fan with floral design, 16½x32", rare, G-, A9 ....$300.00

Moxie, sign, cardboard, die-cut, Drink...Moxie Contains Gentian on shoulder of Frank Archer, 12x16", VG+, A9 ..$95.00

Moxie, sign, cardboard, die-cut, hand holding bottle, 20x10", NM, D30 ....$100.00

Moxie, sign, cardboard, die-cut, He's Got Moxie 5¢ on red sign above baseball boy with bottle, 18x8", NM+, D30..$250.00

Moxie, sign, cardboard, die-cut, Invigorating As An Ocean Breeze, girl at ship's wheel, Frank Archer... below, 40x30", EX, D30 ....$325.00

Moxie, sign, cardboard, die-cut, Moxie on large dot behind upper part of bottle, hanger, 10½x6", EX, A16 ....$80.00

Moxie, sign, cardboard, die-cut, Over 50 Years Of Popularity on sign above pointing Moxie man with bottle, 40x34", VG+, D30..$350.00

Moxie, sign, cardboard, die-cut, pointing Moxie man seated on box with bottle at his feet, 32x24", M, D30 ..$650.00

Moxie, sign, cardboard, die-cut, She's Got... on circle above tennis girl with bottle, Drink It Ice Cold 5¢, 39x27", G, A9..$155.00

Moxie, sign, cardboard, die-cut, The Swing Is To Moxie on oval above girl on swing, Sparkling Drink... below, 40x26", G-, A9 ....$150.00

Moxie, sign, cardboard, die-cut, The Swing Is To Moxie on oval above girl on swing, Frank Archer Invites You..., 11x7", VG, A9 ....$145.00

Moxie, sign, cardboard, Drink in black above Moxie in white shadowed in black, orange background, 24x30", M, D30 ....$45.00

Moxie, sign, cardboard, Drink Moxie on carton with girl peaking over the top, 24x20", VG, D30 ....$135.00

Moxie, sign, cardboard, Drink...A Nickel For Your Thirst! on post beside bathing beauty with bottle, 1930s, 50x30", VG, A9 ....$350.00

Moxie, sign, cardboard, Learn To Drink Moxie, Very Healthful... above girl admiring herself in the mirror, 1892, NM+, D4 ....$1,000.00

Moxie, sign, cardboard, Let's Get Aquainted...Moxie Six-Pack 5¢, Limited Time Only! below, red, white & blue, 15x18", M, D30 ....$55.00

Moxie, sign, cardboard, Moxie girl leaning on back of chair with glass & bottle, hanger, 1905, 13x10", rare, EX+, A15..$1,150.00

Moxie, sign, cardboard, Moxie girl leaning on back of chair with glass & bottle, 1905, hanger, 13x10", rare, G, A21 ....$630.00

Moxie, sign, cardboard, stand-up, Shall I Send A Case Of Moxie To Your Home?, Moxie man displays case of bottles, EX, A3 ....$360.00

Moxie, sign, cloth, Family Size Moxie, 3 For 36¢ at right of 1¢ Sale..., red, black & white on yellow, 36x48", NM+, D30..$250.00

Moxie, sign, counter-top, It's A Hit Says Ted Williams & tilted bottle on sign behind image of Ted Williams, 9x14", G+, A9 ....$450.00

Moxie, sign, flange, Drink Moxie in white shadowed in black on red background, oval, 10x18", NM, D30 ....$195.00

Moxie, sign, porcelain, Drink Moxie on emblem at left of hand holding bottle, cream ground with blue border, 34x44", EX, D8 ....$375.00

Moxie, sign, reverse-painted glass, Ice Cream Soda 10¢, College Ices 10¢ above Moxie, framed, image: 24x32", VG, A9 ....$600.00

Moxie, sign, sidewalk, tin, Drink Genuine above Moxie on diagonal band, 5¢ Delicious, Healthful... below, 36x20", rare, G, A9 ....$425.00

Moxie, sign, tin, die-cut, girl with glass & bottle atop Moxie panel, 7x6", rare, VG, A9 ....$300.00

Moxie, sign, tin, die-cut Moxie man atop Drink Moxie on red sign, hanger, 6", EX, A21 ....$470.00

Moxie, sign, tin, Drink Moxie, Braces First — Chases Thirst, embossed, 7x20", VG, A16 ....$80.00

Moxie, sign, tin, Drink Moxie, Distinctively Different on red oval with yellow & orange border, blue ground, 1920s, NM+, A4..$650.00

Moxie, sign, tin, Drink Moxie, embossed, 19x27", VG, A9..$175.00

Moxie, sign, tin, Drink Moxie, embossed, 6½x19", VG, A16..$95.00

Moxie, sign, tin, Drink Moxie on striped emblem at left of hand holding bottle, 12x28", NM+, D30 ....$145.00

Moxie, sign, tin, Drink Moxie Very Healthful surrounded by To Eat Better, To Sleep Better..., embossed, 22" dia, G, A9 ....$550.00

Moxie, sign, tin, Drink Moxie 100%, embossed, 5¼x19", G+, A9..$85.00

Moxie, sign, tin, Drink Moxie 100% on red circle, 24x24", VG+, D30 ....$85.00

Moxie, sign, tin, Eclipses... above people rushing up steps to bottle at the Moxie Hall of Fame, self-framed, 53x18", EX, A6..$500.00

Moxie, sign, tin, girl on horse in touring car in front of billboard, ...Distinctively Different, self-framed, 19x27", G, A6 ....$350.00

Moxie, sign, tin, Moxie ? Certainly I Just Love It, man pouring some for lady on bike, embossed, wood frame 28x19", EX, A6..$1,600.00

Moxie, sign, tin, Moxie girl with bottle & glass leaning on back of chair, embossed, 27½x19½", rare, G-, A9 ....$550.00

Moxie, sign, tin, Of Course You'll Have Some above woman pouring glass, framed, image: 28x20", rare, EX+, A6..$4,000.00

Moxie, sign, tin, Of Course You'll Have Some above woman pouring glass, framed, image: 28x20", rare, G, A9..$1,950.00

Moxie, sign, tin, Old Moxie & New Moxie on bottle caps above Drink Moxie, red background, 24x28", NM+, D30..$195.00

Moxie, sign, tin, The Drink That Made The Name Famous, horse in touring car at left, Drink... on circle at right, 12x36", G, A9..$450.00

Moxie, sign, tin, The Drink That Made The Name Famous above Drink... on circle, pointing Moxie man at top, 42x15", G, A9..$150.00

Moxie, sign, tin, Yes! We Sell above Moxie on diagonal band, Very Healthful, Feeds The Nerves below, 28x30", EX, D30................................$1,200.00

Moxie, sign, tin, Yes! We Sell above Moxie on diagonal band, Very Healthful, Feeds The Nerves below, oval, 30x22", NM, D30..$1,200.00

Moxie, thermometer, tin, Drink Moxie on oval above Frank Archer, It's Always A Pleasure To Serve You below, 28", NM, D30..$450.00

Moxie, thermometer, tin, Drink Moxie on oval above Frank Archer, It's Always A Pleasure To Serve You below, 28", VG, A9..$300.00

Moxie, thermometer, tin, Old Fashion Moxie above bulb flanked by vignettes, Remember Those Days below, EX, A16..$55.00

Moxie, thermometer, tin, We've Got Moxie above bulb & Old Fashion Moxie, yellow background, 15", NM+, D30..$75.00

Moxie, thermometer, tin, Ya Gotta Have Moxie above Frank Archer & lettering on circle, 28", NM+, D30........$450.00

Moxie, thermometer, tin, Ya Gotta Have Moxie on yellow with boy holding bottle with boxing glove, 14x6", NM, A19..$70.00

Moxie, tip tray, I Just Love Moxie Don't You? & green leaf decor on rim around Moxie girl with hand on hip, 6" dia, EX+, A21..$385.00

Moxie, tip tray, I Just Love Moxie Don't You? on wood-grain rim at right of Moxie girl with glass, 6" dia, EX+, A21..$275.00

Moxie, tip tray, Moxie I Like It on white rim above & below Moxie girl with glass on blue, 6" dia, EX, A21..$360.00

Moxie, tip tray, Moxie Makes You Eat, Drink & Feel Better on label in center, simulated wood-grain background, 6" dia, NM, D30..$225.00

Moxie, tip tray, 5¢ Moxie Feeds The Nerves on rim around brunette girl leaning on chair with bottle & glass, 6" dia, VG, A21..$685.00

Moxie, toy car, tin, blue version with rider on white horse, ca 1917, 6½x8½", VG+, A9..$2,000.00

Moxie, tray, Drink Old Fashion Moxie on red background, 12" dia, NM, D30..$55.00

Moxie, tray, glass & metal, I Like It at left of Moxie girl with glass, handled, 12" dia, VG+, D30..$375.00

Moxie, tray, reverse glass, straight perforated handled rim, 'I Like It' & girl with glass on yellow, 1910-15, 10" dia, VG, A13..$130.00

Moxie, see also Pureoxia Ginger Ale

Moza de Fiesta, cigar box label, outer, belly dancer in king's court, 4½x4½", M, D5..$25.00

Mr Boston Fine Liquors, see Old Mr Boston

Mr Clean, figure, Mr Clean, hard plastic, 1961, EX, D27..$95.00

Mr Pear, crate label, Washington pear, cartoon image of pear with top hat & cane on blue background, yellow logo, 8x11", M, D12..$3.00

Mr Therrien Artistic Hair Care Center, sign, image of father & son grooming in bathroom, ...Family Grooming Is What It's All About, 41x31", EX, D8..........$125.00

Mrs AE Sparks Millinery, trade card, floral design on front, 1880s, EX, D23..$20.00

Mrs FW Winckley Millinery & Lace Goods, trade card, colorful litho of bird & flowers with ship in the distance, 1880s, EX, D23..$20.00

Mrs Rodeback's Eczema Salve, tin, name above bust image of Mrs Rodeback, round with dome slip lid, 2¼x1½" dia, EX, D37..$35.00

Mrs Winslow's Soothing Syrup, fan, cardboard with wood handle, colorful image of mother & baby, ad text on back, 8" dia, EX, D22........................$25.00

MS Kaplan Co Scrap Iron, paperweight, Your Chicago Broker on center design surrounded by company name, M, D13...............................$25.00

Mt Cabin, sign, embossed tin, Drink... 5¢ A Bottle, Just Sweet Enough Just Tart Enough, red & black on white, 1940s, 14x19", VG+, A3..............................$40.00

Mt Hamilton Brand Red Plums, can label, product name above & below branch of plums/product name above farm scene, EX, A7...........................$2.00

Mt Whitney Brand Yellow Cling Peaches, can label, product name above & below large peach with daisy border/mountain scene, 4½x13", NM, A7..............$3.00

Muehlebach Beer, sign, tin, hanger, company crest above product name, gold border, 9" dia, NM, A19.......$60.00

Mueller-Keller Candy Co/Rosary Chocolates, pocket mirror, colorful image of wrapped box, round, EX+, D18......................................$35.00

Muenchener Kindl, label, Kessler Brewing Co, pre-prohibition, EX, A10 ....$70.00

Muessel Silver Edge, bottle opener, metal, shaped like butter knife, 5", EX, A8 ....$50.00

Mug Ale/Burkardt Brewing Co, display, plaster, figural frosty mug, EX, A8 ....$35.00

Mug Old Fashioned Root Beer, soda glass, white logo, footed, 6x3", M, D16 ....$12.00

Mugs Up Root Beer, baby mug, glass, red logo with image of mug & drive-in, M, D16 ....$15.00

Muhlhauser/Hammond Brewing Co, drinking glass, straight-sided with flat bottom, etched lettering with logo upper left, 4", NM, A8 ....$100.00

Mule Beer, label, McGovern Brewing Co, U-type permit number, Internal Revenue Tax Paid statement, 1933-36, 12-oz, EX, A10 ....$10.00

Munchner Beer, label, Frankenmuth Brewing Co, U-type permit number, Internal Revenue Tax Paid statement, 1933-50, 12-oz, M, A10...........................$20.00

Mundus Beer/West Side Brewery Co, drinking glass, straight-sided with applied raised white lettering, 4", NM, A8 ....$20.00

Munsing Union Suits, sign, cardboard stand-up, In All Styles — For All Ages, shows little girl sitting on bench with chalkboard, NM, A13 ....$95.00

Munsing Union Suits, sign, cardboard stand-up, Munsingwear Gives Complete Satisfaction, shows 6 kids in touring car, 11x9", NM, A13 ....$160.00

Munsing Union Suits, sign, cardboard stand-up, shows little girl standing in front of round mirror, NM+, A13...$65.00

Munsing Wear, display, litho tin, container for free Fashion Books, back panel shows mother & daughter, 15x12x15", EX+, A6..............................$875.00

Munsingwear, figure, penguin, vinyl, 1970, VG, D27...$20.00

Munsingwear, sign, oil painting on canvas, 2 girls modeling for grandma, Perfection In Munsingwear, framed, image: 22x30", G+, A9 ....$300.00

Munsingwear, sign, self-framed tin, 'The Munsing Twins,' little girl looking at her reflection in mirror, 38x26", G, A9..............................$400.00

Murad, pocket tin, short vertical, name above colorful painted image, gold lid, EX+, A18 ....$95.00

Murad Cigarettes, sign, Everywhere Why? in script & The Turkish Cigarette flank pack & Murad in large block letters, 22x4", EX+, A18.............................$65.00

Murad Cigarettes, sign, image of the Vanderbilt Cup Race with 3 cars racing down track, copyright 1909, framed, 10½x14", EX, A6.............................$550.00

Muratti's After Lunch Cigarettes, tin, flat, pictures product name & man seated at table, square with square corners, VG+, A18..............................$35.00

Muratti's Gold Tipped Ariston Cigarettes, pocket tin, vertical, gold lettering against diagonal red & black background, EX, A18 ....$90.00

Murphy's Concentrates, sign, tin, Heart Of The Ration on heart with farm animals atop, For Livestock... below, yellow ground, 32x23", NM, D8 ....$375.00

Murphy's Oil Soap, tin, sample, round, lid shows Cleans Everything on receding banner below product name, ¾x2" dia, EX, D37 ....$15.00

Murray & Lanman's Brilliantine Deluxe Lavendar, pocket mirror, colorful image of product tin, The Ideal Pomade, round, EX+, D18 ....$35.00

Murray's Hair Dressing Pomade, tin, sample, Now 25¢ above black couple looking in each others eyes, National Can Co, ¼x1⅝", EX, D37......................$22.00

Murry's Old-Fashioned Root Beer, dispenser, ceramic, embossed barrel shape atop tree stump, lid missing otherwise NM, A4................................$350.00

Musgo, gas globe, encircled Indian chief in center, Michigans Mile Maker below, dated Sept 1928, 1-pc, 14" dia, rare, NM, A6 ....$4,750.00

MW Savage Co, catalog, Fall/Winter, 1927, 486 pgs, EX, D17...$80.00

Myopia Club Beverages, sign, tin, yellow with Indian head in profile at left of Drink & Enjoy... & image of bottle, horizontal, G-, A16 ....$70.00

Nabisco Chips Ahoy, figure, Chips Ahoy girl, 1983, EX, D27 ....$15.00

Nabisco Log Cabin Brownies, container, cardboard, cabin shape with images of the Palmer Cox Brownies, string handle, NM, D22 ....$175.00

Nabisco Shredded Wheat, box, pictures Niagara Falls, 1939, NM, D6..$35.00

Nabob Coffee, tin, Vacuum Packed on center design, **Steel Cut emblem & Always Fresh emblem flank Coffee, key-wind lid, 1-lb, NM, A3** $70.00

Nally's Popcorn, pail, red name above boy's face with full bowl, All Popt Delicious at right, slip lid, bail handle, 8x7" dia, EX+, A18 ....$215.00

Nan's Kitchen, matchbook, Boston, 20 strike, front strike, NM, D28 ....$3.50

Nandora, cigar box label, printer's proof, woman playing guitar through a window, NM, A5 ....$45.00

Napoleon Cigar, sign, self-framed tin, portrait image with name below, 19x16", G+, A21.............................$185.00

Napoleon 10¢ Cigar, window decal, portrait flanked by Powell & Goldstein & Oneida-New York, 8" dia, M, A5..$18.00

Narragansett Ale, tray, The Famous Old in white script above gold product name on red, brewery logo above, decorative rim, round, EX, A19 ....$45.00

Narragansett Gold Label Ale, tap knob, chrome ball shape with gold, red & white enamel insert, VG+, A8...$85.00

Narragansett Lager Beer, can, flat-top, 12-oz, top missing otherwise NM, A19..$35.00

Nash Service & Parts, sign, die-cut porcelain shield, red on white with line design top & bottom, 46x46", NM, D8................................$750.00

Nash Service Station, sign, porcelain, Service above & Station below Nash on circular emblem, white on blue, 2-sided, 28x34", EX, A1..$800.00

Nash's Drip Grind Coffee, tin, Nash's in script, key-wind lid, NM, A3..$25.00

Nash's Jubilee Coffee, pail, red with product name above & below oval image of men's meeting flanked by trumpeters, slip lid, 5-lb, EX, A18 ....$248.00

Nash's Toasted Coffee, pail, Guaranteed Quality in center, product name in script, slip lid & bail, EX, A3.....$50.00

Nation's Reliance Cigars, box label, salesman's sample, portrait of William McKinley, Smoke... below, 1898, NM, A5...$150.00

National Ale, label, National Brewing Co, U-type permit number, Internal Revenue Tax Paid statement, 1933-36, 12-oz, M, A10..$12.00

National Bank of Monticello, paperweight, bronze on marble, NIB logo above ...We're Here To Help You, square, M, D13......................................$25.00

National Beer, tray, cowboy on horse bursting through paper, National Brewing Co lettered on rim, oval, 16½x14", VG+, A9..$900.00

National Bella Hess, catalog, Christmas, 1966, EX, D17...$35.00

National Biscuit Co, tin, Favorite Assortment, pictures various cookies, hinged lid, 7x13x2", EX, D14 ....$36.00

National Biscuit Co, see also Barnum's Animals and O-So-Good Pretzels

National Biscuit Co/Uneeda Bakers, jar, glass, globe shape with side opening, tin knob lid, embossed lettering, 11" dia, EX, A2...$145.00

National Bohemian Pale Beer, can, cone-top, white & black on orange, 32-oz, VG+, A19.......................$100.00

National Brewing Co, tray, National Lager Beer, Best In The West above 2 cowboys trying to lasso each other, ca 1903, oval, 14x16", VG+, A9........................$1,200.00

National Commercial Travelers Association, sign, porcelain, Official Member above silhouette of North America, Supervised Service below, octagon, 18x15", NM, A1..$170.00

National Cycle Mfg Co, pin-back button, celluloid, eagle atop patriotic shield, round, EX+, A11.................$32.00

National Farm Loan Association, sign, porcelain with iron bracket, ...Low Interest Rates, Long-Term, white on blue, 37x41", VG, A9..$50.00

National Lead Co, paperweight, 'Dutch Boy' in high relief in center, 1940s, 3¼" dia, minor scuffs, A6 .... **$20.00**

National Orange Co, crate label, orange grove & wrapped Sunkist orange, Riverside, 10x11", M, D3 .... **$2.00**

National Premium, tray, product name on banners with lions on center logo, ivory background, 11" dia, EX, A19 .... **$25.00**

National Premium Beer, tap knob, black ball shape with silver & blue on yellow background enamel insert, G+, A8 .... **$45.00**

National Seal, cigar box label, inner lid, seal of the US Supreme Court, 6x9", M, D5 .... **$4.00**

National Tailoring Co, display figure, man in tuxedo on lettered base, hard rubber, 36", VG, A9 .... **$625.00**

National Tea Co, end label, color photo image of Yogi Berra, red border, EX, D29 .... **$150.00**

National Trailways System, sign, porcelain, Bus Depot above silhouette map of USA lettered National Trailways System, 2-sided, 18x22", VG, A1 .... **$190.00**

Natural Chilean Soda, sign, tin, product name left of black man, Yassuh! Uncle Natchel, white & yellow on green, 1940s-50s, 15x21", NM+, A13 .... **$180.00**

Natural Product Beer, label, Schutz & Hilgers J Brewery, U-type permit number, Internal Revenue Tax Paid statement, 1933-36, 12-oz, M, A10 .... **$16.00**

Nature's Remedy Tablets, pocket mirror, product name lettered across nose of face viewed close-up, lettered border, 2⅛" dia, EX, A8 .... **$20.00**

Nature's Remedy Tablets, sign, cardboard stand-up, It Only Costs A Quarter To 'Feel Like A Million,' man with product, ...NR-Tablets-NR, NM, A18........$45.00

Nature's Remedy Tablets, sign, self-framed porcelain, ...The All Vegetable Laxative, ...Tomorrow Alright, 1930s, green frame, 18x24", NM, A13 .... **$375.00**

Nature's Remedy Tablets, tin, flat, All-Vegetable Laxative & encircled NR upper left of name on diagonal band, 25¢ & NR lower right, EX, D37 .... **$10.00**

Nature's Remedy Tablets, tin, vertical, NR Juniors, Candy Coated, 2¾x2⅛x1", EX, D37 .... **$10.00**

Nature's Remedy Tablets, tin, vertical, Price $1.00 on slip lid, 180 Tablets, 3⅜x2¾x1", EX, D37 .... **$5.00**

Nature's Remedy Tablets, tin, vertical, Price 50¢ on slip lid, Sixty Tablets, 1¾x2x1", EX, D37 .... **$10.00**

Navy Smoking Tobacco, see Gail & Ax

NBC Bread, end label, Donald Duck In Canada, red background, EX, D29... **$3.00**

NBC Bread, end label, features Pinocchio on blue background, EX, D29... **$7.00**

Neasco Oils, wagon cabinet, wood, black with gold & red highlights, metal latches, late 1800s-early 1900s, 25x52", rare, EX, A6 .... **$500.00**

Nebraska Blossom Cigars, tin, white paper label with red Nebraska Blossom arched above image of cowgirl, gold lid, round, EX, A18................................... **$375.00**

Nebraska Girl Cigars, label, product name above woman on prancing horse with dog running beside them, embossed, 1902, 4x4", NM, A3..$22.00

Necco Sweets, calendar, 1907, months of the year surround image of Puritan lady embroidering Necco logo by fireplace, 12x8", EX+, A3 .... **$50.00**

Necco Wafers, dispenser, 5¢, rotates on pedestal, colorful graphics with lettering, NM, A18......................... **$205.00**

Necco Wafers, sign, paper, 5¢ Refreshing above Assorted Necco Wafers candy roll & Deco girl in bathing suit, 12x20", EX, A2........................$330.00

Nectar Beer, sign, cardboard, A logo & Seal Of Quality above Nectar, The Beer Excellent below, red & white, round, EX, A19 .... **$75.00**

Nectar Beer, tray, deep-dish, Seldom Equalled...Never Excelled, pictures 3 red-robed figures enjoying brew, red rim, EX, A19 .... **$50.00**

Negro Head Oysters, tin with paper label, black man with mouth open wide ready to eat an oyster, 4¾-oz, NM, A3 .... **$150.00**

Nehi, bottle carrier, cardboard, holds 4 bottles, Family Package..., NM, A7 .... **$15.00**

Nehi, bottle topper, keyhole shape with 2 bathers appearing to sip from bottle, NM, A7 .... **$115.00**

Nehi, calendar, 1935, Rolf Armstrong girl standing in yellow gown with white fur cape, dark background, 24x12", EX+, A13... **$140.00**

Nehi, calendar, 1938, Rolf Armstrong sailor girl at the helm, sailboats beyond, 24x12", EX+, A13.................... **$190.00**

Nehi, calendar top, 1932, Rolf Armstrong girl with sweater knotted over shoulders holding bottle, 18½x11½", EX, A13 ....$90.00

Nehi, coupon, Drink Nehi 'For Health & Happiness Too!' In Your Favorite Flavor, bottle pictured at right, NM+, A16 ....$65.00

Nehi, menu board, Drink... on yellow panel above Special Today in yellow script on black menu area, 1930s-40s, 28x20", EX, A13 ....$95.00

Nehi, pocketknife, Remington, metal engraved boot-shaped handle, EX, A16......................................$110.00

Nehi, sign, cardboard, Drink Genuine... on oval behind bottle & lady's legs, green background, framed, 14x21", NM+, A13..$270.00

Nehi, sign, cardboard stand-up, Take A Good Look..., Be Sure You Get..., lady in green seated with bottle, 41", EX, A2 ....$990.00

Nehi, sign, flange, Drink Nehi in beveled letters above Ice Cold, bottle on white panel at left, 1940s, 13x18", NM, A13 ....$525.00

Nehi, sign, tin, Curb Service above Nehi, Sold Here Ice Cold below, black & red on yellow, black trim, 1940s, 28x20", NM+, A13...$140.00

Nehi, sign, tin, Drink Nehi above Gas Today & chalkboard dot, Ice Cold...Sold Here below, 42x15", EX+, A1 ....$380.00

Nehi, sign, tin, Drink Nehi Beverages left of bottle on white oval, embossed, 17x45", NM+, A13.....$190.00

Nehi, sign, tin, Drink Nehi Beverages left of tilted bottle, 18x54", VG+, D30 ....$125.00

Nehi, sign, tin, Drink Nehi Root Beer at left of bottle & Pure Natural Flavors, bright yellow ground, 12x32", NM, D30...$195.00

Nehi, trade card, Don't Let Them Fool You!, shows girl in bathtub, fold down top & she is serving Nehi to 2 men, VG+, A16 ....$82.00

Nehi, tray, shows bathing beauty caught up in ocean wave, orange bottle lower right, labeled rim, vertical, 13", VG+, A21 ....$145.00

Nehi, see also Rums Dry Ginger Ale

Neilson's Jersey Cocoa, tin, sample, product name & other lettering on crisscross design, slip lid, 2½x1¾" dia, EX, D37...$40.00

Neptune Seafood, letter opener, celluloid, fish logo on both sides, 6" long, EX, D22.............................$18.00

Nesbitt's, dispenser, clamp-on type with original cardboard box featuring Orange, M, A16......................$138.00

Nesbitt's, door push bar, porcelain, bottle cap at right of ...Take Home A Carton, yellow background, 32½" long, VG, A6 ....$150.00

Nesbitt's, picnic cooler, aluminum, rectangular with name embossed on front, G, A16 ....$100.00

Nesbitt's, sign, cardboard, die-cut, Made With Real Oranges, lady in hat & gloves with bottle, 1950s, 23x21", VG, A4 ....$50.00

Nesbitt's, sign, tin, bottle shape, 84x24", NM+, A13 ..$850.00

Nesbitt's, sign, tin, Drink & 5¢ above & below Nesbitt's on white band over bottle neck, black background, 1940s, 49x16", EX+, A13...$375.00

Nesbitt's, sign, tin, Drink & 5¢ above & below Nesbitt's on white band over bottle neck, black background, 1940s, 49x16", G, A13..$190.00

Nesbitt's, sign, tin, Drink Nesbitt's... on black left of tilted bottle & 5¢ dot, white border, 1940s, 19x55", VG, A13..$140.00

Nesbitt's, sign, tin, Drink...Made From Real Oranges & tilted bottle on black dot, yellow ground, curved corners, 24x24", NM, A13.............................$200.00

Nesbitt's, sign, tin, Nesbitt's on orange above tilted bottle on blue, curved corners, 26x7", EX, A8...............$80.00

Nesbitt's, sign, tin, Nesbitt's on white band over bottle neck, black background, 1940s, 48x16", EX+, A13........$300.00

Nesbitt's Hot Chocolate, warmer, stainless steel base, blue & white sign with yellow lettering on windmill blades that rotate, 16", EX+, A1......................................$85.00

Nestle Crunch, figure, bendable, 1967, VG, D27....$150.00

Nestle Quik, mug, molded plastic bunny head with ear handles, 1980s, 4½", M $15.00

Nestle Quik, pitcher, brown plastic with name embossed on side, bunny with twisted ears sits atop lid, 9½", M..$18.00

Nestle's Hot Cocoa, bank, metal & cardboard, shaped like cocoa container with allover graphics & lettering, VG, D24...$6.50

Nette Jung's, cigar box label, outer, 2 clowns playing tennis with cigars, 4½x4½", M, D5 ....$45.00

Neuman's Ice Cream, tray, woman eating ice cream with strawberry topping, lettering on decorative rim, 13½" dia, G, A9 ....$70.00

Neuweiler Beer & Ale, plaques, plaster relief, gents with frosty mugs leaning on kegs marked Beer & Ale, 12x10", EX, A8..**$110.00**

New Bachelor, cigar box label, printer's proof, man playing cards & having visions of lady in upper left, Victor Thorsch Co, EX, A5..**$75.00**

New Currency/P Lorillard Co, cigar cutter, metal with reverse-painted glass front, wood base, name flanked by 5¢ symbols, 4½x8", VG, A6................................**$450.00**

New Day, cigar box label, inner lid, sunrise over tobacco field, 1935, 6x9", M, D5..**$5.00**

New Departure Coaster Brake, postcard, King Of Them All arched above lion with bicycle brake in his mouth, EX+, D26..**$60.00**

New England Plug Smoke, tobacco tag, Martin's, EX, D35..**$4.00**

New Home Sewing Machine, sign, paper, comical image of boy hanging upside down while woman sews his pants, framed, image: 40x26", EX+, A9............**$1,200.00**

New Home Sewing Machine, sign, paper, plantation scene with women using machine, ...In The Sunny South upper right, framed, image: 22x16", VG, A9........**$450.00**

New Home Sewing Machine, sign, paper, woman holding up veil picturing the 'Light-Running' sewing machine, framed, 29½x21½", G-, A9................................**$150.00**

New Home Sewing Machine, tip tray, amusing image of mother sewing up pants of boy while he is still in them, lettering on rim, 4" dia, EX, A21.............**$210.00**

New King Snuff, pocket mirror, celluloid, pictures crock of snuff, 3x2", G+, A9..**$35.00**

New Lebanon Brewing Co Weiner Export Beer & Porter, sign, paper litho, company name arched above lady with glass & fan in seductive pose, framed, EX, A19..**$500.00**

New Method Book Bindery Inc, paperweight, celluloid, 'Bound To Stay Bound' above kitten, yellow, white & black, EX, A11..**$20.00**

New Orleans Brewing Ass'n, sign, paper, New Year's Greeting 1895 on building above bearded man on barrels with dogs at his feet, 28x17½", VG, A9....**$1,525.00**

New Orleans Minstrels, poster, Old Reliable... above encircled image of Lollypop & Sparky, 30x22", G, A6..**$60.00**

Newport Cigarettes, hat, embroidered name & insignia, 1980s, MIB, D24..**$8.00**

Newsboy, tobacco tag, Continental Tobacco Co, EX, D35..**$4.00**

Niagara Shoes, sign, tin over cardboard, oval inset of Niagara Falls above product name & For Youthful Feet..., 19x9", NOS, A6..**$150.00**

Nichol Kola, sign, tin, America's Taste Sensation, long-legged waiter serving 5¢ bottle, red & black on cream, 1936, 36x12", EX, A8..**$65.00**

Nichol Kola, sign, tin, America's Taste Sensation, long-legged waiter serving 5¢ bottle, red & black on cream, 1936, 36x12", VG, A8..**$45.00**

Nichol Kola, sign, tin, Drink above large bottle & America's Taste Sensation, 20x8", NM, D30................**$30.00**

Nick Thomas Bock Beer, label, Miami Valley Brewing Co, Internal Revenue Tax Paid statement, 1933-50, EX, A10..**$15.00**

Night Club Beer, label, Wayne Brewing Co, Internal Revenue Tax Paid statement, 1933-50, 12-oz, NM, A10.........**$25.00**

Nightingale, crate label, California apple, bird in apple tree with moon in dark sky, Watsonville, 9x11", M, D12..**$10.00**

Nine O'Clock Washing-Tea, sign, embossed tin, woman beside large box of product pointing to grandfather clock, 13½x14", rare, VG, A9................................**$4,250.00**

Nip Cigar/Jacob Stahl Jr & Co, tray, A 'Nip' Havana 5¢ above dog with plug of tobacco in mouth, decorative & lettered border, 12" dia, EX, A2................**$60.00**

No-Nox, sign, porcelain, New above No-Nox, 4-point star graphics with geometric border above, 18x11", NM, A7..**$35.00**

Nofade Shirts, matchbook, Boston Store, 20 strike, front strike, NM, D28..**$5.00**

Nokes & Nicolia, catalog, 1910, 96 pgs, EX, D17....**$100.00**

Nokomis Shoe, sign, Indian maiden at left of 2 styles of shoes, The Newest...Boots $2.50, Oxfords $2.00, framed, image: 17x14", G-, A9................................**$300.00**

Non-Chattering Oil for Old Style Ford, pail, black with yellow lettering, Sears, Roebuck & Co, press lid & bail, 13x12" dia, VG+, A6..**$30.00**

None Such Mince Meat, sign, tin, trademark image of stoic Indian Chief, Merrell & Soule, Syracuse NY, framed, image: 28x20", EX+, A9................................**$7,500.00**

None Such Mince Meat, thermometer, dial-type, degrees around name & 'Like Mother Used To Make' on pie-crust face, 9" dia, VG, A2................................**$145.00**

None Such Mince Meat Pumpkin & Squash, clock, tin & cardboard, numbers around name & 'Like Mother Used To Make' on pumpkin image, 9" dia, VG+, A2..**$525.00**

None Such Pumpkin, Concentrated Soup..., lantern, tin frame with glass inserts depicting lady holding a pie, a pumpkin & the American flag, tin roof, 18", EX, A2 ....**$2,310.00**

Nordia Fleur Sauvage (Wildflower) Poudre, tin, sample, lady among flowers against sky blue background, gold trim, ¼x1⅝" dia, EX, D37, minimum value.........**$40.00**

Nordlinger-Charlton Fireworks Co, canister, tin, red with black graphics, slip lid, 3x1¾" dia, EX+, A15......**$140.00**

North Star Lager Beer/Mathie-Ruder Brewing Co, label, oval with North Star arched above cavalier flanked by Lager & Beer, company name below, VG+, A19..**$15.00**

North Star Oil Limited, drinking glasses, clear with blue & red logo, set of 6, 5", MIB, D21.............................$70.00

North Ward Cigar, box label, outer, photo image of a bank, 1901, 4½x4½", EX, D5...............................$30.00

North Western Brewery/Allmalt & Bohemian Beer, mug, ceramic, circular logo with serrated edge above company name in script, product name below, black & maroon, EX+, A8........................$110.00

North Woods Egg Coffee, tin, Egg Coffee on oval center flanked by evergreen trees & coffeepot, key-wind lid, NM, A3 ....$30.00

North-Maid Rolled Oats, container, cardboard, yellow with North-Maid arched above standing girl, Rolled Oats on red band below, 3-lb, EX+, A3...............$45.00

North's Hams, Bacon & Lard, ruler, celluloid folding-type, A Good Rule, Use..., black & white, 12", EX, A11 .$12.00

Northeastern Lumber Co, pocket puzzle, celluloid, You Will Get Fair Treatment At The Old Fair Grounds..., blue on white, round, EX, A11 ....$25.00

Northern Beer, sign, self-framed tin, Remember...Northern Beer, We Made It Good...You Made It Famous, 6x13", VG+, A8 ....$45.00

Northern Trust Co Bank Chicago, bookmark/calendar, 1907, black & white key shape, 5x2", EX+, A11 ..$35.00

Northwest Airlines, flight bag, EX, D6 ....$20.00

Northwestern Mutual Life Insurance Co, sign, tin, city of Milwaukee with sailboats & steamboats entering & exiting busy port, framed, image: 20x28", G+, A9 ...$950.00

Norton's Pilsener Beer, label, TM Norton Brewing Co, Internal Revenue Tax Paid statement, 1933-50, 12-oz, NM, A10 ....$16.00

Norwalk Jewelry Co, calendar, 1907, die-cut image of cherub playing the violin surrounded by green leaves, complete, framed, 10x8", NM, A3 .....$105.00

Norwalk Lock Co, catalog, 1935, 287 pgs, EX, D17..$50.00

Nosegay, tobacco box label, image of woman with nosegay, 14x7", EX+, D9..$20.00

Nosler Premium Big Game Bullets, display sign, name above image of large moose in marsh with circular display of real bullets at right, 10x17", EX+, A3......$165.00

Nourse Friction Proof Heavy Duty Oil, can, image of Viking above product lettering, orange, black & white, 1-qt, EX, A1..$20.00

Nourse Friction Proof Homogenized & Reinforced Motor Oil, can, Viking above product lettering, green, black & white, 1-qt, EX+, A1 ....$40.00

Nourse Motor Oil, can, image of Viking above product lettering, green, yellow, black & brown, pour spout & handle, 1-gal, EX, A6 ....$100.00

Nourse Oil Co, can, image of Viking on green & white checked background, flat-sided with small screw cap, 1-qt, NM, A1 ....$20.00

Nourse's Hard Oil, pail, product lettering above & below Viking graphic flanked by rows of Vikings, bail handle, slip lid, 5-lb, NM, A1 ....$50.00

Nu-Icy, fan, cardboard, Cool Off! Drink... & Any Flavor Anytime... Anywhere flank bottle against water, EX, A16 ....$45.00

Nuchief, crate label, apple, Indian boy holding apple on blue background, M, D3....................................$3.00

Nucreme by Langfords, sign, porcelain, Hairdressing... New Tonic Hair Cream, 2-sided, 18x24", G+, A9 ....$100.00

Nugget, sign, tin, Double Size 5¢ above bottle, white background, 24x18", M, D30....................................$165.00

NuGrape, bottle opener, shows bottle, EX+, A16......$12.00

NuGrape, clock, light-up, black numbers around yellow logo over tilted bottle, metal frame, 15" dia, EX+, A13..$225.00

NuGrape, sign, cardboard, die-cut, bottle at left of sandwich & product name, 20x18", NM, D30.............$65.00

NuGrape, sign, tin, Drink at left of colorful bottle on yellow background, embossed, 31x12", VG, A9.....$200.00

NuGrape, sign, tin, Drink at left of colorful bottle on yellow background, 1930s, 12x4½", NM, A13........$180.00

NuGrape, sign, tin, Drink...A Flavor You Can't Forget above hand-held bottle, Demand It... on yellow, 1930s, 36x14", VG+, A13 ....$220.00

NuGrape, sign, tin, You Need A on ribbon banner around neck of bottle, green background, raised border, 1940s, 44x18", G+, A13 ....$180.00

NuGrape, tray, hand-held bottle against bright light on oval with yellow border, green ground, lettered rim, 1940s, 13x9", VG+, A..**$50.00**

Nun Nicer, cigar box label, outer, pictures a nun, 1905, NM, A5..**$110.00**

Nuso Crank-Case Flushing Service, sign, porcelain flange, lettering on diamond in center with We Extend above, Standard Oil Co below, 24x24", VG+, A6............**$325.00**

Nustad's Pointer Brand Coffee, tin, product name above pointer dog, key-wind lid, EX, A3........**$60.00**

Nut Brown Ale, label, Bartels Brewing Co, Internal Revenue Tax Paid statement, 1933-50, 12-oz, M, A10..........**$12.00**

Nut House of Lynn, tin, sample, shaped like house with trademark image of house on side, Home Of Good Nuts on roof, 2¼x2½", EX, D37............................**$75.00**

Nut Tootsie Rolls, product box, full unused box of large foil wrapped Nut Tootsie Roll logs, 1920s (?), EX, A15..**$375.00**

Nutmeg State Ale, label, Eastern Brewing Corporation, Internal Revenue Tax Paid statement, 1933-50, 12-oz, M, A10..**$22.00**

Nyal's Toilet Talcum & Baby Powder, tin, shows encircled photo image of young girl, yellow with red & gold trim, shaker top, VG, A3......................................**$45.00**

✺✺✺ O ✺✺✺

O! Boy Peanut Butter, pail, tin, children's scenes in black, white & green on green, slip lid & bail, 1-lb, NM, A15 ....**$925.00**

O-Cedar, can, O-Cedar above woman spraying for bugs, text lower left, flip top, copyright 1929, ½-pt, NM+, A1 ....**$35.00**

O-So-Gud Butter Pretzels/National Biscuit Co, store tin, Good & Salty above pretzel at right of sea captain & boy in slicker, product name below, 18x12" dia, EX, A2 ....**$135.00**

O-So-Gud Pretzels/National Biscuit Co, sign, paper, Good & Salty... & pretzel twists at left of sea captain & boy in yellow slicker, framed, 14x23", VG+, A2.....**$155.00**

O'Baby Chocolate Dairy Drink, sign, cardboard, ...Ain't Dat Sumptin!, colorful image of black boy holding bottle & licking his lips, 22½x14", G, A6 ....**$65.00**

O'Keefe's Ale, thermometer/sign, tin on cardboard, O'Keefe's above dial & bottle, Ale & Imported From Canada below, 9x13", VG+, A19 ....**$30.00**

O'Sullivan's Heels, trolley sign, cardboard, 8000 Times A Day... above text, man's pant leg & shoe at left, heel at right, 11x21", EX+, A1 ....**$10.00**

O'Sullivan's Heels, trolley sign, open touring car with driver meeting horse-drawn buggy above text & large heel, 1920s, 10x20", EX+, A1 ....**$75.00**

Oak Hill Coffee, tin, oval image of mansion & trees, no lid, VG, A3 ....**$110.00**

Oakite, sign, die-cut cardboard, Here It Is! on circle behind woman & sign, ...Cleans A Million Things, 36x22", EX, D8 ....**$450.00**

Oakland Service Pontiac, sign, porcelain, white lettering on blue background, 2-sided, 24x35½", EX+, A6......**$350.00**

Oakley's Corilopsis of Japan Talc Powder, tin, sample, Japanese lady with parasol, blue & green with gold trim, 2⅛x1⅛x⅞", EX, D37 ....**$60.00**

Oasis Cigarettes, store bin, wood & glass, repeated images & lettering, elongated rectangle, VG+, A18..........**$65.00**

Occident Flour, thermometer, wood, product & company name encircled above bulb, ...Makes Better Bread below, 15", VG, A6 ....**$160.00**

Ockwork Metal Polish/Texas Co, can, Texaco star logo above name & image of man using product, company name below, green, 1-gal, EX, A8 ....**$1,500.00**

Octagan Scouring Cleanser, can, sample, cardboard & tin, with contents, 2½", NM, A7 ....**$55.00**

Oertels '92 Beer, display figure, plaster, bear on icy rocks with base reading Cheerful Refreshment & Oertels '92 Beer, 14", EX, D14..**$95.00**

Oertels '92 Beer, sign, tin over cardboard, round with red, white & black product name on gold ground, 9" dia, EX, A8 ....**$55.00**

Oertels '92 Beer, tray, shows bottles & full glasses with tray of cold cuts & other party food, plain rim, 12x17", VG, A8 ....**$20.00**

Oertels '92 Lager Beer, can, cone-top, filigree border around product name, NM, A8............................**$35.00**

Oertels '92 Old Style Bock Beer, sign, paper, product name over goat & circle with geometric lined background, framed, 9x11", EX, A8 ....**$75.00**

Oertels Bock Beer, label, product name above & below goat's head on yellow circle, 12-oz, VG+, A19 ....**$12.00**

Oertels Lager Beer, label, Just A Nip in diagonal script over brown jug against spider web, 12-oz, VG+, A19..**$6.00**

Oh Boy Gum, sign, tin, fairy whispering in boy's ear, his hand fanning 4 sticks of gum, 1¢ It's Pure! below, 15½x7", EX, A6..**$220.00**

Oh Boy Gum, sign, tin, fairy whispering in boy's ear, his hand fanning 4 sticks of gum, 1¢ It's Pure! below, 15½x7", VG, A9..**$150.00**

Oh Boy Gum, sign, tin, It's Pure Elle Est Pure diagonally above product name & gnomes on diagonal band, 1¢ below, 13x16", G, A6 ....**$175.00**

Oh Mama Louisiana Porto Rican Sweet Potatoes, label, shows product name at right of black mother with 2 children & goat hanging out the laundry, 9x9", NM, A7 ....$22.00

Ohio Blue Tip Matches, pocket mirror, factory scene with large box of matches in the foreground, 3½" dia, EX+, A3 ....$80.00

Oil Cabinet Co, oil cabinet, wood with tin interior, stenciled lettering on front, 48x31x22" missing slant top front otherwise EX, A6 ....$425.00

Oil Creek Petroleum Products, can, product name & creek in center, orange, green & black, 1-qt, EX, A6.....$160.00

Oildag/Gredag, ad, Oildag Increases Mileage..., shows open-cab truck hauling boxes, large Gredag can below, framed, 20x12", VG+, A2 ....$265.00

Oildag/Gredag, ad, Oildag Makes A Motor Boat Run Like Velvet, shows speeding boat, large Gredag can below, framed, 20x12", EX, A2 ....$330.00

Oilzum, can, Oilzum man's face within the O of Oilzum, shaped to fit under car seat, pour spout & handle, 5x13x3", VG+, A6 ....$600.00

Oilzum, charts, each picture Oilzum man's face at top, set of 7, D8............................$600.00

Oilzum, patch, Oilzum man's face with lettering on cap, orange, white & black, 5½x5½", EX+, A6 ....$135.00

Oilzum, sample cylinders, glass with cork stoppers, complete set of 6 in vinyl case with velvet interior, EX, A6 ..$275.00

Oilzum, see also Winter Oilzum

Oilzum Motor Oil, can, triangular logo with Oilzum man's face, Choice of Champions below, full, 1-qt, 5½x4" dia, EX+, A6 ....$50.00

Oilzum Motor Oil, clock, light-up, Oilzum man's face & Choice Of Champions logo in center, blue, orange & white, 14" dia, NM, A6..............$650.00

Oilzum Motor Oil, clock, plastic with metal back, 12-3-6-9 clock above tilted oil can & Choice Of Champions, electric, 19x12", NOS, A6...................................$300.00

Oilzum Motor Oil, patch, inverted triangle with product name above Oilzum man, orange, white & black, EX+, A6 ....$20.00

Oilzum Motor Oil, sign, tin, Oilzum lettered vertically above Motor Oil on black, Oilzum man in letter O, decal letters, 61x13", EX, A6..........................$775.00

Oilzum Motor Oil, sign, tin, Oilzum man logo at left of Motor Oil, Choice Of Champions! on band below, self-framed, 15x36", NM, A1 ....$185.00

Oilzum Motor Oil, sign, tin, product name above Oilzum man on inverted triangle with curved top, orange, dated 4-49, 21x19", EX+, A1 ....$360.00

Oilzum Motor Oil, sign, tin, product name above Oilzum man on inverted triangle with curved top, orange ground, 21x19", VG, A6 ....$180.00

Oilzum Motor Oil, thermometer, Choice Of Champion Race Drivers above Oilzum man & bulb, company name below, 15x7½", VG, A9 ....$375.00

Oilzum Motor Oils & Lubricants, pail, Oilzum man with product name & lettering on his cap, yellow, black & cream, wire bail, 5-gal, 15x10" dia, G, A6 ....$20.00

Oilzum Motor Oils & Lubricants, sign, porcelain, Oilzum man with product & company name on hat above America's Finest Oil, 28x20", G-, A9 ....$300.00

Oilzum Special Motor Oil, can, waxed cardboard, triangular logo with Oilzum man's face, Special in script, 1-qt, VG, A6 ....$40.00

Ojibwa Fine Cut Tobacco, tin, yellow with red & white lettering above image of Indian holding tobacco leaves, 2x6" dia, NM, A18 ....$240.00

Old Abe Chewing Tobacco, tin, eagle on shield above portrait of Abraham Lincoln, 2x8" dia, EX, A18 .$550.00

Old Abe Chewing Tobacco, tin, eagle on shield above portrait of Abraham Lincoln, 2x8" dia, G+, A9.$400.00

Old Baldy Mild Blended Stogie, tin, white with red & blue lettered label, ...Broad Leaf Wrapper, 2 For 5, Berdan & Co, vertical square, EX, A18 ....$275.00

Old Barbee Whiskey, tray, deep-dish, 'College Widow,' girl in plaid coat & feathered hat, lettering on rim, oval, 16x13", VG, A9 ....$150.00

189

Old Bavarian Beer & Hoot-Mon Ale/Sunbury Brewing Co, fan, fold-out type, bird & flower motif, Keep Cool Drink..., VG+, A8.................................**$85.00**

Old Black Joe Speckled Butter Beans, can label, both sides show name above black man with large bowl of beans, 4x9¾", NM, A7.................................**$5.00**

Old Bond Cigars, tin, oval portrait of George Washington flanked by As Good As A Bond, Now 2 For 5¢ below, slip lid, 5½x6", G+, A9.................................**$35.00**

Old Chum Tobacco, sign, paper, sketched image of lady in large hat resting face on muff, Smoke... below, framed, 30x19", EX, A18...............$165.00

Old Cincinnati Lager Beer/Old Jackson Brewery, display label, Old Cincinnati lettered on brick entryway to cask room, other product lettering below, VG+, A19.................................**$355.00**

Old Colony Beverages, sign, celluloid, Enjoy in diagonal letters above Old Colony, Beverages below, 9" dia, NM, A13.................................**$45.00**

Old Colony Beverages, sign, tin, Old Colony in white on red wavy banner, Beverages in black, blue background, 18x54", NM, D30.................................**$120.00**

Old Colony Beverages, sign, tin, tilted bottle & Ask For Your Favorite Flavor flank sign, 1948, 17x47", NM+, A13.................................**$125.00**

Old Company's Lehigh Anthracite, sign, die-cut porcelain, product name on circle above It Lasts Longer!, red, white & blue, 12x12", EX, A6.................................**$160.00**

Old Crow Whiskey, decanter, Royal Doulton ceramic, dapperly-dressed black crow on base, 1955, 13½", EX, A8.................................**$45.00**

Old Crow Whiskey, display figure, molded plastic, dapperly-dressed black crow on gray base marked Old Crow, 11", VG+, A21.................................**$40.00**

Old Crown Ale & Beer, sign, composition, simulated wood emblem with Lazy & Aged flanking elf on cloud above product name, 12x16", EX, A8.................................**$70.00**

Old Dad Cigars, tin, paper label with name above oval portrait, round with slip lid, ca 1900, EX, A18...**$170.00**

Old Derby Ale, label, Peoples Brewing Co, Internal Revenue Tax Paid statement, 1933-50, 8-oz, NM, A10..........**$20.00**

Old Derby Ale, label, Ripon Brewing Co, U-type permit number, Internal Revenue Tax Paid statement, 1933-36, 12-oz, M, A10.................................**$22.00**

Old Dutch, sign, tin on cardboard, Time For above Old Dutch On Tap on red oval above clocks indicating business hours, EX, A19.................................**$150.00**

Old Dutch Cleanser, can, sample, cardboard & tin, 3", NM, A7.................................**$75.00**

Old Dutch Cleanser, sign, curved metal, can shape with Dutch girl logo on yellow, product name on red below, 1910s-20s, 32x19", VG+, A13.......$625.00

Old Dutch Lager Beer, can, flat-top, red, Metropolis Brewing Co, 12-oz, EX, A19.................................**$12.00**

Old Dutch Premium Beer, menu board, tin, ...Order Old Dutch 'Low In Calories' & winking man with mug above blackboard, red on white, EX+, A19..........**$40.00**

Old English Curve Cut Pipe Tobacco, charger, tin, name above image of Englishman in red jacket smoking long-stemmed pipe, green ground, 24" dia, EX, A21.**$275.00**

Old English Curve Cut Pipe Tobacco, store bin, tin, red with white panels, oval portrait flanked by product name on front, rectangular, flat top, VG+, A18..**$270.00**

Old Export Beer, thermometer, dial-type with numbers encircling Old Export emblem, red & black on white, 6" dia, EX+, A8.................................**$25.00**

Old Faithful Beer, ashtray, tin rim with glass bottom, company name & town on rim, product name below frothy glass in center, round, G+, A8.................................**$80.00**

Old Faithful Beer, coaster/dish, clear glass with blue advertising in center, 4" dia, NM, A8.................................**$60.00**

Old Faithful Pale Beer, label, Old Faithful on diagonal blue band, geyser in oval upper left, company name lower right on yellow, 24-oz, EX, A19.................................**$30.00**

Old Fashion Beer/Billings Brewing Co, ashtray, metal with glass insert, red with white & black lettering, 4½" dia, EX+, A8.................................**$325.00**

Old Fashion Beer/Billings Brewing Co, label, product name above scene with 2 men being served flanked by 4 oval vignettes, red background, 12-oz, VG, A19.....**$30.00**

Old Fashion Beer/Billings Brewing Co, tip tray/coaster, red with white & black lettering, 4" dia, EX, A8 ..**$380.00**

Old Georgetown Beer/Christian Heurich Brewing Co, can, flat-top, 12-oz, EX+, A19.................................**$25.00**

Old German Beer, label, Burkhardt Brewing Co, Internal Revenue Tax Paid statement, 1933-50, 12-oz, M, A10..$15.00

Old German Bock Beer, sign, paper, The Original Old German above ram's head, record marked Best On Record Bock Beer below, 22x17", VG+, A8.........$20.00

Old German Lager, drinking glass, barrel shape with etched lettering & graphics, Independent Brewing Co, NM, A8..$40.00

Old German Lager, tray, deep-dish, pictures half-length cavalier holding up mug, lettered rim, Independent Brewing Co, EX, A19 ....$155.00

Old Glory Tobacco, pocket tin, flat, red with black lettering & graphics with circular eagle logo, rounded corners, VG+, A18.............................$450.00

Old Gold Beer, can, flat-top, Internal Revenue Tax Paid statement, 12-oz, G+, A19...................................$55.00

Old Gold Beer, label, Imperial Brewing Co, Internal Revenue Tax Paid statement, 1933-50, 12-oz, M, A10............$10.00

Old Gold Cigarettes, bridge scorer, 1933, NM, A18..$10.00

Old Gold Cigarettes, sign, cardboard, Old Gold Cigarettes, Not A Cough, red & blue on yellow, 2-sided, 19x30", EX, A18 ....$305.00

Old Gold Cigarettes, sign, porcelain, Old Gold Cigarettes, Not A Cough In A Carload, red & blue on yellow, 1930s, 12x36", EX+, A13 ....$250.00

Old Gold Cigarettes, Riled By A Raccoon Rah-Rah? ...Light An Old Gold, For Young Ideas! above, 1920s, 43x32", EX, A6 ....$375.00

Old Gold Cigarettes, tin, holds 50 cigarettes, 2¾" dia, NM, A7 ....$75.00

Old Gold Special, sign, paper litho, Not A Cough In A Carload, passengers enjoy Old Golds at rear of train, Earl Christy, 31x21", EX, A12 ....$700.00

Old Grand-Dad Whiskey, display, rubber, bust of eldery gent on lettered base, 12", VG, A8.....................$20.00

Old Heidelberg, sign, die-cut cardboard, bottle, glass & sandwich on elegant serving tray, 9x11", VG+, A8.........$30.00

Old Hill Side/RC Owen Co, tobacco pouch, cloth, paper label, with contents, EX, A7 ....$20.00

Old Homestead Ale, label, Commercial Brewing Co, U-type permit number, Internal Revenue Tax Paid statement, 1933-36, 12-oz, M, A10 ....$15.00

Old Honesty, tobacco tag, pictures a dog, round, EX, D35..$18.00

Old Honesty Plug Tobacco, sign, paper, elderly couple looking at letter with caricature drawing, Calvert Litho Co, framed, 20x20", VG+, A18 ....$165.00

Old India Pale Ale, label, Commercial Brewing Co, U-type permit number, Internal Revenue Tax Paid statement, 1933-36, 12-oz, M, A10...............................$15.00

Old Jackson Beer/Squibb-Pattison Brewers Inc, display label, round with product lettering around image of rider on rearing horse, VG+, A19.......................$350.00

Old Judge Cigarettes, trade card, die-cut, white-bearded face with monacle, product name on collar, Goodwin & Co, 6x4", G, A5..$55.00

Old Judge Coffee, tin, 'Settles The Question,' red with product name above & below round image of owl, slip lid, 1-lb, EX+, A18 ....$115.00

Old Judge Coffee, tin, encircled owl flanked by Vacuum Packed in center, key-wind lid, EX+, A3.............$45.00

Old Judson Whiskey/JG Stevens, match holder, tin, colorful image of girl offering dad a glass, rounded corners, 5x3½", EX, A6 ....$180.00

Old Kentucky 'Sport-Work' Shirts, sign, Old Kentucky in script above log cabin, 'Sport-Work' Shirts below, 14x10", VG, A7 ....$15.00

Old Kentucky Root Beer, mug, brown barrel shape with black hands & logo, 4x3", EX, D16....................$10.00

Old Kentucky Root Beer, pitcher, image of man & horse, brown & black, 8½x4", NM, D16........................$65.00

Old King Beer, label, Southwestern Brewing Co, Internal Revenue Tax Paid statement, 1933-50, 12-oz, NM, A10..$15.00

Old King Cole Beer, label, Pittsburgh Brewing Co, Internal Revenue Tax Paid statement, 1933-50, 12-oz, M, A10..$22.00

Old King Cole Beer, sign, tin over cardboard stand-up, logo above product name, red, black & white on brown, beveled edge, 9x11", G+, A8....................$95.00

Old King Cole Genuine Key West Havana Cigars, box label, inner lid, Old King Cole on throne, Maxfield Parrish, rare, VG+, A5 ....$365.00

Old King Cole Lager, label, Pittsburgh Brewing Co, Internal Revenue Tax Paid statement, 1933-50, 12-oz, M, A10..$14.00

Old King Quality Beer, sign, paper litho, Drink... above outdoor night scene with gentleman & 2 ladies at table on terrace, gold frame, EX, A19 ....$260.00

Old Loyalty Smoking Tobacco, cigarette papers, NM, A7 ....$35.00

Old Manor Chili Powder, tin, image of mansion & trees on red background, 2-oz, NM+, A3 ....$35.00

Old Manor Coffee, tin, image of mansion & trees in center, key-wind lid, EX+, A3 ....$65.00

Old Master, cigar box label, inner lid, red, blue & bronze, 6x9", EX, D5..$4.00

Old Master Coffee, tin, gold & yellow with oval portrait, round with pry lid, 1-lb, EX, A18........$175.00

Old Mill Smoking Tobacco, cigarette papers, NM, A7 ..$60.00

Old Milwaukee Beer, hat, baseball-type, corduroy with embroidered front, EX+, D24 ....$5.00

Old Milwaukee Beer, salt & pepper shakers, bottle shape, NM, A8 ....$100.00

Old Milwaukee Beer, sign, tin, Old Milwaukee above bottle, Real Beer Flavor below, dark blue background, red border, 1930, 40x14", NM+, A19 ....$480.00

Old Milwaukee Beer, sign, tin, Tastes As Great As It's Name, can shape with early-looking label, 1971, 23x15", EX, A8..**$30.00**

Old Milwaukee Beer, sign, tin, Tastes Like Draught Beer, ...At A Popular Price, glass, bottle & can on keg, beveled edge, 16x11", EX+, A8 ....**$175.00**

Old Mission, crate label, California orange, padres gathering to squeeze oranges, Fullerton, 10x11", M, D12.......**$18.00**

Old Mountaineer Beer, label, Pioneer Brewing Co, Internal Revenue Tax Paid statement, 1933-50, ½-gal, NM, A10 ....**$26.00**

Old Mr Boston Fine Liquors, clock, wood with key-wind mechanism, bottle shape with jigger cap, lettering above & below clock face, 23", G, A21 ....**$55.00**

Old North State Smoking Tobacco, pouch, paper label, with contents, 1 ½-oz, NM, A7...............................**$22.00**

Old North State Smoking Tobacco, sign, embossed tin, name above tilted pack, 2 men looking up, Always Fresh, Mild & Mellow, 1920s-30s, 28x20", EX, A13.......**$1,250.00**

Old Overholt Rye, sign, oilette on canvas, jolly fellow pouring glass of whiskey, framed, image: 30x18½", G+, A9 ....**$90.00**

Old Port Lager, label, product name above multiscene label, 12-oz, VG+, A19 ....**$30.00**

Old Ranger Beer & Ale/Hornell Brewing Co, tray, deep-dish, product name above & below Davy Crockett-type figure on 2-color background, 12" dia, VG+, A8..**$35.00**

Old Reading, sign, light-up, reverse glass, Relax With- above 2 gents with mugs & Old Reading on wood- grain arched panel, NM, A19.....................$1,900.00

Old Reading 'PR' Juniors, sign, tin, product name lettered on blackboard with wood-looking & rope border, 10x13", EX, A19 ....**$25.00**

Old Reading Beer, sign, cardboard, men visiting couple at table by fireside, Old Reading Beer lower right, wood frame, 27x34", G+, A8....................................**$20.00**

Old Reading Beer, sign, porcelain, Good... on plus-shaped sign, Traditionally Pennsylvania Dutch below, brown on white, 12x15", EX, A8 ....**$40.00**

Old Reading Beer, tray, deep-dish, Say!, pictures dog begging for mug of beer from bartender atop product name, round, EX+, A19 ....**$80.00**

Old Reading Cream Ale, label, green with 2 old barkeeps atop product name, 12-oz, EX+, A19...................**$16.00**

Old Reliable, tobacco tag, EX, D35 ....**$3.00**

Old Reliable Coffee, pocket mirror, product name arched above dock worker resting on coffee crate, round, VG+, A8 ....**$40.00**

Old Reliable Coffee, sign, cardboard, man with pipe above lettering & product box, Always The Same & Always Good, 1920s, 21x11", NM, A3..................**$85.00**

Old Reliable Coffee, sign, tin, Always Good upper left of old sea merchant with pipe above product box, 1910-12, 9x6½", NM+, A13 ....**$350.00**

Old Reliable Coffee, sign, tin on cardboard, product name & Always The Same-Always Good on wood-grain, beveled edge, 6x13", EX+, A13 ....**$45.00**

Old Reliable Coffee, tip tray, colorful image of lady ready to sip from cup, gold lettering around rim, 1911, 4" dia, EX, A21 ....**$120.00**

Old Reliable Pilsner Beer, label, lighthouse image with product name on green, 12-oz, VG+, A19.............**$5.00**

Old Rockford Beer, label, Warsaw Brewing Co, Internal Revenue Tax Paid statement, 1933-50, 12-oz, M, A10....**$20.00**

Old Schenley Whiskey, sign, tin, 'I've Struck the Trail,' hunter with rifle beside tree, framed, image: 27½x19½", G, A9 ....$375.00

Old Sport, cigar box label, printer's proof, smiling man with cigar, Three For Five Cents, American Stogie Co, EX, A5 ....**$45.00**

Old Squire Pipe Tobacco, see Tucketts

Old Statesman Cut Plug Smoking Tobacco, tin, lettering around stern-looking bust portrait, Buffalo Tobacco Works, rectangular, square corners, EX+, A18...**$425.00**

Old Style Brew, label, Schutz & Hilgers J Brewery, Internal Revenue Tax Paid statement, 1933-50, 12-oz, M, A10 ....**$15.00**

Old Style Lager, cigarette dispenser/sign, exterior monk scene with product name below, slots for cigarette packs, 13x22", VG, A8...**$35.00**

Old Style Lager, coaster, 'Paul Revere' on horse shouting I'm Asking For The Beer With A 'Snap' To It, orange & black, 4¼" dia, EX, A8 ....**$40.00**

Old Style Lager Beer, can, cone-top, scene of men working above product name on red & black bands, G+, A3 ....**$22.00**

Old Tap Ale-Bohemian Beer, tray, deep-dish, Select & Stock flank encircled gent with glass above product names, 12" dia, EX+, A19......................................**$75.00**

Old Timer, lug box label, various fruit, prospector's donkey loaded with mining supplies, Tracy, M, D12...**$3.00**

Old Timer Lager Beer, tap knob, chrome ball shape with red & gold on blue enamel insert, EX, A8 ....**$155.00**

Old Topper Ale, tap knob, black knob with black, brown & gold on cream enameled insert, EX, A8 ....**$65.00**

Old Town Beer, label, Denmark Brewing Co, Internal Revenue Tax Paid statement, 1933-50, 12-oz, M, A10 .**$10.00**

Old Town Canoe Co, salesman's sample, green canoe with red lettering, original decals on both sides, 50" long, EX+, A9......**$8,500.00**

Old Town Lager Beer, coaster, The Beer Of Good Cheer above Old Town..., Denmark Brewing Co below in brown on octagon, EX, A8 ....**$35.00**

Old Union Beer, label, New Orleans Brewing Co, Internal Revenue Tax Paid statement, 1933-50, 12-oz, M, A10 ....**$12.00**

Old Virginia Catsup, fan, die-cut cardboard, mammy's face with lettering on turban, nose cut out for thumb, framed, image: 10x9", VG, A9 ....**$250.00**

Old Virginia Cheroots, cigar box, 3 For 5¢, Beware Of Imitations, 7x12", VG, A7....................**$75.00**

Old Virginia Cheroots, sign, cardboard, white-bearded black man reciting The Rose Is Red, The Violets Blue..., 10½x6½", NM, A13 ....**$350.00**

Old 76 Distilling Co, sign, paper, woman handing a drink to soldier on horse, 28½x20", G, A9....................**$50.00**

Oldbru Bock Beer, label, Detroit Brewing Co, Internal Revenue Tax Paid statement, 1933-50, 12-oz, EX, A10....................**$25.00**

Olds Gasoline Engine Works, thermometer, dial-type, glass with metal frame, pictures early engine, 6" dia, VG+, D22....................**$150.00**

Oldsmobile Six & Eight, brochure, has all available Oldsmobiles, accessories, services, etc, full color, 9½x7", VG+, A6....................**$40.00**

Oliver Chilled Plow Works, pocket mirror, celluloid, image of James Oliver (founder), oval, EX, A11 ..**$85.00**

Oliver Chilled Plows, sign, self-framed embossed tin, store owner talking to man on horse in front of business, wood frame, 33x22", VG, A2 ....**$880.00**

Oliver Typewriter Ribbon, tin, vertical, dark green lettered label with decorative border, slip lid, 2x1⅝x1⅝", EX, D37, minimum value....................**$75.00**

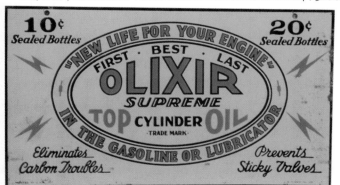

Olixir Supreme Top Cylinder Oil, sign, tin, product name & other lettering on oval with lettering in each corner, red & black on yellow, 9x16", NM, D8 .....$400.00

Olo Soap Powder, string holder, Take Home above product box on blue, You Use Less Because It's Concentrated below, 17", VG+, A2....................**$440.00**

Olson Rug Co, catalog, 1937, 58 pgs, EX, D17..........**$30.00**

Olt's Cream Ale, label, Olt Bros Brewing Co, Internal Revenue Tax Paid statement, 1933-50, 12-oz, M, A10....................**$15.00**

Olt's Superba Beer, label, Olt Bros Brewing Co, U-type permit number, Internal Revenue Tax Paid statement, 1933-36, 12-oz, M, A10....................**$40.00**

Olympia Beer, sign, light-up, reverse-painted glass, Olympia Beer & It's The Water left of waterfall within horseshoe, 12x26", NM, A1....................**$135.00**

Olympia Beer, tray, deep-dish, pictures serving girl with tray through hole in end of wooden keg, round, VG+, A19....................**$100.00**

Olympia Beer, tray, deep-dish, shows cavalier with bottle & full glass, round, VG, A8....................**$30.00**

Olympia Light Beer, sign, plastic, trout on wood-grain shield, oval label below, Keep Our Forests Green..., 23", G+, A8....................**$25.00**

Olympia Motor Oil, can, pictures spilling oil can, 2500 Mile Guarantee, yellow, white & black, screw cap & handle, 2-gal, 11x8", EX+, A3....................**$100.00**

Olympic Club, cigar box label, outer, winged oval, 4½x4½", EX, D5....................**$10.00**

Olympic Cola, sign, tin, snow skier above Olympic on red diagonal band, white background with blue border, NM+, D30 ....**$225.00**

Omaha Brewing Ass'n Export Beer, mug, ceramic, Omaha Brewing Ass'n arched above large leaf with circular elf inset, Export Beer below, 6", EX, A8....**$100.00**

Omar, cigar box label, inner lid, Arab on prayer rug, camels & bay, 6x9", M, D5....................**$7.00**

Omar Turkish Blend Cigarettes, sign, cardboard, 'The Joy Of Life,' shows 2 dapper gents smoking, 20 For 15¢, framed, 21x15", VG+, A21....................$220.00

Omar Turkish Blend Cigarettes, sign, tin, All That A Perfect Cigarette Should Be flanked by unopened pack & 20 For 15¢, name above, 8x14", EX+, A18 ....**$115.00**

Omega Tobacco, canister, tin, product name on diagonal red field above smoking pipe on diagonal blue field, slip lid with knob, EX, A18 ....**$170.00**

Omega Watch, sign, tin, logo at left of The Omega Watch Of Matchless Merit, C Shonk litho, EX+, A3........**$75.00**

On Parade Fine Tobacco, box label, On Parade above profile of soldier with sword, Fine Tobacco & Made in America below, Hone litho, 14", NM, A7..............**$30.00**

On Rush Vegetables, crate label, girl with skirt blowing in the breeze, 7x9", M, D12....................**$6.00**

One-Eleven Cigarettes, cigarette carton, unformed panel for top & ends, VG+, A18 ....$40.00

Oneida Ale, label, oval, 12-oz, EX+, A19 ....$10.00

Oneida Lager, label, oval, 12-oz, EX+, A19 ....$10.00

Ontario Brand Peanut Butter, pail, ocean view with product name above & below, geometric band top & bottom, EX+, A3 ....$155.00

Opaline Motor Oil/Sinclair Refining Co, can, race car with logo on grille above product & company name, green, cream & black, pour spout & handle, 1-gal, EX, A6 ....$650.00

Opel, sign, neon, yellow & white, in original crate, 24" dia, no transformer, scarce, NOS, A6 ....$230.00

Open Manor Pipe Mixture, pocket tin, short vertical, white product lettering over gold & brown image of large estate, EX+, A18 ....$150.00

Opler Brothers Breakfast Cocoa, tin, sample, Opler Brothers on band encircling boy sitting on cocoa bean, slip lid, 3¼x2¼x1⅜", EX, D37 ....$60.00

OPM The Perfect Pipe Tobacco, pocket tin, vertical, black with white lettering above blue & white label with triangular logo & company name, EX, A18 ....$200.00

Orange Blossoms, sign, tin, oval image of bottle at left of Drink...In Bottles Only, horizontal, EX+, A16 ....$125.00

Orange Julep, window display, It's Julep Time, bathing beauty with glass & parasol flanked by 2 glasses on signs, 1920s-30s, EX+, A13 ....$750.00

Orange Julius, sign, die-cut masonite, Cool & Smooth flank devil logo above product sizes & prices on white, 36x24", EX, A13 ....$150.00

Orange Julius, sign, porcelain, product name above orange devil logo, A Devilish Good Drink below, 1920s, 34x24", rare, EX+, A13 ....$800.00

Orange Kist, sign, die-cut cardboard stand-up, image of elves working hard to fill large bottle, Drink... Ice Cold..., 11x9", NM, A13 ....$65.00

Orange Kist, sign, tin, Drink Orange Kist & Other Kist Beverage, pictures bottle & oranges, 1940s-50s, 28x10", EX+, A13 ....$120.00

Orange Kist, see also Kist Beverages

Orange Pekoe & Pekoe Jack Sprat Tea, tin, image of Jack Sprat on front & back, oriental scenes on sides, slip lid, 8-oz, 5x3x3", EX, A3 ....$155.00

Orange Special Soda, bottle topper, emblem surrounded by flowers, 7½x7¼", NM, A7 ....$5.00

Orange Squeeze, sign, tin, Drink Orange Squeeze above unopened bottle, In Bottles Only below, 1930s, 36x12", EX+, A13 ....$90.00

Orange Squeeze, sign, tin, tilted bottle flanked by product name, With The True Fruit Flavor below, yellow background, 12x28", NM+, D30 ....$135.00

Orange-Crush, bottle opener, metal Crushy figure, NM+, A16 ....$16.00

Orange-Crush, bottler opener/spoon, metal, EX, A16 ....$40.00

Orange-Crush, card hanger for phone numbers, lined board with Telephone Numbers above Crushy & bottle, vertical, EX+, A16 ....$40.00

Orange-Crush, decal, large amber bottle, 30x9", EX+, A16 ....$35.00

Orange-Crush, dispenser, steel with porcelain sides, Drink...Fruit Flavored Drink Ice Cold, Crushy knob atop, 20x17", NM, A13 ....$2,100.00

Orange-Crush, door plate, porcelain, French, Revenez Merci in yellow above & below Orange-Crush on red circle, 9x3½", NM, D21 ....$175.00

Orange-Crush, sign, cardboard, die-cut, Hi! Have An Orange-Crush on orange behind bathing beauty with bottle, 1920s, 40x30", VG, D36 ....$500.00

Orange-Crush, sign, cardboard, New! & bottle left of Glorious Golden Orange-Crush & text, Crushy & Served Here below, 14x11", EX, A16 ....$80.00

Orange-Crush, sign, cardboard hanger, amber bottle with enlarged diamond-shaped label, 9", NM+, A16 ....$60.00

Orange-Crush, sign, cardboard stand-up, New Bigger Flavor Guarding Bottle, frowning sun above bottle holding umbrella, 23x17", VG+, A1 ....$190.00

Orange-Crush, sign, celluloid, Orange-Crush Carbonated Beverages, Crushy singing a tune, 9" dia, EX, A8 ....$500.00

Orange-Crush, sign, celluloid button, Enjoy Orange-Crush on orange band, white background, 9" dia, EX, A3 ......$50.00

Orange-Crush, sign, flange, Drink upper left of Orange-Crush & bottle in snow mound, orange sky, 1930s-40s, 14x22", EX, A13 ....$250.00

Orange-Crush, sign, flange, There's Only One Orange-Crush, We Sell It! 5¢, 1930s, 8x18½", EX, A4 .....$225.00

Orange-Crush, sign, neon, Drink... on round glass lens arched above bottle & oranges, Made With... below, 1930s, 18" dia, NM, A13 ....$1,800.00

Orange-Crush, sign, paper, As Wholesome As Sunshine, product name above ballerina, 1936, 32x14", EX, A16 ....$300.00

Orange-Crush, sign, paper, As Wholesome As Sunshine, product name above ballerina, 1936, 32x14", NM+, D30 ....$450.00

Orange-Crush, sign, paper, It's Here! upper left of Orange-Crush & 6-pack, In The Big New Bottle below, 11x29", NM, A16 ....$45.00

Orange-Crush, sign, paper, Tonight... over vase of roses at left of bottle, glass & cake, Orange Sherbet lower right, 14x22", NM, D21 ....$30.00

Orange-Crush, sign, tin, bottle cap, Enjoy Orange-Crush, 18" dia, EX, A6 ....$195.00

Orange-Crush, sign, tin, bottle cap, Enjoy Orange-Crush, 36" dia, NM, A13 ....$525.00

Orange-Crush, sign, tin, die-cut, New Flavor Guarding Bottle on neck label, ribbed bottle with diamond-shaped label, 1930s, NM+, D4 ....$650.00

Orange-Crush, sign, tin, Drink Orange-Crush Carbonated Beverage & bottle on circle over perforated background, 1938, 36x30", VG+, A13 ....$850.00

Orange-Crush, sign, tin, Drink... on orange diamond above tilted bottle, Flavor Sealed In Brown Bottles below, 1940s, 48x18", NM, A13 ....**$750.00**

Orange-Crush, sign, tin, Enjoy & Orange-Crush on oval above tilted bottle on blue & white, beveled edges, 1950s-60s, 54x18", NM, A13 ....**$275.00**

Orange-Crush, sign, tin, Feel Fresh! & Crushy singing a tune above ...Carbonated Beverage, 2-color background, 1940s, 16x12", NM, A4 ....**$210.00**

Orange-Crush, sign, tin, Feel Fresh! Drink Orange-Crush Carbonated Beverage, curved corners, 1939, 20x28", EX+, A13 ....**$130.00**

Orange-Crush, sign, tin, Feel Fresh! Drink...Carbonated Beverage above Crushy, diamond shape, 16x16", EX+, A13 ....**$220.00**

Orange-Crush, sign, tin, Feel Fresh! Drink...Carbonated Beverage right of Crushy & bottle, 1930s, 18x48", EX, A13 ....$400.00

Orange-Crush, sign, tin, Orange-Crush on orange above bottle & Ice Cold Here, embossed, 1930s, 35x8½", EX+, A13 ....**$900.00**

Orange-Crush, sign, tin, There's Only One...Carbonated Beverage, white & yellow on orange, gold border, 1939, 20x28", NM, A13 ....**$180.00**

Orange-Crush, sign, tin over cardboard, Like Oranges? above encircled girl & orange branch, lettering below, 1920s-30s, 6x9", EX, A13 ....**$500.00**

Orange-Crush, thermometer, dial-type, Taste Orange-Crush & daisies on orange background, 12" dia, NM+, D30 ....**$125.00**

Orange-Crush, thermometer, tin, Naturally It Tastes Better & product name above bottle & bulb, rounded ends, 15", EX, D8 ....**$275.00**

Orange-Crush, thermometer, wood, Crushy above bottle & bulb, Rush Rush & diamond logo below, rounded top, EX, A16 ....**$415.00**

Orange-Crush, tray, bottles alternating with diamond logos to form a kaleidoscopic design in center, 12" dia, VG, A4 ....**$110.00**

Orange-Crush, tray, Drink Orange-Crush Carbonated Beverage, raised rim, decorative border, round, G, A16 ..**$45.00**

Orange-Crush, tray, Es Tan Delicioso!, Crushy & product name on orange & white background, lettered rim, Mexican, EX, A16 ....**$65.00**

Orange-Crush, yo-yo, wooden, reads Crushy Ski Top Drink Orange-Crush, EX+, A16 ....**$50.00**

Orange-Crush, see also Crush Carbonated Beverage
Orange-Crush, see also Ward's

Orange-Julep, bottle topper, die-cut, It's Julep Time, features couple sharing a glass with straws, Drink... on emblem, NM, A13 ....**$65.00**

Orange-Julep, sign, cardboard hanger, It's Julep Time lower right of couple sharing bottle, product name above, 1930s, 11x8", NM+, A13 ....**$140.00**

Orange-Julep, syrup bottle, glass with paper label, aluminum measuring cap, 12", EX, D22 ....**$160.00**

Orange-Julep, syrup dispenser, ceramic potbelly shape, Drink..., gold trim on base, original pump, 14x9", VG, A9 ....**$650.00**

Orange-Julep, tray, pictures seated bathing beauty holding parasol & glass, lettered rim, vertical rectangle, 13", VG, A21 ....$90.00

Orange-Julep, see also Howel's

Orangeine (Powders), sign, cardboard, Orangeine Girl in bonnet flanked by lettering, ...'Makes You Well-Keeps You Well' above, 30x20", G, A9 ....**$350.00**

Orchard, crate label, Washington pear, vista with orchard & mountains on dark blue background, Yakima, 8x11", M, D12 ....**$5.00**

Orchard King, crate label, California orange, big orange wearing a crown on blue background, Covina, 10x11", M, D3 ....**$2.00**

Orchard Queen, sign, embossed tin on cardboard, Drink Sparkling...Nothing Quite So Good, white, brown & green, 1920s, 5x9", NM+, A13 ....**$100.00**

Orinoco, see Tuckett's Orinoco

Orinogo Blended Roast Coffee/Chicago Spice Co, tin, gold round shape with product & company name above & below oval lake scene, slip lid, 3-lb, VG, A18 ....**$75.00**

Oriole Coffee, pail, product name above & below bird image on paper label, bail handle, Browning & Bainer litho, 5-lb, EX+, A15 ....$375.00

Orkideer, crate label, Florida citrus, 2 men in dugout full of oranges with curious deer on shore, 9x9", M, D3 ....**$3.00**

Orosi, crate label, Sunkist oranges, diminishing white logo on dark blue background, Orosi, 10x11", M, D12 .**$2.00**

Orphan Boy Smoking Tobacco, pouch, cloth, paper label, with contents, NM, A7 ....**$22.00**

Orphan Boy Smoking Tobacco, sign, paper, image of man, boy & dog at the corner of store front with product sign on side of building, 12x10", VG, A2 .... **$75.00**

Ortlieb's Lager Beer, can, crown-top, Internal Revenue Tax Paid statement, 12-oz, EX+, A19 .... **$85.00**

Ortlieb's Lager Beer & Ale, tray, bust image of elegant lady with glass above product name on divided 2-color background, 12" dia, VG+, A8 .... **$90.00**

Ortlieb's Premium Beer, display, chalkware, half barrel with Since 1869 above product name on red oval, Brewery-Fresh Taste!, 9x11", EX+, A19 .... **$20.00**

Ortlieb's Premium Lager Beer, bank, beer can, white with Ortlieb's on red diagonal band, 12-oz, EX, A19 .... **$22.00**

Ortlieb's Premium Lager Beer, thermometer/sign, tin on cardboard, Ortlieb's on diagonal red band with dial thermometer above, EX, A19 .... $35.00

Ortlieb's Wet Beer, thermometer, tin on cardboard, circular with product name on red oval above dial, NM, A19. **$40.00**

Oscar Mayer, bank, Weinermobile, plastic with paper label, 10" long, M, A **$15.00**

Oscar Mayer, whistle, red plastic weiner shape with yellow & red painted-on label, 1950s, 2¼", NM, A .$10.00

Osceola Brand Tobacco, box label, Hone litho, 14", NM, A7 .... **$40.00**

OshKosh B'Gosh Union Made Overalls, sign, self-framed tin, bust of Uncle Sam in overalls left of Buy..., dealer's name below, 1920, 14x30", NM+, A13 .... **$1,000.00**

Osmundo, cigar box label, printer's proof, portrait flanked by logo, EX, A5 .... **$35.00**

Osterloh's Fine Mixture, canister, plastic, yellow with gold name above & below $ symbol flanked by 100, gold banded top & bottom, EX, A18 .... **$75.00**

Ottawa Chief Tomatoes, can label, product name above & below Indian in full headdress/product name & tomato, 4¼x13", NM, A7 .... **$2.00**

Otto Huber Brewery, tray, Bavarian family around table with little boy taking sip of beer, oval, 17x14", G, A9 ...... **$95.00**

Otto Young & Co Resilient Mainsprings, tin, flat, red & gold with coiled spring & lettering surrounded by decorative border, ⅝x2¾x5⅛", EX, D37 .... **$40.00**

Our Defender Fitzhugh Lee Cigars, box label, salesman's sample, portrait flanked by patriotic images, 1898, NM, A5 .... **$75.00**

Our Family Rolled Oats, container, cardboard, blue over yellow with Our Family above white cameo image, Rolled Oats below, 3-lb, EX, A3 .... **$50.00**

Our Family Rolled Oats, container, cardboard, blue over yellow with Our Family above white cameo image, Rolled Oats below, 1-lb, VG+, A3 .... **$45.00**

Our Next Door Neighbor, cigar box label, salesman's sample, oval image of couple looking through peep hole at each other, EX, A5 .... **$250.00**

Our Pride Pilsener Beer/White Eagle Brewing Co, bottle, amber glass with thick neck, oval logo on label, short, rare, EX, A8 .... **$45.00**

Our Uncle, cigar box label, outer, Uncle Sam straddling a chair & smoking a cigar, 1887, EX, A5 .... **$145.00**

Ovaltine, tin, sample, 2", VG, A7 .... **$20.00**

Ovaltine, tumbler, Beetleware plastic, features Little Orphan Annie & Sandy, decal reads Leapin Lizards..., 1931, 4", EX, D14 .... **$45.00**

Over the Water/Watson & McGill, tobacco label, name above & below image of couple embracing at water's edge, matted & framed, image: 10x10", EX, A18 . **$55.00**

Overland Service/Genuine Parts, sign, porcelain, Overland in script on center band, Service & Genuine above & below, 2-sided, oval, 30x40", EX, A6 .... **$350.00**

Owl Cigar Store, sign, reverse-painted glass, owl on a tree branch, silver, black & gold, brass-bound frame, 80x30", EX, A9 .... **$2,000.00**

Owl Drug Co, matchbook, 20 strike, front strike, NM, D28 .... **$6.00**

Ox Head Beer, sign, die-cut cardboard stand-up, product name encircles hand pouring from can into glass, In Cans Keglined, 15", VG, A8 .... **$20.00**

Ox Head Stock Ale, thermometer/sign, tin on cardboard, product name above dial & The Aristocrat Of Fine Ales, beveled, EX, A19 .... $10.00

Oxo Bouillon Cubes, tin, name on diamond background, rectangular, rounded corners, ¾x1x2¾", EX, D37 . **$6.00**

☙ P ❧

P Lorillard, see also Lorillard

P Lorillard & Co, cabinet, wood with 2 etched glass paneled doors, inlaid gallery top marked 1760 & 1883, 43x35x19", VG, A9 .... **$1,750.00**

P Lorillard & Co Red Cross Cut Plug, insert card, features actress Ada Rehan, 1889, VG+, A5 .... **$18.00**

P Lorillard & Co Sensation Cut Plug, insert card, features actress Jennie Joyce, 1889, G, A5 ....$8.00

P Lorillard & Co Tobacco, label, sailors in center circle entwined with vignettes, Neptune & mermaid below, 10x½x10½", G+, A9 ....$300.00

P Lorillard Fine Cut, sign, paper, name above seated Indian accepting tobacco leaf from angelic figure, 11x8½", rare, EX, A2 ....$220.00

P Schoenhofen Brewing Co's Edelweiss, mug, ceramic, black product name above Chicago USA & Omaha Branch Tel 877, 4¾", EX, A8 ....$485.00

P Schoenhofen Brewing Co's Edelweiss Maltine, tray, company & product name above Chicago, decorative border, gold & silver on black, Shonk litho, oval, 15x19", VG, A8 ....$140.00

Pabst Blue Ribbon Beer, can, flat-top, red & blue on silver, Internal Revenue Tax Paid statement, 12-oz, NM, A19 ....$15.00

Pabst Blue Ribbon Beer, cup & saucer, white with blue ribbon logo & blue rim band, NM, A19.....................$65.00

Pabst Blue Ribbon Beer, display, ...At Popular Prices, Original... sign on brick wall behind bottle & driver in early car, 17x16", VG+, A19 ....$120.00

Pabst Blue Ribbon Beer, display, barbershop quartet flanked by bottle & barber pole, molded plastic, EX, A19 ....$50.00

Pabst Blue Ribbon Beer, display, Old Time Beer Flavor, Original..., train engine w/engineer & bottle against station background, 1961, NM, A19 ....$190.00

Pabst Blue Ribbon Beer, display, We Serve The Finest People Everyday, 3-D metal light-up bartender scene w/glass bottle, EX, A8.....................$75.00

Pabst Blue Ribbon Beer, display, What'll You Have? ...Finest Beer Served Anywhere, chalkware bust of girl in a bonnet, 12x10", NM, A19 ....$100.00

Pabst Blue Ribbon Beer, display/lamp, On Tap sign above bottle on lettered trapezoid base with boxer, VG+, A19 ....$80.00

Pabst Blue Ribbon Beer, print, paper litho, 'Pabst Famous Blue Ribbon Winners,' shows wagon with 6-horse team & running dog, 15x31", VG+, A8 ....$65.00

Pabst Blue Ribbon Beer, sign, cardboard, Quality above smiling black waiter with tray saying Yes-Suh-h, cream background, framed, 36x27", EX, A6.....................$650.00

Pabst Blue Ribbon Beer, sign, porcelain, Pabst upper left of Blue Ribbon on diagonal wavy band, Beer lower right, blue & white, 30x42", VG+, A8 ....$225.00

Pabst Blue Ribbon Beer, sign, tin, Pabst above embossed bottle flanked by curly-Q design, 1930s, self-framed, 18x12", G, A8.....................$85.00

Pabst Blue Ribbon Beer, sign, tin on cardboard, Pabst above Blue Ribbon on ribbon with tilted bottle, In Bottles & 15¢ dot below, 9x13", EX+, A8.....................$55.00

Pabst Brewery, booklet, shows brewery scenes & properties, 1907, 40 pgs, VG, A8.....................$55.00

Pabst Export Beer, sign, tin, product name right of orange, blue & white circular Pabst Milwaukee B logo on white, 13½x6½", EX, A19 ....$110.00

Pabst Extract, calendar, 1907, 'Yard Long Girl' in red dress & plumed hat looking over her shoulder, framed, 37x10", NM, A8.....................$330.00

Pabst Extract, calendar, 1908, 'Jewel,' months with gemstones before provocative lady in black behind red drape, framed, 41x10", EX, A8 ..$575.00

Pabst Extract, calendar, 1910, lady in white dress & plumed hat looking over her shoulder, red ground, 2-sided, framed, 35x10", NM, A8 ....$360.00

Pabst Extract, calendar, 1914, 'American Girl' in gold dress holding black plume, gold background, framed, 41x11", VG+, A8.....................$245.00

Pabst Extract, calendar, 1915, 'Panama Girl' in gold dress & feathered headband holding bouquet & closed fan, framed, 36x10", VG+, A8 ....$155.00

Pabst Extract, calendar, 1916, 'American Girl' in purple dress, yellow background, framed, 41x11", EX, A8.....................$325.00

Pabst Milwaukee, mug, ceramic, features Brigham Young with 1847 & 1897 above & below round Pabst leaf logo, Utah seal on reverse, EX+, A8.....................$140.00

Pabst Milwaukee, mug, elves enjoying mugs of brew around barrel with logo on end, 'Pabst Perfected Brewing...,' EX, A8 ....**$90.00**

Pabst's Okay Specific, sign, embossed tin, You Know on banner above product name, other text with Pabst Chemical Co below, 9x6", NM, A13 ....**$85.00**

Pacer, cigar box label, outer, harness racer, 1909, 4½x4½", M, D5 ....**$45.00**

Pacer 200 Hi-Test, pump sign, porcelain, 200 Pacer lettered diagonally on red above Hi-Test on black, 14x8½", NOS, NM+, A1 ....**$185.00**

Pacer 400 Ethyl, pump sign, porcelain, 400 Pacer lettered diagonally on red above Ethyl logo on black, 14x8½", NOS, NM+, A1 ....**$550.00**

Pacific, crate label, Washington pear, shield inset of white fleet on red & black background, 2 pears, Seattle, 8x11", M, D12 ....**$15.00**

Pacific Brewing & Malting Co, art plate, 'Fruehlings Kinderlust,' shows 2 children playing, decorative rim, VG, A8 ....**$135.00**

Pacific Brewing & Malting Co, calendar, 1913, litho image of lady in large hat with roses, calendar below with partial pad, framed, 33x19", VG+, A1 ....**$500.00**

Pacific Chemical Co, tape measure, celluloid, Janitor's Supplies... arched above company name & Los Angeles, blue & white, 38mm, EX, A11 ....**$20.00**

Pacific Power & Light Co, sign, porcelain, Reddy Kilowatt on yellow at left of white name on green, white border, 24x48", EX, A6 ....**$325.00**

Pacific Power & Light Co, sign, porcelain, Reddy Kilowatt surrounded by company name, red, white & black, 36" dia, NM+, A1 ....**$750.00**

Packard, banner, silk-like cloth with fringe, Ultramatic Drive...Golden Anniversary, burgandy on gold & cream, 60x41", EX, A6 ....**$170.00**

Packard Automotive Cable, display rack, metal, red & black lettering on gold at top, 10 sections for various cable, 36x18", VG, A6 ....**$50.00**

Packard Battery Cables, display rack, metal, Faster Cranking Speeds-Quicker Starts above ribbon & product name, hooks at bottom, 8x20", EX+, A6............**$125.00**

Pacoast, crate label, California orange, aerial view of southern California coast, highway & groves, Los Angeles, 10x11", M, D3 ....**$2.00**

Page's Ice Cream, folding chair, oak with embossed tin back, Eat More...Every Day in white on blue, 32½x20x16", VG+, A9 ....**$300.00**

Page's Seeds, display rack, wood fold-up type with metal racks, advertising above, 50x20", VG, A6 ....**$210.00**

Paige Sales & Service, globe, milk glass with Paige on diamond, Sales & Service above & below, late 1920s, NM, A1 ....**$1,100.00**

Pal Ade, calendar, 1950, Babe Ruth from the heavens urging 'Let's Go Pal' to baseball boy at bat, framed, 23x11", NM+, A13 ....**$525.00**

Pal Ade, push plate, tin, Drink lettered diagonally above unopened bottle, stripes above & below, vertical, NM, A13 ....**$75.00**

Pal Ade, sign, die-cut cardboard hanger, orange bottle shape with 2 packages of marbles attached at bottom, 24", EX, A8 ....**$30.00**

Pal Hollow Ground Razor Blades, display, cardboard, animated man with 4 For 10¢ on hand pointing to Man...What A Blade!!, 20 packs below, 12x9", NM, A7 ....**$45.00**

Palace Garden Golden Pumpkin, can label, product name above & below pumpkin & product name above & below flowers, 4½x11½", NM, A7 ....**$2.00**

Pall Mall Cigarettes, sign, tin, product pack upper right of sexy lady with cigarette in hand, 1950s, 21x15", NM, A13 ....**$230.00**

Pall Mall Famous Cigarettes, box, red with Christmas motif left of product name, 2x8½x7", EX, A18.....**$60.00**

Pall Mall Famous Cigarettes, tin, red with Christmas motif in upper left corner, product name in lower right, gold border, square corners, NM, A18 ....**$150.00**

Palm Cigars, sign, embossed tin, pictures cigars & 3 For 5¢, 6½x19", NM, D35 ....$65.00

Palm Leaf, tobacco tag, embossed die-cut, EX, D35 ...$3.50

Palmer & Goodrich Tires, print, paper litho, portrait of 'Aida' from Verdi's opera, rich color, artist signed, dated 1900, framed, 24x18", NM, A1 ....$300.00

Palmer's Root Beer, barrel sign, porcelain, Drink above ...It's Better, Root Beer below, red center with orange border, 14x19", NOS, A6....................................$350.00

Palmolive After Shaving Talc, tin, sample, oval inset on lined background, EX+, A3.................................$25.00

Palmolive Soap, sign, cardboard stand-up, Keep That Schoolgirl Complexion above cute little girl, ...3 For 25¢ below, 15x10", EX, D8.....................$230.00

Palmolive Soap, sign, paper, Keep Clean above image of little girl washing behind her ear, poem below, matted & framed, 28x17", EX+, A13 ....$900.00

Palo Alto, lug box label, various fruit, tall redwood tree on red background, white lettering, M, D12 ....$4.00

Pan-Am Airlines, cosmetic bag, soft nylon, blue with Pan-Am emblem in lower corner, zipper closure, NM, D24 ....$5.00

Pan-Am Gasoline & Motor Oils, sign, porcelain, Pan-Am on center band, Gasoline & Motor Oils arched above & below, red, white & blue, 42" dia, EX+, A6 ....$210.00

Pan-Am Quality Gasoline, pump sign, porcelain, torch logo above Quality Gasoline in bold letters, red & black on cream, 12½x10½", NM, D8 ....$165.00

Panama, crate label, California lemon, map of US & Mexico showing trade routes from Santa Barbara through Panama, 12x9", M, D3 ....$2.00

Panco Soles & Heels, display rack, metal & wood, open front with shelves, lettering & logo on all sides, yellow, black & red, 35x15", VG, A6 ....$160.00

Panhandle, gas globe, inverted triangle logo, red & black on white, red metal body, 15" dia, NM, A6.....$1,000.00

Panther Oil & Grease Mfg Co, pail, fierce-looking panther's head encircled by company name, black & red on silver, bail handle, 10-lb, VG, A1 ....$40.00

Panton Plows, watch fob, nickle-plated, round with scalloped edges, name above & below plow intertwined with initials P&O, EX, A20 ....$125.00

Pape's Diapepsin Compound, tin, name lettered diagonally on elongated octagon, hinged lid, ⅜x1⅜x3", EX, D37...$10.00

Parade, crate label, California lemon, rank of drummers following drum major, Saticoy, 9x12", M, D12.......$3.00

Paris Millinery Shop, pocket mirror, colorful image of lady surrounded by gold lettering, oval, EX+, D18.....$165.00

Parisian Novelty Co, brush, company name above factory image & Makers Of Advertising Specialties, 3½" dia, EX, A8...$100.00

Parisian Novelty Co, pocket mirror, celluloid, multicolored factory image surrounded by lettering, round, EX, A11 ....$75.00

Parke's Dry Roast Coffees, tin, sample, red & gold with name above star & moon logo, Unmatchable, rectangular, rounded corners, 1x2x2⅜", EX, D3 ......$115.00

Parker's Cold Cream, sign, cardboard hanger, embellished oval bust image of woman against red background, 11½x7½", EX, A21 ....$120.00

Parkes Baking Powder, tin, paper label, with contents, 4-oz, NM, A7..$20.00

Parrot Baking Powder, tin, paper label, with contents, 4-oz, NM, A7..$90.00

Parrot Superior Steel Needles, tin, flat, Loud Tone, blue with image of 2 parrots perched on a single branch, silver border, ¼x1¼x1¾", EX, D37 ....$40.00

Pastum/J Sarubi Co, sign, flange, Pastum flanked by barber poles & busts of a man with before-&-after hairdos, 7x18", EX, A8...$100.00

Pastum/J Sarubi Co, sign, flange, Pastum flanked by barber poles & busts of a man with before-&-after hairdos, 7x18", G, A8...$25.00

Pat Hand/Globe Tobacco Co, pocket tin, vertical oval, product name above hand flanked by Cube Cut Granules & Price Five Cents, VG+, A3........................$100.00

Paterson's Cough Drops, tin, Here's The Cure For That Cough above Paterson's on oval & Cough Drops on banners, gold & red, 8x6x4", VG+, A18................$55.00

Pathfinder Coffee, watch fob, coffee can on celluloid center, EX, A20..$35.00

Patterson's Seal Cut Plug, canister, product name above & below tilted tobacco pack surrounded by lettering, EX+, A3...$75.00

Patterson's Seal Cut Plug, tobacco pouch, cloth, 2-oz, NM, A7 ....$10.00

Patterson's Tuxedo Tobacco, canister, product name above round inset of man in tuxedo, Specially Prepared For Pipe Or Cigarette, screw top, EX+, A3.........$125.00

Patton's Ice Cream, tray, oval image with parfait glass & dish of Rich & Delicious ice cream, 13x13", G+, A9........$95.00

Patton's Sun-Proof Liquid Paints, display cabinet, oversized metal pail with back doors opening to shelves, includes 6 sample cards, EX, A21 ....$825.00

Paul Diller, Watchmaker & Jeweler, pocket mirror, birthstone-type with tan background, oval, M, D18....$25.00

Paul Jones, cigar box label, outer, continental soldier, 1909, EX, A5 ....$65.00

Paul Jones & Co, sign, tin, 'The Temptation Of Saint Anthony,' gent choosing whiskey over watermelon, curled corners, 12x20", VG, A21 ....$550.00

Paul Jones & Co, sign, tin, dead game & rifles hanging on cabin wall with bottle & glass on floor, framed, image: 45x31", EX, A9..$400.00

Paw-Nee Olde Style Rolled Oats, container, cardboard, yellow with red product name above & below Olde Style lettered on fancy shield, 14-oz, NM, A3.......$30.00

Pay Car Scrap Chewing Tobacco, sign, cardboard, Hey There Get Your Chewing Tobacco, railroad man holding up product while pointing down, 20x13", EX, A7 ....$65.00

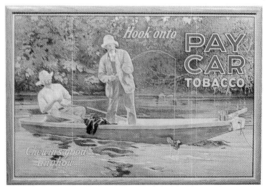

Pay Car Tobacco, sign, cardboard, Hook Onto Pay Car Tobacco, Chews Good Anyhow, 2 fishermen in boat, 1920s-30s, framed, 27x40", NM+, A13 .$700.00

Payn's Spanish Tobacco, sign, die-cut paper, To Make A Hit... & name on either side of base line, batter ready to bat, 11x15", EX, A21 ....$250.00

Payson's Indelible Ink, sign, paper, young black boy holding package in raised hand, framed, image: 6x7½", EX, A2 ....$275.00

Peach Snuff, tin, sample, with contents, VG, A7.........$8.00

Peachey Double Cut Tobacco, pocket tin, vertical, pictures large colorful peach, EX+, D22 ....$125.00

Peachey Ribbon Cut Scrap, tobacco pack, product name above & below large peach on original wax paper wrap, full, 5x3", EX+, A3 ....$35.00

Peacock Blue Ink, tin, glass interior, gold with colorful peacock graphics, 8-sided with smaller round lid, 3x2¼", NM, A18..$70.00

Peacock Brand Coffee, tin, product name above & below colorful peacock on white paper label, slip lid, 1-lb, EX+, A15..$170.00

Peak Coffee, tin, mountain scene, slip lid, EX+, A3 ..$45.00

Pear's Soap, sign, die-cut cardboard, colorful image of mother scrubbing boy's ear, framed, 12½x6½", VG+, A21 ....$75.00

Pearl Lager Beer/Griesedieck Brewing Co, drinking glass, stem with embossed logo, NM, A8 ....$90.00

Pearl Oil, sign, die-cut metal flange, can shape, We Sell...For Heating, Lighting & Cooking, Standard Oil Co, 19x12", NM, A6...$500.00

Pears' Soap, ad from Ladies Home Journal, He Won't Be Happy 'Til He Gets It!, baby crawling out of tub, 1912, framed, 10x14", NM, A3 ....$90.00

Pears' Soap, sign, paper, bar of soap above young girl holding candle, 1905, matted & framed, image: 15x12", EX+, A3..$605.00

Pedro Cut Plug Smoking Tobacco, lunch pail, yellow with red & black product lettering around king-of-spades logo, wire handle, 4x8x5", NM, A18.......$180.00

Peerage, cigar box label, printer's proof, knight on horse with castle beyond, EX, A5....................................$40.00

Peerless, tobacco tag, die-cut P, EX, D35.....................$6.00

Peerless Beer, cigarette holder/dispenser for backbar use, metal, For Your Enjoyment above product name, 14x19", G, A8...$35.00

Peerless Beer, label, La Crosse Brewing Co, Internal Revenue Tax Paid statement, 1933-36, ⅓-gal, NM, A10 ....$15.00

Peerless Chew or Smoke, see FF Adams & Co

Peerless Dyes, cabinet, wood with tin front picturing gypsy girl with camel train below, 32x18½x11", rare, G-, A9...$450.00

Peerless Harvester Beer, label, 1933-50, La Crosse Brewery Co, Internal Revenue Tax Paid statement, ½-gal, NM, A10 ....$15.00

Peerless Weighing Machine Co, scale sign, porcelain emblem, Did You Weigh Yourself To Day? above company name, red, white & blue, EX+, A13..........$170.00

Peerless Weighing Machine Co, scale sign, porcelain emblem, Did You Weigh Yourself To-Day? above scale balancing Weight & Health, 9x5½", NM, A13 ....$230.00

Peg Top, door push plate, porcelain, The Old Reliable above product name on cigar, 5¢ lower right, brown on cream, 13x4", EX, A6 ....$135.00

Pen Point, tobacco tag, die-cut, gold, EX, D35...........$6.00

Pengo, cigar box label, inner lid, black natives dancing in jungle, 6x9", M, D5..................................$25.00

Penn Airliner Motor Oil, can, airplane flying through circle with product name above 100% Pure..., screw cap, 2-gal, 11x8½", EX, A6 ....$160.00

Penn Beer, calendar, 1912, paper, girl in green & black outfit & hat with muff, full pad, framed, image: 30½x15½", EX, A9 ....$300.00

Penn Dutch Ale, label, 1933-36, Bellmont Ale Brewing Co, U-type permit number, Internal Revenue Tax Paid statement, 12-oz, M, A10 ....$35.00

Penn Franklin Motor Oil, can, Ben Franklin & quill pen above product name, green, white & black, full, 1-qt, NM, A1..................................$100.00

Penn Harness Oil, can, encirlced Quaker man flanked by arrowheads above lettering with fancy border, screw lid, 1 Imperial-gal, VG, A6 ....$60.00

Penn Maid Sour Cream, clicker, tin, 2½", EX, A7 ....$20.00

Penn-Beel Motor Oil, can, Pure Pennsylvannia above bees on hive with product lettering below, yellow, black, red & white, full, 1-qt, EX+, A1 ....$210.00

Penn-Rad Motor Oil, can, product name on diamond above Guaranteed 100% Pure Pennsylvania Oil on emblem, screw cap, 2-gal, 10x10", VG+, A6 ....$35.00

Penn-Valley Gasoline, gas globe, red wings on black triangle lettered Independent Oil, red metal body, 15" dia, NM, A6..................................$400.00

Penn-Valley Motor Oil, can, Penn-Valley above encircled Quaker man & scroll design, pink, blue & black, screw lid & handle, 2-gal, 10", VG, A6 ....$85.00

Penn's Cigars, store bin, red with Penn's Spells Quality above gold pen tip, gold border, holds 12 30¢ plugs, 6½x6½", EX+, A18 ....$20.00

Pennfield Motor Oils, sign, embossed tin, Pennfield Motor Oils over silhouette of oil derrick on hill, red & blue on cream, 12x20", EX+, A1 ....$220.00

Pennsyline Motor & Tractor Oils, can, Quaker man atop lettered shield in center, ...Staunch As A Quaker, blue, red & cream, screw lid, 5-gal, VG, A6 ....$20.00

Pennsylvania Dutch Old German Beer, sign, tin hanger, 2 hands toasting with tankards above product name in center, decorative border, oval, NM, A19..................................$105.00

Pennsylvania Oilproof Vacuum Cup Tires, sign, tin, Non Skid logo at left of product name, 12x35½", G, A6 ....$120.00

Pennsylvania Railroad, calendar, 1929, colorful image of train car & 2 airplanes, 3 small pads below, 30x29", VG, A6 ....$210.00

Pennsylvania Resilient Mainsprings/Heeren Bros, tin, flat, red with cream lettering, decorative border, rectangular, rounded corners, ⅝x2¾x5⅛", EX, D37......$40.00

Pennsylvania Tires, ashtray, rubber tire shape with logo cast in green glass insert, 6" dia, NM, A1.............$75.00

Pennsylvania Transformer, sign, porcelain, PT logo surrounded by lettering, blue & white, 12" dia, NM, D30..................................$75.00

Penny Post Cut Plug, lunch pail, gold lettering & black & gold ornate graphics on orange, Strater Bros Tobacco Co, bail handle, EX, D35 ....$350.00

Pennzip Gasoline, sign, embossed porcelain, ...A Pennzoil Product, yellow, black & red, 25x46", VG+, A6 ..$210.00

Pennzoil, can, 'Be Oil Wise' upper left of 3 owls sitting atop oval Pennzoil logo, yellow, red & black, 1-qt, NM+, A1..................................$50.00

Pennzoil, clock, numbers encircle Pennzoil Sound Your Z on white face, 20" dia (scarce size), NM+, A1....$300.00

Pennzoil, license plate attachment, die-cut tin, Pennzoil owls preaching We Are For Safety, 1930s, 6x5", NM, NOS, A1 ....$220.00

Pennzoil, sign, embossed tin, oval logo above Pennzoil in black letters shadowed in red, 58x10", VG+, A6..$120.00

Pennzoil, sign, neon, die-cut plywood back, black name on yellow marquee with red & black trim, 36x92", NM, A6..................................$850.00

Pennzoil, sign, porcelain, bell logo, yellow, red & black, 2½x8", EX+, A6 ....$300.00

Pennzoil, sign, porcelain, oval bell logo on lined background, black, yellow & red, 15x27", EX, A6.....$260.00

Pennzoil, sign, porcelain, oval bell logo on yellow with red & black border, 13x20", NM, A1...................$390.00

Pennzoil, sign, porcelain flange, early logo with brown bell surrounded by Supreme Pennsylvania..., 2-sided, 24" dia, EX, A6 ....$1,500.00

Pennzoil, sign, tin, Pennzoil above Sound Your Z, oval logo below, vertical, raised rolled rim, 60x12", NOS, EX+, A1 ....$200.00

Pennzoil Bonded Dealer, sign, tin, We Are Bonded For $1000 above pedestal sign, To Give You Tough-Film..., dated 1933, 2-sided, 11x14", NM, A1 ....$245.00

Pennzoil Motor Oil, bank, tin, can shape, 2" dia, NM, A7 ....$35.00

Pennzoil Safe Lubrication, can, Mainliner airplane above oval bell logo, red, yellow & black, 9½x7" dia, 5-qt, VG, A6 ....$110.00

Pennzoil Safe Lubrication, display rack, Sound Your Z in black above red bell logo on yellow sign above rack, marked AM-8-49, 39", VG+, A6 ....$180.00

Pennzoil Safe Lubrication, sign, die-cut tin bell, gold with red & cream lettering, 1 of 3 known, 2-sided, 24x22", VG+, A6 ....$1,300.00

Penoka, crate label, Canada apple, red apple with crown above early vista of orchards, 9x11", M, D12........$3.00

Penotol Extra Quality Motor Oil, can, product name above 100% Pennsylvania on white band, screw lid & handle, 2-gal, 10¼x8¼", VG, A6 ....$15.00

Penreco, gas globe, Penreco superimposed over Wm Penn on monument, metal body, 1920s-30s, 15" dia, rare, VG+, A6 ....$700.00

Penrod Tomatoes, can label, early, 3 children in costumes & little dog, M, D3 ....**$2.00**

Pensupreme Ice Cream, menu board, embossed metal on cardboard, small circular portrait below product name, green, red & white, 20½", VG, A6 ....**$70.00**

Peoples Beer, tray, deep-dish, Hits The Spot! above Peoples on arrow pointing to bull's-eye, Beer lettered below, 12" dia, A19 ....**$60.00**

Pep, cigarette papers, NM, A7 ....**$80.00**

Pep Boys, see also Pure as Gold Grease

Pep Boys, catalog, original envelope features various products & prices, Pep Boys at top, 1932, NM, A6 ......**$80.00**

Pep Boys Hand Soap, tin, image of Manny, Moe & Jack, red & gray border at top, red, white & blue border at bottom, red slip lid, 6", EX+, A1 ....**$450.00**

Pep Boys Handy Bulb Kit, tin, lid with Pep Boys lettered at left of the 3 as soldiers, red, black & white, flat rectangle, 2½x4", EX+, A1 ....**$55.00**

Pep Boys Lighter Fluid, can, image of the Pep Boys, black, red, gray & cream, metal squirt top, ca 1934, 8-oz, EX+, A6 ....**$275.00**

Pep Boys Western Motor Oil, can, western theme with Manny, Moe & Jack on bucking horse, 2-gal, rare, EX/VG+, A6 ....**$355.00**

Pep Boys 600 Transmission Oil, can, gold with gold, black, red & white geometric graphics & lettering, 1-gal, EX, A6 ....**$160.00**

Pepper's Hygrade Ginger Ale, sign, celluloid, blue Let Us Serve You With above product name on orange, blue border, oval, 6½", NM+, A13 ....**$110.00**

Pepsi-Cola, ashtray, ceramic, Pepsi-Cola bottle cap on round center, square with bowed sides, M, A16 ..**$65.00**

Pepsi-Cola, banner, canvas, Drink above Pepsi=Cola, Double Size 5¢ below, mid-1930s, 2-sided, 36x33", rare, EX, A13 ....**$275.00**

Pepsi-Cola, belt buckle, embossed Pepsi-Cola above Hits The Spot, NM, A16 ....**$15.00**

Pepsi-Cola, blotter, Drink Pepsi-Cola Delicious Healthful, black on brown, EX+, A13 ....$120.00

Pepsi-Cola, blotter, Drink Pepsi-Cola Delicious Healthful, black on brown, G, A16 ....**$70.00**

Pepsi-Cola, book cover, Think Young- Say 'Pepsi Please,' above basketball player talking to girl, referee signals below, NM, A7 ....**$6.00**

Pepsi-Cola, bottle, clear glass, straight-sided, Wilmington NC, early, NM, A13 ....**$25.00**

Pepsi-Cola, bottle carrier, cardboard, oval Pepsi-Cola & bottle-cap logo against striped background, Please Return..., 1951, VG, A16 ....**$170.00**

Pepsi-Cola, bottle carrier, tin, oval Pepsi-Cola logo against stripes on narrow bands, open bottom sides, rounded handle, VG+, A16 ....**$40.00**

Pepsi-Cola, bottle carrier, wood, Buy Pepsi=Cola stamped on front, bottle images on sides, cut-out handle, 1940, EX, A16 ....**$80.00**

Pepsi-Cola, bottle crate, wood with stamped Pepsi=Cola logo, EX, A16 ....**$70.00**

Pepsi-Cola, bottle opener, bottle shape, bare flat metal embossed with Pepsi=Cola 5¢, 1930s, VG, A16 ..**$25.00**

Pepsi-Cola, bottle opener, bottle shape, litho tin w/Sparkling Satisfying Pepsi=Cola logo, 1930s, 4¼", EX+, A3 ....**$90.00**

Pepsi-Cola, bottle opener, metal triangular shape w/Drink Pepsi-Cola engraved on handle, 1950s, EX+, A16 ..**$17.00**

Pepsi-Cola, bottle opener, wall mount, embossed Pepsi-Cola, G, A16 ....**$20.00**

Pepsi-Cola, bottle opener, wood handle lettered Buy The 6 Bottle Carton & Served Iced Pepsi-Cola, metal opener, EX+, A16 ....**$75.00**

Pepsi-Cola, bottle stopper/pourer, plastic, white with Pepsi=Cola, cork stopper, NM+, A16 ....**$40.00**

Pepsi-Cola, calendar, 1920, signed Rolf Armstrong, shows 1919 & 1921 calendar on back, 7x5", EX, D32 ..**$2,600.00**

Pepsi-Cola, calendar, 1941, Pepsi-Cola Hits The Spot, girl with bottle on red above pad flanked by logos on blue, 23x15", EX+, A13 ....**$250.00**

Pepsi-Cola, calendar, 1945, Pepsi-Cola Competition For American Artists, complete, EX+, A16 ....**$40.00**

Pepsi-Cola, calendar, 1946, The Portrait of America For 1946, complete, EX+, A16 ....**$45.00**

Pepsi-Cola, calendar, 1947, Paintings Of The Year, complete, EX+, A16 ....**$40.00**

Pepsi-Cola, calendar, 1950, January/February sheet shows girl ice skater taking break with a Pepsi, complete, 22x13", EX+, A13 ....**$300.00**

Pepsi-Cola, calendar, 1952, 1 page with 12 months, VG, A4 ....$65.00

Pepsi-Cola, calendar, 1956, The Light Refreshment & bottle cap above date pad flanked by glass & bottle, 12½x8½", EX+, A13 ....$325.00

Pepsi-Cola, calendar, 1960, Pepsi-Cola Bottling Co, art by Lawson Wood, complete, EX+, A16 ....$110.00

Pepsi-Cola, can, cone-top with cap, 1940s-50s, 12-oz, EX, A13...$240.00

Pepsi-Cola, can, flat-top, slanted Pepsi-Cola bottle cap on diagonal stripes, 1960s, VG+, A16........................$40.00

Pepsi-Cola, can, pull-tab, 1st aluminum can, stylized Pepsi logo on white diamond, 1960s, VG+, A16............$60.00

Pepsi-Cola, cash register topper, cardboard, Deco-style billboard, identification of counterfeit bills on back, 1930s-40s, EX+, A13...$550.00

Pepsi-Cola, chairs, metal folding, Relax Have A Pepsi & slanted bottle cap on yellow backs, blue frames, 1960s, VG, A13, pair...$225.00

Pepsi-Cola, cigarettes, sealed pack shows Pepsi=Cola above Pepsi cap logo, M, A16...............................$40.00

Pepsi-Cola, clock, light-up, Drink Pepsi-Cola Ice Cold on stylized bottle cap, numbered 1-12, metal frame, round, 1950s, NM, A16 ....$375.00

Pepsi-Cola, clock, light-up, Drink Pepsi-Cola Ice-Cold on bottle cap in center surrounded by numbers & dots, 1950s, 12" dia, EX+, D30 ....$350.00

Pepsi-Cola, clock, light-up, Drink Pepsi=Cola Ice Cold on embossed bottle cap on plastic front, metal frame, 1945, square, VG, A16 ....$180.00

Pepsi-Cola, clock, light-up, Pepsi logo at 12 with lines between numbers 3-6-9, 1969, square, VG+, A16...$55.00

Pepsi-Cola, clock, light-up, Pepsi over bottle-cap logo right of clock with numbers & dots, horizontal rectangle, 1960s, EX, A16..$80.00

Pepsi-Cola, clock, light-up, Pepsi=Cola on stylized bottle cap surrounded by smaller numbers, metal frame, 1940s, 15" dia, NM+, A13......................................$400.00

Pepsi-Cola, clock, light-up, Pepsi=Cola on stylized bottle cap surrounded by large numbers, metal frame, 1940s, 15" dia, EX+, A13 ....$325.00

Pepsi-Cola, clock, light-up, Think Young Say Pepsi Please! & bottle cap surrounded by numbers, double glass, 1950s, round, EX+, A13 ....$800.00

Pepsi-Cola, clock, light-up counter, Drink Pepsi Anytime, square clock left of Pepsi logo, 1970s, G+, A16...$20.00

Pepsi-Cola, clock, light-up counter, Thank You Call Again, square clock left of Pepsi logo, 1967, 8x13", NM, A4..$40.00

Pepsi-Cola, concentrate drum, metal, Nickel Drink — Worth A Dime above Pepsi=Cola, Bigger & Better 5¢ below, 1941, 10-gal, EX, A7................................$85.00

Pepsi-Cola, cooler, counter-top, deep blue chest-type with embossed Pepsi-Cola bottle caps on sides, 1940s-50s, 17x22x17", EX+, A13..$1,350.00

Pepsi-Cola, cooler, green Glascock-type with red Pepsi=Cola 5¢ & green Double Size on white panels, 1920s-30s, 34x31x22", VG, A13............$1,200.00

Pepsi-Cola, cooler, metal, Ice Cold above Pepsi=Cola 5¢ on wavy band, Sold Here below, bottle opener in upper right, 14x27", VG, A6 ....$500.00

Pepsi-Cola, cooler bag, vinyl, Disneyland Fun/NY World's Fair, round with straps & zipper top, NM, A16 ....$30.00

Pepsi-Cola, cuff links, square with Pepsi-Cola logo, M, A16 ....$20.00

Pepsi-Cola, dispenser, cylinder with figural Pepsi=Cola bottle-cap front, musical, NM, A16......................$275.00

Pepsi-Cola, dispenser, decorated china, stylized flowering tree motif with embossed lettering, 1900-05, G+, A13 ....$3,700.00

Pepsi-Cola, dispenser, white rectangular container with bottle cap above Pepsi-Cola (block letters) on sides, 1960s, NOS, NM+, A13..$500.00

Pepsi-Cola, display, die-cut cardboard with 3-D plastic bottle, New Single Drink Size on triangle behind bottle & cap, 10x14", M, A4 ....$215.00

Pepsi-Cola, display bottle holder, cardboard, 'I Make Sure...,' 'I Protect...,' Pepsi cops measuring bottle with ruler, EX+, A16 ....$725.00

Pepsi-Cola, display rack, metal, 2-case rack designed for stacking or counter-top use, 1930s, scarce, EX, A13 ....$500.00

Pepsi-Cola, display rack, tin, Drink Pepsi-Cola Ice Cold on bottle cap at top, NM, D30 ....$255.00

Pepsi-Cola, display rack, 2-sided sign with slanted bottle cap above Take Home... atop rack with 4 shelves, folds up, 65x18", NM, A1 ....$145.00

Pepsi-Cola, door plate, tin, Pick A Pepsi in black on yellow, Pepsi=Cola bottle cap above & below, 13½x3½", EX, D21 ....$165.00

Pepsi-Cola, door pull handle, Enjoy on blue above red Pepsi=Cola on contour band, Bigger & Better below, 1940s, 12x3", EX+, A13 ....$210.00

Pepsi-Cola, door push bar, porcelain, Have A Pepsi in black flanked by logo, yellow background, 3x30", EX, D21 ....**$100.00**

Pepsi-Cola, drinking glass, flared top, with syrup line, early 1910s, NM, D32 ....**$750.00**

Pepsi-Cola, drinking glass, oval Pepsi=Cola logo, with syrup line, NM, A7 ....**$15.00**

Pepsi-Cola, envelope, Pepsi=Cola logo, NM, A7 ....**$6.00**

Pepsi-Cola, fan, America Keeps Cool With..., shows Pepsi cops, contour logo & 5¢ bottle on reverse, 1930s, EX+, A16 ....**$100.00**

Pepsi-Cola, fan, Drink Pepsi-Cola, girl sipping from straw, 1912-13 calendar on reverse, 1912, round, 9x8", VG, A13 ....**$1,000.00**

Pepsi-Cola, Frigerator Bag, insulated heavy paper with image of bottle cap on refrigerator, wire handle, EX+, A16 ....**$125.00**

Pepsi-Cola, game, Big League Baseball, 1950s-60s, EX, A13 ....**$95.00**

Pepsi-Cola, game, Vest Pocket Baseball, 1941, EX+, A13 ....**$145.00**

Pepsi-Cola, handkerchief, allover bottle-cap design, M, A16 ....**$25.00**

Pepsi-Cola, hat, soda jerk's, white cloth with Pepsi=Cola logo, NM, A16 ....**$75.00**

Pepsi-Cola, lighter, musical pocket-type, white with bottle cap, Drink Pepsi-Cola on reverse, 1950s, EX+, A13 ....**$160.00**

Pepsi-Cola, matchbook, Pepsi-Cola logo, 20 strike, front strike, NM, D28 ....**$3.00**

Pepsi-Cola, menu, full Pepsi glass & food scene with Menu lettered on banner above, bottle & bottle cap below, 10½x7", NM, A7 ....**$7.00**

Pepsi-Cola, menu board, tin, Drink...Bigger-Better above board, wood-look frame with rope-like border, round corners, 1930s, G, A16 ....**$100.00**

Pepsi-Cola, menu board, tin, Have A Pepsi & bottle cap above board, yellow border, 1950s, 30x20", NM, D30 ....**$95.00**

Pepsi-Cola, menu board, tin, Say Pepsi Please & slanted bottle cap on yellow above board, rounded corners, 1950s, 30x19", G, A21 ....**$60.00**

Pepsi-Cola, miniature bottle, clear swirl with red & white label, 4½", NM, D21 ....**$12.00**

Pepsi-Cola, miniature bottle, Pepsi=Cola paper label, NM, A16 ....**$25.00**

Pepsi-Cola, notebook (grocer's ?), Get The Flavor 'There's A Difference,' above Pepsi=Cola logo, stapled binding, early, EX, A16 ....**$65.00**

Pepsi-Cola, paper cup, Pepsi's Best, Prove It For Yourself above Pepsi=Cola bottle cap against red, white & blue band, NM, A16 ....**$18.00**

Pepsi-Cola, paper cup, white with repeated bottle-cap logo, with lid, NM, A16 ....**$50.00**

Pepsi-Cola, paperweight, glass, round with Pepsi-Cola in center, decorative rim, M, A16 ....**$40.00**

Pepsi-Cola, pocketknife, Pepsi-Cola in block letters, 'Clinton's Ditch' on reverse, NM, A16 ....**$30.00**

Pepsi-Cola, pocketknife, Pepsi-Cola 5¢ in blue on bone-colored handle, 3", EX, D21 ....**$60.00**

Pepsi-Cola, rack, metal with painted-metal sign, Take Home A Carton & Pepsi-Cola bottle cap, 65x18x18", VG, A6 ....**$95.00**

Pepsi-Cola, radio, Bakelite bottle on round base, 1940s, 24", EX, D21 ....**$400.00**

Pepsi-Cola, radio, Bakelite bottle on round base, 1940s, 24", restored, EX+, A13 ....**$500.00**

Pepsi-Cola, recipe booklet, 'Hospitality Recipes,' shows tilted bottle on wavy band, 1940, NM, A16 ....**$25.00**

Pepsi-Cola, salt & pepper shakers, clear swirl with red & white label, blue & yellow screw caps, 5½", NM, D21 ....**$30.00**

Pepsi-Cola, score sheet, Pepsi=Cola flanked by the Pepsi cops above, 8x4¼", NM, A7 ....**$5.00**

Pepsi-Cola, sign, aluminum, Drink above red Pepsi=Cola 5¢ on textured wavy band, Bigger-Better below, 1930s-40s, 5x14", EX, A13 ....**$285.00**

Pepsi-Cola, sign, aluminum, More Bounce To The Ounce! above bottle bursting through blue paper, self-framed, 1940s, 48x18", VG+, A13 ....**$325.00**

Pepsi-Cola, sign, cardboard, Be Sociable, Have A Pepsi, image of people conversing & dalmatian dog, 1960s, framed, 26x38", EX+, D30 ....**$145.00**

Pepsi-Cola, sign, cardboard, Be Sociable...Serve/Have A Pepsi, bottle cap & lady with glass/6-pack, 2-sided, 1960s, 26x37", EX+, A13 ....**$130.00**

Pepsi-Cola, sign, cardboard, Certified Quality, lady with tray by picnic spread, Drink... bottle cap, 1940s, 18x21", EX+, A13 ....**$275.00**

Pepsi-Cola, sign, cardboard, Certified Quality By US Testing Co Inc & lady in strapless gown filling glasses, 1940s, 28x38", G, A16 ....**$80.00**

Pepsi-Cola, sign, cardboard, Here's Energy says man with bottle left of oval Pepsi=Cola logo, 1940s, 11x28", G-, A16 ....**$105.00**

Pepsi-Cola, sign, cardboard, Hot Popcorn at left of slanted bottle cap, embossed, foil back, EX+, A13 .... $95.00

Pepsi-Cola, sign, cardboard, Merit!, More Than 30 Years Of Continued Success, shows 5¢ 12-oz bottle, 1930s, framed, 16x8", NM, A13 .... $300.00

Pepsi-Cola, sign, cardboard, Pepsi-Cola bottle cap above ocean shore above bottle & seashell, self-framed, 1950s, NM+, D4 .... $575.00

Pepsi-Cola, sign, cardboard, Pepsi-Cola Hits The Spot left of oval Pepsi=Cola logo, 4 ladies singing, 1940s, 11x28", G, A16 .... $155.00

Pepsi-Cola, sign, cardboard, Pepsi=Cola oval lower left of portrait of girl in hat holding bottle, self-framed, 30x20", VG+, A13 .... $800.00

Pepsi-Cola, sign, cardboard, Reputation Follows High Quality, shows 5¢ 12-oz bottle, 1930s, framed, 16x8", NM, A13 .... $270.00

Pepsi-Cola, sign, cardboard, Say Mix Mine With Pepsi=Cola ...For A Grand Rum Drink, white contour band on blue, 1941, 6x12", NM, A13 .... $450.00

Pepsi-Cola, sign, cardboard, 3-D, New Single Drink Size on yellow emblem at left of Pepsi bottle & cap, foil back, 1960s, NM, A4 .... $215.00

Pepsi-Cola, sign, cardboard (?), Obey That Impulse! Drink Pepsi=Cola..., lady at cooler, Canadian, 1940s, 36x60", rare, EX, A13 .... $2,000.00

Pepsi-Cola, sign, cardboard die-cut, Pepsi-Cola bottle cap above hand pouring from bottle into glass, self-framed, 1950s, NM+, D4 .... $850.00

Pepsi-Cola, sign, cardboard die-cut, Take Home Six!, lady with bottle at window with green shutters, 1940s, 27x28", EX, A13 .... $800.00

Pepsi-Cola, sign, cardboard die-cut hanger, Drink Pepsi=Cola Iced on oval above hanging 12-oz bottle, 1940s, 16x9", NM, A13 .... $800.00

Pepsi-Cola, sign, cardboard die-cut hanger, Refreshing Big Big Bottle 5¢, beach girl with bottle under umbrella, 1930s, NM+, D4 .... $1,100.00

Pepsi-Cola, sign, cardboard die-cut stand-up, Pepsi cops inpecting Bigger & Better 6-Pack, 1930s, 15x21", restored, VG+, A13 .... $375.00

Pepsi-Cola, sign, cardboard stand-up, Say Pepsi-Cola above girl in bonnet at table with glass (no bottle), 1910s, 30x20", EX, A16 .... $4,125.00

Pepsi-Cola, sign, cardboard stand-up, We Use...Exclusively In Making Rum Drinks, blue & white contour logo, 1940s, 6x12", NM, A13 .... $425.00

Pepsi-Cola, sign, cardboard stand-up, We Use...Exclusively In Making Rum Drinks, blue & white contour logo, 1940s, 6x12", VG+, A16 .... $310.00

Pepsi-Cola, sign, cardboard trolley, Big OK From USA on white map of US with tilted bottle, blue ground, 1940s, 11x26", EX, A13 .... $400.00

Pepsi-Cola, sign, cardboard trolley, Big Shot, cartoon image of boy offering girl large bottle, oval logo at right, 11x28", NM, A13 .... $240.00

Pepsi-Cola, sign, cardboard trolley, Cross Country Favourite!, ski girl left of tilted bottle, 1942, framed, 11x42", NM+, A13 .... $850.00

Pepsi-Cola, sign, cardboard trolley, More Bounce To The Ounce left of party couple & bottle cap, 1940s, NM+, A13 .... $270.00

Pepsi-Cola, sign, cardboard trolley, Pepsi's Best, Drink It At The Fountain Too! left of glass & bottle cap, 1940s, 11x21", G+, A13 .... $550.00

Pepsi-Cola, sign, cardboard trolley, Why Take Less...Pepsi's Best!, 6-pack, receding row of glasses & crown, 1940s, 11x25", NM, A13 .... $775.00

Pepsi-Cola, sign, celluloid, Ice Cold Pepsi=Cola Sold Here on red, white & blue emblem, 1940, 9" dia, VG+, A13 .... $250.00

Pepsi-Cola, sign, celluloid, More Bounce To The Ounce on tag with ribbon, bottle cap above, beveled edge, 1950s, 9" dia, EX+, A13 .... $225.00

Pepsi-Cola, sign, celluloid, Now It's Pepsi... Perfect Any Time! above black couple, oval hanger or stand-up, 1960, 12x8", M, A4 .... $65.00

Pepsi-Cola, sign, celluloid, Pepsi=Cola crown, 1945, 9" dia, EX, A8 ....**$175.00**

Pepsi-Cola, sign, celluloid, Refresh Without Filling & slanted cap right of lady with hand on hip, oval, EX+, A16 ....**$75.00**

Pepsi-Cola, sign, fiberboard, Drink Pepsi=Cola A 5¢ Nickel Drink Worth A Dime left of slightly tilted bottle, 1930s, 15x13", EX, A13 ....**$140.00**

Pepsi-Cola, sign, flange, Ice Cold on blue above red Pepsi=Cola on white contour band, Sold Here on blue below, 1940s, 10x15", EX+, A13 ....**$475.00**

Pepsi-Cola, sign, flange, Pepsi bottle cap, 1940s, 14x15", EX, A13 ....**$625.00**

Pepsi-Cola, sign, light-up, counter-top, Drink Pepsi-Cola on red, white & blue contour logo, 1950s, 14" dia, restored, EX, A13 ....**$175.00**

Pepsi-Cola, sign, light-up, Drink Pepsi Cola, The Light Refreshment, round contour logo, glass lens, 1950s, 16" dia, NM+, A13 ....$1,250.00

Pepsi-Cola, sign, light-up, Drink Pepsi-Cola Ice Cold, molded plastic bottle cap, 1950s, 16" dia, EX, A13 ....**$500.00**

Pepsi-Cola, sign, light-up, Ice Cold Drinks, bear & bottle cap logo against northern lights, 3-D effect, 1950s-60s, 20x16", NM, A13....................$1,750.00

Pepsi-Cola, sign, paper, Listen To 'Country-Spy' above Pepsi=Cola crown, Pepsi's Radio Thriller!...On Your ABC..., 8x19", EX+, A8 ....**$55.00**

Pepsi-Cola, sign, paper, Standard Summer Uniforms For Salesmen, Pepsi-Cola bottle cap above ad text, 18x12", NM+, D30...**$75.00**

Pepsi-Cola, sign, plastic, ...Say Pepsi Please, 3-D Pepsi-Cola glass in snow mound at left of Pepsi bottle cap, 1970s, VG, A13...**$65.00**

Pepsi-Cola, sign, porcelain, Drink upper left of bottle cap, Iced lower right on yellow, curved corners, 1949, 12x30", EX+, A13..**$150.00**

Pepsi-Cola, sign, porcelain, Enjoy A Pepsi in black on white at left of bottle cap, yellow background, 10x30", VG, A1 ....**$310.00**

Pepsi-Cola, sign, porcelain, Enjoy Pepsi on bottle cap, 12x29", M, D11 ....**$195.00**

Pepsi-Cola, sign, porcelain, Enjoy Pepsi on white field receding to slanted bottle cap on yellow, 1950s, 12x30", EX+, A13 ....$250.00

Pepsi-Cola, sign, porcelain, Have A Pepsi right of slanted bottle cap on yellow, curved corners, 2-sided, 1950s, 26x28", VG/VG+, A13 ....**$60.00**

Pepsi-Cola, sign, porcelain, Pepsi=Cola on red on white, black border, 8x20", EX, A1 ....**$365.00**

Pepsi-Cola, sign, tin, Drink & bottle bursting through yellow background & bottle cap, curved corners, Canadian, 1950s, EX+, A13 ....**$250.00**

Pepsi-Cola, sign, tin, Drink above 5¢ Pepsi=Cola 5¢ on contour band, America's Biggest... below, embossed, 1940, 10x36", NM, A13..**$575.00**

Pepsi-Cola, sign, tin, Drink Delicious Refreshing in green on white Pepsi=Cola on green, red trim, embossed, 1910-15, 4x10", NM, A13.................................**$275.00**

Pepsi-Cola, sign, tin, Drink Pepsi-Cola bottle cap above & behind tilted bottle on white, 48x18", NM, A13.**$475.00**

Pepsi-Cola, sign, tin, Drink Pepsi=Cola, Double Size 5¢, A Nickel Drink Worth A Dime, embossed, 28x20", EX, D11...**$175.00**

Pepsi-Cola, sign, tin, Drink Pepsi=Cola Iced, 2 Pepsi bottles on ice, self-framed, 17½x55", EX, A6...........**$750.00**

Pepsi-Cola, sign, tin, Drink Pepsi=Cola Iced right of icy-looking bottles on yellow & blue ground, Canadian, 1941, 18x54", G, A13..**$230.00**

Pepsi-Cola, sign, tin, Drink Pepsi=Cola 5¢, Refreshing & Healthful, blue & red on white, blue border, 1930s, 6x17", EX+, A13...**$325.00**

Pepsi-Cola, sign, tin, Drink Pepsi=Cola 5¢ flanked by Pepsi cops on white contour band, embossed, 1940, 3½x21", VG, A8...**$215.00**

Pepsi-Cola, sign, tin, hanger, Have A Pepsi & slanted bottle cap inset left of bottle, beveled edge, 1940s, 9x11", EX+, A16..**$40.00**

Pepsi-Cola, sign, tin, Have A Pepsi above bottle & bottle cap on yellow, self-framed edge, 1960s, NM+, A13.....**$160.00**

Pepsi-Cola, sign, tin, Hot Dogs/Hamburgers/Pepsi=Cola Ice Cold 5¢/Bigger-Better, red, white & blue, 1930s, 28x20", VG+, A13..**$325.00**

Pepsi-Cola, sign, tin, Pepsi-Cola, slanted bottle cap on yellow band, embossed, rounded corners, 1950s, 48x42", NM, A13...**$100.00**

Pepsi-Cola, sign, tin, Pepsi-Cola Bottle cap on blue background, gold & black border, 1940s, EX+, A **$400.00**

Pepsi-Cola, sign, tin, Say 'Pepsi Please,' pictures bottle & cap, 1965, 46x17", M, D32.................................**$150.00**

Pepsi-Cola, sign, tin, Say 'Pepsi Please,' cap & bottle on yellow, gold beveled edge, stand-up/hanger, 1960s, 9x11", NM, A13..$45.00

Pepsi-Cola, sign, tin, Say 'Pepsi Please' below Pepsi bottle & cap, yellow background, 1950, 46x16", NM, D8 ....**$295.00**

Pepsi-Cola, sign, tin, You'll Enjoy...Take Home A Carton Today!, red, white & blue, for drink rack, 10x15", EX+, D21..$50.00

Pepsi-Cola, sign, tin die-cut, slanted bottle cap on yellow circle atop white & gray courtesy panel, 1950s, 56x42", EX+, A13..$260.00

Pepsi-Cola, sign, tin die-cut bottle, Pepsi=Cola Refreshing-Enjoyable label, 5¢ dot above octagon label, 1930s, 45", EX, A13..$625.00

Pepsi-Cola, sign, tin die-cut bottle, Pepsi=Cola Refreshing-Enjoyable label, 5¢ dot above octagon label, 1930s, 45", EX+, A13..$825.00

Pepsi-Cola, sign, tin die-cut bottle, Sparkling Pepsi=Cola label, embossed, 1940s, 44½x12", NM, A1......$1,250.00

Pepsi-Cola, sign, tin die-cut bottle cap, Drink Pepsi-Cola, 32" dia, EX+, A13..$210.00

Pepsi-Cola, sign, tin die-cut bottle cap, Pepsi-Cola, embossed, 1950s, 26", dia, NM, D8....................$375.00

Pepsi-Cola, sign, tin die-cut bottle cap, Pepsi-Cola, 1960s, 20" dia, EX, A13 ....$225.00

Pepsi-Cola, sign, tin die-cut bottle cap, Pepsi-Cola, 30" dia, NM, A1..$425.00

Pepsi-Cola, sign base, heavy cast iron, round red, white & blue Pepsi-Cola logo, for patrol boy or other sign, 1950, EX+, A13..$150.00

Pepsi-Cola, stadium cushion, blue with Pepsi logo, M, A16..$30.00

Pepsi-Cola, stick pin, bottle shape, 1940s, M, D32....$70.00

Pepsi-Cola, tap knob, musical, bottle cap inset, 1940s, EX+, A13..$275.00

Pepsi-Cola, thermometer, tin, Any Weather's Pepsi Weather on card with ribbon, bottle cap above, 1950s, 25x9", EX, A13..$230.00

Pepsi-Cola, thermometer, tin, Bigger & Better, large bottle at right of bulb, raised border, 1940s, 16x6", EX+, A13..$525.00

Pepsi-Cola, thermometer, tin, Have A Pepsi on white field receding down to bottle cap, embossed, round corners, 1950s, NM, A13..$270.00

Pepsi-Cola, thermometer, tin, Pepsi-Cola bottle cap above & below bulb, red, stepped sides, curved ends, 1950s, 27", EX, A8..$90.00

Pepsi-Cola, thermometer, tin, Say 'Pepsi Please,' slanted Pepsi-Cola bottle cap, yellow, square corners, 1967, 28", EX+, A16..$110.00

Pepsi-Cola, thermometer, tin, Say 'Pepsi Please,' stylized Pepsi bottle cap logo, yellow, square corners, 1967, 28", EX, A16..$75.00

Pepsi-Cola, thermometer, tin, The Light Refreshment, embossed bottle cap above bulb, 27", VG, A6.....$80.00

Pepsi-Cola, thermometer, tin, Weather Cold Or Weather Hot..., girl drinking from straw in bottle above Pepsi=Cola, 27", NM, A1..$1,125.00

Pepsi-Cola, tip tray, bouquet of roses in center, decorative rim, rectangular, NM, A16..$100.00

Pepsi-Cola, tip tray, Compliments Of Pepsi-Cola in center, banded rim, rectangular, NM, A16..$35.00

Pepsi-Cola, tip tray, Pepsi=Cola in red on white milk glass, serrated edges, NM+, A13..$200.00

Pepsi-Cola, tip tray, Pepsi=Cola 5¢, girl with roses lifting glass, ornate border, 1907, NM+, D4...$1,200.00

Pepsi-Cola, tip tray, woman in plumed hat lifting glass, plain rim, 1909, 6x4", NM+, A4..$1,079.00

Pepsi-Cola, toy hot dog wagon, wooden cart with tin umbrella, incomplete, G, A16..$45.00

Pepsi-Cola, toy truck, Marx, plastic double-decker, open bed w/ad marquee, Drink Pepsi=Cola bottle cap decals on doors, EX+, A16..$350.00

Pepsi-Cola, toy truck, Marx, plastic flatbed with cases of bottles, Pepsi=Cola decals on sides of bed, 7½", NM, A7..$195.00

Pepsi-Cola, toy truck, Marx, plastic flatbed with wood wheels, no cases, bottle cap decals on doors, EX+, A16..$75.00

Pepsi-Cola, toy truck, Marx, plastic flatbed with 3 rows of cases with bottles, bottle cap decals on doors, 9", NMIB, A4 ....**$310.00**

Pepsi-Cola, toy truck, Nylint, snub-nose cab with white walls, roof over open-sided bays, 4 cases, original box, 1950s, EX+, A13 ....**$400.00**

Pepsi-Cola, trash can, shaped like a Pepsi can, early 1970s, 16", EX, D24 ....**$20.00**

Pepsi-Cola, tray, bouquet of stylized flowers on black background with connected dots, 1940s, 11x14", VG+, A16 ....**$25.00**

Pepsi-Cola, tray, deep-dish, large Pepsi=Cola bottle cap in center, 12" dia, EX, A6 ....**$150.00**

Pepsi-Cola, tray, Enjoy Pepsi=Cola, Hits The Spot, musical notes below, 1940, 11x14", VG+, A **$150.00**

Pepsi-Cola, tray, large bottle cap image in center, 13¼" dia, EX+, A4..**$225.00**

Pepsi-Cola, umbrella, red & white beach type with bottle caps alternating with Pepsi's Best in block letters, 1950s, EX, A13 ....**$120.00**

Pepsi-Cola, vending machine, Vendorlater model 3D-33, 1950s, working, EX, D32 ....**$400.00**

Pepsi-Cola, see also Evervess Sparkling Water

Pepto-Bismol, jar, clear glass, 4-sided with label under glass, ground glass stopper, 9", NM, A13 ....**$85.00**

Pepto-Bismol, sign, die-cut cardboard, Upset Stomach? Take Soothing..., man rubbing his tummy & holding bottle, 30x20", NM, D30..**$65.00**

Peptomalt/Atlas Brewing Co, sign, tin on cardboard, King Of All above Peptomalt in script, Invigorating on tail, company name below, 7x10", VG, A8..................**$80.00**

Percival Mainsprings/DC Percival & Co, tin, flat, red with embellished gold lettering, red & gold decorative border, square corners,¾x3x3⅜", EX, D37..........**$40.00**

Perfect Circle Piston Rings & Piston Expanders, sign, embossed tin, Don't Drive An Oil Hog above image of 'oil hog' pulling car into garage, name below, 36x30", VG+, A6..$700.00

Perfection Beer, sign, cardboard, Aged Nine Months..., bottle with sign before 2 elves in forest with barrel, framed, 27x22", EX, A8 ....**$255.00**

Perfection Brew, label, gold on white, gold border, 11-oz, EX, A19 ....**$7.00**

Perfection Distilled Water Co, sign, porcelain, 15x26", NM, D11..**$90.00**

Perfection Dyes, cabinet, wood with tin insert, ...For Silk, Woolen, Cotton & Feathers, W Gushing & Co, 24x17x6", EX+, A9..**$900.00**

Perfection Oil, sign, tin, product name above 3 oval inserts of families using product flanked by Brilliant & Odorless, 13x19", EX, A9..................................**$325.00**

Perfection 9 Months Old Beer, sign, tin on cardboard, product lettering & In Bottles Only on wood-grain background, beveled edge, 5x7", NM, A19........**$155.00**

Perma-Grip Adhesive Powder, tin, sample, 2¼", NM, A7 ....**$12.00**

Perma-Grip Denture Powder, tin, sample, with contents, 2¼", NM, A7 ....**$14.00**

Permalube Motor Oil, see Standard

Perry's Beverages, push plate, tin, product name above glowing tilted bottle, vertical, NM, A13 ....**$55.00**

Pet Cigarettes, trade card, girl on rock, ...Are The Best, Allen & Ginter, 9x4", EX, A5 ....**$115.00**

Pet Cigarettes, trade card, girl with wagon, ...Are The Best, Allen & Ginter, 9x4", EX, A5 ....**$115.00**

Pet Cigarettes, trade card, monkey standing on donkey, ...Are The Best, Allen & Ginter, 6½x4", VG, A5..**$25.00**

Pet Cigarettes, trade card, smiling boy, ...Are The Best, Allen & Ginter, 9x4", EX, A5 ....**$115.00**

Pete Hagens 100 Proof Rye Liquor, sample bottle, glass with metal screw cap, 5", EX, D24......................**$10.00**

Pete's Best, crate label, Washington apple, handsome blond boy on pale yellow background, black & red logo, 9x11", M, D12..**$5.00**

Peter Barman Lager, Ale & Porter, calendar, 1914, shows George Washington's inauguration above full pad, 20x15", EX+, A8..**$50.00**

Peter Bock Beer, label, William Peter Brewing Co, Internal Revenue Tax Paid statement, 1933-50, 12-oz, M, A10..**$15.00**

Peter Doelger, tray, pictures factory scene flanked by bottles, decorative rim, oval, G, A19........................**$250.00**

Peter Doelger, tray, shows 2 bottles & frothy stemmed glass with country lake scene beyond, decorative border, pre-1920s, oval, G+, A19............................**$250.00**

Peter Doelger Bottled Beer, tip tray, eagle surmounting medallions, product name on rim, 4" dia, VG, A9..**$60.00**

Peter Doelger First Prize Beer & Ale, tray, deep-dish, product name above & below factory scene, round, VG+, A19 ....**$45.00**

Peter Pan Ice Cream, sign, tin, Demand...Take Home A Pint, image of Peter Pan, 28x24", NM+, D30......**$155.00**

Peter Pan Peanut Butter/Derby Foods Inc, tin, image of Peter Pan left of lettering & logo, 11-oz, EX, A3..**$60.00**

Peter Pan Peanut Butter/Kelly Confection Co, tin, round with colorful graphics depicting bunnies having a picnic in the park, pry lid, 4", extremely rare, EX, A2..**$2,100.00**

Peter Rabbit Baby Powder, tin, 6-sided, pictures bunnies & animal friends crossing stream, 4x4", VG, A2......**$165.00**

Peter 1859 Beer, tray, deep-dish, Peter in script above 1859 & Beer on blue, lettered rim, 12" dia, VG, A8.....**$100.00**

Peters Big Game Ammunition, sign, paper, encircled P above moose, 29x18", G-, A9............................**$700.00**

Peters Cartridge Co, calendar, 1910, Goodwin illustration of bull moose in stream, incomplete pad, framed, image: 25x½x15½", EX, A9 ....$1,250.00

Peters Diamond Brand Shoes, sign, cardboard stand-up, name & list of 5 Service Points at left of cut-away view of shoe, 1910, 10x18", EX+, A3 .....$65.00

Peters Shells & Cartridges, pin-back button, P logo surrounded by product name & The Perfect Ammunition, EX, A20 ....$10.00

Peters Weatherbird School Shoes, thermometer, wood, shows boy & product lettering above bulb, curved top, square bottom, 8½x2¼", NM, A7 ....$70.00

Peters Weatherbird Shoes, bank, tin & cardboard, oblong can shape, 2x1¼", NM, A7............$25.00

Peters Weatherbird Shoes, clicker, tin, NM, A7 ......$20.00

Peters Weatherbird Shoes, pencil holder, cardboard, shaped like a large pencil, 10½", NM, A7 ....$45.00

Peters Weatherbird Shoes, toy spinner, tin, shaped like 4-leaf clover, 1½" dia, NM, A7............$25.00

Peters Weatherbird Shoes, whistle, tin, cylindrical, 2", EX, A17 ....$15.00

Peters Weatherbird Shoes, whistle, tin keyhole shape, Best For Boys — Best For Girls, 2½", EX, A17 ....$15.00

Petoskey Chief 5¢ Cigar, sign, paper, Indian chief with bear claw necklace, Try A... above, Our Best... below, framed, image: 28x21", G+, A9 ....$2,500.00

Pettijohn's Rolled Wheat, container, bear on cliff flanked by wheat, Rolled Wheat With All The Bran... below, Quaker Oats Co, 22-oz, NM+, A3 ....$185.00

Pevely Super Test Ice Cream, sign, die-cut porcelain, **Pevely Super Test on red oval above Ice Cream & logo on blue, 2-sided, 30x36", NM, A1..........$220.00**

Pfeiffer's Beer, label, illustrated elephant with blanket reading Pfeiffer's Beer Jumbo Full Quart..., company name below, 32-oz, VG, A19............$10.00

Pflueger Fishing Tackle, sign, die-cut cardboard stand-up, Ask For..., 3 large fish going for bait, copyright 1937, 23x22", EX, A12............$460.00

PH Zang Brewing Co, match safe, sterling silver with applied circular enamel logo, rectangular with rounded corners, EX, A8............$230.00

Pheasant, crate label, citrus, strutting pheasant on black background, 9x9", M, D3 ....$4.00

Phenix, sign, tin shield with chain hanger, Drink Phenix on red above For You Thirst... & 5¢ on white, 1910s-20s, 6x5", EX+, A13............$250.00

Philadelphia Brewing Co, print, paper litho, company name on matte around country scene with sheep, pre-1920s, wood frame, 15x19", EX, A19 ....$52.00

Philgas, doll, Buddy Lee in gray uniform, pipe in mouth, no hat, EX+, A13 ....$350.00

Philip Morris Cigarettes, can, holds 50 cigarettes, 2¾" dia, NM, A7............$30.00

Philip Morris Cigarettes, cigarette carton, bellboy calling for Philip Morris, America's Finest Cigarette on light brown, EX, A18 ....$40.00

Philip Morris Cigarettes, display, cardboard stand-up, bellboy with pack of cigarettes standing atop ad panel, 5-ft, NM, D22 ....$165.00

Philip Morris Cigarettes, sign, cardboard die-cut, Call For Philip Morris Cigarettes, bellboy above sign, framed, 15x6", EX, A18............$125.00

Philip Morris Cigarettes, sign, cardboard stand-up, All Parties Vote For Philip Morris, bellboy holding sign, crown behind, 14", EX, A18 ....$55.00

Philip Morris Cigarettes, sign, paper, Safety First on band above bellboy calling 'Call for Philip Morris,' 23x40½", NOS, M, A1 ....$115.00

Philip Morris Cigarettes, sign, tin, Buy 'Em Here! shouts bellboy with pack, Call For... on black band, King-Size... below, 14x12", VG+, A1............$195.00

Phillips Petroleum Co Capitol Site, sign, porcelain, shield logo at left of lettering, 6x18", M, D11.....$125.00

Phillips 66, doll, Buddy Lee in tan shirt & brown pants, no hat, EX, A13 ....$275.00

Phillips 66, gas globe, red & black shield shape, 15½", EX+, A6............$375.00

Phillips 66, sign, die-cut porcelain shield, orange & black, 29½x29½", NM+, A6............$250.00

Phillips 66, slide tile puzzle, plastic, Puzzled/Technology Licensing The Solution, cream, beige, black & red, 5x4", NM, A6............$5.00

Phillips 66 Ethyl, sign, die-cut porcelain shield, orange & black with yellow, black & white Ethyl logo over 66, 2-sided, 29x29", VG, A6............$425.00

Phillips 66 Farm Service, picnic cooler, red metal box with lift-off lid & swing handle, white emblem & lettering, 14x19x12", EX, A6............$75.00

Phillips 66 HDS Motor Oil, can, Phillips 66 emblem on white circle on black with white stripes above HDS & Motor Oil on white band, 1-qt, NM+, A1..............**$30.00**

Phillips 66 Trop-Artic, bank, tin & cardboard, can shape, 2" dia, NM, A7 ....**$18.00**

Phillips 66 Trop-Artic, can, shield logo in circle on lined background, Trop-Artic in bold lettering below, 5-qt, 9½x7" dia, G, A6 ....**$10.00**

Phillips 66/Lee Tires, Mapsac, vinyl, orange with black graphics & text, Lee Tires advertising at bottom, US map on back, 9½x6", EX, A6 ....**$35.00**

Phillips' Milk of Magnesia Tablets, tin, sample, 30 Tablets Price 25¢, Complimentary Package, Not To Be Sold, rounded corners, ¼x2⅜x2¾", EX, D37 ....**$8.00**

Phoenix Fire Extinguishing Compound, container, metal with painted label, red, black & gold, 22", scratches & paint chips, A6 ....**$50.00**

Phoenix Harburg Bike Tires, sign, German, porcelain, 2 tires around road & logo, 21x33", NM+, D11 .....**$575.00**

Phoenix Rolled Oats, container, little girl with bowl of oats on front, trademark image of phoenix rising from flame on back, 4-oz, NM, A3........................**$110.00**

Physician's Beef Peptonoids, tin, sample, lettering on fancy oval with rounded decorative borders, ½x1⅝x2¾", EX, D37 ....**$90.00**

Picant, cigar box label, outer, woman seated on half moon, 4½x4½", M, D5.......................................**$25.00**

Piccadilly Little Cigars, sign, self-framed tin, loving couple above product name & open cigar box, 10 Minute Havanas lower left, 22x13", VG, A9 ....**$150.00**

Piccadilly Smoking Mixture, box, product name on decorative background, Wm S Kimball & Co, American Tobacco Co... lower left, square corners, EX, A3..**$40.00**

Pickwick Ale, sign, composition, product name on oval, With The Sparkling Clean Taste on base, red & brown, 7½x14", NM, A19..**$80.00**

Pickwick Ale, sign, tin over cardboard, product name on sign at left of 2 horses pulling barrels with buildings beyond, 7x23", VG, A6 ....**$45.00**

Pickwick Ale, tray, product name in sky above 2 horses pulling barrels with buildings beyond, 'Ale That Is Ale,' 12" dia, EX, A6...**$95.00**

Pickwick Coffee, tin, product name flanked by Flavor Fresh & oval portrait on plaid background, key-wind lid, 1-lb, EX, A3 ....**$50.00**

Picobac, pocket tin, vertical, tobacco plant (hand-held) above name on diagonal band, 10¢ & Very Mild below, short, NM, A18..**$85.00**

Picobac, pocket tin, vertical, tobacco plant (hand-held) above name on diagonal band, Very Mild below (no 10¢), tall, NM, A18..**$90.00**

Picobac, pocket tin, vertical, tobacco plant (no hand) above name on diagonal band, 10¢ & Very Mild below, short, EX+, A18..**$50.00**

Picobac Sliced Plug, pocket tin, flat, product name on diagonal center band flanked by tobacco leaf & 5¢, 2x3", EX+, A3..**$25.00**

Picobac Tobacco, sign, tin with cardboard insert, ...Pick Of Pipe Tobacco above hand holding pipe, 10x3", G, D21 ....**$20.00**

Piedmont Cigarettes, box, paper over tin, holds 100 cigarettes, rectangular, EX, A13............................**$40.00**

Piedmont Cigarettes, display, oversized box featuring lady in plumed hat, ca 1910, 17½x10x4", VG, A13...**$400.00**

Piedmont Cigarettes, folding chair, wood with porcelain back, For Cigarettes Virginia Tobacco Is The Best above Piedmont, 32x21x16", G-, A9 ....**$115.00**

Piedmont Cigarettes, sign, cardboard, Piedmont The Cigarette Of Quality, lady in plumed hat & product pack, 25x19", EX, A13..**$325.00**

Piedmont Cigarettes, sign, cardboard, Piedmont The Cigarette of Quality, man-in-the-moon image, 20x14", VG+, A13 ....**$425.00**

Piedmont Cigarettes, sign, porcelain, Piedmont, For Cigarettes Virginia Tobacco Is The Best below, shows pack, blue ground, 46x30", VG+, A21 ....**$415.00**

Piedmont Cigarettes, sign, porcelain, Piedmont The Cigarette Of Quality, blue on white, 12x35½", VG+, A18 ....**$200.00**

Piedmont Cigarettes, sign, porcelain, Piedmont The Cigarette Of Quality, unopened 5¢ pack, white lettering on blue, 46x30", EX, A13 ....**$475.00**

Piels Beer, bar caddy, metal figures of Bert & Harry, 8½", EX, D25...**$90.00**

Piels Beer, display, hard rubber, Bert & Harry in blue suits on base with slots for bottles, 12x7", NM, A19.....**$50.00**

Piels Beer, sign, light-up, Enjoy Piels Beer Now!, glass lens featuring animated Bert & Harry figures, metal body, 13" dia, NM, A13 ....**$180.00**

Piels Light Lager Beer, clock, diamond shape with numbers & dots surrounding name & Bert & Harry at 3 & 9, glass front, 13x13", EX+, A3................................**$35.00**

Pierce Hardware Co, calendar, 1896, elegant woman holding floral branch flanked by lettering, full pad below, 21½x14", NM, A3 ....**$220.00**

Piggly Wiggly, sign, porcelain, smiling pig flanked by stars, red lettering on white, 24" dia, NM+, D11..........**$450.00**

Piggly Wiggly, whistle, tin, paper label, NM, A7.......**$28.00**

Pillsbury A, cigar box label, outer, factory image, 1903, M, A5 ....**$55.00**

Pillsbury's Best Flour, pin-back button, celluloid, eagle atop barrel with logo, The Flour That Sells Around The World, round, EX+, A11..**$25.00**

Pillsbury's Turk's Head Restaurant, matchbook, Trenton/Princeton, 20 strike, front strike, NM, D28.......**$4.00**

Pilot Beer, label, Louis Ziegler Brewing Co, Internal Revenue Tax Paid statement, 1933-50, 12-oz, M, A10 . **$18.00**

Pilot Boy Tobacco, trade card, Chappies's Cane, mechanical wheel with 4 faces, Boykin, Seddon & Co, Richmond VA above, 4½x2½", EX, A5 .... **$85.00**

Pilot Brand Typewriter Ribbon, tin, flat, red with lettering around single-engine plane, square, rounded corners, ¾x2½x2½", EX, D37 .... **$75.00**

Pilot 10¢ Plug Chewing Tobacco, tin, green with white product name around CF-ARO aircraft, round, EX+, A18 .... **$115.00**

Pimlico Course, sign, paper, racehorses running past clubhouse, framed, 18x25", G-, A9 .... **$650.00**

Pinch Hit Chewing Tobacco, sign, paper, 'Wow! It's A Homer,' excited baseball fan against green dot with pack & The Hit Of The Day, 27x42", G, A2 .... $525.00

Pioneer Valley, miniature bottle, green with applied color label, NM, A16 .... **$25.00**

Pipe Major English Smoking Mixture, pocket tin, vertical, tan with product name on plaid band above man in kilt serving seated man, NM, A18 .... **$255.00**

Pipe Major English Smoking Mixture, pocket tin, vertical, tan with product name on plaid band above man in kilt serving seated man, VG, A3 .... **$165.00**

Piper Heidsieck Chewing Tobacco, pocket tin, flat, product name above exploding champagne bottle, hinged lid, 3x3x½", NM, A1 .... **$20.00**

Pippins 5¢ Cigars, tin, 5¢ Cigars above Pippins apple, H Traiser & Co Inc, Boston below, tall, EX, A18 ..... **$75.00**

Pirate Cigarettes, alarm clock, colorful ad with swordsman aboard ship on face with Roman numerals, round footed case, 1890, 6", EX, A2 .... **$358.00**

Pirelli, sign, porcelain, star & P logo above Pirelli, Reifen below, blue, yellow, black & red, 29x29", NM, A1 .. **$195.00**

Pittman Streamlined Gasoline, gas globe, Pittman arched above airplane flying through cloud, blue rippled Gill body, 13½" dia, NM, A6 .... **$7,000.00**

Pitts Farm Machinery, pin-back button, Put Me On To arched above image of a white buffalo, Pitts Farm Machinery below, EX, A20 .... **$75.00**

Pittsburgh Brewing Co, mug, salt-glazed stoneware, barrel shape with pointed handle, Pittsburg... above Darlington in blue, 1860-80, VG+, A8 .... **$155.00**

Pittsburgh Pretzel Co Ltd, jar, glass, ball shape with embossed lettering, round knob lid, 12" dia, rare, EX, A2 .... **$440.00**

Pittsburgh Utility Enamel, display, 15 color samples for enamel, EX, 25", A6 .... **$20.00**

Pittston Gazette, sign, porcelain, Read The...And Keep Posted, Bright, Clean, Newsy in white on blue, 8x16", EX, A6 .... **$100.00**

PJ Cray's Old Fashioned Root Beer, bottle, stoneware, tan with brown neck & black logo, crown top, 8", EX, D16 .... **$125.00**

Placer, crate label, California pear, classic gold-mining scene with prospectors panning river, Auburn, 8x11", M, D12 .... **$10.00**

Planet Jr Garden Tools & Farm Implements, banner, canvas, Garden Tools above Buy Planet Jr It Pays!, Farm Implements below, 2½x47", EX, A6 .... **$40.00**

Planters, ashtray, metal, Mr Peanut standing in center, marked Planters Peanuts 1906-1956, 6x6" dia, EX, A6 .... **$25.00**

Planters, bank, plastic Mr Peanut figure, M, A16 .... **$20.00**

Planters, cocktail glasses, red plastic with figural Mr Peanut stems, set of 6, 5", EX, A21 .... **$155.00**

Planters, container, papier-mache, Mr Peanut figure with tan body, black hat, arms, legs, cane, hand-dated 1940, 12½", NM+, A13 .... $525.00

Planters, container, papier-mache, peanut shape with Planters in script, original string, 12", EX+, A13 ... **$65.00**

Planters, container, papier-mache, peanut shape with Planters in script, no string, 10", NM, A13 .... **$35.00**

Planters, costume, Mr Peanut, fiberglass body with removable hat, arm holes, open bottom for legs, 50", VG+, A13 .... **$900.00**

Planters, cup, blue plastic, shaped like Mr Peanut's head, NM, A7 .... **$10.00**

Planters, figure, Mr Peanut, painted wood, yellow body with jointed black arms & legs, gray hat, with cane, 8", VG+, A21 .... **$185.00**

Planters, jar, blue glass, 3-D peanut in each corner, 14", NM, D24..$55.00

Planters, jar, glass, barrel shape with embossed images of Mr Peanut, Planters Salted Peanuts label, peanut finial, 10", EX, A6..$275.00

Planters, jar, glass, barrel shape with embossed images of Mr Peanut, peanut finial, 12x9" dia, EX, A2 ....$175.00

Planters, jar, glass, barrel shape with embossed product name & Mr Peanut images, NM, A13..................$200.00

Planters, jar, glass, flat-sided fishbowl shape, no label, knob lid, 12", EX, A2..$55.00

Planters, jar, glass, flat-sided fishbowl shape with ...Pennant Brand Salted Peanuts 5¢ label, peanut finial, 12", EX, A2...$150.00

Planters, jar, glass, flat-sided fishbowl shape with embossed Planters Salted Peanuts, peanut finial, 9", EX, A2...$275.00

Planters, jar, glass, flat-sided fishbowl shape with Planters Salted Peanuts 5¢ label, peanut finial, 13", EX, A2...$230.00

Planters, jar, glass, octagon with embossed Pennant Peanut 5¢ & Mr Peanut figures, decal label, knob lid, 12x9" dia, EX, A2 ....$230.00

Planters, jar, glass, Planters embossed vertically between raised peanuts on each corner, peanut finial, 14x8" dia, VG, A9 ....$175.00

Planters, jar, glass, slant front with Planters Peanuts painted on, tin screw lid with Mr Peanut & advertising, EX+, A13...$150.00

Planters, jar, glass, square with Planters embossed on all 4 sides, round lid with peanut finial, 7x7", EX, A2 ..$135.00

Planters, lighter, plastic, Mr Peanut figure above Planters, disposable, M, A19..$20.00

Planters, night light, cream-colored plastic Mr Peanut figure on brown round beveled base, 10", NM+, A13..$250.00

Planters, pencil, Mr Peanut floating at end, 6", EX, A6...$20.00

Planters, salt & pepper shakers, plastic, figural Mr Peanut, EX, A16 ....$15.00

Planters, scoop, plastic, figural Mr Peanut handle, NM, A7...$20.00

Planters, spoon, silver plate, with figural Mr Peanut on handle, round spoon bowl, NM, A16 ....$20.00

Planters, toothpick holder, china, Mr Peanut sitting on peanut behind holder, black, brown & cream, 4", appears EX, A6...$100.00

Planters, walker, plastic wind-up Mr Peanut figure, 8½", VG+, A13 ....$300.00

Planters Chocolate Covered Peanuts, box, The World Gone Nuts, Mr Peanut graphics & product lettering, holds 24 packs, 1937, NM, A13..........................$800.00

Planters Cooking & Salad Oil, display, mechanical, Mr Peanut atop actual cans of product pointing to can & ad, 1940s-50s, 56x56", NM, A13....................$11,500.00

Planters Fresh Roasted Salted Peanuts, display box, die-cut circle on back shows smiling lady with pack, holds 24 packs, NM+, A13..$450.00

Planters Hot Roaster Fresh Peanuts, peanut bag, product name above Mr Peanut standing next to large peanut, more text below, large, NM, A7 ....$10.00

Planters Pennant Brand Salted Peanuts, tin, product name above & below Pennant logo, black with blue, silver, red & black detail, pry lid, 10½", VG+, A1......$85.00

Planters Salted Peanuts, box, waxed cardboard, product name on arched band above 5¢, Mr Peanut on oval, peanuts on background, VG+, A13......................$40.00

Planters Salted Peanuts, can, square 1-lb size with pry lid, 1920s, G+, A13 ....$90.00

Planters Salted Peanuts, dispensing cup, tin, blue cone shape with red & black lettering around red pennant, 2½", NM, A18 ....$100.00

Planters Suffolk Brand Salted Peanuts, can, gold with 10 Pounds Net above blue, white, black & gold label, Planters Nut & Chocolate Co, original lid, G, A13 ....$1,500.00

Planters Whole-Blanched Salted Peanuts, tin, product image & lettering on green background, square with curved corners, pry lid, ca 1920, 1-lb, VG, A13 ...$85.00

Plantista Cigars, tin, white & gold paper label with Plantista above woman in profile, slip lid, VG+, A18...........$45.00

Platinum Plus Super Premium, pump sign, porcelain, red & blue product lettering with diamond on white field, 12x12", NM+, A1..$60.00

Platteville Beer, label, Platteville on red diagonal band, white background with blue border, 12-oz, EX, A19.......$135.00

Player's Cigarette Papers, dispenser, French lettering & product on blue & white diagonal background, vertical with opening at bottom, EX+, A18......................$45.00

Player's Country Life Cigarettes, pocket tin, flat, blue with silver emblem, holds 50 cigarettes, NM, A18..........$60.00

Player's Please, playing cards, each showing clown, full deck, original box, EX, A18..................................$25.00

Player's Weights, playing cards, each showing clown, full deck, original box, EX, A18..................................$25.00

Plee-Zing Coffee, tin, Plee-Zing on oval inset above steaming cup of coffee, slip lid, rare, EX, A3................$65.00

Plenti Grand, crate label, vegetable, blond girl posing in sunsuit, M, D3...$2.00

Plow Boy Chewing & Smoking Tobacco, container, cardboard & tin, boy resting on plow in field, pry lid, round, EX+, A18...$55.00

Plow Boy Chewing & Smoking Tobacco, pail, boy resting on plow in field, slip lid & bail, EX, A18.......$30.00

Plow Boy Chewing & Smoking Tobacco, sign, die-cut tin, shaped like product pack with boy resting on plow in field, 13x9", VG, A2 ....$525.00

Plow Boy Chewing & Smoking Tobacco, tin, boy resting on plow in field, Liggett & Myers Tobacco Co, slip lid, 6x5" dia, EX, A6...$50.00

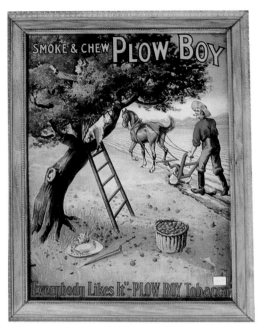

Plow Boy Tobacco, sign, cardboard, Everybody Likes It, farmer watching girl in apple tree while plowing, framed, 20x15", EX+, A18 ....$410.00

Plug Crumb Cut, pocket tin, vertical, brown with gold name above E in diamond flanked by Extra & Fine, lettering below, VG, A18 ....$180.00

Pluto Water, sign, celluloid, Safety First on red bordering devil image on white, Drink...America's Physic, 1940s, 6" dia, EX+, A13 ....$100.00

Plymouth Beer, tap knob, black ball shape with red & gold on red enamel insert, VG, A8 ....$30.00

Plymouth Rope, sign, tin, pictures various dimensions of rope, ...Extra Strength, Yardage & Service above, 18x26", G, A9....................$125.00

Plymouth Sea Fire, tin, yellow with black product name above square image of log on fire, Shake Lightly Over The Fire, oval, 6x2", EX, A18................$10.00

Pocono Cream of Tarter, tin, paper label, 3½", NM, A7 ....$35.00

Pocono Tobacco, box, horizontal, VG, D35.............$25.00

Point Bock Beer, sign, paper, Point above ram's head, Bock Beer below, red & black on yellow, Philipp Litho Co, 32x21½", VG+, A8 ....$85.00

Point Special Beer, tray, deep-dish, Point Special on diagonal scrolled banner, Beer below, black & red, 12" dia, EX, A19 ....$45.00

Pointer Beer, foam scraper, gold lettering on black, VG, A8 ....$30.00

Poker Club Mixture, tin, name above & below poker hand, SF Hess & Co, square corners, EX, A18 ....$1,000.00

Poker Cut Plug, tin, name above embellished circular image of 4 men playing poker, The Rock City Tobacco Co, rectangular, EX, A18.....................$225.00

Pola-Kiss Grapes, lug box label, Pola-Kiss formed in ice, blue on red, Lodi, M, D12.....................$2.00

Polar Bear Allspice, tin, paper label, 3", NM, A7......$35.00

Polar Bear Tobacco, store bin, blue with gold graphics & lettering, slant top, EX, A18 ....$395.00

Polar Beer, paper cup, waxed, 1970s, NM, A19 ....$3.00

Polar Methanol Anti-Freeze, can, pictures a polar bear surmounting a car, green, white & black, with contents, 5½x4" dia, 1-qt, VG, A6 ....$210.00

Polar Methanol Type SC Anti-Freeze, can, Polar above other lettering on polar bear's back, red, white & blue, 1-gal, 9½x7", VG+, A6....................$85.00

Polar Ware, ashtray, enamel, polar bear & product name in center, blue on white, 1939, 4½" dia, NM, A3.......$40.00

Polar-Maid Ice Cream, tray, mother feeding son & daughter ice cream, lettering on decorative rim, 13½" dia, G+, A9 ....$200.00

Polarine Frost & Carbon Proof Motor Car Oil, sign, embossed tin, oil can pictured at left of product lettering, 9¼x19⅝", EX, A1 ....$525.00

Polarine Motor Oil, can, open car driving from summer to winter scene, 2 pour spouts & handle, 1-gal, 10x3x8", G+, A1....................$250.00

Polarine Motor Oil, can, open car driving from summer to winter scene on front, Semidac Liquid Gloss ad on sides, 1910s, ½-gal, EX, A1.......................$375.00

Polarine Motor Oil, can, The Perfect Motor Oil on tail of P above family in open car, pour spout & handle, 1-gal, 11x8", VG+, A6....................$475.00

Polarine Motor Oil, watch fob, polar bear above product name & Adds Life To All Types & Makes Of Motor Cars, VG+, A6 ....$65.00

Poll-Parrot, sign, die-cut porcelain, parrot with neon outline perched on branch above product name in red, 41x21", EX, A6 ....$950.00

Poll-Parrot All Leather Shoes, whistle, paper, 2½", EX, A7 ....$15.00

Poll-Parrot Shoes, bank, tin & cardboard, can shape, 2" dia, NM, A7.....................$15.00

Poll-Parrot Shoes, bank, tin & cardboard, short can shape, 1½" dia, NM, A7 ....$15.00

Poll-Parrot Shoes, clicker, tin, 2", NM, A7 ....$15.00

Poll-Parrot Shoes, display, parrot standing between 2 shoe holders with leather shoes, product name on base, 12", EX, A2....................................$285.00

Poll-Parrot Shoes, toy spinner, 1½" dia, NM, A7......$25.00

Pollack Wheeling Stogies, thermometer, porcelain, product name above bulb, Crowns Melo Crowns Experts below, 39x8", EX, D11 ....**$175.00**

Polo, crate label, California orange, polo player on horse in action, green background with red border, 10x11", M, D12..**$10.00**

Polo Beer, coaster, silhouette of polo player encircled by product name, blue & black, 4", EX+, A8.............**$60.00**

Poly Oxide Lubricating Oil, bottle, glass with diamond-shaped paper label, lettering above & below man in motorboat, 1-qt, NM+, A1 ....**$45.00**

Pompeian FG Co, calendar, 1909, 'Pompeian Beauty,' elegant lady in purple dress & plumed hat, gold background framed, 38x11", EX, A8 ....**$375.00**

PON Feigenspan, tap knob, black ball shape with white, gold & red on blue enamel insert, VG+, A8.........**$20.00**

PON Feigenspan, tap knob, black ball shape with white, gold & red on green enamel insert, EX, A8.........**$30.00**

PON Feigenspan Quality Beer, sign, embossed tin on cardboard, hanger or stand-up, gold lettering on blue, beveled edge, 6x13", NM+, A19 ....**$125.00**

Pond Brand Peanut Butter, tin, product & company name on oval inset, pry lid, EX, A3 ....**$50.00**

Pond's Extract, mirror, beveled with etched lettering, oak frame, diagonal product name, See Landscape Trademark..., 12x12", VG, A9 ....**$130.00**

Pond's Extract, trade card, Sold Only In Bottles... above little girl on pony with dog running beside them, ca 1885, EX, D23 ....**$15.00**

Pontiac, calendar, 1931, encircled portrait of Chief Pontiac flanked by various symbols, incomplete, framed, image: 27x19", G, A9...**$300.00**

Pontiac, sign, neon, Chief Pontiac on circle, blue & red, new, 18x26", NM+, A6 ....**$185.00**

Pontiac, see also Oakland Service Pontiac

Pontiac Sales & Service, sign, porcelain, Chief Pontiac in red on white circle, white letters on black, red band top & bottom, 28x51", NM, D8 ....**$1,225.00**

Pop Kola, sign, tin, Drive In in bold letters at left of Drink Pop Kola on red oval, orange background, 6x33", NM+, D30...**$95.00**

Popeye Paints, sign, litho tin, shows Popeye & Olive Oyl making over Sweet Pea's painting of Popeye, red ground, 1933, 5x6", NM, A3 ....$65.00**

Popeye White Hulless Pop Corn, tin, Popeye holding sign above product name, pry lid, ca 1949, 12 ½-oz, 11½x3x2", EX+, A3..**$80.00**

Popeye Yellow Pop Corn, tin, Pour Spout lettered on arrow above Popeye, product name on paper label, 1949, 1-lb 4-oz, EX, A7 ....**$23.00**

Popeye Yellow Pop Corn, tin, Popeye behind sign above product name, 'Arf Arf', unopened, ca 1939, 10-oz, 5x2½" dia, EX+, A3 ....**$120.00**

Popper's Ace, pocket tin, vertical, 10¢, cream with metallic gold & black lettering around single-engine biplane, EX, A18 ....$675.00

Popper's Ace Cigars, dispenser, tin box with slanted glass top, Popper's Ace & 10¢ on top panel, biplane & text on sides, 9x6x7", EX, A6....................................**$500.00**

Porico Brand Coffee, tin, product name above & at side of Uncle Sam holding flag, square with round lid, 6½", scarce, VG, A2..**$275.00**

Portage Cord Tires, sign, self-framed tin, tire rolling down country road with sheep & colorful scenery, signed RJ Kennedy, 26x38", EX+, A6 ....**$1,400.00**

Portage Paprika, tin, paper label, 3½", NM, A7........**$40.00**

Porter's Antiseptic Healing Oil, sign, thin fabric, For Cuts, Sores & Burns, lettering above & below oval image of prancing horse, 36x20", G, D38..........**$900.00**

Porto Rico Extras, cigar box label, outer, pictures 4 elegant women, 4½x4½", M, D5...........................**$18.00**

Portola Tuna & Sardines, display box, cardboard, die-cut image of tuna can atop back of box, Insist On Portola, 12x10x7", NM, A7..**$8.00**

Portsmouth Ale, tray, red, white, blue & gold, 12", G, D7...**$35.00**

Post Toasties, car mug, ceramic, EX+, D24 ....**$8.00**

Post Toasties, sign, cardboard, A Message For You! & box on fence messenger is pointing to, billboard behind, framed, 41", EX, A21 ....**$800.00**

Post Toasties, string holder, mechanical, Post Toasties in bold letters above box of Corn Flakes, ca 1916, 12" dia, VG, A9 ....**$625.00**

Postal Telegraph, sign, Postal Telegraph The International System in white on blue above Here in blue on white, 16x30", EX+, A1...**$300.00**

Postmaster Smokers, tin, red with white name above & below image of man smoking pipe flanked by 2 For 5¢, round, slip lid, EX+, A18..**$80.00**

Postum, string holder, tin, Drink Postum, 'There's A Reason,' Health First above & below, ca 1916, 11½" dia, G, A9 ....**$275.00**

Postum, tin, sample, Instant, with contents, 1¾", NM, A7 .... **$20.00**

Postum, tin, sample, Instant, with contents, 3½", NM, A7 .... **$30.00**

Poth's Beer, tray, deep-dish, Poth's in diagonal script above beer, 12" dia, VG+, A19 .... **$48.00**

Poth's Cream Ale, label, Poth Brewing Co, Internal Revenue Tax Paid statement, 1933-50, 12-oz, EX, A10 .... **$28.00**

Poth's Pilsener Beer, label, Poth Brewing Co, Internal Revenue Tax Paid statement, 1933-50, 1-qt, M, A10 .... **$10.00**

Poth's Special Pilsner Beer, tray, deep-dish, product name over triangle logo, NM+, A19 .... **$110.00**

Potosi Beer, sign, cardboard, Drink above Potosi on diagonal band, 'Made With Spring Water' below, embossed tin frame, 8x10", NM, A3 .... **$116.00**

Potosi Brewing Co, sign, self-framed tin, 'The Cockfight,' oval image of 2 gents watching cockfight in barn, copyright 1912, 24x20", G, A6 .... **$155.00**

Pounce, tin, yellow, red & black with ornate graphics, ...For Tracing Cloth, Keuffel & Esser, slip lid with dome top, 5", EX, A6 .... **$40.00**

Powell Muffler, sign, tin over cardboard, Carbon Monoxide left of Danger on creepy hand over car, Free Inspection..., 10x13", EX+, A6 .... **$300.00**

Power-lube Motor Oil, can, product name above & below stalking tiger outlined in white, blue, orange & white, 1-qt, EX, A1 .... **$850.00**

Power-lube Motor Oil, sign, painted tin, yellow product lettering & tiger logo on reflective blue background, wood frame, 25x48", G+, A1 .... **$550.00**

Powow Brand Salted Peanuts, tin, green product name on red encircles Indian head & company name, green background, pry lid, 10-lb, VG+, A2 .... **$600.00**

Practical School Supply Co, catalog, 1934, 136 pgs, EX, D17 .... **$40.00**

Prairie Kid Cigars, box label set, cowboy with pistol on horse running through large horseshoe, 1887, 2 pcs, VG, A5 .... **$440.00**

Pratt & Lambert Paint, sign, porcelain, logo on 3-color band left of product name in blue & red, blue & yellow border, 2-sided, 24x36", EX, A6 .... **$75.00**

Pratt & Lambert Varnish Makers, sign, paper, girl on dock unveiling framed sign with 2 more at her feet, product barrels & boxes on dock, 20x13", EX, A2 ...**$880.00**

Preferred, crate label, California orange, huge orange & official red seal, Covina, 10x11", M, D3 .... **$2.00**

Preferred Auto Fuses, tin, flat, EX, D37 .... **$15.00**

Premier Beer, label, Premier-Pabst Corp, U-type permit number, Internal Revenue Tax Paid statement, 1933-36, 12-oz, NM, A10 .... **$18.00**

Premona/Kamm & Schellinger Br'g Co, sign, tin on cardboard, name above bottle on oval inset, company name below, beveled edge, pre-1920s, 19x9", VG+, A19 .... **$210.00**

Pres-Ope Powdered Toilet Soap, tin, sample, Press Here lettered on center dot surrounded by product name, ovoid, ¾x3x3", EX, D37 .... **$215.00**

President Suspenders, tip tray, bust portrait of girl encircled by ...Absolute Comfort, Reynolds & McKinsey, glass cover, 4" dia, EX, A8 .... **$100.00**

Prest-O-Lite Hi-Level Batteries, door push, porcelain, The Battery With A Kick, shows horse atop battery, 4x36", VG, A6 .... **$160.00**

Prestone Anti-Freeze, clock, metal, silver numbers & product name on blue, 10" dia, EX+, A6 .... **$40.00**

Prexy Plug Cut Tobacco for Pipe & Cigarette, pocket tin, vertical, red with white & yellow name around oval image of college official, EX, A18 .... **$1,200.00**

Prexy Tobacco for Pipe & Cigarette, pocket tin, vertical, red with white & yellow lettering above & below college official, EX+, A18 .... **$1,700.00**

Pride of Reidsville, cigarette papers, green, NM, A7 ..**$60.00**

Pride of the Indies, cigar box label, salesman's sample, 2 maidens surrounded by medallions & trees, M, A5 ..**$86.00**

Pride of the River Asparagus, crate label, sternwheel steamer on Sacramento River, Locke, M, D12 ....**$6.00**

Prima Beer, drinking glass, stem with screened pebble-type lettering, 7", NM, A8 .... **$20.00**

Prima-Tonic, tray, The Food Drink, lettering around full-length image of waitress with tray, decorative rim, vertical, 15", VG+, A21 ....$138.00

Primo Bock Beer, label, Hawaii Brewing Co, U-type permit number, Internal Revenue Tax Paid statement, 1933-36, 1-pt, NM, A10 ....$45.00

Primo Gassosa, sign, embossed tin, bottle on tilted oval at right of Sparkling...First For Thirst & Quality, horizontal, VG+, A16 ....$36.00

Prince Albert Crimp Cut, tin, product name above & below oval 3-quarter portrait, slightly domed slip lid, 5½x4" dia, VG, A7 ....$28.00

Prince Albert Crimp Cut, tobacco pouch, cloth, 1909 tax stamp, with contents, unopened, NM, A18 ....$115.00

Prince Albert Tobacco, charger, tin, jolly fellow smoking pipe, ...The National Joy Smoke, 24" dia, G+, A9 ..$375.00

Prince Albert Tobacco, pocket tin, with contents, unopened, 3x4¼", NM, D35 ....$10.00

Prince Albert Tobacco, sign, cardboard, 'From Now On It's — Prince Albert,' The National Joy Smoke!, man & product at left, 15x58", G, A21 ....$12.00

Prince Albert Tobacco, sign, tin, image of Chief Joseph, Nez Perce above tobacco tin & ...National Joy Smoke, 25½x19½", G-, A9.....................$225.00

Prince Albert Tobacco, sign, tin, image of Chief Joseph, Nez Perce above tobacco tin & ...National Joy Smoke, 25½x19½", VG, A2.....................$440.00

Prince Hamlet Club Cigars, tin, wood-grain, embossed name above image of prince leaning on red-draped podium, kingdom in background, round, EX, A18 ....$50.00

Prince of Pales, label, Mitchel Brewing Co, Internal Revenue Tax Paid statement, 1933-50, ½-gal, NM, A10.....................................$15.00

Prince Spaghetti House, matchbook, pictures chef with spaghetti, Spaghetti At It's Best across sticks, 20 strike, front strike, NM, D28.....................$5.00

Princess Rolled Oats, container, bust image of princess looking over her shoulder, Goebel-Reid Grocer Co, 42-oz, rare, VG+, A3 ....$160.00

Princeton Farms Hybrid Pop Corn, can, 10-oz, NM, A7.....................................$65.00

Prior Beer, sign, neon, green Prior with red dot above I, red Beer below, VG+, A19 ....$215.00

Prior Beer, sign, tin on cardboard, product name above & below can flanked by Liquid Luxury, round with raised rim, NM, A19 ....$165.00

Prior Lager Beer, sign, tin on cardboard, name on circle flanked by lion & unicorn, Liquid Luxury on scrolled banner, white & gold, EX, A19 ....$150.00

Priscilla #37 Hexagon Crayons, sign, litho tin, name & image of hand-held crayons on black background, white & red border, 1937, 5x6", NM, A3.....................$40.00

Prize Shot, cigar box label, outer, pictures a wounded mallard, 1901, EX, A5.....................................$90.00

Proctor Never Lift Irons, display iron, wood replica with functioning buttons & knobs, 35" long, VG, A21...$880.00

Professional Razor Blades, display, cardboard, Professional & other advertising above 2 rows of 5 packs each, 12x5", EX, A7.....................$30.00

Progress Beer/Indianapolis Brewing Co, tray, shows 3 gentlemen by open hearth, lettered rim, pre-1920s, G+, A19 ....$40.00

Progress Bock Beer/Progress Brewing Co, label, U-type permit number, Internal Revenue Tax Paid statement, 1933-36, 12-oz, M, A10.....................$16.00

Prosperity Ranges/Sears, Roebuck & Co, bank, metal barrel with blue, orange & white celluloid top, product name arched above range, EX, A11 ....$52.00

Prost/Ph Kling Brewing Co, tip tray, Drink Prost, A Beer For Guest & Host, company name below, orange background, decorative rim, 4" dia, VG+, A8 ....$40.00

Prudential, sign, paper, '1904 Prudential Girl,' 3-quarter image of bare-shouldered girl against yellow background, 12x9", EX, A2.....................$220.00

Prudential Insurance, postcard, 'Paid For By Your Prudential Protection When Dad's Not Here,' shows milk bottle, meat & other food, NM, D26 ....$40.00

Prudential Insurance Co of America, paperweight, glass, company name above home office building, ...Claims Paid Over $17,000,000 below, rectangular, M, D13..........$55.00

Prune Nugget Fruit Flavor Plug, tin, lettering around dish of fruit, blue ribbon with lettered bow surrounds tin, square corners, EX+, A18.....................$55.00

Puck Virginia Cigarette Tobacco, tin, Puck & 25¢ flanked by 2 hockey players, Virginia Cigarette tobacco on band below, round, slip lid, EX, A18 ....$250.00

Pullman, cigar box label, inner lid, train car on tracks, 6x9", M, D5.....................................$50.00

Pulver Chewing Gum, sign, porcelain, product name lettered vertically above The Tasty Chew, 23x5", EX, D11.....................................$115.00

Punxy Special Beer/Punzsutawney Brewing Co, tray, 'Hearts Are Trump,' tavern scene in center, lettered rim, rectangular, 12x17", G+, A8.....................$175.00

Pur-ox, fan, cardboard, name arched above family watching baby climb onto chair, VG+, A16 ....$20.00

Pur-ox Syrups & Beverages, thermometer, wood, Pur-ox above girl with glass, curved top, 1910s, 21x5", NM+, A13 ....$400.00

PurAsnow Enriched Flour/General Mills Inc, sign, tin, white product lettering right of hand-held 'Valuable Coupon' emerging from flour sack, 12x14", NM, A3 ....$140.00

Purdue, cigar box label, printer's proof, university scene with lettered flags above, 1892, EX, A5 ....$65.00

Pure, sign, porcelain, Be Sure With Pure arched above & below Pure, fancy border, wrought-iron frame, 2-sided, 42" dia, EX, A6 ....$150.00

Pure As Gold, see also Pep Boys

Pure As Gold Cup Grease, can, product name above circular image of the Pep Boys, 1933, 1-lb, 2½x4¼" dia, VG, A6 ....$40.00

Pure As Gold Cup Grease, pail, product name above circular image of the Pep Boys, slip lid & bail, 1933, 5-lb, 6½x6" dia, VG, A6...$80.00

Pure As Gold Motor Oil, can, product name above circular image of the Pep Boys, screw lid & handle, 1933, 2-gal, EX, A6..$165.00

Pure Beer, label, pre-prohibition, North Lake Brewery, M, A10 ....$16.00

Pure Canadian Honey, tin, product name above beehive on front, silhouette of man guiding horse-drawn plow on sides, pry lid, EX, A3 ....$20.00

Pure Oil Co, gas globe, Products Of The arched above Pure... with geometric border, blue & white, metal body, 15" dia, NM/VG, A6..................................$300.00

Pure Oil Co, license plate attachment, metal, round logo above Drive Safely, blue, cream & orange, 6", VG, A6...$65.00

Pure Oil Co, license plate attachment, metal, round logo flanked by Drive Safely on banner, 4", EX, A6 ..$130.00

Pure Premium, pump sign, porcelain, product name above round logo & Be Sure With Pure, red, white & blue, dated 1948, 12x10", NM, A1 ....$120.00

Pure Premium, pump sign, porcelain, product name above round logo & Be Sure With Pure, red, white & blue, marked IR 52, 12x10", EX, A6....................$110.00

Pure Quill Spice Honeydew, tin, paper label, 3¼", NM, A7 ....$35.00

Pure Quill Tumeric, tin, paper label, 4", EX+ A7 .....$22.00

Pure Stock Quality 5¢ Cigar, tin, initialed emblem flanked by tobacco leaves above product name, repeating logo on lid, EX+, A18 ....$25.00

Pure-Pep, pump sign, porcelain, Pure-Pep above circular logo & Be Sure With Pure, red, white & blue, marked IR 53, 12x10", EX, A6..$65.00

Purebay Oysters/BJ Rooks & Son, tin, blue lettering & graphics on white, pry lid, 7¼x6¾", EX, A18 ....$195.00

Pureoxia Beverages, sign, tin, ...Made With Distilled Water, 7x23", VG+, A9..$90.00

Pureoxia Ginger Ale, menu board, tin, small boy & bottle at top, Special Today on board, 29x23", G, A9 ..$250.00

Pureoxia Ginger Ale, sign, cardboard, Drink... above elephant standing in car, Frank Archer Invites You To Moxieland, 28x39", rare, NM, D30 ....$500.00

Pureoxia Ginger Ale, sign, tin, Drink Pureoxia Ginger Ale on red horizontal oval in center, green ground with yellow border, 1920s, NM+, A4............$650.00

Pureoxia Ginger Ale, sign, tin, Drink... on octagon in center, A Product Of The Moxie Company below, framed, image: 19x27", G-, A9 ....$140.00

Purina Eggs, sign, paper, Guaranteed halo around smiling egg pointing to For Sale!..., checkered border below, 1954, 19x26", NM, A7 ....$20.00

Purina Poultry Chows, sign, Produced On... above Fresh Eggs For Sale, checkered border below, 1942, 19x26", NM, A7 ....$15.00

Puritan Crushed Plug Mixture, pocket tin, vertical, gray with black & white product name above & below image of Puritan man smoking pipe, EX+, A18 ....$185.00

Puritan Dairy Ice Cream, whistle, tin, 2½", NM, A7 ..$20.00

Puritan Motor Oil, sign, embossed tin, policeman with Stop on oversized hand at left of product & company name, 11x35", EX, A6 ....$230.00

Purity Brand Rolled Oats, container, cardboard, product & company name above & below floral image, 1940s, 10x6", VG, A4 ....$15.00

Purity Cigarettes, sign, cardboard, Smoke Purity Cigarettes, bust portrait of lady in stole with rose border, 1880-90s, 14x9", G+, A13 ....$50.00

Purity Cigars, box label, salesman's sample, Indian family looking into trunk, VG+, A5 ....$65.00

Purity Fruit, sign, paper, Purity above cameo of 2 Victorian girls, This Fruit Is Warranted... below, ca 1880, framed, 20x13", EX, A3 ....$315.00

Purity Kiss/National Biscuit Co, sign, tin, 2 children kissing in large wicker chair, ...Everybody Likes It, 8" dia, G, A9..$450.00

Purol Gasoline, gas globe, arrow in center, blue on white, white porcelain body, 15" dia, NM+, A6 ....$800.00

Purolator Oil Filters, display, die-cut cardboard stand-up, close-up of station attendant holding up filter & Valvoline can, 22x26", NM, A1 ....$180.00

Pursuit Gasoline, decal on glass, product name & airplane, framed, 13½x17", EX+, A6 ....$70.00

Putnam Fadeless Dyes, cabinet, wood with tin front, trademark image of General Putnam escaping the Red Coats, G, A6...$185.00

Putnam Fadeless Dyes, fan, cardboard with wooden handle, Charm Of Color above peacock, Putnam Fadeless Dyes & Tints below, 1930s, 7", VG, D14 ....**$18.00**

Pyramid Brand/TC Williams Co, tobacco box label, product name above display of fruit, company name below, 1872, 14", NM, A7 ....**$16.00**

Pyramid Resilient Mainsprings/Cha's HO Bryon, tin, flat, lettering surrounds pyramids & coiled spring, decorative border, rounded corners, ½x2¾x5⅛", EX, D37 ....**$45.00**

Q

Q Boid Cube Cut Pipe Tobacco, pocket tin, vertical, wide, shaded tan, brown lid, large tobacco plant with cabin beyond, NM, A18 ....**$210.00**

Q Boid Finest Quality Granulated Plug, pocket tin, vertical, concave, red on tan, product lettering above tobacco plant flanked by round symbols, EX+, A................**$55.00**

Q Boid Pipe Tobacco, pocket tin, vertical, wide, shaded tan, blue lid, large tobacco plant with cabin beyond, with contents, NM+, A18 ....**$275.00**

QR Cough Drops, tin, red with gold lettering, gold slip lid, 8½x5" dia, EX, A18 ....**$115.00**

Quail, crate label, California pear, quail walking through grass, NM, D3 ....**$5.00**

Quail Brand Quick Cooking Rolled Oats, container, quail in center, Quaker Oats Co, 3-lb, EX+, A3..............**$65.00**

Quaker Cigar, box label, outer, image of young Quaker lady, 4½x4½", M, D5..**$4.00**

Quaker Corn Meal, container, Quaker man on triangle in center, 8-oz, EX+, A3 ....**$25.00**

Quaker Foods, sign, cardboard, framed oval image of 'The Quaker Girl' holding can on yellow & white striped ground, 22x18", EX+, A3..................**$112.00**

Quaker Maid Baking Powder, tin, paper label, 4-oz, EX+, A7 ....**$20.00**

Quaker Maid Non-Detergent Motor Oil, can, waxed cardboard, oval bust image of Quaker lady in center, 1-qt, 5½x4" dia, VG, A6 ....**$35.00**

Quaker Maid Outboard Motor Oil, can, waxed cardboard, oval inset of Quaker woman left of pennant above product name, green, white & black, 1-qt, VG, A6 ....**$35.00**

Quaker Oats, see Mother's Toy Oats & Quail Brand

Quaker Ranges, pin-back button, name above & below profile image of Quaker man, EX, A20.................**$20.00**

Quaker Ranges, sign, paper, product name arched above little girl hugging bulldog, 21½x14", G, A9........**$400.00**

Quaker Rolled White Oats, container, cardboard, Quaker man on rectangular inset, 7x4½" dia, rare, NM, A3 ..**$80.00**

Quaker Rolled White Oats, container, cardboard, Quaker man on rectangular inset, 7x4½" dia, rare, VG, A6 ..**$30.00**

Quaker State, mechanic's creeper, wood with metal wheels, green lettering, 36x15", NOS, A6.............**$10.00**

Quaker State Cold Test Oil, sign, porcelain, Use...For Winter Driving, 6x26½", VG, A9 ....**$95.00**

Quaker State Duplex Outboard Oil, sign, tin, Quaker State within large Q at left of 100% Pure Pennsylvania Oil..., 12x24", NOS, D11 ....**$75.00**

Quaker State Motor Oil, can, product name on center circle, logos & company name below, green, white & black, 9½x7" dia, 5-qt, VG+, A6 ....**$20.00**

Quaker State Motor Oil, clock, metal & glass, 4-leaf clover above product name in center, It's A Lucky Day... around border, 15" dia, VG, A6 ....**$175.00**

Quaker State Motor Oil, clock, plastic, Ask For... in center, numbered 1-12, green & black on white, 16x16", NM, A6 ....**$60.00**

Quaker State Motor Oil, sign, metal, Ask For..., green & white, marked AM Sign Co Lynchburg, VA 5-54, 24" dia, EX+, A6..**$75.00**

Quaker State Motor Oil, sign, paper, Keep 'Em Rolling... above traffic cop, Change Now To...For Summer Driving below, 34x58", NOS, NM, A1 ....**$155.00**

Quaker State Motor Oil, thermometer, metal, 4-leaf clover & It's A Lucky Day For Your Car above bulb, When You Change To... below, 39", EX, A6.................**$120.00**

Quaker State Summer Oil, banner, paper, Time For That Lucky Change... left of robin on branch with pink flower, 34x57½", EX+, A6.....................................**$65.00**

Quaker State Winter Oil, banner, paper, It's A Lucky Day... left of snow scene with car traveling through horseshoe, 34x57½", EX, A6.................................**$50.00**

Quality Enamel Ware, sign, light-up, reverse-painted curved glass panel with arched top on round base, US above tea kettle, 14x7", EX, A13 ....**$550.00**

Quandt Brewing Co, tray, colorful image of cavalier in red plumed hat & cape holding up frothy stein, 12" dia, VG, A21 ....**$110.00**

Quandt Dark Beer, label, Quandt Brewing Co, U-type permit number, Internal Revenue Tax Paid statement, 1933-36, M, A10..**$25.00**

Queed, tin, Queed in red on white diamond in center, green background, slip lid, 4x4½x6", EX, A18.....**$28.00**

Queen Esther, crate label, California orange, regal queen with crown & turquoise jewelry, Placentia, 10x11", M, D3 ....**$5.00**

Queen Hair Dressing, tin, sample, with contents, rectangular, NM A7 ....**$10.00**

Queen Hair Dressing, tin, sample, with contents, round, NM, A7 ....**$8.00**

Queen Quality Shoes, pocket mirror, bust portrait of lovely young woman, logo below, oval, EX+, D18 ....**$150.00**

Queen Quality Shoes, pocket mirror, image of patriotic lady on steps before building, vertical oval, 2¾", VG+, A21 ....**$65.00**

Queen Skin Whitner, tin, sample, with contents, round, NM, A7 ....**$10.00**

Quick Meal Ranges, tip tray, name & Ask Your Dealer on rim around image of newborn chicks in landscape, oval, 3½x4½", EX, A3 ....**$45.00**

Quick Mother's Oats, see Mother's Oats

Quinlan's Butter Pretzel, tin, Readings'-Original... above farm boy with basket of pretzels, slip lid, 1920s, 8", EX, D8 ....**$80.00**

Quinlan's Butter Pretzel, tin, Readings'-Original... above farm boy with can of pretzels, slip lid, 15½x12" dia, VG+, A9 ....**$75.00**

❧ R ❧

R Dougherty's Carriage Works, sign, paper, horse-drawn carriages in front of factory, company name arched above, framed, image: 12x14½", VG, A9............**$150.00**

R&H Beer & Ale, foam scraper, smoky tan with black lettering, EX, A8 ....**$20.00**

R-B Cigars, sign, tin, Daddy Wants An R-B, bare-bottom child reaching into a box of cigars, beveled edge, 19x13", EX+, A15...**$650.00**

R-B Cigars, sign, tin over cardboard, Daddy Wants An R-B above bare-bottomed child reaching into box of cigars, 19x13", VG, A1 ....**$200.00**

R-Pep, sign, die-cut tin bottle, 1940s-50s, 48x12", NM+, A13 ....**$225.00**

R-Pep, sign, embossed tin, Drink R-Pep above 5¢ & tilted bottle, cream & green lettering shadowed in black, 17½x36", G, A6 ....**$100.00**

Radiant Roast Coffee, tin, mountain scene on back, key-wind lid, NM, A3 ....**$30.00**

Raid, toy bug, plastic wind-up, 1980s, 4", M **$40.00**

Railway Express, sign, porcelain, white lettering on red arrow with green border, white background, 6½x23", NM, D11 ....**$200.00**

Railway Express Agency, sign, fiberboard with metal frame, Railway in white arched above Express, Agency below on red, diagonal, 14x14", VG+, A1 ....**$45.00**

Rainbo Bread, door push bar, porcelain, white panel with red Rainbo outlined in yellow above Good Bread on blue, EX+, A13 ....**$150.00**

Rainbow Sweet Snuff, tin, sample, paper label, with contents, VG, A7 ....**$9.00**

Rainbow/Peerless Rubber Manufacturing Co, sign, shows the battleship Oregon & graphics of gaskets & packing & how they were used, 15x21", VG+, A3.................**$140.00**

Rainier, display, plaster, bald brewmaster in white coat with R initial holding mallot on white base, 16x7x5", EX, A8 ....**$140.00**

Rainier, sheet music, 'There's Something Else Goes With It,' front pictures 2 ladies in open car, 1907, matted & framed, VG+, A19 ....**$110.00**

Rainier, tap knob, chrome with Rainier in white script on red celluloid insert, 2" dia, EX, A8 ....**$70.00**

Rainier Ale, can, flat-top, oval logo, NM, A8.............**$25.00**

Rainier Ale & Beer, sign, embossed brass plaque, Since 1878 banner above product name lettered over mountain scene, 8½x13", EX, A1 ....**$60.00**

Rainier Beer, can, flat-top, Not-So-Light... label, M, A8..**$25.00**

Rainier Beer, can, flat-top, Special Export label, Sicks' on mountain peak below, M, A8...........................**$100.00**

Rainier Beer, corkscrew, wooden cylinder-type handle, EX, A8 ....**$45.00**

Rainier Beer, letter opener, cream with red & black graphics & lettering on both sides, Seattle Brewing & Malting Co, 8½", NM, A1 ....**$115.00**

Rainier Beer, mug, ceramic, company name on circular logo above product name on white, 4½", EX+, A8.......**$115.00**

Rainier Beer, tray, girl in ruffled bonnet with hands to chin flanked by circular logos, product name on rim, 1903, 12" dia, VG, A9..**$325.00**

Rainier Beer, tray, pictures girl leaning against ferocious-looking bear, lettered & decorative rim, G, 13" dia, A21...**$120.00**

Rainier Club Beer, sign, tin, Rainier over bottle, Club Beer below, red ground with Drink... on gray rim, 12x7", VG+, A19...$150.00

Rajah Motor Oil, sign, die-cut tin, Arab's face above Double Mileage...A Penn-O-Tex Product, blue & yellow, 28x20", rare, EX+, A6..$1,400.00

Raleigh Cigarettes, sign, cardboard, Save B&W Coupon above couple dancing, open pack & name on oval, Now At Popular..., 18x12", EX, A7 ....$10.00

Raleigh Cigarettes, sign, paper, Playing Cards Free, Save The Coupon..., Now 15¢ with image of pack & cards, Reedemable..., 20x14", NM+, A18 ....$85.00

Raleigh Cigarettes, sign, paper, Raleigh above woman in seductive pose against circle, product lower right, 15x10", EX, A7 ....$35.00

Raleigh Cigarettes, sign, paper, Now At Popular Prices Raleigh Cigarettes above shoulder view of woman, 1939, 18x12", VG, A7 ....$10.00

Raleigh Cigarettes, tin, holds 50 cigarettes, 3" dia, NM, A7...$75.00

Ralph's, crate label, Washington apple, map of Washington & apples on blue background, Yakima, 9x11", M, D12...$3.00

Ralston Leather Wing Tip Shoes, display shoe, leather, Smart Shoes For Men, They Need No Breaking In, sole marked Foot Joy, 25½" long, EX, A21 ....$660.00

Ralston Purina, ashtray, heavy pottery, shaped like dog's feeding bowl, colorful graphics on white, 6" dia, EX, D25...$30.00

Ralston Purina, toy chuck wagon, vinyl, horse-drawn covered wagon with red & white checked top, 8" long, EX, A21..$15.00

Ram Head, tobacco label, sample, lady's portrait above name, matted & framed, image: 12x6", EX, A18 ..$50.00

Ram's Horn Suncured, tobacco tag, EX, D35.............$3.00

Rambler Parts & Service, sign, porcelain, Rambler on center band, white on red, 42" dia, NM, D8.$450.00

Ramco Motor Overhaul, sign, porcelain flange, rocking chair on 1 side, piston uniform centered within cylinder on back, 19x25½", EX+, A1 ....$450.00

Ramon's Brownie Pills & Pink Pills, thermometer, metal, image of doctor at right of bulb, Diuretic Stimulant To The Kidneys..., 21x8½", EX, A6 ....$325.00

Rams Head Ale, sign, embossed composition, product name above ram's head, The Aristocrat Ale below, inverted corners, 8x8", VG+, A8..........................$30.00

Rams Head Ale, sign, neon, green lettering with fancy pink border, EX+, A19.......................................$240.00

Rams Head Ale, sign, tin on cardboard, product name above crest logo flanked by Aristocrat Of Ales! on brown, rectangular, EX, A19 ....$150.00

Rams Horn Tobacco, pouch, tobacco, EX, A7 ....$12.00

Ramseses Cigarettes/Stephano Bros, sign, celluloid, oval 20¢ emblem above open pack with cigarettes around, The Largest Selling..., beveled, 11x8", EX, A18 ....$85.00

Rand McNally Pocket Maps, display bin, pasteboard, slanted with 6 slots, product name on front, 6x9x7", EX, A12 ....$190.00

Ranger Beer, label, Ahrens Brewing Co, Internal Revenue Tax Paid statement, 1933-50, 12-oz, M, A10.........$18.00

Rapid Transit Hoosac Tunnel Route, poster, locomotive entering & exiting tunnel, East & West below, 1870s, framed, image: 29x22", G-, A9 ....$500.00

Rasche Yeast & Vinegar Co, bill hook, round celluloid insert with green lettering on white, EX, A11 ......$15.00

Rat-Tox, sign, die-cut cardboard stand-up, Pied Piper lures rats with open tube of Rat-Tox, ...A Nibble Kills, 19x24", EX, A12..$410.00

Rathskeller Brew, label, A Gettleman Brewing Co, Internal Revenue Tax Paid statement, 1933-50, 12-oz, NM, A10..$12.00

Rathskeller Gettleman Brew, tap knob, chrome ball shape with gold & blue on yellow enamel insert, EX, A8..$100.00

Rawleigh's Aspirin, tin, flat, rectangular with rounded corners, EX, A7 ....$12.00

Rawleigh's Baking Powder, tin, paper label, with contents, 1¾-oz, EX, A7...$18.00

Rawleigh's Good Health Cocoa, tin, product name above circular portrait inset over tropical scene, 6", NM, A18...$40.00

Rawleigh's Good Health Cocoa, tin, sample, Free Sample & name above circular portrait inset over tropical scene, slip lid, 1¾x1⅛x¾", EX, D37 ....$70.00

Rawleigh's Good Health Cocoa, tin, sample, Free Sample & name above circular portrait inset over tropical scene, slip lid, 2¼x1¾x1¼", EX, D37 ....$50.00

Rawleigh's Good Health Talcum, tin, various nursery rhyme scenes, product & company name on emblem in center, 7½", EX, A6..$110.00

Raybestos, thermometer, painted tin, Check Brakes! above man pointing up & bulb, advertising below, sharp corners, 30½", EX+, A1 ....$80.00

Raybestos Brake Service, sign, tin flange, Stop Here For Silver Edge..., man's arm with hand on brake, yellow ground, 14x18", VG, D8......................................$450.00

Rayette GDT Dandruff Lotion, decal, It Pays To Look Well on yellow banner, bottle image on barber pole, 1930, 18x4", NM+, A3 ....$200.00

RC Cola, see Royal Crown Cola

RCA, sign, reverse-painted glass light-up, Tubes Tested Free, RCA Radiotrons flanked by good tube & bad tube, framed, VG, A6..$100.00

RCA Radiola Dealer, sign, scroll-shaped hanger with fancy bracket, Radio Dealer in yellow above red & white RCA logo, 15x19", NM, A1 ....$800.00

RCA Radiotrons, display figure, man with lettering on hat & chest banner, wood, 1950s, 15", M, D8.......**$1,500.00**

RCA Victor, salt & pepper shakers, Nipper figures, Lenox-type earthenware with glossy white glaze, approx 3", EX, D14 ....**$55.00**

Re-Ma, tin, pictures vehicles on highway running through patched inner tube, PKWI lower right corner, ⅝x2¼x3½", EX, D37.................................**$30.00**

Reader's Digest & Campbell's Soup's, alarm clock, Reader's Digest & Campbell's Soups Go Together, dial spins with more wording, square case, 1950, 3", EX, A2..**$45.00**

Reading Beer, sign, cardboard, Welcome upper left of bar scene, Reach For Reading, The Friendly Beer..., 17x29", EX+, A19 ....**$25.00**

Reading Beer, sign, plastic, Get Modern above hand pouring from can into glass, inverted triangle with clear top, EX+, A19..**$460.00**

Reading Premium, sign, tin on cardboard, For Friendly Flavor, round with bands of gold & white around lettered blue center, NM, A19.........................**$70.00**

Real Kill Bug Killer, clicker, tin, 2", NM, A7 ....**$15.00**

Real Penn Motor Oil, can, pictures Quaker man on diamond in center, product name in red, green background, 1-qt, NM, A1..**$100.00**

Rebecca, tobacco tag, hexagonal, EX, D35 ....**$3.00**

Recruit Cigarettes, folding chair, wood with spindle back, 32½x20x17", G-, A9 ....**$30.00**

Recruit Little Cigars, sign, die-cut cardboard stand-up, Civil War soldier holding pack with 5¢ pack between legs on labeled base, 20", VG, A2..........**$175.00**

Red & White Brand Foods, clock, light-up, black numbers on white around name on red dot, glass face, metal frame, 14" dia, EX, A6..**$235.00**

Red & White Quick Cooking Oats, container, Red & White encircled at top, Oats on large red band at bottom, plaid background, 42-oz, NM, A3.................**$40.00**

Red Ace Beverages, bottle, NM, A7........................**$15.00**

Red Bell Motor Oil, can, product name above & below encircled bell, screw cap, 2-gal, 11x8½", G+, A6.**$75.00**

Red Bird, crate label, California orange, red phoenix-type bird in wreath, Porterville, 10x11", M, D12.............**$3.00**

Red Buoy, cigar box label, inner lid, woman in red on red buoy, 1903, 6x9", EX, D5.....................................**$100.00**

Red Cap Wine, postcard, girl with bottle of wine & town of Freyburg in the distance, signed Mailick, 1913, VG+, D26..**$50.00**

Red Chief Plug Cut/H Bohls & Co, tin, red with product name & image of George Washington, 4x6", scarce, VG+, A18 ....**$85.00**

Red Comb Poultry Feeds, sign, tin, rooster encircled by band with product name above 'Quality Results At Low Cost,' black ground, 27x20", EX, D8.................**$375.00**

Red Crest Cut Plug, lunch box, cardboard, black with product lettering & rooster's head, slip lid, NM, A18 ..**$230.00**

Red Cross Coffee, tin, sample, orange with allover lettering & graphics, slip lid, 3x2" dia, EX, D37 ....**$450.00**

Red Cross Mills Steel-Cut Coffee, tin, product name above & below corner view of large brick building, oval, slip lid, 1-oz, VG+, A18................................**$75.00**

Red Cross Stoves, Ranges & Furnaces, pocket mirror, celluloid, Co-operative Foundry Co arched above logo, red, white & blue, round, EX+, A11....................**$45.00**

Red Crown Ethyl, gas globe, white crown shape with product name in red raised letters on both sides, 1-pc, EX+, A1...**$800.00**

Red Crown Gasoline, sign, porcelain, crown logo surrounded by product name, 14" dia, NM, A1 ......**$550.00**

Red Crown Gasoline, sign, porcelain, crown logo surrounded by product name, 2-sided, 30" dia, VG+, A6..**$275.00**

Red Crown Gasoline, sign, tin, Coupons Accepted Here at right of crown logo, red & blue on cream with red border, 9x24", VG+, A1 ....**$200.00**

Red Crown Gasoline/Polarine, thermometer, porcelain, crown logo & For Power Mileage at top, Polarine logo below, bulb missing, 73", EX+, A6......................**$850.00**

Red Crown Grapes, lug box label, red crown & lettering on orange background, Sanger, M, D12.................**$2.00**

Red Devil's Lighter Fluid, thermometer, metal, can of lighter fluid above bulb, The Fluid With A Thousand Lights below, 11½", EX, A6 ....**$180.00**

Red Diamond Overalls & Shirts, watch fob, man in overalls in front of elongated diamond logo, EX+, A11 ....**$20.00**

Red Feather, cigar box label, salesman's sample, Indian in full headdress flanked by buffalo & bird, NM, A5.........**$530.00**

Red Fox Ale & Beer/Largay Brewing Co, coaster, shows fox with front paws on lettered drum, lettered border, red & brown, 4¼", EX, A8.................................**$20.00**

Red Fox Cigarette Tobacco, pouch, cloth, paper label, NM, A7 ....**$15.00**

Red Fox Motor Oil, can, Red Fox above encircled fox head flanked by Five US Gallons, cream, black & red, screw lid & handle, 15x9", VG, A6.......................$50.00

Red Fox Pale Ale, label, Largay Brewing Co, U-type permit number, Internal Revenue Tax Paid statement, 1933-36, 12-oz, M, A10.......................$12.00

Red Fox XXX Ale, keg label, round with red product name above fox logo, Largay Brewing Co on white, blue border, VG+, A19.......................$18.00

Red Giant Oil, can, Red Giant arched above image of giant holding engine, Oil lettered below, cream, red & black, 1-qt, G, A1 ....$30.00

Red Goose Shoes, bank, cast iron, 3¾", EX, A7........$85.00

Red Goose Shoes, display figure, chalkware, product name lettered on red goose, 11½x9x5", VG+, A9 ....$175.00

Red Goose Shoes, mechanical pencil, 5½", G, A7 ....$10.00

Red Goose Shoes, pencil, with pocket clip, NM, A7..$20.00

Red Goose Shoes, pencil box, top shows ruler with 'Half The Fun Of Having Feet' & dealer name left of goose logo, 1½x8", VG, A7 ....$25.00

Red Goose Shoes, store display, revolving rack with red cardboard goose applied to side, pictures monkey & organ grinder, 36x32", VG, A9 ....$300.00

Red Goose Shoes, string holder, die-cut tin, product name on red goose, 26x18", VG+, A9 ....$1,500.00

Red Goose Shoes, thermometer, painted wood, It Takes Leather To Stand Weather, goose logo above bulb & advertising, 22", VG, A2.......................$240.00

Red Goose Shoes, top, tin, 1¼", NM, A7 ....$20.00

Red Goose Shoes, whistle, tin, round, 1¼", NM, A7.$20.00

Red Goose Shoes, whistle, wood with paper label, cylindrical, 'Blow To Beat The Band,' 3½", EX, A7 .....$15.00

Red Hat Motor Oil, can, product lettering encircles red top hat with 3 stars on band, red, black & white, 1-qt, NM, A1.......................$750.00

Red Hat Motor Oil & Gasoline, gas globe, top hat flanked by Top Hat, red, white & black, black metal body, 15" dia, NM+, A6 ....$2,100.00

Red Horse Chewing Tobacco, sign, cardboard, Good Friends, man with product in squatting postion talking to dog, 19x14", NM, A7.......................$40.00

Red Indian Aviation Motor Oil, can, profile of Indian in full headdress above product name, 1 Imperial-qt, 6½x4" dia, VG+, A6.......................$50.00

Red Indian Cut Plug Tobacco, pouch, cloth, 1½", VG, A7.......................$40.00

Red Indian Motor Oils, can, profile of Indian in full headdress above product name, full, 1 Imperial-qt, 6½x4" dia, EX+, A6.......................$175.00

Red Indian Motor Oils, sign, porcelain, product name above Indian in full headdress, red, black & white, 18x20½", scarce, VG+, A6 ....$1,400.00

Red Jacket Smoking Tobacco, pocket tin, vertical, red with cream lettering above & below oval image of jockey on horse, EX+, A18 ....$120.00

Red Keg, syrup dispenser, ceramic, red keg with black bands, Drink... above 5¢ Refreshing 5¢, original pump, 15", VG+, A2.......................$935.00

Red Keg Beer, label, Midland Brewing Co, U-type permit number, Internal Revenue Tax Paid statement, 1933-36, 12-oz, EX, A10 ....$40.00

Red Letter, cigar box label, outer, Roman coin, crown & mystical symbols, 4½x4½", VG, D5 ....$15.00

Red Lion, tobacco tag, oval, large, EX, D35..............$10.00

Red Man Chewing Tobacco, display box, cardboard, blue, red & white Red Man emblem on front, 15", EX, A2.......................$120.00

Red Man Chewing Tobacco, sign, cardboard, Buy above band reading ...America's Best Chew, Big New Pack Lasts Longer & pack below, 14x11", NM, A7........$10.00

Red Man Chewing Tobacco, sign, cardboard, Dad Asked Me To Get Him Some Red Man..., shows man & woman standing, 20x15", NM+, A7.......................$75.00

Red Man Chewing Tobacco, sign, cardboard, First In America above circular view of the Fulton Steamship, 21x14", EX, A7.......................$30.00

Red Man Chewing Tobacco, sign, cardboard, Get Hold Of This...The Flavor Lasts, shows 2 iron workers on Red Man beam, 19x14", NM, A7 ....$55.00

Red Man Chewing Tobacco, sign, cardboard, If It's Good Taste You Want..., policeman with product, 20x12", NM, A7 ....$55.00

Red Man Chewing Tobacco, sign, cardboard, Man — Here's Flavor That Stays With You!, utility lineman reaching into pocket, 20x15", NM+, A7 ....$70.00

Red Man Chewing Tobacco, sign, cardboard, Now That's Something To Write About..., shows reporter talking to editor, text below, 19x14", NM, A7 ....$50.00

Red Man Chewing Tobacco, sign, cardboard, Sure — More Men Ask For It Every Day, shows hotel desk clerk talking on the phone, 20x15", NM, A7..................$50.00

Red Man Chewing Tobacco, sign, cardboard, That Good Chew, Here Jim — Put A Smile In Your Face, shows 2 railroad porters, 19x15", NM, A7 ....$60.00

Red Man Chewing Tobacco, sign, cardboard, That Good-Tasting Chewing Tobacco, Red Man on Railroad signal above brakeman, 20x14", NM, A7 ....$50.00

Red Man Chewing Tobacco, sign, paper, Fresh! & Red Man above Cigar Leaf product pack, Two Sizes 10¢ & 15¢, yellow ground, 1915, 22x12", NM, A3 ....$50.00

Red Man Chewing Tobacco, sign, paper, Fresh! Red Man Wax Wrapped left of man in vest & tie holding product in both hands, framed, 8x18", EX, A8...................$65.00

Red Moon, crate label, California pear, red moon rising over Mendocino County mountains, Ukiah, 8x11", M, D12..$5.00

Red Owl Harvest Queen Coffee, tin, owl's face above ...Finest Quality, key-wind lid, NM, A3................$45.00

Red Raven, tray, nude child reaching for bottle with red raven looking on, ...Ask The Man & logo on rim, 12" dia, EX, A13...$475.00

Red Raven, tray, nude child reaching for bottle with red raven looking on, ...Ask The Man & logo on rim, 12" dia, G+, A9 ....$300.00

Red Raven, tray, pictures red raven, glass & bottle, For Headache & For Indigestion in upper corners, 1910, 13x13", EX, A13 ....$90.00

Red Raven Splits, sign, paper roll-down, shows backside of nude child climbing onto product box to reach bottles, 25x14", EX, A13 ....$450.00

Red Rock Cola, sign, cardboard, girl fishing flanked by lettering, bottle in lower left, 18x12", EX, D30.........$75.00

Red Rock Cola, sign, paper, elegant girl with flowers on oval above bottle, 24x20", EX+, D30 ....$85.00

Red Rock Cola, sign, tin, Drink above bottle, yellow on red with white border, late 1930s, 32x8", NM+, A13 ..$200.00

Red Rock Cola, sign, tin, Enjoy Red Rock Cola in red on white, 4x19", NM+, D30 ....$35.00

Red Rock Ginger Ale, calendar top, 1900-10, bust of girl with flowers & holding flared glass by table with bottle, framed, 12x10", VG+, A13 ....$160.00

Red Rock Ginger Ale, sign, reverse-painted glass, product name & text above Annie Oakley-type cowgirl, chain border, 1904, 10x5", EX, A1................................$550.00

Red Rooster Coffee, tin, crowing rooster at left of product name, key-wind lid, EX+, A3.........................$40.00

Red Rooster Fruit & Produce, sign, porcelain, name on red band around crowing rooster against morning sun, 20" dia, EX, A6..$1,300.00

Red Rooster Fruit & Produce, sign, porcelain, Red Rooster on border above red rooster in front of sun, Fruit & Produce on blue band, 20" dia, EX+, A1 ....$1,600.00

Red Rose Coffee, sign, tin, Red Rose Coffee Is Good Coffee in red & black on cream, orange & cream striped background, 19x27", EX+, D21 ....$60.00

Red Rose Coffee, tin, Vacuum Packed above product name & red rose, pry lid, VG+, A3 ....$50.00

Red Rose Tea, door plate, die-cut porcelain, product name in bold letters above 'Is Good Tea,' white on red, 9x3", NM, D21..$290.00

Red Rose Tea, sign, tin, colorful box of tea on black background, embossed, 19x29", EX, A6....................$100.00

Red Rose Tea, sign, tin, colorful box of tea on black background, embossed, 19x29", NM, A3......$220.00

Red Rose Tea, sign, tin, Red Rose Tea For Sale Here in white on red, 1940s, 18x24", VG+, D21...............$75.00

Red Seal Dry Battery, sign, embossed tin, pictures upright battery with product name on orange background, 19¼x9¼", NM, A1 ....$100.00

Red Seal Dry Battery, thermometer, porcelain, pictures a battery at top, The Guarantee Protects You below, rounded ends, 27", VG, A6...................................$95.00

Red Seal Peanut Butter, pail, depicts Old King Cole nursery rhyme scenes, slip lid & bail, 3", EX, A2......$185.00

Red Seal Snuff, tin, paper label, with contents, EX, D35 ....$15.00

Red Swan Pumpkin Pie Spice, tin, 2¾", NM, A7.....$20.00

Red Top Beer, sign, die-cut tin, shaped as toy top with embossed product name, white on red & black, 21x14½", NOS, NM+, A1..............................$110.00

Red Wagon Grapes, lug box label, little boy with red wagon, red diagonal logo, Reedley, M, D12..........$3.00

Red Wolf Coffee, tin, oval inset of wolf in center, red lettering above & below, key-wind lid, 1-lb, VG, A3....$75.00

Red Wolf Coffee, tin, oval inset of wolf in center, red lettering above & below, key-wind lid, 1-lb, NM, A15...$220.00

Red Wolf Coffee, tin, oval inset of wolf in center, red lettering above & below, slip lid, 3-lb, VG, A18 ......$95.00

Red-Top Flour, sign, curved porcelain, red & white background with name above & below image of boy climbing fence, 22x16", EX, A13 ....$700.00

Redbreast Flake Tobacco, box, horizontal, VG, D35.$35.00

Reddy Kilowatt, display figure, plastic, red & cream figure on black base, Reddy Kilowatt Inc, copyright 1959, 5½", EX, A6 ....$130.00

Reddy Kilowatt, earrings, on cardboard card, ...Your Favorite 'Pin-Up,' EX, A7 ....$45.00

Reddy Kilowatt, see also Pacific Power & Light Co and Massachusetts Electric

Redford's Celebrated Tobaccos, sign, cardboard, plantation image of landowner smoking cigar while watching workers in fields, 1900-10, 20x25", NM, A3........**$195.00**

Redhill Beer, label, St Clair Brewing Co, Internal Revenue Tax Paid statement, 1933-50, 11-oz, M, A10.........**$40.00**

Redlands Best, crate label, California orange, 4 arrows pointing to big orange, Redlands, 10x11", M, D3...**$7.00**

Redlands Joy, crate label, California orange, fancy glass of orange & big orange, deco designs, 1934, M, D3 ..**$8.00**

Redman, crate label, Washington apple, Indian & cave drawings on blue background, 9x11", M, D12.......**$4.00**

Reed & Bell Root Beer, mug, glass, red logo & mug, Ice Cold Reed & Bell Root Beer, 4½x3", NM, D16 ....**$20.00**

Reed & Bell Root Beer, mug, glass, red print oval logo & mug image, 6x3", NM, D16.........................**$18.00**

Reed & Bell Root Beer, sign, porcelain, product name & frothy mug on oval flanked by 5¢ above Frosted Glasses, 30x39", NM, D11 ....**$375.00**

Reed's Tonic, clock, oak with glass front, Reed's Tonic Cures Malaria on bottom glass panel, 36x15x4", VG+, A9 ....**$170.00**

Regal Ale, sign, tin on cardboard, gold lion logo above gold product name on black, gold border, 9" dia, NM+, A19 ....**$265.00**

Regal Beer, sign, paper, 'Let's All Get That Regal Feelin!,' black lady at piano surrounded by piano keys, 1950s, 21x27", EX, A19 ....**$35.00**

Regal Beer, thermometer, metal, Better Change To Better Taste! above embossed bottle & bulb, white, curved corners, 14x6", EX, A8 ....**$55.00**

Regal Beer, tray, deep-dish, Prince Regal Salutes You on ribbon beneath bust of man in plumed hat & holding glass, 13" dia, EX+, A8 ....**$30.00**

Regal Boots, display sign, cast-aluminum boot, Regal lettered vertically down side which used to contain neon, 78", VG, A21 ....**$770.00**

Regal Cube Cut Smoking Tobacco, pocket tin, vertical, cream with red & blue name above & below encircled lion emblem, gold trim, flip top, EX, A18.........$450.00

Regal Ice Cream, sign, tin flange, pictures strawberry ice-cream cone, EX, D34 ....**$145.00**

Regal Oil Co, badge, #87, metal with red, black & white truck in center, 2½x2", EX, A6 ....**$35.00**

Regal Pale Beer, sign, cardboard hanger, name above cowboy serenading girl on fence before full moon, Mellow As..., 12x18", VG+, A8 ....**$60.00**

Regal Pale Beer, sign, flange, product name on wavy bands on oval, red, white & blue, 19x14", VG, A8 ....**$60.00**

Regal Pale Beer, sign, reverse-painted glass, large bottle on black background, curved ends, 11½", VG, A8 ...**$35.00**

Regal Premium Beer, tray, plastic, palm tree & product name on vertical rectangle with bowed sides, EX+, A19...**$50.00**

Regal Remtico Ribbon/Remington Typewriter Co, tin, vertical, red with black lettering, decorative slip lid, ¾x1¾", EX, D37 ....**$40.00**

Regal-Amber Ale, sign, embossed tin hanger, We Recommend above Regal-Amber on diagonal band, Ale flanked by Nut Brown below, 6x9", EX, A8.......**$100.00**

Regent Beverages, sign, embossed tin, bottle left of You'll Like Regent Beverages Better, horizontal, EX, A16..**$35.00**

Regoes Rubbed Sage, tin, 3¾", NM, A7 ....**$40.00**

Reis Lavender Label Union Suits, trolley sign, cardboard, Come On Along...I'll Show You Where To Get... at left of 2 WWI-era soldiers, 11x21", EX+, A1 ....**$20.00**

Reis Union Suits, trolley card, cardboard, shows conductor shouting 'Passengers On This Car Will Please Change To — ...,' 11x21", EX+, A1 ....**$10.00**

Reisch's Wiener Style Special Bottle Beer, sign, tin, red & gold lettering on black, beveled edge, pre-1920, 13x6", VG+, A8 ....**$50.00**

Remington Arms Co, sign, paper, Get Your Game With... above 3 divided images of various rifles & large game, framed, 22x16", EX+, A3.....................................**$230.00**

Remington Firearms Ammunition, catalog, 1955, 12 pgs, EX, D17 ....**$15.00**

Remington Game Loads, display, 3-fold, product box & birds flanked by various game & hunt scene, signed Lynn Bogue Hunt, 18x48", VG, A6 ....**$230.00**

Remington Game Loads, print, pictures a buck surrounded by various game birds, by Lynn Bogue Hunt, framed, 29½x21½", EX+, A6 ....**$160.00**

Remington Grand Prize Modern .22 Caliber Rifles & Cartridges, sign, die-cut cardboard, Some American Boys Who Are...They All Shoot..., How To Aim Your Rifle below, 10x15", EX, A12..............................**$400.00**

Remington UMC, sign, cardboard, Spaniel sitting on box surrounded by guns & Nitro ammunition, Let's Go!, framed, 26x20", VG, A9 ....**$325.00**

Remington UMC, sign, cardboard, woman holding rifle at left of product name on large circle, framed, image: 15x18", VG+, A9 ....**$300.00**

Remington UMC, sign, cardboard stand-up, shows man checking out shotgun in front of gun case, 20x14", EX, A7 ....**$600.00**

Remington UMC, sign, paper, The Remington Idea, Solid Breech Hammerless above 4 images of various guns, ammo & animals, 24x13", EX, A3........................**$395.00**

Remington UMC Auto Loading & Repeating Firearms, sign, cardboard stand-up, man trying out rifle in front of display case, ...Sold Here below, 20x14", EX, A12...............**$625.00**

Remington Visible Writing, sign, paper, girl using early typewriter, framed, image: 32x22", VG, A9 ....**$325.00**

Rene Cigars, sign, paper, girl with fan, Smoke... on original frame, oval, 26½x19½", VG+, A9.................**$425.00**

Repeater Fine Cut Tobacco, tin, flat, Mountie on horse & product name, Smoking Tobacco upper right, round corners, 4x3x1", VG, A1.................................**$45.00**

Repetti Cocoa, tin, sample, pictures Oriental girl, slip lid, 2x1¼x1¼", EX, D37................................**$150.00**

Repetti Tabs, sign, paper, True Fruit Flavor...5¢ Everywhere on black with open pack & branch of lemons, 10x19", EX, A2........................**$145.00**

Republic Lumber & Millwork, sign, die-cut porcelain, red, white & blue shield with eagle atop, 23x17", NM, D8................................**$380.00**

Resinol Soap & Ointment, tip tray, bust image of girl in see-through wrap against white floral & green ground, gold lettering, 4" dia, EX, A21.................**$175.00**

Restylers Gilt Edge Lager, tray, 'California Invites The World,' girl in gold dress standing before San Francisco Exhibition, 12" dia, VG+, A21....................**$135.00**

Revelation Nail Polish, tin, decorative kaleidoscopic-type background, short oval with small round top, 1¾x2¼x1¼", EX, D37............................**$20.00**

Revelation Smoking Mixture, pocket tin, sample, cream & red with name above & below black oval, 'It's Mild & Mellow' below, NM, A18..............$95.00

Rex Beer, label, Standard Brewing Co, Internal Revenue Tax Paid statement, 1933-50, 12-oz, EX, A10.......**$25.00**

Rex Mild Cool Burning Pipe & Cigarette Tobacco, pocket tin, vertical, dark green with name above & below oval bust portrait flanked by torches, EX, A18............**$145.00**

Rex Mild Cool Burning Pipe & Cigarette Tobacco, tin, dark green with name above & below oval bust portrait flanked by torches, vertical square, EX, A18........**$35.00**

Rexall, sign, porcelainized steel, product name in white script on blue background, gold border, 72" long, EX, A21...........................**$55.00**

Reymann Brewing Co, calendar, 1897, frothy mug surrounded by wheat & hops, Wheeling W VA below, 1-sheet calendar, 22x14", NM, A9...............**$1,050.00**

RG Sullivan's 7-2 0-4 Cigar, sign, porcelain, RD Sullivan's on black banner against 7-2 0-4 on red, white & black border, 1930s, 11x23", NM, A13...................**$260.00**

Rheingold (Pale) Beer, tray, deep-dish, oval image of 2 men toasting with beer, scrolled background, lettering on rim, 13x10½", G+, A9...................**$50.00**

Rheingold Beer, can, flat-top, gold with product name on diagonal white band, 12-oz, EX, A19................**$10.00**

Rheingold Beer, tap knob, black ball shape with white & gold on blue enamel insert, VG+, A8...............**$35.00**

Rheingold Beer, tray, deep-dish, cartoon image of marching soldier leaving group to have a Rheingold, red & white, 12" dia, VG+, A19........................**$25.00**

Rheingold Famous Scotch Brand Ale, sign, reverse-painted Becco, emblem & leaf design above red foil lettering, 3-sided plaid border, framed, 11x13", EX, A8............**$20.00**

Rheingold Golden Bock Beer, can, flat-top, red, white & gold, 12-oz, EX+, A19.........................**$25.00**

Rheingold Scotch Ale, tap knob, green ball shape with red & green on cream enamel insert, VG+, A8....**$45.00**

Rhinehaus Old German Beer, label, Imperial Brewing Co, Internal Revenue Tax Paid statement, 1933-50, 12-oz, M, A10................................**$10.00**

Rib Mountain Lager, label, Wausau Brewing Co, U-type permit number, Internal Revenue Tax Paid statement, 12-oz, NM, A10................................**$40.00**

Rich & Ripe, tobacco tag, round, EX, D35...................**$3.00**

Richardson Root Beer, door plate, Rich In Flavor, silhouette image of waiter with bottle on tray above & below lettering, vertical, EX, A16..................**$95.00**

Richardson Root Beer, mug, embossed crystal, barrel shape with staves & bands, 6⅝", EX, D14...........**$35.00**

Richardson Root Beer, mug, glass, applied Richardson Root Beer label, M, A16......................**$20.00**

Richardson Root Beer, mug, glass, embossed lettering, M, A16................................**$40.00**

Richardson Root Beer, sign, die-cut tin, frothy wood-grained barrel with product label on front, 26x21", NM, A1................................**$225.00**

Richardson Root Beer, sign, paper, Rich In Flavor & product name on label above tiled bottle & hamburger, Fine With Food, 14x10", NOS, VG+, A1...............**$30.00**

Richardson Silk Company Perfect Knitting Silk, spool cabinet, for counter-top or wall, reverse-painted glass front, 9 rows of pegs, EX+, A13.........................**$170.00**

Richardson's Silk, spool cabinet, oak with 7 glass front drawers & 1 solid drawer with product name, 22x18x19", VG+, A9................................**$575.00**

Richelieu Coffee, tin, product name above & below Our Best Grade on banner, pry lid, 3-lb, EX, A3.........**$45.00**

Richelieu Coffee, tin, product name above & below Our Best Grade on banner, slip lid, 1-lb, EX, A3........**$25.00**

Richfield, gas globe, yellow lettering on blue band across circle, blue metal body, 15" dia, NM, A6............**$800.00**

Richfield, radiator front, cardboard, 2 shield logos over race car scene, Choice Of The World's..., framed, 13x20", EX+, A1................................**$275.00**

Richfield, salt & pepper shakers, plastic gas pumps, yellow with eagle & shield logo, 1 marked Ethyl, 1 Hi-Octane, 3", NM, A1 ....$170.00

Richfield, weathervane, painted metal, eagle atop arrow & directional letters, 43x28", M eagle/EX accessories, A1................................**$1,000.00**

Richfield Ethyl, gas globe, product name & logo on shield, yellow & blue on white, silver metal body, 15" dia, NM, A6 ....$1,600.00

Richfield Hi-Octane, gas globe, logo & product name on shield, blue, orange & white, blue metal low-profile body, 15" dia, EX+, A6.........................$375.00

Richfield Motor Oil, can, eagle atop shield below product name, yellow, cream & black, 10x7" dia, G, A6...$30.00

Richford Grinding Compound, tin, product name above emblem reading Always Ready No Mixing Required, slip lid, 2⅜x1⅜" dia, EX, D37 ....$20.00

Richlube Motor Oil, sign, metal, Longer Wear Without Repair, 2-sided w/attached Richlube can that spins, 21x36", VG+, A6 ....$120.00

Richmond Maid Coffee, tin, encircled image of smiling girl in center, key-wind lid, 1-lb, VG+, A3 ....$100.00

Richmond Mixture, tin, box-type with square corners, lid reads The Richmond Mixture For Smoking, 2¼x4½", VG, A7 ....$30.00

Richmond Service Station, sign, embossed tin, ...Electrically Hammered Rings above box flanked by rings, Stops Oil Troubles below, 18x12", VG, A6........$160.00

Richmond Straight Cut Cigarettes, cabinet card, Denmark flag with blue border, ...Are The Best, 9x6", VG, A5 ....$40.00

Richmond Straight Cut Cigarettes, cabinet card, Sweden flag with blue border, ...Are The Best, 9x6", VG, A5........$45.00

Richmond Straight Cut Cigarettes, sign, paper, name & product box on blue at right of 3-quarter image of young woman, dark red border, 15x12", G, A2...$35.00

Ridges Food, sign, die-cut cardboard stand-up, black & white child ready to spar, ad text on back, 10x5", EX, A3..$250.00

Rieck's Ice Cream, sign, paper, It's So Delicious I'll Take Home A Brick Of... says lady to soda jerk, purple ground, 12x22", G, A2 ....$175.00

Riley's Bunny-Bons, tin, product name above animated bunnies, The Tastiest Toffies below, slip lid, 8½x6½x4", EX, A18 ....$175.00

Riley's Creamy Toffee, sign, cardboard, colorful image of little boy with box of Riley's Creamy Toffee Rolls, matted, 20½x14", EX, A6 ....$45.00

Riley's Creamy Toffee, tin, product name above & left of Dutch boy & girl on boardwalk before sailboats, gold lid, rectangular, 6x7x4", EX, A18.......................$80.00

Rimmon Rock, cigar box label, inner lid, photo image of waterfalls over dam, 6x9", M, D5 ....$15.00

Rinso Soap, trolley sign, cardboard, A Whiter Wash In Half The Time, pictures product box & clothesline, framed, 11x21", G, A6......................................$80.00

Rising Sun Stove Polish, store card, Uncle Sam & other people watching crowds run toward store, 7x11", G, A9 ....$35.00

Rislone, thermometer, tin, Ask About... on yellow above product can & bulb on red, 25½x9½", EX, A6.....$85.00

Ritz Crackers/Nabisco, tin, allover graphics of crackers with Nabisco logo upper left of product name, slip lid, 1974, 13-oz, NM, A7...............................$10.00

Ritz Lager Beer/Pacific Brewing & Malt Co, label, product lettering & graphics against light green background, 11-oz, EX+, A19...$12.00

Rivals, label for tobacco barrel, paper, The Rivals above lady surrounded by men, The Only Single Lady... below, 6x13", NM+, A1...............................$100.00

River Lad Asparagus, crate label, Dutch lad & windmill, M, D3 ....$2.00

Rivera Brand Coffee/Sears, Roebuck & Co, milk can, lime green with darker green lettering, bail handle, 5-lb, 12", G-, A2...$45.00

Road Queens, cigar box label, outer, 2 women riding bicycles, 1896, M, A5...............................$275.00

Road Runner Non-Detergent Motor Oil, can, waxed cardboard, road runner on circle above product name, yellow, orange, red & blue, with contents, 1-qt, NM, A6.....$50.00

Road Runners, cigar box label, outer, elegant couple in carriage, EX, A5...............................$145.00

Rob Roy Coffee, tin, logo between Rob Roy, Donald Company, Grand Island Nebraska on band below, plaid background, pry lid, 1-lb, EX+, A3.....................$85.00

Robert Burns 10¢ Cigar, charger, tin, bust-portrait of Robert Burns & open box of cigars on Scottish plaid background, 24" dia, VG, A9................$200.00

Robin Brand Coffee, tin, paper label with robin perched on branch on emblem flanked by Steel Cut, Scudders-Gale Co, 3-lb, rare, EX, A3.........................$245.00

Robin Hood Beer/Fontenelle Brewing Co, label, product name on diagonal band over image of Robin Hood pulling back bow, 12-oz, EX+, A19.....................$5.00

Robin Hood Flour, watch fob, red & blue porcelain shield with various logos, EX, A20.................................$25.00

Robin Hood Shoes, bank, tin & cardboard, 2¼x2", NM, A7..$30.00

Robin Hood Shoes, display, die-cut cardboard, Hal Roaches character 'Farina' holding chalkware display, 12", rare, EX+, A3...$330.00

Robin Hood Shoes, display, plaster figure of Robin Hood with arms crossed on base lettered with product name, 12", EX, A2...$210.00

Robinson Crusoe Brand Salted Peanuts, tin, black, yellow & red island scene with lettering, round, 10-lb, VG+, A18 ....$375.00

Rochester Beers-Ales, sign, wood, On Tap above product name in outlined rectangle, 5 slots to show brands, 16x10", VG+, A8 ....$75.00

Rochester Journal, sign, embossed tin, Inspring-New-Complete above Rochester Journal, Make It A Daily... below, 1920s-30s, 5x20", NM+, A13 ....$95.00

Rochester Photo Supply Co, pocket mirror, black & white view of a city block, oval, EX+, D18 ....$75.00

Rochester Root Beer, mug, glass, straight-sided with flared bottom, embossed lettering, 7", M, A16 ....$30.00

Rochester Root Beer, syrup dispenser, ceramic barrel on tree stump, embossed product name on front & back, 12x6½", VG+, A9 ....$100.00

Rochester Root Beer, syrup dispenser, ceramic barrel shape on tree stump, embossed product name on front & back, 12x6½", NM+, A4 ....$450.00

Rochester Yacht Club, license plate attachment, porcelain on metal, R logo in center, red, white & blue, 1947, 5¼x3½" dia, EX, A6 ....$25.00

Rock-Co Pure Cocoa, container, cardboard & tin, product name above & below illustrated image of man with steaming cup, 2-lb, VG+, A18..................$40.00

Rocket Motor Oil, can, Rocket lettered above flying rocket & Motor Oil on emblem, screw cap & handle, 2-gal, 11x8", VG, A6 ....$55.00

Rockford Watch, sign, tin, Incomparable..., elegant girl holding pocket watch on oval inset surrounded by clocks, 23x17", G, A9 ....$550.00

Rocky Hill, crate label, California orange, bronze Indian on horseback at top of rock, Exeter, 10x11", M, D12...$6.00

Rocky Mountain Beer, label, product name in diagonal script on red band across mountain scene, company name below, 12-oz, EX, A19 ....$40.00

Rocky Mountain Beer, matchbook, Anaconda Brewing Co, 20 strike, front strike, NM, D28..................$5.00

Rode-O-Cuba Cigars, tin, product name arched above portrait of lady on gold oval, round, EX+, A18 ....$110.00

Rodeo, crate label, Washington apple, cowboy on bucking pinto horse, 9x11", M, D12 ....$6.00

Roe Feeds, sign, tin, comical image of man wearing feed sack walking with farm animals, embossed, 28x23", EX, A6..........................$230.00

Roe Feeds, sign, tin, red & cream striped feed sack on green background, 12x7", EX, A6 ....$30.00

Roelofs Hats, pocket mirror, pictures colorful image of billboard, horizontal oval, 2¾", EX, A21..................$110.00

Rofelda, cigar box label, outer, woman crowned in red roses, 4½x4½", M, D5..........................$8.00

Roi-Tan Cigars/Sophie Tucker Roi-Tan Radio Show, toy car with 2-sided sign, tin, red 1939 Wyandotte Chevy, store promotion, 4x4½", NMIB, A3 ..$220.00

Rolling Rock Beer, sign, wood composition, Kaiai King, horse above product advertising, 19x10", VG+, A19..........................$50.00

Rolling Rock Beer, sign, wood composition, Lucky Debonail, horse above product advertising, 14x10", VG+, A19..........................$55.00

Rolling Rock Premium Beer, display, horse & 7-oz bottle with painted label on lettered base, 10x11", EX, A19..........................$230.00

Rolling Rock Premium Beer, golf putter, 'The Original' Arnold Palmer putter, engraved with product name, special corporate gift, MIB, A8..................$220.00

Rolling Rock Premium Beer, sign, light-up box, plastic panel, metal frame, We Serve... above name right of tilted bottle, green on white, EX+, A19..................$50.00

Rosa de Oro, crate label, California orange, view of ranch with fancy lettering above oranges & a rose, Thermalito, 10x11", M, D12..........................$20.00

Rose Leaf, pocket tin, flat, imprinted design around compass in center, rounded corners, EX+, A18 ....$70.00

Rosenbloom's Linens & Rubber Collars, display case, glass with oak top & 3 shelves, marble base, 63x18x21", G, A9..........................$350.00

Roth's Hy-Quality Coffee, sign, die-cut cardboard, girl on swing enjoying a cup of coffee, framed, 42½x24", EX, A6..........................$550.00

Rothchilds Bros Hat Co Star Hats, sign, print on textured hardboard, close-up of man in hat with city beyond, name below, framed, 16x12½", VG, A6 ....$180.00

Rothenberg's Mixture, pocket tin, short vertical, red with product name above & below framed oval portrait, gold lid, VG, A18 ....$275.00

Rothenberg's Mixture, pocket tin, short vertical, red with product name above & below framed oval portrait, gold lid, NM, A18..........................$595.00

Rothman's Speedboat Mixture, tin, oval image of 1930s-style speedboat in lower right, red with white lettering, 3x6", EX, A6..........................$230.00

Rough Diamond, crate label, California lemon, large L in diamond on lime green background, Santa Paula, 12x9", M, D3 ....$2.00

Rough Rider Baking Powder, tin, paper label, with contents, 4¼-oz, NM, A7 ....$75.00

Round Oak Stoves, Ranges & Furnaces, mug, ceramic, light tan glaze shading to dark brown with encircled image of 'Doe-Wah-Jack,' 1900s, 4¾", EX+, A1 ..$85.00

Round Oak Stoves, Ranges & Furnaces, sign, tin, embossed 'Doe-Wah-Jack' emblem at left of product advertising & dealer name, 10x27½", NOS, EX+, A1 ....$200.00

Roundtree Cocoa, tin, sample, lid pictures encircled images of people of different nationalities, gold border, 2½x1¾x¾", EX, D37..$155.00

Roundy's Coffee, tin, The Peak Of above steaming cup on triangle, red, white & blue, key-wind lid, 2-lb, NM, A3 ....$55.00

Rover Cut Plug, tin, name above & below ship with yellow sails against sunset, slip lid, 4x4" dia, rare, EX, A18..$560.00

Rowley & Hermace Co, catalog, 1894, working machinery, EX, A12 ....$100.00

Royal, gas globe, white crown shape with red lettering, 1-pc, 13x11" dia, NM, A6 ....$1,000.00

Royal, pump sign, die-cut porcelain, product name on band across triangle, red & white, 10x8½", EX+, A6 ....$50.00

Royal Ale, label, Royal on blue diagonal scrolled banner against yellow background, American Brewing Co Ltd, 11-oz, EX, A19..$15.00

Royal Amber Beer, tap knob, yellow ball with gold & black on white & gold metal insert, EX, A8.......$100.00

Royal Arms, crate label, citrus, gladiator with sword & shield, 9x9", M, D3 ....$3.00

Royal Baking Powder, store poster offering free Fairy Book, gingerbread man with product & booklet, pre-1914, framed, 30x20", rare, EX+, A3 ....$250.00

Royal Baking Powder, tin, paper label, with contents, 2-oz, NM, A7 ....$16.00

Royal Baking Powder, trolley sign, cardboard, Only With Royal Can You Make Cakes Like This, pictures cake & product, framed, 10x21", G-, A6.............................$40.00

Royal Banner Cigars, sign, tin, open box of cigars on crossed flags, 23½x17½", EX, A9 ....$650.00

Royal Beer, mug, ceramic, 'Admires Blondes Until He Marries A Brunette,' product name on logo above company name, gold trim, EX, A8.......................................$95.00

Royal Beer, mug, ceramic, barrel shape, 'The Art Of A Long Life,' product name on logo above company name, gold trim, EX, A8.......................................$95.00

Royal Blue Line Motor Oils, brochure, Royal Blue Line Service Boston, colorful image of tour bus & mountain scene, copyright 1929, EX+, A6.............................$15.00

Royal Club Cut Plug, tin, embossed lion & crown emblem left of name, company name below, rectangular with rounded corners, EX, A18 ....$195.00

Royal Club Peanut Butter, pail, green with white product name above & below gold & red crown & lion logo, slip lid, bail handle, 1-lb, EX+, A18 ....$145.00

Royal Crown Cola, bottle, RC on shoulder, 1936, NM, A7.$20.00

Royal Crown Cola, calendar, 1950, RC Tastes Best! Says Wanda Hendrix, oval image of Wanda with bottle, complete, 25x12", EX, A7 ....$30.00

Royal Crown Cola, calendar, 1953, features Arlene Dahl with bottle, full pad, 24x11", EX+, A13...............$210.00

Royal Crown Cola, can, flat-top, blue with RC on white dot, open, EX+, A16...$35.00

Royal Crown Cola, clock, reverse-painted glass light-up, RC above Royal Crown Cola on red emblem, 15x15", NM, A18..$175.00

Royal Crown Cola, ice chest, steel with embossed tin panels, 2 with bottles & 2 with pyramid logo, double-door lift top, 30x31", G-, A9 ....$250.00

Royal Crown Cola, lighter, aluminum flip-top, crown above product name, VG, A16.............................$25.00

Royal Crown Cola, matchbook, pictures big bottle with pyramids, 20 strike, NM, D28 ....$3.00

Royal Crown Cola, playing cards, oval image of bottle, scalloped border, NMIB, A16 ....$30.00

Royal Crown Cola, sign, cardboard, 'RC Tastes Best!' Says Barbara Stanwyck, shows Barbara with bottle, 11x28", VG, A13 ....$100.00

Royal Crown Cola, sign, cardboard, 'RC Tastes Best!' Says Bing Crosby, shows Bing holding bottle, 26x31", NM, A16..$250.00

Royal Crown Cola, sign, cardboard, Go Fresher...Go RC, girl on swing & 6-pack carton, colorful scenery beyond, 12x34", VG, D30...$30.00

Royal Crown Cola, sign, cardboard, Take Home RC For Your Family!, mom & kids in store, 1950s, 11x28", NM, A13 ....$110.00

Royal Crown Cola, sign, cardboard, You'll Flip At the ZZZip In RC Cola, couple on sailboat, 22x34", VG, A16 ...$30.00

Royal Crown Cola, sign, cardboard stand-up, die-cut, 'RC Tastes Best!' Says Hedy Lamarr, Hedy at table, 1940s-50s, 9", EX, A13..$100.00

Royal Crown Cola, sign, cardboard stand-up, die-cut, Nothing Sparkles Like A Royal Crown, crowned girl in gown, 1950s, 30x16", VG, A13 ....$120.00

Royal Crown Cola, sign, Glo Glas, We Serve RC Cola Highballs, Smooth-Mellow left of bottle, 10x12", EX+, A13........................$1,100.00

Royal Crown Cola, sign, tin, bottle, 1951, 60x16", NM, A13........................$400.00

Royal Crown Cola, sign, tin, die-cut, Royal Crown Cola, Best By Taste, bottle on dot, red & yellow ground, 2-sided, 1940, 16x24", EX, A13........................$475.00

Royal Crown Cola, sign, tin, die-cut, Take Home A Carton, Six Big Bottles 25¢, shows 6-pack, black ground, 2-sided, 1940, 16x24", EX+, A13......$600.00

Royal Crown Cola, sign, tin, Drink Royal Crown Cola, Best By Taste-Test left of bottle, 12x28", EX+, D30.......$85.00

Royal Crown Cola, sign, tin, Drink Royal Crown Cola & tilted bottle on red & yellow, 1939, self-framed, 22x34", NM, A13........................$375.00

Royal Crown Cola, sign, tin, Drink...Best By Taste-Test flanked by bottles, embossed, marked A Product Of Nehi...12-51, 18x54", EX, A6........................$185.00

Royal Crown Cola, sign, tin, large bottle on white background, self-framed, 1940s, 36x16", NM, A13 ....$225.00

Royal Crown Cola, sign, tin, We Serve...Best By Taste-Test, Ice Cold, red & green, 1940s, framed, NM, A13..$250.00

Royal Crown Cola, sign, tin hanger, Take Home A Carton next to 6-pack, Six Big Bottles 25¢ on green emblem, 1941, NM, A13........................$1,550.00

Royal Crown Cola, spare tire cover, canvas & cardboard, Drink..., Drive Carefully, mountain graphics, 1940s, 29" dia, VG, A13 ....$70.00

Royal Crown Cola, tap knob, chrome over steel, bottle shape with red labels, 1940s, 15", EX+, A13 ......$200.00

Royal Crown Cola, thermometer, tin, blue, Drink..., Best By Taste-Test, bulb on arrow pointing up, vertical, rounded corners, EX, A16........................$75.00

Royal Crown Cola, thermometer, tin, blue, Royal... on diamond above bulb on arrow pointing up, vertical, rounded corners, earlier, VG+, A $75.00

Royal Crown Cola, thermometer, tin, white, Royal Crown Cola (crown logo), The Fresher Refresher, rounded corners, 28", NM+, D30 ....$95.00

Royal Crown Motor Oil, can, product name & 100% Pure Pennsylvania logo, Crown Oil Co, orange, cream & blue, easy pour, 5-gal, 16" dia, G+, A6..............$130.00

Royal Delight of Virginia, label for tobacco barrel, shows onlookers watching man on bended knee offering gift to queen, ca 1880, 6x13", NOS, M, A1.................$15.00

Royal Egypt, cigar box label, outer, Egyptian dancer beside tiger, 1900, M, A5 ....$170.00

Royal Knight, crate label, California orange, castle scene with knight in armor on horseback, yellow ground, Redlands, 10x11", M, D3 ....$2.00

Royal Palm, seltzer bottle, palm tree flanked by product name, Coca-Cola, Terre Haute Ind, 1930s, 12", NM, A13 ....$150.00

Royal Palm, sign, cardboard, All Flavors, Drink Royal Palm... By The Coca-Cola Bottling Co, bottle at right, 1930s, 11x17", VG, A13........................$60.00

Royal Purple Stock Specific, tin, Royal Purple above encircled building with street scene, Stock Specific on emblem below, pry lid, 8", VG, A1 ....$20.00

Royal Snowdrift Oil, pump sign, porcelain, lion atop emblem with product name, green, white & black, 12" dia, NM, A6........................$180.00

Royal Sugar Cones, bucket, red with black detail, slip lid & wire side handles, Yohay Baking Co, Brooklyn NY, 15½x12" dia, EX, A1 ....$145.00

Royal Tailors, sign, die-cut tin, tiger atop sign, Authorized Resident Dealer...Chicago-New York, 9x20", EX, A9 ....$250.00

Royal Triton Motor Oil, sign, porcelain, America's Finest in script above product name, purple & white, 2-sided, 39x25", EX+, A6........................$165.00

Royal 76 Marine Gasoline, pump sign, porcelain, product lettering on white field, orange banded border, 11½" dia, EX, A1........................$240.00

Royal 99, pump sign, die-cut porcelain shield, Royal in red diagonal letters on white, logo & 99 in white on blue, 9x7", NM, A1 ....$325.00

Royale Republic Regular, pump sign, porcelain, Royale in script above Republic on shield, Regular below, red, white & blue, 11x10", EX+, A6........................$250.00

RPM Heavy Duty Motor Oil, sign, porcelain, product name over bull's-eye type field, red, white & blue, 2-sided, 34" dia, EX, A1 ....$250.00

RPM Motor Oil, sign, porcelain flange, Thermo-Changed...100% Pure Paraffin Base, blue, red, white & black, 22x22½", NM, A6 ....$700.00

Rubber Manufacturing Co, see Rainbow Packing

Rubsam & Horrmann Bottled Beers, tray, bare-chested woman flanked by R&H Bottled Beers & Bottled At The Brewery, 12½" dia, EX, A9 ....$650.00

Ruby Mocha & Java, pail, sample, fancy lettering on yellow, gold slip lid, bail handle, 3x2½" dia, EX, D37 .....$200.00

Ruff's Pilsner Beer, label, Ruff-Riedel Brewing Co, Internal Revenue Tax Paid statement, 1933-50, 12-oz, M, A10 ....$10.00

Ruhl's Bakery, matchbook, double-wide cover with 40 matches, 2 loaves of bread & slogans on front, bakery on back, NM, D14 ....$2.50

Ruhstaller's, tip tray, California Invites The World, girl with city beyond, decorative rim, 4" dia, EX+, A8.......**$225.00**

Ruhstaller's, tip tray, lady seated in profile posed with dove on her knee, Sacramento California on rim, 5" dia, VG+, A8 ....**$100.00**

Ruhstaller's Gilt Edge, tray, product name on billboard behind man serving 2 ladies in open car, black rim, pre-1920s, 13x13", G, A19 ....**$65.00**

Ruhstaller's Lager & Gilt Edge Steam Beer, tray, product name in sky above factory scene, decorative rim, oval, VG, A19 ....**$600.00**

Rumford Baking Powder, tin, 6-oz, EX, A7 ....**$5.00**

Rummy, sign, die-cut cardboard, Get Chummy With Rummy, 2 flowers in bottle flanked by lemons, 24x12", NM+, D30..**$35.00**

Rummy, sign, die-cut cardboard, The Master Mixer, bathing beauty beside large bottle on beach, 18x12", NM+, D30..**$85.00**

Rums Dry Ginger Ale, pocket mirror, black lettering on gold, rectangular, M, A16......................................**$60.00**

Runkel's Cocoa, tin, sample, crest emblem above product name, vertical rectangle with slip lid, 1½x1⅛x¾", EX, D37...**$115.00**

Runkel's Cocoa, tin, sample, name above & below oval image of lady flanked by Pure & All Purpose, 2½x1¾x1¼", EX, D37 ....**$90.00**

Runkel's Cocoa, tin, sample, name above & below oval image of lady flanked by Founded... & Registered US..., 2½x1¾x1¼", EX, D37..............................**$130.00**

Runkel's Essence of Chocolate, tin, tall white shouldered square shape with white, gold & red graphics, small round screw lid, EX, A18 ....**$125.00**

Runkel's Pure Cocoa, tin, sample, name & Serial No 5 above & below Pure lettered on shield, slip lid, 1½x1⅛x⅞", EX, D37..............................**$115.00**

Runkel's Pure High Grade Cocoa, tin, sample, vertical square with screw lid, 1⅝x1⅛x1⅛", EX, D37 ......**$95.00**

Ruppert Ale, sign, mirrored etched glass, shaped like police shield with eagel & ribbon logo above product name, 10x12", VG, A8..............................**$85.00**

Ruppert Beer, sign, glass, chain hanger, blue shield with eagle & ribbon logo above product name, recessed lettering, NM+, A19 ....**$75.00**

Ruppert Beer & Ale, see also Jacob Ruppert

Ruppert Knickerbocker Beer, sign, tin on cardboard, cream & gold on blue, gold beveled edge, 9x13", VG+, A8.**$95.00**

Ruppert Old Knickerbocker Beer, sign, light-up, Ben Franklin-type gent at left of etched & gold-leafed product name on glass panel, metal base, EX, A8 ....**$130.00**

Ruppert's Beer, globe, light-up, red lettering above & below eagle & shield logo on blue lens, rippled body, 1920s, 16" dia, NM, A13 ....**$425.00**

Rurales, cigar box label, outer, man flirting with Spanish senorita, 4½x4½", M, D5 ....**$6.00**

Russell Emulsion, trolley sign, cardboard, A Food That Restores..., product bottle, box & steaming cup flanked by text, 11x21", EX+, A1 ....**$10.00**

Russell-Miller Milling Co, see Occident

Ruth Shoes, tape measure, celluloid, Ask For The Ruth Shoe, It Has Character arched above & below image, round, EX+, A11..**$45.00**

Ryder Furniture & Carpet Co, tape measure, celluloid, You Will Like Trading At Ryder's, black & white, round, EX, A11 ....**$15.00**

Ryzon, sign, die-cut metal hanger, white colonial-style emblem, name above box, Results Sure below, 1930s-40s, 16x12", NM, A13 ....**$525.00**

∽ S ∾

S Bolton's & Sons, tray, colorful image of jolly fellows conversing while testing ale, lettering on decorative rim, oval, 15x19", G, A9......................................**$50.00**

S&H Fro-joy Ice Cream, curb sign, tin in cast-iron frame, Fro-joy on diagonal oval above logo & 'Finer Flavor,' 33x20", VG, A6 ....**$80.00**

S&H Green Stamps, tip tray, bust image of girl in profile with feather, lettering & stamps around rim, 1911, 4½" dia, VG+, A21 ....**$35.00**

S&H Root Beer, syrup jug, ...Manufactured By Simmons & Hammond, Portland, Maine in black, shows hand with German mug, 12", NM, D16 ....**$150.00**

S-Bro-Co Red Pepper, tin, 2½", NM, A7 ....$100.00

Sachs Bros & Stern Children's Clothing & Utility Knee Pants, calendar, 1899, paper with metal strips, boy in chair holding paint pallette with advertising, 20x15", VG+, A3 ....$155.00

Safe Deposit Cedar Chests, sign, cardboard hanger, We Sell Guaranteed... lettered around image of chest, white on wood-grain, 8x12", EX+, A3 ....$30.00

Sailor's Hope, tobacco label, name above backside view of girl on dock, decorative border top & bottom, framed, 13x7", EX, A21 ....$35.00

Sailor's Pride, tobacco tag, EX, D35 ....$6.00

Sakrete Concrete & Mortar Mixture, sign, embossed tin, product name on diagonal center band with man saying Gosh! above & Ahh!! below, 18x29", VG, A9 ....$25.00

Salada Tea, dispenser, counter-top, black & yellow porcelain sign on oak base, ...Always Delicious, cast-iron cutter, 16x29", EX, A6 ....$235.00

Salada Tea, door push bar, porcelain, 'Salada' Tea flanked by Delicious & Flavour, yellow with black lettering, 3x32", VG, A6 ....$125.00

Salada Tea, door push bar, porcelain, Fresh & Delicious in diagonal script flank 'Salada' Tea, EX+, A13 ....$85.00

Salada Tea, door push bar, porcelain, The 'Salada' Tea, EX, A13 ....$70.00

Salada Tea, wrapping paper dispenser, oak & cast iron with porcelain sign atop, ...Always Delicious, 17x26x9", EX, A6 ....$110.00

Salem Beer, see also Schmidt's Salem Beer

Salem Beer/Salem Brewing Association, label, product name above red seal logo, company name below, metallic gold border, 11-oz, EX, A19 ....$8.00

Sally Clover Coffee, tin, Sally Clover in script above cameo & lettering, 1-lb, EX+, A3 ....$40.00

Salmon Trout, cigar box label, salesman's sample, 2 fishing scenes above large trout, VG, A5 ....$120.00

Salon Cigarren, cigar box label, inner lid, train puffing down track, 6x9", EX, D5 ....$25.00

Sam Sloan High Grade Cigar, sign, die-cut cardboard hanger, name & 5¢ on red band around locomotive with image of Sam Sloan, framed, 14x10", VG, A2 ....$85.00

Samoset Chocolates, banner, full-color image of Indian in canoe on black background, 9x14", NM, D15....$150.00

Samoset Chocolates, display, cast plaster, Indian in canoe flanked by Trade Mark, product name on oak leaf base, 19", NM, D15 ....$700.00

Samoset Chocolates, sign, aluminum, product name & 'Chief Of Them All' flanked by Indian in canoe, 1940s, 4x22", NM, D8 ....$265.00

San Antonio, crate label, California lemon, brook from snowy mountains running through meadow, Ontario, 9x12", M, D12 ....$10.00

San Bartolo, cigar box label, salesman's sample, bust portrait at left of ship, cigar band at right, M, A5 ......$50.00

San Benito Wines, corkscrew, metal with wood handle, 1950s, 4", EX, D23 ....$18.00

San Blas Cocoanut, tin, red, vertical square with smaller round lid, Ginna, VG, A18 ....$15.00

San Blas Cocoanut, tin, yellow, vertical square with smaller round top, Ginna, EX+, A18 ....$70.00

San Blas Cocoanut, tin, yellow, vertical square with smaller round top, Somers, VG, A18 ....$15.00

San Blas Golden Crown Cocoanut, tin, tall green shouldered square shape with round lid, VG+, A18.....$30.00

San Blas Golden Crown Cocoanut, tin, tall red shouldered square shape with round lid, EX, A18 ....$50.00

San Diego Quality Beer, pennant, red & white felt, San Diego The Quality Beer In Bottles, encircled bird & hops logo, pre-1920s, 29", VG+, A8 ....$85.00

San Francisco, crate label, California orange, view of Oakland Bay Bridge with city beyond, 1940s, 10x11", M, D12...$45.00

San Francisco World's Fair 1939, license plate attachment, tin, silhouette of Golden Gate & skyline with lettering above, red, white & blue, 11", VG+, A1.....$75.00

San Rey, cigar box label, outer, lion atop shield, 4½x4½", M, D5 ....$4.00

San-Tox After Shave Talcum, tin, pictures a maid pointing toward product name, EX, A3 ....$40.00

Sana-Dermal Talcum Powder, tin, embossed image of Victorian mother powdering child in bathroom, shaker top, oval, 5½", EX, A2...$360.00

Sandy Hook Cigars, box label set, lighthouse surrounded by ships, 2-pc, NM, A5 ....$60.00

Sanford's Inks, display case, counter-top, oak & glass with 2 glass shelves, 16x12x½x11", EX, A9 ....$500.00

Sanford's Inks & Mucilage, sign, embossed tin, Faultless!... above various product bottles & jars, Kaufmann & Strauss, 13½x19½", VG, A9 ....$2,600.00

Sanguinette Grapes, lug box label, white block letters on blue background, Lodi, M, D12.............................$2.00

Sani-Flush, tin, pictures woman using product, contains some contents, pry lid, EX+, A3............................$14.00

Sanitary Milk, tray, 'Right To The Point,' shows bust image of lady pointing, lettered rim, oval, 16", VG, A21 ..$90.00

Sanitol Violet Elite Talcum Powder, tin, sample, oval image of lady surrounded by pink flowers & lettering against sky blue, 2⅛x1¼x¾", EX, D37..............$110.00

Santa Maria Vegetables, crate label, steam train chugging reefer cars past vegetable field, Santa Maria, 7x9", M, D12 ....$4.00

Santovin, sign, self-framed tin, 'Santovin' above sun & sheep graphics with list of remedies, dealer name below, 27x20", VG+, A1 ....$145.00

Sapolio Cleaning Products, booklet, women doing household chores & 2 black women scrubbing the floor, 1880s, 14 pgs, VG, D23 ....$20.00

Sarony Cigarettes, roulette table box, EX+, D35 ....$110.00

Sarony Cigarettes, tin, shaped like roulette game with game materials, holds 200 cigarettes, EX, A18 .....$40.00

Satin Gloss Liquid Stove Polish, banner, canvas, product name above can flanked by lettering, Non-Inflammable below, 48x40", G-, A9 ....$200.00

Satin Skin Cream & Powder, sign, die-cut cardboard stand-up, Caucasian lady in Oriental dress holding fan above 2 product boxes, 27x24", EX, A21 .$145.00

Satine Washing Powder & Satin Gloss Soap, sign, die-cut tin, woman washing clothes in tub supported by product boxes, DS Brown & Co, 13½x9½", G-, A9 ....$900.00

Satisfaction Cut Plug, lunch pail, red with gold lettering above & below red S on white circle, hinged lid with wire handle, EX, A18 ....$135.00

Sauer's Flavoring Extracts, cabinet, wood with glass front, gold Sauer's on black band across gold medallion, lettering below, 21x15x11", VG+, A13 ....$550.00

Savage Arms Co, catalog, pictures machine gun & uses for guns on planes, motorcycles, etc, 48 pgs with blueprint, 1916, rare, G+, A9 ....$125.00

Savage Rifles & Ammunition, sign, paper, 2 hunters in canoe shooting at wild dogs chasing deer, framed, image: 26x20", EX+, A9 ....$1,900.00

Savage Smokeless Rifle Powder, tin, black lettering on red, Savage Arms Co, small screw cap, 6x4", EX, A15 .$375.00

Savage/Stevens/Fox, sign, cardboard hanger, Rifles, Shotguns & Accessories For Every Shooter..., photo image of 2 hunters, 22x20", EX+, A3....................$50.00

Savage/Stevens/Fox, sign, cardboard hanger, World's Most Complete Line Of Rifles, Shotguns..., photo image of duck hunters, 22x20", EX+, A3 ....$50.00

Savarin Normal-ized Coffee, sign, celluloid hanger, We Serve...The Coffee Of Distinction in white on red disk, 6" dia, NM, A13 ....$90.00

Sayman's Allspice, tin, paper label, 3", NM, A7 ....$25.00

Scandinavian American Lines, sign, self-framed tin, colorful image of ocean liner with cloudy skies above, 31x41", EX, A6....................................$475.00

Scarless Gall Remedy, tin, with contents, round, NM, A7 ....$15.00

Schaefer Beer, foam scraper holder, red container inserted in red base shaped like bar with chrome foot rail, EX, A19 ....$85.00

Schaefer Bock Beer, label, red & black with product name & goat's head, 12-oz, EX, A19 ....$6.00

Schaefer Irish Brand Cream Ale/F&M Schaefer Brewing Co, can, flat-top, green shamrock on yellow, 12-oz, NM, A19 ....$35.00

Schafer's Bread, end label, features Gene Autry, yellow border, EX, D29.....................................$10.00

Scheidt's Rams Head Ale, tray, deep-dish, winter colonial scene with lettered rim, 11½" dia, EX+, A1.........$25.00

Scheidt's Valley Forge Beer, sign, light-up, reverse glass, product name on panel with Deco style metal case, EX, A19 ....$75.00

Scheidt's Valley Forge Bock Beer, sign, paper litho, red product name above & below goat's head, On Draught-In Bottles, matted & framed, EX, A19................$500.00

Schenley, sign, counter-top light-up, glass, rooster at sunrise pointing to Schenley above, Mellow As A... on base, 13", EX+, A1..................................$110.00

Schepp's Cake Box, store bin, tin with slant top, Victorian-type lettering & graphics on deep yellow, EX, A18 ....$50.00

Schepp's Cocoanut, pail, orange, tapered sides, slip lid, bail handle, VG, A18.............................$55.00

Schepp's Shredded Cocoanut, tin, sample, The Old Standard, rectangular with oval LS Trade Mark logo & product name, square corners, EX, D37....................$75.00

Schiller Beer, keg label, Schiller Brewing Co, Internal Revenue Tax Paid statement, 1940-41, M, A10..........**$16.00**

Schinasi Bros Natural Cigarettes, sign, cardboard, The Original Egyptian Cigarettes, name above close-up Egyptian & white horse, framed, 24x16", VG+, A18 .....**$35.00**

Schlaich Locks for the Boyce Motometer, display box, tin litho, lettering over driver behind wheel, A Complete Line Of Interchangeable Initials..., VG+, A6........**$450.00**

Schlitz, calendar, 1941, self-framed tin, The Beer That Made... above calendar flanked by bottle & couple, 11x21", EX, A1 ....$70.00

Schlitz, clock, light-up, round clock with Roman numerals in ball-shaped coach-light-type case on lettered bracket, EX, A8 ....**$20.00**

Schlitz, coaster, cardboard, The Beer That Made Milwaukee Famous, 1940s, 4x4", EX, D23 ....**$6.00**

Schlitz, display, counter-top light-up, glass bottle on base marked Have A Bottle Now, globe logo on backdrop, 20", VG+, A1 ....**$60.00**

Schlitz, display, 3-tier pyramid base displays 6 glass bottles with Internal Revenue Tax Paid labels, 22x12", EX, A19.....................**$45.00**

Schlitz, drinking glass, older fluted mug with grain-screened design, NM, A8 ....**$30.00**

Schlitz, lamp, hanging, 2-color stained-glass shade with every fourth panel lettered, chain hanger, 14" dia, VG+, A8 ....**$45.00**

Schlitz, mug, ceramic, classical girl sitting atop Schlitz globe within fancy border, The Beer That Made..., pre-1920s, VG+, A8 ....**$30.00**

Schlitz, mug, salt-glazed ceramic, blue on gray with embossed logo & lettering, German text on side, EX, A8 ....**$95.00**

Schlitz, sign, composition, No Bitterness, Just The Kiss Of The Hops, bottle, hops & wheat on wood-look plaque, 17x11", EX, A8....................**$75.00**

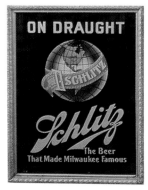

Schlitz, sign, reverse-painted glass, On Draught above Schlitz globe, Schlitz The Beer That Made..., framed, 17x13", VG+, A8..........$180.00

Schlitz, sign, tin, Drawn To Perfection...Served With Pride, hand scraping foam from 4 glasses, The Beer... below, 27x19", VG, A8 ....**$155.00**

Schlitz, sign, tin, Drink... & hops & world logo on folded card behind 15¢ bottle, The Beer That Made... below, 13x9", VG+, A8....................**$95.00**

Schlitz, sign, tin, Never A Bitter Note above singing bird beside bottle, self-framed, 16x11", VG, A9 ....**$50.00**

Schlitz, sign, tin, Real Gusto In A Real Light Beer, man with sandwich drinking from glass, 1962, 16x13", EX, A8....................**$55.00**

Schlitz, sign, tin on cardboard, bottle, can & full glass on table with lamp & upright books, beveled edge, 1950, VG+, A8 ....**$40.00**

Schlitz, sign, tin on cardboard, bottle & glass on table by window with fishing scene beyond, beveled edge, 1952, VG+, A8 ....**$45.00**

Schlitz, sign, tin on cardboard, opened bottle with frothy glass & opener on map table, beveled edge, 16x11", EX, A8 ....**$65.00**

Schlitz, stained glass window, ripple & patterned glass with banner circling globe, ornate background pattern, 36x67", EX, A9....................**$1,550.00**

Schlitz, stein, embossed world logo on sides, EX, A8 ..**$20.00**

Schlitz, tray, deep-dish, For Great Occasions lettered diagonally flanks bottle, gold trim, 13" dia, VG+, A8.....**$20.00**

Schlitz, tray holder, cast metal, handle with elf atop sphere with hops & grain design, pre-prohibition, VG+, A8....................**$155.00**

Schlitz Brewery, pin-back button, world globe flanked by 10% War Bond Buyer, EX, A20 ....**$12.00**

Schlitz Famous Gold Label Malt Syrup, sign, tin, product name on yellow left of red can with gold label, red border, horizontal rectangle, VG, A19 ....**$65.00**

Schlitz Famous Malt Syrup, sign, tin, product name on yellow left of can with brown label, red border, horizontal rectangle, VG, A19....................**$110.00**

Schlitz Light Beer, tray, red & white, 1965, 12", NM, D7....................**$5.00**

Schlitz Tonic, sign, tin on cardboard, Have You Tried It? flanked by bottle & frothy glass, beveled edge, VG+, A19....................**$250.00**

Schmidt's Beer, art plate, metal, Norman Rockwell scene with 4 gents at card table under tree, dog resting, 1984, 10" dia, NM, A8 ....**$65.00**

Schmidt's Beer, sign, light-up, reverse glass panel on metal base, product name above None Better Since 1860, 9x12", EX+, A19....................**$45.00**

Schmidt's Beer, tray, deep-dish, ...Quarts-Pints-Draught, girl pouring from bottle into glass, red, black & yellow, 12" dia, VG+, A19....................**$65.00**

Schmidt's Beer & Ale, display figure, bronze, bartender holding 2 beer mugs in front of barrel, embossed lettering on base, 8", EX, A6....................**$150.00**

Schmidt's Bock Beer, label, product name & goat's head on red, 12-oz, VG, A19 ....**$14.00**

Schmidt's City Club Beer, drinking glass, heavy glass mug with etched product name, EX, A8.....................**$75.00**

Schmidt's City Club Beer, foam scraper, black lettering on ivory, VG+, A8....................**$35.00**

Schmidt's City Club Beer, label, Jacob Schmidt Brewing Co, U-type permit number, Internal Revenue Tax Paid statement, 1933-36, 64-oz, NM, A10......................**$10.00**

Schmidt's City Club Beer, sign, cardboard, product name on red sign next to girl on bicycle with basket full of bottles, VG+, A19......................**$145.00**

Schmidt's City Club Beer, sign, celluloid, Schmidt's in diagonal script above star logo flanked by City Club, Beer below, 9" dia, EX, A8......................**$100.00**

Schmidt's Cream Ale, can, cone-top, 32-oz, EX+, A19..**$75.00**

Schmidt's Kloster Brau, sign, paper, product name upper right of jolly tavern scene, Brewed At... below, 1930, matted & framed, EX+, A19......................**$60.00**

Schmidt's Malta, sign, embossed tin, Drink above Schmidt's (diagonal script), Malta lower right, bottle at left, 1930s, 9x20", NM+, A13......................**$170.00**

Schmidt's of Philadelphia Beer-Ale, sign, reverse glass light-up, Schmidt's logo on arched panel, Beer-Ale lettered on bracket, NM, A19......................**$65.00**

Schmidt's Salem Beer, label, product name left of polar bear atop round logo against orange & black background, 22-oz, EX, A19......................**$10.00**

Schocney's Garage, calendar, 1955, draped nude sitting in front of bathtub, full pad below, with original mailer, M, A7......................**$25.00**

Schoenling Beer, tap knob, chrome with celluloid cover, white & gold on red & black, 2" dia, VG+, A8.....**$65.00**

Schoenling Little Kings Cream Ale, sign, light-up, framed sign against geometric wire background, name changes colors, red, blue & white, 10", VG+, A8......................**$40.00**

Schoenling Old Style Bock Beer, label, orange, black & red, 32-oz, NM, A19......................**$55.00**

Schoens Old Lager, tap knob, red plastic with gold insert, round, EX, A8......................**$75.00**

School Boy Peanut Butter, tin, red with School Boy above oval portrait, Peanut Butter on blue band below, pry lid, 5-lb, EX, A18......................$275.00

Schooner Beer, label, Dakota Brewing Co, U-type permit number, Internal Revenue Tax Paid statement, 1933-36, 12-oz, M, A10......................**$40.00**

Schrade Walden, knife case, wood with slanted glass front, 8x12x15½", EX+, A18......................**$110.00**

Schrafft's Chocolate, portrait, chromo litho, 'Schrafft's Chocolate Girl,' pretty girl in wicker chair in landscape, framed, 32x23", EX, A12......................**$425.00**

Schrafft's Chocolate, sign, cardboard, 'Schrafft's Chocolate Girl,' bust-portrait, framed, 29x23", EX+, A8 ......**$215.00**

Schrafft's Chocolates, trolley sign, The Fairest Of Spring's Buds..., 'Daintiest Of Dainty Sweets,' scholar in profile, 11x21", EX, D8 ....**$195.00**

Schramm Bottling & Creamery Co, calendar, 1931, image shows hunters coming upon bears seeking honey, lake beyond, NM+, A3 ....**$120.00**

Schreiber's Manru Lager, display, light-up, flat bottle against arched backdrop atop curved base, Make Mine Manru & company name, 13", VG, A8......................**$85.00**

Schultz, tap knob, black ball shape with black Schultz on cream celluloid insert, EX, A8......................**$155.00**

Schuster Bock Beer, label, Canton Brewing Co, U-type permit number, Internal Revenue Tax Paid statement, 1933-36, 12-oz, M, A10......................**$10.00**

Schuster's Orange-Pineapple Rickey, sign, tin, Try...A Delicious Combination, colorful lettering & images of fruit & full juice glass, 10x6", VG+, A21 ....**$330.00**

Schwab's Pure Gold/Cincinnati Brewing Co, drinking glass, straight-sided with flat bottom, etched lettering with hops logo, 3½", NM, A8......................**$100.00**

Schwartz's Homogenized Peanut Butter, pail, white S above name bordered by red line against white beach scene, tapered sides, bail handle, slip lid, EX+, A18......................**$35.00**

Schwartz's Peanut Butter, pail, white product lettering against blue sky & ocean, tapered sides, bail handle, slip lid, 4-lb, EX, A18 ....**$15.00**

Schweppes, lighter, name lettered on side, M, A16 ..**$25.00**

Schweppes Dry Ginger Ale, door push bar, porcelain, Ask For... in white & yellow on green, 3x30", NM, D21......................**$100.00**

Schwinn-Built Bicycles, sign, reverse-painted glass, Schwinn-Built in diagonal script in center, circular logo upper left, image: 9x19", EX, A9 ....**$90.00**

Scientific Model Co, catalog, 1941, 40 pgs, EX, D17..**$50.00**

Scissors Mild Cut Plug, pocket tin, vertical, Smoke...Something New For Pipe Or Cigarette, yellow with scissors image, EX, A18......................**$2,200.00**

Sclarine Metal Polish, tin, sample, with contents, VG, A7 ....**$18.00**

Scotch Brand Oats, container, bagpipe player flanked by lettering, product name on band below, Quaker Oats Co, 3-lb, NM, A3 ....$145.00

Scotch Laddie, cigar box label, inner lid, little boy & his dog, EX, A5......................**$35.00**

Scotch Lassie Jean, crate label, California orange, young woman in kilt with castle beyond, Strathmore, 10x11", M, D12......................**$5.00**

Scott Miller Co, pocket mirror, celluloid, photo image of a battleship, round, EX, A11......................**$25.00**

Scott-Powell 'A' Milk, brochure, die-cut paper, delivery truck with product name & Fresher By A Day, orange & green cover, 4x9", EX, A6 ....**$80.00**

Scott's Emulsion, trolley sign, Keep Your Boy In The Game... flanked by boy in catcher's uniform & product, 12x24", NM, D8 ....**$200.00**

Scotten, tobacco tag, blue on yellow, rectangular, EX, D35 ....**$3.00**

Scotty, crate label, California pear, white lettering & 2 pears on Scottish plaid background, Walnut Grove, 8x11", M, D12 ....**$4.00**

Scotty Mild Little Cigars, pocket tin, flat, square corners, EX, A18 ....**$60.00**

Scuffy Shoe Polish, box with contents, features Mickey Mouse, ...For All White Shoes, EX+, D21 ....**$25.00**

Sea Bird, crate label, California lemon, large white flying sea gull, yellow lettering on blue, Carpinteria, 12x9", M, D3 ....**$4.00**

Sea Bound, crate label, California lemon, 3-masted ship with orange-colored sky beyond, Oxnard, 9x12", M, D12 ....**$15.00**

Sea Robin, cigar box label, embossed fishing motif, ca 1908, EX, D23 ....**$16.00**

Seagram's Rare Old Whiskies, sign, tin on cardboard, We Recommend above product name & 'Time Works Wonders' flanked by curly-Qs, 9x13", EX+, A19 ....**$25.00**

Seagull Baking Powder, tin, paper label, with contents, 4-oz, NM, A7 ....**$80.00**

Seal of Minneapolis Cigar, tip tray, En Avant arched above emblem with falls & cityscape beyond flanked by encircled 10¢, 4" dia, EX, A8 ....**$65.00**

Seal of North Carolina Plug Cut, box, wood, 1909 tax stamp, 2x4x6½", NM, A18 ....**$100.00**

Seal of North Carolina Plug Cut, cabinet cards, features actress Agnes Folsom & actor Henry Dixey, 13x7½", A5 ....**$55.00**

Seal of North Carolina Plug Cut, tin, red & yellow lettering around oval coastal image of 2 ladies by brick wall, round with smaller round lid, EX+, A18.$450.00

Seal of North Carolina Plug Cut, tobacco pouch, cloth, EX, A7 ....**$15.00**

Seal of North Carolina Plug Cut, trade card, backview of nude little girl conducting birds in song, 4x2½", G, A5 ....**$8.00**

Seal of North Carolina Smoking Tobacco, sign, paper, Look Out Dar, I Is Comin, comical black man on wagon with large bag of tobacco, 13x10", VG, A9 ....**$475.00**

Seal Rock Cut Plug, tin, gold & black lettering & graphics on red, rectangular with square corners, EX, A18......**$135.00**

Sealed Power, sign, die-cut tin flange, Authorized Service, stylized nude divides lettered circle, 32x22", NOS, NM+, A1 ....**$525.00**

Sealed Power Piston Rings, clock, nude logo divides Sealed Power & Piston Rings on numbered dial, red & blue on white, 15" dia, NM+, A1 ....**$420.00**

Sealtest Ice Cream, curb sign, tin in cast-iron frame, Enjoy... above logo, red & cream on gray, cream & red background, 28x20", G, A6..............................**$75.00**

Sears, catalog, Christmas, 1958, EX, D17..............**$100.00**

Sears, catalog, Craftsman Power Tools, 1952, 50 pgs, EX, D17...**$20.00**

Sears, catalog, Summer, 1965, EX, D17 ....**$20.00**

Sears, Roebuck & Co, see also Non-Chattering Oil..., Rivera Brand Coffee, or Silvertone Phonograph

Sears, Roebuck & Co Roasted Coffee, store bin, fancy design on lined background, VG, A3 ....**$75.00**

Sears Kenmore Vacuum Cleaners, jigsaw puzzle, cartoon story showing 'If Hubby Did The Housecleaning He'd Buy A New Kenmore...,' 1933, 10x14", EX, D10 ....**$75.00**

Seaside Gasoline, sign, die-cut porcelain, inverted triangle with product name above bird, orange, blue & yellow, 2-sided, 38x38", VG+, A6..............................**$1,000.00**

Security Lightning Rod Co, tape measure, depicts Uncle Sam in center, sepia tone with blue lettering, EX, A11 ....**$200.00**

Security School Shoes, sign, embossed tin, ...Look Best, Wear Longest flanked by shoes, Bagstad & Aaseth below, 14x19", EX+, D11 ....**$115.00**

Seekamp, crate label, Washington apple, orange coat-of-arms on white between blue panels, Seattle, 9x11", M, D12 ....**$2.00**

Seiberling Tires, ashtray, tire shape with green glass insert lettered with dealer's name & address, 3¾" dia, EX+, A1 ....**$130.00**

Seitz Beer/HJ Osterstock, tray, deep-dish, product name & eagle logo on green, lettered rim, G+, A19 ......**$40.00**

Seitz Brewing Co, puzzle, Compliments Of The... above bust image of Indian girl in profile, 1909, NM+, A19....**$400.00**

Select Brand Grade-A Milk/Sheffield Farms Co, trolley sign, cardboard, A Growing Child Should Have A Quart Of... at left of 2 smiling faces, 11x21", VG+, A1...**$10.00**

Select Lily of the Valley Talcum Powder, tin, light blue with embossed lettering & flower image, shaker top, EX, A3 ....**$25.00**

Selmer Joint Grease, tin, flat, Buckeye Stamping Co, ½x1½" dia, EX, D37....................**$10.00**

Selsun Blue Dandruff Shampoo, snow globe, half-length man in suit & tie in glass globe on plastic base, 4", EX, A21 ....**$285.00**

Selva, crate label, California lemon, view of Sespe Canyon with stream, trees & flowers, Fillmore, 9x12", M, D12...........**$4.00**

Selz Good Shoes, print, elegant girl in front of flower garden, small logo at bottom, framed, 36x11", EX, A6........**$850.00**

Selz Shoes, sign, porcelain flange, name on diagonal band over Make Your Feet Glad on circle, black & white, 1915-25, 8x18", NM, A13....................**$200.00**

Sem FS 12 Needles, tin, flat, shows couple dancing, rectangular, rounded corners, EX, D37....................**$35.00**

Semdac Liquid Gloss, can, product name above woman using product, advertising below, cream, blue & orange, screw-on cap, 1-gal, 11x8", EX, A6..........**$50.00**

Sen-Sen Assorted Gum, display box, inside lid label shows product name above list of flavors right of image, 7x6", VG, A7....................**$25.00**

Sen-Sen Gum, sign, die-cut cardboard stand-up, shows woman & 2 children in Japanese attire, name lettered on base, 7x4½", NM, A7....................**$115.00**

Senate, door push, Thank You above large bottle, Call Again below, curved corners, 11", VG, A8...........**$75.00**

Senate, door push, We Recommend above large bottle, Buy It Here below, curved corners, 11", VG, A8..........**$75.00**

Senate Bock Beer/Chr Heurich Brewing Co, label, white product name on red circle flanked by white goats facing each other, 12-oz, EX, A19....................**$10.00**

Senator Smoking Tobacco, pocket tin, upright, portrait flanked by Virginia Cut Plug, 4½x2½", EX+, D21..**$45.00**

Seneca Cameras, calendar, 1927, product name above side view of Indian princess, full pad, framed, image: 22½x10½", VG+, A9....................**$350.00**

Sensation Steel Cut Coffee, tin, Sensation in script above logo, pry lid, 1-lb, VG+, A3 ....$65.00

Sensation Tobacco, lunch pail, yellow & black lettering & graphics on yellow basketweave design, rounded corners, swing handles, EX, A18 ....**$65.00**

Sensible, lunch pail, yellow with Sensible lettered in red, double swing handles, EX+, A18 ....**$82.00**

Sentinel, cigar box label, outer, woman flanked by giant cigars, 4½x4½", M, D5....................**$15.00**

Sentinel, tobacco tag, octagonal, EX, D35 ....**$4.50**

Sergeant's Dog Medicines, display, litho tin counter-top, 2 puppies with product name, 'No Mother To Guide Them,' Ask For Free Dog Book, EX+, A1...........**$250.00**

Seroco Cure, pocket tin, flat, tobacco leaf at left of lettering, ...For The Tobacco Habit above, 2x4", VG+, A3...**$35.00**

Serv-Well Coffee, tin, waitress with tray on emblem flanked by Vacuum Sealed, key-wind lid missing, 1-lb, VG+, A3 ....**$55.00**

Service Merchandise, catalog, 1975, EX, D17 ....**$35.00**

Service Motor Oil, can, Service arched above gas station scene, red, silver & blue, screw cap & handle, 2-gal, 11x8", VG, A6....................**$40.00**

SET Valve Hydrant Co, replica of man hole cover, cast aluminum, 5x5" base, EX, A21 ....**$286.00**

Seven-Up, ashtray, brown glass with white lettering, 'Fresh Up' With Seven-Up, It Likes You, 3 rests, 5½" dia, NM, D21 ....$15.00

Seven-Up, bank, can shape, NM, D22 ....**$25.00**

Seven-Up, bottle carrier, aluminum, basket shape with embossed logo, round handle, rare, NM, A16......**$60.00**

Seven-Up, bottle carrier, cardboard, features Fresh Up Freddie, EX, A16....................**$40.00**

Seven-Up, bottle opener, heavy brass, M series, VG, A8 ....**$20.00**

Seven-Up, bottle opener, metal with wood handle lettered 'Fresh Up' above logo, VG+, A16....................**$25.00**

Seven-Up, bottle topper, Easter 'Fresh Up,' shows bunny in a dress holding a parasol, NM, A7 ....**$6.00**

Seven-Up, bottle topper, Enjoy A 7-Up 'Float'! on curved banner with logo in center, 7-Up With Your Favorite Ice Cream, NM, A7 ....**$6.00**

Seven-Up, bottle topper, Top O' The Mornin', shows leprechaun with pipe in profile encircled by shamrocks & logo, NM, A7 ....**$12.00**

Seven-Up, bottler carrier, cardboard, large 7-Up logo with Take Some Home on dot, punch-out handle, G, A16 ....**$40.00**

Seven-Up, bottler carrier, cardboard, You'll Like It — It Likes You, 7-Up flanks 3-hole handle, EX, A16...**$35.00**

Seven-Up, bottler carrier, tin, 'Fresh Up' With left of 7-Up, tall wire handle, VG+, A16 ....**$75.00**

Seven-Up, calendar, 1940, pin-up girl, complete, 12x7", NM, A16....................**$160.00**

Seven-Up, calendar, 1942, pin-up girl, complete, 12x7", G, A7....................**$55.00**

Seven-Up, calendar, 1942, pin-up girl, complete, 12x7", NM, A16....................**$175.00**

Seven-Up, calendar, 1943, General McArthur, complete, 12x7", EX+, A13....................**$70.00**

Seven-Up, can, flat-top, bubble logo, EX, A16..........**$25.00**

Seven-Up, clock, light-up, die-cut plastic flower design with exaggerated numbers, 7-Up logo at number 7, VG+, A16 ....$70.00

Seven-Up, clock, light-up, You Like It...It Likes You!, square with wood frame, EX+, A16....................$100.00

Seven-Up, clock, plastic, 7-Up logo in center of vertically rectangular face with lines between numbers 12-3-6-9, G-, A16..$40.00

Seven-Up, display, cardboard, die-cut, We Proudly Serve..., large peacock with loop to hold bottle & logo, NM+, A16 ....$55.00

Seven-Up, door push bar, porcelain, 'Fresh Up' Seven-Up! flanked by logo on white background, 3x30", EX, D21 ....$60.00

Seven-Up, door push bar, porcelain, 'Fresh Up' With & Ca Ravigote between 3 logos on white background, 3x31½", NM, A1..$45.00

Seven-Up, door push bar, tin, 7-Up flanked by multicolored designs on white background, 3x30", NM, D21 .....$60.00

Seven-Up, drinking glass, green with white logo, ribbed, 5", NM, D21 ....$20.00

Seven-Up, drinking glass, slightly tapered, Don't Drink Water, Drink 7-Up, shows boy in stream, 5", NM, A8..$20.00

Seven-Up, drinking glass, straight-sided, applied gold lettering, syrup line, EX+, A16..$65.00

Seven-Up, key chain, bottle shape featuring the bubble girl, NM, A16..$25.00

Seven-Up, lighter, aluminum, white with logo above The All-Family Drink, plain aluminum flip-top, EX+, A16...$20.00

Seven-Up, lighter, bottle on white background, MIB, D21 ....$45.00

Seven-Up, matchbook, Nothing Does It Like 7-Up, square logo, 20 strike, front strike, NM, D28.....................$2.00

Seven-Up, menu board, tilted logo with green & white menu slots at sides & bottom, stepped border, 1950s-60s, 16x27", VG, A13..$95.00

Seven-Up, menu board, tin, 'Fresh Up' & 7-Up logo on striped background above board, Nothing Does It Like Seven Up below, EX, A16..$60.00

Seven-Up, menu board, tin, hand-held bottle at left of logo above chalkboard, 27x19", EX+, D21....................$70.00

Seven-Up, menu board, wood, First Against Thirst & 7-Up logo above 3 rows of menu spaces, EX, A16.......$45.00

Seven-Up, miniature bottle, paper label, NM, A16.....$20.00

Seven-Up, picnic cooler, vinyl, 'Fresh Up' With 7-Up, white with green straps, EX+, A16 ....$15.00

Seven-Up, ruler, celluloid, 'Fresh-Up' Freddie & bicycle safety, M, D6..$15.00

Seven-Up, salt & pepper shakers, plastic bottles with applied color 7-Up label with bubbles, M, A16, pair $40.00

Seven-Up, salt shaker, plastic bottle with applied Bubble girl label, NM, A16 ....$30.00

Seven-Up, sign, bottle, tin, 1950s-60s, 44x13", EX+, A13..$230.00

Seven-Up, sign, cardboard, die-cut, Proudly We Serve on emblem above oval logo, It Likes You below, 9x6", EX, A16..$60.00

Seven-Up, sign, cardboard, die-cut stand-up, Here's Your Family 'Fresh Up,' grocery man offers a case of 7-Up, 1948, 12x9", NM, A7..$65.00

Seven-Up, sign, cardboard, die-cut stand-up, Morning, Noon & Night 7-Up Likes You, round map behind logo, G-, A16a..$40.00

Seven-Up, sign, cardboard, die-cut stand-up, 7-Up It Likes You, eccentric circles on base, G, A16 ....$40.00

Seven-Up, sign, cardboard, Enjoy A Seven-Up 'Float', bottle & float on tray with price dot, Made With..., 1952, 16x12", EX, A3..$25.00

Seven-Up, sign, cardboard, Go Steady...Cool Clean Taste!, teen couple at jukebox, bottle at right, 7-Up frame, 21x33", EX, A13..$300.00

Seven-Up, sign, cardboard, We're a 'Fresh Up' Family! above kids in pajamas & father reading, 1950s, vertical, EX+, A16..$20.00

Seven-Up, sign, drink rack, tin, white logo on red square in center, 12x19", EX, D21 ....$30.00

Seven-Up, sign, flange, die-cut, We Proudly Serve 7-Up on sign behind hand-held tray with bottle, 19½x16", VG, A6..$400.00

Seven-Up, sign, flange, Real 7-Up Sold Here & bubbles on round disk, G, A16..$95.00

Seven-Up, sign, flange, 7-Up Sold Here & bubbles on square panel with rounded corners, G+, A16....$100.00

Seven-Up, sign, paper, 'A Cooling Sight — A Cooling Drink' tilted bottle in snowy mountain scene with logo, 10x21", EX+, A16..$40.00

Seven-Up, sign, porcelain, 'Fresh Up' With above bottle tilted toward logo, green band below, 1951, 16x40", VG+, A13..$210.00

Seven-Up, sign, porcelain, 'Fresh Up' With left of logo, You Like It..., It Likes You, white, green band, 1948, 20x28", NM+, A13..$375.00

Seven-Up, sign, porcelain, bold logo on orange, black border top & bottom, 36x30½", EX, A6 ....$150.00

Seven-Up, sign, tin, 'Fresh Up!,' It Likes You, set of 2 triangular screen door signs, bubbles around logo, VG, A16..$60.00

Seven-Up, sign, tin, 'Fresh Up!' With 7-Up, It Likes You, orange background, raised rim, oval, 39½x30", rare, EX, A6..$1,000.00

Seven-Up, sign, tin, 'Fresh Up' With above hand-held bottle, marked 31-10-51 Made In USA Stout Sign Co..., 12x30", VG, A6 ....$95.00

Seven-Up, sign, tin, 'Fresh Up' With above hand-held bottle, white background, 28x20", VG, D30 ....$65.00

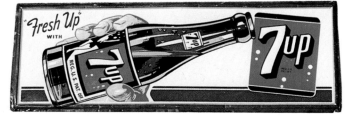

Seven-Up, sign, tin, 'Fresh Up' With above hand-held bottle & logo, embossed, 19x54", EX+, D11 ..$175.00

Seven-Up, sign, tin, 'Fresh Up' With above 6-pack, The All-Family Drink! below, raised rim, Canadian, 1950s, 60x36", NM, A13..$500.00

Seven-Up, sign, tin, 'Fresh Up' With at left of logo, black & red on white with black border, 12x19", EX+, D21 ....$90.00

Seven-Up, sign, tin, 'Fresh Up' With at left of logo, embossed, 12x30", VG+, D11 ....$50.00

Seven-Up, sign, tin, 'Fresh Up' With The All-Family Drink!, lettering above & below 6-pack, green frame, 1950s, 60x36", NM+, A13 ....$550.00

Seven-Up, sign, tin, First Against Thirst at right of logo, 10x28", NM, D30 ....$85.00

Seven-Up, sign, tin, Real 7-Up Sold Here, 9" dia, VG, A16 ....$80.00

Seven-Up, sign, tin, Sold Here on embossed 7-Up label, scalloped, ribbed border, 1949, 18x21", NM, A13 ....$220.00

Seven-Up, sign, tin, You Like It, It Likes You in bottom corners, bubble logo on circle over emblem, 24x36", EX, D30 ....$250.00

Seven-Up, sign, tin, Your 'Fresh Up', hand-held bottle & 7-up logo on white & green, raised border, 1947, 20x28", EX+, A13 ....$225.00

Seven-Up, sign, tin, 7-Up Your Thirst Away, green, orange, white & black, embossed, dated 7-63, 12x30", VG+, A1 ....$10.00

Seven-Up, sign, tin on cardboard, stand-up, 7-Up above Some Mixer, beveled edge, 6x6", NM, A13 ....$110.00

Seven-Up, syrup jug, glass with paper label, 7-Up logo left of Seven-Up Syrup, screw cap, 1-gal, NM, A16....$25.00

Seven-Up, thermometer, dial-type, logo on green background, 12" dia, NM+, D30 ....$95.00

Seven-Up, thermometer, dial-type, Nothing Does It Like 7-Up & logo in center, glass front, 12x12", EX+, A13 ....$170.00

Seven-Up, thermometer, porcelain, 'Fresh Up' above bottle & bulb, You Like It..., ...It Likes You below, 1950s, 14", EX, D21 ....$100.00

Seven-Up, thermometer, tin, Ca Ravigote beside large bottle, Agreable A Tous below, rounded ends, 15", G, A6 ....$40.00

Seven-Up, tie bar, oval celluloid emblem with 7-Up logo, M, A16 ....$18.00

Shac, trolley sign, cardboard, Quicker Than Tablets...Used Wherever Heads Ache right of globe man with product, 13x22", EX, A6 ....$120.00

Shaker Tamar Laxative, sign, paper, cascade of fruit surrounded by lettering, ...Fruit Compound For Constipation..., image: 11x9", rare, NM, A9 ....$1,300.00

Shakey's Pizza, doll, Pizza Chef, vinyl, red lettering on base, 9½", VG, A21 ....$35.00

Shamrock Trail Master Regular, pump sign, porcelain, green & yellow shamrock above Trail Master on brown & green bands, cream ground, 13x11", NM, D8 ..$225.00

Sharp's, clock, neon, Sharp's Great Beer Taste Anytime, triangles indicate 12-3-6-9, battery-operated, 16" dia, EX, A $25.00

Sharp's Super-Kreem Toffee, tin, orange with cartoon image of dapper man standing with legs crossed leaning on cane above name, oval, 6", VG, A18 ....$25.00

Sharples Separator Co, sign, self-framed tin, oval image of milkmaid using the 'Tubular A' separator, little girl helping, 39x28", VG+, A6 ....$850.00

Sharples Tubular Cream Separator, sign, tin, product name above separator & Used On This Farm, yellow ground with red border, 1920s, 19½x14", VG, D19 ....$200.00

Sharples Tubular Cream Separators, match safe, die-cut tin, pictures cows above mother & child using separator, 'Pet Of The Dairy,' 7x2", NM, A6 ....$375.00

Sharples Tubular Cream Separators, pocket mirror, pictures child watching mother using separator, lettered border, vertical oval, 2¾", EX, A21 ....$30.00

Sharps Super-Kreem Toffee, bank, orange tin-can shape with product name on blue diamond, 4x3" dia, VG+, A18 ....$60.00

Shawano Club Beer, tap knob, black ball shape with red lettering on buff enamel insert, VG+, A $135.00

Shawmut Rubbers, pocket mirror, celluloid, Buy...OL Nelson, Vienna, birthstones around edge, EX, A11...$18.00

Sheldon, sign, die-cut porcelain, white Sheldon on blue panel across red circular field, white edge, 16¼x30", EX+, A1 ....$55.00

Shell, flag, cloth, Shell lettered in black over large red shell, yellow background, 48x72", NOS, NM+, A1 ....$400.00

Shell, gas globe, shell shape with baked-on paint, black on white, Chance Brothers, Smethwick on bottom, 20x19", EX+, A1 ....$1,000.00

Shell, pin-back button, Shell Curb The Limit Club arched above logo, EX, A20...................................$6.00

Shell, radiator guard, cardboard, Shell lettered twice vertically above shell logo, red & orange, EX, A6.......$25.00

Shell, salt & pepper shakers, plastic gas pumps, yellow & red with shell logo, 1 marked Gasoline, 1 Premium, 3", NM, A1...$160.00

Shell, sign, porcelain, yellow shell with red lettering on black background, 6" dia, scarce, NM, A1......$1,600.00

Shell, sign, reverse-painted glass light-up with metal frame, Garage Shell Spirits & Oils, 2-sided, 23x35½", EX+, A6...$1,500.00

Shell, winter front, waxed die-cut cardboard, Shell logo flanked by Starts Quickly, red on yellow, 2-sided, 12x19", VG, A1...$130.00

Shell, see also Aeroshell, Golden Shell, or Silver Shell

Shell Anti-Freeze, can, with contents, product name above shell logo, Shell Oil Co, 1-qt, 5½x4" dia, EX+, A6 ..$75.00

Shell Co of California, sign, cardboard, die-cut shell, Help Prevent Forest Fires..., forest scene, framed, 32x32", VG, A1..$300.00

Shell Gasoline, postcard, features Mutt & Jeff, Shell logo at bottom, signed Fisher, 1934, VG, D26.................$35.00

Shell Gasoline, sign, porcelain, die-cut shell, red on yellow, stamped Property Shell Petroleum Corp, 25x25", EX, A1...$500.00

Shell Gasoline, sign, tin flange, die-cut shell, red on yellow, 17½x22", VG, A1..$230.00

Shell Gasoline & Motor Oil, painting, watercolor, scene of Crater Lake, Oregon with 2 logos at right, signed Eli Sinnors, 1920s, 14x27½", NM, A1....................$400.00

Shell Huile Pour Moteurs, can, shell in center, red, yellow & black, screw cap & handle, 9x6", VG+, A6.....$100.00

Shell Motor Oil, sign, porcelain, die-cut shell, red on yellow, 2-sided, 25" dia, EX, A1.............................$600.00

Shell NH3, sign, porcelain, die-cut shell, embossed NH3, 36x36", NM+, D11 ....$400.00

Sherer, Shirk & Co Tobacco, label, comical image of black man on mule, Git On in upper right, company name below, framed, image: 11x11", VG+, A9 ..$375.00

Sheridan Coal Co, paperweight/desk mirror, celluloid, pictures Hanna the mammy, rare, M, D6 ....$250.00

Sherwin Electric Service, sign, porcelain, 9x15", NM, D11 ....$45.00

Sherwin-Williams, sign, porcelain hanger, Paint Headquarters..., Cover the Earth logo at left, wrought-iron frame, 15x15½", EX, A6.......................................$130.00

Sherwin-Williams Floorlac, display, trifold, shows furniture covered with 'The All Around Varnish Stain,' 1930s, 24x39½", EX, A12.......................................$120.00

Sherwin-Williams Paints, sign, cardboard stand-up, Cover The Earth, paint can pouring over world globe, product name below, 24x14", VG, A6..............................$35.00

Sherwin-Williams Paints & Varnishes, sign, porcelain, Cover The Earth logo, ...Paint Headquarters, blue & white on yellow & blue, 2-sided, 20x28", EX+, A1..$275.00

Shield 100% Wax Free Motor Oil, can, lettered shield on lined background, screw lid & handle, 10¾x8½", VG, A6 ....$5.00

Shiner, tap knob, blue plastic with red & white on blue enameled insert, round, VG+, A8.........................$50.00

Shiner Bock Beer, label, Spoetzl Brewery, U-type permit number, Internal Revenue Tax Paid statement, 1933-36, 12-oz, M, A10...$30.00

Shinola Shoe Polish, shoehorn, metal, colorful image of brushes & product, ...The Wonderful Shoe Polish, 4", EX, A6 ....$90.00

Shoney's, bank, plastic bear dressed in red shirt & blue pants, head turns, 7¾", M.....................................$15.00

Shot Crushed Plug, pocket tin, vertical, EX, A18 ...$200.00

Shot Plug Cut, pocket tin, vertical, name above image of guns crossed over banner, company name below, decorative trim, EX, A18...$155.00

Sick's, see also Emil Sick's or Brew 66 Special Draught

Sick's Select Ale, sign, self-framed tin, The Famous Ale From Seattle on blue sky with tilted bottle against snowy mountain scene, EX+, A19.....................$165.00

Sickle Plug Old Fashion Smoke, tobacco pouch, EX, A7 ....$15.00

Sierra Vista, crate label, California orange, scenic image of groves & snowy mountains, Porterville, 10x11", M, D3...$8.00

Signal Ethyl, sign, metal, Signal above stoplight on diamond at left of Ethyl, black, yellow, orange & white, 9x30", EX+, A6..**$270.00**

Signal Ethyl Gasoline, pump sign, porcelain, product name on black above Ethyl logo, red border, 12" dia, NM, A1 ....**$410.00**

Signal Gasoline, pump sign, porcelain, Signal Gasoline around stoplight, orange & yellow on black with white edge, 12" dia, EX, A1 ....**$530.00**

Signal Penn Motor Oil, can, Signal & circular stoplight logo above Penn lettered on diagonal band above Motor Oil, 1-qt, EX+, A1 ....**$240.00**

Signal Products, winter front, waxed cardboard, circular stoplight logo on yellow background, 2-sided, dated 8-40, 17", NOS, A1..**$100.00**

Signal Products Household Oil, can, stoplight logo above Household Oil on 2-color ground, white, yellow & black, pour top with screw lid, 4-oz, NM, A1 ......**$65.00**

Signal Quality Lubricants, can, stoplight above product name on black emblem on yellow background, pry lid, EX+, A1 ....**$90.00**

Signal Quality Products, can, stoplight logo atop emblem with product name, yellow, black & white, flat-sided with screw cap, 1-gal, VG+, A1............................**$40.00**

Silver Buckle Brand Peanut Butter, tin, product name arched above belt buckle, 'The Kind To Buckle To,' ER Godfrey & Sons Co below, pry lid, VG, A3..........**$35.00**

Silver Dime, tap knob, chrome ball with blue, white & silver enamel insert, EX, A8 ....**$110.00**

Silver Edge Mussel Beer, coaster, emblem encircled by product name, red & black, pre-1920s, 4" dia, VG+, A8...**$80.00**

Silver Foam Beer, label, Power City Brewery, Internal Revenue Tax Paid statement, 1937-40, 12-oz, M, A10...**$15.00**

Silver Ideal Cream, plaque, plaster, image of woman at table with bowl of cream, 18x16x4", G, A9..........**$55.00**

Silver King, crate label, Florida citrus, pictures a large fish, 9x9", M, D3 ....**$2.00**

Silver Label Lager Beer/Lancaster Brewing Co, tap knob, black ball shape with silver & white on black insert, EX, A8...**$90.00**

Silver Medal, crate label, cranberry, scene of Pan-Am Expo, 1901, M, D3...**$2.00**

Silver Shell Motor Oil, can, product name above Shell logo, red & yellow, screw lid & handle, 2-gal, 11½x8½", EX, A6..**$10.00**

Silver Shell Motor Oil, can, product name on large shell on center, silver & blue, 1 Imperial-qt, 6¼x4" dia, EX, A6..**$100.00**

Silver Spur, crate label, apple, large silver spur with lettering in rope script on red background, M, D3........**$3.00**

Silver Tips, crate label, California orange, mother bear with cub looking at bee on flower, dated 1930, Tustin, 10x11", M, D12 ....**$35.00**

Silver Top Old Stock Lager, label, Independent Brewing Co of Pittsburgh, U-type permit number, 1933-36, Internal Revenue Tax Paid, 12-oz, M, A10 ....**$22.00**

Silver Top Premium Lager, sign, cardboard, Real Refreshment in red script above fishing scene with large fish & tilted bottle, 16x23", NM+, A19............................**$25.00**

Silvertone Phonograph/Sears, Roebuck & Co, postcard, With A...The Whole World Of Music Is Yours above scene of family listening to music, NM, D26........**$65.00**

Simon Pure, platter, lobster in center with decorative gold-trimmed scalloped edge, Simon Pure on reverse, oval, 14½", EX, A8..**$25.00**

Simon Pure, tap knob, chrome ball shape with red & gold on white enamel insert, EX, A8.............................**$95.00**

Simon Pure Beer & Ale, sign, composition, plastic buffalo head on oval with arrow atop wood-grain sign, 1950s, 12x14", VG+, A8 ....**$60.00**

Simon Pure Beer & Ale, sign, composition, plastic trout on emblem atop wood-grain sign, ...The Best In Town, 1950s, 12x10", EX, A8 ....**$40.00**

Simon Pure Bottled Beer, plates, lobster in center, scalloped rim with decorative gold trim, 9½", set of 6, EX, A8 ....**$30.00**

Simon Pure Old Abbey Ale, sign, foil label on stand-up partical board, Simon Pure on logo above product name, 5x4", NM, A8 ....**$20.00**

Simon's Roosevelt Cigars, tin, Simon's above Roosevelt on diagonal band, portrait of Teddy Roosevelt below, flat, round corners, 4x5x½", VG+, A1...................**$75.00**

Simonez, store card, Motorists Wise... above photo image of man polishing car while 2 women watch, 12½x10½", M, D8 ....**$30.00**

Simpson Spring Beverages, sign, tin, Ask For above product name on emblem, Famous For Flavor below, embossed, green, red & cream, 13x20", EX, A1....**$160.00**

Simpson Spring Beverages, sign, tin, Best Of All, Ginger Ale, Strawberry..., green, pink & white with fancy scrollwork, 1910s, NM+, D4 ....**$800.00**

Sinclair, sign, cardboard stand-up, A Life Preserver For Your Car..., attendant with car in life preserver, 1950s, 38", EX+, A13..**$225.00**

Sinclair, toy truck, Marx, Sinclair lettered on tanker, Power-X & Super Flame on doors, green & white, 2-pc, 17", EX+, A1 ....**$450.00**

Sinclair Aircraft, gas globe, red airplane in center, fired-on letters with baked-on finish, 1925-28, 16x16", scarce, NM, A6...$4,000.00

Sinclair Extra Duty Motor Oil, can, product name on vertical tapered panel, NM, A7....................................$10.00

Sinclair Gasoline, sign, tin, dinosaur logo on emblem above Gasoline, 13½x12", EX, A6....................$45.00

Sinclair Gasoline, sign, tin, product name in red on cream, green border, embossed, 11¾x19½", NOS, NM+, A1..$195.00

Sinclair Harness Oil, can, wood & metal cylinder form with cone-shaped top, black lettering, screw lid & handle, 18½x10" dia, VG+, A6 ....$25.00

Sinclair H-C Gasoline, bank, tin, gas pump, 4x1¾", NM, A7...$40.00

Sinclair H-C Gasoline, gas globe, etched glass, red & green, 1-pc, 16½" dia, NM, A6 ....$900.00

Sinclair H-C Gasoline, clock, neon, white with red numbers 12-3-6-9 around name in center, glass face with metal frame, 20" dia, VG+, A6....$1,300.00

Sinclair Motor Oil, can, product name on emblem above circular logo on green & cream pinstripe background, 5x4" dia, rare, EX, A6................................$285.00

Sinclair Motor Oils, sign, metal, New Advanced Formula... above 4 quarts of various Dino brand oil cans, 9½x18", NM, A6 ....$60.00

Sinclair Motor Oils, sign, paper, From Oldest Crudes & product name above dinosaur image & Lasts Longer, 42x28", VG+, A9 ....$260.00

Sinclair Oils, clip, brass with green & white circular logo, Sinclair Cuba Oil Co Havana embossed at bottom, 2½x2½", EX+, A6 ....$300.00

Sinclair Oils, pump sign, porcelain, product name lettered around vertically striped center, 6" dia, NM, A6 ..$600.00

Sinclair Opaline Motor Oil, can, Sinclair arched above Opaline on lined background, Motor Oil below, easy pour spout, 5-gal, 14" dia, G+, A6 ....$130.00

Sinclair Opaline Motor Oil, sign, porcelain, Authorized Dealer above product name on rectangle, can at right, Seals Power... below, 20x48", VG, A6 ....$250.00

Sinclair Opaline Motor Oil, sign, porcelain, Opaline on center band with Sinclair... arched above & below, 2-sided, 24" dia, EX+, A6 ....$700.00

Sinclair Opaline Motor Oil, sign, tin, product name in green on cream with red border, 11¾x19½", EX+, A1...$200.00

Sinclair Pennant, gas globe, Sinclair above Pennant lettered on pennant, red, black & white, Gill body, 13½" dia, NM+, A6 ....$600.00

Sinclair Pennsylvania Motor Oil, can, Mellowed 100 Million Years, product name on circle above dinosaur, 5-qt, VG, A6...$30.00

Sinclair Pennsylvania Motor Oil, can, Mellowed 100 Million Years, product name superimposed over dinosaur, 5-qt, EX, A6..$85.00

Sinclair Pennsylvania Motor Oil, can, Premium Grade..., dinosaur logo at bottom, red & white, 10x7" dia, 5-qt, VG, A6 ....$40.00

Sinclair Power-X, gas globe, ...Over 100 Octane, red & green lettering, plastic body, 13½" dia, NM, A6...$200.00

Sinclair Power-X, gas globe, ...The Super Fuel, green & red lettering, glass body, 13½" dia, NM, A6.......$300.00

Sinclair Shamrock Lubricant, can, product name on white ground in center, logo on striped ground top & bottom, screw cap, 15x4" dia, scarce, EX, A6 ...$350.00

Sinclair's Chlorinated Lime, paperweight, glass, product can flanked by Standardized & Guaranteed, Sinclair Manufacturing Co below, oval, M, D13 ....$55.00

Singer's Diplomat, box label, outer, man & gold coins, 1925, 4½x4½", EX, D5 ....$8.00

Sioux City Stock Yards, pin-back button, celluloid, Indian in full headdress, Home Market For The Great Northwest below, round, EX+, A11...............................$60.00

Sir Haig Cigars, tin, round with name flanking portrait, slip lid, 5x3½" dia, EX, A18 ....$55.00

Sir Walter Raleigh, pocket tin, sample, cut-down vertical, red with white lettering on black, NM, A18 ....$65.00

Sir Walter Raleigh, tin, product name above & below circular portrait, key-wind, 3½" dia, EX, A7 ....$30.00

Sir Walter Raleigh Tobacco, display, 3-D cardboard stand-up, name plate atop green shadow box with image of fisherman, 1940s, 17x10", EX+, A13 ....$500.00

Siren Delicious Hot Chocolate, container, aluminum, 8x7" dia, EX, A3 ....$110.00

Six Horse Beer, label, Capital Brewing Co of Milwaukee, Internal Revenue Tax Paid statement, 1933-50, 12-oz, EX, A10 ....$12.00

Skelly Aromax Ethyl, sign, porcelain, Skelly logo above Aromax on large center band, Ethyl logo below, red ground, 2-sided, 30" dia, EX+, A6..................**$1,000.00**

Skelly Tagolene Hypoid Lubricant, can, Skelly logo above product lettering, red, white & blue, 3-lb, EX, A1 ....**$20.00**

Ski Soda, sign, tin, Drink...Say Skee-E-E, comical image of bottle on skis, 12x32", M, D11 ....**$125.00**

Ski-Club Beverages, sign, tin, product name above & below image of snow skiers, 10x14", NM, D30 .**$140.00**

Skipper Pop Corn, box, product name above boy feeding begging dog, 6¾x4½", VG, A7..............................**$8.00**

Skookum, crate label, cartoon image of Indian mascot on blue background, Chelan, M, D12 ....**$3.00**

Skooner Beer, label, Blumer Brewing Co, Internal Revenue Tax Paid statement, 1933-50, 12-oz, M, A10.........**$15.00**

Sky Chief, see Texaco

Sky Maid Coffee, tin, Sky Maid in script above woman with coffee cup in front of airplane, key-wind lid not original, EX+, A3 ....**$65.00**

Sky Ranger, pump sign, porcelain, product name above airplane, 10" dia, rare, NM+, A6..........................**$950.00**

Sky-Trak, gas globe, Sky-Trak lettered diagonally in green with white shadowing, red plastic body, NM, A6 .**$70.00**

Skyway Motor Oil, can, product name above & below twin-engine DC-3 type plane, black, orange & yellow, 1-qt, NM, A1 ....**$270.00**

Slade's Mustard, tin, 3¾", NM, A7.............................**$28.00**

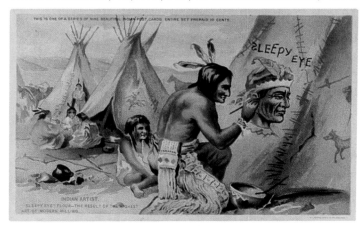

Sleepy Eye Flour, postcard, 'Indian Artist,' Indian painting portrait of Sleepy Eye on side of teepee, 1 in series of 9, NM, D26..................................**$100.00**

Sleepy Eye Milling Co, barrel label, trademark image of Old Sleepy Eye flanked by Strong & Bakers, 16" dia, EX, A9 ....**$250.00**

Slidewell Collars, display cabinet, wood with Slidewell decal on glass front, contains 8 original collars, 30x12", EX, A2 ....**$1,000.00**

Slinger Keg Beer, label, Storck Products Co, U-type permit number, Internal Revenue Tax Paid statement, 1933-36, ½-gal, NM, A10...**$18.00**

SM Hess & Brother Fertilizers, calendar, 1907, paper with metal strips, little girl with white flowers, gold letters on green, full pad, 22x15", EX, A6 .....**$140.00**

Smile Orange Drink, sign, celluloid, small, NM+, D32...**$95.00**

Smile Orange Drink, sign, flange, small, NM, D32 ..**$285.00**

Smile Orange Drink, sign, tin, die-cut, small, NM, D32 ....**$90.00**

Smile Orange Drink, sign, tin, embossed, 28x10", NM+, D32...**$300.00**

Smiles, tin, flat, white, holds 50 cigarettes, very scarce, VG, A18...**$100.00**

Smith & Richards Druggists, bottle, glass with cork top, dated 5/17/34 on label, EX, D24 ....**$5.00**

Smith Bros Commission Co, calendar, 1913, lady seated in blue dress draped with gold shawl, flowers in foreground, framed, 40x10", EX+, A8......................**$225.00**

Smith Brothers Cough Drops, dispenser, tin, wall mount, white lettering on dark blue background, 15½x3¾", G+, A21..**$410.00**

Smith Brothers Cough Drops, display, metal, black with orange & cream boxes on lid & sides, cream lettering, 10½x4", VG, A6..**$165.00**

Smith Brothers Cough Drops, trolley sign, cardboard, man chasing trolley car, product name flanked by boxes below, framed, 10½x20½", VG, A6 ....**$110.00**

Smith Guns, sign, paper, crossed rifles with hunting dog in center, 1906, framed, image: 19x25", EX, A9......**$600.00**

Smith Premier Brand Typewriter Ribbon, tin, vertical, pictures early typewriter left of product & company lettering, 2x1⅝x1⅝", EX, D37 ....**$35.00**

Smith Premier Typewriter, pocket mirror, celluloid, product name above typewriter, other lettering below, round, EX, A11 ....**$50.00**

Smith's Rose Bud Salve, tin, product name in red surrounds blue rosebud wreath, blue scroll design & other lettering below, 2" dia, EX, D14 ....**$15.00**

Smith's Stock Ale, label, product name lettered diagonally on red, 12-oz, VG+, A19 ....**$5.00**

Smokeless Cartridges, box, product name above man with shotgun in front of house, D Kirkwood, 23 Elm St, Boston below, rare, VG+, A3 ....**$215.00**

Smoky Jim's Sweet Potatoes, crate label, Smoky Jim's above seated black man flanked by text, framed, 9x11", EX, A8 ....**$65.00**

Smoky Jim's Yams, crate label, black man emptying sweet potato crate, Sunset, 9x9", M, D12 ....**$5.00**

Snag-Proof, see Lambertville Rubber Co

Snap Shot Gunpowder, tin, black with Canadian Explosive Limited & Snap Shot on band around wounded fowl, NM, A18..............................**$60.00**

Snap Shots Crushed Cubes for Pipe & Cigarettes, pocket tin, vertical, yellow with red & black name above & below initialed shield flanked by Positively Cool, EX+, A18 ....**$720.00**

Snow Ball Brand Oranges, crate label, name at right of black boy with orange, diagonal corners, 3½x9", NM, A7 ....**$8.00**

Snow Ball Citrus, lug box label, black boy holding half-peeled orange on green background, Leesburg, 3x9", M, D12..**$5.00**

Snow King Baking Powder, sign, die-cut cardboard, 2 reindeer pulling Santa in sleigh, Use...One Trial Convinces, ca 1900, 20x36", EX, D8 ....**$550.00**

Snow King Baking Powder, tin, paper label, with contents, 5-oz, NM, A7 ....**$25.00**

Snow King Baking Powder, tin, sample, paper label, with contents, 3-oz, NM, A7...........................**$60.00**

Snow-Maid, sign, artist's proof, painted hardboard, Snow-Maid candy bar on red background, 1920, matted & framed, NM, A3 ....**$50.00**

Snowball, crate, label, Florida citrus, black child holding a peeled orange, 5x9", M, D3 ....**$2.00**

Snowcrest Syrup, tin, coffee flavor, with contents, 3", NM, A7 ....**$20.00**

Snowflake Axle Grease, sign, cardboard, product lettering & can encircled with dogwood blooms, For Sale Here below, early 1900s, 12x14", EX, A1 ....$170.00

Snowman Anti-Freeze, can, Snowman in script above traveling cars & snowman, Completely Denatured... below, screw lid & handle, 2-gal, VG+, A6........**$220.00**

Snowman Cand-Ice, can, Cools Everything Faster! & product name lettered on snowman in top hat, red, blue & white, 1-pt, 5x4" dia, EX, A6 ....**$230.00**

Snyder's 331 Crushed Plug, pocket tin, vertical, product name above Joseph T Snyder, EX+, A18............**$720.00**

Society Brand Mocha, Java & Mexican Coffee, tin, sample, product name above & below oval image of 2 couples at table, slip lid, 2x2½" dia, EX, D37 ....**$195.00**

Society Snuff, tin, paper label, with contents, NM, A7..**$10.00**

Socony, gas globe lens, Socony in red shadowed in blue on white, 15" dia, NM, A1 ....**$85.00**

Socony, soap dispenser, cast iron on wood base, GH Packwood Mfg Co, St Louis MO, Pat Pending, pull handle, 5½x6", EX, A6 ....**$150.00**

Socony, thermometer, porcelain, Pegasus & product name above bulb, Friendly Service below, red, white & blue, 34½", VG+, A6................................**$225.00**

Socony Air-Craft Oils, sign, porcelain, airplane image with Air-Craft on wings, Standard Oil Co... below, red, white & blue, 20x30", NM+, A6...........................**$1,400.00**

Socony Air-Craft Oils, sign, porcelain, airplane image with Air-Craft on wings, Standard Oil Co... below, red, white & blue, 20x30", VG, A6..............................**$450.00**

Socony Asphalt Oils, knife/corkscrew/bottle opener, metal, 3" closed, EX, D22 ....**$50.00**

Socony Chassis Lubricant, sign, porcelain, (Pressure Gun Grease) below product name, red, white & blue, 18x30", NM, D8 ....$500.00

Socony Gasoline, pump sign, porcelain, Uniform Quality...Best Results, red, white & blue, 7½x11½", EX+, A6 ....**$120.00**

Socony Gasoline, Polarine Oil & Greases, brush, red-stained wooden handle with applied decal, red, cream & blue, 2x7", VG+, A1............................**$60.00**

Socony Gasoline & Motor Oils, calendar, 1926, round logo above buildings (Executive Offices), Standard Oil Co Of New York, full pad, 24x14", EX, A6..........**$75.00**

Socony Gear Oil, can, product name above logo & company name, red, white & blue, pour spout & handle, 1-gal, 11x8", G+, A6 ....**$50.00**

Socony Household Lubricant, can, bicycle & sewing machine above lettering, scrolled border, yellow & black, screw lid & handle, 5-gal, 15x9", VG, A6 ..**$55.00**

Socony Household Oil, can, blue, red & cream, screw cap with long spout, 4¾", VG, A6 ....**$65.00**

Socony Kerosene Oil, can, We Sell... on emblem in center, Safest & Best below, blue, red & cream, pour spout & handle, 1-gal, 11x8", G+, A6............................**$50.00**

Socony Kerosene Oil, can, 40th Anniversary, embossed emblem, 1-gal, 14½x4x4", EX, A6......................**$125.00**

Socony Lubricote Handy Oil, can, Lubricote on diagonal band in center, orange, cream & blue, squirt top, 4-oz, EX, A6 ....**$110.00**

Socony Motor Gasoline, pocket mirror, celluloid, red, white & blue, 3½" dia, NM, A1 ....**$140.00**

Socony Motor Gasoline, sign, porcelain flange, We Sell on die-cut emblem above product & company name, 24x20", EX, A6................................**$700.00**

Socony Motor Oil, can, Socony Dewaxed Paraffine Base... above logo & company name, pour spout & handle, 1-gal, 11x8", G+, A6 ....**$35.00**

Socony Motor Oil, pump sign, porcelain, SO above product name on emblem flanked by N&Y, red, white & blue, 15" dia, VG, A6 ....**$175.00**

Socony Motor Oil, sign, porcelain, Crank Case Service Drain & Refill With Socony Motor Oil, 1930s, 18x36", EX+, A4 ....**$300.00**

Socony Oil Co, padlock & key, Trademark XLCR AAE 285, Patented Nov 5-07, 4x2", minor scuffs, EX, A6 ....**$70.00**

Socony 990 Motor Oil For Ford Cars, can, encircled emblem above company name, red, white & blue, pour spout & handle, 1-gal, 11x8", G+, A6 ....**$80.00**

Socony-Vacuum, license plate attachment, die-cut metal winged horse, red, 4½x6¼", EX, A1 ....**$120.00**

Soft Thing, cigar box label, salesman's sample, man with arms around maid, G, A5 ....**$715.00**

Sohio Farmex, bank, tin, Sohio logo above Farmex & text, red & blue on white, 2¾x2" dia, VG+, A6...........**$40.00**

Sohio Gasoline, sign, die-cut porcelain shield, Ethyl logo flanked by Anti-Knock in center, red background, 2-sided, 30x25", VG, A6 ....**$425.00**

Solarine Metal Polish, match holder, metal, Wise Wives Work Wonders With at left of image of product can, holder below, 5x4", VG, A6..............................**$125.00**

Solitaire Coffee, tin, knight on rearing horse at left of product name with Regular Grind on center band, key-wind lid, EX+, A3.....................................**$40.00**

Solo, sign, tin, Drink Solo above airplane & pilot, 2 Large Glasses 5¢ on circle, 6 Fruity Flavors below, 30x15", EX, A6 ....**$400.00**

Somersworth Ranges & Parlors, sign, wood, red & black lettering on yellow, ...Sold By Seth Walker, Bethel, 5½x42", VG, A9 ....**$100.00**

Somervill'e Red Hand Chewing Gum, sign, tin with hinged center, Somerville's Red Hand above hinge, red hand & Chewing Gum below hinge, 9½x12", VG, A7 ....**$200.00**

Something Rare Cigars, box label, outer, couple watching over 4 children in bed, Smoke Them..., VG, A5 ..**$50.00**

Songster Bronze Pick-Up Needles, tin, flat, blue & orange, with gold border, rectangular, rounded corners, ⅜x1¼x1¾", EX, D37 ....**$40.00**

Songster Soft Tone Needles, tin, flat, blue, yellow & white, with gold trim, rectangular, rounded corners, ⅜x1¼x1¾", EX, D37 ....**$40.00**

Songster Spear Point Needles, tin, flat, orange & gold, rectangular, rounded corners, ⅜x1¼x1¾", EX, D37 .....**$40.00**

Sooner Queen Motor Oil, can, Sooner Queen above & below circle showing cowgirl & mountains, Motor Oil below, striped backgound, 1-qt, EX+, A1..........**$650.00**

South Bend & Oreno Fishing Tackle, sign, die-cut cardboard foldout, Fish & Feel Fit!, fisherman with arms raised surrounded by jumping fish, 29x48", EX, A2.........**$580.00**

South Fork Beer, label, South Fork Brewing Co, U-type permit number, Internal Revenue Tax Paid statement, 1933-36, 12-oz, NM, A10......................................**$18.00**

South Fork Special Beer, label, South Fork Brewing Co, Internal Revenue Tax Paid statement, 1933-50, 12-oz, NM, A10 ....**$10.00**

South Mountain, crate label, California orange, mountains, groves & ranch house, Santa Paula, 10x11", M, D3..**$2.00**

South Omaha Brewing Co, mug, tan with white interior, multicolored eagle & barrel logo with lettering above & below, EX, A8..**$435.00**

Southdown Tobacco, label, landscape scene with sheep beside stream, Maclin-Zimmer-McGill Tobacco Co, 1870s, 10½x10½", NM+, A3........**$30.00**

Southeastern Utilities Service Company, sign, porcelain, poles surrounded by lettering, green, yellow & black, oval, 11x16", NM, A6 ....**$235.00**

Southern All Butter Bread, menu board, Better Say Southern... with loaf of bread & 2 sticks of butter above Special Today, 24x18", EX, A1............................**$50.00**

Southern Enriched Bread, sign, embossed sign, Pick The Loaf With The 'Bright' Yellow End, shows boy pointing at large loaf, 14x28", NOS, NM, A1 ....**$100.00**

Southern Flour Mills Premium Enriched Flour, sack, linen, blue, red & yellow front with wreath & lettering, cut & sew doll on back, 50-lb, NM, A6.................**$15.00**

Southern Plantation Pure Georgia Ribbon Cane Syrup, can label, shows brick wall with product lettering & vignettes of plantation life, 6½x20", NM, A7 ....**$18.00**

Southern Tier Beer, label, Jos Laurer Brewing Co, pre-prohibition, NM, A10 ....**$65.00**

Southland, cigar box label, inner lid, Southern homestead & green garden, 1934, 6x9", M, D5 ....**$6.00**

Southwestern Bell Telephone, sign, brass with embossed bell logo & lettering, 21x16½", tarnished, A6.....**$130.00**

Sozodont Powder, tin, gold with product lettering around portrait, curved sides with rounded corners, Ginna, pre-1901, 3 pcs, EX+, A18 ....**$225.00**

Sozodont Powder For The Teeth, tin, product name on banners flanking man brushing teeth, rectangular with concave sides, 1x2x2¾", EX, D37 ....**$65.00**

Spalding Baseball Goods, sign, paper, baseball player on crossed bats flanked by baseballs & lettering, text below, framed, image: 10x13", G, A9............**$1,300.00**

Spalding Cork Center Ball, sign, paper, The First Choice, group of boys choosing first at bat, metal strip top & bottom, 1912, 28x20", NM, A15.....................$6,250.00

Spanish Blacking, clock, Baird regulator, figure-8 with embossed lettering & design around dial & open glass pendulum window, 27", G+, A9.......................$850.00

Spark Plug Chewing Tobacco, sign, cardboard, large open box with tobacco packs & 5¢, Liggett & Myers Tobacco Co, 1930s, 15x18x½", EX+, A3..........$65.00

Sparkle Cleaners, Launderers & Furriers, sign, porcelain, boy running at left of Sparkle in bold letters at top, 24x57", NM, D11.........................$295.00

Sparks' Perfect Health For Kidney & Liver, platter, ceramic, somber-faced woman in center, 16½x11", G-, A9.....................................$65.00

Spear Head, tobacco tag, die-cut, American Tobacco Co, EX, D35..$2.00

Spear Head Plug Chew, sign, embossed tin, Indian with raised spear right of & facing product name, 10x28", EX, A13...$500.00

Spearman Ale, sign, tin, logo on band above Spearman, Ale with outlined scrolled border on band below, 4x8", VG, A8..$35.00

Spearman Bavarian Style Beer, sign, tin, The Beer Man's Beer above Spearman Beer on crossed spears, Bavarian Style on oval below, 4x8", VG+, A8.....................$30.00

Spearman Bock Beer, label, Spearman Brewing Co, Internal Revenue Tax Paid statement, 1933-50, 12-oz, NM, A10.....................................$25.00

Special Brew, can, flat-top, instructional, 12-oz, G, A19..$18.00

Special Select Beer, label, White Eagle Brewing Co, Internal Revenue Tax Paid statement, 1933-50, ½-gal, EX, A10...$18.00

Speckled Sports, cigar box, 5x8", EX, A7...............$30.00

Speedway Motor Oil, can, Speedway & race car on yellow & white checked flag above Motor Oil, screw lid & handle, 2-gal, 11½x8", VG+, A6....................$190.00

Sphinx Mixture, pocket tin, yellow, rounded corners, EX, D35...$65.00

Spiegel, catalog, Fall/Winter, 1954, EX, D17.............$50.00

Spiegel, catalog, Spring/Summer, 1945, EX, D17.......$60.00

Spiffy, sign, tin, smiling boy with large bottle at left of Make Mine Spiffy & 5¢ over glasses on circle, 12x32", EX, D30...$275.00

Spirit of Camphor/Larkin Co Inc, bottle, clear glass with cork top, 5", EX, D24...............................$12.00

Splendid, crate label, California lemon, colorful country scene with home, orchard & mountains, Ivanhoe, 12x9", M, D3.....................................$2.00

Sportsman, crate label, Washington apple, silhouette of hunter with mountains & lake beyond, Chelan, 9x11", M, D12...$9.00

Sportsman Cigarettes, sign, tin, product name in blue & red on yellow above Extra Douces in white on orange, 20x27", EX, D35...............................$95.00

Spring Blossom, cigar box label, salesman's sample, elegant girl with cigar in front of large fan, VG, A5 ..$25.00

Springeez Oil, can, Lubricant Supreme over lightning bolt on circle, For Better Lubrication below, cork top, 5-gal, 14x9", VG+, A6.......................................$5.00

Sprite, sign, tin, Taste It's Tingling Tartness above tilted bottle & Sprite in bold letters, 12x32", NM+, D30 .....$125.00

Square Deal, cigar box label, inner lid, rectangular portrait flanked by Justly & Popular, VG, A5..................$110.00

Square Deal, cigar box label, outer, hand holding scale above cards, chips & money bag, EX, A5...........$75.00

Squaw Choice Sifted Peas, can label, product name above & below pea pods/squaw left of product & company name, 4¼x11¼", NM, A7.........................$8.00

Squeeze, bottle carrier, cardboard, G, A16.................$15.00

Squeeze, fan pull, cardboard, Drink...Delightfully Refreshing on blue disk against posed bathing beauty, 1940s, 11x8", NM, A13..................................$300.00

Squeeze, fan pull, cardboard, Drink...The Snappy Drink on yellow disk against posed bathing beauty, 1940s, 11x8", VG+, A13...$175.00

Squeeze, sign, cardboard, die-cut, Will You Please Have Squeeze, So Refreshing, bathing beauty beside bottle, 30x20", EX, A16.....................................$525.00

Squeeze, sign, cardboard, Drink Squeeze on yellow circle above girl in red dress holding bottle, 24x18", NM, D30...$300.00

Squeeze, sign, cardboard, Had Your Squeeze Today? left of bathing beauty leaning on diving board, 24x18", EX, D30...$200.00

Squeeze, sign, cardboard, Squeeze Scores Again... on sign & tilted bottle above boy running toward home plate, 20x15", NM+, D8...............................$360.00

Squeeze, sign, tin, keyhole design with backside of 2 girls on bench & tilted bottle, Squeeze below, 20x28", NOS, NM, A1...$300.00

Squeeze Orange Drink, sign, flange, trademark image of 2 girls from behind above Squeeze The Satisfying Orange Drink, 12x13", EX, A6 ....$450.00

Squire's, see also John P Squire & Co

Squire's Arlington Hams-Bacon-Sausage, sign, self-framed tin, wreath of corn surrounds oval image of pig, name above & below, 24½x20", restored, VG, A2..........$415.00

Squirrel Brand Fancy Salted Nuts, tin, yellow with red name above image of squirrel, Fancy Salted Nuts & company name below, pry lid, 5-lb, EX, A2......$415.00

Squirrel Brand Peanut Butter, pail, yellow with name above & below trademark image of squirrel, slip lid, bail handle, 1-lb, VG, A6..........................$300.00

Squirrel Brand Peanut Butter, tin, red, gold & black with product name above & below encircled squirrel, pry lid, 6½x5" dia, VG+, A18 ....$240.00

Squirrel Brand Peanut Butter, tin, yellow with cartoon image of a squirrel holding a peanut flanked by lettering, pry lid, 48-oz, NM, A3 ....$65.00

Squirrel Brand Peanut Taffy, display stand, tin, die-cut squirrel atop yellow sign with red lettering, 4 rows of slots for product, 25", VG+, A2 ....$685.00

Squirrel Brand Salted Peanuts, jar, clear glass, black & yellow decal label with squirrel, square with round black & yellow lid, 10", EX, A2 ....$185.00

Squirrel Confections, tin, top pictures 2 squirrels in tree & a bird, A Piper & A Pair Of Nutcrackers, 5x8", EX+, A3 ....$25.00

Squirt, calendar, 1948, complete, EX+, A16 ....$45.00

Squirt, drinking glass, Squirt boy on red & yellow applied label, 1952, M, A16 ....$35.00

Squirt, menu board, tin, Switch To on circle pointing to bottle & Squirt boy above chalkboard, 27x19", NM+, D30 ....$75.00

Squirt, miniature bottle, applied label, EX, A16.........$20.00

Squirt, sign, cardboard, die-cut hanger, Switch To..., Never An After-Thirst, boy & bottle on dot, 1955, VG, A16 ....$25.00

Squirt, sign, cardboard, die-cut hanger, Why Monkey? Drink Squirt, 2 monkeys with bottle, 1941, EX, A16 ....$80.00

Squirt, sign, cardboard, stand-up, Squirt Gives You Go! above girl on swing, bottle & grapefruit at left, 1944, 28x38", NM, A1 ....$130.00

Squirt, sign, tin, Enjoy Squirt on yellow design at left of bottle & Never An After-Thirst, red background, 12x28", NM+, D30 ....$125.00

Squirt, sign, tin, You'll Love Squirt left of partial bottle, yellow background, framed, 13x36", G, D31 ....$110.00

Squirt, sign, tin on cardboard, Squirt in embossed script over splash design, 5x7", EX+, A13 ....$100.00

Squirt, thermometer, tin, Squirt on band above bottle & bulb, Put A Little Squirt In Your Life below, 15", NM, D30..$65.00

St Andrews/Alex Cameron & Co, tobacco box label, 1872, 14", NM, D8 ....$20.00

St James Coffee, tin, red with gold name above & below image of Gimbel's department store, square, round lid, bail handle, 5-lb, VG, A2 ....$275.00

St Johns Motors, calendar, 1939, Indian princess on mountain top, full pad, framed, image: 45x22", EX, A9 ....$550.00

St Leger Flake Cut Smoking Tobacco, tin, yellow with name around image of jockey on horse racing around track, rectangular, rounded corners, 4x6", VG, A18.........$155.00

St Louis Lager Beer, label, pre-prohibition, Anheuser-Busch Brewing Assoc, M, A10..............................$85.00

St Marys Ale, label, St Marys Beverage Co, U-type permit number, Internal Revenue Tax Paid statement, 1933-36, 12-oz, M, A10..$14.00

St Marys Bock Beer, label, St Marys Beverage Co, Internal Revenue Tax Paid statement, 1933-34, 12-oz, M, A10 ....$12.00

St Regis Brew, label, Jetter Brewing Inc, U-type permit number, Internal Revenue Tax Paid statement, 12-oz, EX, A10 ....$25.00

Stafford's Hot Choclate, container, aluminum with product name in red, EX, A18....................................$95.00

Stag Beer, matchbook, triangular pattern with bottle, glass & stein, Stop For..., 20 strike, front strike, NM, D28 ....$4.00

Stag Tobacco, canister, tin, red with white name above & below image of stag, square, round lid, EX, A18..$195.00

Stag Tobacco, door push plate, porcelain, image of pocket tin above Ever-lasting-ly Good For Pipe Or Cigarette on white, 7x4", VG, A21..$300.00

Stag Tobacco, pocket tin, vertical, red with product name above & below oval image of stag against lake & mountains, EX+, A18..$85.00

Stagecoach, crate label, pear, colorful stagecoach scene, M, D3 ....$2.00

Staley's Baking Powder, tin, paper label, with contents, 4-oz, A7 ....$25.00

Staley's Baking Powder, tin, sample, paper label, with contents, 2-oz, NM, A7....................................$55.00

Standard, thermometer, metal with glass front, logo at right of vertically arched degrees, red, white & blue, 22x15", EX+, A6 ....$90.00

Standard Ale, sign, cardboard, Standard Ale truck hauling 2 brown & white oxen, framed, 12½x16", G, A6.....$80.00

246

Standard Brewing Co, tray, center depicts the execution of 38 Sioux Indians in 1862, company name & Mankato Minnesota in rim, 12" dia, EX, A1 .$465.00

Standard Brewing Co Pure Lager Beer, Ale & Porter..., tray, pictures tavern scene with men playing cards & dog on floor, lettering on rim, pre-1920s, oval, EX, A19 .....$400.00

Standard Clothing Co, store card, portrait of President Grover Cleveland with text & company name above, framed, image: 10x7", G, A9................................$60.00

Standard Dry Ale Genuine Draught, can, Party Barrel..., 1-gal, EX+, A19..$35.00

Standard Ethyl Gasoline, sign, die-cut porcelain, product name above encircled logo, 28x21", G+, D11......$90.00

Standard Heating Oils, sign, die-cut porcelain, product lettering on panel with serrated ends across diamond shape, 14¾x23¾", VG+, A1....................$250.00

Standard Lager, label, Kessler Brewing Co, pre-prohibition, M, A10...$45.00

Standard Licorice Lozenges, tin, Standard arched above glass window, red & black Oriental motif on sides, SV&FP Scedder, slip lid, 8x5", G-, A9 ....$85.00

Standard Lubrite Motor Oil, can, Pegasus logo on shield below product name, Socony-Vacuum Oil Co Inc, red, white & blue, 5-qt, VG, A6 ....$40.00

Standard Oil, bottle, embossed glass with metal cap & spout, 15", EX, A6 ....$55.00

Standard Oil, checkers game, w/orig box, EX, A1...$100.00

Standard Oil Co Household Lubricant, can, early, product text with graphics of early bicycle & sewing machine, dome top with small screw cap, 8-oz, EX+, A1 ....$85.00

Standard Oil Co Thresher Hard Oil, see Thresher Hard Oil

Standard Oil Indiana, gas globe, crown-shaped milk glass with blue detail, painted metal screw base, EX+, A1...$700.00

Standard Permalube Motor Oil, bank, metal, product name above Standard logo, red, white & blue, EX+, A6...$20.00

Standard Porter, label, Standard Brewing Co of Scranton, Internal Revenue Tax Paid statement, 1933-50, 12-oz, M, A10..$18.00

Standard Sewing Machine Co, ad card, snow scene with little boy pulling sled while baby girl watches, 4x3", VG, D14 ....$6.00

Standard Tobacco, sign, paper, soldier on charging horse in front of lettered flag, Chew Or Smoke..., 5¢... below, image: 20x15", NM, A9 ....$350.00

Standard Tru-Age Beer, interior streetcar sign, Season's Greetings left of red-gloved girl with glass, product name at right, 13x29", NM, A19........$65.00

Standard Varnish Works, sign, self-framed tin, The Man Who Knows... above painter standing behind row of products, ca 1909, 10x17", VG, A9.....................$100.00

Standard Water Closets, sign, paper, Quieter Action With..., pictures a toilet seat & see-thru tank, framed, image: 26x20", G-, A9 ....$300.00

Standard-Kaffe, tin, young girl with can sitting next to black gentleman in early car, VG, A6................$325.00

Stanfield's Unshrinkable Underwear, box, image of 2 men in long johns conversing in front of window, 14x11", G+, D21 ....$25.00

Stanley, tool caddy, wood with black lettering, Stanley Helps You Do Things Right, 1940s, 20x36", EX, A6..........$40.00

Stanley Electrical Power Tools, catalog, 1939, 52 pgs, EX, D17..$25.00

Stanley Garage Door Holders, sign, tin, shows product in use with auto in garage, HD Beach litho, 1920s, 27x35", EX, D8..$850.00

Stanley Hardware, sign, cardboard, gold lettering on red & blue, 5x12", EX, A6 ....$50.00

Stanley Powerlock II, radio, shaped like chrome '25 ft' tape measure with round yellow emblem, plastic, Hong Kong, M $30.00

Stanley Tools, sign, die-cut cardboard, product name & various tools above town scene featuring Henry Brown Hardware, 32x33", G, A9 ....$450.00

Stanocola Gasoline, sign, porcelain, We Sell Nothing But..., black & white lettering on red & white, 1906-08, 14x24", rare, EX+, A6...$1,200.00

Stanocola Petroleum Products, sign, porcelain, product name on emblem surrounded by Standard Oil Co Of Louisiana, 30" dia, rare, EX+, A6.....................$2,300.00

Stanton Beer & Ale, tray, maroon & gold, 12", G, D7....$20.00

Stanwix Ground Plug, pocket tin, vertical, The Ace Of Them All, black with white lettering, EX+, A18..$210.00

Staple Brand Peanut Butter, pail, Trade Mark logo flanked by product name on elongated diamond shape, Valley Preserving Co, 25-lb, 9x10" dia, EX, A6.....**$20.00**

Staple Grain Plug Cut, pocket tin, vertical, yellow with blue name around star encircled with MA Gunst & Co... on blue band, short, EX+, A18.........................**$1,320.00**

Staples-Hildebrand Co, paperweight, glass, company name arched above Building Materials, Builders Specialties... in red & black, oval, M, D13.................**$50.00**

Star & Crescent Quality Beverages/Waupun Bottling Works, sign, self-framed tin on cardboard, Star & Crescent & logo above Lemon Soda & Ginger Ale..., 6x11", EX, A8 ....**$45.00**

Star Ales, thermometer, dial with mirror center, numbers around upper half, product name around bottom half, 9" dia, VG+, A19..**$65.00**

Star Bottling Works, sign, tin, star logo above Sudbury Ont, blue, orange, yellow & cream, 35½x11", EX, A6 ....**$95.00**

Star Brand Shoes, alarm clock, round gold face reads Star Brand Shoes Are Better, pink case, Lux Clock Co, 1920s, 3½", EX, A2 ....**$80.00**

Star Brand Shoes, racer, diecast tin, The Winner, Star Brand Shoes Are Better, red with blue driver, ca 1917, 8½" long, rare, VG, A6 ....**$550.00**

Star Brand Shoes, racer, diecast tin, The Winner, Star Brand Shoes Are Better, red with blue driver, ca 1917, 8½" long, rare, EX+, A6.....................................**$1,800.00**

Star Chewing Tobacco, pocket tin, flat, red with lettering & logo, Old Chicago Stamping Co, VG+, A18....**$410.00**

Star Double Edge, display, cardboard, Wotta Shave! spoken by man shaving with 20 packs of razors, 4 For 10¢, 12x9", NM, A7...**$40.00**

Star Egg Carriers & Tray Mfg Co, pocket mirror, celluloid, Costs You Nothing, Makes Profit Besides above open carton of eggs, round, EX+, A11 ....**$80.00**

Star Lager Beer, label, Star Brewing Co, U-type permit number, Internal Revenue Tax Paid statement, 1933-36, 12-oz, M, A10...**$12.00**

Star Lager Beer, label, Star-Peerless Brewing Co, U-type permit number, Internal Revenue Tax Paid statement, 1933-36, 12-oz, EX, A10 ....**$16.00**

Star Lager Brewing Co Fine Ales & Lager, tray, deep-dish, shows colonial tavern scene on blue background, lettered rim, VG+, A19 ....**$20.00**

Star Maid Salted Peanuts, tin, product name above & below maid with tray against star emitting rays, blue on white, 10-lb, VG, A18...**$200.00**

Star Malton Beer, label, Star Union Products Co, Internal Revenue Tax Paid statement, 1933-50, 12-oz, NM, A10...**$10.00**

Star Plug, tobacco pouch, leather, EX, A7.................**$18.00**

Star Safety Razor, tin, flat, black lettering over 2-tone gold star logo, hieroglyphics-type border, ¼x1x2", EX, D37, minimum value..**$80.00**

Star Safety Razor, tin, image of man shaving on 1 side, razor on the other, VG+, D22.............................**$50.00**

Star Scotch Sniff, container, cardboard, Clarksville Tenn 1898 tax stamp, unopened, 2x3", D35.................**$18.00**

Star Soap, sign, curved porcelain, Extra Large above product box, Extra Good below, green background, 26x21½", G, A9 ....**$550.00**

Star Stogies, sign, cardboard, product name left of open pack & Smoke Easy As Breathing & 5 For 10¢, blue ground, 10x20", VG+, A3 ....$55.00

Star Tobacco, pocket tin, vertical, Star lettered in white on red lid, Tobacco on red band below, star images in center, EX, A18...**$160.00**

Star Tobacco, sign, porcelain, Star above tobacco plugs & star logo, Sold Here & Tobacco below, blue on yellow, 12x24", EX, A18...**$135.00**

Star Union, cigar box label, outer, lady above clouds holding American flag, NM, A5.....................................**$95.00**

Starin's Excursions, sign, paper, black & white image of woman with fruit basket & business card, steamship vignettes above, 22x15", G, A9 ....**$100.00**

Starkist Tuna, alarm clock, Charlie Tuna & Sorry Charlie sign, white round dial, blue numbers, 2 bells, 1969, footed, 4" dia, EX, A6..**$65.00**

Starkist Tuna, alarm clock, Charlie Tuna & Sorry Charlie sign, white round dial, blue numbers, 2 bells, 1969, footed, 4" dia, EX+, A2 ....**$100.00**

Starkist Tuna, squeeze toy, Charlie Tuna, 1974, Product People, EX, D27 ....**$40.00**

Starrett Fine Mechanical Tools, catalog, 1930, 383 pgs, EX, D17...**$50.00**

Stars & Stripes/Willow Springs Brewing Co, drinking glass, straight-sided with flat bottom, etched logo with 'My Country 'Tis Of Thee,' 3½", NM, A8 ....**$40.00**

State Flyer, cigar box label, outer, locomotive surrounded by vignettes, NM, A5...**$85.00**

State Life Insurance Co, pocket mirror, smiling baby surrounded by lettering, round, NM, A20.................**$18.00**

State Mutual Assurance Co, letter folder, tin, frontal view of the building, Kellogg & Bulkeley, 12x3", rare, G+, A9 ....**$75.00**

State of Maine Potatoes, display, 3-D cardboard, Victory Food For You & Uncle Sam, farm boy seated behind patriotic hat, 1960s, 44", NM, A13 ....**$275.00**

Stay Ready Automatic Transmission Fluid, can, Type A above woman on back of a mallard duck, product name below, red, black & white, scarce, 1-qt, EX+, A1 ..**$200.00**

Steamro Red Hots, sign, porcelain, Spicy on hot dog at left of product name & Star Mfg Co..., red & black on white, 2x17", G, A6 ....$180.00

Stearn's Root Beer, dispenser, ceramic, embossed barrel shape on tree stump, NM+, A4 ....$550.00

Stearn's Root Beer, dispenser, wood, barrel shape with decals, 1920s, EX+, A4 ....$400.00

Stegmaier Beer, tip tray, factory scene with lettering around rim, oval, 6", NM, A8................................$165.00

Stegmaier Brewing Co, tray, deep-dish, colorful image of 3 kittens playing around product bottle & box, lettered rim, 12" dia, G+, A21 ....$395.00

Stegmaier Brewing Co, tray, image of woman with long brown hair & draped shoulders, 13" dia, VG+, A21 ..$65.00

Stegmaier Gold Medal Beer, clock, light-up, white round face on red plaque lettered Stegmaier, Gold Medal Beer on beveled base, EX+, A19....................................$80.00

Stegmaier Gold Medal Beer, sign, tin on cardboard, product name & In Steinies on diagonal gold & black bands left of bottle, 9x13", EX+, A19 ....$100.00

Stegmaier Gold Medal Beer, tray, deep-dish, Cool Blended For Clean Taste Clear Through, product label with bottle & glass, 12" dia, VG+, A8....................$25.00

Stegmaier's Gold Medal Beer, tray, Drink... above factory scene, lettered rim, round, EX, A19 ....$50.00

Steinbrau Beer, label, St Claire Brewing Co, Internal Revenue Tax Paid statement, 1933-50, 11-oz, M, A10...$20.00

Steinhaus Beer, sign, embossed tin, Everybody Likes above product name, white on orange, 17x35", NM+, A19 ....$75.00

Stephenson Underwear, sign, stamped brass, product name on rectangle at left of Certified For Health & Comfort, 3x16", EX, A3 ....$40.00

Sterling Beer, label, Sterling Brewers Inc, Internal Revenue Tax Paid statement, 1933-50, 12-oz, M, A10.........$10.00

Sterling Beer, sign, tin on cardboard, We Serve upper left of Sterling logo, One Of America's Finest..., beveled edge, 9x13", NM+, A19 ....$85.00

Sterling Bock Beer, label, ram's head above product name, yellow background, 12-oz, NM, A19 ....$6.00

Sterling Gasoline, pump sign, porcelain, Sterling symbol in center, yellow, red, black & white, oval, 8½x11", EX, A6..$375.00

Sterling Light Fine Cut/Spaulding & Merrick, tin, red Sterling on gold above white tilted pack on red, 5¢ Packages 5¢ below, round with square lid, VG, A18 ....$55.00

Sterling Mellow Beer, display, metal, statue of 'Tinkerbell' with arms up on base with Sterling banner over Mellow Beer oval, 15", EX, A8...$70.00

Sterling Motor Oil, sign, tin, Sterling arched above round logo, Motor Oil below, 2-color field, black wood frame, 36x72", NM, A1.....................$460.00

Sterling Oil, sign, tin, Sterling in red vertical letters on white band, round logo below, yellow ground, wood frame, 72x12", NM, A1..$375.00

Sterling Oil, sign, tin, Sterling in red vertical letters on white band, round logo below, yellow ground, wood frame, 72x12", VG, A6 ....$125.00

Sterling Pepsin Gum, sign, cardboard, girl's face & package of gum above product name & Pure Mint Flavor on red, framed, 35x25", G, A9 ....$300.00

Sterling Salt, thermometer, dial-type, Service & Research Are The Extras In... on diamond in center, NM, D11 ..$125.00

Sterling Super-Bru, sign, tin, vertical pennent with We Serve above bottle, Leisurely Aged Always below, red & blue on green, 18x9", VG+, A8 ....$115.00

Sterling Work Shoes, sign, reverse-painted glass with metal frame, red & green lettering on black, 7x16", EX, A6 .$25.00

Sterno Double Burner Cook-Stove, sign, die-cut cardboard trifold, cooking scene above text, Free Practical Toaster... on outer panels, 27x36", EX, A12 ......$110.00

Stetson Pipe & Cigarette Smoking Tobacco, pocket tin, vertical, red with lettering around oval bust image of John B Stetson, EX+, A18 ....$5,000.00

Stevens Arms, sign, shows couple in hunting scene, metal strip top & bottom, Kaufmann & Strauss litho, 1906, framed, 20x15", NM, A15...................................$2,200.00

Stewart Ball Bearing Clipping Machine, sign, self-framed tin, oval image of men grooming horse, 20x24", G, A9 ....$85.00

Stewart's Drive-In, mug, glass, black & orange diamond logo, 4x3", M, D16 ....$20.00

Stewart's Root Beer, mug, glass, embossed lettering, high-rise handle, 4½x3", M, D16 ....$35.00

Stickney & Poor Spice Co, sign, wood, name above 3 product packages, Founded 1815, wood-grain background, framed, 28x19½", VG+, A21 ....$320.00

Stoddard-Dayton, ad, 1910, Stoddard-Dayton on 4 sides of band bordering open touring car, text below, framed, 17x13", EX, A8...$20.00

Stoddard's Harness Soap/Stoddard & Hellier, sign, product & company name above & below black stable hand tending to harness with horses in stalls, 21x13", EX, A2 ....$660.00

Stoffel Bros Dry Goods, tape measure, celluloid, multicolored image of Cupid with bow & arrow, round, EX, A11 ....$35.00

Stollwerck's Chocolates & Candies, display case, wood with beveled & etched glass front, Stollwerck's in diagonal script, None Nicer above, 23x15", VG, A9 ....**$150.00**

Stone Malt Company, mug, stoneware, yellow with company name & 5 listed cities on rectangular field, blue bands above & below, EX+, A8 ....**$55.00**

Stoneware Food Container, sign, self-framed tin, We Sell All Sizes, boy & dog getting donut from crock, 19x13", G, A9.................................**$950.00**

Stoney's Beer, display, chalkware, Nothing Tops It But The Foam! bust of smiling man in top hat on base, 10x8", EX+, A19..................................**$55.00**

Stoney's Beer, tray, red, yellow & white, 13", EX+, D7..**$20.00**

Storck's Ice Cream, sign, reverse-painted glass, We Serve above stork at left of product name, A Pure Food Product below, 14x22", NM+, A1.........................**$250.00**

Stradella, cigar box label, outer, elegant woman & red fan, 1887, 4½x4½", M, D5.................................**$10.00**

Straiton & Storm's Owl Cigar/Frankle Bros Co, sign, reverse glass & gold foil, product name & Now 5¢ above & below owl on cigar, 58x22", EX, A2 ....**$3,630.00**

Strathmore Cigars, sign, tin, 2 elderly gents sharing box of cigars, original frame, 15x17½", VG, A9 ....**$200.00**

Straub Beer, sign, tin on cardboard, circular with gold band bordering product name, 9" dia, EX+, A19.........**$320.00**

Strawbridge & Clothier, catalog, Spring/Summer, 1909, 96 pgs, EX, D17.................................**$90.00**

Strength, crate label, California orange, elephant with tusks on yellow background, Santa Paula, 10x11", M, D3.................................**$28.00**

Strick Co, paperweight, glass, The Truck That Carries Weight... above truck image, company name below, rectangular, M, D13.................................**$25.00**

Strickler's Strictly Fresh Oysters, tin, 1-pt, EX, A7..**$10.00**

Strikes & Spares Cigars, box label set, pictures 2 men bowling & spectators, 2 pcs, EX, A5...................**$300.00**

Stroh's, sign, glass, You'll Like It, It's Lighter!, 3-D plastic pilsner glass right of food scene, 13x16", VG+, A19 ....$110.00

Stroh's Bohemian Beer, sign, cardboard, man in top hat with glass of beer, 1940s, framed, image: 23x15½", G, A9.................................**$140.00**

Stroh's Bohemian Beer, sign, tin on cardboard, America's Only Fire-Brewed Beer upper right of tray with bottle, glass & opener, 12x15", EX, A19 ....**$60.00**

Stroh's Bohemian Beer, sign, Where Quality Counts on banner flanked by lion emblems, product name on gold oval above, 1950s, framed 15x17", EX, A8...**$50.00**

Stroh's Bohemian Beer, tap knob, black ball with insert, VG+, A8.................................**$100.00**

Stroh's Bohemian Beer, tray, product name above young girl in red hooded coat carrying a box, 13x13", A19.....**$120.00**

Stroh's Pure Hopped Malt Syrup, sign, embossed tin, It's Best By Test on tail of S in Stroh's, product can at right, framed, image: 17x23", G, A9.................................**$400.00**

Stromberg Carburetors, sign, porcelain, Authorized Sales & Service...Bendix Product, red, white & black, wrought-iron hanger, 36" dia, EX, A6.............**$2,750.00**

Stromeyer's Grape Punch, syrup bottle, clear glass with label & metal cap, VG, A13 ....**$60.00**

Stuart's Handy Cloves, tin, 3¾", NM, A7 ....**$65.00**

Stubby, palm press, die-cut tin, ...Zip In Every Sip, winking man with round body atop sign, Canadian, 1950s, 9x4", VG, D36 ....$150.00

Stubby Beverages, door push bar, tin, Enjoy Stubby Beverages in red & black on white, 3x30", VG, D21 ....**$60.00**

Stubby Orange, sign, tin, Enjoy Stubby Orange in black, red & orange on cream, 4x30", NM+, D21 ....**$110.00**

Studebaker, mirror, yellow car & oval logo at top, company name below, beige & black lettering with blue border, 11x6", VG+, A6.................................**$125.00**

Studebaker Service Station, sign, Studebaker in diagonal script, Service upper left, Station lower right, white on blue, G+, A6.................................**$155.00**

Student Prince Beer, label, Heidelberg Brewing Co, U-type permit number, Internal Revenue Tax Paid statement, 1933-36, 12-oz, NM, A10 ....**$10.00**

Student Prince Beer, tray, shows glass & bottle with sandwich & other food, plain rim, round, VG, A8 ......**$75.00**

Sturdy Motor Oil, can, product name above encircled tree flanked by lettered banner, green, black & white, screw cap, 2-gal, 11x8", EX, A6.................................**$65.00**

Success Manure Spreader, ashtray, farmer driving team pulling manure spreader, lion-head logo upper left, lettered rim, rectangular, 3x5", NM, A8.................**$175.00**

Success Manure Spreader, tip tray, shows horse-drawn spreader in use, lettered rim with fluted design at corners, horizontal rectangle, EX, A21.................**$165.00**

Sudan Ginger, tin, paper label, 3¾", NM, A7.........**$12.00**

Sudan Sage, tin, paper label, 4", NM, A7..................$12.00

Sultana, cigar box label, inner lid, woman, star & crescent moon, 6x9", EX, D5.................................$25.00

Sultana All Purpose Cocoa, container, cardboard & tin, red Sultana on white band above full cup on brown, vertical square, 1-lb, EX, A18 ....$10.00

Sultana Cinnamon, tin, product name on band around image of family, round, VG, A18 ....$25.00

Sumaba Coffee, container, cardboard, decorative oval image of woman in profile with steaming cup, Wm Steinmeyer Co, 3-lb, rare, EX, A3................$140.00

Summer Girl Pure Cocoa, container, cardboard with tin lid, girl in bonnet above 2 crossed stemmed yellow roses, 10x4x3", EX, A3 ....$180.00

Summer-Time Long Cut Tobacco, container, cardboard, name above & below couple with boardwalk scene beyond, round, pry lid, EX+, A18 ....$85.00

Summit, crate label, California apple, snow-covered mountains & forest, Colfax, 9x11", M, D11 ....$4.00

Sun Crest, calendar, 1941, shows pretty girl enjoying bottle of Sun Crest, incomplete, 27x17", VG, A13 ....$70.00

Sun Crest, calendar, 1955, complete, EX+, A16........$22.00

Sun Crest, clock, light-up, blue numbers surround Drink...Beverages on orange sunset graphics, Swihart, 1950s-60s, 16x13", EX, A13................................$180.00

Sun Crest, clock, light-up, bottle bordered by black numbers, 1950s, round, NM, A13 ....$300.00

Sun Crest, sign, cardboard, You Can't Lose With Sun Crest above baseball boy & bottle, orange on blue, 1950s, 12x9", NM, A13.......................................$120.00

Sun Crest, sign, drink rack, tin, Drink...It's Best in black & white over white sun on red background, 9x17", EX, D21..$40.00

Sun Crest, sign, tin, Get Tingle-Ated Drink Sun Crest Beverages on bottle cap, 35" dia, NM+, D11............$225.00

Sun Crest, sign, tin, Get Tingle-Ated With at left of close-up of label portion of tilted bottle, bottle cap lower right, 12x30", EX+, A16......................................$100.00

Sun Crest, thermometer, embossed tin bottle shape, NM, D21..$100.00

Sun Cured Extra Mild Smoking Tobacco, pocket tin, vertical, Crushed, Ready For Pipe, name above barrel full of tobacco leaves, EX, A18 ....$800.00

Sun Oil Co, display, copper & bronze derrick on wood base, Follow The Sun... engraved on plaque on base, 15", NM, A6...$70.00

Sun Prince, crate label, California orange, big smiling sun on blue background, Orange Grove, 10x11", M, D3......$2.00

Sun Spot, sign, embossed tin, Drink America's Favorite above 3 bottles & round logo, Made With Real Juice!, 1940s, 15x12", EX, A13.......................................$70.00

Sun-Maid Raisins, trolley sign, Delicious Nutricious..., shows little girl being offered raisins & spilling box over 5¢, 13x23", EX, D8..........................$100.00

Sun-Maid Raisins, trolley sign, Makes A Good Pudding Complete, shows various desserts & 2 boxes of raisins, 11x21", VG, D8...................................$80.00

Sun-Maid Raisins, trolley sign, We Always Use Them..., shows 2 boxes & bowl of cereal, framed, 11x21", VG, A6...$90.00

Sun-Maid Raisins, trolley sign, We Recommend Them, Good Grocers, Bakers..., shows 2 boxes, framed, 11x21", G, A6...$40.00

Sun-Rise Beverages, sign, tin, Discover Refreshing Pure... over smiling sun & orange half, 28x20", EX+, D30.........$140.00

Sun-Rise Beverages, sign, tin, Discover Refreshing Pure... over smiling sun & orange half, 28x20", EX, D30..$120.00

Sunbeam Bread, end label, color photo of Hopalong Cassidy with white border, EX, D29 ....$15.00

Sunbeam Bread, end label, features Esther Williams, red background, EX, D29 ....$15.00

Sunbeam Bread, end label, features Gene Autry, red border, EX, D29 ....$10.00

Sunbeam Bread, end label, features William Tell, blue background, EX, D29...$4.00

Sunbeam Bread, end label, pictures man & monkey fighting over a hat, yellow background, EX, D29 ....$3.00

Sunbeam Bread, end label, pictures man carrying bass drum, yellow background, EX, D29.....................$3.00

Sunbeam Bread, end label, pictures Oscar the Ostrich, Oscar Orders, red border, EX, D29 ....$3.00

Sunbeam Bread, sign, tin, ...It's Batter Whipped!, trademark image in white & red on yellow, red rolled rim, 1960s, 12x30", NM, A13 ....$180.00

Sunbeam Bread, sign, tin, Bread With A Bonus, EX, D34 ....$195.00

Sunbeam Bread, sign, tin, Reach For...Energy-Packed..., Sunbeam girl above text on red, curved corners, 55x19", NM, A13..$575.00

Sunbeam Bread, sign, tin, Reach For...It's Batter-Whipped, loaf of bread in center, 1950s, 36x72", NM, A13 ..**$400.00**

Sunbeam Bread, sign, tin, Sunbeam girl atop product name, red ground with yellow border, diamond shape, 1956, 48x48", NM+, A13.................................**$400.00**

Sunbeam Bread, sign, tin, Sunbeam girl atop product name on red oval, yellow ground with red border, diamond shape, 48x48", EX, A13.............................**$225.00**

Sunbeam Bread, thermometer, dial-type, Reach For... above Sunbeam girl flanked by Let's Be Friends, 1950s, 13" dia, EX, D8 ....$225.00

Sunbonnet Spices Cream of Tartar, tin, pictures girl in bonnet, VG, A3.....................................**$75.00**

Sunday Best, crate label, Oregon pear, silhouette of couple going to church, Medford, 8x11", M, D12..............**$4.00**

Sundial Shoes, clicker, tin, 2", NM, A7 ....**$25.00**

Sunflush Oil, sign, embossed tin, ...Cleans The Inside Of Your Motor, 15¢ Quart in lower right, 11½x46", EX, D11 ....**$95.00**

Sunkist, sign, paper, I'll Tell You A Secret, Sunkist Orange Juice Everyday! above girl with glass, 1910s-20s, 42x28", NM, A13 ....**$600.00**

Sunkist Lemons, trolley sign, cardboard, ...In Hot Tea Aids Digestion, Enhances Flavor, pictures lemons & teapot, framed, 13x23", EX, A6 ....**$55.00**

Sunkist Oranges, sign, die-cut cardboard, shows a smiling Santa holding a box of oranges, 1930s-40s, 36x28", VG+, A13 ....**$110.00**

Sunkist Oranges, trolley sign, cardboard, California's Gift To The Nation's Health, family looking at oranges, framed, 12x22", EX, A6 ....**$95.00**

Sunland Frictionized Motor Oil, sign, die-cut porcelain, can shape, white, orange & green, 2-sided, 18x12", NM, A1...**$350.00**

Sunlight Oil, tip tray, Use... on sun in center, 92 Different Oil Products... around rim, 4" dia, VG+, A6 ....**$55.00**

Sunlight Soap, sign, curved metal, yellow & blue can shape with blue & white lettering, 24x16", NM+, A13 ....**$775.00**

Sunny Boy Peanut Butter, pail, product name above & below image of boy surrounded by rays, red on white, slip lid, bail handle, 1-lb, EX+, A15 ....**$190.00**

Sunny Cove, crate label, California orange, view of 1930s style house overlooking groves & mountains, Redlands, 10x11", M, D12 ....**$6.00**

Sunnybrook Pure Rye, match holder, metal, shows bottle & advertising, Bred In Old Kentucky, Should Be In Every Home... on holder, VG+, A8.....................**$150.00**

Sunnyside Quick Rolled Oats/Great Atlantic & Pacific Tea Co, container, children at play around bottom, EX, A3 ....**$40.00**

Sunnyside Tobacco, label, woman with parasol passing plug to gent, product name in graduated letters, Tho's Hoyt & Co, 9½x11", G+, A9 ....**$250.00**

Sunoco, ashtray, metal, blue & yellow with logo in center, 8" dia, EX, A6 ....**$20.00**

Sunoco, bottle, glass with blue plastic top & lid, blue & yellow fired-on logo, 14", EX+, A6.....................**$90.00**

Sunoco, calendar, 1936, shows girl with dreamy eyes, Wishing You A Happy New Motoring Year on front of calendar, 16x10", EX, A6.......................................**$75.00**

Sunoco, container, glass jar with yellow & blue diamond-shaped paper label, new metal cap with pour spout, 1-qt, 14½", VG, A6...**$50.00**

Sunoco, hat, cloth with vinyl bill & brass Sunoco badge, VG+, A6 ....**$210.00**

Sunoco, radio, yellow & blue gas pump shape, transistor, 4", EX, A6 ....**$50.00**

Sunoco, see also Blue Sunoco

Sunoco Automotive Lubricant, can, yellow, blue & white, pry lid, 1-lb, VG+, A1.....................................**$10.00**

Sunoco DX, lighter, Zippo, yellow, red & blue logo, 2⅛x1⅛", NOS, A6 ....**$40.00**

Sunoco Dynafuel, gas globe, product name in blue on yellow elongated diamond, metal body, 15" dia, NM, A6...**$700.00**

Sunoco Gasoline, bank, tin, gas pump, 4x1¾", NM, A7...**$40.00**

Sunoco Mercury Made Motor Oil, pump sign, porcelain, logo above product name, black on yellow with black border, 12x10", NM, D8 ....$400.00

Sunoco Motor Oil, pump sign, porcelain, Distilled on elongated triangle above product name, yellow, blue & red, 12x10", EX, A6 ....**$180.00**

Sunoco Motor Oil, sign, porcelain flange, Sun Oils on diamond above large product name, yellow & red on blue & yellow, 20x26", EX+, A6 ....**$600.00**

Sunoco Oil Co, blotter, features Donald Duck, Reinforced For Rationed Driving..., marked A-981 700M 4-43, Printed In USA, 4x6", EX, A6 ....**$60.00**

Sunoco Winter Oil & Transep, sign, cardboard, features Mickey Mouse shooting at bird, For Trigger-Quick Starting!..., 28x20", rare, NM+, A6 ....**$2,500.00**

Sunray Ethyl, gas globe, bright yellow sunray logo on orange with Ethyl logo on green below, red plastic body, NM+, A1 ....$850.00

Sunray Mid-Continent Oil Co, sign, porcelain, company name above logo & Sanders Well No 5, 10x18", NM, D11...$175.00

Sunrise Lager Beer, sign, tin hanger, Sunrise on Draught around Lager Beer on sunrise image in center, 1940s, NM+, A19..$200.00

Sunrise Light, beer label, Sunrise Brewing Co, U-type permit number, Internal Revenue Tax Paid statement, 1933-36, 12-oz, EX, A10.......................................$25.00

Sunset Beer/Golden West Brewing Co, label, blue product name above white Fully Aged on red circle against golden orange background, 11-oz, VG+, A19......$20.00

Sunset Brand, lug box label, various fruit, colorful sunset in streaked sky, Fresno, M, D12.............................$2.00

Sunset Trail, tin, name arched above couple on horseback flanked by 5¢, vertical oblong with rounded corners, slip lid, VG, A18..$165.00

Sunshine & Othello Enameled Ranges, pocket mirror, celluloid, product name over sunrise scene, Reading Stove Works Orr, Painter & Co below, round, EX+, A11 ..$22.00

Sunshine Biscuits, product display, wood with 5 slanted shelves, vertical stenciled lettering on legs, 57x21½x17", VG+, A9 ....$50.00

Sunshine Cigarettes, sign, embossed tin, Twenty above & For 15¢ below tilted open pack on yellow background, framed, 18x14", EX+, A18..................................$110.00

Sunshine Hydrox, sign, paper, product lettering casting a shadow above cookies & ice cream, A Biscuit Bon Bon, 10x19", EX, A2 ....$185.00

Sunshine Krispy Crackers, tin, pictures a cracker & product name on fancy design, chefs on band below, orange, cream & blue, 1-lb, 7x6" dia, G, A6.........$35.00

Sunshine Premium Beer, beer can, flat-top, Internal Revenue Tax Paid statement, 12-oz, EX+, A19...........$15.00

Sunshine Premium Beer, display, plaster relief plaque, barrel shape with applied plater 'Peacemaker 45' gun & logos, 11x15", VG+, A8..$45.00

Sunshine Premium Beer, sign, cardboard, Get 1/3 More Beer... on yellow diamond left of Half Quart 16-oz... on brown over white, 22x27", NM, A19.....................$15.00

Sunshine Premium Beer, sign, tin, Fun-Time Favorite, Sunshine Premium Beer left of overview of bottle & frothy glass, 21x27", EX, A19..................................$20.00

Super Flash, gas globe, product name above Ethyl logo, red, yellow & black, clear ripple body, 13½" dia, NM, A6...$1,200.00

Super Frigidtest Anti-Freeze, can, arctic scene with 2 polar bears & twin-engine plane flying in front of sun, red, green & white, 1-qt, EX+, A1........................$50.00

Super Shell, signs, die-cut cardboard, 4 Toonerville Town People advertising Super Shell, copyright HC Fisher/Fontaine Fax, 1934, 24", EX+, A6.........$1,700.00

Superba Coffee, tin, Superba arched above Puritas Trade Mark logo, A Perfect Coffee below, slip lid, VG+, A3.........$45.00

Superior Bock Beer, label, Superior Brewing Co, U-type permit number, Internal Revenue Tax Paid statement, 1933-36, 12-oz, M, A10..$14.00

Superior Cleanser, can, sample, cardboard & tin, with contents, 2¼", NM, A7 ....$65.00

Superior Mainspring, tin, flat, blue with decorative border surrounding knight on horse, square, rounded corners, ¾x2¾x2¾", EX, D37...$55.00

Superior Vegetable National Dry Hop Yeast, trade card, product name arched above The Ladies Favorite & lady serving bread, 1880s, EX, D23.............................$18.00

Superlative Cigarettes, sign, paper, girl with grapes, Cigarettes lettered vertically at right, framed, image: 17x12", NM, A9..$150.00

Superlative Cigarettes, sign, paper, pretty girl in bonnet holding pansies, WS Kimball & Co, Rochester NY below, framed, image: 17x12", VG, A9..............$200.00

Supertone/Foster Oil Co, gas globe, Supertone in diagonal script over flames, orange & blue, glass Gill body, 13½" dia, NM, A6..$500.00

Supporter, cigar box label, outer, soccer player kicking ball, 4½x4½", M, D5 ....$10.00

Suprema (Stearns) Face Powder, tin, sample, lady with folded fan touching lips, fancy gold border, oval, ½x1¾x2⅜", EX, D37, minimum value.................$85.00

Supreme Auto Oil/Gulf Refining Co, sign, porcelain flange, ...Leaves Less Carbon in blue on orange circle, white background, 18x22", EX+, A1 ....$275.00

Supreme Auto Oil/Gulf Refining Co, sign, porcelain flange, round logo at left of product name, company name below, black on yellow, 11x15", VG, A6 ..$325.00

Supreme Court Fancy Red Salmon, can label, courthouse & 2 salmon on red background with gilt highlights, M, D5...$5.00

Suprex Coffee, tin, product name flanked by lancers, yellow background, key-wind lid, 1-lb, EX+, A18...$75.00

Surbrug's Golden Sceptre, pocket tin, vertical, Burley Floss Cut, white with red arm holding sceptre, gold lettering & trim, EX, A18...$330.00

Sure Shot Chewing Tobacco, store bin, tin, shows kneeling Indian shooting bow & arrow, It Touches The Spot, rectangular, 5x10x15", EX+, A18.........................$650.00

Surety, crate label, Washington apple, steamship sailing down Columbia river, Yakima, 9x11", M, D12.....$15.00

Surtro Bath, sign, paper, 2-panel image of people swimming in various pools with spectators watching from balconies, 80x82", EX, A9................................$2,100.00

Swain, Earle & Co Coffee, tin, sample, Swain, Earle & Co Boston Mass within fancy gold border, slip lid, 2¼x2½" dia, EX, D37 ....$210.00

Swamp Root, display, cardboard, Thousands Have Kidney Trouble..., 2 3-D boxes flank crowded cityscape, 27x36", EX+, A15 ....$1,050.00

Swan, crate label, pear, white swan on black background, M, D3 ....$4.00

Sweet Bouquet Extra Fine Smoking Tobacco, pocket tin, flat, pictures card game, rounded corners, 1¾x5x3½", rare, EX, A18 ....$550.00

Sweet Burley Dark Tobacco, canister, tin, red with gold tobacco leaf wreath & lettering, round, square lid, 10-lb, 12", G, A2 ....$200.00

Sweet Burley Light Tobacco, canister, yellow with tobacco leaf wreath & red & gold lettering, round, square lid, 10-lb, 12", EX, A2..$110.00

Sweet Caporal, tray, pressed cardboard, 'Compliments Kinney Bros,' pictures lady in red gown by fireplace, oval, 20x11", EX+, A18..$35.00

Sweet Caporal Cigarette, sign, paper, Old Reliable... above satisfied man at dinner table, ca 1898, framed, image: 27½x16", G+, A9 ....$350.00

Sweet Caporal Cigarettes, cabinet card, die-cut cardboard, military man, Standard Of The World..., 15x5", rare, G, A5..$160.00

Sweet Caporal Cigarettes, charger, cardboard, elegant girl in Victorian interior, 20x11", G+, A9 ....$35.00

Sweet Caporal Cigarettes, pocket tin, flat, square, EX, D35 ....$35.00

Sweet Caporal Cigarettes, sign, cardboard, product name above girl clown, Standard For Years below, original frame, 31x22", EX, A21 ....$690.00

Sweet Caporal Cigarettes, sign, cardboard, product name above majorette on cloud of smoke, For 40 Years..., 37x21", G, A6..$165.00

Sweet Cuba Dark Tobacco, store bin, brown, cream & gold graphics, round, NM, A18 ....$150.00

Sweet Cuba Fine Cut, lunch pail, silver-tone metal, product name on red oval with rectangular green border, EX, A18 ....$50.00

Sweet Cuba Fine Cut, store bin, cardboard & tin, tall square with product & company name above & below oval image of fort & ocean, VG+, A18 ....$200.00

Sweet Cuba Fine Cut, store bin, lady in profile on front, product name in red on slant top, VG+, A18.....$360.00

Sweet Cuba Fine Cut Chewing Tobacco, store bin, tin, yellow with red & black product lettering, slanted hinged lid with black knob, 12x14x18", EX, A2..$375.00

Sweet Cuba Light Fine Cut Tobacco, tin, light green with black & red lettering, decorative border, One Pound Full Weight, 2x8" dia, EX+, A18...........$15.00

Sweet Cuba Light Tobacco, store bin, tin, brown & metallic gold canister with square lid, EX, A18...........$120.00

Sweet Girl Fresh Roasted Coffee, container, paper on cardboard, bust portrait of little girl in center, tin pry lid, VG, A3 ....$55.00

Sweet Heart Products, door push, porcelain, red heart shape with white lettering, Hard Wheat Flour, White Corn Flour..., 5x5", NM, D8 ....$365.00

Sweet Lilacs, cigar box label, salesman's sample, photo album with bouquet of flowers at left, EX, A5.....$35.00

Sweet Mist Chewing Tobacco, store bin, tin & cardboard, yellow with red name above & below encircled image of 3 children by fountain, G, A9 ....$85.00

Sweet Mist Chewing Tobacco, store bin, tin & cardboard, yellow with red name above & below encircled image of 3 children by fountain, EX+, A18 ....$200.00

Sweet Mist Fine Cut Chewing Tobacco, pail, oval image of children playing in fountain, 6½x5½", scarce, VG+, A3 ....$55.00

Sweet Patootie Vegetables, crate label, oval vignette of 1920s-style flapper girl, white lettering on blue, Los Angeles, 7x9", M, D12..$5.00

Sweet-Orr Overalls, sign, curved porcelain, product name in white above & below tug-of-war image on yellow, blue ground, 15x20", EX, D38..$600.00

Sweet-Orr Overalls, Pants & Shirts, sign, porcelain, product name above & at right of men playing tug of war, Clothes To Work In at left, 8x30", NM, D8.........$650.00

Sweet-Orr Overalls-Pants-Shirts, sign, cardboard, product name above men playing tug of war, Have Stood The Test For 50 Years below, 12x22", VG, A1 ....$185.00

Sweet-Orr Pants, Overalls & Shirts, sign, porcelain, product name surrounds oval image of men playing tug of war, red & black on cream, 10x24", EX+, A1.....$315.00

Sweet-Orr Union Made Shirts, box, product name above & below Deco-style image of men playing tug of war, 11x19x2½", EX, D8 ....$150.00

Sweetie, sign, tin, Drink above Sweetie on wavy band & circle above tilted bottle, cream ground with orange border, 12x5", NM, D8 ....$110.00

Sweetie, sign, tin, Drink Sweetie on circle & wavy band in center, For Real Pleasure below, 20x24", NM, D30 ....$125.00

Swift's Oz Peanut Butter, pail, white, red & yellow with cartoon images, lettering on red slip lid, 2-lb 2-oz, EX+, A3 ....$25.00

Swift's Premium Bacon, sign, tin, Three Convenient Ways above 3 product packs, product name on blue below, 1930s-40s, 6½x9½", NM, A13 ....$375.00

Swift's Premium Ham, sign, cardboard, Broil Or Fry...Without Parboiling, shows packaged products & little chef frying, 1900, 18x10", NM, A3 ....$730.00

Swift's Premium Ham, stickpin, shaped like a ham, EX, A20 ....$15.00

Swift's Pride Cleanser, can, sample, cardboard & tin, with contents, 2½", NM, A7 ....$40.00

Swift's Pride Soap, sign, curved porcelain, product name above bar of soap & Save Your Clothes..., blue, black & white, 14x11", G+, A9 ....$350.00

Swift's Washing Powder, sign, paper, metal strips, ...For General Use... above black family in cart racing past plantation, 42x27", EX, A2..............................$2,860.00

Swifty Genuine Ethyl, pump sign, porcelain, product name & Ethyl logo in yellow & black, red ground with yellow border, 10x12", NM, D8 ....$225.00

Syke's Comfort Powder, tin, oval image of 2 small girls with product name above, shaker top, 4x2¼", EX, A18 ....$215.00

Symington's Tomato Soup, postcard, tomatoes & bowl of steaming soup flanked by lettering, EX+, D26 .....$40.00

Syrup of Figs, mirror, etched glass with silver & gold, ...Nature's Own True Laxative..., 12x12", VG, A9..$450.00

 **T**

T Mongenon Pure Spices, store bin, tin, oval portraits & product name above 6 side-by-side spice compartments, 21x24x14", G, A9....................................$775.00

T&T (Tried & True) Coffee, tin, red with black lettering outlined in gold, slip lid, 1-lb, VG+, A18............$100.00

Ta-che, crate label, California orange, Indian in profile on yellow background, Santa Paula, 10x11", M, D12..$30.00

Table King Coffee, tin, ...Makes A Good Meal Better, pry lid, rare, EX+, A3 ....$85.00

Table King Coffee, tin, pry lid, EX, A3 ....$60.00

Table King Tea/Green Japan, tin, picture of Japan on back, screw top, 8-oz, NM, A3 ....$50.00

Tacoma Brewing Co, note holder, celluloid with metal hook, For Your Beverage Wants Call...Main 2835 in blue on white, EX, A11 ....$50.00

Tacoma Cigars, sign, paper, product name above Indian princess with feathers & jewels in her hair, framed, image: 20x12", VG+, A9......................................$650.00

Taka-Cola, tray, deep-dish, lady holding bottle at 12 o'clock, ...Every Hour, Take No Other on rim, 13" dia, VG, A9 ....$225.00

Talisman, crate label, California orange, 3 talisman roses on blue & black background, Redlands, 10x11", M, D3 ....$2.00

Tally-Ho Beer & Ale, tray, stagecoach scene, white, red & black, 12", EX+, D7 ....$40.00

Tally-Ho Beer/Ale/Porter, tray, deep-dish, shows horse-drawn coach with Tally-Ho Beer in script, white background, 12" dia, EX+, A8 ....$40.00

Tam o' Shanter Ale/American Brewing Co, sign, light-up, reverse-painted glass, Ale Sir! above Tam o' Shanter On Tap & Scotsman, 1930s-40s, framed, VG+, A8 ......$75.00

Tam o' Shanter Ale/Apollo Lager Beer, sign, reverse glass, white with red Two Fine Brews above Tam o' Shanter... on black & Apollo... on red, 8x16", EX, A19................................$55.00

Tampanola, cigar box label, inner lid, goddess holding flowers & tobacco, 6x9", M, D5..........................$25.00

Tannenbaum Beer, label, Marathon City Brewing Co, U-type permit number, Internal Revenue Tax Paid statement, 1933-36, 12-oz, M, A10 ....$25.00

Tannhaeuser/Claussen Brewing Association, drinking glass, straight-sided with gold rim (worn), etched logo & lettering, 3½", EX, A8................................$65.00

Target Cigarette Case, pocket tin, vertical, red with name on black triangle above bull's-eye with arrow, 'It's Blended' below, short, EX, A18 ....$25.00

Tarr Beer, label, Tarr Brewing Co, U-type permit number, Internal Revenue Tax Paid statement, 1933-36, 12-oz, M, A10................................$15.00

Tartan, crate label, California lemon, pictures a lemon on green & blue plaid pattern, Corona, 9x12", M, D12..$3.00

Tavern Beer, can, cone-top, coach scene above product name, M, A8 ....$120.00

Taylors Natural Leaf, tobacco tag, EX, D35 ....$3.00

Taystee Bread, end label, features Range Rider & Dick West, orange border, EX, D29 ....$10.00

TÉ Tigre Tobacco, store bin, rectangular with front & back showing tigers trying to kill an elephant, woman on each end, 5x5x9", EX, A18 ....$125.00

Tech Beer, sign, self-framed tin, Too Good To Forget, outdoor scene with hunter behind dog, 18½x26½", VG, A6 ....$140.00

Tech Beer, tray, cream, black & red, 12", NM, D7 .....$25.00

Tech Premium Beer, display, plaster relief, circle logo at left of 3 men standing at bar with bartender, 10x14", VG, A8 ....$100.00

Teddy Bears Brand Lemons, sign, paper, comical image of 2 bears carrying branch of lemons, Francesco Zito... below, framed, image: 18x12", G, A9 ....$500.00

Teddy Cigarettes, pocket tin, flat, black & white diagonal bands with Roosevelt's image & product name, holds 50 cigarettes, VG+, A18 ....$80.00

Teem, sign, tin, Enjoy on black emblem above lemon & tilted bottle, An Ice Clear Lemon-Lime Drink below, 1963, 19x27", NM, D21 ....$50.00

Teem, sign, tin, Enjoy Teem in green on white, A Lemon-Lime Drink & lemon on green at right, 12x32", NM+, D30 ....$125.00

Teen Queen Mustard Seed, tin, 2¾", NM, A7 ....$50.00

Teen Queen Nutmeg, tin, 2¼", NM, A7 ....$40.00

Telechron, clock, light-up, reverse-painted glass, dots around lettered square field, brown & white, wood frame, 16x15", EX, A18 ....$200.00

Tellings Ice Cream, sign, die-cut cardboard stand-up, photo image of child with ice-cream cone leaning on lettered table, 14", NM, A2 ....$175.00

Temple Bar New Cut, tin, white & black lettering & graphics on red, ¾x6½x3", EX+, A18 ....$65.00

Temple Bar Wave Cut Tobacco, box, horizontal, G+, D35 ....$25.00

Tenk's Clipper Tools & Cutlery, baseball score keeper/fob, celluloid, mechanical, red, black & white, round, EX+, A11 ....$45.00

Texaco, ashtray, Division Sales Meeting, January 9, 1968, china, logo above company logo, green on cream, 7" dia, EX+, A6 ....$45.00

Texaco, ashtray/thermometer, metal with paper thermometer, logo in center, 3½", VG, A6 ....$70.00

Texaco, attendant's cap, green, black & red, VG+, A6 .$210.00

Texaco, book, 'Petroleum & It's Products,' Texas Co, black & white photos of Texaco plants, ships, etc, 1910, NM, A6 ....$75.00

Texaco, booklet, 'Texaco Helps,' black & white photos inside, 10x13¾", NM, A6 ....$200.00

Texaco, booklet, 'The Last Question Answered,' guide that shows how to select the right lubricants for your car, 6x3", NM, A6 ....$50.00

Texaco, brochure, 'Painted Bulletin Designs,' Spring 1983, several designs with some in color, EX, A6 ....$60.00

Texaco, calendar, 1940, Hustling To Serve You, litho of Hal Roach's Our Gang, Texas Co & logo above pad, framed, 29x21", EX, A6 ....$850.00

Texaco, gas globe, milk glass star shape with fired-on red, green & black, made for Australian market, 1930s, 17x16x8", EX, A6 ....$8,500.00

Texaco, gas globe, red star logo with green T, Texaco & border in black, 1-pc, EX, A1 ....$600.00

Texaco, gas globe, Texaco above star logo, red, green & black, red ripple body with copper base, 13½" dia, NM, A6 ....$2,200.00

Texaco, gas globe, Texaco above star logo, red, green & black on white, Gill body with metal base, 13½" dia, EX, A6 ....$400.00

Texaco, lamp, cast iron, pair of black Scotty dogs on base embossed Listen, pleated shade, 1930s, 12½x8½" base, NM, A1 ....$455.00

Texaco, map, 'Tour Florida With Texaco,' colorful image of 2 men conversing in front of car on front, NM, A6 ...$250.00

Texaco, pump sign, large Texaco & star logo, rounded for post, 15" dia, VG, A6 ....$180.00

Texaco, restroom key tags, marked Ladies & Men with 6-sided Texaco logo, red & black on white, 5½", NOS, M, A1 ....$135.00

Texaco, sign, cardboard, for Metropolitan Opera Broadcasts, opera scene above The Texas Co & star logo, 20x18", NM, D30 ....$55.00

Texaco, sign, porcelain, For Your Safety above No Smoking & Stop Motor in bold letters, 8x13", NM+, D11 .....$40.00

Texaco, sign, porcelain, No Smoking in black flanked by red, green & black star logo, 1963, 4x23", EX+, A6 ....$210.00

Texaco, sign, porcelain, red star logo with green T on white with black border, dated 10-8-46, 8" dia, NM+, NOS, A1 ....$375.00

Texaco, sign, porcelain, red star logo with green T on white with black border, dated 4-30, 8" dia, EX+, A1 ....$350.00

Texaco, sign, stained-glass panel, star logo above large T, Reg TM below, 21¾" dia, EX+, A1 ....$1,500.00

Texaco, toy truck, Buddy-L, red with Texaco decals, 24" long, VG+, A6 ....$120.00

Texaco, winter cap, green, black & red, EX+, A6 ......**$80.00**

Texaco Aircraft Engine, can, 2-color background with product name above winged star logo, red, white & green, 1-qt, NM, A1 ....**$160.00**

Texaco Axle Grease, cup, green with red star logo & black lettering, Texas Co, Port Arthur Texas on lid, 1910s, 1-lb, VG, A1 ....**$325.00**

Texaco Chassis Lubricant W, can, product lettering on band above star logo, green, red & white, screw lid, full, 3-lb, NOS, A1 ....**$120.00**

Texaco Diesel Chief (Diesel Fuel), pump sign, porcelain, star logo over design of fuel spraying from nozzle above product name, 18x12", NM, D8 ....**$300.00**

Texaco Diesel Chief (Diesel Fuel), pump sign, porcelain, star logo over design of fuel spraying from nozzle above product name, 18x12", VG, A1 ....**$120.00**

Texaco Diesel Chief L, pump sign, porcelain, star logo over design of fuel spraying from nozzle, dated 3-10-62, 18x12", scarce, NM, A1 ....**$530.00**

Texaco Diesel Fuel, gas globe, star logo over design of fuel spraying from bottle, plastic body, 13½" dia, NM, A6 ....**$1,450.00**

Texaco Diesel Fuel 2, pump sign, porcelain, star logo over design of fuel spraying from nozzle, dated 3-4-54, 18x12", EX, A6 ....**$210.00**

Texaco Farm Lubricants, sign, porcelain, star logo above Farm Lubricants Sold Here, dated 10-8-46, 30x42", VG+, A6 ....**$200.00**

Texaco Fire-Chief, banner, cloth, A Greater... above fireman's hat & lettered circle, 100% Anti-Knock, No Extra Price, 30x17", VG+, A6 ....**$160.00**

Texaco Fire-Chief Gasoline, pump sign, porcelain, product name above fireman's hat & star logo, dated 3-10-62, 12x8", NM, D8 ....**$250.00**

Texaco Fuel Chief 1 (Diesel Fuel), pump sign, porcelain, logo over design of fuel spraying from nozzle, dated 3-1-62, 18x12", rare yellow variation, NM, A6 ...$1,700.00

Texaco Gaviota Gasoline Plant, sign, porcelain, star logo at left of lettering, 12x48", NM+, D11 ....**$140.00**

Texaco Kerosine, sign, tin, product name above line of flames, Clear Burning below, marked AM 2-58, 12x20", VG+, A6 ....**$130.00**

Texaco Lubrication Guide, full of text, 9½x4", NM, A6 ..**$50.00**

Texaco Marfak Lubrication, sign, tin, Marfak on diagonal center band, star logo above, Lubrication below, dated 11-55, 24x40", NOS, NM, A1 ....**$300.00**

Texaco Marine Lubricants, booklet, black & white photos of ships, 1926, 8x5½", NM, A6 ....**$175.00**

Texaco Marine Lubricants, sign, porcelain, pictures 3 types of boats at left of product & company name, 15x30", NM, A6 ....**$1,500.00**

Texaco Marine Motor Oil, can, product name above ocean scene & star logo, birds flying around top, Texas Co, 1-qt, 5½x4" dia, VG, A6 ....**$150.00**

Texaco Marine Motor Oil, sign, porcelain, logo & product name above ocean liners & various boats, birds in flight above, 2-sided, 11x21", G+, A6 ....**$650.00**

Texaco Marine White Gasoline, pump sign, porcelain, star logo on ship's wheel above Marine White Gasoline, green & black ground, 18x12", NM, D8 ....**$750.00**

Texaco Motor Oil, blotter, early car with passengers & star logo on side, country town scene in background, 3x6", NOS, A6 ....**$140.00**

Texaco Motor Oil, blotter, pictures attendant pointing out different brands, Let Us Tell You What Brand..., 3x6", NOS, A6 ....**$120.00**

Texaco Motor Oil, blotter, pictures man putting oil in woman's car, The Easy Pour Two Quart Can... upper left, 3x6", NOS, A6 ....$110.00

Texaco Motor Oil, booklet, 'For Ford Owners,' shows oil pouring from container, Important! on white diagonal band, 1925, 6x3½", NM, A6 ....**$95.00**

Texaco Motor Oil, brochure, 'Modern Packaging,' shows 2 tilted cans, black & white photos & sketches inside, 1935, 12x9", EX+, A6 ....**$220.00**

Texaco Motor Oil, brochure, 'The Tourist's Companion,' Easy-Pour Can... at left of hand holding product at top, map inside, NOS, A6 ....**$120.00**

Texaco Motor Oil, can, Improved... above encircled star logo, red, white & green, 5-qt, 9½x7" dia, G, A6 ..**$15.00**

Texaco Motor Oil, pail, star logo above product name & Insulated Against Heat, Against Cold, wire bail with wooden handle, 5-gal, VG+, A6 ....**$20.00**

Texaco Motor Oil, sign, flange, die-cut, Clean, Clear, Golden..., star logo & oil pouring above, rounded top, 23x18", EX+, A6 ....**$160.00**

Texaco Motor Oil, sign, porcelain, Easy Pour can above oil pouring from hand-held can, 2 Qts Texaco Motor Oil below, 16x15", EX, A6 ....**$1,400.00**

Texaco Motor Oil, sign, porcelain, Free Crankcase Service... at top, oil pouring above star logo & lettering on octagon, 30x30", EX, A6 ....**$300.00**

Texaco Motor Oil, sign, tin, Stays Full Longer left of smiling man & tilted can of New Texaco Motor Oil, dated E-2-37, 18x30", VG+, A6 ....**$325.00**

Texaco Motor Oil, see also Golden Texaco Motor Oil

Texaco Motor Oil F For Ford Cars, blotter, gas station scene with Your Ford & oil pouring from can at top, product name below, 3½x6", NOS, A6.............$120.00

Texaco Motor Oil Free Crankcase Service, sign, porcelain, oil pouring over Clean, Clear, Golden & logo on black octagon on white with red border, 30x30", NM, A1..$450.00

Texaco Outboard Lubricants, sign, aluminum, product lettering on white T-shaped field flanked by logos on striped fields, dated 3-58, 10x20", EX, A............$220.00

Texaco Outboard Motor Oil, bottle, green glass with red & white painted label, product lettering above star logo, boat scene below, 1-pt, NM, A1 ....$55.00

Texaco Petroleum Products, bottle, clear glass with red, green & black painted label, 6¼", NM, A6.........$375.00

Texaco Products, brochure, pie-shaped image on cover with 6 different pictures, star logo in center, color pgs, 1932, 11x8", NM, A6...$300.00

Texaco Products, tea towel, linen, farm scene with Texaco truck traveling toward farm house, 1940s, 27½x15½", NM, A6...$145.00

Texaco Refrigerating Machinery Lubrication, booklet, black & white pictures, 1925, 33 pgs, 8x5½", NM, A6...$75.00

Texaco Roofing, blotter, pictures man pointing to product with factory scene in background, text at right, 3½x6", NOS, A6 ....$80.00

Texaco Sky Chief Gasoline, pump sign, porcelain, product name on band above star logo, Gasoline below, 18x12", EX, A6...$75.00

Texaco Sky Chief Gasoline, pump sign, porcelain, product name on band above star logo, ...Super-Charged With Petrox below, 22x12", EX, A6 ....$110.00

Texaco Sky Chief Marine, pump sign, porcelain, Sky Chief Marine on large band above star logo, Super-Charged With Petrox below, 18x12", NM, D8...$650.00

Texaco Sky Chief Su-preme Gasoline, pump sign, porcelain, product name on band above star logo, ...Super-Charged with Petrox below, 18x12", NM, A6.......$80.00

Texaco Spica Oil, can, shows product name & star logo, vertical with small round lid, 1-pt, VG+, A18.......$50.00

Texaco Starfak Grease, pail, product lettering on white panel above star logo, green, red, white & black, slip lid & bail, 5-lb, EX, A1 ....$90.00

Texaco Thuban Compound, brochure, red, gray & green pictures, copyright 1920, 6¼x3½", NM, A6 ....$85.00

Texaco Tractor Lubricants, foldout, shows models & what kind of lubricant to use, 6¼x3" folded, NM, A6....$80.00

Texaco Valor Motor Oil, can, product name above star logo, screw cap, 2-gal, 11x8½", VG, A6 ....$55.00

Texas Gas Corporation, sign, porcelain, elongated diamond shape, red, white & blue, 7x12", EX+, A6..............$125.00

Texas Neon Adv Co, sign, porcelain, inverted triangle with black lettering on yellow with black border, 7", NM, D8..$75.00

Texas Pride Beer, label, San Antonio Brewing Co, U-type Permit number, Internal Revenue Tax Paid statement, 1933-36, 12-oz, M, A10..................................$20.00

Texas Pride Beer, tray, image of a Texas city on horizon, Keg & Bottle & Texas' Own on yellow rim, 11x13", NM+, A19..$240.00

Texas Punch, door push plate, tin, Hello! You'll Love It, tilted bottle on yellow background, 1940s-50s, NM+, A13 ....$150.00

Texcomo Coffee, tin, product name & swastica within scroll design flanked by This Symbol Stands For Purity, press lid, 8x6" dia, G, D14...................................$150.00

The Enchanter, cigar box label, romantic couple, 7x14", EX+, D9..$20.00

The News, cigar box label, outer, ...Established 1842, Dallas & Galveston above building with horse-drawn carriages in front, A5..$60.00

The Queen, tobacco box label, name above queen's image, 1882, Knapp litho, 14", NM, A7.................$60.00

The Sun Garter, display cabinet, oak with convex glass front, Pat'd 1902, advertising on leg with garter, 11", EX, A12..$430.00

Thea Nectar Tea, see Atlantic & Pacific Tea Co

Thermo Alcohol Anti-Freeze, can, Publicker Commercial Alcohol Co, red, black & cream, pour spout & handle, 1-gal, 9½x9½", G+, A6..$20.00

Thermo Anti-Freeze, can, prancing snowman above product name, 1945, 1-qt, VG+, A6 ....$65.00

Thistle Brand Pure Lard, pail, product name above & below logo on yellow design, white background, press lid & bail, 6x5½" dia, VG, D21............................$45.00

Thomas J Webb Coffee, tin, small portrait & product name on large center band, pry lid, with contents, 1920s, 1-lb, EX, A3..$65.00

Thomas J Webb Coffee, tin, The Winning Cup on band above coffee cup, key-wind lid, 1-lb, EX+, A3 ....$25.00

Thomas Moore Whiskey, tray, nude girl reclining on red blanket in woodland scene, Take A Little Moore... on rim, 10" dia, rare, G, A9......................................$600.00

Thomas Ryan's Ales & Lager, tray, porcelain, Indian chief in center, Consumer's Brewing Co, Syracuse NY, red, white & blue, oval, 13x16", VG+, A9.................$400.00

Thompson Boats, catalog, 1937, 32 pgs, EX, D17....$60.00

Thompson Products, display, 3-D composition, squatting Indian pointing to logo on teepee, product name on base, 17x19½", VG+, A6....................................$120.00

Thompson's Malted Milk, canister, porcelain, dome top with knob, 9½x7" dia, NM, A18.............**$500.00**

Thorsen Ice Cream, sign, porcelain, ...Ellsworth, Maine, blue on cream, 17x24", EX, D8 ....**$150.00**

Three B & Royal Polish, alarm clock, twins holding oversized product cans on round face, ring handle at top, footed, ca 1895, EX, A2......................................**$95.00**

Three Castles Cigarettes, display, wood & cardboard, name on marquee above displayed product pack on stand, 11x10x3", EX, A18 ....**$45.00**

Three Crow Ginger/Atlantic Spice Co, tin, oval image of 3 perched crows, with contents, 1.50-oz, NM+, A3...**$60.00**

Three Feathers Choice Granulated Plug Cut, pocket tin, vertical, 3 feathers in crown on circle, yellow & red background, EX, A18 ....**$260.00**

Three Kings Cigarettes, sign, paper, biblical kings with maids in laden boat, Wm L Kimball & Co, 21½x17½", G+, A9..**$200.00**

Three RRR's Motor Oil, can, product name above encircled horse head, Russell Oil Co, green, black & white, 1-qt, rare, VG+, A3..........................**$375.00**

Three States Mixture, tin, Kentucky, Virginia & Louisiana on banner around 3 coins, Harry Weissinger Tob Co, square corners, 2x5x3", EX+, A18 ....**$60.00**

Three Twins Smoking Tobacco, see 3 Twins on page 283

Thresher Hard Oil, tin, lettering above & below threshing machine, Standard Oil Co at bottom, black on yellow, square, 25-lb, VG, A1 ....**$50.00**

Thumper Sun Cured Tobacco, pouch, cloth, NM, A7 ..**$5.00**

Tick-Tock Peeled Apricots, label, apricots above name flanked by bust portrait of girl, 8½x6", NM, A7 .....**$8.00**

Tide Water Approved Dealer, sign, porcelain in cast-iron frame, black on white with orange border, curved bottom, 2-sided, 1930s, 21x18", NM, A1 ....**$675.00**

Tide Water Associated Oil Co, plaque, bronze with raised lettering & winged A logo, Our Creed..., stair-step relief on border, 11½x9", EX, A1................................**$250.00**

Tide Water Associated Oil Co, pump sign, porcelain, company name with Tydol Veedol logo, rectangular with slightly V-shaped bottom, 8x11", EX+, A1 .**$600.00**

Tidex, gas globe lenses, pair of blue lenses with black Tidex on thick white band, thin vertical band forms cross, 15", NM, A1 ....**$325.00**

Tidex Motor Oil, can, Tidex on encircled plus sign above 'Full Bodied' Motor Oil, screw cap, 2-gal, 11x8½", VG+, A6 ....**$80.00**

Tiger Bright Chewing Tobacco, canister, tiger's face on gold circle, product name above & below, red background, tall rectangle with slip lid, G, A2 .....**$110.00**

Tiger Bright Chewing Tobacco, tin, tiger's face on gold circle, red background with gold crosshatch design, 4x6", EX, A1..**$40.00**

Tiger Bright Chewing Tobacco, tin, tiger's face on gold circle, red background with gold crosshatch design, 4x6", G, A18..**$15.00**

Tiger Bright Sweet Chewing Tobacco, pocket tin, short vertical, running tiger & 15¢ above product name, P Lorillard & Co, EX, A18......................................**$170.00**

Tiger Dark Chewing Tobacco, canister, tiger's face on gold circle, product name above & below, black background, round with slip lid, EX, A18..................**$440.00**

Tiger Dark Chewing Tobacco, tin, tiger's face on gold circle, black background with gold crosshatch design, 4x6", NM, A18..**$75.00**

Tiger Rolled White Oats/Quaker Oats Co, container, inset of roaring tiger in center, 6-oz, VG+, A3...**$165.00**

Tillman Quality Coffee, tin, Quality on red emblem in center, key-wind lid (unopened), 1-lb, EX+, A3 ..**$80.00**

Time Premium Gasoline, pump sign, porcelain, U-shaped with Time above clock showing 10 'til 1, Premium Gasoline below, 14x9", NM+, A1 ....**$330.00**

Time Super Gasoline, pump sign, porcelain, U-shaped with Time above clock showing 10 'til 1, Super Gasoline below, 14x9", NM+, A1................................**$350.00**

Times Square Smoking Mixture, pocket tin, vertical, night scene at Times Square, ...Mellowed In Wood, slip lid, 4½x3", VG, A9 ....**$250.00**

Times Square Smoking Mixture, pocket tin, vertical, night scene at Times Square, ...Mellowed In Wood, slip lid, 4½x3", EX+, A18 ....$310.00

Timur Brand Coffee, tin, gold product name above night scene with Mongol warrior on horse, pry lid, 3-lb, EX, A18 ....$430.00

Tintex, display cabinet, tin, Tints & Dyes Anything Any Color... & product boxes above woman using product, 23x22x7", G, A9..$100.00

Tiolene Motor Oil, can, with contents, ...100% Super-Pennsylvania above target logo, Pure Oil Co, screw lid & handle, 11x8", EX, A6 ....$55.00

Tiolene Motor Oil, oil drum with pump, heavy metal, decals with 100% Pure... & product name with target logo, 54x23" dia, EX, A6 ....$150.00

Tiopet Motor Oil, can, 3-banded field with Tiopet above encircled Indian chief, Motor Oil below, red, white & blue, 1-qt, EX, A1 ....$460.00

Tip Top Bock Beer, label, Tip-Top Brewing Co, Internal Revenue Tax Paid statement, 1933-50, 12-oz, NM, A10 ....$18.00

Tip Top Bread, end label, black & white image of Cisco Kid on horse, Cisco Kid's Choice, red border, EX, D29 .$10.00

Tip Top Bread, end label, black & white photo image of Gil Hodges, red border, EX, D29.........................$150.00

Tip Top Bread, end label, features Gene Autry, yellow border, EX, D29 ....$10.00

Tip Top Bread, wallet, tortoise shell, full of movie star photos, EX, D6 ....$20.00

Tip-Top Bread, spinner, plastic & paper, Enriched Tip-Top Is Better Bread, EX, A20 ....$6.00

Tipper's 3 Tips! sign, paper, raging bull attacking Quack Medicines with various Tippers products in the foreground, image: 45x34", G, A9 ....$200.00

Tivoli Brewing Co, clothes/shoe brush, slight hourglass shape with paper label showing man in knickers pouring a glass of beer, 7", VG, A8 ....$35.00

TJ Martin Brewer, sign, paper, Successor To George W Gray..., 1864, oval, decorative frame, 12x14", EX+, A19 ....$500.00

Toddle House Restaurant, plate, chef motif & Good As The Rest, 7" dia, EX, D25.....................................$48.00

Tokheim Gasoline Pumps, sign, porcelain, Quality on extended T in Tokheim, Authorized Service, white letters & border on red, 13x19½", EX, A6 ....$350.00

Tokio Cigarettes, sign, die-cut cardboard, girl holding box of cigarettes, ...10 For 5¢ below, framed, 19½x14", G, A9 ....$85.00

Toledo, tobacco tag, pictures a frog, oval, EX, D35...$10.00

Tom Cigars, box label set, black man playing banjo, 2-pc, VG+, A5 ....$60.00

Tom Hendricks, cigar box label, printer's proof, portrait on shaded ground, Wm A Stickney Cigar Co, 3 pcs on 1 sheet, VG, A5...$30.00

Tom Sawyer Apparel For Real Boys, sign, counter-top, composition, image of Tom Sawyer painting fence, 6½x21½", VG, A9..$75.00

Tom's, sign, embossed tin, Time Out For Tom's above 3 product packs on red, white & black background, 28x20", NM, A13..............................$500.00

Tom's Toasted Peanuts 5¢, store jar, glass with painted lettering, with lid, NM, A13................................$55.00

Tomahawk, tobacco tag, die-cut, P Lorillard Co, EX, D35...$6.00

Tomahawk Beer, label, Garden City Brewery, Internal Revenue Tax Paid statement, 1933-50, 1-qt, M, A10 ....$18.00

Tommy Atkins, cigar box label, outer, soldier standing at attention, 1910, NM, A5.....................................$35.00

Tommy Slick, cigar box label, outer, cat sitting next to cigar box, 4½x4½", G, D5 ....$20.00

Ton-Gors, sign, die-cut porcelain, hog & hens surrounded by Protector Sales... on red, ...For Sale Here above & below, 36", EX, A1 ....$275.00

Tonka Smoking Mixture, pocket tin, flat, large lettering above scene with 2 soldiers by tent, McAlpin Tobacco Co, rounded corners, EX+, A18......$200.00

Tooke Kum-Sealed Handkerchief, display, wood with glass front, back opens to fill 5 compartments, gold & green with white lettering, 12x22", EX, A6........$140.00

Tootsie Rolls, see Nut Tootsie Rolls

Top Card, crate label, California pear, ace of spades showing on stack of 4 cards, blue background, Suisun, 8x11", M, D12 ....$2.00

Top Peak, crate label, California apple, silhouette of San Gorgonio Peak, Redlands, 9x11", M, D12..............$2.00

Topic Cigars, tin, wood-grain with embellished image of couple, B/B on diagonal black & white shield below, 7x6x5", VG, A18 ....$15.00

Topsall Beer/Bismark Brewing Co Ltd, label, ...Tops In Beer on red upper left of illustrated hand-held glass on black, 64-oz, VG+, A19 ....$15.00

Torrey Safety Razor, tin, flat, green & gold, Blade Box above name on embellished scroll, decorative border, ¼x1x2", EX, D37, minimum value $120.00

Tortoise Shell Cut Roll, tobacco box, white with red name above & below fishermen on beach, rounded corners, scarce American version, VG, A18..........$55.00

Tortoise Shell Smoking Mixture, tin, product name arched above & below turtle on tortoise shell background, rounded corners, 3½x5", EX+, A3..........$45.00

Totem Tobacco, pocket tin, vertical oval, orange with blue name above & below totem pole & pipe-smoking Indian, EX+, A18 ....$1,200.00

Touchet Valley, crate label, apple, apples & ranch scene with blue border, M, D3 ....$2.00

Towel's Log Cabin Maple Syrup, tin, sample, cabin shape, 2½x1¼x1⅞", G, D37.................................$400.00

Towel's Log Cabin Syrup, bank, tin, cabin shape with mother & children at doorway & window, 12-oz, EX+, A18 ....$72.00

Towel's Log Cabin Syrup, pull toy, tin, cabin shape, Log Cabin Express, 5x4½x3½", VG, A9 ....$350.00

Towel's Log Cabin Syrup, tin, cabin shape with people seated on bench waiting to see Dr RU Well, EX+, A3 ....$300.00

Towel's Log Cabin Syrup, tin, red cabin shape with white product name, 12-oz, EX, A18.................................$40.00

Toxaway Coffee, tin, sample, product name above & below lake scene, square, round lid, 3x2½x2½", EX, D37.................................$200.00

Trailing Arbutus Talc, tin, sample, oval with shaker top, 3x1½", EX, A18 ....$60.00

Train Master Cigars, pocket tin, vertical, white with product name above & below yellow ticket, gold lid, EX+, A18 ....$80.00

Transo Envelope Co, pocket mirror, celluloid, Transo in diagonal script above Original One-Piece Window..., black & red, round, EX, A11 ....$10.00

Trapuhu Tea, tin, green with red lettering above white horizontal bust image of Indian chief, square with slip lid, 1-lb, EX, A2 ....$265.00

Traveler Leading Cigar, canister, The National Smoke above Traveler surrounded by fancy scroll design, NM, A3 ....$22.00

Traveler's Insurance Co, letter folder, tin, Kellogg & Bulkeley, Manufacturer of Tin Signs on reverse, gold on red, 2-sided, 13x3", G+, A9.................................$225.00

Traveller's Club Cigars, box label set, group of men conversing with luggage behind them, 2-pc, EX, A5..$110.00

Treasure Island Honey, tin, product name on bands above cartoon image of boy & girl on island digging for treasure, pry lid, 5x4" dia, EX+, A18 ....$30.00

Trenton Old Stock Beer/Peoples Brewing Co, tray, deep-dish, orange & white product name on white center, company name on rim, 12" dia, EX, A19.......$80.00

Triangle Brand Shoes, clicker, tin, 2", NM, A7.........$12.00

Triangle Club Ground Spice White Pepper, container, cardboard, product name on inverted triangle on lined background, Montgomery Ward Co, 4-oz, NM, A3..........$35.00

Triangle Filling Station, calendar, 1944, embossed hunting scene, full pad, 15½x9½", VG, A6.................................$40.00

Triple A Artesian Water, sign, porcelain, product name on emblem above Pure, Soft, Delicious, 24x30", EX, D11.................................$135.00

Triple AAA Root Beer, sign, self-framed tin, Just Say & product name on emblem with diagonal corners at left of tilted bottle, 33x57", EX, A1 ....$125.00

Triple AAA Root Beer, sign, self-framed tin, Just Say & product name on emblem with diagonal corners at left of tilted bottle, 19x28", NM+, A1 ....$170.00

Triple AAA Root Beer, sign, tin, die-cut bottle, 1940s-50s, 45x12", NM, A13.................................$190.00

Triple Cola, sign, tin, It's Bigger It's Better at left of tilted bottle, 16 Ounces in lower right, 32x12", NM+, D30 ....$75.00

Triple Ex Family, sign, cardboard, Triple Ex Family above girl with basket of bread, The Standard Flour... below, framed, 23x16", VG+, A13 ....$375.00

Triple 16 Cola, sign, embossed tin, product name on white circle on red field pointing down to tilted bottle on white, 31x11", NM+, A19 ....$25.00

Tripoli Quinine Tonic, sign, cardboard, Tripoli above Quinine Tonic on band above Has Merits Of Its Own...For Sale Here, 5x8½", NM, A7 ....$15.00

Trisco Flour, thermometer & decal under silvered glass, Famous Because It's Good above bulb, factory scene & flour bag, 14x10", NM, A3 ....$100.00

Triton 76 Premium Motor Oil, sign, porcelain, Only 2 Changes A Year, tilted oil can on red above white lettering on blue, 2-sided, 30" dia, EX, A1.................................$800.00

Triton 76 Union, sign, porcelain, Extra Margin of Safety, tilted oil can with shadow above, 2-sided, 30" dia, VG+, A1 ....$325.00

Triumph Cycle Bath, can, shows man looking at motorcycle in claw-footed bathtub, lettering above & below, blue & white, full, 1-pt, NM, A1 ....$80.00

Trixy Root Beer, alarm clock, white numbered face showing picaninny's face, twin bells atop round footed case, Lux Clock Co, 1942, EX, A2 ....$410.00

Trojan Motor Oil, can, white silhouette profile of Trojan head above product name on circle, white on red & black, 1-qt, EX+, A $35.00

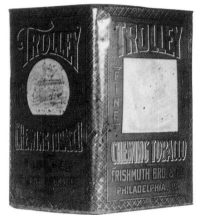

Trolley Chewing Tobacco, store bin, square with gold lettering on dark blue background, gold checked border, very rare, VG, A18 ....$1,150.00

Trommer's Genuine Ale, sign, tin on cardboard, white product name on green background, beveled edge, 6x9", VG+, A19 ....$75.00

Trommer's Malt Beer, sign, tin on cardboard, gold product name with black outline on red, beveled edge, 6½x9½", EX, A19 ....$50.00

Trommer's Malt Beer, tap knob, black ball shape with white lettering on blue enamel insert, EX, A8.....$20.00

Trommer's Malt Beer, tray, deep-dish, product name flanks 2 full pilsner glasses on bar, 12" dia, VG+, A19 ....$15.00

Trommer's Malt Beer & Genuine Ale, calendar, 1939, animated depiction of elves with bottles & cans above full pad on green background, 12x9", EX, A8.....$45.00

Trommer's Prize Winners, tray, deep-dish, pictures 4 different bottles of brew, pre-1920s, oval, G+, A19$145.00

Trommer's White Label Beer, tray, pictures a beer glass, white & brown, 12", NM, D7 ....$28.00

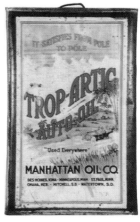

Trop-Artic Auto Oil, can, split image of arctic scene & tropical scene, Manhattan Oil Co, 5-gal, EX+, A6......$800.00

Trop-Artic Auto Oil, cup, tin, split image with touring car in arctic scene & in tropical scene, ca 1915, 2½x4" dia, VG, A6 ....$140.00

Trop-Artic Motor Oil, thermometer, wood, star logo & Your Motor Deserves above bulb, product name below, 21x6½", scarce, VG, A6.............$85.00

Trophy Balanced 40 Below Motor Oil, can, Trophy in curved letters over loving cup above rest of product name lettered over winter scene, 1-qt, NM, A1..$490.00

Trophy Beer, can, cone-top, Internal Revenue Tax Paid statement, 12-oz, EX, A19 ....$60.00

Trophy Coffee, tin, B Trade Mark logo above product name, pry lid, EX, A3.............$55.00

Trophy HD Motor Oil, can, Trophy in curved letters over loving cup above HD Motor Oil, red & blue on white, 1-qt, NM, A1 ....$110.00

Tropical Curry, tin, paper label, 3¼", NM, A7.........$12.00

Tropical Ginger, tin, paper label, 2¾", NM, A7........$12.00

Trout-Line Smoking Tobacco, pocket container, cardboard & tin, vertical, product name above & below encircled fisherman, green ground, EX+, A18....$485.00

Tru-Ade, sign, flange, Drink A Better Beverage on wavy band below tilted bottle & circle logo, 1951, 14x20", NM+, A13 ....$230.00

Tru-Ade, thermometer, metal, Drink above bottle & bulb, A Better Beverage & Tru-Ade on dot below, rounded ends, EX+, A16 ....$95.00

Tru-Age Beer, foam scraper holder, blue glass on gold plastic base with enameled insert, Special Light lettered below, EX+, A8 ....$110.00

Tru-Age Beer, label, Standard Brewing Co of Scranton, Internal Revenue Tax Paid statement, 1933-50, 12-oz, M, A10.............$22.00

Tru-Test Pocketknives, display case, wood with glass front & 3 shelves, logo across top, opens from back, 17½x14", chips on shelves, A6.............$45.00

True Blue Tobacco, sign, cardboard stand-up, Smoke Or Chew... above tobacco pack, arched line design above & below, 1920, 13x10", NM, A3 ....$30.00

True Fruit Soda, sign, cardboard, 'True Fruit' lettered above fruit flanked by Delicious Soda, ca 1905, 16x9", EX+, A13 ....$90.00

Trunk Line, tobacco tag, die-cut trunk, EX, D35.........$8.00

Tube City Beer, can, cone-top, 12-oz, VG, A19........$50.00

Tube City Beer, pipe, ceramic, VG+, A8.............$20.00

Tuckahoe Plug, tobacco tag, EX, D35.............$4.00

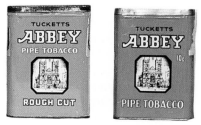

Tucketts Abbey Pipe Tobacco, pocket tin, vertical, blue with white & black lettering & graphics (with 10¢), EX, A18.............$235.00

Tucketts Abbey Rough Cut Pipe Tobacco, pocket tin, vertical, blue with white & black lettering & graphics (no 10¢), 4½", EX+, A18 ....$195.00

Tucketts Abbey Rough Cut Pipe Tobacco, pocket tin, vertical, blue with white & black lettering & graphics (with 10¢), 4½", VG+, D21 ....$125.00

Tucketts Marguerite Cigar, sign, self-framed tin, bust portrait of lady in gold gown with red flower in her hair, 28x22", EX, D21 ....$1,850.00

Tucketts Old Squire, pocket tin, vertical, orange with name above encircled image of old man smoking pipe, A Rich Blend..., VG+, A18 ....$140.00

Tucketts Old Squire Pipe Tobacco, pocket tin, vertical, orange with name above & below encircled image of old gent smoking pipe, 10¢, short, VG+, A18....$105.00

Tucketts Orinoco Cut Fine, tin, Orinoco Cut Fine upper left of fisherman on bank, blue border, small rectangle, rounded corners, EX+, A18 ....$55.00

Tucketts Orinoco Long Cut Mild, tin, Tuckett's Orinoco upper left of fisherman on bank, gold border, oblong, rounded corners, EX, A18.....................$85.00

Tucketts T&B Cut Fine, tin, red & gold with lettering above & below T&B encircled by tobacco leaves & beaver with myrtle plant, 4x6", EX, A18........$45.00

Tue'Namba, sign, embossed tin, black man & product pack flank name on yellow, decorative gold border, framed, horizontal, VG+, A18................$110.00

Tulare Chief, lug box label, various fruit, Indian in full headdress, shaded red lettering on blue, Cutler, M, D12 ....$3.00

Tums, fan, cardboard, For Health & Beauty, Crystal Drugstore, Oroville, Cal, bust portrait of elegant girl, 11x6", EX, A6 ....$40.00

Tums, fan, cardboard, You Get The Best At The Drug Store..., young boy with lollipop, advertising on handle, VG, A3 ....$15.00

Turkey Brand Coffee, watch fob, metal round shape with name on band around embossed image of turkey, M, A20 ....$85.00

Turkey Coffee, tin, turkey & fancy scrolls in center, slip lid, G+, A3 ....$85.00

Turkish Cross-Cut Cigarettes/W Duke Sons Co, sign, paper with metal hanger, pictures Leilla Farrel & other dignitaries, inverted triangle, EX+, A3 ....$145.00

Turkish Dyes, cabinet, wood, state seal on paper front, product name above moon & star logo on marquee, 27½x17x9", G-, A9 ....$200.00

Turkish Trophies Cigarettes, sign, paper, product name above Turkish maiden, framed, 36x26", EX, A9..**$300.00**

Turnbull's Scotch Whiskey, sign, embossed tin, bottle of whiskey flanked by Extra Special, black letters shadowed in gold, 18x12", VG, A6....................$70.00

Turret Cigarettes, sign, porcelain, Canada's Choice!... in red & black on green, geometric design around border, 18x30", NM, D21 ....$210.00

Tustana, crate label, California orange, pictures a palomino horse, groves & yellow logo on black, Tustin, 10x11", M, D12 ....$35.00

Tuxedo Tobacco, pocket tin, sample, cut-down vertical, EX+, A18 ....$75.00

Tuxedo Tobacco, pocket tin, vertical, encircled image of man in tuxedo, Specially Prepared For Pipe Or... below, unopened, NM, A18.....................$60.00

Tuxedo Tobacco, tin, encircled image of man in tuxedo, Specially Prepared For Pipe Or... below, square with round screw lid, EX, A19 ....$250.00

Tuxedo Tobacco, tin, encircled image of man in tuxedo flanked by Specially Prepared For Pipe Or..., oval slip lid, EX+, A18 ....$140.00

TWA, see also Lucky Strike

TWA Airlines, clipboard, TWA logo & printing on clip, standard size, VG+, D24 ....$12.00

Tweed Tobacco, tin, product name & Made For Pipes left of Scotty dog, other product lettering below, 1926 stamp, 16-oz, NM, A7.............................$25.00

Twenty Grand Double Edge, display, 20 packs of blades shaped like horseshoe around advertising in center, 5 Blades 10¢, 12x9", NM, A7....................$65.00

Twin Brothers Co, paperweight, glass, red & white image with company name arched above twin baby boys, Waco Texas below, oval, M, D13 ....$50.00

Twin City Garage Association, sign, tin, pictures head-on image of '40s car above U-shaped lettered emblem, yellow, black & white, 28x16", NOS, EX, A1 ....$185.00

Twin Kiss Root Beer, mug, glass, applied color label, frothy mug flanked by Twin Kiss, Root Beer below, small, M, A16 ....$30.00

Twin Oaks Mixture, box, gold casket shape with embossed design around product name on red emblem, EX+, A18..$125.00

Twin Oaks Mixture, jar, ceramic, white barrel shape with black bands & logo, knobbed lid, NM, A18.......$100.00

Twin Oaks Mixture, pocket tin, vertical, flat lid, silver-tone with embossed trees flanking red & silver double acorn logo, EX+, A18 ....$180.00

Twin Oaks Mixture, pocket tin, vertical, flip lid, silver-tone with embossed trees flanking red & silver double acorn, NM, A18................................$60.00

Twin Ports Steel Cut Coffee, tin, 'Where Sail Meets Rail,' pictures encircled ships, company name on band below, 1-lb, VG, A3 ....$230.00

Two Patriots Cigars, box label, salesman's sample, 2 soldiers with flags shaking hands, Smoke... below, 1898, EX, A5 ....$135.00

Two Wheeler, cigar box label, outer, girl flanked by 2 mules, 4½x4½", M, D5 ....$15.00

Tydol, gas globe, Tydol in bold letters on bordered circle, orange, black & white, black metal body, 14½" dia, EX+, A6 ....$350.00

Tydol, license plate attachment, embossed metal, running Tydol man, cream & black, 6½", VG, A6 ....$50.00

Tydol Ethyl, gas globe, Tydol above Ethyl logo, orange, black & yellow, cast face with black metal body, 15" dia, EX+, A6 ....$750.00

Tydol Ethyl, sign, porcelain, Tydol above Ethyl logo within bordered circle on black square, 13x13", G+, A1 ..$130.00

Tydol Flying A, gas globe, winged A logo, red & black on white, glass body with metal bands, 3-pc, 3½" dia, NM, A6 ....$475.00

Tydol Flying A, pump sign, porcelain, Tydol Flying above winged A on band over white field, black-banded border, 10" dia, EX, A1 ....$200.00

Tydol Motor Oil, sign, tin, product lettering on arrow pointing to oil can, 2-sided, 11x21½", VG, A1 ...$130.00

∽ U ∽

U-No Coffee, tin, Good Vacuum Packed & line designs in center of product name, key-wind lid, EX+, A3...$50.00

U-S-A- Lubricant, can, product name above eagle, Richardson Lubricating Co, Quincy, Ill below, slip lid, 4x3" dia, VG, A6 ....$40.00

U-Ta-Ka, tobacco pouch, cloth, EX, A7......................$10.00

Ultra-Sonic Knox, pump plate, Ultra-Sonic above Knox on oval, Super Regular below, white on red, 12x12", rare, NM, A1 ....$350.00

UMC Steel Lined Shells, sign, cardboard hanger, UMC circle with Nitro Club & Arrow Shells above flying ducks, Steel... below, 7x12", EX, A7 ....$425.00

Una Co Gloves, sign, cardboard, colorful image of Loretta Young with horse, 14x11", VG+, A21 ....$40.00

Uncle Daniel Fine Cut Tobacco, tin, round, red with gold & black lettering & graphics, pictures Uncle Daniel, Scotten-Dillon Co, 2x8", EX+, A18 ....$125.00

Uncle Jake's Nickel Seegar, box label, inner lid, cartoon character & cat, 1925, 6x9", M, D5 ....$6.00

Uncle John's Syrup, sign, paper, large syrup can at right of man guiding oxen through snow, early 1900s, 11x21", EX+, A3..............................$110.00

Uncle Remus Syrup, can label, product name above & below black man, 1924, 6½x20", NM, A7............$45.00

Uncle Sam, crate label, Washington apple, Uncle Sam holding top hat on red background, Wapato, 9x11", M, D12..............................$6.00

Uncle Sam Smoking Tobacco, pocket tin, vertical, Uncle Sam & product name on red, white & blue shield, EX, A18 ....$1,210.00

Underwood Typewriters, still bank, ivory-painted pot metal typewriter shape, Underwood impressed on paper label, NM, D14..............................$45.00

Uneeda Bakers, canister, square with hinged glass front with name & logo on black panel, 10x10", VG, A2........$65.00

Uneeda Bakers Snaps, sign, paper, product name upper right of 4 boxes pouring different flavored cookies onto plate, 11x21", NM+, A1 ....$65.00

Uniform Cut Plug, pocket tin, flat, product name above & below portrait of sailor encircled by wreath, rope border, 4x6", EX+, A18 ....$165.00

Union Beer, tray, pictures Dutch boy carrying large food tray with frothy mug, 13x19", EX, A19..................$65.00

Union Biscuit Co, bookmark, heart shape, product name above encircled shield, High Grade Goods below, 2¼x2", EX, A11..............................$30.00

Union Certified Motor Oil & Gasoline, sign, embossed tin, We Use above Union Certified on oval above Motor Oil & Gasoline, 12x18", VG+, A1 ....$90.00

Union Leader, pocket tin, sample, cut-down vertical lettered Union Leader, EX+, A18..............................$45.00

Union Leader, sign, cardboard, tilted pocket tin & The 10¢ Tin at right of ...The Best Tobacco Value, blue ground, 10x23", VG+, A3..............................$230.00

Union Leader Cut Plug, lunch pail, name in gold lettering surrounds eagle atop product pack, red ground, wire handle, paper banded, EX+, A18 ....$40.00

Union Leader Cut Plug, lunch pail, name in gold lettering surrounds eagle atop product pack, red ground, wire handle, EX, A18..$25.00

Union Leader Cut Plug, sign, cardboard, Take Uncle Sam's Advice above his image flanked by The Best..., 5¢ Size & pack, oval, 12x10", VG+, A2..............$285.00

Union Leader Cut Plug, sign, cardboard, Uncle Sam holding package with naval armada beyond, original frame, 46x36", EX, A9..$7,500.00

Union Leader Cut Plug, sign, cardboard, Uncle Sam reading The Naval Review, National Smoke & Chew below, original frame, 43x36", G+, A9........................$2,500.00

Union Leader Cut Plug, sign, cardboard, Uncle Sam reading The Naval Review, National Smoke & Chew below, original frame, 43x36", NM, A9......................$7,500.00

Union Leader Cut Plug, tin, eagle atop product box above product name in gold, red & gold basketweave background, EX+, A18...$25.00

Union Leader Redi Cut Tobacco, canister, oval image of Uncle Sam on red, white & blue band, red background, slightly domed slip lid, 6x5" dia, EX+, A18........$120.00

Union Leader Redi Cut Tobacco, pocket tin, vertical, oval image of Uncle Sam on red, white & blue band, red background, EX, A18...................................$75.00

Union Leader Smoking Tobacco, pocket tin, sample, vertical, Complimentary in script over oval image of perched eagle, red ground, unopened, EX+, A18..............$95.00

Union Leader Smoking Tobacco, sign, tin, oval image of perched eagle, product name above & below, 15½x10½", NM, A3..$140.00

Union Leader Smoking Tobacco, sign, tin, tilted pocket tin at left of Union Leader For Pipe Or Cigarette, yellow background, 10x22", EX+, A3..........................$115.00

Union Made Pants & Overalls, sign, cardboard, conductor in overalls standing on platform with train approaching, fancy gold border, 20x16", EX, A2 ....$2,420.00

Union Metallic Cartridge Co, sign, paper, product name above battle scene with woman loading cannon, framed, 26x22", EX+, D21.................................$625.00

Union 76, pin-back button, I'm Fast! lettered diagonally below running & smiling man in white, orange field, 2" dia, NM, A1...$180.00

Union 76, salt & pepper shakers, plastic, shaped as gas pumps, blue sides with decals on white fronts, 2¾", EX+, A1...$220.00

Union 76, sign, porcelain, Please For Your Safety above serviceman & No Smoking, Stop Your Motor, 12x15", M, D11...$250.00

Union 76, telephone, gas pump shape, EX, D25.......$65.00

Union 76 Certified Car Condition Service, sign, porcelain, Certified Car Condition Service around Union 76 symbol, serrated-looking border, 22" dia, NM, A1.............$275.00

Union 76 Underground Cable, sign, porcelain, 76 logo above ...Union Oil Co Of California, 14x10", D11 .$65.00

Unis Cigarette, sign, tin, man in tuxedo in front of stage door, ...The One You've Been Waiting For, Ten For 15 Cents, 27x19", G+, A9...................................$200.00

United Airlines, timetable, Hawaii, August-September 1952, surfer on cover, EX, D23 ....$15.00

United Motors, sign, neon, Service on car outlined with neon in center, United Motors above & below, neon border, oval, 24", NM, D8 .....$2,800.00

United Motors Service, sign, porcelain, Service in white on black car, United Motors above & below, yellow background, oval, 28x48", NM, D8 ....$1,150.00

United Solvenized Gasoline, sign, porcelain, running figure & Chases Carbon above United on center band, Solvenized... below, 30" dia, EX, A6...................$225.00

United States Auto Club, sign, metal flange, Approved Service Station above patriotic shield, 18x16", EX+, A6..$80.00

United States Brewing Co, drinking glass, straight-sided with etched logo & name, 4", NM, A8.................$45.00

United States Royal Cord Tires, display, rubber tire on metal stand with painted metal sign as hub, porcelain light socket in center, 35x27", VG, A6.................$70.00

United States Savings Bonds, sign, die-cut cardboard stand-up, Lady Liberty in front of flag holding gold box & savings bond, 60x40", EX, A6.......................$600.00

United States Tires, display rack, metal, cream & blue lettering on orange & blue, ...Royal & Usco Cords, 9½x18½", EX, A6 ....**$90.00**

United States Tires, fan, cardboard, patriotic logo above early car surrounded by tires, ...Are Good Tires, 9½x8", VG+, A6 ....**$90.00**

United Utilities System, sign, porcelain flange, U logo in center of circle bordered by Public Telephone, white on blue, 11x11", NM, A13................................**$160.00**

Unity Mixture, pocket tin, vertical, green with red lettering on yellow graphics, gold lid, short, EX, A18..$330.00

Universal Blend Coffee, pail, Uncle Sam standing on Phillipines & Cuba with Universal Commerce flag, knobbed slip lid, VG+, A3................................**$220.00**

Universal Credit, sign, reverse-painted glass in metal frame, Buy On..., red, gold & white lettering, 9x19", EX, A6 ....**$375.00**

Universal Mainsprings, tin, flat, winged spring atop globe, The Universal below, square, rounded corners, ¾x2½x2½", EX, D37................................**$50.00**

Universal Vanishing Cream, jar, milk glass, paper label, NMIB, A7 ....**$15.00**

University Club Beer, label, Louis Eckert Brewing Co, Internal Revenue Tax Paid statement, 1933-50, 11-oz, M, A10..**$32.00**

Unoco Motor Oils/Union Oil Co, sign, embossed tin, ...Cleveland, Ohio, Established 1877, black on orange, 13½x20", VG+, A6................................**$125.00**

Upland Pride, crate label, California orange, red rose on navy blue background, Upland, 10x11", M, D3 .....**$6.00**

Upper Ten, tobacco tag, EX, D35 ....**$3.00**

Urbana Wine Co, sign, tin, elegant colonial gentleman toasting while seated at dinner table, C Shonk litho, 15x11", VG, A7 ....**$90.00**

US Borax, sign, porcelain, team of horses pulling wagons above product name in red & black letters, white ground, 27x48", NM, D11................$300.00

US Cartridge Co, sign, die-cut cardboard trifold, duck hunting scene with cartridges displayed in the foreground, 34x48", EX, A7 ....**$1,400.00**

US Marine Cut Plug, tin, red paper label with name around circular US logo bordered by gold rays, round & shouldered, slip lid, EX, A18................**$185.00**

US Marine Flake Cut, pocket tin, vertical, red with yellow product name above & below US on blue circle, with contents, EX, A18................................**$400.00**

US Navy Success Cigars, box label, salesman's sample, US Navy ships with fancy scroll design, Smoke... below, 1898, EX, A5..**$210.00**

US Royal Tempered Rubber Boots, display boot, felt-lined rubber, bear logo, 36", G, A21................**$165.00**

US Royal Tempered Rubber Boots, display boot, molded rubber, 36", EX, A21................................**$440.00**

US Royal Tempered Rubber Galoshes, display boot, molded rubber with metal clasps, 26", VG, A21 ..**$195.00**

US Royal Tires, sign, porcelain, 2-sided, blue, yellow & white, 33½x26", NM, A6................................**$150.00**

US Tires, clock, numbers surround man's smiling face, U&S lettered on goggle lenses, 'Tire-ly Satisfied' below, 18" dia, EX, A21................................**$1,650.00**

US Tires, jigsaw puzzle, man by auto tells boy lying by overturned cart 'New US Tires Saved Your,' 1933, 10x10", EX, D10..**$65.00**

US Typewriter Ribbon Mfg Co, tin, vertical, allover star design around lettered inset, slip lid, 1¾x1⅝x1⅝", EX, D37..**$25.00**

USCO/United States Tires/US Royal Tube, display, tin, 3 hinged & framed panels, tire in country scene, product name on each panel, 2-sided, 31x19", EX, A1 ....$1,350.00

USCO/United States Tires/US Royal Tube display, tin, 3 hinged & framed panels, tire in country scene, product name on each panel, 2-sided, 31x19", NM, A6 ..**$2,500.00**

USL Batteries, sign, porcelain, ...Power To Spare, orange, blue & white, 18x60", EX+, A6................................**$65.00**

USL Battery Service, sign, metal, red, black & cream, 38½x12½", VG, A6..**$15.00**

USS American Fence & Posts, thermometer, porcelain, ...Buy The Fence With 3-Way Protection Against Rust, red on cobalt, 19", EX, A3................................**$110.00**

USS Tiger Brand Wire Rope, sign, metal, 2-sided, product name & roaring tiger above America's No 1 Wire Rope, red, black & yellow, 26x31", EX, A6................**$25.00**

Utica Club, stein, ceramic, 'Dooley' character lid with shamrock on side of stein, 1960, EX+, A19................**$80.00**

Utica Club Beer, sign, 3 die-cut foil hangers, Big Brew 12 ozs (bottle), Old Timer On Draught (mug), Short Snort 7 oz (bottle), EX+, A3................................**$35.00**

Utica Club Beer, tray, The Famous Utica Beer above factory scene encircled by product & company name, 12" dia, NM, A1 ....$35.00

Utica Supreme Pocket Knives, display, wood with glass front, metal label with blue lettering at bottom, 13x18x5½", G, A6.....................................$35.00

❧ V ❧

V-Line Clothes for Stouts, sign, easel-back, EX, D6 ..$20.00

Val Blatz Brewing Co, booklet, color scenes on 1 side of page with black & white etching of brewery scenes on the other, 1914, 8x6", EX, A8.................................$65.00

Val Blatz Brewing Co, match safe, engraved metal rectangular shape with decorative rounded corners, VG+, A8...$60.00

Val Roma, cigar box label, outer, Roman couple flanked by pillars, 4½x4½", M, D5....................................$6.00

Valiant, strip label, citrus, pictures large swordfish, M, D3...$2.00

Valley Boy Cherries, lug box label, little boy with fruit basket, Victor, M, D12..$2.00

Valley Brew Beer, label, El Dorado Brewing Co, Internal Revenue Tax Paid statement, 1933-50, 11-oz, M, A10 ....$20.00

Valley Brew Gold Medal Beer, sign, tin, girl seated at table with glass flanked by Awarded...In Competition With Beers Of The World, 14" dia, NM, A9........$400.00

Valley Forge Beer, display, molded plastic, boxers on labeled bases, 1 black & 1 white, EX, A19, pair ..$50.00

Valley Forge Beer, display plaques, plastic, baseball pitcher in red uniform throwing Valley Forge ball to batter in blue, 3-pc, EX, A19 ....$265.00

Valley Forge Beer, sign, neon, red Valley Forge on red trapezoid background, yellow Beer & company name lettered on base, EX, A19 ....$350.00

Valley Forge Beer, sign, tin on cardboard, product name in gold left of can, Pilsener Of America on gold scroll, 9x15", VG+, A19 ....$90.00

Valley Forge Beer, tap knob, black plastic with red enamel insert, round, EX, A8...$25.00

Valley Forge Beer, tap knob, chrome with red & white enamel, ball shape, VG+, A8.............................$35.00

Valley Forge Special Beer, pocket mirror, product name above bottle, Adam Scheidt Brewing Co below, oval, EX+, D18...$125.00

Valley Forge Special Beer, sign, porcelain, Valley Forge & Special on black above & below bottle flanked by Ice Cold on red band, VG+, A19.............................$175.00

Valley Forge Special Beer, tip tray, product name & A Beer Of Unsurpassed Quality flank bottle, 4" dia, VG, A8 ....$50.00

Valley Forge Special Beer, tray, As Good As It Looks & product name on red & gold rim around server with tray, pre-1920s, vertical, VG+, A19.......................$55.00

Valvoline Go-Mix Outboard Fuel, gas globe, black boat moving across center band, light blue with red & white lettering, plastic body, 14" dia, NM, A6 ....$250.00

Valvoline Motor Oil, clock, Ask For Valvoline Motor Oil in center, numbered 12-3-6-9, blue & red, 14½" dia, EX+, A6...$180.00

Valvoline Motor Oil, sign, tin, Pennsylvania 100% Pure above logo, Light Medium on band below, green background, 2-sided, 7" dia, NM, A1............$220.00

Valvoline Motor Oils, sign, tin, Pennsylvania 100% Pure above logo, green background, 2-sided, 30" dia, EX+, A1 ....$350.00

Valvoline Oil, can, Costs Less To Use above product name, 50¢ Per Quart, Canadian, white on black & green, prewar, VG, A1 ....$80.00

Valvoline Outboard Motor Oil, can, World's First Motor Oil in script above product name & 2 men in boat, red & white, screw cap, 7x4½", EX, A6 ....$15.00

Van Bibber Little Cigars, pocket tin, vertical, silver-tone with embossed name above & below oval bust image, NM+, A18...$150.00

Van Bibber Sliced Plug Pipe Tobacco, pocket tin, flat, lettering right of oval portrait, rounded corners, EX+, A18...$40.00

Van Camp Hardware & Iron Co, display, life-size die-cut man behind 3-D wooden work bench, various hooks & holes to display tools, 62x42", EX, A21..........$1,760.00

Van Camp Hardware Co, catalog, 1933, 2,423 pgs, EX, D17...$125.00

Van Camp's Concentrated Soups, sign, die-cut tin stand-up, Dutch girl with can of soup standing next to boy with soup tureen, 32x23", EX, A2.....................$5,720.00

Van Curler Chili Powder, tin, 3½", NM, A7............$25.00

Van de Kamp's Bakery, sign, porcelain, windmill above lettering, 48x22", EX+, D11.................................$100.00

Van Dyke's Peanut Butter, pail, round with straight sides, depicting story line & images from Mother Hubbard, 4", very rare, no lid, EX, A2.................................$1,155.00

Van Fleet-Mansfield Drug Co, paperweight, glass, Our New Home, Largest & Most Modern... above building, company name below, rectangular, M, D13.........$65.00

Van-Loo Cigars, tin, round with product name above profile image of cavalier, 5¼x5½" dia, EX+, A18......$75.00

Vandalia, crate label, California orange, large peacock & moonlit sky, Deco style lettering, Porterville, 10x11", M, D12 ....$4.00

Vander Bies Ice Cream, sign, die-cut Santa with bag of toys & tree, Ask For... on base, embossed, ca 1890, framed, 9½x5", NM, A3......................................$225.00

Vanity Coffee, tin, peacock on circle at right of product name, key-wind lid missing, 1-lb, EX, A3............$65.00

Vanko Cigars, tin, encircled horse head above Vanko on diagonal scrolled banner, slip lid, round corners, 6x5½x4", VG+, A1......................................$50.00

Vantine's Kutch Sandalwood Talcum Powder, tin, sample, lettering over archway, bronze-colored shaker top, 1⅞x1⅛x¾", EX, D37 ....$65.00

Vaseline Cold Cream, tin, sample, For The Skin & Complexion, company name & city on fancy border around product name, ½x1⅜" dia, EX, D37 ....$25.00

Vaseline Mentholated Petroleum Jelly, trolley sign, cardboard, product flanked by encircled lady with tube & encircled text, 1920s, 11x21", NM, A1 ....$60.00

Veach Oysters, can, white with lettering above & below image of oyster, 3½", VG, A21 ....$50.00

Veedol, pump sign, embossed tin, The New Veedol 30¢ A Quart, black, orange & cream, 9x9", EX, A6 ......$210.00

Veedol Gear & Chassis Lubricants, can, product name on black, pry lid, full, EX+, NOS, A1 ....$20.00

Veedol Motor Oil, bank, tin, can shape, 3", EX, D25 ..$20.00

Veedol Motor Oil, can, High Detergency above encircled product name & winged V, orange, black & cream, 9½x6½" dia, 5-qt, VG+, A6 ....$60.00

Veedol Motor Oil, can, product name above winged V logo, 100% Pennsylvania below, orange, black & cream, 1-qt, EX, A1 ....$40.00

Veedol Motor Oils, sign, porcelain, Buy... on circle above 100% Pennsylvania At It's Finest, curved top, orange, white & black, 28", NM, A6 ....$275.00

Veedol 10-30 Motor Oil, bank, tin, blue can shape, 2" dia, NM, A7 ....$20.00

Vegederma, sign, tin, Prevents Baldness, Cures Dandruff above bare-chested girl with flowing hair, 13x9", VG+, A9 ....$900.00

Vegetine, trade card, girl leaning over fence, The Great Blood Purifier, 1880s, EX, D23 ....$20.00

Veltex Gasoline, pump sign, porcelain, blue Veltex over large V on orange keyhole design, Gasoline below, white field, 15x13", VG+, A1 ....$300.00

Veltex Penn Motor Oil, can, product name on band over large encircled V, 100% Pennsylvania below, orange, blue & white, 1-qt, EX+, A1 ....$120.00

Velvet Tobacco, canister, red emblem on square shape with beveled corners, flared bottom, slip lid with knob, NM, A18 ....$140.00

Velvet Tobacco, pocket tin, cut-down sample, red with Velvet lettered in white, EX+, A18 ....$60.00

Velvet Tobacco, pocket tin, sample, vertical, red with product name above & below burning pipe, EX, A18 ....$165.00

Velvet Tobacco, sign, die-cut cardboard stand-up, Joy Ride above 2 men in car with product name & pipe on front, 9x7", VG, A6 ....$175.00

Velvet Tobacco, sign, tin, 2 men with child & dog enjoying pipe, A Man That Loves Kiddies An' Dogs... above, image: 28x21½", EX, A9 ....$575.00

Velvet Tobacco, watch fob, enamel, shows pipe with smoke forming the word Velvet, Tobacco lettered below, 1¼x1", VG, A7 ....$45.00

Venable Tobacco Co, sign, paper, Gettysburg on banner above battle scene, company name below, 11x10", G, A2 ....$200.00

Ventura Maid, crate label, California lemon, young blond woman holding lemons, Ventura, 1930s, 9x12", M, D12 ....$20.00

Venus/Alex Cameron & Co, tobacco label, name above image of Venus, decorative border, company name below, matted & framed, image: 10x10", EX, A18 ..$75.00

Ver-ba, syrup dispenser, ceramic urn, Drink on emblem above Ver-ba, Safe 5¢ Sane on emblem below, original pump, 15", VG, A9 ....$750.00

Vernor's Ginger Ale, dispenser tab knob, embossed chromed metal, Ice Cold upper left of Vernor's in script, Ginger Ale lower right, NM, A13 ....$60.00

Vernor's Ginger Ale, display figure, automated, Quaker man holding sign, 36" figure on 16" square base, rare, A6 ....$4,500.00

Vernor's Ginger Ale, drinking glass, tapered sides, applied lettering, ...Deliciously Different, M, A16 ....$20.00

Vernor's Ginger Ale, sign, self-framed tin, Drink... above man with large bottle sitting on barrel, Deliciously Different! below, 54", EX, A6 ....$250.00

Vernor's Ginger Ale, tray, Deliciously Different above Vernor's in diagonal script, From Extract... below, yellow on green, 11x13", EX, A6 ....$15.00

Vess, miniature bottle, embossed & applied color label, NM, A16 ....$15.00

Vest Pocket, cigar box label, inner lid, man with vest pocket full of cigars, 6x9", M, D5 ....$8.00

Veteran Brand Coffee, tin, product name above & below profile portrait, striped top & bottom, round with screw lid, 1-lb, EX, A18 ....$300.00

Veteran Paprika, tin, paper label, 3", NM, A7 ....$30.00

Viccola, syrup dispenser, ceramic urn shape, 5¢ Drink...The Famous Drink in red on white, gold trim, original pump, 16", EX, A2.............................$1,760.00

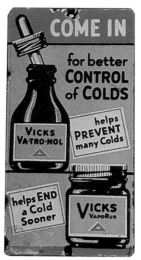

Vicks Va-Tro-Nol/Vaporub, door plate, porcelain, Come In on red band above 2 product jars, green background, 7½x4", VG, A6 ....$220.00
Vicks Va-Tro-Nol/Vaporub, sign, painted metal flange, Vicks For Symptomatic Control Of Colds above 2 signs with product images, 9x9", EX, A6 ....$120.00
Vico Iodine Ointment, jar, sample, milk glass, paper label, with contents, NM, A7 ....$20.00
Victor Duck Decoys, display, pressed cardboard & papier-mache, 3-D duck atop base lettered Victor Duck Decoys, 6x7", NM, A15 ....**$650.00**
Victor Guaranteed Traps, thermometer, wood, pictures a skunk above When The Mercury Is Low Furs Are High, advertising below, 15", EX, A6............................$150.00

Victor Needles, tin, flat, Extra Loud Tone, green with gold trim, trademark image of Nipper, rounded corners, ½x1½x2½", EX, D37 ....$50.00

Victor Needles, tin, flat, Full Tone, red with gold trim, trademark image of Nipper, rounded corners, ½x1½x1½", EX, D37 ....$60.00

Victor Needles, tin, flat, Half Tone, light blue with gold trim, rounded corners, ½x1½x2½", EX, D37 ....$65.00
Victor Needles, tin, flat, Soft Tone, green with gold trim, trademark image of Nipper, rounded ends, ½x1¼x1½", EX, D37...$60.00
Victor Records, trolley sign, cardboard, 'After I've Called You Sweetheart,' romantic couple within heart, framed, 13x23", EX, A6..$150.00
Victor Records, trolley sign, cardboard, 'Invitation To The Waltz,' The Gift That Keeps On Giving above candle, framed, 12x22", EX, A6 ....$75.00
Victor Records, trolley sign, cardboard, 'Together, We Two,' Irving Berlin's Latest above romantic couple, framed, 12x22", EX, A6 ....**$165.00**
Victor Sewing Machine, sign, paper on canvas, product name & medallion above 2 women using machines & other lettering, 20x25", G, A9 ....$275.00
Victor Traps, sign, cardboard, pictures a skunk, Make Mr Skunk Pay You A Profit, Get Him With..., orange & black, 13x10", VG, A6 ....$45.00
Victoria Needles, tin, flat, blue, red or aqua, 1x2", NM, A7, each..$20.00
Victoria Records, clock, tin, black record shape with numbers around red label, 15" dia, very rare, EX, A2.........**$1,045.00**
Victorious Yams, crate label, cowgirl riding white horse, M, D3 ....**$2.00**
Victory Footwear, display, painted composition, roosters standing together after a fight on rectangular base, 24x13x10", VG+, A9 ....**$550.00**

Victory Liberty Loan, poster, Sure! We'll Finish The Job, man in bib overalls & hat reaching into pocket, dry mounted, 1918, 38x26", EX, A13 ....$60.00
Victory Sanitary Wax Dressing/Victory Chemical Co, sign, paper, product name above girl on fancy oval flanked by text, company name below, framed, 13x11", EX, A8 ....$50.00
Victrola Record Co, display, papier-mache figure of Nipper the dog with head cocked & 1 ear up, with collar, 36", EX, A2...$850.00
Vienna Bock Beer, label, Vienna Brewing Co, Internal Revenue Tax Paid statement, 1933-50, 12-oz, M, A10...$25.00
Vienna Coffee, tin, sample, lettered Not To Be Sold, round with screw top, 3x2¾" dia, VG+, A18..................$35.00
Vienna Select Beer, label, Southern Indiana Ice & Beverage Co, U-type permit number, Internal Revenue Tax Paid, 1933-36, 12-oz, M, A10 ....$10.00

Vigoral, sign, product name in script above woman running hands through her hair, The Most Delicious..., image: 18x14", EX, A9......................................$400.00

Vigorator Foaming Hair Tonic & Head Rub, sign, tin hanger, product name above & left of Dissolves Dandruff atop oval with person washing hair, 5x9", EX+, A13......................................$80.00

Viking Beer/White Seal Brewing Co, label, product name in red & white above Viking ship on diamond inset, black background, 12-oz, EX+, A19......................................$12.00

Viking Line Typewriter Ribbon, tin, flat, pictures Viking ship at sea with lettering on border, ¾x2½x2½", EX, D37......................................$40.00

Violet, crate label, pear, large cluster of violets on black background, M, D3......................................$4.00

Violet Talcum Powder, tin, product name above encircled baby with decorative border, tax stamp on back, 3½-oz, EX, A3......................................$55.00

Virgin Leaf Tobacco, alarm clock, Chew... on yellow around white numbered band encircling man's face, round footed case, 1885, EX, A2......................................$1,760.00

Virginia Brewing Co, tray, lettering around seductive bust image of a pretty girl, green & gold decorative rim, 10" dia, EX+, A13......................................$450.00

Virginia Dare Carbonated Beverages, sign, celluloid, head image upper left of blue product name, red Thanks For Your Business at bottom rim, 9" dia, NM, A13......................................$75.00

Virginia Dare Extra Fine Cut Plug, tin, embellished name at right of standing draped nude & goose against landscape, rectangular, square corners, NM, A18......$235.00

Virginia Dare Extra Fine Cut Plug, tin, embellished name at right of standing draped nude & goose against landscape, rectangular, rounded corners, VG, A18......$50.00

Virginia Dare Ginger Ale, sign, cardboard, small bust portrait of girl at left of product name, Quality In Flavor..., yellow ground, 5x8", EX, D30......................................$20.00

Virginia Whole Salted Picnic Peanuts, tin, Fresh From The Plantation, shows man & child riding peanut, orange, cream & black, pry lid, 10-lb, EX, A15..$475.00

Virginity Smoking Tobacco, sign, paper, sepia image of young girl reclining on pillow, product name upper left, framed, image: 14x19", G, A9......................................$200.00

Visible Gasoline, gas globe, black repainted lettering, 1-pc, 14" dia, EX+, A6......................................$850.00

VJ Plewa Up-To-Date Shoe Store, calendar, 1926, cute image of mother & daughter hugging, full pad below, framed, image: 19x12", NM+, A3......................................$385.00

Vogue Pure White Papers, dispenser, tin, product name above cigarette papers, 7x3", NM, D21......................................$30.00

Vogue Pure White Papers, dispenser, tin, product name above cigarette papers & 5¢, 7x3", scarce, EX, D21......................................$35.00

Volk Beer, label, Volk Brewery, U-type permit number, Internal Revenue Tax Paid statement, 1933-36, 12-oz, M, A10......................................$80.00

Volk Cream Ale, label, Volk Brewery, Internal Revenue Tax Paid statement, 1933-50, 12-oz, M, A10......................................$60.00

Volumo, cigar box label, outer, tobacco field & port with town beyond, 1907, 4½x4½", M, D5......................................$12.00

Vulcan Automobile Springs, sign, tin, 2-sided, Quality on banner across Vulcan, In Stock For Your Car below, red, black & cream, 9x24", EX+, A6......................................$180.00

Vulco Insured Tires, sign, tin, Vulco lettered vertically above Insured Tires, blue, red & cream, 1920s, 49x19½", G+, A6......................................$50.00

W Baker & Co's Breakfast Cocoa, tin, sample, Absolutely Pure...Costs Less Than One Cent..., slip lid, 1¾x1¼" dia, EX, D37......................................$150.00

W/WH Baker or Walter Baker & Co, see also Baker's

Wabasso Fine Cottons, display figure, Wabasso rabbit, papier-mache, white with product name in raised gold letters on base, 28", EX, A6......................................$275.00

Waconia Pure Sorgum, tin, paper label, 2¼", NM, A7..$60.00

Wagner Lager Beer, label, Wagner Brewing Co, U-type permit number, Internal Revenue Tax Paid statement, 1933-36, 12-oz, NM, A10......................................$18.00

Wagner's Ice Cream, sign, tin, Eat... 'It's Good,' Freeport Ill above tray of ice-cream desserts, 1920s, 13½x19½", EX+, A13......................................$95.00

Wake Up Cut Plug Tobacco, tin, red & gold paper label, name above & below round image of rooster, round & shouldered with slip lid, rare, EX, A18......................................$700.00

Wake Up Viz Motor Oil, can, Wake Up Viz on crowing rooster above Motor Oil on 2 bands, screw cap, 2-gal, 11x8½", NM, A6......................................$100.00

Wake Up/El Gallo, tobacco label, 'Wake Up!' in red letters above rooster in barnyard, fancy border, metal frame, EX+, A18......................................$80.00

Wake-Em-Up Coffee, canister, tin, encircled Indian flanked by symbols in center, gold highlights, 15x12" dia, rare, VG+, A3......................................$300.00

Wake-Em-Up Coffee, pail, encircled Indian flanked by symbols, slip lid & bail, 9½x9" dia, EX, A3......................................$330.00

Waldorf Towers Hotel, flier, 1941, illustrated, EX, D23..$10.00

Walk Over Cigars, box label, salesman's sample, man walking through banner with sporting equipment tied to 1 side, VG+, A5......................................$280.00

Walker Products, bill hook, celluloid & tin, Ask For... & small portrait above 3 product cans, EX, A3 ...$30.00

Walkover Shoes, display figure, plaster, turn-of-the-century gentleman on base, 12", VG+, A21...............**$16.00**

Wall Flower, cigar box label, outer, woman on ladder reaching across wall to light man's cigar, VG+, A5...........**$50.00**

Walla Walla Pepsin Gum, jar, glass, embossed with name & bust of Indian chief, square with round frosted rim lid, 13", EX, A2...**$285.00**

Wallen's Special Coffee, tin, sample, screw top, ¼-lb, EX, A18...**$90.00**

Walsh Shoe Repair System, sign, porcelain, Trademark High Quality Shoe Repairing above figure working on shoe, 17x25", M, D11...**$295.00**

Walter A Wood Mowing & Reaping Machine Co, trade card, fold-out, 1880s, colorful farm scene, For Sale By Enoch Bridges in upper right, EX, D8.................**$80.00**

Walter Baker & Co Breakfast Cocoa, sign, tin, Pure/Delicious/Nutritious, Costs Less Than One Cent A Cup, girl standing with tray, framed, 19x14", EX+, A21...**$1,045.00**

Walter Baker & Co Limited, tin, sample, La Belle Chocolatiere above full-length profile of chocolate girl with tray, 1¾x1⅜x1", EX, D37.............**$115.00**

Walter Bros Brewing Co, drinking glass, straight-sided, gold rim, etched company name above factory scene, 3½", NM, A8...**$90.00**

Walter Field Fashions, catalog, Fall/Winter, 1957, 60 pgs, EX, D17...**$15.00**

Walter Neilly & Co, trolley sign, cardboard, elegant couple in doorway at right of dish of Pineapple Snow, 'Smilin' Through,' 11x21", NM, A1.........................**$45.00**

Waltham & Warfield Pianos & Players, whetstone, celluloid, High-Grade...HD Strauch, Alexandria, SD, sepia tones, oval, EX, A11...**$12.00**

Wampole's Antiseptic Solution, bottle, sample, paper label, cork top, with contents, VG, A7.................**$40.00**

War Chief Motor Oil, can, War Chief diagonally above 100% Pure & Paraffine Base on ribbon & shield, screw cap, 2-gal, 11x8½", NM, A6.........................**$35.00**

War Eagle Cigars, tin, black with white product name above & below yellow image of eagle, slip lid, round, EX, A18...**$120.00**

War Eagle Cigars, tin, red with white product name above & below yellow image of eagle flanked by 2 For 5¢, slip lid, EX+, A19...**$165.00**

Warco Penn, can, shows waving station attendant & product name, green, red, white & pink, 1-qt, scarce, VG+, A1...**$410.00**

Ward's Lemon-Crush, syrup dispenser, porcelain, embossed product name on lemon with flowers on oval base, original pump, 13x10", EX+, A1.....**$1,145.00**

Ward's Lime-Crush, syrup dispenser, ceramic, embossed product name & Color Added on lime with flowers on base, original pump, 15", VG, A9...................**$1,100.00**

Ward's Orange-Crush, sign, tin flange, Ice Cold on orange above Ward's... on black wavy band, ...Sold Here on orange below, 9x11", EX+, A13.....................**$650.00**

Ward's Orange-Crush, syrup dispenser, ceramic, embossed product name on orange with flowers on base, original pump, 15", VG, A9....................**$550.00**

Ward's Orange-Crush, syrup dispenser, ceramic, embossed product name on orange with flowers on base, original pump, 15", NM, A2...................**$1,925.00**

Ward's Orange-Crush, see also Orange-Crush

Ward's Vitovim Bread, thermometer, tin, Keeps Him Smiling..., shows smiling baby with bread above name & bulb, arched top, 1915, 21", G, A2.................**$275.00**

Wards Ice-Guard Concentrated Anti-Freeze, can, lettering above & below on pink-to-gray horizon with graphic of a land sailer, pour top, screw lid, 1-gal, EX, A1....**$35.00**

Wareco Ethyl, gas globe, serviceman saluting behind product name, oval Capcolite body, 10½x15½", NM, A6...**$1,300.00**

Warner's Log Cabin Sarsaparilla, broadside, pictures log cabin with 2 portrait inserts above, ...Greatest Blood Purifier below, image: 42x28", G+, A9.................**$600.00**

Warner's Safe Cure, sign, Cures All Kidney, Liver, Urinary & Female Diseases, Stanley & group of natives, framed, 19x15", VG+, A8...**$1,155.00**

Warren County Twist, tobacco tag, EX, D35.............**$4.00**

Washington, cigar box label, inner lid, sailor lighting cigar & US flag, 6x9", M, D5...**$45.00**

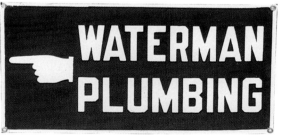

Waterman Plumbing, sign, porcelain, hand pointing finger at left of lettering, white on blue with white border, 8x16", M, D11.........................**$200.00**

Waterman's Ideal Fountain Pen, display, counter-top, wood & glass, white lettering on front, wood display tray at top, 17½x16", EX, A6.............................**$555.00**

Waterman's Ideal Fountain Pen, display pen, stenciled wood with metal filigree trim, black & cream detail with lettering, 42" long, VG, A21...................**$1,210.00**

Waterman's Ideal Fountain Pen, thermometer, shaped like fountain pen with point up, bulb on handle with blue & white sign, 1920s, 19½x3¼", NM, A4.....**$975.00**

Watkins Baking Powder, tin, paper label, with contents, 4-oz, NM, A7...**$25.00**

Watkins Baking Powder, tin, sample, Watkins above lady with tray of biscuits, ...Purity Guaranteed below, pry lid, 2-oz, NM, A3...**$45.00**

Watkins Baking Powder, tin, Watkins above lady with tray of biscuits, ...Purity Guaranteed below, pry lid, 16-oz, NM, A3 .... $30.00

Watkins Cinnamon, tin, profile portrait against striped background, 4¼", NM, A7 .... $22.00

Watkins Cocoa, tin, portrait flanked by leaves at top, workers gathering beans below, blues & gold on cream, pry lid, 5x3½", NM, A3 .... $40.00

Watkins Ginger, tin, striped, 3½", NM, A7 .... $20.00

Watkins Menthol Camphor Ointment, tin, 3½" dia, EX+, D24 .... $8.00

Watkins Sweetened Malted Milk Chocolate Flavor, tin, sample, image of full glass with straw & product name, round, 2½x1¾", EX, D37 .... $60.00

Watson's Cough Drops, tin, gold & orange, vertical square, slip lid, McDonald-Canada, 5-lb, VG, A18 .... $30.00

Watson's Matchless Cleanser, sign, porcelain, 2-sided, ...Is The Best Soap For All Purposes, 14x12", VG, D11 .... $125.00

Wausau Oil-savr, sign, cardboard, die-cut Indian head & piston ring on red, black & white sign hangs from tomahawk, 21x14", EX, A1 .... $145.00

Waverly Oils & Gasoline, sign, porcelain flange, barrel with product name & lettering on ends, red, white & blue, 10x16", NM+, A6 .... $2,200.00

Wavine Skin-Whitner & Ointment, tin, product name left of encircled image of lady in profile, ¾x1⅞", EX, D37 .... $30.00

Wayne Brew, tray, deep-dish, shows Mad Anthony Wayne blockhouse, product name below, lettered rim, 14" dia, NM+, A19 .... $50.00

Wayne Lager Beer, Ale & Porter, ashtray, tin, cartoon image of family at table with man entering house with case of beer, 4½" dia, VG, A9 .... $130.00

Weather-Bird Shoes, sign, porcelain neon, chicken on weathervane, Weatherized... in red & white, 25½x17", EX, A6 .... **$1,700.00**

Weber Waukesha Beer, tap knob, black ball shape with name on maroon & cream celluloid-covered insert, VG+, A8 .... $95.00

Weber's Pioneer, tap knob, black ball with red & silver painted aluminum insert, VG+, A8 .... $80.00

Weber's Star Ginger Ale, tray, deep-dish, portrait of Gypsy-type girl, lettering inside rim, 12" dia, VG+, A9 .... $75.00

Weber's Superior Root Beer, mug, glass, 10-panel, white logo, 5x3", EX, D16 .... $18.00

Webster, crate label, Oregon apple, spider web stretched over dark blue background, 9x11", M, D12 .... $2.00

Webster Cigars, postcard, court scene with Daniel Webster arguing the famous Dartmouth College case, ad text on back, 1817, VG+, D26 .... $40.00

Webster Non-Filling Typewriter Ribbon, tin, vertical, lettering around star trademark, slip lid, 11½x1⅝x1⅝", EX, D37 .... $30.00

Wedding Breakfast Roasted Coffee, tin, wedding party seated at table flanked by Gas Roasted on paper label, embossed slip lid, rare, NM, A3 .... $175.00

Weed American Chains, box, town scene with car on front, signed S Werner, VG+, A6 .... $180.00

Weed Anti-Skid Chains, gas price chart, cardboard, ...Necessary As Gasoline, Prevent Skidding, American Chain Co, Buckstown..., 3" dia, VG+, A6 .... $80.00

Weed Chains, brochure holder, tin, Take One above image of early chained tire, light grays & blue with gold lettering, 6x4", G+, A6 .... $60.00

Weger Bros Export Dark, mug, ceramic, circular logo with leaf & hops border above product name & Philadelphia, mulicolored, EX+, A8 .... $260.00

Wehle Bock Beer, label, round with side tabs, BO & CK flank goat's head against yellow background, black & green border, 12-oz, VG+, A19 .... $15.00

Wehle Brewing Co, see Ox Head Beer or Mule Head Ale

Weidemaier Beer, sign, tin, shows elk with head up at water's edge with bottle on other side, pre-1920s, wood frame, 31x43", G+, A19 .... $200.00

Welch Guaranteed Motor Oil, can, metal, Welch above Guaranteed lettered diagonally above '30s sedan & map of Illinois, Motor Oil below, 1-qt, NM, A1 .... $295.00

Welch Juniors, sign, embossed tin, Drink A Bunch... above bottle & grape cluster, From...10¢, raised rim, 1930s, 14x20", EX+, A13 .... **$400.00**

Welch's, sign, celluloid, The National Drink, Capitol rotunda above, grape cluster below, diagonal, 10x10", NM+, A13 .... $625.00

Welcome Cigarettes, sign, die-cut cardboard, patriotic lady at attention with broom & dust pan, copyright 1883, framed, 11x16", EX+, A18 .... $250.00

Weldon Cube Cut Smoking Tobacco, pocket tin, vertical, wood-grain with white & black lettering above & below crest logo, short, EX+, A18 .... $340.00

Welle-Boettler Bakery Co, calendar, 1899, die-cut cardboard, wicker basket with movable flowers, each displaying a month, NM, A18 .... $140.00

Welle-Boettler Bakery Co, calendar, 1901, cardboard, girl in red hooded cape surrounded by flowers, 12 months on leaves, EX, A18 ....**$50.00**

Welle-Boettler Bakery Co, calendar, 1902, cardboard, 3 angels surrounded by Happy New Year with each letter indicating a month, EX, A18..................................**$65.00**

Welle-Boettler Bakery Co, calendar, 1906, die-cut cardboard, sailing ship with floral motif, sails open to reveal months, NM+, A18 ....**$140.00**

Wellington London Mixture, pocket tin, vertical, orange with name arched above encircled crown, body EX+/lid VG, A18...**$225.00**

Wellman Foods/Coffee, tin, sample, product name above & below filigreed image of Mercury standing on globe, 2½x2" dia, EX, D37 ....**$115.00**

Wells Fargo, key chain, metal coach, ca 1950, 1", EX, D23 ....**$10.00**

Welsbach, tip tray, Welsbach Assures Dependable Lighting Service on rim around home scene with woman & child, 4" dia, EX, A8.......................................**$100.00**

Wenoka, crate label, Washington apple, profile of Indian brave on arrowhead on blue background, yellow logo, 9x11", M, D12 ....**$5.00**

Wernet's Powder, tin, sample, with contents, EX, A7 .**$10.00**

West Beach & Motor Hair Net, display, counter-top, pictures early car & bathing beauty on inside of lid, 1918, 5½x6½", EX, A6 ....$250.00

West End Ales & Lager, sign, tin, product name above & below oval image of girl smelling rose, wood-grain background, 10x13½", EX, A21...........................**$300.00**

West End Brewing Co, tip tray, patriotic image of lady Liberty surrounded by lettering, 4" dia, EX+, A21...**$275.00**

West End Brewing Co, tray, deep-dish, patriotic image of lady Liberty surrounded by lettering, 13" dia, VG, A9 ....**$275.00**

West Hair Nets, display, tin, 4-sided with images of young ladies & lettering on all sides, dome top, 18½x12½x12½", G+, A9 ....**$300.00**

West Moor Blend Coffee, tin, 4-sided with round screw top, 5-lb, EX, A7 ....**$65.00**

West Virginia Pilsner Beer, sign, brown velvet on cardboard, bust image of woman with red & pink flower, gold lettering, 22x14", EX, A6..............................**$85.00**

Westclox Pocket Ben, sign, cardboard, name above schoolboy glancing at pocket watch with school beyond, matted & framed, 13x9½", VG+, A2.......**$65.00**

Western Ammunition, calendar top, 1932, pictures English setter Champion Mars Guy, original metal strip at top, 22x15", EX+, A3..**$195.00**

Western Ammunition, sign, paper, features Super-X loads, hunter in tall grass aiming shotgun at ducks, framed, image: 35x20", EX, A9...........................**$925.00**

Western Auto, catalog, Fall/Winter, 1967, 220 pgs, EX, D17 ....**$25.00**

Western Auto Associate Store, sign, die-cut tin arrow, Home Owned..., 9x33", EX+, D11 ....**$145.00**

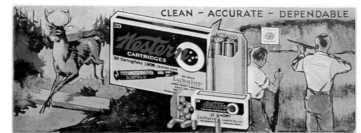

Western Cartridges, sign, cardboard stand-up, Clean-Accurate-Dependable above elk, box of cartridges & men shooting at target, 4x11", NM, A3.....$170.00

Western Lubaloy Big Game Cartridges, sign, cardboard stand-up, running deer above box & large cartridge, product name lower left, 1920s, 18x14", NM, A3..**$245.00**

Western Lubaloy Rifle & Pistol Cartridges, sign, cardboard trifold, Clean, Accurate, Hard Hitting..., product boxes against fall scene, 1920s, 14x13", EX, A3..**$135.00**

Western New Chief, sign, paper, 'Power Behind The Blind,' ducks flying over water, shotgun shell below, framed, image: 17x13", NM, A9...........................**$900.00**

Western Shells, sign, paper, image of ducks landing near decoy, display of cartridges above, matted & framed, image: 32x16½", VG, A9.....................................**$750.00**

Western Super-X Lubaloy, sign, cardboard stand-up, Clean Kills At Long Ranges above large box & hunter aiming rifle at birds, 4x11", NM+, A3.................**$170.00**

Western Super-X Shells, sign, cardboard stand-up, 1930s, product name above large tilted shell & box, 15 To 20 Yards..., 21x11", EX+, A3.................................**$370.00**

Western Union, sign, porcelain, product name on yellow background, 17x30", NM, D11 ....**$145.00**

Western Union, sign, porcelain flange, product name in white on cobalt blue, 6½x35½", EX, A1............**$165.00**

Western Union, sign, porcelain flange, Telephone Telegrams From Here above candlestick phone & Ask Operator For..., 20x18", EX, A13 ....**$300.00**

Western Union Telegraph, sign, porcelain flange, Telegraph Here above Western Union lettered diagonally, 17x25", EX+, A9...**$150.00**

Western Xpert For Field, Trap & Skeet, sign, die-cut stand-up, grouse & rabbit in field above box of ammo & shell, 1920s, EX+, A3......................................**$260.00**

Western Xpert Shells, sign, stand-up, Popular Prices — Top Quality, distant hunter taking aim at rabbit & grouse, 1929, 7x18", EX, A3.................................**$70.00**

Westinghouse, license plate attachment, porcelain, orange & black, 5x10", VG, A6 ....**$20.00**

Westinghouse, salt & pepper shakers, washer & dryer shape, M, D6 ....**$35.00**

Westinghouse Batteries, globe, milk glass with black etched lettering, Solar Elec Co, Chicago cast in neck, 16" dia, NM, A1 ....$400.00

Westinghouse Kitchen-Proved Refrigerator, sign, light-up, wood, metal & plastic on cardboard, orange & yellow lettering, 9x25", EX, A6................................$170.00

Westinghouse Mazda Lamps, sign, paper with cardboard stand-up, product name above girl with book, light bulb in the foreground, 41½x29", NM, A6 ....$55.00

Westminster Virginia Diamond Size, pocket tin, vertical, oval, deep blue with Trade Mark logo above cream & white product lettering, British, EX+, A18 ....$75.00

Westside, crate label, California pear, orchard vista with palm tree at left & road in center, 8x11", M, D12 ..$3.00

Wet Weather Goods, sign, cardboard, red with white name above & Satisfaction For... below oval image of duck marked Brand, 11x18", VG, A2.................$275.00

Wetherill's Atlas Paints, clock, neon, black & yellow with lettering in center, ornate border, octagon, 18x18", EX, A6 ....$375.00

Wetmore's Best, tobacco tag, EX, D35 ....$3.00

Weyman's Cutty Pipe Chewing & Smoking Tobacco, store bin, tin, red & yellow lettering & graphics on lime green background, slip lid, 13⅓x10x9", EX, A13.............$400.00

WH Baker & Co's Cocoa, tin, sample, name above & below lady in profile sipping cocoa, square, round screw lid, 2¾x2½x2½", EX, D37 ....$95.00

WH Baker Chocolate & Cocoa, sign, cardboard, girl with lilies flanked by various product boxes, 23½x13½", G, A9 ....$100.00

WH Crissman Moving Van Service, thermometer, company name above truck & Champion Coal Coke Disco Stoker, 116 Climax St... below, 38½x8", G+, A6 ..$85.00

WH Killian Co Sea Lite Baltimore Oysters, pail, white with red product name above & below encircled image of mermaid, bail handle, 7½x6¾", no lid, VG+, A18........$215.00

Whale White Ale/National Brewing Co, can, pull-tab, white, 12-oz, EX+, A19 ....$30.00

Wheat's Ice Cream, sign, self-framed tin, Home Of Quality on gold plate above factory image & large block of ice cream, 18x26", VG, A6....................................$425.00

Wheaties, cereal bowl with lid, milk glass with red silhouettes of Joe DiMaggio & other athletes, 2x5" dia, EX, A6 ....$60.00

Wheeler Lumber Bridge & Supply Co, tape measure, celluloid, company name arched above lettering, black & white, EX, A11...$35.00

Whip Ready Rolled for Pipe & Cigarette, pocket tin, vertical, green with red name above & below encircled man in riding habit standing by horse, short, EX, A18..$500.00

Whippet & Willys-Knight Genuine Parts, sign, porcelain, 2-sided, Authorized Service..., 24x35½", G, A9..$275.00

Whist Club Mixture, tin, lettering above & below row of playing cards, SF Hess & Co, square corners, VG, A18 ....$825.00

Whistle, ad, paper, shows cannibal prodding victim towards pot of boiling water, logo & text below, 1941, 13x10", EX+, A1..$100.00

Whistle, clock, die-cut masonite & wood, Golden Orange Refreshment Time on round face flanked by bottle & cartoon face, EX, A16....................................$550.00

Whistle, menu board, tin, Thirsty? Just Whistle above board with elves in each corner, embossed, 27x20", EX+, A9...$260.00

Whistle, sign, arrow, tin, Whistle in block letters, 27", EX+, A16..$165.00

Whistle, sign, cardboard, boy behind fence lettered Whistle & large bottle with straw, outlined border, 11x14", EX+, A8 ....$35.00

Whistle, sign, cardboard, Golden Orange Refreshment, elf beside bottle & orange, blue background, 21x16", NM+, D30...$100.00

Whistle, sign, cardboard, 12 Ounces & 5¢ flank bottle neck, black background, cropped upper corners, 1939, 31x9", NM+, A1.......................................$70.00

Whistle, sign, cardboard die-cut, seated girl in black & white flanked by oversized 5¢ bottles in color, 34x26", EX+, A1 ....$330.00

Whistle, sign, cardboard stand-up, Golden Orange Refreshment above elf with large bottle, 14x19", VG, D21..$70.00

Whistle, sign, cardboard stand-up, Thirsty? Just Whistle & Golden Orange Goodness above girl & train, 14x11", EX+, A16..$100.00

Whistle, sign, cardboard stand-up, Thirsty? Just Whistle & Golden Orange Goodness above table setting, 14x11", NM+, A16...$55.00

Whistle, sign, light-up, Thirsty? Just Whistle, Golden Orange Goodness, 5-sided case with blue border, 9x14", EX+, A13...$900.00

Whistle, sign, tin, Thirsty? Just above hand holding bottle, Demand The Genuine, 10x24", M, D30.............$295.00

Whistle, sign, tin, Thirsty? Just above hand holding bottle, On Ice, The Only Handy Bottle, 9x10", NM, D30 ....$255.00

Whistle, sign, tin, Thirsty? Just above hand holding bottle, The Choice Of Orange Drinks 5¢, 1930s, self-framed, 10x30", NM, A13...............................$675.00

Whistle, sign, tin, Thirsty? Just above hand holding bottle, The Genuine...Help Yourself, 22x26", VG+, A1.$200.00

Whistle, sign, tin, Thirsty? Just on white banner above Whistle on sign being carried by elves, embossed, 18x54", VG, A6.................................$600.00

Whistle, sign, tin, Thirsty? Just Whistle above encircled image of elf pushing bottle on cart, 30x26", EX+, A13 ....$475.00

Whistle, sign, tin, Thirsty? Just above Whistle on diagonal band, Morning, Noon... & large 5¢ below, 1939, 24x12", NM, A13 ....$450.00

Whistle, sign/thermometer, plaster, Anytime..., Any Weather..., elf with bottle right of thermometer, 13x12", EX, D8.................................$425.00

Whistle, soda glass, Thirsty? Just Whistle in white, slightly tapered with flared bottom, 4", NM, D16 ....$18.00

Whistle, whistle, plastic, NM, A7 ....$14.00

White Ash, tin, White Ash above oval bust image flanked by 5¢, Genuine Sumatra Wrapped below, wood-grain field, slip lid, EX, A18 ....$15.00

White Banner Brew, label, Pabst Corporation, L-type permit number, 1920-28, 12-oz, NM, A10 ....$28.00

White Bear Steel Cut Coffee, container, paper on cardboard, White Bear arched above bear on oval inset, Durand & Kasper Co below, no lid, VG+, A3......$85.00

White Cap Baking Powder, tin, with contents, 4-oz, VG, A7 ....$10.00

White Cap Beer, drinking glass, barrel shape with brown & white logo, 3", NM, A8......................................$40.00

White Cap Beer, label, Vienna Brewing Co, Internal Revenue Tax Paid statement, 1933-50, 1-qt, M, A10 ..$34.00

White Crown, tap knob, chrome ball with white on red enamel insert, EX, A8..$110.00

White Crown Beer & Ale, tray, deep-dish, crown above White Crown in diagonal script, Beer & Ale below, red, black & white, 12" dia, EX, A8 ....$65.00

White Crown Pale Lager Beer, display, light-up, cylinder on base showing crown atop White Crown emblem with curled corners, VG+, A8.............................$230.00

White Eagle, gas globe, figural milk glass eagle, NM+, A1 ....$1,600.00

White Eagle Fruit Beverages, sign, embossed tin, Ask For & Fruit Beverages in script above & below product name, 9x24", EX+, A19 ....$25.00

White Eagle Gasoline & Oil, sign, porcelain, 2-sided, White Eagle on center band, Gasoline & Oil above & below, red, white & black, 30" dia, EX, A6........$500.00

White Horse Grapes, lug box label, white galloping horse & lettering on black background, Sanger, M, D12..$2.00

White House Coffee, tin, White House arched above image of the White House, key-wind lid, 1-lb, VG+, A3..$40.00

White King Washing Machine Soap, sign, tin, Granulated above pouring box, It Takes So Little & It Goes So Far below, 1920s-30s, 14x10", EX, A1 ....$100.00

White King Washing Machine Soap, sign, tin, Granulated above pouring box, It Takes So Little & It Goes So Far below, 1920s-30s, 14x10", NM+, A13..$230.00

White Laundry Co, pocket mirror, woman's smiling face (has laundry done at White's) flips to frowning face (I Wish I Did), round, VG+, A8................................$20.00

White Manor Pipe Mixture, pocket tin, vertical, name above & below image of plantation house, short, EX+, A18..$200.00

White Mountain Refrigerator, sign, embossed cardboard, 'The Chest With The Chill In It,' For Sale Here, image left of lettering, 18½x10", G, A21 ....$75.00

White Rabbit Easter Egg Dye, sign, paper, image of Easter bunny coloring eggs that hen & duck are laying, lettering above & below, 13x7", G, A2 ....$185.00

White Rock, sign, paper, lady in red with pool cue behind back standing on horizontal bottle, green field, framed, 21x15", EX+, A13...$375.00

White Rock, sign, tin, circular image of topless nymph kneeling on rock at water's edge, curled corners, 13½" dia, VG, A21 ....$275.00

White Rock, sign, tin hanger, Drink White Rock The Leading Mineral Water, rectangular with rounded corners, EX+, A16 ....$55.00

White Rock, tip tray, product name above & Spanish lettering below nymph at water's edge, green border, 6x4", EX, A18 ....$110.00

White Rock, tray, pictures lady & tiger in profile, decorative border, round, G+, A19 ....$55.00

275

White Rolls Cigarettes/Ware-Kramer Tobacco Co, watch fob, nickle-plated round shape with white porcelain cigarette pack in center, filigree border, EX, A20..**$100.00**

White Rose, gas globe, white rose on yellow center circle, red lettering, Gill body with metal base, 3-pc, 13½" dia, NM, A6..**$1,000.00**

White Rose Bock Beer, label, Dallas Brewery Inc, U-type permit number, Internal Revenue Tax Paid statement, 1933-36, 12-oz, M, A10...**$30.00**

White Rose Huile A Moteur, radio, waxed cardboard & metal oil can shape, white rose above lettering, 6½x4½" dia, scarce, G+, A6 ....**$70.00**

White Rose Motor Oil, can, large rose above product name, Canadian Oil Companies Limited... around bottom, 1 Imperial-qt, 6¾x4" dia, EX, A6 ....**$40.00**

White Sewing Machine, sign, paper, mother at sewing machine with little boy crying because of bulldog, 28½x20", VG+, A9..**$150.00**

White Slave Cigars, box label, salesman's sample, oval interior scene with woman slave, VG, A5 ....**$220.00**

White Star/Andrew Lohr Bottling Co, sign, cardboard, encircled image of girl holding rose, floral design in each corner, logo on back, 1890s, 11x11", NM, A3 ....$365.00

White Top Beer, label, Capital Brewing & Ice Co, pre-1920, M, A10...**$55.00**

White Villa Coffee, tin, pictures a villa above product name lettered diagonally, America's Finest below, keywind lid, VG+, A3 ....**$35.00**

White Witch Talcum Powder, tin, EX, D6 ....**$75.00**

White Wonder, tin, sample, with contents, EX, A7...**$15.00**

White's Specific Face Cream (Bleach), tin, sample, Prepared Only By White's Specific Toilet Co..., ¼x1⅛" dia, EX, D37 ....**$22.00**

Whitman & Lord Beer, can, flat-top, 12-oz, EX+, A19...**$35.00**

Whitman's Chocolates, desk lamp, black ornamental metal pedestal frame with white product name on blue glass panel, 20", G, A2..**$330.00**

Whitman's Chocolates, sign, paper, elegant girl seated on bench with box of chocolates, oval, framed, image: 13x10", EX, A9..**$175.00**

Whitman's Chocolates & Confections, sign, porcelain, Agency above Whitman's in diagonal script, Since 1842 in lower left, white on green, 14x40", EX, A1....**$200.00**

Whiz, sign, cardboard hanger, Whiz above bottle, The Certified Drink below, red & white, 1940s, 10x5", NM, A13..**$45.00**

Whiz Gear-Life Transmission & Differential Grease, pail, lettering above & below the 'Whiz Kids' dancing around open transmission case, bail handle, pry lid, 10-lb, VG, A1...**$60.00**

Whiz Hush-Shak Lubricates, can, Whiz encircled above Hush-Shak over bird, text below, screw lid & handle, 2-gal, 10½x6½", VG+, A6 ....**$100.00**

Whiz Metal Polish, can, pictures early car, RM Hollingshead Co, cone-top with pour spout & handle, 8", G+, A6..**$160.00**

Whiz Motor Oil, bank, tin, can shape, 2½" dia, NM, A7 ..**$40.00**

Whiz Neats Foot Compound, can, Whiz in bold letters above other lettering on triangle, screw cap, 6½x3½" dia, VG, A6 ....**$55.00**

Whiz Nickel Polish, can, product lettering above & below image of early sedan, black & white on silver, pour top with screw lid, 1-qt, G, A1....................................**$65.00**

Whiz Radiator Stop Leak, display, cardboard holder with 3 cans, colorful image of gnomes carrying can toward car, We Guarantee..., 7x14", EX, A6....................**$750.00**

Whiz Reflector Polish, tin, shows 'Whiz Kids' in front of car, For Burnishing Lamp Reflectors below, text on bottom, 3½" dia, VG, A6...**$90.00**

Whiz Service Center, display case, metal, pictures babies in diapers & crowns working on car below 4 stair-type shelves, 40x24x20", VG, A6 ....**$350.00**

Whiz Spring Leaf Lubricant, display, cardboard with several boxes of lubricant, colorful image of the 'Whiz Kids' using product, NM, A6 ....**$600.00**

Whiz Stop Leak Radiator Compound, display box, complete with original full tins, lid shows elves bringing tin to stranded touring car, 6x14", EX, A15 ..$1,225.00

Whiz Tar Remover, can, product name above & below the 'Whiz Kids' using product on old car, flat-sided with small screw lid, 1-pt, G+, A1.........................**$35.00**

Whiz Wax Auto Finish, can, Whiz above triangle on front, Restores the Lustre... & gnomes beside car on back, 5x4" dia, EX, A6..**$85.00**

Whiz/Davies Young Soap Co, tin, sample, Enter Wiz — Exit Dirt above product & company name, Free Sample on slip lid, 1½x1¼" dia, EX, D37 ....**$45.00**

Whizoil for Automobiles, can, pictures early car & scroll design, RM Hollingshead Co, blue, cream & black, screw cap, 5-gal, 13" dia, G+, A6....................**$400.00**

Wiedemann's, see also Geo Wiedemann

Wiedemann's Fine Beers, sign, tin, product name flanked by bottles within filigree border, W & eagle logo above, pre-1920s, framed, EX, A19........$575.00

Wiedemann's Royal Amber Beer, sign, product name & pheasant in flight embossed on copper panel applied to wood plaque, 15x19", EX, A8 ....$40.00

Wieland's Beer, tray, 'Congratulations,' elegant girl seated with flowers in her lap reading a note, wood-grain rim, 13x10", VG, A21 ....$90.00

Wieland's Beer, tray, elegant girl writing a letter, product name & San Francisco USA on rim, 1908, 13x10", VG+, A9...$275.00

Wieland's Extra Pale Lager, tray, Indian princess in center, product name & scroll design on rim, 13" dia, VG, A9...$300.00

Wieland's Extra Pale Lager, tray, Indian Princess surrounded by Indian artifacts, Kaufmann & Strauss, 13" dia, VG, A9...............................$400.00

Wiggle Stick Wash Blue, string holder, blue tubular shape, white lettering & hooks for paper bags or related items, chain hanger, 26", G-, A2 ....$635.00

Wigwam Allspice, tin, paper label, 3", NM, A7.........$50.00

Wigwam Coffee, tin, Wigwam above square image of Indian in profile & Patent Cut, Indian on horse & teepees at bottom, NM, A3................................$225.00

Wil-Flo Motor Oil, can, product name above At 30 degrees Below on snow scene with car at left, 5-qt, VG+, A1 ....$210.00

Wild Indian Slot Machines, doll, Cal-Neva Indian brave, flexible rubber, marked Copyright Fred Reinert, 1950s, 6½", G, A21...$6.00

Wild West, cigar box label, outer, cowboy on horse aiming rifle, 4½x4½", EX, D5 ....$40.00

Wild West Toilet & Bath Soap, box, pictorial label inside lid with 2 cowboys lassoing longhorns, colorful end label, 4x16x12" closed, G, A9..............................$525.00

Wildroot, sign, tin, tilted barber pole at right of Barber Shop, Ask For..., red, white & blue, 14x40", VG, A6..........$50.00

Wilko, crate label, Washington apple, yellow apple on red background, white script logo, 9x11", M, D12.......$5.00

Willard Battery Cables, display rack, pressboard back with 12 metal hooks, battery image above product name, black, red & cream, 12x17", VG, A6..........$60.00

Willard Dry Batteries, display case, metal, product name above 5 shelves, logo on sides, cream on red, 17x11x11", EX, A6...$80.00

Willfommen Thr Bruder/August Schell, drinking glass, etched barrel with lettering above & below mounted Viking with raised sword, dated Sept 1897, 3", NM, A8...$250.00

William Hollenberg Blacksmith, sign, die-cut cardboard, child couple in early car moving along fence & billboard, EX+, A18 ....$90.00

William's La Tosca Rose Talc Powder, tin, sample, product name surrounded by pink stemmed roses, gold shaker top, 2¼x1¼x¾, EX, D37, minimum value $110.00

Williams Bread, door push, It's Fresh on arrow pointing to Williams Bread on porcelain panel with wrought-iron brackets, NM, A13..$230.00

Williams Khosh-Amadit Talc, tin, dark blue with fairy standing on lily pad surrounded by colorful flowers, gold shaker top, oval, 5", NM, A2....................$2,420.00

Williams Radiator Co, pocket mirror, celluloid, Steam Heat Without A Boiler arched above Gas For Fuel..., brown, white & black, round, EX, A11................$25.00

Willoughby Taylor Personal Blend, pocket container, cardboard, vertical, product name in gold above logo on red & white band, black background, NM, A18 ....$30.00

Willow Spring Brewing Co, tray, deep-dish, 'In Old Kentucky,' girl in pink feeding horse at fence, 13" dia, G+, A8 ....$65.00

Willys Jeep, sign, porcelain shield, ...above Jeep flanked by Sales & Service & Fort Plain Motor, red, white & blue, 26x24", NM, D8...................................$400.00

Wilmington Speedway Big Car Auto Races, poster, Big Car Auto Races surrounds race car at top, Sat July 4th, 2:30 PM, 26x17", EX, A6 ....$210.00

Winchester, calendar, 1907, pictures 2 hunting dogs, full pad, matted & framed, image: 14½x13½", EX+, A9.......$600.00

Winchester, window display, 4-fold, front shows various products, reverse shows craftsman using tools, 48", rare, EX, A6 ....$440.00

Winchester Cartridges & Guns, calendar, 1913, hunters holding horses to avoid scaring rams, incomplete pad, framed, image: 21½x13½", EX, A9 ....$2,050.00

Winchester Factory Loaded Shotgun Shells, sign, cardboard, Do You Shoot? We Have A New Stock Of above puppies with shotgun & product name, 9x13", EX+, A13 ....$900.00

Winchester Gun Advisory Center, sign, die-cut tin shield, lettering on 2 sections & checked design on 2, copyright Olin Mathieson..., 16x15½", NM, A6 ....$70.00

Winchester Gun Oil, can, product name above text, squirt top, 3-oz, 5x2½", EX, A6................$60.00

Winchester Guns & Ammunition, display, die-cut cardboard stand-up, A Good Harvest..., hunter & dog at corner of fence, ca 1934, 2-pc, 42", EX, A12...$2,000.00

Winchester New Gun Oil, tin, red with yellow & white bull's-eye graphics, 1968, NM, A3 ....$45.00

Winchester Roller Skate Rolls, box, cardboard, green, red & cream, contains 11 rollers, NOS, A6...........$55.00

Winchester Shotgun Shells, sign, cardboard hanger, Ask For... on sign above Sold Here, pictures a snipe & product boxes, 12½x9", NM, A7 ....$1,325.00

Winchester Shotgun Shells, sign, cardboard hanger, Factory Loaded Shotgun Shells..., pictures dog flushing snipe, 12x8", EX, A7..$550.00

Winchester Sporting Rifles & Ammunition, sign, die-cut cardboard, product name above hunter shooting at large deer & rabbit, framed, 27½x19", EX+, A9 .$350.00

Winchester Super Speed Silvertip Cartridges, decal on glass, mountain scene with large bear & product in foreground, Shoot... upper left, 7½x9", EX, A6..$110.00

Winchester Tires, sign, embossed tin, ...Customer Satisfaction Guaranteed, red, white & blue, 18x54", G-, A9.......$145.00

Winchester W Shot Gun Shells, sign, cardboard, die-cut hanger, Ask For... on sign above grouse perched on fence, product boxes below, 13x9", EX, A13 .....$950.00

Windsor Wear, box, image of man running & waving in long johns, The Aristocrat Of Undergarments, 13x10", VG+, D21 ....$30.00

Winenot, sign, cardboard, Drink...5¢ encircled by moon with glass against starry sky, Delicious & Refreshing..., 14x11", VG, A7 ....$15.00

Wings King Size Cigarettes, sign, cardboard, Free! Piper Cub Airplane... & yellow plane above Wings advertising on red, 1940, 15x10", NM+, A3 ....$140.00

Wings Motor Oil, sign, porcelain, 2-sided, product name in white above 3 geese in flight, red background, curved top, 35x27", NM, A1 ....$950.00

Winner Cut Plug Smoke & Chew, lunch pail, colorful racing scene on front, blue & brown lettering, hinged lid & wire handle, 4x8x5", G-, A6 ....$130.00

Winner Cut Plug Smoke & Chew, lunch pail, colorful racing scene on front, blue & brown lettering, hinged lid & wire handle, 4x8x5", EX+, A18.......................$225.00

Winner Plug Tobacco, box label, horses & riders jumping through horseshoe, 12x12", EX+, D9 ....$30.00

Winnie Winkle, cigar box label, inner lid, blond cartoon character, 6x9", EX, D5 ....$75.00

Winston Cigarettes, mug, red plastic with logo on 2 sides, handled, 8x4" dia, NM, D24..................................$5.00

Winter Bock Beer, label, Internal Revenue Tax Paid statement, 1933-50, 12-oz, A10 ....$35.00

Winter Oilzum, sign, die-cut tin, Oilzum man's face within the O of Oilzum, Cream of Pure Pennsylvania... below, 12x20", EX, A6..$825.00

Winterton's Satsuma Wafers, tin, 1½" dia, EX, A7....$40.00

Wirthbru Beer, label, Standard Brewing Co, U-type permit number, Internal Revenue Tax Paid statement, 1933-36, 12-oz, EX, A10 ....$10.00

Wisconsin Pilsner Beer, label, Bloomer Brewery Inc, Internal Revenue Tax Paid statement, 1933-50, 64-oz, NM, A10 ....$14.00

Wisconsin's Best Beer, label, La Crosse Brewing Co, Internal Revenue Tax Paid statement, 1933-50, 12-oz, M, A10 ....$10.00

Wisdom Toothbrushes, display toothbrush, painted wood, red with Wisdom in yellow lettering, ca 1910, 38" long, G+, A21...$525.00

Wise Potato Chips, sign, die-cut cardboard, product name on owl perched on branch, 32", VG+, D30..........$45.00

Wish Bone Coffee, tin, pictures a steaming cup of coffee & wish bone in center, key-wind lid, EX, A3...........$50.00

Wishing Well Orange, door push bar, porcelain, We Sell Wishing Well Orange on bright yellow background, 3x30", EX, D21..$80.00

Wiss Scissors, display scissors, die-cut tin, Genuine Wiss in top handle grip, Stay Sharp in bottom handle grip, 36", EX, A21...$495.00

Wissahickon Tomato Pulp, can label, 1 end shows product name & diamond logo, other shows Indian, 3½x9", NM, A7 ....$10.00

Wisteria Talcum, tin, sample, 2 Japanese ladies, 1 with parasol, 1⅞x1⅛x¾", EX, D37, minimum value .$135.00

Witherill's, pocket mirror, black & white view of store, ...The Busy Corner, oval, EX, D18 ....$45.00

Wixon Brand Chili Spice, container, cardboard, Trade Mark ram in center, Strictly Pure, 1½-oz, EX, A3...$24.00

Wizard of O's, doll, vinyl, Campbell Soup Co, 1970s, 7", EX, A9 ....$50.00

Wm Deering & Co Grass Cutting Machinery, sign, paper, kids & couples watching man use horse-drawn grass cutter from bungalow, framed, image: 22x29", EX, A9 ..$3,000.00

Wm Gillette, cigar box label, inner lid, portrait flanked by man working & man relaxing, AG Kauffman, 1903, NM, A5 ....$400.00

Wm Kraas Celebrated Root Beer, bottle, 12-sided, pumpkin & gray-colored with embossed lettering, blob top, 10", EX, D16 ....$95.00

Wm S Kimball & Co, insert cards, Goddesses of the Greek & Romans series, 1889, set of 8, all EX, A5........**$187.00**

Wm S Kimball & Co's Cigarettes, insert cards, Ballet Queen series, 1889, set of 5, all VG-EX, A5 ....**$85.00**

Wm S Kimball & Co's Cigarettes, insert cards, Butterflies series, 1888, set of 16, all VG-EX, A5..................**$300.00**

Wm S Kimball & Co's Cigarettes, trade card, library setting with older man & younger woman exposing her legs, EX, D23 ....**$85.00**

WNAE Betty Lee Restaurant, clock, neon, black & white lettering, numbered 1-12, 21" dia, EX, A6 ....**$325.00**

Wolf Co Machinery, sign, paper, depicts Little Red Riding Hood & Wolf, vignettes of flour milling machinery below, image: 21x14", NM, A9 ....**$650.00**

Wolf's Head Marine Oils, sign, tin, lettering over 2-color field with sea waves, 100% Pure Pennsylvania, dated A-M 2-55, 9x18", EX+, A1 ....**$165.00**

Wolf's Head Oil, can, wolf's head & product name on horizontal oval above Motor Oil 100% Super..., screw lid & handle, 5-gal, EX, A6 ....**$65.00**

Wolf's Head 100% Pennsylvania Motor Oil, sign, tin, wolf's head on band above product name, oval, 30x23", G+, D11 ....**$70.00**

Wolverine Toys, tip tray, early, EX, D6 ....**$100.00**

Wonder Bread, end label, shows Howdy Doody in top hat promoting Free Wonder Circus Album, EX, D29 ..**$12.00**

Wonder Bread, sign, porcelain, yellow product name outlined in gold on dark blue, 1930s-40s, 9x20", EX+, A13 ....**$180.00**

Wonder Orange, sign, paper, Drink Refreshing Appetizing above product name flanked by oranges, blue background, 10x20", NM+, D30 ....**$18.00**

Wonder Orange, sign, tin, Drink...5¢ & bunch of oranges, Always On Ice-From Grove To You, orange on green, 1930s, 14x20", NM+, A13 ..$225.00

Wonder Orange, sign, tin, For Fresh Fruity Flavor Drink...Delicious-Refreshing, black, yellow & red, 1930s, 6x9", NM, A13...**$300.00**

Wood, Taber & Morse's Steam Engine Works, sign, paper, horse-drawn steam engine above vignettes with various equipment, framed, image: 22x17", EX+, A9...**$2,500.00**

Wood Bros Steel Self-Feeder & Band Cutter, pin-back button, product image flanked by lettering, EX, A20 ....**$35.00**

Woodbury's Facial Soap, box, small inset of John Woodbury above product name, green & cream, contains 3 bars of soap, EX, A6...**$50.00**

Wooden Shoe Lager Beer, tray, deep-dish, 2 Dutch girls with harbor scene beyond, product name on rim, oval, 15¼x12½", VG+, A1..**$95.00**

Woodfield's Oysters, can, sailing ship in center, Packed By Woodfield Fish & Oyster Co..., yellow background, press lid & bail, 1-gal, G, A6 ....**$120.00**

Woodlake Nymph, crate label, California lemon, nude blond lady dancing beneath eucalyptus tree, black ground, Woodlake, 12x9", M, D3........................**$12.00**

Woodsworth's Trailing Arbutus Talcum Powder, tin, sample, pink with name surrounded by pink decorative floral border, 2¼x1¼x¾", EX, D37, minimum value......**$150.00**

Wool Soap, thermometer, metal frame, bar of soap with degrees arched above, Toilet & Bath below, black & white, 6" dia, EX, A6..**$200.00**

Woolsey Cawlux Marine Finish, thermometer, tin, Best For Topsides above can at top, Tops For Bottoms above can at bottom, 28x8", EX, D8 ....**$295.00**

Worcester Salt, pin-back button, celluloid, product name above bag of salt, The Standard For Quality on band below, round, EX+, A11 ....**$30.00**

Worcester Salt, pin-back button, Worcester Salt, The Standard For Quality, shows big sack of salt & train, VG+, A20.**$6.00**

Worcester Salt, sign, paper, pictures a bag of salt, matted & framed, image: 20x14", G+, A9........................**$100.00**

Worker Cut Plug, lunch box, green with look of alligator skin, gold trim, wire handle, EX, A18................**$100.00**

World Oil Co, banner, cloth, Season's Greetings & Santa with bulb ornament wrapped in World Oil Co 24 Hr Service banner, 58", EX, A1 ....**$30.00**

Wrigley's, ad, American Flag offer, flag left of ad text, 5x8", NM, A7 ....**$22.00**

Wrigley's, ad, Great Three-Way Truck offer, 3¼x5¾", NM, A7...**$75.00**

Wrigley's, ad, Jr's Scale offer, 3¼x5¾", NM, A7 ....**$15.00**

Wrigley's, ad, Jumbo Scale offer, name left of scale, 3¼x5¾", NM, A7 ....**$18.00**

Wrigley's, ad, Lantern offer, lantern left of ad text, 3½x5½", NM, A7 ....**$18.00**

Wrigley's, ad, Rain-Coat/Wagon Umbrella, man in raincoat right of ad text above umbrella ad, 10x8", NM, A7..**$22.00**

Wrigley's, ad, Safety Razor offer, name above man shaving, 8x5", NM, A7 ....**$30.00**

Wrigley's, ad, Wrigley's Advertising Fan offer above display of 4 different images, ordering details below, 15x8½", NM, A7 ....**$110.00**

Wrigley's, ad, Wrigley's Ice Saving Refrigerator Assortments, pictures 3 refrigerators with ad text, 7x10", NM, A7 ....**$22.00**

Wrigley's, letter, Wm Wrigley Jr & Co letterhead with Sterling Nail File coupon below, 1898, NM, A7 ....**$30.00**

Wrigley's, sign, cardboard, Wrigley's sign above smiling lady behind register, 29x21", VG+, A1................**$460.00**

Wrigley's, sign, tin, pictures 3 packs of various flavors in vertical row, 16x12", EX, A7 ....**$50.00**

Wrigley's, sign, tin, pictures 3 packs of various flavors in vertical row, 16x12", NM+, D11............................**$80.00**

Wrigley's, trolley sign, cardboard, 'Mite' Makes Right..., elderly lady giving gum to girl over counter, 11x20", G, A2...**$110.00**

Wrigley's, trolley sign, cardboard, Help Yourself!... above Good For You on arrow flanked by displays, 1927, 12x22", NM, A7 ....**$290.00**

Wrigley's, trolley sign, cardboard, Wrigley's on banner above joker's & various gum packages, framed, 12x21", EX, A6 ....$350.00

Wrigley's, see also Juicy Fruit

Wrigley's Doublemint Gum, change mat, U-shaped with twins & product pack flanking Double Good Doublemint Gum, EX, A7 ....$25.00

Wrigley's Doublemint Gum, matchbook, Enjoy above Healthful-Delicious Doublemint on arrow pointing to girl, 20 strike, front strike, NM, D28......................$2.00

Wrigley's Doublemint Gum, trolley sign, cardboard, Cooling Refreshing, Be Sure It's Wrigley's, pack of gum riding a wave, framed, 11x21", VG, A6 ....$90.00

Wrigley's Doublemint Gum, trolley sign, cardboard, Take Your Choice Of Flavor... above Santa handing large gum pack to girl, 11x21", rare, VG, A1 ....$100.00

Wrigley's PK Chewing Sweet, sign, cardboard stand-up, Wrigley's PK Chewing Sweet on sign in front of girl in bonnet, 1920s, 15x9", VG, D22 ....$275.00

Wrigley's PK Chewing Sweet Peppermint Flavor, change felt, After Every Meal above name & Wrigley man with body initialed PK & double arrows, 1930s, 5x7½", EX+, A13 ....$130.00

Wrigley's PK Chewing Sweet Peppermint Flavor, sign, tin, Wrigley's PK in bold letters above & right of Wrigley boy pointing to pack of gum, 6x13", EX, A21 ....$525.00

Wrigley's Soap, tip tray, image of black cat on product boxes, yellow background, 3½" dia, EX, A21 ....$165.00

Wrigley's Spearmint & Doublemint Gum, sign, porcelain, After Every Meal above 2 packs, Aids Digestion... below, yellow & black, 1920s, 14x36", NM, A13...........$1,350.00

Wrigley's Spearmint & Doublemint Gum, sign, porcelain, Ice Cream on large band above product name (1 on each side), ca 1912, 9x30", EX+, A13.........$1,200.00

Wrigley's Spearmint Gum, calendar, 1935, simulated oil painting of 2 female radio stars, full pad, 15½x9", EX+, A6 ....$140.00

Wrigley's Spearmint Gum, display box, The Perfect Gum, The Flavor Lasts, Wrigley man pointing to advertising, 1927, NM, A16 ....$75.00

Wrigley's Spearmint Gum, license plate reflector, reverse image of gum pack on celluloid, oval, 4x6", rare, NM, A1..$125.00

Wrigley's Spearmint Gum, sign, cardboard, Pure, Wholesome, Inexpensive, tiny gent with oversized hand holding large gum pack, 11x21", VG+, D21 ....$35.00

Wrigley's Spearmint Gum, trolley sign, A Famous Flavor above Wrigley boy displaying large pack, Sweetens The Breath lower right, 11x21", EX, A7......................$55.00

Wrigley's Spearmint Gum, trolley sign, cartoon image of 'Dave Squeegee Famous Window Washer' talking to lady about Wrigley's, 11x21", EX, A7.....................$30.00

Wrigley's Spearmint Pepsin Gum, sign, cardboard, die-cut stand-up, features boy holding oversized pack of gum, 1920s, 14x10", VG, A13 ....$675.00

Wrigley's Spearmint Pepsin Gum, sign, cardboard, die-cut stand-up, features girl holding oversized pack of gum, 1920s, 14x10", G, A13.................................$400.00

Wrigley's Spearmint Pepsin Gum, sign, cardboard stand-up, The Flavor Lasts & gum pack on arrow at top & above row of packs, 8x9", EX, A6 ....$220.00

WT Grant Stores, doll, Bucky Bradford, vinyl, holding lollipop reading It's Yum Yum Time, name on round base, 9½", EX, A21 ....$55.00

Wunder Beer, sign, cardboard, product name above Full Alcoholic Strength, hops logo & company name, pre-1920s, 6x9", EX, A8 ....$45.00

Wunderbar Pilsener Beer Supreme, display, hollow plaster stein with lid, Oktoberfest scene with lettering on oval emblem & base, 16½", EX, A8 ....$40.00

Wurlitzer, sign, light-up, bubbling letters atop wood base marked Musical Fun For Everyone, limited edition, 1990, 6x19", NM+, A13..$425.00

Wurzburger Beer/AB Co Brewers, tip tray, product name on scrolled banner over castle landscape, company name on rim, 4" dia, VG+, A8 ....$60.00

Wyandotte Cleaner & Cleanser, sign, paper, Use...For All Cleaning Purposes above Indian brave with bow & arrow, framed, image: 39x18", VG, A9 ....$750.00

Wynola, door plate, tin, 'You'll Enjoy' above bottle & Good Any Time, 1950s, 14x4", EX, D21 ....$65.00

Wynola, sign, cardboard stand-up, 3 tiers of bottles, Wynola, Good Any Time 5¢ on front panels, 26x15", EX, D21 ....$55.00

Y

Yacht Club Coffee, tin, encircled yacht in center, key-wind lid, EX+, A3...$35.00

Yacht Club Smoking Tobacco, pocket tin, vertical, red with bust image & name on white cross, gold trim, VG, A18 ....$290.00

Yacht Club Straight Bourbon Whiskey & London Dry Gin, matchbook, 20 strike, front strike, NM, D28..$3.50

Yacht Cut Plug, pocket tin, flat, name on ribbon flanking circular image of sailing ship with anchors & helm, EX+, A18...$225.00

Yakima Chief, crate label, apple, scowling Indian chief, 10x10", M, D3 ....$5.00

Yako Chief Beer, label, Yakima Brewing & Bottling Co, U-type permit number, Internal Revenue Tax Paid statement, 1933-36, 12-oz, M, A10 ....$35.00

Yale, tire rack, cast iron, yellow & green repaint, 7x13½", NM, A6 ....$60.00

Yale Coffee, tin, sample, blue & gold with Yale on pennant upper left of product & company name, slip lid, 2¼x2½ dia, EX, D37 ....$145.00

Yale Mocha & Java Coffee, tin, sample, pennant left of product & company name, slip lid, 2¼x2½" dia, EX, D37 ....$130.00

Yale Shirts, display, miniature oxford shirt in celluloid easel display, 9", EX, A21 ....$120.00

Yale Tobacco, cabinet card, photo image of actress Louise Montague, Smoke Yale Mixture Tobacco, Marburg Bros, 13x7½", VG, A5 ....**$20.00**

Yankee Boy Plug Cut, pocket tin, vertical, pictures blond baseball boy at bat on shield against red & white checked background, VG, A18 ....**$465.00**

Yankee Doll, crate label, Oregon apple, 1940s girl in red sweater on blue background, white logo, Hood River, 9x11", M, D12 ....**$30.00**

Yankee Doodle Root Beer, chalkboard, image of Yankee & product name at top, 27x19", NM+, D11 ....**$100.00**

Yankee Girl, tobacco tag, EX, D35.............................**$5.00**

Yankee Safety Razor Blade Box, tin, flat, rounded corners, ¼x1x2⅛", EX, D37....................................**$110.00**

Yankee Standard, cigar box, wood, inner lid label pictures girl in Yankee hat flanked by flags & product name, EX+, A3 ....**$85.00**

Yara Tobacco/Bendixen Tobacco Co, sign, cardboard trifold, interior schoolroom scene with man teacher paddling boy student, 20x30", EX+, A18 ....**$440.00**

Yeast Foam, sign, paper, ...Makes Delicious Buckwheat Cakes, image of young girl at table eating pancakes, 15x10", EX, A6 ....**$110.00**

Yeast Foam, wall dispenser, Eat Yeast Foam For Health, 5 Cakes 10¢ above vertical row of boxes, red on yellow, 18x3", EX, A18 ....**$65.00**

Yello Bole Pipes, display rack, rotates on pedestal, smiling woman on lettered sign above, name flanked by $1 below, 18", EX+, A18 ....**$135.00**

Yellow Bonnet Coffee, tin, girl in bonnet flanked by Vacuum Packed, key-wind lid, 1-lb, EX+, A3 ....**$170.00**

Yellow Bonnet Coffee, tin, sample, girl in bonnet flanked by Steel Cut, pry lid, 2½x3" dia, EX, D37 ....**$495.00**

Yellow Bonnet Pumpkin Spice, tin, paper label, 3¼", NM, A7 ....**$30.00**

Yellow Bonnet Pure Ground Cloves, container, cardboard, tin top & bottom, white with trademark image above name on blue band, 1.50-oz, EX+, A3.......**$45.00**

Yellow Cab, cigar box, shows early cab above Takes The Right Of Way on emblem, 2 For 15¢ at right, G+, A6 ....**$55.00**

Yellow Cab, driver's cap, black leather with brass cloisonne badge featuring back end of taxi, Yellow Cab below, VG+, A1..**$100.00**

Yellow Cab, thermometer, painted wood, Call a Yellow above sedan, bulb & advertising below, curved top, square bottom, 4x15", EX, A1..............................**$250.00**

Yellow Cap, cigar box label, outer, woman wearing Turkish costume, 4½x4½", M, D5 ....**$12.00**

Yellow Strand Rope, watch fob, porcelain, product name on band across spool of rope, EX, A20 ....**$60.00**

Yocum Brothers Y-B Quality Cigars, box, Y-B flanked by portraits, EX+, A3 ....**$35.00**

Yodora Deodorant Cream, tin, sample, product name in 3 different styles of lettering above Banishes Body Oders, ¼x1¼" dia, EX, D37.............................**$18.00**

Yokohl, crate label, California orange, Indian brave fishing by stream, Exeter, 10x11", M, D3 ....**$2.00**

York County Garagemen's Association, sign, porcelain flange, Member above spoked wheel with logo surrounded by lettering, blue & white, 24x18", EX+, A1...............**$80.00**

Yosemite Beer, sign, paper, profile of girl wearing feathered shawl, Enterprise Brewing Co, ca 1898, framed, image: 19x15", VG, A9.......................................**$800.00**

Young Fritz, tobacco tag, oval, VG, D35 ....**$2.00**

Your Treat, cigar box label, ca 1910, EX, D23..........**$25.00**

Yuengling's, see also DG Yuengling

Yuengling's Beer, sign, tin, hands pouring from bottle into glass against product name on blue, Since 1829 on red dot, 19x27", G+, A19 ....**$200.00**

Yuengling's Beer, tip tray, bust image of girl in wide-brimmed hat, lettering on rim, 4" dia, EX, A21 ..**$230.00**

Yuengling's Ice Cream, tray, maid carrying tray with ice cream, 13½" dia, G+, A9..**$200.00**

Yuengling's Ice Cream, tray, shows children gathered around woman with tray, lettered & decorative border, vertical rectangle, VG+, A19.............................**$25.00**

Yuengling's Porter, sign, tin, Drink!..., Made In Pottsville PA on blue, horizontal rectangle, EX+, A19 ....**$75.00**

Yukon Permanent Anti-Freeze, can, product name above huskies pulling Eskimo on sled, Clark-Lurton Corp, red, white & blue, 1-gal, 9½x7", EX, A6......................**$85.00**

❧ Z ❧

Zanol Cocoa, tin, Quality First above oval logo flanked by leaves in center, text below, ½-lb, 5x3x2", VG+, A3..**$40.00**

Zanol Military Foot Powder, tin, product name & advertising on emblem flanked by officers shaking hands, 4½x2½", EX+, A3 ....**$75.00**

Zanol Spices, tin, 4", NM, A7 ....**$10.00**

Zanzibar Brand Cocoa, tin, product name above & below native village, shouldered square shape with round lid, EX, A18 ....**$65.00**

Zanzibar Brand Ground Black Pepper, tin, product name above & below native village, shouldered square shape with round lid, 1927, 10-lb, EX, A18........**$140.00**

Zatek Chocolate Billets, store container, glass jar with embossed lettering, footed, 16x7" dia, EX, A9 ...**$750.00**

ZBT Baby Powder, tin, with contents, 2", NM, A7 ....**$20.00**

Zecol Wax, license plate attachment, metal, Drive Safe, Zecol Wax Your Car, red, cream & yellow, 4½", VG+, A6 ....**$35.00**

Zeigler Coal, sign, tin, EX, D34 ....**$65.00**

Zelman Rawlston, cigar box label, outer, young boy in formal attire, 4½x4½", M, D5 ....**$20.00**

Zemo Clean Antiseptic Liquid, sign, paper, yellow with lettering at right of product box, For Itching Skin..., 35¢ & $100 Bottles, 12x19", EX, A2 ....**$100.00**

Zeneda, crate label, Florida citrus, glass of orange juice, whole grapefruit & orange half, 7x7", M, D3 ....**$1.00**

Zeno Chewing Gum, display box, tin, inside lid label shows man leaning over fence to grab large pack, 5x10", EX, A7..$135.00

Zeno Chewing Gum, trade card, I Keep My Nerves Steady..., frontal view of lady driving early open car, 5½x3½", EX, A7......................................$125.00

Zeno Chewing Gum, vendor, 1¢, oak with embossed lettering, Off Boys Old Zeno & portrait on label in upper left, 17x10", restored, A9......................$400.00

Zephyr Gasoline, gas globe, High Octane above Zephyr on large center band, red, white & blue, plastic body, oval, 12x15½", NM, A6..........................$275.00

Zeppelin Motor Oil, can, zeppelin flying over the ocean above product name, pour spout, 2-gal, 11x8½", VG+, A6..$110.00

Zerolene, sign, porcelain, product name on band above bear, Standard Oil For Motor Cars arched above & below, 24" dia, VG, A6..............................$800.00

Zerolene No 5, can, circular bear logo above No 5, Standard Oil Co of California below, pour spout & handle, 1-gal, EX, A1...$165.00

Zett's, sign, paper litho, shows Bavarian street scene, pre-1920s, matted & framed, EX, A19 ....$125.00

Zett's Par-Ex Beer, calendar, 1915, paper litho, shows joyful tavern scene, small pad below, matted & framed, 22x26", NM, A19..$150.00

Ziegler Bavarian Lager, label, product name above innkeeper by hearth, 12-oz, NM, A19....................$8.00

Ziegler's Beer, sign, tin, Drink..., Beaver Dam Wisconsin & round logo left of bottle on blue, beveled edge, 8x11", EX, A8..$100.00

Ziegler's Beer, sign, tin, Drink..., Beaver Dam Wisconsin & round logo left of bottle on blue, beveled edge, 8x11", VG, A8..$45.00

Zig-Zag Cigarette Papers, dispenser, gold with white label, vertical rectangle with opening at bottom for dispensing, NM, A19..$45.00

Zingo Sweets, tin, product name & #2 racer on emblem, blue, orange & brown with gold slip lid, 10x12" dia, VG, A6..$175.00

Zip Oil, can, Zip Oil in bold letters above Spring Lubricant & Rust Solvent, blue, orange & cream, 7", G+, A6.....$20.00

Zipp's Cherri-o, drinking glasses, Zipp's Cherri-O etched below circular bird logo, flared tops, ca 1920, set of 3, NM, A13...$290.00

Zipp's Cherri-o, syrup dispenser, ceramic barrel shape with product name & bird logo flanked by 5¢, gold trim, 1910s-20s, EX, A13.................................$1,500.00

Zipp's Cherri-o, syrup dispenser, name & bird logo on footed metal canister with gallon glass jug atop, 1920s, 18x13" dia, VG, A13......................................$165.00

Zipp's Root Beer, mug, black logo, handled, 6x3½", M, D16..$95.00

Zippo Lighters, display case, vertical box rotates on pedestal, displays various advertising lighters: Amoco, Ford, etc, 13", VG, A6..$160.00

Zira Cigarettes, box, cardboard, with contents, holds 10, NM, A18..$35.00

Zira Cigarettes, sign, embossed tin, Winning On Merit & 5¢ flank open pack on yellow oval on black, red & yellow border, 24x12", VG, A18..............................$60.00

Zoller's Famous Beer, label, product name above factory scene, gold background, 12-oz, VG+, A19.............$8.00

Zonweiss for the Teeth, alarm clock, girl spooning powder & product lettering on face, round footed case with ring atop, 1880, EX, A2....................................$600.00

1000 Mile Motor Oil, can, It's All Oil, Pure Paraffine... encircled in center, blue, yellow & red, screw cap & handle, 2-gal, 11x8", VG+, A6............................$30.00

102 Beer, trolley sign, cardboard, California's Finest Beer above '102' with bottle next to lady with glass, 11x22", VG, A8..$40.00

18K Coffee, tin, 18K encircled above Coffee on center band, steaming cup below, 1-lb, VG+, A3 ....$26.00

18K Coffee, tin/bank, sample, 18K encircled above Coffee on center band, steaming cup below, A Penny Saved..., EX, A3 ....$75.00

1860 Old Virginia Smoke, tin, gold square shape with 2 gentlemen next to 1860, EX, A18......................$230.00

20 Grand Select Cream Ale, can, cone-top, oval logo with gold border, Select in script above 20 Grand on diagonal band, Cream Ale below, NM, A8...................$60.00

20th Century Rheumatic Oil, sign, die-cut cardboard stand-up, shows couple in very early open car, 14x14", EX+, A15...$925.00

3 Twins Fine Cut Smoking Tobacco, tin, flat, 3 head portraits of girls above product name, rounded corners, 4x6", EX, A18..$100.00

3 V Cola, thermometer, dial-type, bottle flanked by product name & Giant 16 Oz Bottle, Makes Any Weather Better, 12" dia, EX+, D30..$125.00

30 Below, sign, tin, Drink above 30 Below on circle at left of penguin, 11x9", NM+, D30............................$155.00

36 Pilsner, sign, tin hanger, Drink '36' Pilsner, Altoona Brewing Co, black & white, 6x18", EX, A8 ....$100.00

4-X Junior Beer, label, New Orleans Brewing Co, Internal Revenue Tax Paid, 1933-50, 12-oz, M, A10 ....$16.00

4-X Pilsener Beer, label, New Orleans Brewing Co, U-type permit number, Internal Revenue Tax Paid statement, 12-oz, M, A10...$12.00

76, sign, tin, America's Favorite Soft Drink & boy flank red & white bottle cap, 10x24", NM, D30 ....$130.00

7-Up, see Seven-Up on page 236

AD RATE CARD FOR HUXFORD'S COLLECTIBLE ADVERTISING

PLEASE CONTACT HUXFORD ENTERPRISES *IMMEDIATELY* TO RESERVE YOUR SPACE FOR THE NEXT EDITION

RATES (Ad Size)

FULL PAGE	7½" wide x 9¾" tall	— $750.00
HALF PAGE	7½" wide x 4½" tall	— $400.00
QUARTER PAGE	3½" wide x 4½" tall	— $250.00
EIGHTH PAGE	3½" wide x 2¼" tall	— $150.00

*Note: These rates are for **camera ready copy only**— add $50.00 if we are to compose your ad. These prices are net—no agency discounts allowed. Payment in full must accompany your ad copy.*

All advertising accepted under the following conditions:

1. The Publisher will furnish advertising space in sizes and at rates as set forth in this rate sheet upon full payment in advance of its annual advertising deadline as set forth herein.

2. *Submission of Copy.* The Publisher shall have the right to omit any advertisement when the space allotted to Advertiser in a particular issue has been filled. In addition, the Publisher reserves the right to limit the amount of space the Advertiser may use in any one edition.

3. *Content and Design.* Publisher reserves the right to censor, reject, alter or refuse any advertising copy in its sole discretion or disapprove any advertising copy in accordance with any rule the Publisher may now have, or may adopt in the future, concerning the acceptance of advertising matter, but no intentional change in advertising copy will be made without the prior consent of the Advertiser.

4. *Publisher's Liability for Deletions.* Publisher's liability for failure of the Publisher to insert any advertisement in their books shall be limited to a refund of the consideration paid for the insertion of the advertisement or, at Advertiser's option, to such deleted advertisement being inserted in the next edition.

5. *Copyright and Trademark Permission.* Any Advertiser using copyrighted material or trademarks or trade names of others in its advertising copy shall obtain the prior written permission of the owners thereof which must be submitted to the publisher with the advertising copy. Where this has not been done, advertising will not be accepted.

Half Page

Quarter Page

Eighth Page

Make checks payable to:

HUXFORD ENTERPRISES
1202 7th Street • Covington, IN 47932

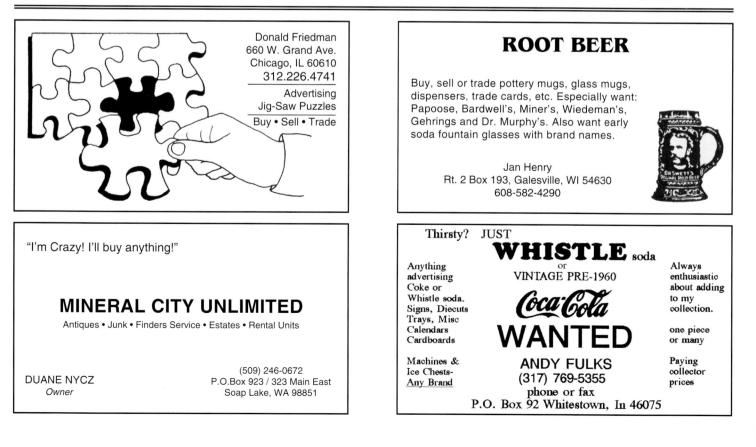
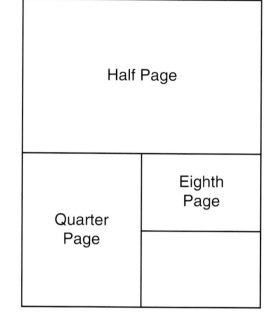

Leila & Howard Dunbar
76 Hauen Street
Milford, MA 01757

508-634-8697 *(Days)*
508-473-8616 *(Evenings & Weekends)*

20-yr. Collectors and Dealers. Advertising Signs & Posters. Buy, Sell, Appraise.
All Items Guaranteed. Mail Order Our Specialty.

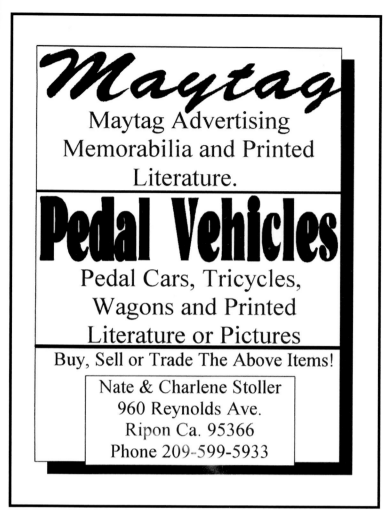

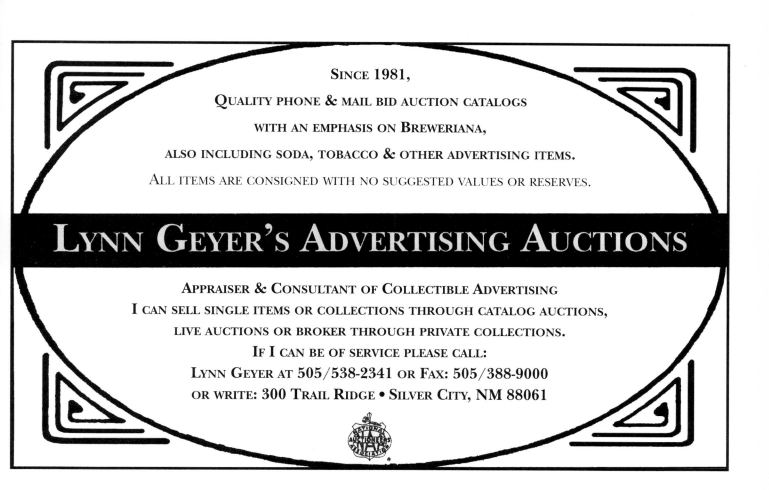